THE
LABYRINTH
OF
EXILE

THE
LABYRINTH
OF
EXILE

A Life of Theodor Herzl

ERNST PAWEL

Farrar, Straus & Giroux

NEW YORK

Library of Congress Cataloging-in-Publication Data
Pawel, Ernst.
The labyrinth of exile : a life of Theodor Herzl / by Ernst Pawel.
—1st ed.
p.   cm.
Bibliography: p.
Includes index.
1. Herzl, Theodor, 1860–1904.   2. Zionists—Austria—Biography.
I. Title.
DS151.P39   1989
320.5'4'095694092—dc20   89-7905
[B]

To the Spiritual Heirs of Ahad Ha-Am

PREFACE

*M*any people have helped to make this book possible. I am profoundly grateful to all of them, not least for having proved that civility and generosity survive even in the age of greed and mindless competition.

No one exemplified these qualities more graciously than the late Dr. Alex Bein, whose own 1934 Herzl biography remains a classic of its kind. In his many years as head of the Herzl archives in Jerusalem he set the standards and laid the foundations for all serious work in the field. He gave unstintingly of himself, and the youthful enthusiasm he preserved into the ninth decade of his life served as an inspiration to everyone who had the good fortune to know him. I am deeply in his debt.

His successors at the Central Zionist Archives in Jerusalem were equally generous with their time and counsel. Moshe Schaerf and Pinchas Selinger lit the way for me through the archival maze, and Shulamit Nardi was kind enough to give me the benefit of her long, hard-earned expertise in Zionist history. My heartfelt thanks also to Dr. Karyn Moses and the staff of Mishkenot Sha'ananim, whose hospitality made my wife and me feel truly at home.

The Austrian National Library in Vienna provided valuable information, and in New York the Leo Baeck Institute, the library of the Herzl Foundation, the YIVO Institute, and the Austrian Information Service proved uniformly helpful and efficient. My special thanks to Dr. Michael Riff, Ms. Esther Togman, and Ira Brophy.

A number of photographs appear courtesy of the Herzl Foundation in New York and the Picture Archive of the Austrian National Library in Vienna.

David Rieff helped to shape this book, not only as an editor but as a friend, and Jenny Plath handled the technical aspects with awe-inspiring competence. All translations, errors, and opinions are strictly my own.

Key to Abbreviations

CZA   Central Zionist Archives, Jerusalem

D   Theodor Herzl's Diaries. All excerpts translated from the original German of the latest and most authoritative edition: *Theodor Herzl, Briefe und Tagebücher, Vols. 2 and 3*. Berlin: Ullstein GmbH, 1983–1985

F   Theodor Herzl. *Feuilletons*, 2 vols. Berlin: Verlag Benjamin Harz, 1903

L   *Letters*

PB   Theodor Herzl. *Das Palais Bourbon*. Leipzig: Dunker & Humblot, 1895

TD   *Travel Diaries*. In Vol. 1 of the Diaries

THM   *Theodor Herzl Memorial*. Ed. by Meyer W. Weisgal. New York: The New Palestine, 1929

YD   The so-called *Youth Diary*, or *Jugendtagebuch*, in Vol. 1 of the Diaries

THE
LABYRINTH
OF
EXILE

ONE

*A*t the age of thirty-five, the fashionable Viennese playwright and journalist Theodor Herzl fantasized about the collective conversion of the Jews in a mass ceremony at the Cathedral of St. Stephen. By the time he died, a mere nine years later, he had redefined Jewish identity in terms of a modern secular faith and created a national movement which, within less than half a century, led to the foundation of the Jewish state.

It was a momentous achievement, but one which owed far less to the originality of his ideas than to the power of his personality. Zionism existed long before Herzl appeared on the scene; the dream of Zion is as old as the Diaspora. He brought to it leadership, organization, and a unique blend of fantasy and practical realism, but his most important contribution by far was the messianic image of himself, his stature in the eyes of the Jews and in the eyes of the world. The mid-life metamorphosis of the dandified littérateur, the dramatic rise of the charismatic leader, and the apotheosis of the prophet mourned at his death as the uncrowned King of the Jews defy all plausibility and raise provocative questions. What turned this Budapest-born German patriot into a Jewish nationalist? How, within a scant two years and without the benefit of modern mass media, was he able to impose himself as the spokesman for the Jewish people? To what extent did his spirit shape the state he helped to found, and how much of it survives today, for better and for worse? What, ultimately, is his place in history?

The key to the answers must be sought in the man and in his life—

a man of vast complexity, and a life tragic and turbulent, full of paradox and contradictions, and yet all of a piece; the inner consistency that links the truculent teenager to the messianic prophet far outweighs the apparent contrast. Who was he, and what made him who he was?

Herzl's life, especially in its later public phases, has been abundantly documented in often conflicting testimony that ranges from venomous vituperation to frank hagiography; he inspired strong emotions and left few people indifferent. Yet in the end, he himself remains the most important source and witness. Though barely forty-four years old at the time of his death, he left behind a truly staggering volume of writings which, in ways both deliberate and unwitting, provide vital clues to the enigma of his personality. The literary fame to which he aspired eluded him, but he was nonetheless a writer by vocation, avocation, and compulsion—playwright, journalist, essayist, novelist, pamphleteer, diarist, and indefatigable correspondent. The bulk of this prolific output has been lovingly preserved, a tribute to the politician rather than the artist, but an inexhaustible challenge to those trying to discover the human being encapsulated in the legend.

Like most of the avatars of Vienna's *fin de siècle*, Herzl was not a native Viennese. Born in Budapest on May 2, 1860, he spent the first eighteen years of his life in the Hungarian capital, a fact whose major significance to his emotional and intellectual development he consistently tended to minimize or deny. Yet the cultural diversity of his native environment, along with the identity problems it engendered, surfaced almost at birth; he was duly circumcised eight days later and given the Hebrew name of Zeev, along with the Hungarian Tivadar and the German Wolf Theodor. And since German was the language spoken in the Herzl home, he started out in life as Dori, little Theodor.

No childhood is ever quite as idyllic as it appears in retrospect, but little Theodor's early years appear to have been a tranquil enclave within one of the century's most turbulent decades, a time of high hope and despair, of heady new freedom and savage repression. The Habsburg Empire—with help from the Czar's Cossacks—had survived the nationalist insurrections of 1848, drowned them in blood, but failed to defeat the cause that inspired them. Its foundations were crumbling even while a revolution of an altogether different kind, bloodless but far more profound in its long-range effects than any confrontations on the barricades, doomed the archaic feudalism of the monarchy. Industrialization, long overdue and hence all the more disruptive, put an end to the old order; capitalism triumphant brought chaos, anarchy, and progress, created great wealth and even greater misery. It also opened the gates of the ghetto; in 1849—a mere eleven years before Herzl's birth—the residence restrictions were removed, and the Jews of Austria-Hungary began a mass exodus from rural ghettos to the faceless urban centers of the realm.

Thanks to the affluence and solicitude of their parents, the Herzl children—Dori and his sister, Pauline, older by a year—were well protected from the icy winds of change. Their childhood Eden was a spacious apartment on Dohany-utca (Tabakgasse, or Tobacco Lane) in one of the choicest sections of town, within a few minutes' walk of the National Theater, the National Museum, and the magnificent shoreline promenade along the Danube. The house stood right next door to the fancy and fanciful new Dohany Street Synagogue, an extravagant monument to bad taste and rising affluence which—unlike the apartment house itself—survives to this day. Its eclectic mix of pseudo-Moorish architecture and nouveau riche pretentiousness, complete with two minarets topped by spiked globes, celebrated among other things the ascendance of the liberal, middle-class Reform wing in the Jewish community over traditional Orthodoxy. Consecrated just a year before Herzl's birth, it became an integral part of the landscape of his childhood; its contribution to his spiritual growth is much more problematical.

A formal studio portrait taken when he was about six years old shows a Hungarian Little Lord Fauntleroy standing at attention, a vision of conspicuous if pathetic elegance in his fancy suit, ruffled shirt, and high boots, toes turned out, right hand by his side, and the left placed with studied nonchalance on a heavy folio which, like the ornate armchair, testifies to the photographer's artistic pretensions.

A grotesque pose for any six-year-old, but struck here with remarkable aplomb; the boy seems totally at ease with the world and already somewhat disdainful of it. Or perhaps disdainful merely of the photographer, who for all his manifest limitations managed not only to freeze a moment in time but also to capture something of its spirit—a child of the mid-century bourgeoisie, well fed, well-bred, sheltered, and sure of himself, living in the best of all possible worlds.

The world of his parents.

*　　*　　*

The emancipation of the Jews in Austria-Hungary fizzled within two generations. Its initial promise enabled young men like Dori's father to break out of the ghetto; less than half a century later, the son was to pronounce the emancipation a dismal and calamitous failure.

Jakob Herzl, who rose from penniless apprentice in 1850 to president of the Hungaria Bank in 1870, was typical of the tough, ghetto-smart ex-peddlers and petty tradesmen who supplied the drive, the contacts, and the money for the mid-century boom that propelled the monarchy out of the Middle Ages. Born in 1835 in the border town of Semlin (the present Zemun), across the Sava River from the capital of Serbia, he grew up in an impoverished but strictly Orthodox family and, with barely four years of elementary schooling and some brief exposure to the traditional cheder, left home at seventeen to make his way in the outside world just opening up for the likes of him. By 1856, he had established himself as a "transport and commission agent" in Budapest, and two years later he married Jeanette (Johanna Nanette) Diamant, the daughter of a wealthy textile merchant.

It seemed an unlikely match; in background, breeding, and temperament the couple were a study in contrasts. The bride, at nineteen, was four years younger than the groom, but light-years ahead of him in self-assurance and what passed for sophistication. Raised in a wealthy home, accustomed to its comforts and conveniences, she had acquired all the fashionable social vices, including a trendy addiction to German belles lettres and to German—as opposed to Austrian—culture in general that was rampant at the time among the freshly minted Hungarian–Jewish bourgeoisie. Harmless enough, as addictions go, but probably responsible for some genetic damage to her son's taste in literature and the arts.

Her own parents, both born in Budapest, were totally assimilated and shared the prevailing pro-German bias, although in her father's case any such sentiments were inevitably tempered by a notoriously cynical wit. In fact, the textile tycoon Hermann (Hersh) Diamant made no attempt to disguise his enlightened skepticism about all aspects of religion and politics, an attitude which, by the same token, also made him scorn any formal conversion; unlike most of his relatives, he retained his ties to the Jewish community.

But he quite uncynically worshipped his bright and self-willed little daughter, the youngest of five children, and the shy but able upstart from the boondocks, fingered by some amateur or professional match-maker as a solid marriage prospect, may well have struck him as just

innocuous enough a rival for his daughter's affections. He turned out
to be wrong. Methodical to the point of pedantry, enormously good-
natured in his fussy way, Jakob Herzl proved fully capable of taking
Daddy's place. He was a good provider, he adored his wife, and he
stood in awe of her culture and refinement. She, in turn, seems to
have cared for him, but it hardly mattered—they had their children.
And the children had their parents. A charmed circle, whose charm
made escape all but impossible.

The model husband also became an affectionate father, the rare
example of a hard-driving businessman who remained close to his
children. In the early years he traveled a great deal, and five short
notes he received from his then six-year-old son are the earliest known
samples of Herzl's literary genius. Only the first is in German; in the
later ones he switched to Hungarian, an indication that the outside
world had begun to intrude, after all.

But the child's love for his "sweet darling Papa," which comes
through in even these few simple lines, was to remain untroubled and
unchanged throughout his lifetime. The oedipal turmoil of adolescence, the conflict between the generations, the dramatic and oft-
dramatized tensions between the uneducated Jewish "founding fathers"
and their hyperintellectual offspring so characteristic of the period
never seem to have arisen, or even so much as been noted in this
particular family. In later years, with Jakob staunchly supporting what
most of his friends and acquaintances derided as Theodor's madcap
schemes, relations between them grew, if anything, even closer. This
son never rebelled against the father, and the father never gave him
reason to do so.

Yet for all the conventional deference paid the father as the nominal
head of the family, the tone in the Herzl home was set by the mother.
Jakob's lack of formal education was no handicap in the business world,
where he trusted his instincts—more so, it turned out, than was warranted—and never doubted his competence. But in all other matters
he cheerfully deferred to his wife's judgment and taste. He never ceased
to be impressed by her moral rectitude and intellectual pretensions,
and it was only natural for him to leave her in full charge of the
children's upbringing.

She is reputed to have been a great beauty in her youth, but the
early portraits merely show a statuesque young woman with a resolute
expression and strong, masculine features bearing a marked resemblance to those of her son. Everything known about her suggests that

she was highly intelligent, but her education in a society that treated the female brain as a troublesome and potentially malignant appendage was deliberately designed to stunt the intellect and avert any danger of independent thought. Jeanette's tastes in everything, from fashion to literature, were rigidly conventional, her opinions strictly Budapest-bourgeois; yet her husband, family, and social circles would have been deeply shocked had they been anything more original. For a woman of Jeanette Herzl's brains, energy, and ambition, the emotional price of conformity came high; unfortunately, part of it was paid by her son.

She had a daughter as well, an appealing and affectionate child much beloved by everyone who knew her. The last photograph of Pauline, taken shortly before her sudden death at nineteen, captures the poignant beauty of the young woman, the look of melancholy resignation that seems almost tragically prescient. Relations between mother and daughter have been described as very close, and while piety is bound to color all such recollections, there is no reason to doubt them.

But Pauline was a girl, and as such fated and slated to repeat the cycle of marriage and motherhood; there was no way in which she could have satisfied her mother's thwarted ambitions. That burden fell upon the son.

Whatever the elemental nature of the ties between mother and son, the passion with which Jeanette involved herself in every aspect of his life derived much of its thrust from her broader frustrations as a human being. What locked a Jeanette Herzl into lifelong motherhood was not mere biology but a social order she accepted as given. Her boy, unlike the girl, had a chance to succeed in the real world; his success would in some measure validate her role as a mother and redeem her own dreams and ambitions. And so she smothered him with a relentless devotion that outlived him and in which love became hopelessly entangled with possessiveness.

The mix, though poisonous, is said to be the recipe for breeding heroes. Growing up in the smug certainty of being his mother's favorite, of having her unconditional love and acceptance, gave the child a self-confidence and sense of security that were never to leave him. And it probably goes a long way toward explaining the remarkable absence of friction between father and son. There was no conflict because there was no contest.

*　*　*

Jeanette's own family, the Diamants and the Abeleses, had settled in Hungary in the eighteenth century, their more distant origins lost in the chaotic history of Jewish migrations in the Middle Ages. But for the Herzl side of her son's ancestry she was able to contrive a more imaginative family tree, extending all the way back to King David.

The known facts are more prosaic. When Jakob Herzl left Semlin in 1852, he was making his escape from a brackish provincial backwater in which his family had stagnated for generations. In 1739, when Belgrade reverted to Turkish rule, some thirty Jewish families chose to cross the Sava River and settle on the Austrian shore. The Herzls may have been among them, but the first ancestor of record was one Moses Herzel, a glazier born in Semlin in 1751. (Herzel is a diminutive of Herz, German for "heart," the equivalent of the Hebrew *Lev*, or Loeble by analogy; the second *e* was later dropped.)

Herzl's Grandfather Simon was born in 1805. Two of his brothers converted to Christianity, changed their names, and skipped town (the grandson of one of them, Jenö Heltai, became a well-known novelist and secretary of the Hungarian PEN Club), but Simon stayed put, married the daughter of a Sephardic rabbi, and lived a life of genteel poverty increasingly devoted to the rigorous observance of Orthodox Jewish ritual. Unhappy though he may have been about the quasi-apostasy of his son Jakob, who had drifted into the lukewarm liberalism of a Reform movement which in Simon's eyes hardly qualified as Jewish, the two nonetheless remained on good terms, and Grandfather Simon was for many years a frequent though perhaps not always comfortable guest in the Herzls' non-kosher Budapest home.

As it happened, in his day the small, close-knit community of Semlin Jews was led by a charismatic figure whose influence on Herzl's grandfather is a matter of conjecture but who, in word and deed, anticipated many of the ideas of his grandson Theodor by about half a century. Yehuda Alkalai, the Semlin rabbi since 1826, preached Jewish nationalism, called for the restoration of the Jewish homeland in Palestine, and actively promoted the revival of Hebrew as a language of daily discourse. In 1839, following a stay in Jerusalem, he published a Hebrew grammar (after persuading the Serbian government's printshop in Belgrade to acquire a Hebrew type font for the purpose). In 1841 he went to Constantinople, where, much like Herzl some fifty-five years later, he tried and failed to obtain Turkish territorial concessions for Jewish settlements. His *Goral le-Adonai* (*A Lot for the Lord*), published in Vienna in 1857, proposed the systematic acquisition of land parcels in the Holy Land, and in 1862 he founded a Society for the Colonization of Palestine in Jerusalem, where he settled permanently in 1874 and where he died four years later.

Alkalai was a man of great moral and intellectual force, for decades an impressive if perhaps controversial figure in his tiny congregation; it seems hard to believe that Simon Herzl, who only died in 1879, when Herzl was already in law school, would never have talked about him to his grandson.

And yet, in the thousands of obliquely or overtly self-revelatory pages of Herzl's diaries and letters, there is only one glancing reference to his paternal grandfather, and none at all to Rabbi Alkalai: at a moment of great triumph in 1896, when a crowd at the Sofia railroad station hailed him as the King of the Jews, Herzl noted "an old man in a fur cap" who "resembled my Grandfather Simon."

Too much can be made of a stray remark, yet the fact remains that free associations of this sort are seldom as free as they seem, and his invoking, for the first and only time, the ghost and spirit of the grandfather at this emotional high point in his life may not have been entirely accidental. Simon Herzl had, after all, been the one and only unapologetic Jew in the family, probably the only one he had known as a child. The more pertinent question is why he so relentlessly repressed the memory of his father's father in the first place.

As a child, Herzl apparently accompanied his father fairly regularly to services at the Dohany Street Synagogue. What, if anything, he made of them is hard to say, the more so since Jakob Herzl's Judaism, while assuaging his sense of guilt and satisfying his own pietistic nostalgia, was no longer robust enough to be passed on to the next generation. At the same time, Jeanette Herzl's passionate Germanophilia, coupled with disdain for Jewishness in general and her own in particular, made for a conflict of loyalties in the hypersensitive child which, whether conscious or not, had certain inevitable consequences. And here, too, there was no contest; the mother won hands down.

Loyalties aside, the ambiguities of the situation had an inherent dynamic of their own. Even in the most assimilated and secular home, no Jewish child could long escape the awareness of being different. That difference, incomprehensible, imposed from the outside, wholly devoid of inner meaning and increasingly defined in racial rather than religious terms, itself became the sum and substance of Jewishness.

Being Jewish meant being different; and the more desperately the child strove to be what he was not, the more desperate the confusion. The struggle to escape a self-image riddled with anti-Jewish stereotypes required an enormous capacity for repression and denial, and it may well be that burying this embarrassing ancestor, the shabby old Jew from Semlin, and everything he stood for, in the deepest, most inaccessible layers of the unconscious was part of Herzl's earliest efforts to cope with these conflicts.

Compulsory school attendance started at age six, but Jeanette decided to hire a private tutor for the child a year ahead of time so as to give him a head start over the competition.

Whatever her motives, the idea was sound. Uncommonly bright but pampered, isolated, and overprotected, the five-year-old seems to have been more than ready for solid brain food. Many years later, Dr. Alfred Iricz, the young law student chosen to initiate the already bilingual Theodor along with his older sister into the arcane mysteries of reading, writing, and conversational French, reminisced about his pupils:

> Within a very short time both children made great strides in their studies. In less than two weeks they learned to read and write, and after a month they passed with flying colors an examination administered to them by their parents. Especially Theodor absorbed things very easily and excelled with his quick power of perception. Only a few weeks after he started to study he composed a little speech in which he expressed happy new year wishes to his parents in German as well as in French. . . . I taught the children only one hour every day in order not to overburden them with studies. They spent much more time walking. When Theodor strolled in the street, strangers, and especially young women, would admire his charm and try to engage him in conversation. [Reuben Brainin, *Chay Herzl*, New York, 1919. Quoted in Patai, "Herzl's School Years," *Herzl Yearbook*, Vol. III, pp. 53–54]

Dr. Iricz, by that time a distinguished lawyer, recorded these impressions some years after Herzl's death. But even allowing for posthumous

reverence, the account sounds convincing enough in the light of everything known about his erstwhile pupil.

In the fall of 1866, the splendid isolation came to an end. Herzl
entered the Pest Jewish High Elementary School—Pesti Izraelita Föe-
lemi Iskola—a grade school despite its pretentiously oxymoronic name,
which it justified by conferring titles such as headmaster and head
teacher upon its staff and dividing the school year into "semesters."
In a curious way, the school owed its existence to the 1848 Hungarian
rebellion against the Austrians: over half the fine—1,200,000 forints
out of a 2 million total—levied by the imperial government upon
Hungary's Jews as punishment for their pro-rebel sympathies and activities was returned to the Jewish community in 1850, on condition
that the money be used to establish a community-controlled school
system. By the end of the 1850s this system, of which Herzl's school
was a part, had grown into a nationwide network of over three hundred
schools which, because of their largely justified reputation for excel-
lence, became the prime choice of even the most assimilated segments
of the Jewish bourgeoisie.

Herzl's own references to this institution are playfully obfuscating.
In a brief autobiographical sketch first published in the London *Jewish
Chronicle* of January 14, 1898, he wrote: "I cannot deny that I went
to school. At first I was sent to a Jewish elementary school, where I
enjoyed a certain standing because my father was a wealthy merchant.
My earliest memory of this school was the caning I received for not
remembering the particulars of the Exodus of the Jews from Egypt.
Nowadays many a schoolmaster would like to cane me for remembering that Exodus rather too well."

The tone is still that of the Viennese playwright straining for wit
and whimsy, given to twisting plain facts into more dramatic shapes.
For one thing, the "wealthy merchant" father happened to be far from
exceptional; many of his classmates came from similarly affluent
homes, so that only scholastic achievements or personality traits could
have earned him whatever privileged status he may have enjoyed. But
if such was indeed the case, his getting caned for not remembering
details of the Exodus would seem all the more implausible; and in
fact, Joseph Patai, who himself taught in the Budapest Jewish schools,
flatly states that "the teachers in his [Herzl's] school did not administer
physical punishment" (Patai, "Herzl's School Years." In *Herzl Yearbook*, Vol. III, p. 55). To his biographer Reuben Brainin Herzl gave
a somewhat different account of the incident, according to which he

had simply been led to believe that the teacher had made up the whole fantastic story of the flight from Egypt.

At issue, in either version, is not the tale as such but what it tells about the teller and his sense of self in the later years of his life. The adult Herzl's references to his childhood frequently bear the mark of such creative touches, most of which have become part of his legend. Yet he himself did not invent that legend; he merely succumbed to it, and its spell had a way of reshaping the memories of a distant past that at best tend to be a mixture of fact and fantasy.

Thus, the elementary school he attended from 1866 to 1869 seems to have been both much more Jewish and much more Hungarian in its orientation than he later chose to recall. The headmaster, Solomon Kohn, was himself a Hebrew scholar who enthusiastically endorsed and supported the publication of two new Hebrew journals—*Hatse-firah* (*Epoch*) and *Havatselet* (*Lily*) launched in Jerusalem. The curriculum included biblical Hebrew as well as "religious studies," in both of which Herzl consistently received above-average marks. And while it may be taken for granted that neither the subject matter nor the customary methods of instruction were likely to provide much by way of inspiration, four years of even routine exposure to Jewish subjects must have left their mark; the young Herzl could not possibly have been as unfamiliar with the exploits of his spiritual ancestors as he later claimed.

Judging from the report cards that have been preserved, Herzl was a model pupil in elementary school, though according to his teachers this did not prevent his mother from frequently dropping in to check on his progress. He received top grades in the four major subjects, i.e., Hungarian, German, science, and arithmetic. His efforts in drawing and singing were considered "very good," and only in penmanship and Hebrew did he and his mother have to content themselves with a mere "good." His "moral conduct" was judged exemplary.

The historic significance of the 1867 Compromise, which gave Hungary a measure of administrative independence and finally codified the full legal emancipation of Hungary's Jews, was probably lost on the seven-year-old; but a more spectacular event, the opening of the Suez Canal in 1869, seems to have fired his imagination and provided him with his first hero image in the person of Ferdinand de Lesseps. The feat supposedly inspired him to search his atlas for another spot offering a similar chance for glory, and in his 1898 autobiographical sketch he actually mentions having hit on the idea of digging a canal across the Isthmus of Panama. "At that time," he wrote, "de Lesseps was the hero of the day."

He was also a more personal idol to the nine-year-old. The opening of the Suez Canal, hailed as a victory of technology over nature, vindicated—albeit briefly—the peculiar genius of the man who built it. And it was this aspect of the drama, the triumph of one man's will in the face of all the odds against him, that stirred something in the young hero worshipper. Lesseps was a practical visionary, an idealistic wheeler-dealer who dreamed big dreams and went about realizing them with single-minded determination, though in his case not overly constrained by moral scruples. In him, the dreamer and the schemer coexisted in an uneasy alliance (he died convicted, paroled, and destitute in 1894, at the age of eighty-nine). And in his own later career Herzl came to display a not too dissimilar blend of quixotic idealism and relentless drive, although in money matters not even his enemies could ever accuse him of conduct less than scrupulous.

TWO

*T*he school system run by the Jewish community did not extend beyond primary education, and after completing his four years of elementary school, Herzl in the fall of 1870 enrolled in a six-year technical high school rather than the academically and socially far more prestigious Gymnasium, whose eight-year classical curriculum was a prerequisite for admission to the university. Even making allowances for his Panama plans and his infatuation with Lesseps, this was still a rather odd choice for a child of the Jewish bourgeoisie.

The Municipal High Secondary Modern School—the Pest Városi Förealtonada—was the only institution in town with a heavy emphasis on science and mathematics. Enrollment had skyrocketed ever since it opened in 1855, at the very start of the industrial era; the squat, dismal building, a mere five minutes' walk from the Herzl apartment, was badly overcrowded by the time Herzl first set foot in it, and temporary substitutes far outnumbered the small teaching staff struggling to cope with huge classes and inadequate facilities.

The prevailing patriotic fervor also demanded some drastic readjustments on his part. Even the Jewish schools had been increasingly Magyarized following the transfer of administrative authority over public education from Vienna to Budapest in 1860; by the time Herzl entered first grade, Hungarian was already the exclusive language of instruction, a move that reflected the broader trends within the community and was being vigorously pushed by the influential Jewish Magyar Society (Izraelita Magyar Egylet) in close cooperation with the government. But the technical high school fostered a much more militant brand of Magyar racism. The technical trades and applied sciences for which it prepared its graduates were for the most part still closed to Jews, who therefore constituted only a small fraction of the student body. And while Herzl could hardly have been unaware of anti-Semitism—an inexhaustible topic of conversation in his parents' circles, if nothing else—he now for the first time had to confront it as a personal challenge. In the autobiographical sketch he refers to this initiation with mere casual irony:

"But I soon lost my former love for logarithms and trigonometry, because a distinctly anti-Semitic trend prevailed at the technical high school. One of our teachers explained the meaning of the word "heathen" as referring to idolators, Mohammedans, and Jews. After that peculiar definition I was fed up with this school and wanted to transfer to a classical Gymnasium."

The encounter with anti-Semitism—and with real-life anti-Semites —may well have been traumatic but hardly accounts for Herzl's disenchantment with logarithms and trigonometry. In any case, what he lost was not his "former love" but merely a few illusions. The would-be canal builder turned out to have trouble with basic math, he was hopeless in drawing and sculpting, and he had no taste for physics. The report cards track the uneasy compromise between reality and wishful thinking. After a near-disastrous start, his grades began to pick up somewhat, but he remained a mediocre student and seldom attained higher than passing grades even in subjects more congenial than geometric drawing (in which he failed on more than one occasion). And if his teachers' anti-Jewish bias contributed to the fiasco, what explains the mere passing grade in religion, taught by a rabbi?

Stubborn even in childhood, reluctant ever to acknowledge defeat, he for three more years floundered among the technocrats before letting himself realize that he was not cut out to be one of them. By that time, he was outgrowing not only his childish self-delusions but his childhood altogether; and with the onset of adolescence, his interests began to shift in the direction of his true potential, literature rather than logarithms. He was nothing if not verbal—immensely articulate, already fluent in three languages, an avid reader as well as perpetrator of high-minded poetry. By 1871, he had given up on the Isthmus of Panama, discarded the fast-fading Lesseps along with other childhood mementoes, and replaced him with a new and radically different ego ideal: the arch-Junker Count Otto von Bismarck, founder of the German Reich and spirit of Prussia incarnate.

The choice was not quite as outlandish as it may seem in retrospect. Bismarck's Machiavellian genius dominated European politics throughout the second half of the nineteenth century. In 1866, he tricked Austria into a war that lasted just long enough to demonstrate the overwhelming superiority of Prussian arms, thereby removing the Habsburgs from any further consideration in the imperial power game. In August 1870, he was not above provoking a French attack by means of outright forgery. Six weeks later, the French Army surrendered at Sedan, and the last obstacle to German unification—in effect, Prussian rule over the rest of the country—had been cleared. In a dramatic ritual, staged by Bismarck and performed on January 18, 1871, in the Hall of Mirrors at Versailles, the Hohenzollern King Wilhelm I of Prussia was crowned Emperor of the newly united German Reich.

Except for the apprehensions of a few perceptive observers, the German victory and the founding of the Reich were greeted with universal enthusiasm not only within the boundaries of the new empire but also among sizable groups in Central Europe who, for one reason or another, regarded Germany as their spiritual homeland, most notably the Jewish bourgeoisie of Austria-Hungary. They may not have been fully aware of the enormous gap that already separated Bismarck's Reich—and Bismarck himself—from the land of *Dichter und Denker* and the humanism of the German enlightenment, but whether such awareness would have made much of a difference seems highly doubtful. They mistook the new Reich for the New Jerusalem and hailed its wily founder with all the passion and reverence due a modern Messiah.

This makes it easier to understand how an eleven-year-old youngster of Herzl's background would have been swept up in this tidal wave of Teutonic mush. Remarkable only is the length to which he carried the identification with his new idol and his tribe, one particularly telling example being an ode apparently inspired by this idolatry. Its title, "To Canossa We Won't Go"—referring to the humiliation inflicted upon the German Emperor Henry IV at Canossa in 1077 by Pope Gregory VII—was the slogan Bismarck adopted in the so-called *Kulturkampf*, the confrontation between Protestant power and the Catholic Church immediately following Germany's unification; the final two stanzas convey the flavor:

Es ist aus langer Nacht
Durch Luther's gewaltige Kraft
Der deutsche Geist erwacht.

Und der Freiheit goldnes Licht
Bestrahlt der Erwachenden Angesicht
Nach Canossa gehn wir nicht.

[Out of a long-lasting night
The force of Luther's might
Has awakened the German spirit.

And freedom's golden light
Illumines the faces come to life
To Canossa We Won't Go.]

Rather weird sentiments, coming from a little boy in Budapest getting ready for his bar mitzvah, but by no means out of character.

Though he remained formally enrolled at the technical high school, Herzl attended no classes during the 1872–73 school year. Instead, he studied at home, probably with the aid of a tutor. The unorthodox arrangement may have been intended as a temporary compromise, allowing him to avoid the problems that had plagued him in the classroom; he was, in fact, able to pass the requisite final examinations with grades that showed marked improvement over his earlier ones.

It was also the year in which he prepared for his bar mitzvah, the traditional rite de passage by which a Jewish male, upon reaching the age of thirteen, assumes the full duties and obligations incumbent upon him under Mosaic law. According to the invitations sent out to relatives and friends, the "confirmation" was scheduled to take place on May 3, 1873, at 11 a.m. No record of it has been found in the archives of the Dohany Street congregation, of which his father was a prominent member, nor did he himself ever allude to the ceremony.

It was, in any case, not a propitious time for festivities. To begin with, the severe cholera epidemic which had been raging in Hungary for nearly a year reached its most deadly intensity precisely in the early days of May 1873; fear of contracting the disease made most people wary of public gatherings. But less than a week later, on Friday the ninth, the Vienna stock market collapsed and Jakob Herzl lost the better part of his fortune.

To the child, it meant an end to illusions of parental omnipotence and inviolate safety. Black Friday and its aftermath may simply have obliterated the memory of the celebration six days earlier; they almost certainly robbed it of what sentimental significance may have attached to it.

It was a spectacular end to a spectacular boom—the record loss of over 700 million guilders within a period of hours, signaling the onset of a deep and stubborn depression which was to have devastating political as well as economic consequences for the country as a whole, and for its Jews in particular. It was also entirely foreseeable, given the mounting pressure of an overheated and overexpanded economy whose productive capacity had outrun its markets, and perhaps even foreseen by a good many of Jakob Herzl's fellow speculators and entrepreneurs who, though ignorant of the as yet to be formulated theories of cyclic depressions, must have known in their more sane and sober moments that bust follows boom as night does day.

In the Budapest of the late sixties and early seventies, however, it was easy to lose sight of such elementary wisdom. The uneven pace of capitalist development had opened up wide gaps and fissures in the structural foundations of the Dual Monarchy. But while segments of the Austrian economy as a whole were falling behind and state finances struggled with huge budget deficits every year since 1848, Hungary remained an enclave of conspicuous prosperity, and the explosive vitality of her capital cities Buda and Pest—formally joined in 1872— made even hard-nosed realists believe in miracles.

In Budapest the 1860s, for all their manifest problems, were years of free-spending entrepreneurial optimism and faith in everlasting progress translated into a wild scramble for fun and profit. Ornate monumentalism—of which the Dohany Street Synagogue was but one example—transformed the face of the city; gaslight was introduced in 1856, but sanitary conditions remained abysmally poor, and wild speculation flourished along with even wilder corruption. Baron Prottmann, Pest's police chief from 1853 to 1865, justified his hands-off attitude toward prostitution and crime by the not unfounded belief that "if people are having fun, they won't give a damn about politics" (Bristow, p. 67). His successor, Alexis von Thaiss, who held the post until 1885, went one step further: he married the notorious Fanny Reich, a Jewish ex-prostitute with a heart of diamonds and a passel of criminal relatives, most of whom found uncommonly gainful employment in her husband's police department. The city also became an important link in the international white-slave trade, which had its local headquarters at the Café Farber.

An ideal time and place for speculators, crooks, and other enterprising spirits, but while their role in the ensuing debacle may have been blown out of proportion, the corruption uncovered in its wake proved even more extensive than had been suspected; it compromised three ministers, along with the director-general of the new Galician Railway, as well as several prominent politicians and parliamentarians. By the end of the year, eight banks, two insurance companies, one railroad, and twenty-seven industrial enterprises had gone bankrupt, and few were the family fortunes that had not at least been seriously affected. But as in most such man-made disasters, the real losers were not those who lost a fortune but those who had none to begin with and who merely lost their job, their pension, or their shop—the petite bourgeoisie and equally petite aristocracy, small tradesmen, and the recently urbanized peasants-turned-proletarians. They were the ones left out in the cold, bleeding, baffled, and above all seething with rage and resentment, seeking revenge against those whom they blamed for their misery.

In that sense, the crash of 1873 marked the end of an era. Liberalism, which had dominated Austrian politics up to that point, received a blow from which it never recovered; its economic program had proved a failure, and the personal integrity of many of its leaders had been severely compromised. And quite a few of them happened to be Jews.

The virulence of anti-Semitism relates in only the most tenuous fashion to objective phenomena; it can survive even the total absence of Jews. But the crash of 1873 and the depression that followed mark the debut of populist anti-Semitism as an organized force in national politics. To be sure, the medieval lynch-mob mentality had not faded in the age of reason; the demagogues who denounced the "stock-exchange Jews" for poisoning the economy, feeding on Christian misery, and plotting to rule the world appealed to the same primitive instincts that had triggered pogroms through the ages, and all too often to the same effect. But on the face of it, at least, the manifest content of the new accusations against the Jews seemed far more plausible and realistic than the ancient superstitions. Jews had, in fact, played a crucial role in the country's economic development. They were a highly visible presence in commerce and industry, and their grip on international finance, as symbolized by the many-mansioned House of Rothschild, was incontrovertibly real.

At some time during the building boom, Jacob Herzl had invested a substantial part of his fortune in timber. Unlike his son, he was not a gambler by instinct, and he had already reached a point where he could seriously contemplate retirement, but the lure of one last great financial coup apparently overcame his natural caution. When the dust settled after Black Friday, he—along with countless others—found himself ruined, as his son later put it.

Although ruin may seem a somewhat melodramatic hyperbole—it does not seem to have affected the family's standard of living in any significant way—Jacob Herzl no doubt lost a great deal of money. Fortunately he was only thirty-eight, still young enough for a comeback, but he never again attained the degree of affluence he had enjoyed before the crash. His son, for his part, acquired a lifelong contempt for *Boersenjuden*—stock-exchange Jews—that probably owed its venom as much to the anti-Semitic stereotypes of popular German fiction—the best-selling novels of Gustav Freytag, Wilhelm Raabe, Theodor Fontane, among others—as it did to his father's misfortunes. In any event, the idolized father himself remained beyond censure, the blameless victim of unscrupulous speculators.

In the fall of 1873, Herzl returned to the technical high school as a regular student; the decidedly mediocre marks he collected in the course of the next year and the unusually high number of absences (a total of sixty-seven) point to a certain degree of reluctance, if not outright resistance, on his part. Tensions at home may have added to his troubles. As in any proper bourgeois home, money was never discussed in the presence of children; but with the father gone much of the time trying to recoup his losses and the mother grimly striving to keep up appearances, Herzl must have had Dickensian nightmares of going to work in a blacking factory.

While money was taboo but boring, sex, though equally taboo, became increasingly fascinating and a great deal more troubling as the hormonal surges of puberty began to assert themselves. In his relations with his parents, the teenager remained a child, but a child now burdened with shameful secrets and a sense of guilt, strapped by his mother's adulation into a harness that provided firm support and at the same time stunted his emotional growth.

The immediate effect was a striking gap between emotional infantilism and intellectual precocity. Intellectually, the thirteen-year-old was way ahead of himself, even by the standards of his day. Always a voracious reader, he now began to devour poetry as well as prose, his favorites being Lenau and Heine, an intriguing combination of literary lodestars that left distinct traces in his own later writings. Lenau (Nikolas Franz Niembsch von Strehlenau, 1802–50) was a German-Hungarian poet whose inner demons inspired effusions of lugubrious fantasy and, after a brief, frustrating interlude in America, eventually drove him insane. The appeal of his tortured romanticism to a youngster in the throes of adolescent *Weltschmerz* is understandable, though in Herzl's case it may also have tapped a deeper vein of melancholy, which eventually proved to be a much more permanent affliction.

In contrast to Lenau—a private vice probably passed on to him by his mother—Heine was a rather public passion shared by thousands of other young readers and writers, who worshipped him for precisely the reasons that led Karl Kraus in later years to denounce the poet as a literary rapist who had "uncorseted the German language and enabled anyone to fondle its breasts." Kraus was right in his way, although stripping the German language of its whalebone pomposities struck others as an achievement rather than a crime. And Kraus was right again when he accused Heine of having popularized the feuilleton, a type of journalism more reprehensible in his view than necrophilia. The corrosive brilliance, self-irony, and muted lyricism of Heine's prose did indeed create a whole new literary genre—one, as it happened, in which Herzl himself was soon to make his mark.

His emotional development, on the other hand, proceeded at a far slower pace, impeded by rigid defenses and suspiciously devoid of dramatic turbulence. He fell in love with a girl named Madeleine Kurz, who died in early adolescence. Although by his own admission he never so much as exchanged a word with her, Herzl in his mature years repeatedly, and in dead earnest, referred to this teenage infatuation as the one and only true love of his life—a confession of whose pathetic implications he seems to have remained characteristically unaware.

It was during this developmentally critical period that he later claimed to have had a dream whose manifest content obviates the need for interpretation.

One night I had a wonderful dream: King Messiah came and he was old and glorious. He lifted me in his arms, and he soared with me on the wings of the wind. On one of the clouds, full of splendor, we met the figure of Moses (his appearance was like that of Moses hewn in marble by Michelangelo; from my early childhood I liked to look at the photographs of that statue), and the Messiah called to Moses: "For this child I have prayed." Then he turned to me: "Go and announce to the Jews that I will soon come and perform great miracles for my people and for the whole world." I woke up and it was only a dream. I kept this dream a secret and didn't dare to tell it to anybody. [Brainin, *Hayye Herzl*, pp. 17–18. Quoted in Patai, "Herzl's School Years," *Herzl Yearbook*, Vol. III, New York, 1960]

This dream was never mentioned until late in life, when Herzl described it to his biographer Reuben Brainin. Whether it was an authentic memory or a dubious product of his imagination, the sense of being chosen, the underlying emotion as distinct from the details, may well have been accurately recalled. But regardless of what messianic dreams may or may not have lain buried in Herzl's unconscious for the first thirty-five years of his life, his early goals and ambitions were far more prosaic than the liberation of the Jews.

He wanted to be a writer.

It was an eminently conventional ambition for a young Jew of his generation in the waning days of the Habsburg Empire. In Vienna, Prague, and Budapest, the descendants of Torah scribes and Talmud sages turned to literature with much the same passion and ferocity with which their ancestors had searched the Holy Scriptures for their meanings beyond meanings. At times it seemed as though almost every young Jew in these three cities, no matter how he made his living, spent his real life either writing or wanting to write. Talent obviously differed, and genius was as rare in this as in any other age; but it was the aggregate of this communal obsession that not only shaped the consciousness of what has since become banally stereotyped as *"fin de siècle* Vienna" but in fact revolutionized science as well as literature and the arts throughout the German-speaking world.

The disproportionately prominent role played by the Jews offers some clues to this extraordinary phenomenon: social discrimination

and political impotence, the patricidal rage of a generation delivered
from bondage into affluent futility, and the retreat into extremes of
solipsism by marginal men without roots, faith, or community. Literature, as Flaubert pointed out, became the sacrament of those who
believed in nothing, an outlet for the vast energies that in times past
went into shoring up faith by reason, and it lent despair an edge of
divine creativity.

At the superficial level, the initial inspiration in Herzl's case may
not have differed significantly from that which motivated most youngsters of his day and age, but where his poetizing never rose above the
painfully puerile, his prose almost from the very beginning displays a
polish distinctly out of the ordinary. As a teenager he already wrote
with much of the flair and seemingly effortless ease that later enabled
him to function with such relentless efficiency. Innate talent alone
cannot account for his level of productivity; it took vast ambition,
energy, self-discipline, and work habits bordering on the compulsive.
But talent, a natural or unnatural aptitude for turning out smooth
prose at breakneck speed, was amply evident from the very beginning,
though it proved a dubious blessing; for while it helped to establish
Herzl's reputation as a brilliant journalist, it also allowed him to skitter
gracefully over the surface of things without ever having to venture
into uncharted depths, most particularly those of his own self. He
became a prolific writer, but neither quantity nor stylistic elegance can
quite make up for superficiality.

The year of relative freedom made the return to the grind and ambiance
of the trade school doubly painful. He felt more lost and lonely than
ever among classmates and teachers who not only failed to share his
newfound interests but would have mocked them as downright
freakish—or as typically Jewish. Aesthete among the barbarians, he
defended himself with a contemptuous arrogance that is not likely to
have enhanced his popularity, while his absences multiplied and his
marks continued their relentless downward slide.

The school reinforced not only his sense of isolation but also his
mistrust of "the vulgar herd" that was part of his heritage as a child
of the Jewish bourgeoisie, threatened both as a Jew and as a member
of the rising middle class by the sullen hostility of the lower orders.
But it also taught him to turn that mistrust born of apprehension into

a stance of aristocratic disdain, faithfully reflected in the political outlook of his later years.

Unlike most teenage poets determined to shield their secret vice
from the sneers and arrows of a cruelly prosaic world, this budding
genius even at age thirteen was already eager to be read and heard.
He had nothing to hide. He neither searched nor bared his soul, then
or ever; he merely flaunted his brilliance and wanted to be admired
for it. And in the absence of a congenial environment at school, he
resolved to create one for himself by organizing his own circle of
kindred spirits. In February 1874 he founded WIR (We), a literary
society consisting of his sister, Pauline, their cousin Wilhelm Diamant,
and a few close friends, with himself formally elected president. The
lapidary name of their short-lived venture suggests an "us against them"
mentality of which its youthful participants may have remained
unaware.

The idea itself was not wildly original; literary clubs and societies
had a long tradition in Hungary. Basically dedicated to the defense of
Hungarian culture, many of them became centers of intellectual and
political ferment throughout the nineteenth century, and in the wake
of the 1860 Compromise, school-sponsored literary societies began to
flourish among older high-school students. In fact, the only somewhat
unusual features of WIR—and probably the ones chiefly responsible
for its early demise—were the relative youth of its members and the
absence of adult supervision.

WIR provided an antidote to the indignities of the classroom and
gave Herzl his first chance to write for an audience. It also remains
one of the few well-documented episodes of his youth, thanks to the
meticulous care with which he squirreled away every scrap of paper
of any conceivable significance. The compulsive sense of order that
characterized all his dealings with the outside world was to evolve into
a highly effective defense against the persistent stirrings of inner chaos,
but it also goes a long way toward accounting for the fabled efficiency
he later displayed as an organizer and leader.

On that score alone, the evidence of WIR is intriguing. The statutes
of this high-minded organization, its "ground rules," as drawn up by
the president and adopted at the first meeting on February 22, 1874,
call for the "founding of an association dedicated to enriching our
knowledge by writing short stories or fairy tales which would enhance
our mastery of the language." The duties of the elected officers—

president, secretary, and archivist—were described in minute detail, and at the insistence of the president, all members were obliged to address each other by the formal *Sie*, the third person plural rather than the customary informal *Du*. Games of make believe, but not much different in substance from Herzl's attitude some twenty-three years later, when at the first Zionist congress in 1897 he insisted on formal attire, complete with top hat and black tie. In fact, the whole record of his stewardship at age thirteen suggests that Herzl's organizational talents, his prickly self-importance and near-fanatical sense of propriety had deep roots in his early childhood; the abiding horror of rebellion, disorder, and what he regarded as moral laxness reflected in his conduct as well as in his work were an integral part of his being.

Along with firm guidance and most of the requisite enthusiasm, however, the president also supplied the bulk of the contributions that were read at the meetings—most, like those of the other members, written in German, but with a substantial number in at least equally elegant Hungarian. The sheer volume of work inspired by this captive audience is awesome, even if some of the compositions—notably the Hungarian ones—were probably written for school and thus served a double purpose. Even more impressive, however, is the intellectual precocity and sure sense of style that mark many of these youthful efforts, ranging from lyrical and epic poetry to legends, fairy tales, short stories, and essays. The poetry never rises above the normal level of banal juvenilia, but the prose is remarkably self-assured and clearly anticipates the concision, narrative drive, and tight organization characteristic of Herzl's mature writings.

Not surprisingly, it also contains early hints of the self-righteous pomposity, priggishness, and sententious moralizing that crop up in his later work and express the rigid conservatism of his background and outlook. An example is the boy president's detailed critique of an essay on Greek mythology submitted by one of WIR's younger members: "Greek mythology, and its faithful imitation, the Roman, are poetic; we find in them the most enchanting ideals of the beautiful and the good, of the ugly and the evil; we see in them the limitless fantasy of the happy peoples of antiquity; but a moral tendency . . . cannot be found in them. . . . I cannot imagine that the honorable author has not heard of those adventures which—as an outcome of anthropomorphism—the Greeks attributed to their gods. Out of these radiates, not a moral tendency, but—licentious lascivity" (quoted in Patai, pp. 64–65). And in the same vein he goes on to pontificate that "no people can be young and at the same time cultured. A people can attain its culture only after it has struggled for its existence for hundreds of years; but by the time it reaches a high degree of culture it has already lost its youth" (ibid., p. 65).

Heroes and conquerors, from the ancient Romans to Napoleon, his special idol, fire the young teenager's imagination, while his rhetoric is inspired by the lofty ideals of a rising bourgeoisie touched by delusions of incipient nobility. Absent, interestingly enough, are Jewish themes of any kind; the recent bar mitzvah boy allegedly singled out in his dreams by Moses and the Messiah could write with passion and intelligence about Luther and Savonarola but remained eloquently silent about the idols of his own tribe.

WIR folded after a mere eight meetings—the last one held on April 26, 1874—presumably due to parental pressures, because, like Herzl himself, many of the members had begun to neglect their schoolwork. But for him it had served its purpose, helped him discover where his talents lay and spurred him on to a furious productivity that continued unabated throughout the remaining years of his adolescence and for the rest of his life.

THREE

*I*n the fall of 1874, Herzl began his fifth year at the Realschule with all the enthusiasm of an escaped prisoner being returned to his cell. His marks at the end of the first semester reflected these feelings, and this time his parents got the message; in February 1875 they again took him out of school and hired a private tutor to prepare him for a transfer to the classical Gymnasium.

Although Herzl in his "autobiography" refers to it as the Evangelische Gymnasium, it was a thoroughly Hungarian institution founded in 1822 as the *evangéelikus fögymnásium*. The building, which still exists, was attached to the main Protestant church on Süto Street, in the central district of Pest, but Jews constituted the majority of the student body. They did not have much of a choice; in the absence of Jewish secondary schools, the only alternative would have been Catholic high schools, informed by the spirit of Pope Pius IX, declared infallible in 1870, who in his *Syllabus of Errors* had condemned "progress, liberalism, and modern civilization" and denounced the very concept of tolerance for religions other than Catholicism. The spirit of Protestantism seemed understandably far more congenial by comparison, the result being a rare example of interfaith cooperation that redounded to their mutual benefit: the school educated the children of the Jewish middle class, and the Jewish middle class helped to support the school through generous contributions.

For a while, Herzl thrived in the new environment. He entered the Gymnasium in the fall of 1875, and the very first report card the following February documents a remarkable change. He received top grades in Latin, Greek, Hungarian, German, algebra, and religion. His marks in history, science, and psychology were good, and only his neatness, of all things, dropped to a mere "satisfactory." He had evidently put the six months of private tutoring to excellent use, but his ability in so short a time to catch up on four years of Greek and Latin—neither of them taught at the technical high school—again testifies to his extraordinary gift for languages. In any case, the entire classical curriculum, with its disdainful neglect of science and mathematics, was much more in line with his own emergent tastes and talents and put an end to the terrors of trigonometry.

Even more propitious was the change of atmosphere. "At the Evangelische Gymnasium the Jewish boys formed the majority, and therefore we did not have to complain of any anti-Semitism" was his terse way of summing up four years of social ostracism and hostility. He was sufficiently resilient to have survived this diaspora within a diaspora, but the experience left scars. While it may have steeled him for future trials, it also reinforced that defensive arrogance and snobbism for which he became notorious in his long-drawn-out adolescence.

At the Gymnasium, on the other hand, he was among his own— a group of boys drawn largely from the same layer of the Jewish upper middle class, and with teachers who, on the whole, seem to have been not only uncommonly indulgent but also competent in their respective fields and clearly impressed by their new pupil.

The attitude of his new classmates seems to have been more ambivalent. Alex Bein quotes one of them, the Budapest attorney Szécsi, as remembering

> a dark, slender youth, always fashionably dressed, forever in a good mood and ready for jokes and pranks, but mostly superior, ironic, even downright sarcastic. These qualities did not, of course, contribute to his popularity. On the other hand, he was not unpopular, either, and his gay, sprightly nihilism always made him look interesting in the eyes of his teachers and classmates. This was confirmed to me by many a colleague and teacher at the Budapest Evangelical Gymnasium, even by those who had often been the butt of Herzl's jokes, which were usually good-natured but always witty and in good taste. . . . He was almost always unprepared in class, but an uncanny quick grasp and a fabulous memory helped him, more often than not, to bluff his

way out of a tight situation. He kept his distance from Judaism
and referred to all matters religious with jocular cynicism. [P.
34]

Many other sources, including Herzl himself, convey a similar portrait of a brilliant, aggressive, but essentially solitary youngster who,
despite a show of urbane sociability, carefully kept his distance. He
had countless acquaintances and, in his final years, masses of worshipful admirers, but—with one single exception—no truly close
friend. Real intimacy both frightened and repelled him, and his often
caustic wit served as an effective deterrent to unwelcome approaches.

Nevertheless, he obviously felt comfortable at the Gymnasium,
moderately challenged by the syllabus, and relatively at ease among
classmates whom the conjunction of affluence and Jewishness struck
as neither remarkable nor reprehensible. At the same time, he was in
many ways intellectually far ahead of them and increasingly determined to live up to his self-image of the literary prodigy. One inevitable
result was that he again began to neglect his schoolwork in favor of
his private pursuits. He was never a model student, and his classmate's
observation is doubtless correct—what saved him from the ultimate
ignominy of outright failure was brash self-assurance, a quick grasp,
and a photographic memory, assets which in later life he drew upon
time and again to extricate himself from far more ominous
predicaments.

But he was deadly serious about his writing and prolific in his output,
enough of which survives to give a fair notion of its range and quality.
There are fragments of an impassioned essay on Girolamo Savonarola,
the fifteenth-century Church reformer burned at the stake for his opposition to Pope Alexander VI. Herzl saw him as one in a long line
of "martyrs to their conviction"—Peter Walde, Arnold of Brescia, Jan
Hus, Martin Luther—who rebelled against the tyranny of papal absolutism: "We can and must pay tribute to their virtues, acknowledge
their firm and unshakable loyalty and the manly courage that made
them resist a vastly superior power. For what today would be mere
daring was in those days a contemptuous defiance of death itself."

There is something decidedly odd about a young Budapest Jew's
fascination with the fanatical Florentine monk. But the subject had
topical relevance. Whatever else Herzl may have seen in that sinister
figure, the struggle between Church and state, between the Catholic
hierarchy's embittered resolve to cling to its secular prerogatives and

the imperial bureaucracy's equally stubborn determination to assert its supremacy was still an acutely sensitive issue in the Dual Monarchy, and the chance to glorify an opponent of papal power must have seemed tempting to an impassioned teenage liberal.

Just how far he carried his increasingly militant rationalism is evident from an essay on "the human mind," in which he exalts reason as having "wrested from the past all that which it concealed . . . brought land and sea under its dominion, forced the savage lightning into a harmless path and provided rational explanations for the so-called miracles performed by swindlers who cunningly exploited natural phenomena, men such as Moses, Jesus, and all the way to the Count of St. Germain" (Bein, p. 39).

There also exists a fragment of what was evidently conceived as an epistolary novel in the spirit of Goethe's *The Sorrows of Young Werther*, that nineteenth-century bible of teenage melancholia. The eerie aspect, in this instance, is its prophetic plot, the hero being a German journalist stationed in Paris whom the French climate, the futility of human existence, and the faithlessness of his beloved drive to the verge of suicide. And while these youthful efforts seldom rise above what one would expect from a gifted and literate adolescent, they demonstrate that Herzl even at this early age knew exactly what he wanted and spared no effort to get it. Given their background and the spirit of the times, most of his classmates at the Gymnasium must have dreamed of literary fame, but Herzl set out to realize this dream with the kind of single-minded concentration and willpower that were to mark all his endeavors. He wrote articles, essays, poems, stories—none up to the standard of a young Heine or Rimbaud, but they taught him the elements of his craft and helped him find a voice of his own: that detached, cool, faintly supercilious irony that was to blend so well into the dominant mode of liberal journalism in Central Europe.

The tone spills over into his private correspondence, as shown by this excerpt from a letter to his father written on June 9, 1877:

> Here, that is at home, a festive excitement is already brewing. Ominous clouds of feverish activity are gathering, and while Mamma still vacillates between red-white-black on the one hand and gray-green-blue on the other (I am talking about the colors of her eventual dress as the Matron of the Ball), Pauline absolutely and under no circumstances wants to yield to Mamma on certain nuances while brooding over the dances she already promised

and those for which she has not yet decided on a partner. Every so often the thunder-laden arguments come to a head in splut- tering verbal fireworks and lightning flashes of indignation, while I, wisely and cautiously, slink off to the side like a timid terrier, tail between my legs, so as to keep the approaching storm from discharging its shattering and tragic blows upon an innocent by- stander. . . . One would almost be tempted, as a man, to intone a hymn of praise for being in the fortunate position of the Lords of Creation, our own sex. For if they don't let us stay at home, we get into a black tuxedo, a feat which even the slowest among us can manage within about two seconds. If, on the other hand, they do permit us to stay home, as is the case with a person extraordinarily close to me, one follows the example of the old stoics and says: "Have a great time; I'll be fine." With which indubitably classical quotation I have the honor to bring this impermissibly long epistle to its blessed conclusion. [L, 1/9/87]

Remarkable about this youthful oeuvre is the almost total absence not only of the emotional surges, the soul-searching, despair, exu- berance, and confusion that normally feed and fan such adolescent creativity, but the absence of authentic firsthand emotion altogether. It is as though the very features that made this particular teenage author seem so startlingly precocious—the arch irony, the sometimes windy but often impressive erudition, the polished sentimentality in lieu of crude sentiment—had all grown out of the need for distance, from himself as well as from others, an elaborate stratagem to ignore in- admissible feelings and avoid self-confrontations. The young Herzl wrote not to express himself but to impress others.

And he went about it with characteristic tenacity and verve. Ad- dressing the editor of the *Pester Lloyd*, one of the most important German-language newspapers in Budapest, the seventeen-year-old would-be contributor displayed no undue humility:

Further to the invitation which, on the occasion of my visit the day before yesterday to your office, you were kind enough to extend to me, I take the liberty of enclosing a feuilleton essay, the same one Dr. Lasky was good enough to show you. Since, from your question about it, dear Sir, I feel justified in assuming that you did not read it, I am herewith submitting it once again. It is not as though I were dazzled by the perfection and flawlessness of this firstling from my pen. On the contrary, I see the weaknesses and faults of this essay rather clearly, but I believe that it will serve the purpose of giving you an opportunity to judge my way of writing.

And, in what was evidently a follow-up:

Dear Sir:
If your opinion concerning my abilities is unfavorable, I might as well spare you the remainder of this letter and not take up any more of your precious time. If, on the other hand, your recent amiable and encouraging words about my "talent" were more than mere kindness meant to sweeten the first bitter taste of failure for a novice, I should like to come to the point of this letter by imposing upon you once again with a request: Could you, if your busy schedule allows it, spare a quarter of an hour to give me, in brief, a few hints as to the perfection of form whose secret has obviously eluded me in my past two attempts and also—in broad outline, of course—indicate some of the topics in line with your editorial policy and likely to interest your readership. . . . I shall make every effort to write a good essay, and I hasten to add, in full confidence of my own abilities, that I hope to succeed once I know the shoals of which I must steer clear. And I shall succeed without lapsing into a slavish imitation of other authors. Like Grillparzer's lyric-pathetic hero, I insist that

> Nought I am, but be I shall,
> Fast and high is the hero's flight
> What on this earth others can do
> That, by God, I can do, too.

Please, Sir, do not read into this quote the ridiculous self-aggrandizement of an unjustifiably vain fool but rather the quiet self-confidence of a man who knows his own worth and disdains any display of false modesty. [L, May 1877]

Youthful arrogance verging on juvenile megalomania, but it seems to have worked: a few weeks later, the *Pester Lloyd* published Herzl's first contribution, though the editors chose not to disclose the identity of the author—possibly at his own request. In his "autobiography," at any rate, Herzl asserts that "when I was in the seventh grade, I wrote my first newspaper article—anonymously, of course, else I would have got punished with after-school detention." A rather doubtful explanation; his teachers were a tolerant lot, and even a few hours of detention would seem a cheap price to have paid for the heady rush of instant fame. Be that as it may, the topic Herzl chose for his public debut proved singularly appropriate: the future champion of the breed delivered himself of a disquisition on the nature of the feuilleton and on the kind of writer likely to be successful in this genre.

He also placed several book reviews in the *Pester Journal* and—again anonymously—published a short, biting sketch in the Vienna weekly *Das Leben* about demagoguery and horse trading in the Hungarian parliament, another preview of things to come; a few years later his sketches from the Palais Bourbon—the French parliament—were to make him famous as a diplomatic correspondent. In addition to this lively literary activity, Herzl also participated in the Deutsche Selbstbildungsverein, the German Society for Self-Improvement officially promoted by the Gymnasium, though what survives of his efforts amounts to only a few fragments of bad poetry and portentous literary criticism.

Given these manifold outside activities, his fast-fading interest in schoolwork and the corresponding slump in grades could hardly have been surprising. He was now entering his final year at the Gymnasium; looming a few months down the road was the dread *Matura*, the comprehensive oral and written examination on which his admission to a university, and hence his future, depended to no small extent. But despite an undistinguished report card in the fall of 1877, there is no record of his having been unduly worried by either prospect. He had supreme confidence in his ability to clear any scholastic hurdles—or sneak around them, if need be; as for his future, it was all settled as far as he was concerned.

For his loving parents, on the other hand, the end of their son's high-school days called for some hard decisions. They approved of his literary ambitions, as they approved of anything and everything he ever did. At the same time, they were realistic enough—or bourgeois enough—to see the literary life for what it was, a rather precarious way of making a living. At the very least, they wanted to make sure that their son, like any son of the enlightened Jewish middle class, would have the advantages of a good education as well as a respectable profession to fall back upon. A law degree—law and medicine being basically still the only professions open to Jews—seemed a sound hedge against the vagaries of a career in the arts, not to mention the respectability it conferred upon the possessor in this title-conscious society.

That Herzl himself shared these expectations can be inferred from a copybook he kept in his last year in high school. In the margins, along with caricatures of his teachers and classmates, he practiced his signature in numerous versions, Hungarian, German, French, always preceded or followed by the title of Dr., Dr. Phil., Dr. Iur., Doctor utriusque juris, etc. (Patai, p. 75). It seems unlikely, however, that he ever seriously considered studying in Budapest. The university was a notorious hotbed of anti-Semitism, and the faculty of law, in particular, had the reputation of an intellectual wasteland. Furthermore, by the late 1870s, cultural life in Hungary had become almost totally Magyarized, even among the new generation of Jewish intellectuals. As a German writer, Herzl would soon have been without a public; as a Hungarian writer, he would have had to settle for what crumbs of glory the Budapest intelligentsia was willing to bestow upon its local celebrities.

His sister, Pauline, may have faced similar problems, although educational opportunities were not an issue in her case. Education beyond bare literacy and a smattering of the arts was still regarded as harmful to women's prospects of preordained self-fulfillment in marriage and motherhood, and there is no evidence that the Herzl family or any of its members ever questioned this prevailing view. But Pauline, a strikingly good-looking young woman with a great deal of natural charm, was very active in amateur theatricals and is said to have entertained hopes of a professional acting career. If so, the Hungarian stage with its fervently nationalist orientation, which had largely replaced the once dominant German theaters of Budapest, offered few opportunities. Taken together, these were powerful arguments in favor of a fresh start in Vienna. Jakob Herzl's business was neither bound nor confined to Hungary, and letting the children go alone would have seemed out of the question in this close-knit family.

By the end of 1877, the Herzls were thus faced with some weighty decisions. But before they ever had a chance to make their first move, fate struck a blow that put an end to all rational planning: on February 7, 1878, their daughter Pauline died of typhus at the age of nineteen after a three-day illness.

*   *   *

Four years later, Herzl recalled the tragedy in a sketch in which, despite some of his habitual literary posturing, he was for once forced to confront authentic feelings of grief and of guilt. "In My Hometown" was written on the occasion of a brief visit to Budapest in 1882, penned in evident haste on tiny scraps of notebook paper, an obvious effort to cope with the onrush of emotions triggered by this encounter with the past; it was never published and probably never meant for publication.

After indulging in some conventional nostalgia and recalling a childhood which, in retrospect, seemed to him fraught with bittersweet though often artificial sadness, he evoked the vision of his sister's flower-bedecked coffin.

The first true great grief of my life. But I had wasted myself too much in small and imaginary suffering to feel the pain in all its searing force. I screamed something, as is customary on such occasions, I sobbed a great deal, but I edited the obituary with a clear head and an eye for oratorical effects. My pain was somewhat histrionic. I felt very sorry for myself, but mostly, I think, because I noticed that other people were feeling sorry for me. I thought of the black tie and matching gloves; the situation did not find me completely overcome. Nor did I fail to appreciate the chance to stay out of school. I also felt flattered by the attention our sad case received in the newspapers. I must have been one miserable cur. Thus while my beloved sister was already dying I still frequented the coffeehouse where, albeit with a serious mien appropriate to the occasion and with a certain studied sadness—my sister's illness was known—I played dominoes. I did not cover myself with glory.

And then came the horrible night of my sister's death. The doctor had given us hope that the crisis might yet have a favorable outcome. I sat talking with my mother and a few aunts, while my father sat at the deathbed of my sister, my beloved Pauline. Suddenly we heard loud sobbing in the sickroom, an unforgettable sound such as only the cruel blow of fate's hammer on a father's twitching heart can evoke. We knew she was dead. The aunts began the spasmodic sobbing called for on such occasions, the omission of which is rightfully regarded as indicative of a lack of feeling. My mother did not cry. Later on she cried for several years, incessantly. The capacity of a mother's tear glands is beyond belief, enough to fill an ocean. I shed a lot of tears, and then I fell asleep. I now was my parents' only child.

During the next two days I was the object of compassionate attention on my own part as well as that of everybody else. I shook a great many hands, accepted the condolences called for, but was not, on the whole, as profoundly sad as I understandably pretended to be. But to be fair, I must admit that at certain moments I did have an inkling of the magnitude of my loss. Ah, but only an inkling. And yet I was almost eighteen years old; that is a bitter reproach.

The funeral took place on a Saturday, February 10, 1878.

My father, mother and I slowly walked behind the slow-moving hearse. In it lay my dead sister, whose mouth I would never again seal with a brotherly kiss to make up after a mock quarrel. I vaguely felt how hard that was going to be, but the people by the wayside stopped to watch us, and somehow that seemed to comfort me a little as I led my father by the arm. He stumbled along, all but doubled over, and he has remained so ever since. And then we stood at the edge of the square hole, and with uncanny speed the gravediggers did their job. . . . They put my beloved only sister into the cold earth, one who had been so used to drift in comfort through a well-heated life, that sweet, young blood. Now she was to lie all alone, outside the city, in wind and storm and rain, she who never even crossed the street by herself. That was hard. Even for me. I dimly began to feel it. Why did you do that? Why did you die?

Eight days later we left town, settled in a large city which I had always been longing for. . . . There my mother at last found the tears she had so long kept back. My father and I finally succeeded in changing her sighs into sobs, her sobs into incessant crying that went on for years. What did my father do with his tears in the meantime? . . . But now that even my mother has calmed down somewhat, it is my turn. Now my tears are flowing, and I am mourning my sister, who certainly deserved to be mourned. My darling Pauline, are we never to see one another again? My last word to you was perhaps not a friendly one—who could have known that you would get sick and die? And yet despite all our squabbling we loved each other so dearly, you and

I. And you no longer hear me as I press my face into the grassy knoll over your grave and try to speak to you. Can it really all be over? Is this innocent, wise, dear heart stilled forever? We'll never meet again. March 1, 1882. Is everything finished?

A mannered essay, yet always teetering on the verge of a primal scream. Despite the labored irony and literary flourishes meant to apologize—to himself more than anyone else—for genuine heartfelt emotion, the piece evokes the pain, the guilt, and the shattering sense of loss. Brother and sister were close enough in age—barely more than a year apart—to be playmates and friends as well as rivals. Pauline attended the meetings of WIR, Herzl shared her interest in the theater, and the few fondly patronizing references to her in his early correspondence do, in fact, confirm the impression of an easy, untroubled intimacy between a younger brother strutting his male superiority and an older sister content in the role assigned her by destiny and her parents.

In contrast to the unpublished memoir, the autobiographical sketch in the *London Chronicle* devotes only one brief and characteristically ironic paragraph to the tragedy: "My only sister, a girl of eighteen, died when I was in my last year at the Gymnasium; my good mother became so devastated by grief that we moved to Vienna in 1878. During the week of mourning, Rabbi Kohn paid us a visit and asked about my plans for the future. I told him that I wanted to become a writer, whereupon the rabbi shook his head with the same disapproval with which he was later to regard Zionism. Writing, he said, was not a proper profession."

In life, Pauline had been his sister, with all the ambivalence this implies in even the happiest of families. In death, she came to represent an ideal of female innocence and purity which no live woman past the age of puberty could ever hope to live up to.

But there is no doubt that her death had dealt him a numbing blow. He is said to have visited her grave every year on the anniversary of her death, though his diaries and schedules fail to bear this out. She clearly inspired his vision of Miriam, the saintly heroine of the novel *Old New Land*, which he dedicated to her memory. He named his first daughter after her.

And barely a week past the mourning period, he and his parents picked themselves up, left Budapest and its memories behind them forever, and headed for Vienna.

FOUR

*T*he milieu into which the Herzls settled in Vienna differed hardly at all from the one they had left behind. About one-fourth of all Jews in the city originally came from Hungary, and the influx continued throughout the 1880s; Hungarian Jews accounted for nearly 50 percent of new arrivals during a decade in which the Jewish population grew from 73,000 to 118,000. What is more, the vast majority of newcomers settled in Leopoldstadt, officially referred to as the Second District, where more than half of Vienna's Jews were already living at the time.

The Herzls did likewise, renting the entire third floor of an ornately elegant building at Praterstrasse 25, a wide street that led from the Danube Canal to the Prater Stern Square, with its pretentious memorial to Admiral Tegetthoff, forgettable hero of a long-forgotten naval victory in 1866. More substantial inspiration to the budding young playwright was provided by the Carl Theater at Praterstrasse 31, just a few steps from the Herzls and second in importance only to the Burgtheater. And what may have added an even greater sense of familiarity was the new Moorish-style synagogue on Temple Street around the corner, designed by the same Ludwig Foerster who had been responsible for the turreted edifice near their Budapest home.

Leopoldstadt, the site of Vienna's ghetto since 1622, had remained a largely Jewish enclave ever since. In a city increasingly segregated according to class, status, and income, Jews came to Leopoldstadt because they were Jewish; the rich, the poor, and the in between lived side by side in a now unofficial ghetto whose housing stock ranged from somber ostentation to decrepit squalor. In time, the steadily expanding population spilled over into the adjacent districts of Alsergrund and the Inner City, where Jewish merchants and professionals formed genteel ghettos of their own that reflected the essential failure of their assimilation. Leopoldstadt itself, however, retained not only its ethnic character but also much of its economic diversity; fully one quarter of those deemed sufficiently well off to pay the *Gemeindesteuer*, i.e., the Jewish community tax, continued to live in the district.

Herzl had little time to adjust to his new environment. Three months after his arrival he had to return to Budapest for the *Matura*, the grand finale of his undistinguished high-school career. This academic variant of the third degree, which quite literally scared any number of students to death, consisted of a comprehensive oral and written examination covering all subjects to which they had been exposed during the preceding eight years of indoctrination. The seven-day ordeal—five for the written part, two for the orals—took place at the beginning of June. Thanks to his superb memory, Herzl managed to pass, albeit far from brilliantly. He did get two top grades, in German and in religion. In German he undoubtedly deserved it; in religion he either had an unusually indulgent examiner or else his knowledge of Judaism was more extensive, after all, than he cared to acknowledge. His grasp of Hungarian, Latin, philosophy, and natural history was judged adequate, and he received passing grades in Greek, math, history, and geography.

Yet all that really mattered was that he had scraped through and thus qualified for admission to the university.

Since Herzl must have spent the rest of the month in Budapest waiting for the official graduation on July 1, it would be interesting to know if he took note of a widely publicized speech delivered on June 24 in the Hungarian Diet, which in some rather uncanny ways anticipated many of the ideas he himself was to formulate some eighteen years later. Győző Istóczy, founding father of Hungarian anti-Semitism and the first deputy to be elected on a purely anti-Semitic platform, proposed what he called an original solution to the Jewish problem—"none other than the restoration of the ancient Jewish state" (Handler, p. 113). The Turkish Empire, he declared, was teetering on the brink of disaster. The Jews—whom, by way of a backhanded compliment, he credited with great intelligence and initiative—could prop up Turkey's finances, revitalize the entire Middle East, and live as free people in a state of their own rather than as parasites in a Christian Europe. According to him, plans for such a scheme already existed but were being sabotaged by the cosmopolitan Jewish financiers bent on world domination. "I appeal not to these conniving parasites, but to the Jewish patriots who have preserved their ancient traditions and love of their ancestral home, to grasp the opportunity for regaining their state" (Handler, p. 114).

Yet even had Herzl been aware of the speech, it is unlikely that he would have recognized a kindred spirit and future ally.

> Herzl [writes Alex Bein] never talked about the impression that Vienna had made on him; but numerous later writings give evidence of the love with which he took to the new city and of his lifelong ties to it, to its ways of life, and above all to its literary style. This is where his love for art and music received their daily stimulus from the noble baroque architecture rooted in a sense of beauty and responsibility, and from the Viennese people known for their playfulness, their love of music, vivacious, inclined to jest and irony yet also thoughtful and brooding, eschewing harsh judgment and preferring instead serene harmony or even the hesitant indecision that characterized the policies of its ruling house. This city tempered young Herzl's tendency toward sharp, pointed criticism and softened his style, which soon acquired that combination of smooth irony and lucid expression that later distinguished his newspaper work. [Pp. 42–43]

That Herzl eagerly plunged into the bracing turmoil of the imperial capital and emerged reborn, an authentic lifelong Viennese, has long been part of the legend. One may assume that a bright eighteen-year-old, fresh out of high school and suddenly transplanted from Budapest to Vienna, would in fact be excited by the opportunities, the challenges, and the temptations of the metropolis. Budapest was no village, by any means; but aside from the persistently provincial atmosphere that accounted for much of its charm, the newly consecrated "second capital" was second after Vienna not only in size but in every other respect as well, and exceedingly self-conscious about it. The cosmopolitan glitter of the imperial capital represented a different world altogether, and chances are that the ambitious young man from Budapest was made keenly aware not only of its thrills but also of the threat it posed to the anonymous outsider bent on making a name for himself.

But this remains conjecture. We simply don't know how Herzl felt about Vienna, not when he first settled there in the summer of 1878, and not in later years, either. He never explicitly made his feelings known about the city or his place in it. To outsiders, he became the quintessential Viennese, a view by no means incompatible with his remaining a perennial outsider himself.

The fiction of young Herzl as an exile home at last seems questionable on many grounds, not least because it is based on a highly romanticized notion of Vienna in the 1880s. True, the glitz and the glory—grandiose displays of imperial splendor, the sweeping vistas of the new Ringstrasse, the frenzied vitality of Viennese culture—were abundantly evident. Music and art, theaters, cafés, newspapers, and sex flourished in promiscuous profusion and provided the upper and middle classes with the varieties of satisfaction that passed for the good life. It also enabled them—at a high price to themselves and the country—to ignore the problems lurking just beneath the surface of this fragile fantasy, piously enshrined in nostalgia ever since.

In crushing the 1848 revolution, Metternich's *Realpolitik* triumphed one last time. Its aftermath opened up a gap between reality and fantasy that undermined the monarchy and ultimately led to its collapse. But for some eighty years, fantasy prevailed, in Vienna more than anywhere else—a boon to the arts, a disaster in government and politics.

The two major consequences of the 1848 debacle were the progressive radicalization of the nationalist movements and the political castration of the bourgeoisie. Where earlier in the century the irredentist movements had fought to change the structure of the multinational state, they now dedicated themselves to its outright destruction. At the same time, the bourgeoisie suffered a defeat from which it never recovered. It lost the support of the students and intellectuals, who had provided the leadership in the 1848 uprisings and now turned to nationalism as a more satisfactory outlet for their youthful passions, and it abandoned all further attempts to translate economic power into radical politics. Instead, the broad range of mutual and common interests promoted a partnership with the establishment which survived liberal as well as conservative governments, despite often violent disagreements as to means, if not ends. The bourgeoisie never again challenged the fundamentals of imperial rule or the divinely ordained social order that sustained it.

On the contrary. In a deliberate retreat from reality, a bourgeoisie infatuated with the aristocracy, its ways and its values, began to develop acute delusions of glory and expended enormous energy and imagination—not to mention money—on efforts to transcend or at least camouflage their prosaic origins. One result, certainly the most conspicuous and the most enduring, was the architecture of the period, the proliferation of pretentious palaces and town houses built by the untitled rich as monuments to fantasy and self-delusion. Equally symptomatic was the profligate generosity with which the Habsburg establishment indulged this fantasy by conferring minor titles of nobility upon large numbers of citizens whose sole merit consisted of being wealthy and well connected. The Jewish bourgeoisie worked even harder at these games, but the reality they had to contend with was also harder to ignore than that of their Gentile confrères.

The same relative freedom—the removal of residence and trade restrictions—that had spurred the rapid growth of an urban Jewish middle class also cleared the way for the Jewish underclass, the destitute masses from the Eastern part of the empire, to head for the fabled fleshpots of the imperial capital. Their life in the small towns and villages of Galicia, Hungary, Moravia, and Bohemia had been difficult in the past; with the rise of militant nationalism, which made few distinctions between German Germans and German-speaking Jews, it became impossible. Half driven, half lured—driven by misery, prosecution, and boycott, lured by the promise of prosperity and the protective anonymity of an urban environment—they abandoned the countryside in ever-increasing numbers, so that well before the end of the century most Jewish communities in the rural areas had ceased to exist as such.

The provincial capitals and industrial centers of the monarchy absorbed part of this mass migration, but it was Vienna, above all, that loomed as by far the most alluring magnet; its Jewish population grew from 6,000 in 1859 to 40,000 in 1870, a rise from 1.3 to 6.1 percent of the total population. And as the influx into the capital continued and the number of Jews nearly doubled in every successive decade—73,000 in 1880, 119,000 in 1890—a sharp split developed within the Jewish community between the new arrivals and their more assimilated precursors. It was a clash of cultures—the *Ostjuden* on the one hand, who in appearance, habits, and language still clung to the traditions of the Eastern *shtetl*, and, on the other, the already Westernized Jews who, in their eagerness to assimilate the attitudes as well as the looks and manners of their Teutonic fellow citizens, had inevitably ingested a hefty portion of their anti-Jewish prejudices as well.

The resultant self-hatred, conscious or unconscious, rendered them exquisitely sensitive to what they perceived as unsavory reminders of their own not all too distant origins, and tensions were further exacerbated by the rise of racial anti-Semitism, which Western Jews were at least initially inclined to blame on the outlandish garb, grating jargon, and blatantly un-German behavior of their Eastern co-religionists. Thus, Heinrich Friedjung, a liberal Jewish historian and editor of the pointedly named *Deutsche Wochenschrift* (*German Weekly*), was constantly denouncing "this tenacious and alien part of the population." Herzl himself, in his early Vienna years, shared the common bias and probably felt much the same embarrassment at the sight of a caftan and skullcap that Arthur Schnitzler later described so eloquently in his autobiography. Even in his youthful writings, however, Herzl blamed not the "aliens" but the ghetto; as he saw it, the way to overcome its baneful heritage, now that the walls had finally come down, was total integration, including most particularly intermarriage by way of improving the deplorable "typically Jewish" physiognomy that had evolved through centuries of inbreeding. "Crossing the Occidental races with the so-called Oriental ones on the basis of a common state religion—that is the desirable, the great solution," he wrote in 1882, commenting on a novel by Wilhelm Jensen (YD, p. 610). The idea, however naïve, was no more than the assimilationist dream carried to its logical conclusion, and he clung to it up to the very eve of his conversion to Zionism.

The aspiring young writer and uninspired law student who entered the University of Vienna in the fall of 1878 was every bit as estranged from reality as any native member of his class, and student life would most likely have widened the gap even if he had been more than marginally interested in his studies instead of preparing for a profession which he never seriously intended to practice. For the university itself typified, more faithfully perhaps than any other institution, the broad retreat from reason and reality that followed the 1848 disaster.

And for good reason. The insurrection that shook the empire, sent Metternich into exile, and forced the abdication of the reigning Emperor in favor of his nephew Franz Joseph was spawned and sparked at the university, a bastion of subversive thought at a time when all thought was deemed subversive. Students and faculty, united in their demand for basic democratic rights and as yet remarkably free of racial, national, and class prejudices—among their top leaders were three Hungarian-born Jews and a liberal Catholic priest—provided the backbone and shock troops of the revolution. True to their ideals, they briefly achieved the kind of fraternal solidarity between intellectuals and workers that was not to be seen again until the Russian Revolution and, in our own day, in the Poland of the early 1980s. They routed the establishment, took over the capital, inflicted a humiliating military defeat on the troops of the regular army, and, for a few heady summer months in 1848, seemed close to realizing their goal of transforming the absolutist regime into a democratic multinational federation.

But unlike the French revolutionaries whom they idolized, they failed to grasp the difference between insurrection and the exercise of power, allowing the forces of reaction ample time to regroup and organize a counterblow. It came at the end of the summer. Carried out with all the brutal efficiency of which even the most incompetent of armies is capable in combat with civilians, it ended in devastating destruction and in a bloodbath that cost hundreds of lives—exact figures were never published—including most of the student leaders.

Understandably enough, the imperial establishment, once restored to absolute power, was determined to snuff out any whiff of academic subversion, even if it meant snuffing out higher learning altogether, a prospect the military, for one, contemplated with cheerful equanimity. For a decade, teaching took place in improvised classrooms scattered throughout the city, and it was not until the liberals took firm hold in Vienna that a new, neo-Renaissance-style university—completed during Herzl's student years—was built as part of the official Ringstrasse monumentalism.

By then, however, the democratic ferment that had corrupted the student body of the 1840s was as safely dead and gone as most of the students themselves. Those who took their place tended instead to regard themselves as a pseudo-aristocratic elite, entitled by divine right to all the privileges that went with their status as *Studenten*. The arrogance of these budding bureaucrats expressed itself in a pervasive contempt for the plebeian masses as well as for liberals, liberal ideas, and anything considered "un-German." One of the most tragic consequences of the events of '48, in fact, was the perversion of academic freedom and the emergence of the university as a hotbed of reaction, a development that had its exact parallel in Germany; in striking contrast to most countries the world over, Austrian and German students up to the end of World War II formed the vanguard of radical right-wing extremism.

Inevitably, this synthetic aristocracy developed the rites and rituals that fed into their primitive fantasies, from the obligatory brawling, boozing, and whoring to the dueling fraternities whose members carved up each other's faces by way of demonstrating courage and masculinity. There were countercurrents, of course—liberals, even socialists, a large contingent of students genuinely interested in their studies and an even larger one concerned only with fun and games. But by the time Herzl arrived on the scene, the dominant trend among the approximately 5,000 students was a strident, xenophobic pan-German nationalism with increasingly anti-Semitic overtones, militantly opposed not only to liberalism but to the very concept of a multinational state. The ideals of '48 had been supplanted by the worship of Wotan, Wagner, and Kaiser Wilhelm II; the new breed of student radicals sought nothing less than union with Bismarck's newly founded German Reich. It was a goal that brought them into sharp conflict with the ruling powers and in effect forced all their opponents, from left to right, to rally to the defense of the Habsburg establishment. Their brief but bloody triumph came some sixty years later with the *Anschluss* of 1938.

There is no reason to assume that the freshman law student was unduly disturbed by these manifestations of political extremism. His own views, a compromise between paternal liberalism and the maternal romance with German culture, favored a constitutional monarchy and a multinational state in which the German element, due to its cultural superiority, would retain a dominant influence. But basically he kept out of politics and regarded zealotry in any cause with the ironic detachment that later marked his style as a political correspondent.

The polarization of the student body, however, made it all but impossible to maintain a stance of Olympian detachment. Early on in his freshman year, Herzl joined the Akademische Lesehalle (Academic Reading Hall), an organization founded in 1870 whose original membership comprised an eclectic mix of German, Slav, Hungarian, and Jewish students. It was politically neutral and dedicated mainly to social and cultural affairs, in contrast to the Leseverein der deutschen Studenten (Reading Club of the German Students), founded a year later for the express purpose of promoting pan-German nationalism.

Following a public demonstration against the Emperor, the authorities dissolved the Leseverein in 1878, a move its members countered by joining the Academic Hall in a body, thus setting the stage for a prolonged internal struggle between pro-Austrians and pan-Germans in which Herzl also saw himself forced to take sides. According to notes for a speech he prepared when running for a seat on the steering committee, he came out for the moderates, promising "always to be the friend and comrade of those who would take a patriotic pro-Austrian stand" (Bein, p. 47).

From the start, he was active on committees, organized literary meetings, and participated in debates, an ever cool, ironic voice, distant and faintly supercilious; humility was never to be among the virtues Herzl practiced or believed in. Years later, in a letter to him, Arthur Schnitzler recalled their first encounter at the Lesehalle: "I still remember the first time I saw you. You were giving a speech and were being 'sharp'—so sharp. You were smiling ironically. If only I could speak and smile that way, I thought to myself."

Above all, however, the Lesehalle was an escape from loneliness, from isolation, and from the largely meaningless cramming for examinations. It was there that Herzl met the two men who were to become his closest friends, probably the only real friends he ever made in his life.

Oswald Boxer, the Viennese-born son of an impecunious and rather shady speculator, was a handsome young man the same age as Herzl, tall and robust, with a keen sense of humor and seemingly inexhaustible energy. The friendship between them may have had less to do with common interests than with temperamental differences. Boxer, like Herzl, wanted to write; unlike Herzl, he was quite frankly interested more in money than in art and tended to deprecate his own talent. Unjustly so, it would seem, since within a very short time he was able to establish himself in Berlin as a highly paid journalist with an outstanding reputation for brilliance and integrity. Ironically, that reputation cost him his life. The Jewish community sent him to Brazil on a mission to explore the possibility of resettling Eastern European refugees in that country; he contracted yellow fever and died at the age of thirty-two.

Boxer's outgoing disposition, his common sense and utter lack of pretentiousness made for an easy friendship devoid of rivalry or emotional entanglements, but mutual admiration and sympathy cannot quite take the place of real intimacy. Boxer appealed to Herzl's public *persona*, to that rakish image of an urbanely sardonic young man-about-town he was anxious to cultivate. There was, however, another side to him—the brooding loner consumed by ambition, unsure of his gifts, and deeply troubled by the still-unresolved conflicts of a chronic adolescence, who was looking not merely for a friend but for a soulmate, someone with whom to share his private dreams as well as his agonizing self-doubts. He came as close to that goal as he ever would when he met Heinrich Kana.

The fact that Kana responded to Herzl's emotional needs in ways in which Boxer neither could nor would made for a much closer relationship. Inevitably, it also turned out to be a much more turbulent one, complicated by strains of ambivalence, jealousy, and sexual tension that probably remained unconscious but that in any case went almost certainly unacknowledged. Financially, Kana's background was quite similar to Boxer's. His parents were poor immigrants from Rumania, he barely managed to support himself by tutoring, and the poverty that continued to dog him to the end of his days was merely one of many sources of sporadic friction between him and Herzl. In every other respect he was Boxer's exact opposite—withdrawn, unworldly, morbidly introspective and touchy, with literary ambitions which, as he must have known, far exceeded the scope of his talents. He was, however, a sharp and perceptive critic whose judgment Herzl, normally hypersensitive to criticism, accepted with good grace, even though it was almost always negative and often downright brutal. But no matter how hard Kana was on others, he was hardest on himself, setting standards he could not possibly live up to. Whether his failure as a writer was the cause or the effect of his self-destructive and ultimately suicidal drives is a matter of interpretation as much as speculation.

Kana's feelings are easy to account for; the intensity with which they were being reciprocated is more difficult to understand. Yet in both tone and content, Herzl's letters to Kana testify to the unique nature of what was undoubtedly the most intimate, in fact, the only intimate relationship of his entire life: "There is only one single human being toward whom I am completely open (silly or vain), and that is you" (L, 5/28/83).

Formal studies, the pretext for leading the life of a student, were seldom allowed to interfere with its pleasures. This may have been less true in the School of Medicine, the largest component of the university and already an institution of world renown. But the Law School, next in enrollment, served different functions altogether. Its student body was divided between future lawyer-bureaucrats, on the one hand, and, on the other, a substantial group who, like Herzl, had drifted into "the law" for want of reasonable alternatives. Most were Jews, and as such they faced a special problem in that, for all practical purposes, medicine and law were the only licensed professions open to them; by 1880, 60 percent of all physicians, over half of all lawyers, and 50 percent of medical students in Vienna were Jews. Most Jewish Gymnasium graduates who felt no special vocation for medicine wound up in law school, where they constituted about 25 percent of enrollment.

It thus became a refuge of sorts for budding *littérateurs*, with one eye on fame, the other on security, and no stomach for heavy scholarship. This did not reflect on the standing of the institution as such; the faculty of the University of Vienna in Herzl's time included some of the most brilliant legal minds in the country, men whose interests and lectures ranged far beyond dry textbook material—Lorenz von Stein, a Hegel disciple and advocate of state socialism; the brothers Carl and Anton Menger, who dealt with the law of marginal utility and the role of the state in social welfare; Adolf Exner, specialist in Roman law; and the charismatic philosopher Franz Brentano, one of the founders of phenomenology. Students in quest of a sound legal education could hardly have found a more auspicious environment. On the other hand, attendance at lectures was optional, and those whose passion for the law was less than ardent did most of their studying in cafés and bordellos, trusting luck, their memory, or their classmates to pull them through the tests.

Herzl had an excellent memory. He also had a very active social life, and many interests more compelling than civil litigation or the criminal code. His legal background is said to have left traces in his later work, especially the juridical concepts derived from Roman law as formulated in *Der Judenstaat*. This may well be so; the whole of Austria-Hungary's literary establishment was shot through with Doctors of Jurisprudence, and even better writers than Herzl had a hard time overcoming the aftereffects of their brush with the law. As usual, he passed all his exams without distinguishing himself, but neither teachers nor subject matter seems to have made much of an impression or contributed noticeably to his intellectual development.

In his own way and at his own pace he was obviously testing the waters during that first year, laboring mightily to shed the inhibitions of a mama's boy raised with suffocating care in an overprotective environment. At the same time, he never lost sight of what he considered his primary goal in life, and he let neither the law nor the obligatory extracurricular activities—"the usual student pranks," as he chastely referred to them in his autobiography—deflect him from it.

Prior to 1860, almost the only way for an Austrian writer to at least be heard if not read was to write for the stage; the prepublication censorship of all print media was so draconian as to make any other literary effort an exercise in futility and frustration. Even the four-page bulletin boards that in those days passed for newspapers often displayed large white patches testifying to the rancorous vigilance of never-napping censors. Their caprice and mindless vandalism made book publishing in Austria-Hungary economically impossible, so that the few intrepid Austrian novelists had to seek German publishers for even the most fulsome demonstrations of patriotic piety.

The theater thus remained as the only forum for expressing ideas, always provided they were not instantly recognizable as such. The need to dissimulate intelligent thought favored satire and slapstick; censors are not famous for their sense of humor and could be relied upon to miss the often barbed point of a joke, but it is also fair to say that stage productions were not subject to the same savage scrutiny as print media. The authorities were well aware that the theater appealed mainly to an educated, well-tamed, and by now quite non-combustible middle class impervious to the occasional spark of subversion.

Sparks were rare, in any case; light even rarer in those innumerable farces mass-produced under constraints that made the threat of mere censorship seem almost benign. Royalties were so small that even Johann Nepomuk Nestroy, the best and most popular playwright of the day, had to turn out at least two plays a year just to make ends meet. Lesser ones, such as Berg and Kaiser, churned out a minimum of three a year, each ending up with something like 150 justly forgotten plays to their credit. In the circumstances, any manifestation of thought, subversive or otherwise, was bound to be purely accidental.

Radical changes came about with the end of prepublication censorship in 1860, the most important being the emergence of an aggressive and articulate press. The privileged position of the theater was further undermined by foreign competition; a tidal wave of—mostly

French—comedy and farce, banned under the earlier puritanical regulations, now all but monopolized the stages of both Vienna and the
provinces.

The press, on the other hand, began to flourish. In a fast-shrinking
world full of uncertainty and risk, information was becoming a vital
commodity in a competitive market. Within limits clearly drawn if
often capriciously applied, newspapers were free at last to report on
public affairs, and those skillful enough to provide broad coverage and
to attract a substantial slice of the rapidly growing and ever more
demanding readership soon turned into highly profitable business enterprises, whose power to manipulate public opinion did not escape
the notice of either politicians or the government.

One consequence of this development was the gradual transfer of
newspaper ownership from private to corporate control; well before the
turn of the century, all metropolitan dailies except the *Fremdenblatt*,
published by the Foreign Ministry, and the Social Democratic *Ar-
beiterzeitung* were owned by banks, with salaried employees replacing
the freelance journalist. Another was the intimate link between papers
and politics, their programmatic effort to shape as well as to cater to
the attitudes and prejudices of the particular readership on which they
had come to depend.

Much the same process took place throughout Western Europe,
and although in the long run it may have done more damage to
objective reporting than overt censorship, it still left considerable room
for competence and professionalism; the leading *Neue Freie Presse*, for
one, compared favorably with the best newspapers anywhere in its
foreign and domestic coverage.

Specific to Vienna, however, was a rising young middle class, the
sons of the founding fathers, much better educated, still liberal, but
politically powerless, resigned to their impotence, wallowing in apocalyptic despair, and far more interested in Wagner's latest opera than
in news from the Balkan wars. In competing for the patronage of this
important and trend-setting group, newspapers began to expand their
coverage of cultural affairs, soon devoting as much space to books,
music, and the arts at home and abroad as they did to politics, finance,
and other crimes. But it was the introduction of the feuilleton, that
eclectic mix of essay, fiction, and commentary, that projected the
newspapers themselves into a key position on the cultural scene. For
the beginning writer, making the front page "below the rule"—the
heavy line separating the news columns on top from the feuilleton

below—meant a first step on the road to fame; the established writer accepted it as a tribute to his reputation. For better or for worse, virtually all the important literary talent in *fin de siècle* Vienna got its first exposure in the pages of the daily press.

Herzl carried on a lifelong love affair with the theater which neither disappointment nor rejection could ever quite discourage. He had natural assets—an imposing stage presence, a flair for the dramatic gesture, and in a sense he was successful beyond his wildest dreams, but on a stage quite remote from the world of the Viennese theater that he set out to conquer as a student. In that world he, in the end, came to consider himself a failure. And rightly so, even though a good many of his plays had long runs and earned respectful notices, testimony to Vienna's insatiable appetite for candied fluff. In the age of Schnitzler, Wedekind, Hauptmann, Ibsen, Strindberg, Herzl wrote boudoir farces.

He was ruefully conscious of it in later years. But when he first came to Vienna, the glamour of the stage still seemed undimmed, and his notion of success—of all-encompassing bliss, in fact—was to have one of his plays produced by a reputable theater. At the same time, Herzl the dreamer always had one foot firmly planted on the ground; he fully realized that making dreams come true took not just hard work but also the right contacts and a bit of luck. He also knew that for a young man in a hurry—in a desperate hurry: "Success won't come," lamented the twenty-three-year-old, "and I need success. I only thrive on success" (YD, 11/27/83)—the path to instant glory led across the front page of a major newspaper.

He set out to write his way to fame. Brilliantly versatile and doggedly efficient, he kept at his beloved plays, while at the same time turning out the elegantly ironic essays, melancholy meditations, and moralizing fiction he hoped would catch the eye of a discerning editor and earn him his place in the sun; it was a division of labor which, at a somewhat more exalted level, he adhered to throughout his career.

Right after the move from Budapest, some time in the summer of 1878, he outlined an ambitious comedy tentatively entitled *The Knights of Platitude,* and although the piece itself remained unfinished, the draft offers a revealing preview of the themes, plot devices, and posturings which the mature playwright never quite outgrew: the moral corruption and intellectual vapidity of the nouveau riche bourgeoisie as against the wisdom, spiritual refinement, and moral purity of the hereditary nobility. This contempt for middle-class values, which Herzl satirizes in play after play as the naked greed and crude manners of pretentious parvenus, represents the son's most outspoken if wholly unconscious gesture of rebellion against a father who, though perhaps lacking in pretension, was indisputably a parvenu.

That the deeper sources of his bias remained inaccessible to Herzl was part of his problem, both as a man and as a playwright, just as he remained manifestly unconscious of the anti-Semitic undertones that colored his outbursts against the money mentality of the very circles in which he had been raised. The inane idealization of the aristocracy, the exaltation of "aristocratic values," and his not altogether unsuccessful effort to live up to what he considered the highest standards of manhood as exemplified by the Prussian Junker can be seen as a defense against the corrosive self-hatred he shared with so many of his Jewish contemporaries. It might, however, have shocked him to discover that his adulation of the aristocracy stamped him indelibly as very much a bourgeois of his time and place.

Even more revealing is the novella "Hagenau," written around the same time, an almost classic compendium of both liberal and adolescent fantasies. Its hero, Count Robert Schenk von Hagenau, the impoverished scion of an ancient noble line, is forced to sell his ancestral home to a wealthy bourgeois with two beautiful stepdaughters and a young nephew who happens to be a law graduate every bit as high-minded as the count himself. The fast friendship between these two effaces all class distinctions; the author's alter ego soon rivals the aristocrat in nobility of both spirit and comportment, and their kinship is sealed for eternity when they each marry one of the conveniently available sisters.

But, as Herzl strives to demonstrate in this description of a ball at the now *embourgeoisé* castle, the leveling of barriers transcends the mere gentrification of the bourgeoisie and involves the redemption of the Jews as well:

Herr Moritz Loewenstein was there, too, escorted by his first-born, Karl, in the uniform of a lieutenant. Sign of the leveling power of time: Karl's nose, in profile, was already altogether straight. And as to the ladies and gentlemen, they seemed quite indistinguishable in dress, in bearing, and in speech. The Baroness Loewenstein, seated next to the Countess von Wortegg, was dressed no less tastefully than her neighbor; her French was just as impeccable, and what is more, so was her German.

The passage, for all its puerile snobbism, stands as one of Herzl's earliest attempts to resolve the Jewish problem—or at least his own problem with being Jewish—by means of fantasy. In a broader sense, it illustrates the persistent identity crisis that was part of the price of admission to the world of the goyim—the Jew in spite of himself, who tried to draw what comfort he could from the thought that even Jews, given their chance, could learn to talk and act like ladies and gentlemen. (In 1900, "Hagenau" was published anonymously in the *Neue Freie Presse*.)

Along with these long-range projects, Herzl went after more immediate goals. The prolific ex-president of WIR had in the meantime greatly sharpened his skill at turning out brief essays, sketches, and stories; he had, after all, written feuilletons long before he ever even knew the word. It was a medium in which style counted more than substance, and style was his strength. His weakness was sentimentality, the scourge of those out of touch with their feelings. But though he participated in every one of the frequent competitions organized to discover new talent, it took him five years before he finally won an Honorable Mention and saw his short story "The Humdrum Life" appear in the *Wiener Allgemeine Zeitung*. In the interim he published some brief pieces in Viennese and provincial dailies, wrote for the student newspaper, worked on his plays, tried to gain access to influential actors or producers, and pitied himself for being a hopeless failure while making the most of "the best time in a man's life."

FIVE

*O*n April 28, 1879, Vienna celebrated the twenty-fifth wedding anniversary of the imperial couple with a monstrous display of hypocrisy and pomp, staged with thousands of actors against the backdrop of the city itself and designed to dramatize a myth that had long since lost all credibility.

For one thing, it was common knowledge that the marriage of the phlegmatic Emperor and his high-spirited bride had been a disaster from the start. Franz Joseph is said to have loved her, in his way, which was that of a pedantic and conscientious train dispatcher. Elisabeth, on the other hand, a buoyant Bavarian princess shoehorned into this ill-fitting marriage for reasons of state, had to contend not only with a singularly dull husband and the stifling formality of a court mired in the ceremonial of medieval Spain but also with a venomous mother-in-law who, having been deposed in the 1848 revolution, was all the more determined to make up for it by asserting her authority. At first Elisabeth—Sissy, as she was popularly known—made dutiful efforts to live up to her part of the contract, but in time her resolve gave way to the impulse to take flight. Bright, unstable, haunted by the perhaps not unfounded fear of a hereditary taint—the Wittelsbach dynasty was notorious for eccentric brilliance and a strain of madness— she spent most of her time abroad and made no secret of her intense dislike of Vienna and of the imperial court.

What further complicated matters was the issue of this mismatch, the then twenty-one-year-old Crown Prince Rudolf, whose increasingly erratic behavior scandalized the court, alarmed the politicians, and raised the hopes of the liberal intelligentsia. He was the very opposite of his father—quick-witted, unpredictable, an inveterate gambler and compulsive womanizer who, in addition to his easy conquests among blue-blooded amateurs, also regularly availed himself of the professional services provided by Vienna's more exclusive establishments and ended up with a syphilitic infection which he spread with impartial generosity, one of the more innocent victims being his own wife. Intelligent but impulsive, driven by a fierce hatred of his father, he may have been involved in conspiratorial intrigues against the government; in any event, his suspiciously close contacts with Hungarian revolutionaries and with the capital's intellectual and artistic elites, including many Jews, sufficed to earn him round-the-clock police surveillance as well as the reputation of a closet radical—one reason why the mysterious circumstances of his supposed suicide at Mayerling ten years later never ceased to exercise the popular imagination.

This, then, was the illustrious couple whose quarter century of domestic bliss the city fathers felt compelled to glorify by means of a giant pageant symbolizing the people united in devotion to their rulers. The task of staging this monumental extravaganza was entrusted to the painter Hans Makart, an inspired as well as an inevitable choice. Makart, known as the "Wizard of the Ringstrasse," was the artist idol of the bourgeoisie. His luxuriantly allegorical friezes decorated many of the arriviste palaces, his huge and busy canvases—*The Triumph of Ariadne, The Five Senses, Charles V Entering Antwerp*—sold for what in his day were astronomical prices, and his *trompe l'oeil* style of decorative illusionism left its imprint on an entire period of Viennese art, not least because Makart, however much he may have prostituted his genuine gifts, retained his genius for self-promotion. The "Makart era" ended in 1884 with Makart's death of syphilis at the age of forty-four, not so the popularity of decorative kitsch, which persisted well beyond his time.

It was Makart who planned the procession from the Prater to the imperial castle as a neo-Renaissance spectacle. Each craft guild contributed a float manned by extras in medieval costumes designed by Makart, who himself headed the parade on a white charger wearing the broad-brimmed hat and velvet cloak of a Renaissance genius. "The citizenry of Vienna has demonstrated its patriotism and its loyalty to the Emperor," proclaimed the *Neue Freie Presse*. "The festively decorated streets of our city have seen a spectacle that no onlooker will ever forget. . . . The manifestation was a poem in motion. The fertile imagination of a great artist, inspired by past centuries, conceived the dream. A sensitive and art-loving people, whose trade and industry have attained the heights of modern civilization, made it come true. . . . The show of devotion organized by the City of Vienna was a triumph of our peaceful and hardworking citizenry" (4/28/79).

A triumph it was, but one of fantasy over the facts of life, the self-apotheosis of the Ringstrasse Wizard. And despite the antagonism between Makart and his successors, this oft-lampooned procession with its Wagnerian overtones prefigured precisely the sort of *Gesammt-kunstwerk*—the total work of art—whose fervent pursuit emerged as the obsession of the next generation of artists.

The parade led up the Praterstrasse right past Herzl's house, and he is not likely to have missed the show. What he made of it has not been recorded, but it may have been his first lesson in the crossbreeding of politics and the theater.

A more old-fashioned game of politics, no less remote from reality, was being played in the chambers of the chancellery and the imperial castle. After the last liberal chancellor resigned in 1878, he was succeeded by the Emperor's childhood friend and hunting companion, Count Eduard Taaffe, an adroit politician who could be counted upon not to rock the leaky boat; his goal, as defined by him in an oft-quoted phrase, was "to keep all nationalities of the monarchy in a state of even and well-modulated discontent." The elections of July 1879, which gave the right-wing coalition a slim majority, consolidated his position; thanks to his skillful high-wire balancing act, his unconditional subservience to the Emperor, and an 1882 electoral reform that greatly strengthened the right-wing parties by enfranchising large numbers of peasants and petit bourgeois, he was able to maintain himself in office for a record fourteen years.

The Taaffe regime, regressive in its agricultural and industrial policies and in its support of clerical interests, was nonetheless pragmatic enough to acknowledge certain late-nineteenth-century realities, though it would not go so far as to do much of anything about them. Taaffe's policy of playing the minorities off against one another by means of largely symbolic concessions may have temporarily kept the pot from boiling over, but in the long run it merely served to exacerbate tensions and strengthen extremism, particularly among the German middle class.

A more immediate and, to the nervous middle classes, seemingly

far more sinister threat had in the meantime arisen in the factories
and in the slums. By now the industrial proletariat comprised some
20 percent of the working population, an army of wage slaves in the
most literal sense of the term, including a large contingent of women
and children. Conditions in the factories combined the worst features
of laissez-faire capitalism with the vestigial practices of feudalism—
starvation wages, 70- to 80-hour work weeks, including Sundays and
holidays, total disregard for health and safety. Workers were denied
the right even to assemble, let alone organize; deprived of voting rights,
they had no representation in parliament.

But if working conditions were bad, living conditions were worse.
The rural immigrants streaming into the rapidly expanding industrial
centers created housing shortages that resulted in some of the most
appalling slum conditions in all of Europe; the population density in
Vienna was nearly double that of Paris, with sanitary conditions to
match. As late as 1910, fewer than one out of ten Viennese apartments
had a bathroom, and only about one in five had an inside toilet.
According to an 1872 study, the average life expectancy of an Austrian
factory worker was thirty-three years.

In the 1860s, several moderate workers' organizations inspired by
the ideas of Ferdinand Lassalle and the illusions of self-help through
education pressed for reforms but were consistently rebuffed by the
Liberal government. As Karl Giskra, a Minister of the Interior later
indicted for graft and corruption, told one of their delegations in 1868,
"Austria is never going to introduce mob rule. General franchise is
not going to pass in Austria, not now, and not ever."

Small wonder that moderate leaders soon lost their credibility and
were replaced by aggressive radicals, especially in the wake of the 1873
crash. By the time Taaffe took charge, the seething discontent of a
disorganized and demoralized urban proletariat exploded in a series of
riots that for the most part were spontaneous eruptions, but for which
the anarchists got most of the blame or the credit.

The specter of revolution, of plundering mobs and of tumbrils full
of headless aristocrats, haunted governments and ruling classes
throughout the nineteenth century; in Austria, those paranoid fears
prompted hysterical reactions to even minor provocations. Thus, the
Taaffe government time and again called out the troops and, in 1884,
proclaimed a state of emergency in Vienna and environs. In 1886, an
"anarchist law" was enacted which suspended trial by jury for crimes
perpetrated "for motives of an anarchist or subversive nature."

But for all their severity, these measures were merely another instance of trying to "muddle through." And even Taaffe himself finally seems to have realized the need to deal with certain fundamentals, although this may be giving him more credit than he deserves; the series of social reforms introduced between 1885 and 1887—the 11-hour workday, Sunday rest, a ban on the employment of children under twelve, the rudiments of accident and sickness insurance—were not only modeled on the German legislation but also inspired by Bismarck's tactics in his own war on the socialists.

Whether or not they proved successful in the long run depends on one's point of view. In both Germany and Austria, the Social Democratic movements emerged stronger than ever and eventually became the majority parties in parliament. In both countries they also scuttled all vestiges of revolutionary élan, supported the First World War, and eventually came to represent a tepid liberalism uplifting in theory and harmless in practice.

As for Herzl, his politics had much in common with his Judaism. Both were legacies passed on to him by previous generations, accepted more out of filial piety than genuine conviction. He was no democrat and made no secret of how he felt about majority rule. He profoundly mistrusted the "plebs" until late in life, when, rather to his surprise, he discovered his own magical gift for manipulating the masses. He watched the power plays of politicians in Austria and later on in France with the detached amusement of an astute and skeptical observer, well informed as to trends and personalities, perversely indifferent to the forces beneath the surface that were transforming European society. His personal outlook on life closely matched the conservative liberalism of the *Neue Freie Presse*—one reason, no doubt, why his position on the paper remained comfortable and secure despite sharp disagreements with its owner-editors on the subject of Zionism. And it was natural for him to share the prevailing middle-class dread of socialism, spiced in his case with a dash of aristocratic disdain that on occasion could short-circuit his brain: "In my opinion, socialism is a purely technological problem. The distribution of nature's forces through electricity will eliminate it" (D, 6/8/95).

Herzl's first year at the university marked the climactic crisis of his adolescence. The embryonic lawyer, going on nineteen in the spring of 1879 and a full-fledged adult in the eyes of the world, was striving with dramatic flair to live up to the Viennese image of the student. He dressed with immaculate taste and subtly understated elegance. He became active in the Lesehalle, earned a reputation for sharp wit and eloquence, acquired a taste for beer and a rather more expensive taste for gambling.

In a town in which appearances counted for everything, the façade worked deceptively well, but the struggle to maintain it imposed an inordinate strain on his meager emotional resources. The typical teen-age mood swings kept tossing him back and forth from wild euphoria to deep depression, or, as he himself described it with a quote from Goethe, "from heavenly jubilation to sadness unto death." His special blend of arrogance and social graces masked morbid shyness and pet-ulant self-involvement; but for the first time in his life he was now reaching out for friendship, risking himself in human contact beyond the tight little circle of his immediate family, breaking loose at last and coming into his own. A process all the more painful for having been long delayed.

These daring forays into reality did nothing to curtail the scope of his fantasies, but they led to more frequent collisions between grandiose dreams and reluctant self-awareness. In April he completed a one-act comedy oddly illustrative of just that clash: two bored dandies, wanting to write a play, decide to first act out its plot in real life so as to assure the proper touch of realism. As a result, one of them finds himself trapped in marriage to an ugly old hag, and the play remains unwritten. Herzl's own future bride was no ugly old hag; but in many other respects, the parallels between the story line of Compagniearbeit—Joint Labor—and the course of Herzl's own courtship and marriage cut rather too close for comfort. Acting out one's fantasies is a sure recipe for disaster.

The play was rejected by the prestigious Stadttheater—the Burg-theater was still under construction—as well as by a number of less exalted institutions and individuals, though it took Herzl some time to acknowledge what his new friend Heinrich Kana had told him from the outset, namely that Compagniearbeit was a dilettantish piece of work. At this point, Herzl had an inspiration that almost wrecked the burgeoning friendship; he proposed an arrangement whereby Kana would doctor the sickly play and share in the royalties. Kana, prickly as a cactus and morbidly sensitive about his poverty, felt himself being patronized and broke off relations. It took all of Herzl's powers of persuasion as well as the joint efforts of several common friends to effect a reconciliation.

Herzl eventually expanded the comedy to four acts and had it privately printed the following year. It was never produced.

He spent July and August with his parents at Bad Vöslau, a spa about an hour's train ride from the capital, where Jakob and Jeanette took the cold-water cure while their son explored literature and life; the exhaustive reports he sent back to Kana suggest that he had some trouble telling one from the other. The July elections, the disastrous defeat of the Liberals, and the reappointment of Taaffe left the future political commentator blissfully indifferent, nor does he ever refer to any current events in politics or the arts. But his consummate lack of interest is understandable: he had far more pressing concerns.

Given the glutinous intimacy of the Herzl family, the relentless rectitude of its presiding matriarch, along with his own priggish attitudes and manifestly unresolved conflicts, it seems safe to assume that he had kept out of the Budapest bordellos, refrained from picking up streetwalkers, and thus missed out on what in his day passed for the normal initiation into the mysteries of sex. His boyhood notions of chaste passion and knightly romance remained curiously untouched by adult sophistication; the love story in *Old New Land*, his last novel, could have been written by the president of WIR. That, being human, he also fantasized about sex may be taken for granted. But sex was the antithesis of love, a matter of sordid lust profaning lofty sentiments— the normal emotions of early adolescence, except that Herzl never outgrew them.

To some extent he was the victim of his times. For even though individual pathology determined the ultimate outcome, the whole social pathology of the Central European middle class fostered this radical split between love and sex through a process of emotional castration whose tragic consequences provided the literature of the period with one of its most abiding themes. Men loved their mothers and their wives—the distinction between these two sacralized and sanitized love objects often being as blurred as the difference between love and hate. But when it came to sex, they turned to the *süsse Mädel*, the underpaid shopgirls, waitresses, and working women whose venal charms contributed so much to the legendary gaiety of Vienna and to its high rate of venereal disease.

The atmosphere of the metropolis, the anonymity afforded by the sheer size of the city, his newfound freedom of movement, and the relative loosening of the constrictive family ties all played a part in helping the nineteen-year-old Budapest virgin to shed some of his inhibitions, including his virginity. Sex was as sordid as ever, and all the more fascinating for it. In later years he repressed and sublimated that fascination by reverting to principled prudery, but the first rush of powerful urges still seemed liberating rather than threatening. In any case, he was under great pressure—self-generated as much as social—to adapt to the manners and morals of his new environment, and the correspondence with Kana bears witness to his conscientious efforts in that direction. They were only partly successful. The snickering references to brothel visits, the puerile boasts about the size of his penis sound more pathetic than persuasive, a high-school sophomore dabbling in mandatory machismo. On the other hand, the dithyrambic rhapsodies he devotes to the climactic sexual experience of his summer vacation—a furtive glimpse of a blue garter on a pair of shapely legs—convey some of the profound unease and confusion he sought to dissimulate.

His confidant was in much the same bind, another victim of ambivalence, fear, and frustration seeking relief in teenage fantasies. "My much beloved Ezzelino," he addressed Herzl in September 1879, "in your last letter you uttered a thought that has really gripped me when you said that what we both needed was a truly overpowering passion, an unhappy love affair. . . . Since here in the country I have nothing better to brood about than my own miserable self, the pertinence of your idea has become clear to me. I need a grand passion that will grab me, shake me out of my self-involvement. But where are we to find her, the unknown one, be she short or tall, brunette or blond?"

Two would-be grownups in need of human warmth as much as sex but afraid to acknowledge it even to themselves lest they betray unmanly weakness. What drew them together, beyond common interests, ambitions, and complementary neuroses was an affection charged with all the ambivalence of a late-adolescent crush. So far as we know, Kana was the only one to whom Herzl ever confided the intimate details of his personal life, and the tone of reckless bravado in which he usually couched his self-revelations never quite masks the anguish that inspired them.

Both, moreover, shared an attitude toward women which, at least in Herzl's case, frequently tipped over into frank misogyny. This from a letter to Kana, also written in the summer of 1879:

I am living in the house of the local mayor, who cancels out whatever minimal contribution he may have made as a physician to the general welfare of mankind by being the owner of three debt-free but ugly daughters whom he permits to roam about freely without regard to people's aesthetic sensibilities. This situation forces me to leave the house if I wish to satisfy my understandable need for the visual enjoyment of female beauty. Which, unfortunately, is not as easy as you might think; in all of Veesloo I have up to now seen only one really beautiful lady and three halfway pretty ones, while Gainfarn cannot boast a single pretty face, with the exception of the innkeeper's daughter at the Black Eagle. . . . When I awoke, in a melancholy mood, and looked out of the window at the yard, all I saw were the three household Furies and two other cows that also belong to the family. [L, 7/8/79]

Unlike the preciously mannered jests about Kana's "minimal philogyn" (nothing like do-it-yourself Greek when it comes to euphemistic vulgarity) and other remarks of like subtlety, the contempt for women—real women, that is, as differentiated from the unsexed creatures populating his fantasy—was heartfelt and wholly genuine, a contempt born of primordial fear and superstition, endemic to the culture, hallowed by tradition, and reinforced by law. But in this respect, Herzl had to do himself no violence in order to conform to prevailing norms: his thoughts and feelings about women were wholly in tune with the spirit of the times.

The spirit of the times was, as always, shot through with hypocrisy.

The reputedly oldest profession is, in fact, merely the oldest form of exploitation, but it took the rise of capitalism to transform it from a cottage industry into a multinational business. It was commercial vice that propped up bourgeois virtue; the whole elaborate structure of sexual repression, with its cult of female chastity, would have collapsed without it. The state legitimized it, while society at large, despite periodic outbursts of sanctimonious indignation, in effect promoted prostitution as a healthy outlet for the unbridled lust of the male animal. An outlet it may have been; as for health, the incidence of venereal disease among Vienna's prostitutes, both registered and freelance, was close to 100 percent.

What drove Herzl to patronize brothels or pick up *süsse Mädel* was not unbridled lust so much as the need to reassure himself about his manhood. Living up to the self-image of gay young blade and man-about-town made these dreary encounters mandatory, but his discomfort with female sexuality is summed up in a four-liner remarkable more for its candor than its poetry:

> Schlangenmädchen, Mädchenschlangen
> Sind ein gefährliches Geschlecht.
> Hüt dich mit ihnen anzufangen,
> Sonst geht es bald dir schlecht.

> [Snakegirls, girl snakes
> Are a dangerous brood.
> Beware of tangling with them,
> Else you will soon be in trouble.] [CZA, H IV B71]

And indeed, he soon did find himself in trouble: sometime in the spring of 1880, he picked up the almost inevitable dose of gonorrhea.

In a letter to Kana of June 8, 1880, he described his embarrassing symptoms in frank and explicit detail, not without a note of boastful triumph; after all, the clap proved him a real man. But lurking beneath the turgid bravado and forced frivolity was an undertone of quiet hysteria, justified enough even though popular myth trivialized gonorrhea as "no worse than a bad cold."

The truth was considerably less reassuring. Though generally self-limited, gonorrhea—whose causative agent had just been isolated in 1879—has the potential for nasty systemic complications, rarely seen in developed countries since the discovery of penicillin but quite common before effective therapies became available. In males, they include infections of the genitourinary tract, crippling arthritis, endocarditis, and damage to the heart valves; gonorrheal infections in females were the most frequent cause of sterility, as well as of blindness in neonates. In Herzl's day, no effective remedies existed as yet; those routinely prescribed—mostly a tincture of zinc sulphate—made doctors feel better but did nothing for their patients.

The Herzl letter documenting at least one venereal infection has given rise to much wayward speculation about possible long-range effects on his health. Could his death at forty-four and his wife's death at thirty-nine have been the result of—or, as some would prefer, punishment for—his youthful indiscretions?

There is no way, and no particular need, to offer conclusive proof to the contrary; the fact that Herzl in his twenties caught a sexually transmitted disease hardly qualifies as either a revelation or a moral blemish. But, in any case, the medical histories of both husband and wife strongly argue against it. One pertinent clue that has received insufficient attention is Herzl's military record.

As a high-school graduate, he qualified for the limited one-year volunteer service rather than the regular two-year stint of the ordinary conscript. On December 21, 1879, he presented himself for his pre-induction medical examination at the barracks of the Infantry Regiment Wilhelm III and was found unfit for service. A second examination on January 10, 1880, confirmed the original findings, and he was granted an indefinite deferment by the Vienna Staff Command two weeks later. He in fact never served.

No reasons were given for the decision of the medical board, but in the absence of any manifest physical disabilities, the most likely—and most frequent—grounds for medical deferment were heart murmurs gross enough to be picked up by the relatively crude techniques then available. (Even the binaural stethoscope did not come into general use until the turn of the century.) Herzl's deferment was almost certainly based on the suspected presence of a congenital heart defect.

Unlike the dubious pleasures of the flesh, gambling was a vice less threatening to body and soul and much more in tune with his basic instincts. The correspondence of his student years abounds in references to debts, pleas for small loans, complaints about lack of funds, none of them addressed to his parents; to infer from them a financial crisis in the Herzl household—as some biographers have done—seems disingenuous. Jakob Herzl, though no longer as affluent as in the early Budapest days, remained eminently solvent and as generous as ever toward his now one and only child. He would certainly have been able—and in all likelihood willing—to cover the relatively trivial sums Herzl kept fussing about, such as the 9.40 guilders he borrowed from Kana to pay the registration fee for his semester finals. The doting parents might, however, have been shocked to discover that their pride and joy regularly gambled away part or all of his monthly allowance, and Herzl was always anxious to spare their feelings.

He himself in later years referred to his gambling as a brief, passing phase, part of his "student pranks," and in the narrow technical sense this was true. He ran up debts, patronized pawnshops, yet ultimately possessed too much self-control to let things get too far out of hand. But in his later career as a prophet and politician, the gambler's instinct reasserted itself; the stakes, however, were of a far different order of magnitude.

He had taken to gambling, learned to swill booze with the worst of them, caught the clap like a regular fellow, but all these efforts combined still fell short of giving him a sense of belonging, of full participation in the legendary student life. The compleat student wore the cap and sash of a dueling fraternity, swore fealty to its colors, and demonstrated his manly courage by acquiring a *Schmiss*—a conspicuous facial scar—in a procedure more akin to mutilation rites than to a fencing match. If he passed muster in the eyes of his elective brothers, he graduated from "young fox" to "active fellow" and eventually retired as an "old boy" to become part of the alumni network.

By the 1880s, the dueling fraternities had come to represent the most extremist element among the student body, militantly pan-German and clamoring for immediate union with Bismarck's Reich. Ultra-reactionary, anti-Semitic by tradition, they were now being further radicalized by a new breed of demagogues who introduced blatant racism as a weapon in the struggle for political supremacy. In spite of which, Herzl, in the spring of 1881, saw fit to join the dueling fraternity Albia.

The immediate impetus may have been provided by the dissolution of the Academic Reading Hall, permanently shut down by police decree in early March after it had sponsored a rabble-rousing speech by the anti-Semitic deputy Georg von Schönerer. The edict left Herzl at loose ends, without an outlet for his social needs and organizational talents. But there is every reason to believe that he also felt strongly attracted to both the chintzy glamour of this self-appointed elite and to the spirit of ostentatious machismo that animated it.

By the standards of the day, Albia at this stage was still relatively more moderate than most of its rival saber rattlers. A contemporary observer described the typical Albia members as "rugged, handsome, high-class fellows, fencers ever ready for sword play; in 1881 they fought no less than seventy-five duels." The fraternity, though staunchly reactionary from its inception in 1871, was somewhat lagging behind the general trend and had not yet entirely succumbed to Schönerer's brand of pan-German racial militancy. At the time Herzl joined it, Albia had two other Jews and several converts on its active rolls, as well as a fair number of Jewish alumni.

Herzl initially flung himself into fraternity life with all the zeal of a true believer. He either chose or was given the fraternity name of Tancred, Prince of Galilee and Antioch. The choice is thought to have been inspired by the hero of Torquato Tasso's *Jerusalem Delivered*, although Benjamin Disraeli's 1847 novel, *Tancred: or the New Crusade*, is another possibility; in any case, this oddly prescient appellation, whether aptly chosen or imposed, suggests that Herzl's "racial origins" were an issue from the outset. He faithfully attended the obligatory drinking bouts, joined in the dirty ditties and the patriotic slush, and took private fencing lessons in addition to the daily ones provided by the fraternity so as to prepare himself properly for the *Mensur* ("measure," presumably of manhood), the duel testing his fitness for becoming a full-fledged member of the brotherhood. It took place on May 11, 1881. Herzl's opponent was another "young fox" from the rival Allemania fraternity, and after hacking away at each other for a while, they both managed to draw blood. Although Herzl's facial gash was minor and required only a single stitch, it was eventually judged sufficient to earn him the coveted admission despite several opposing votes.

He never fought another duel, one of many black marks against him on the Albia books. But the official record noted much more serious charges: "Herzl openly mocked or covertly sneered at everything his fraternity brothers hold sacred. Although his contributions to the fraternity were below average, he demanded special treatment. During the brief period of his active membership, he was unpopular with both his fellow tribesmen as well as with the far more numerous pure-blooded Germans. He did not feel happy among his fraternity brothers and remained for all of them an alien element."

Rather a tribute to Herzl's good sense, which seems to have reasserted itself fairly quickly and led him, in the course of the following year, to distance himself from the Albia's social life and to cease contributing to its official publication. He had no doubt earned the hostile remarks that summed up his brief fraternity career, and his censors told no more than the truth: they did not much like Jews to begin with, and most particularly not those who acted like Jews. What made Herzl a

Jew of the most objectionable sort was not the crooked nose he at that time still so self-consciously fretted about but his biting sarcasm and sense of irony.

The outrage was genuine but in no way original, the issue an old one between Jews and Germans long before Herzl came on the scene. For a century of brief, uneasy coexistence—from 1826, when Heine published his first travel sketches, to Tucholsky's suicide in 1935, which closed the chapter for good—the rebellious, twice-alienated descendants of brooding Talmudists and ever-questioning believers wielded the irony and skepticism of their ghetto ancestors with a merciless ferocity that was altogether without precedent in German letters and badly ruffled the cozy self-assurance of small minds. (The fact that both Heine and Tucholsky were nominal converts proves nothing beyond the illusory nature of the emancipation.) To be sure, many Jews quickly adopted the dominant mode of rhapsodic smugness, while on the other hand some of the best German writers outdid any Jew in strident irreverence and ruthless critique. But the lockstep mentality of Prussian militarism which, after 1848, set the tone in German culture as well as politics and inspired the Teutonic fundamentalism of their Austrian admirers perceived these sniper attacks as a Jewish plot.

What lends a particularly ironic twist to Herzl's troubled relations with his Albia brothers is that, at least at the conscious level, he still shared many of their misbegotten fantasies at a time when most young Jewish intellectuals in Vienna had already shed their illusions. A man like Schnitzler, two years younger than Herzl, would not have been caught dead joining a dueling fraternity. Herzl believed in duels, he believed in Bismarck, and he adopted the Prussian Junker as his ego ideal. Nor did he ever quite outgrow these beliefs. Even in his Zionist phase he still retained his uncritical admiration of the Iron Chancellor, and in outlining the social order of the future Jewish state, he fantasized with majestic megalomania: "I must have the duel in order to have good officers. . . . The saber duel is permitted and will not be punished, whatever the outcome, provided the seconds did their best to reach an honorable settlement" (D, 6/9/95).

And yet, there was always the haughty look in his eyes, the disdainful curl of the lips, the provocative arrogance of intellectual superiority. The sarcasm, in his case, was a matter of form rather than substance; he was no social critic, but he could whip even the most banal platitudes into a soufflé of piquant irony and sardonic asides—a talent that later greatly endeared him to the liberal and largely Jewish readers of the *Neue Freie Presse* but made him no friends among the Albia conservatives. As far as they were concerned, he merely ran true to type—an uppity Jew.

Though increasingly isolated, Herzl formally remained a member until a scandal in the spring of 1883 forced the issue and brought him into open conflict with the fraternity and all it stood for. It was not his first collision with reality, but the first to dent some of his fantasies.

On March 5, 1883, the League of German Students organized a memorial service for Richard Wagner, who had died three weeks earlier in Venice. The league was an umbrella organization expressly dedicated to the promotion of Schönerer's racial and pan-German doctrines, and its sponsorship of the event could have left no doubt as to its purpose, which was to eulogize not the musical genius but the benighted racist and mythopoeic prophet of Teutonic supremacy. The Albia's chief delegate was one Hermann Bahr, at that time still a "young fox" and would-be scribbler, who with the sure touch of the true opportunist gauged the mood of the crowd and seized the moment to deliver himself of an anti-Semitic tirade so violent that the police felt constrained to intervene and disband the meeting. The feat earned Bahr a mild reproof by the Academic Senate and instant celebrity as a hero of the militant extremists.

Herzl, who had not himself attended the meeting, gave the Albia a day's grace for a public disavowal of its representative, something he must have known by then was not likely to happen. The letter he fired off to the steering committee on May 7 offers some clues to the qualities which, in later years, made him an effective leader:

> From press reports I have regretfully learned that the Richard Wagner meeting, whose sponsors included the fraternity to which I have the honor of belonging as an inactive member, turned into an anti-Semitic demonstration. I have no intention to polemicize here against this reactionary fashion of the day, but I would like to mention in passing that even as a non-Jew I would feel compelled by sheer love of freedom to oppose a movement with which, from all appearances, my fraternity has also allied itself. From all appearances; for the absence of protest in such cases spells complicity. *Qui tacet, consentire videtur.* The press reports contain no indignant disavowal on the part of the frater-

nity. Unfortunately I cannot believe that the omission will be corrected as a result of this letter.

It seems rather obvious that, handicapped as I am by Semitism (a term still unknown at the time I joined), I would not today request admission to the Albia, which in any case would probably be refused for the above reasons, and any decent person will understand that in these circumstances I do not wish to remain where I am not welcome.

As an "old boy" I would have to relinquish my rights. As an inactive fellow I request severance of my links to the fraternity. Since, to the best of my knowledge, my record contains nothing dishonorable, I am counting on an honorable dismissal.

The fraternity at the time still included a fair number of Jews and ex-Jews among both student members and alumni. Herzl alone had the backbone to voice his protest.

The steering comittee spent almost a month debating his case. Their initial impulse was not to accept the resignation but rather to punish this flagrant example of Jewish insolence by summary expulsion. Calmer counsel prevailed, however, and in a curt letter of April 3, Herzl was ordered to surrender his blue cap and sash and "permitted" to resign. His subsequent request for a statement to the effect that he had resigned on his own initiative met with renewed outrage: "We will not respond favorably to a demand couched in the deliberately disrespectful tone of your missive."

The incident raised the Albia's simmering anti-Semitism to the boiling point. On a motion by its leading spirit and most dedicated activist, Paul von Portheim—fourteen duels to his credit—it was resolved henceforth to bar all Jews; and although current members were to be exempt for the time being, it took no genius to read the signs in the wind. Portheim was no genius, but he read the signs and killed himself three months later, on July 13. He was, as it happened, himself "of Jewish extraction."

SIX

*T*he break with the Albia was an assault on windmills, executed with a dramatic flair which in this instance came to be appreciated only by posterity. Herzl's own contemporaries, to the extent to which they took notice at all, saw the gesture as one of either Jewish arrogance or Quixotic futility, and he himself was evidently less than happy about it. "On a personal note," he avowed, in a covering letter to the "brother" to whom he was instructed to surrender the Albia sash and insignia, "I would like to add that the decision to resign has not been an easy one." There is no reason to doubt his sincerity; at this stage in his life, membership in a German dueling fraternity must have seemed far more glamorous than the shriveled vestiges of Judaism with which he was congenitally afflicted. At the same time, however, the very traits that led him to exalt the ideals of Teutonic knighthood made it unthinkable for him to compromise on an issue involving dignity and honor. True, "even as a non-Jew" he might have felt compelled to protest against anti-Semitism. But being a Jew, he experienced it as an intolerable and intensely personal insult.

A Jew rather in spite of himself, but a Jew for all that. Some of the most revealing clues to the inner turbulence of those early years in Vienna are provided by a curious journal of sorts that Herzl began to keep in January 1882, about a year before the Albia fiasco. He referred to it as "The Chronicle of My Sufferings." It is more prosaically known as his "Youth Diary," although neither title quite describes the peculiar mix of arrogance and anguish that characterizes much of the contents.

The manuscript consists of 105 pages, the first half of them written in 1882 and mainly devoted to detailed critical comments about Herzl's reading during that period—popular third-rate French and German authors for the most part, whose output he devoured with a gluttonous zeal worthy of more exalted fare.

If escape was the purpose of this frenzy, it seems to have worked. The entries break off in May, and to judge from the suddenly upbeat tone of his letters, the depression began to lift with the start of the summer vacation, which he spent with his parents at the Purkersdorf spa and on a trip to Italy. By late fall, he was involved in two ambitious literary projects of his own, a novel as well as a play, and it was not until after his clash with the Albia that he again took up the journal in April 1883. Unlike those in the earlier section, however, the miseries he sporadically bewailed or railed against over the next four years whenever self-pity got the best of him—the final entry is dated September 7, 1887—conform to the banal patterns of the conventional diary, complete with sticky sentiment and voluble despair; Vienna was teeming with gifted young Jews just like him, arrogant, insecure, with a large dose of *Weltschmerz* and a touch of paranoia, desperate to make their way in the world. A much more sharply focused portrait of this particular young man, on the other hand, emerges from the opinionated book reviews in the first half of the journal, in which Herzl flaunts his convictions with spontaneous candor and reveals a great deal about their emotional roots.

The forty-odd books discussed by Herzl are about evenly divided between French and German authors, none rising above the level of popular entertainment; the sole exceptions, on both counts, are Mark Twain's *Notebooks* and Dostoevsky's *Crime and Punishment*, which he read in German translations. French literature is represented by the likes of Victor Cherbuliez, Arsène Houssaye, Jules Claretie, Jean Richepin, Ernest Feydeau, and Henri Murger, while the German contingent features names such as Carl Reinhardt, Adolf Wilbrandt, Wilhelm Jensen, F. W. Hackbinder, Hans Hopfen, among other luminaries equally obscure and forgotten. The sole woman writer, one E. Werner, alias Elisabeth Bürstenbinder, is accused of having committed prose "even flatter, I presume, than the chest of this bluestocking lady." The selection as a whole reflects an amazing tolerance for ephemeral trash, but Herzl's critical comments make it abundantly clear that what kept him from exploring the more challenging trends in late-nineteenth-century literature was not middlebrow tastes so much as middle-class bias.

The Hungarian-born cosmopolitan polyglot Jew in him may have strained a bit at the lumps of Teutonic chauvinism he made himself swallow and regurgitate. "After all," he notes, "we Germans love our mothers no less than those gentlemen across the Rhine; just the same, here at home we do not indulge in this—I can't put it any other way—high-falutin and pretentious cult of motherhood." Despite his familiarity with the language—Herzl had learned French in childhood and spoke it with near-native fluency—and later on with the country and its people, he never seems to have felt quite at ease, let alone at home among them. During his years as Paris correspondent he came to know all the great names of French culture and politics, but to the extent to which he was aware of it, the literary and artistic ferment of this extraordinarily creative era repelled him. His view of the French remained patronizing and faintly contemptuous, but since his prejudices were widely shared by the readers of the *Neue Freie Presse*, they merely added to his popularity.

The Youth Diary, however, hints at elements of his Francophobia that transcend mere cultural bias: "It is in the lap of the whore that a gifted people dissipates its strength, its spirit and its enthusiasm." France, to the young Herzl—and there is no evidence of the older one ever changing his opinion—was the quintessence of sexual depravity, the land of lust, license, and libertinism. Vice was no less prevalent in Vienna than in Paris, although imperial censorship and bourgeois hypocrisy allowed the Austrians to indulge in illusions of moral superiority. Yet while Herzl engages in some mindless stereotyping, the virulence of his reactions and the vituperative eloquence aroused by the subject of sex suggest that it touched on some very basic inner conflicts. Thus, for example, his review of an 1866 novel by Jules Claretie, a minor French novelist:

> *Une Femme de Proie* . . . is a precursor of Zola's *Nana*, except for being somewhat cleaner, after all, than the obscene abortion of filth and "Spanish" fire concocted by that "naturalistic" speculator. . . . Altogether too much has been written about the whores of the boulevards; what one does with them is pay the standard fee and leave them to their own defiled selves. . . . But

with the French, their entire literature dances endless circles around the soiled couch of the whore. [YD, 1/30/82]

In support of which sweeping conclusion he immediately plunged into another dirty book and a mere four days later was able to report that *La Glu* (*The Lime Twig*) by Jean Richepin (1849–1926), a moderately successful French poet, playwright, and novelist, was

more Zolaesque even than *Nana*. When *Madame Bovary* was published, they hauled its author, Gustave Flaubert, before the morals squad. Compared to Zola's *Nana*, *Madame Bovary* is a mere innocent. . . . *La Glu* seems to me the ultimate of what even a literature such as the French, notoriously accustomed to gamboling around the figure of the whore, can permit itself. Beyond it there is only the bordellotristic. . . . [Richepin] is even more naturalistic than Zola (yes, even more naturalistic), naturalistic like a suppurating boil, naturalistic like a syphilitic sore, naturalistic like a dungheap. . . . He who likes this school of literature can go on reading their books, permeated as they are by the bestial lascivity of the stud and reeking with the stench of sweat and whores. This is naturalism! . . . [The heroine] is a mistress of the "art," or rather "arts," of love. . . . These are the very arts that are about to doom modern French society; these are the arts that, in the manner of Messalina, choke off the growth of its population. [YD, 2/4/82]

It might have made Herzl feel better about the future of French society to know that Richepin was eventually tried for obscenity and actually spent time in jail.

On the whole, German authors got a much more sympathetic reading. Herzl was, of course, far too intelligent not to realize that, intellectually and stylistically, such regional sentimentalists as Adolf Wilbrandt, Wilhelm Jensen, and Otto Buchwald were simply not in the same league with the sex-crazed French romanciers. Yet at the same time he felt incomparably closer to them in spirit, at home in their cozy little world, and moved by their cloying sentimentality even where he saw it for what it was. They spoke to him in his *Muttersprache*—quite literally, one suspects, in the emotional idiom of his mother.

But early that same February he came across one German author whose work—non-fiction at least in intent—upset him far more profoundly than all the salacious Frenchmen put together.

Karl Eugen Dühring owes his modest claim to immortality to the polemical broadside launched against him in 1877 by his archenemy, Friedrich Engels. *Herr Eugen Dühring's Revolution in Science,* commonly known as "The Anti-Dühring," became a Marxist classic, thus unwittingly preserving the ferociously anti-Marxist professor from the well-deserved oblivion he himself might have preferred, in the circumstances.

In life, however, Dühring's notoriety rested on more tangible exploits. A polymath of prodigious intelligence and legendary irascibility, author of works on philosophy, history, and economics, he taught at the University of Berlin from 1863 to 1877, when the Senate fired him for persistently aggressive misconduct. Dühring blamed Jewish intrigues for his downfall and retaliated with a diatribe noteworthy only in that it was one of the first to mark the shift from a predominantly religious to an out-and-out racist brand of anti-Semitism.

The process was inevitable and already well under way by the time Dühring published *The Jewish Question as a Question of Race, Morality, and Culture* in 1880. If anything, the end of physical and legal segregation had exacerbated rather than eased the atavistic hostility against the Jews by generating new points of friction, but religion as such could no longer serve as a plausible rationale for persecution in an age of secularism.

The Christian-Social Labor Party, founded only two years earlier by the imperial court chaplain Adolf Stöcker, still appealed to religious prejudice in its campaign against the Jews. In 1879, a gutter journalist by the name of Wilhelm Marr, himself a converted Jew, coined the term "anti-Semitism" in a pamphlet in which he accused the "Semitic race" of aiming to enslave the Teutons. Dühring, weighing in a year later, had no use for religion generally and Christianity in particular. Like Marr, he hated the Jews for being Jewish; unlike Marr, he possessed impressive if somewhat tarnished academic credentials, which lent an air of scholarly authority to his perverse opinions. His book was a frenzied tirade denouncing virtually every major Jewish contribution to civilization, starting with the Bible and culminating in the demand for the renewed exclusion of Jews from public life along with a ban on mixed marriages so as to prevent pollution of the German race.

In calling for his version of the Nüremberg Laws, Dühring was still about fifty years ahead of his time, but his vituperations upset Herzl in ways which no objective criteria could quite justify.

> An infamous book [he complained, at the start of his detailed and polemical review]. And unfortunately so well written, not at all as if base envy had guided the poison pen of personal revenge. When such infamous nonsense is presented in so straightforward a manner, when so well-schooled and penetrating a mind, enriched by scholarly and truly encyclopedic knowledge such as Dühring undeniably possesses, can write this sort of stuff—what, then, can one expect from the illiterate mob? He treats the Jewish Question as a racial one and sees the "infamous race" as having none but infamous and reprehensible qualities. . . . The early chapters, however, despite exaggerations and clear bias, are rather instructive and should be read by every Jew. The slippery slope of Jewish morals and the lack of ethical seriousness that characterize so many (all, according to Dühring) activities of the Jews are being mercilessly exposed and stigmatized. One can learn a lot from this! But reading on, one gradually comes to realize that, along with some truths, a great deal of falsehood and, in fact, deliberate and mean forgery have gone into this brew. [YD, 2/9/82]

That a mind could be both stuffed with learning and dangerously unbalanced, and that a book could be both well written and thoroughly despicable were obviously notions that Herzl had trouble accepting. A professor—even one fired for paranoid behavior—still merited attention, if not respect, the more so since many of his accusations were not all that different from Herzl's own views about Jews and about the slippery slope of their morals, whatever that meant. But this particular professor had decidedly gone too far.

> He describes the Jews just the way the old witches of either sex used to gossip about them in the Dark Ages. However, since he happens to be a scientifically enlightened and semi-reasonable old witch, he no longer talks about the Passover sacrifice of

kidnapped Christian children. He has kept pace with the times, he knows that one can no longer dish up these stupid old lies that have led to so much bloodshed, and so he thinks up more plausible new ones. Christian children now have turned into Christian money. . . . However, there is hope that someday humanitarian hearts and calm, dispassionate minds will look back upon today's anti-Jewish movements the way any educated person, even the educated anti-Semite, looks back upon those of the Dark Ages.

Herzl did not live to see the real darkness settle over Europe, but a mere two months after he penned these lines, the ancient blood libel in its most primitive form was revived in his own native Hungary. The ritual murder trial at Tisza-Eszlar, skillfully orchestrated and exploited by political demagogues throughout Austria-Hungary, was in fact the opening battle in a broad anti-Semitic offensive, but most Jews preferred to see it as a temporary aberration, the dying echo of medieval superstitions. They clung to their faith in progress and in the eventual triumph of the enlightenment; what else was there for them to believe in? Herzl shared their illusions, and perhaps it was in order to preserve them that he never so much as mentioned Tisza-Eszlar, which for nearly two years made headlines throughout Europe, just as he ignored the bloody Russian pogroms of 1881.

"This rascal," he concludes, "who ought to have his teeth bashed in, sanctimoniously turns up his eyes and demands freedom for all, but emergency laws for the Jews. . . . I was all the more outraged because this book is written in so excellent and pure a German. Furthermore, despite its vicious rantings it contains many an original and reasonable idea. And finally, one senses a certain independence (though far from selfless and probably not unselfish, either), which in spite of everything strikes one as refreshing" (YD, 2/9/82).

Herzl's reaction to Dühring—that peculiar mix of outrage, admiration, and denial—was an attitude rather typical of Austria's assimilated Jews and their refusal to acknowledge the unmistakable changes in the atmosphere. Aside from a pointedly reactionary Prime Minister and government, the most obvious one was the rise of the anti-Semitic, pan-German extremists, who had profited enormously from the 1882 electoral reforms and the enfranchisement of the disgruntled *petite bourgeoisie* that made up their principal constituency. In spite of which the Jewish middle class kept the faith and continued to worship the trinity of progress, enlightenment, and the Emperor Franz Joseph. Vienna's Jewish-owned newspapers, though desperately anxious to avoid even the appearance of ethnic parochialism, reflected a liberal bias in their editorial policies to the very end, although by the 1880s liberalism was a dying cause everywhere except in Vienna, where the agony took a little longer. There may be something admirable in the refusal to abandon lost causes, but in fact no serious alternative presented itself to those still committed to assimilation, even though in the process they increasingly lost touch with reality. The *Neue Freie Presse* may have owed its reputation to comprehensive coverage and a first-rate staff, but it was the liberal outlook of the paper's commentators and columnists, who served up their reassuring fantasies twice every day, six days a week, that made it the bromide of the Jewish bourgeoisie. Herzl at this point still shared all their illusions and persisted in them for some years to come, but Dühring forced him to confront feelings he had successfully managed to suppress since childhood.

SEVEN

*F*laubert's definition of literature as "the mystique of those who believe in nothing" applied with particular relevance to the young Jewish intellectuals of Herzl's generation. Wholly out of touch with their ancestral faith, emancipated past the point of no return but still adrift in largely uncharted waters, they practiced this new form of worship with much the same fervor which their grandfathers had devoted to the study of the Holy Scriptures. Literature had assumed for them the functions of a substitute religion, usurping the place of ritual and tradition.

Not so for Herzl.

He had never seriously contemplated any career other than writing since he gave up on the Panama Canal. And unlike most of his fellow dreamers, whose unwritten masterpieces had a way of going up in smoke and fury at the Café Griensteidl, he had already written several plays and published a fair number of essays. But what set him apart was not his single-minded determination so much as his distinctly utilitarian attitude toward literature. Writing, to him, was not a sacred vocation but a means to an end.

His resolutely conventional tastes may have reflected the philistine prejudices of Jeanette Herzl and the Budapest bourgeoisie, but his conservative bias went way beyond mere taste; Herzl abhorred anarchy and revolution, be it in literature or in life, and he had no use for radical experiments or avant-garde art in any form. Although he was himself living proof of Flaubert's dictum, he would no doubt have ridiculed it just as he scorned both Mme Bovary and her creator. For his avowed aim was not immortality but success—instant success—in the here-and-now. The plays, stories, and essays he churned out at a furious pace were not designed to grapple with eternal verities or social problems; they were quite simply meant to win him the recognition and acclaim he wanted more than anything else in the world.

Herzl's contempt for the "mystique" of literature and its muddle-headed coffeehouse prophets may have been amply justified and rather refreshing in its lack of affectation, but his own down-to-earth approach to writing as the road to fame and fortune led to excesses of a different sort, such as those he so graphically described in a letter whose metaphors should have delighted the early Freudians:

> I feel like the young man "taking his pleasure" [he wrote to his friend Kana]. The first two or three chapters were fun, but now he realizes that the all-too-demanding paramour wants to go on being screwed—all the way to Chapter 12. And although the poor if grateful boy feels his strength giving out, he whips and spurs himself on to ever fresh deeds, so as to help his Muse reach the convulsive orgasm she lusts for. I'll tell you one thing—and here I'm speaking from personal experience: both a love affair and a novel can drain you, and in either case overindulgence is apt to leave you with a case of the clap. And the final insult: love's labour's lost, as often as not; the lady cheats on us, and success eludes us. [L, 8/18/82]

Success eludes us—the eternal refrain, a one-note dirge sounded over and over throughout his brief life. Objectively fatuous, considering his career and achievements. But there is nothing objective about success; what it stood for in Herzl's life was the affirmation of a self-image conceived in heroic proportions yet resting on a very shaky pedestal. Just how shaky comes through in a letter Herzl wrote in May 1883 to the prominent actor Ernst Hartmann:

> One's lack of success always strikes other people as comical. It is, however, a well-known fact that our dear fellow man, ever anxious to poke fun at our mishaps and clumsiness, stops laughing the moment we feign self-irony and pretend to be ourselves greatly amused by the whole thing. He who is first to laugh about his

own pratfalls will be spared other people's laughter. Which is a victory of sorts, even if he did sustain a few bruises. [L, 5/15/83]

This driving ambition, the frank and frankly desperate pursuit of success—of the acclaim and admiration, the tribute to Narcissus that he called success—did indeed make for some embarrassing pratfalls along the slippery road to glory. But its main effect, at this early stage, was to lead him into frustration. Herzl was a facile and competent writer. His irony, cool reason, and powers of observation lent a unique personal touch to his essays and raised his later journalism well above the level of routine reportage, yet his attempts to write fiction—stories as well as plays—invariably proved disastrous. The lucid prose of the essayist turned arch and mushy, streaked with trite moralizing and mawkish sentimentality, but above all, he seemed utterly unable to create characters bearing an ever so remote resemblance to real human beings. He was far too self-absorbed to perceive others in their full complexity, and far too vulnerable to risk the kind of intimacy that alone would have given him an insight into the human soul, his own included. In fact, his grim insistence on writing for the stage was itself a measure of his capacity for self-deception. He clearly did not have what it took, and even the best of actors cannot breathe life into paper dolls cut out of scrap platitudes.

What he did know was that he wanted to "succeed," and that in Vienna the quickest way to instant celebrity and public acclaim led across the stage. The Viennese genuinely loved the theater, which for historical reasons still dominated the cultural life of the city, straddling the gap between art and popular entertainment. Actors were far better known than cabinet ministers, and no mere newspaper scribbler could compete for fame and adulation with a successful playwright.

Given his dream of seeing his name featured on the playbill of the Burgtheater, Herzl's determination to write plays made sense. The fact that his talents lay elsewhere and that his inspiration derived from raw ambition rather than artistic vision presented obstacles which, for a long time, he was able to ignore. They would in any case not have deterred him; Herzl was not the man to let reality interfere with his dreams.

On the other hand, the unremitting struggle took its toll, most obviously in recurrent depressions—another instance of those pratfalls he was always eager to conceal from the world at large, and from his parents in particular. On the whole, he was a far better actor than playwright, always cheerful with his parents, an ever dutiful and loving son in private, a haughty, self-assured, and sarcastic young genius in his public appearances. The pose, cultivated since childhood, effectively kept friend and foe alike at a safe distance.

By 1882, the romance of student life had evidently begun to pall; the staggering number of books he devoured in the early months of the year suggests that he had totally lost interest not only in his studies—which he had never taken very seriously—but also in fraternity affairs and social life generally. He increasingly withdrew into himself, began to hack away again on the ill-starred "Hagenau" novella so aptly compared to joyless copulation in the above-quoted letter to Kana, and after the summer vacation wrote a one-act comedy entitled *The Hirschkorn Case*, in which he himself starred at its premiere in late November before a group of family and friends. Their predictable enthusiasm apparently encouraged him to submit this sophomoric farce about fumbling lawyers, a beautiful young widow, and a contested inheritance to the Burgtheater—nothing but the city's most prestigious would do—which rejected it early in 1883. (Herzl resubmitted the piece in 1899, with the same negative result.)

This disappointment, coinciding as it did with his resignation—or expulsion—from the Albia, sharply intensified an acute sense of despair which he consistently ascribed to his "lack of success." "Some of my acquaintances are just beginning to believe in me, and I simply can't," he lamented in April 1883. "They presumably refer to me as a 'talented fellow' or 'a witty young man.' . . . Alas, they don't know about the invisible burden of misery, pain, and despair he hides under his vest. Doubts, despair. Elegant doubts, perfumed despair—which is why Heinrich Kana, the only one able once in a while to look under the vest, also does not believe them to be genuine. . . . Motto, heading, definition of my current state of mind: *désenchanté!*" (YD, 4/13/83).

Submitting *The Hirschkorn Case* to the Burgtheater had been a gambler's bid to beat the odds; when it failed, Herzl turned to other, more conventional methods of challenging the gods. The orgiastic highs of gambling may have somewhat assuaged the burden of "elegant doubts" and "perfumed despair" that plagued him during the first half of 1883, but it gave rise to problems of another kind. Time and again he found himself short of cash and had to pawn his watch or borrow from friends and acquaintances against next month's allowance, which no doubt was more than adequate. The family's move, in May 1883, from Leopoldstadt to the Zelinkagasse, a much more prestigious address in the Inner City, signaled further improvement in the family finances, and Jakob Herzl was a notoriously generous father. But for all his indulgence and understanding, he nonetheless remained committed to the moral standards of both Judaism and the bourgeoisie. He would have been profoundly upset about his son's gambling, and there was nothing Herzl dreaded more than to inflict pain on his beloved parents. It should be said that the need for filial discretion seems to have strained Herzl's purse more than his conscience; for a Jew of his time, he was remarkably immune to guilt feelings about his youthful transgressions.

In May, a short story he had entered in a contest received an honorable mention and was printed in the *Wiener Allgemeine Zeitung*— a triumph of sorts over his friend Kana, whose acid critique had almost kept him from submitting it. Kana was dead right about the treacly sentimentality of "An Everyday Occurrence," in which a wealthy playboy deliberately sets out to wreck the idyllic love affair of two sensitive youngsters by wooing and winning the girl. But Kana was obviously wrong about the Viennese public, probably because—unlike Herzl— he failed to share its taste for candied cream puffs.

Publication of the feuilleton did little to lift Herzl's spirits. For one thing, an honorable mention in the *Wiener Allgemeine Zeitung* was not the kind of success he dreamed about, and for another, he faced his first comprehensive State Law Boards a month later and was desperately trying to make up for several years of indifference and neglect. In the end, he managed to pass the exam with three votes out of five, a far from brilliant result but good enough to impress his ever-impressionable parents, who by way of reward treated him to his first trip abroad. His mother is reported to have sent him on his way with a flourish of heroic self-abnegation: "My precious child, write to us every day, for in spirit we are always with you and live only through you, but a postcard suffices. Let whatever your impressions, moods, and thoughts along the way inspire your work as a writer, for that work belongs not to us but to the world" (L. Kellner, p. 10). Blind adulation makes the biographer who "quotes" these words more suspect than most ("How many mothers," he adds, "would of their own free will have brought such a sacrifice?"); but he probably caught the spirit of relations between Jeanette Herzl and her twenty-three-year-old "precious child." Herzl, in any case, spurned the mother's sacrifice and instead wrote home at least once, often twice a day, while at the same time keeping a journal. The letters to his parents were full of high spirits and bubbly good cheer; as always, he was determined to keep up appearances. But although some of his customary *Weltschmerz* crops up in the rather cursory journal, his delight rings true; Herzl had discovered the magic power of travel as a means of escape. It was a lesson he never forgot.

Armed with his parents' blessings and with what seemed a respectable purse—200 Austrian guilders, 200 German marks, and 150 Swiss francs,* as he meticulously noted in his journal—he left by train on July 9, 1883, traveling at a leisurely pace, bound to no fixed itinerary and guided only by the whim of the moment, a keen, often acidulous, but detached observer. He spent the first night in Linz, a picturesque old town on the Danube some two hours from Vienna, impressed by the spectacular main square and by a young lady's legs in red stockings. From there he went on to Ischl, a fashionable sulphur spa where, in a densely wooded park, the Emperor Franz Joseph spent his summers in a villa whose lack of ostentation stood in marked contrast to the sumptuous mansions of Vienna's merchant princes. The next leg of the trip, by coach and steamer, took him through the heart of Austria's lake district, one of Europe's most dramatic landscapes, and on to Switzerland via Munich. He spent several days around the Bodensee, where "one night from half past nine to a quarter past ten" he was "madly in love with a blond, delicious French princess with a darling little nose and enchanting little feet in black silk stockings. . . . To be loved by a princess—an old dream of my youth, unlikely ever to come true" (TD, 6/18/83).

After living it up in Switzerland for a few days, he ran out of money. "We live in sobering times," he informed his parents, conveying a vivid idea of his spending habits. "Without money no status, no honor, no pleasure, no comfort, no good dinner, no tasty drinks, no concert and no theater, no raincoats, no bowing waiters, no good cigars, no . . . In a word, nothing without money" (L, 7/22/83). Daddy, as usual, did more than just come to the rescue, and a mere two days later Herzl was able not only to thank him for the remittance but "most particularly for the kindly way in which you took care of it. Dad, you really know about people; some additional cash never does any harm. You undoubtedly felt sure that I would not erupt in righteous indignation at getting more money than I had asked for" (L, 7/24/83).

---

* 1 Austrian guilder (or florin) = approximately 45 cents.
  1 German mark = 24 cents.
  1 franc (Swiss or French) = 20 cents.

He crossed briefly into Bavaria, where the tranquil charm of Augsburg's ancient quarters—the city was founded by the Romans in 15 B.C.—strongly appealed to his own romantic streak: "In Augsburg I'd like to spend the last twenty years of my life; this is where I'd like to die. It should be easy to die in this city, that has seen the death of so much greatness." As fate would have it, twenty years and some months was all he had left from the time he penned these lines. "But," he promised, "I shall return—perhaps to stroll in your ancient lanes arm in arm with my beloved young wife." And, once launched on the topic:

Strange how dreams of intimate marital happiness tend to sneak up on one during travel. The unknown, beloved beauty which I shall one day hold in my violent, tender embrace—I see her as I gaze out of the train window into the fleeting distance. There she drifts in the sky, soaring above the meadows, her luminous beauty intoxicatingly outlined against the forests. I cannot distinguish the features of her lovely face, but what bewitches me is the sweet softness of her figure, the endearing bliss of the apparition. I sense the perfume of her golden hair, and the warmth of her breath caresses my face like the delightful breeze of a summer evening. [TD, 7/26/83]

A day earlier, by way of contrast, he had noted in his diary: "If ever I marry, I am bound to cheat myself horribly" (TD, 7/25/83), while a day later he described "a delightful episode" at the end of his ten-hour trip from Augsburg to Passau:

I was leaning out of the window, and so was a blond, bright-eyed little girl in the next car. And between stations we carried on a lively conversation without being able to hear a word over the clatter of the wheels. But we laughed at one another and both enjoyed ourselves. . . . Thus, at the end of my summer trip, the poetry of travel has for the first time looked upon me out of the eyes of a child. That is why I am dedicating this page to you, my amiable travel companion. I bet that he to whom you will one day belong is going to be happy. You lovely, tender child. Today I understood for the first time that one can fall in love with a child. [TD, 7/27/83]

At the end of July, Herzl returned from his trip and spent the next
six weeks in Baden, a thermal spa near Vienna, where his parents took
up residence every summer in quest of sociability and a cure for
whatever happened to ail them at the moment. The hot sulphur springs
were touted as miraculously effective against a whole host of afflictions,
from gout and gallstones to hysteria, hypochondria, and genitourinary
complaints, although the mind-numbing boredom of the therapeutic
regimen itself probably constituted the main ingredient of the cure. It
was a charming little town, once the favorite retreat of the Emperor
Franz I; Beethoven had spent two summers here, and Mozart wrote
the Ave, verum in the fifteenth-century Church of St. Stephen. But
in Herzl's day, Baden had become a watering place of the middle-
aged middle class, dull to the point of arousing suicidal impulses in
any healthy twenty-three-year-old, and the insipid routine of prome-
nades, band concerts, and card games to which his parents lovingly
constrained him soon pitched Herzl right back into the trough of
depression.

He implored his friend Kana, stuck in Vienna for the summer, to
join him "as soon as possible, as often as possible. Maybe you don't
have the money for the trip. How delighted I'd be to spend the paltry
sum that would buy me the pleasure of having my one and only friend
here with me every week. My friend, my confidant, the only one with
whom I like to watch the clouds drift over the fields and the evening
fade in the sky, without fear of ridicule or affectation. But for some
strange reason a certain unease seems to trouble our relations when it
comes to matters of money. Should you, in the meantime, have had
a change of heart in this respect, please let me know" (L, 8/1/83).

Kana turned down the invitation, offering transparent excuses which
merely confirmed Herzl's suspicions. Pride, poverty, and petit bourgeois prejudice, exacerbated by a paranoid streak, made Kana bristle
at the merest hint of generosity. Herzl could obviously have avoided
the problem by simply joining his friend in Vienna instead, but he
evidently did not want to deprive his parents of his company, be it
only for a weekend.

And so he deprived himself instead and, with the tenacious willpower
he always mustered under stress, spent seven more weeks in Baden
cramming for the next round of exams and writing the first two acts
of his new play, aptly entitled The Disillusioned. In the long run,
however, willpower is no match for a serious depression, and by the

time he got back to Vienna for his final semester, his emotional resources were badly depleted.

Once again I am taking up this confessional of my afflictions [he wrote in November 1883]. Once again, in the stillness of an evening that caps another day of lethal emptiness, I am overcome by the hopelessness of my existence. On the outside I am acquiring stature in the eyes of old and new acquaintances; on the inside I am just one desperately unhappy fellow. Death and damnation, will this go on forever? Success will not come. Yet I need success. I thrive only on success.

Here in my drawer lies *The Disillusioned*, a now completed piece of work that has gorged on my longings, my hopes, on years' worth of struggle, on my blood, a part of my very youth and that now nauseates me. I don't even feel disposed to submit it anywhere. What for? Just to collect another printed rejection slip? No sunbeam lights my way, no goal looms up ahead, no flower blooms by the wayside. I won't go on; even the blank page inspires disgust, my very handwriting strikes me as nauseous. No love in my heart, no longing in my soul, no hope, no joy. [YD, 1/27/83]

His unhappiness was clearly more than just a passing mood. In fact, his letters and diary entries throughout the next few years indicate a recurrent pattern of that characteristic listlessness symptomatic of a genuine depression and for which success is anything but a cure.

Yet at the same time his state of suspended animation—just like his physical illness years later—struck him as a moral defect, a shameful and unmanly weakness which had to be hidden behind an elaborate façade of insouciant self-assurance. He had his youth going for him as well as self-discipline and a faith in his own genius sturdy enough to bounce back after every defeat, but the struggle clearly sapped his strength. On New Year's Eve, 1883–84, he surveyed the damage:

No New Year's Eve party for me. I won't even wait up for the clock to strike midnight, but lie down instead and seek the sleep that will lift me out of the apathy of an empty day in an empty life. Nothing but emptiness. The head empty of hope, the brain empty of thought, the purse empty of money and life empty of poetry. In five weeks I am supposed to pass my finals in Roman law, but I am no longer fit for study.

I have a mistress, an appetizing female made for love, a *bonne fortune*, but I am no longer fit for love. Already no longer fit for love. I have a play in my desk to which I've devoted pieces of my life, a play I dreamed about on summer days and worked on in winter nights—but it won't bring me success. I . . . [YD, 12/31/83]

Here the text breaks off abruptly, with the next few pages missing from the original notebook. The gap is followed by an intriguing explanation: "On later rereading these pages, I tore them out because they reminded me of a base and nefarious female, along with some other things." One must assume that the reference is to the appetizing mistress made for love, but what dark deeds of hers so roused Herzl's shame or anger will never be known; it was not the sort of subject he dealt with in his plays.

A desperate last-minute bout of cramming enabled Herzl to pass his comprehensive orals, and on May 16, 1884, he formally became a Doctor of Law. The doctorate probably meant a great deal more to him than the law—"These lines are written with a trembling hand by Doctor Theodor Herzl" reads a diary entry of May 13, 1884—but in any event he was immensely pleased just to have passed and be done with his studies, the more so since, by way of reward, his parents once again sent him abroad to recover from the strain. At the end of May he left Vienna and, traveling at his usual leisurely pace, with stopovers at Karlsruhe, Baden-Baden, Strasbourg, and Nancy, he arrived in Paris on June 3.

Paris was to be his beat in later years, the place where he made his name as a journalist and which he interpreted and satirized at length for the benefit of his Viennese readers. Yet he never quite recaptured the enthusiasm and the pristine, unaffected sense of wonder with which he first discovered and explored the capital of the Western world.

Paris, with about 2.5 million inhabitants, was twice as large as Vienna, but mood and atmosphere rather than size made for the crucial difference, the immense vitality of a city in perpetual ferment as against the fake placidity of Habsburg provincialism. After a century of triumphs and disasters played out in its streets, from the storming of the Bastille in 1779 to the bloodbath of the Commune in 1871, Paris had emerged more alive than ever, and for once the young tourist dropped his pose of blasé sophistication and responded with simple and unfeigned delight. He roamed the streets and boulevards of the central arrondissements—"In the evening I am tired like a mailman, but I sleep like a god"—spent hours in the Louvre, the Musée de Cluny, the Bibliothèque Nationale, walked from Montmartre to Montparnasse, and rhapsodized about the brilliant displays of elegance and ostentation in the Bois de Boulogne. His familiarity with the language enabled him to catch at least some glimpses of Paris life beyond the tourist circuit. He saw Sarah Bernhardt and Benjamin Constant Coquelin at the Comédie Française, went to the opera several times, heard a lecture by Renan, and attended a trial at the criminal court as well as a rally of the Salvation Army—"a weird, caterwauling sect."

If he also savored some of the less esoteric pleasures for which Paris was famous in his day, he failed to record them for posterity. In one of his daily letters to his parents—the only documentation extant—he describes an outdoor ball where "an emaciated, insipid little girl with 'shopclerk' written all over her dances the quadrille (a euphemism for the cancan). The dancer is poorly dressed and meek-looking, but once the music starts, she lets herself go and dances the most incredible things. And as she gets worked up, the scars on her neck become prominent, some kind of disgusting memento. Please forgive me for talking about this. But every city requires some advance preparation. If you send a man to Rome, he should know something about history. Art history for Venice, and for Paris—a bit of medicine" (L, 6/13/840). A bit of medicine might not have hurt in Vienna, either, as he knew only too well; interesting, though, is not the sanctimonious slur so much as the need to stress the terrors of sex in a letter to his squeamish parents. Just whom was he trying to reassure?

But nothing could dampen his enthusiasm, not even the half dozen rejection slips forwarded to him from Vienna. "For some strange reason I seem to have made a good recovery here—I mean, as far as my nerves are concerned; in other respects I wasn't, after all, ailing even when I left."

On August 4, 1884, a month after his return from Paris, Herzl began his probationary year in the offices of the Vienna District Court, starting in the Department of Criminal Justice and switching in December to civil law, neither of which struck him as very inspiring. The actual workload, however, was nothing to complain about. "In the mornings I fill out forms at the Mercantile Court, but the afternoons are beautiful. I read, I smoke, I write. And so the days follow one after another, and one day I'll be old without ever having been young. But we must remain restless" (YD, 121/31).

He used the time to work on a number of projects, among them the stage adaptation of a story by the French author Catulle Mendès and a new play dramatizing the conflict of the generations. In January he obtained a personal interview with Friedrich Mitterwurzer, a prominent Burgtheater actor who also toured extensively with his own troupe in both Europe and the United States and was always on the lookout for fresh material. *Tartarin*, the Mendès piece turned by Herzl into a brief, melodramatic one-acter, seemed to him of possible interest as a filler; *The Disillusioned*, on the other hand, he rejected out of hand. "Mitterwurzer had me read part of the first act; then he abruptly cut me off with the terse remark that he could take no more of this boredom" (YD, 1/20/85). He also urged Herzl to forget about the generational conflict and find himself a more promising topic—tactful advice, considering that there was nothing wrong with the topic and almost everything wrong with its execution.

Between the dull office work and the constant rebuffs and rejections, frustration piled up that winter like the mounds of snow outside. But instead of sliding into yet another depression, Herzl turned his wrath outward and challenged anyone whose looks or behavior offered an ever so flimsy excuse for taking umbrage. Three times in the course of as many months he was prepared to kill or be killed over some trivial or imaginary slight—twice by saber, once by pistol. Fortunately, all three duels were averted, the first by mutual apologies, the second because the opponent refused to accept the challenge, the third because the illness of his father made it impossible for Herzl to absent himself from home on the agreed-upon day. The issue, in this instance, had been a quarrel over a chair, and for years thereafter Herzl worried that his failure to show up might have been misconstrued as cowardice.

In June, Herzl had himself transferred to the District Court in Salzburg. He wanted to be near his parents, who that year were doctoring themselves in the upper Austrian resort town of Hall; its iodine-rich waters had been recommended as particularly effective against the ear ailment from which his father was suffering. The two towns were at least close enough for regular weekend visits, with daily letters full of mutual solicitude compensating to some extent for the loss of day-to-day intimacy: "How are you, my golden daddy? How are you, my golden momma? The truth! I urgently request a daily report" (L, 6/19/85). "Is the cure beginning to help? Are you looking well, do you feel stronger, my sweet daddy? And you, my dear good momma, are you rid of your sciatica? Are you making good use of the cure? Is it also raining in Hall? Are you getting enough fresh air, and are you comfortable?" (L, 6/21/85). "Your worries, my dear, dear momma, are quite unfounded. There are bars on my windows, and besides, I'm home every day at half past nine. Also, I am eating abundantly and very well: two meat courses for dinner, dessert, and a glass of Bavarian beer" (L, 6/26/85). "Today I did not get a letter from you, which makes me very uneasy. I must urgently ask you once again to mail your letters every day at the exact same time if you don't want to torment me unnecessarily. You know from your own experience how quickly one starts to worry" (L, 6/28/85).

Such hysterical apprehensions in a nominally adult young man hint at some profound ambivalence in his relationship with his parents. Yet in spite of the eloquent anguish, Herzl seems to have been rather happy in Salzburg, at some remove from their ubiquitous presence and smothering round-the-clock concern. Beyond the attractions of the lovely town as such, he found himself in the congenial company of young colleagues who made him feel warmly welcome. The offices were located in a stately old castle, and though the workday was twice as long as in Vienna—three hours in the morning and two and a half in the afternoon—the workload itself proved no more onerous and left him ample time for private pursuits. Fifteen years later he was to assert that, had he been able to count on regular advancement, he might have stayed on in Salzburg for good; but realizing as he did that for a Jew there was no room at the top, he quit.

Fifteen years later, however, the Jewish problem had become the focus of his life and retrospectively invested every aspect of the past with polemical significance. And though it was true that unbaptized Jews did not go far in the Habsburg bureaucracy, it was equally true that Herzl had never given any serious thought to a legal career, in or out of government service. His goal was the Burgtheater, not the Appellate Court, and when his probationary year was up on August 4, 1885, he turned his back on the law and everything connected with it. Everything but the hard-earned title that became part of his signature.

EIGHT

*I*t was part of Herzl's conceit to view himself as a high-minded dreamer, a sensitive and poetic soul struggling to safeguard his ideals in a world awash in greed and corruption. This projection of himself crops up time and again in his fiction as well as in his letters—a self-image patently out of focus though not wholly inaccurate: he did, in fact, have dreams.

Striking about them, however, was their sheer banality. All over Europe—and in Vienna more dramatically than almost anywhere else—young artists and writers rose up in rebellion, determined to smash idols and icons, shock the ruling classes out of their smug complacency, and breathe new life into every aspect of human creativity. That most of them aimed far beyond their reach and, in the end, had to settle for mediocrity or oblivion does not detract from the initial impulse and ideals. Yet here was Herzl, twenty-five years old, in that "dawn when it was bliss to be alive and to be young was very heaven," consciously plotting not to revolutionize the stage or to create literary masterpieces but to write plays and feuilletons tailored to the prevailing middle-class tastes.

The task involved no agonizing compromises on his part; he fully shared those tastes. Even so, he cannot have failed to realize that titillating a Burgtheater audience or charming the readership of Vienna's liberal newspapers was incompatible with exalted literary standards. But his dreams, like everyone else's, grew out of his needs, and what he most needed—what he dreamed about—was approval. He called it success: a Burgtheater premiere, popular enthusiasm, critical acclaim, or a front-page feuilleton that, for an afternoon, became the talk of the coffeehouses along the Graben. Such was the stuff of his dreams, as solidly earthbound in their way as those of the parents he never ceased to worship. And with much the same methodical application with which his father had managed his own rise from poverty to affluence and respectability, the dreamer now began to demonstrate the eminently practical side of his multifaceted self as he set out to make his dreams come true. He had chucked the law in favor of literature; the time had come to justify that decision by proving that he could support himself.

Not that there was any objective urgency about it. His parents, with their boundless confidence in his genius, never exerted the least pressure and were perfectly willing to go on supporting him as long as necessary. But he had his own pride to contend with, not to mention the inevitable self-doubts that required a more objective affirmation of his talents than the adulation of the family. And ten days after resigning his court appointment, he began his new career as a freelance writer by taking a three-week trip through Holland.

It was the first time he purposefully set out to gather material for a newspaper project, but what he discovered was something much more fundamental—a heady sense of freedom, a rush of energy that went far beyond the stimulus of fresh impressions. Herzl's passion for travel was to become a lifelong addiction and the most potent antidote to his recurrent depressions, a routine form of escape which he successfully transformed into a highly individualistic form of self-expression. The moment he boarded a train, he ceased to be the perennial outsider and became simply another stranger among strangers, a tourist taking in the scene, with no obligation or desire to be part of it. The popularity of Herzl's travel sketches owes much to the very qualities that precluded personal intimacy—the ironic detachment and faintly supercilious tone, modulated by an occasional dash of sentiment. At a time when foreign travel was still a relative luxury even among the more affluent middle classes, his reports from abroad struck exactly the right note calculated to inform, intrigue, and amuse the Viennese bourgeoisie— a view of foreigners and foreign lands that reinforced their own complacent sense of superiority. This is not to minimize his obvious talents as a gifted stylist and prolific author; but the decision to use his travels as an entry wedge into journalism was probably instinctive more than rational. It legitimized the anonymity of the voyeuristic loner.

He left Vienna on August 15, 1885, traveling at his usual leisurely pace via Munich to Heidelberg. In the daily communiqué to his parents, he comments on the local scene:

> The old castle, which the French maliciously destroyed two hundred years ago, is delightful. Hundreds upon hundreds of tourists busy themselves at all hours running through this magnificent ruin from top to bottom with the requisite admiration prescribed by the Baedeker. Their shepherds or guides herd and whip them in bunches through the labyrinth of the old edifice, and shadowy figures suddenly pop up in dark tunnels. These are not, however, ancient knights but mustachioed English ladies, class of 1829, and male Britons or Yankees who—probably in order to stress the difference between the sexes—shave their upper lip. . . . Later I made the acquaintance of a Heidelberg student, a gorgeous-looking, charming young fellow, his left cheek hatched like notepaper, who took me to his fraternity house. Most interesting, despite the vacation quiet: the pictures, the precious trophy cups (some twenty made of finely hammered, high-grade gold), drinking horns, student emblems, etc., of the fraternity which I knew about by reputation proved very interesting to a connoisseur like myself. [L, 8/8/85]

In Brussels he discovered Antoine Joseph Wiertz, "that weird original of a painter," who ended up getting his own museum because he would not sell any of his work. Herzl was greatly impressed by the artist-philosopher; and though he criticized him for having philosophized a bit too much in some of his pictures, Wiertz's *La Belle Rosine*, a luscious nude contemplating her own skeleton in the mirror, struck enough of a responsive chord to inspire a melancholy feuilleton some five years later.

In Ghent and Bruges he relished quaintness and medieval architecture while keeping an eye out for female pulchritude—in vain, it seems: "Remembering my latest loves, the blond one in Kammer and sweet red-haired Laure . . ." But "*formosis Bruga puellis?* [Any pretty girls in Bruges?] Not a single one" (TD, 8/25/85). It was beauty of a different sort, the timeless works of art clustered in singular profusion throughout the towns and villages along the way, that caught his imagination and turned the trip into a pilgrimage. He was spellbound by the entire Dutch school, from relatively obscure artists such as Pieter van Anraadt, Jan de Braij, and von der Helst all the way to Frans Hals and Rembrandt, and he spent days amid the inexhaustible riches of the Rijksmuseum in Amsterdam, the high point of the trip. In a letter to his parents, he waxed almost inarticulately rhapsodic: "My trip is beautiful, beautiful, beautiful. . . . At the moment I am fascinated by the splendid beach at Ostend." Still, he felt constrained to add a barbed afterthought: "True, one sees a great many Jews here from Budapest and Vienna, but the rest of the vacation crowd is very interesting." The hairshirt of self-hatred itching beneath the armor.

In his letters to his parents, Herzl often went to absurd lengths trying to feign high spirits, if he had to, even in the face of death itself; the very last notes to his mother, already written in full awareness of the inevitable, still convey a message of hope and good cheer. Even so, the exuberant mood of his letters from Holland and Belgium rings true. He responded with an unspoiled, almost childlike enthusiasm to the visual delights of the Dutch landscape, with its exotically immaculate towns. On the other hand, he kept aloof from day-to-day life; in fact, he seems to have had virtually no human contact at all throughout these three weeks, unless the hatch-marked young nobleman in Heidelberg qualifies as such. He drank in the scenery but paid scant attention to the players and their play, happy in his loneliness as long as he kept on the move.

But he never lost sight of the main purpose of the trip. He took copious notes and completed two articles along the way, at least one of which—describing the fiftieth anniversary celebration of the Brussels–Mechelen railroad—appeared a few days later in the *Neue Wiener Tagblatt*.

His return to Vienna, however, precipitated another crisis. His student years may not have been as happy and carefree as he later chose to remember them, but they had offered adult freedom without adult responsibility—an ideal adolescence, artificially prolonged. Now he faced the task of proving that he had what it took to be a grownup, which in the world in which he had been raised meant being able to make a living. He had staked his future on faith in his talent; what if he was fooling himself?

Torn between cocky self-assurance—or self-reassurance—and recurrent doubts, he went back to his half-finished play, *Momma's Little Boy*, which had been giving him trouble even before he left. Unable to complete it to his own satisfaction, he had asked the prominent Berlin author and editor Paul Lindau to collaborate on the script. Lindau declined. His refusal, which Herzl found waiting for him when he got back on September 8, was not calculated to dispel his dark mood.

Over the next three months, Herzl wrestled with this misbegotten farce, trying to breathe some semblance of life into it. "Hopeless the prospect," he noted in his *Journal of Frustration and Fatigue* on October 11. "Every week I toss off jokes for the *Floh* [*The Flea*, an illustrated Viennese humor magazine] at the rate of 60 florins a month. Mercy! I am stuck in the third act of *Momma's Little Boy*, and everything I write seems insipid, nauseating. This 'age of manhood.' For all its childishness, the age of sentimentality was sweet, after all. . . . Miserable, miserable life" (YD, 10/11/85).

Eventually, however, he not only finished the play but even considered it his major achievement when he took it to Berlin in late November as part of a carefully laid plan to conquer by devious strategy rather than frontal assault. "Whether the play gets staged at the Wallner Theater [in Berlin] or some other place doesn't matter," he explained to his parents. "One way or another, it is certain to make its way. . . . I'll be quite satisfied with it if I conquer a theater on the order of the Carl Theater. So what if I get into the Burgtheater when I'm twenty-seven rather than twenty-six. After all, that is bound to be the high point of my career, and I don't really have to reach it now already. And although the Burgtheater has the most to offer when it comes to glory, Berlin is the only place for financial success, or rather the necessary starting point" (L, 5/12/8).

His contacts and, more importantly, an urbane Viennese charm that could be quite irresistible when he made the effort, gained him quick access to influential circles in both journalism and the theater. On November 25, a mere four days after his arrival in Berlin, he triumphantly reported home that

> the campaign has already been launched. On the whole, people are most amiable. Tonight after the theater I'll be at Michel's. Tomorrow I'll be the Wallners' guest in their box for a premiere at the Residenztheater. I am carefully exploring the terrain, because I want to submit my play only where I have a real chance.

Siegwart Friedmann, whom on the basis of Pollitzer's letter I asked for an interview, gave me an appointment for tomorrow afternoon. Today I'll be meeting Paul Lindau, and sometime soon I'll be having dinner at Wallner's with Oskar Blumenthal and Director Anno of the Residenztheater. [Wallner was a prominent actor, Friedmann a director at the Deutsche Theater, Blumenthal a theater critic and feuilleton editor of the *Berliner Tageblatt*.] Yesterday *grande soirée* at Treitel's [one of his father's business contacts]. Some thirty–forty ugly little Jews and Jewesses. Not a very edifying sight. [L, 11/25/85]

(One must assume that Friedmann and Blumenthal, for their part, were tall and handsome.)

The very next day his social standing as well as his ego received a boost from a wholly unexpected quarter. Friedrich Mitterwurzer, who earlier in the year had accepted Herzl's *Tabarin* for possible use in his repertoire, had staged it as the first offering on his United States tour. Thus it came about that Herzl made his debut as a playwright at the Star Theater on Fourteenth Street in New York on November 23, 1885. The rather favorable review which appeared the next day in the New York *Staats Zeitung* was prominently featured in the Vienna press a few days later and picked up by several Berlin papers. Herzl's impromptu press agents—his father and his friend Oswald Boxer— had obviously done a good job, but it seems fair to say that journalism, in those happy days, had different priorities and that the theater still far outranked murder and mayhem, if only because make-believe seemed more appealing than reality.

Herzl affected a pose of blasé indifference. *"Tabarin* performed in New York. The commodities exchange and the *jours fixes* [i.e., his parents' social and business circles] offer their congratulations. Mbah" (YD, 12/31/85). But whatever his own reaction, the news further heightened suspense among the Berlin contacts he had so assiduously been cultivating for a week without granting them a peek at his actual work. "Already a whole lot of people talk about my *Momma's Little Boy,* but so far no one has read it. Yesterday Mrs. Michels gave a big dinner, to which she invited two prominent journalists for my sake" (L, 11/30/85).

The campaign had indeed been launched, the terrain explored, the forces deployed. But now that the time had come to start shooting in earnest, the metaphorical field marshal found himself in a position not unfamiliar to his real-life counterparts in the imperial Austrian Army: the first shell he fired turned out to be a dud. So did the second and the third. After which he ran out of ammunition.

He had brought what he considered his three best plays, and the Berlin theater people were uniformly polite about them. They masked their consternation by stressing the difference between Viennese and Berlin audiences—a difference very real, to be sure, rooted in a fundamental culture clash between the Danubian capital of make-believe and the dull sobriety of a Prussian garrison town. But what ailed the Herzl plays was not Viennese sparkle and romance, which the dour Berliners had long since learned to put up with or even appreciate in moderate doses, but the lack of simply everything else, from coherent plot and characterization to plausible stage dialogue. The most outspoken response came from Siegwart Friedmann: "I regard your play as hopeless and cannot recommend its submission." The setback, as Herzl reported, left him quite unfazed; what troubled him was that Friedmann "had not said a word about whether he found the play good or bad" (L, 12/2/85).

Less bluntly but in much the same spirit, Franz Wallner persuaded Herzl to desist from further personal efforts and instead turn the entire portfolio over to one Felix Bloch, a seasoned theatrical agent. Bloch expressed guarded hope for *The Hirschkorn Case* and *Tabarin*, but pronounced *Momma's Little Boy* as "too Austrian" and shipped it off to the Burgtheater, which turned it down in due course. (Four years later, and unbeknownst to Herzl, his father on his own initiative resubmitted the play, along with a personal plea for reconsideration based on his son's now secure reputation. The director of the Burgtheater, in his reply of December 18, 1889, pointed out that staging the play might go a long way toward undoing that reputation.)

In his letters home, Herzl summed up his Berlin experience as immensely valuable. "I learned all about the theater here, which was vitally necessary, in fact indispensable. I made good and useful contacts. I am in great spirits and full of high hopes for success" (L, 12/4/85). In private, however, he saw the trip as a fiasco. "I was in Berlin. Came back. No success. How much longer?" (YD, 12/31/85). To Heinrich Kana he complained about the humiliations to which he had been subject, the shameful self-abasement and "groveling in excrement." The outburst elicited a stinging reply from the far less successful but in many ways all too clear-sighted friend:

Is it "groveling in excrement" if one has to socialize with a few ugly and unpleasant people? . . . How would your overblown rhetoric strike someone who, unlike myself, didn't know that at bottom you are a kindhearted and modest person? There goes a young man who has written a good play. His life's goal is to get it produced and to have it earn glory and success. Quite as it should be. But now he demands that everyone else also take up the cause of his play as their supreme goal in life, to the exclusion of everything else. And because they quite rightfully refuse to do so, the young man grows bitter. . . . He sees excrement everywhere. He is disgusted. There are 1,300 million people in the world—1,300 million centers of the universe. And here is one tiny 1,300 millionth, insisting that all the others stop functioning. . . . [Bein, pp. 86–87]

In fact, the results of the trip were about evenly divided between success and failure. People praised his talents but turned down his plays, and even Herzl must have had a hard time accepting their often transparent excuses. His plays were evidence not of talent but of dogged determination, and for all his manifest bravado, he himself must have begun to suspect as much. It did not stop him. For better or for worse, he never outgrew his infantile delusions of omnipotence; all his life he clung to the belief that by sheer force of will he could make any dream come true. In 1885, his dream was to "get into" the Burgtheater. Years later—in 1902—he prefaced his visionary novel about a Jewish state with the motto "If you will it, it won't be a fairy tale." Different dreams, same dreamer.

On the other hand, the failure of his plays obscured the more positive results of the trip, most notably some valuable contacts in the field of journalism, where he was beginning to make a name for himself. He had for some time already been contributing feuilletons and travel pieces to the *Pester Lloyd*, the *Wiener Allgemeine Zeitung* and the Vienna *Presse*, although he complained that "the good feuilletons are rejected, the bad ones accepted and never published" (YD, 10/10/84). But shortly after his return from Berlin he received two tempting offers, both of which he in the end rejected for reasons that reveal a solid core of self-respect beneath the often puerile bluster.

The first came from Heinrich Friedjung, a Jewish historian and rabid German nationalist who was about to assume the editorship of the right-wing, pan-German *Deutsche Zeitung*. He accepted one of Herzl's feuilletons and cordially solicited further contributions—which, in view of his paper's sponsorship and orientation, he proposed to publish under a "less Jewish-sounding" pseudonym. Herzl, the assimilationist proponent of mixed marriages, responded so vehemently that Friedjung felt constrained to apologize.

Of potentially far greater interest was a proposal from Moritz Szeps, the editor of the *Neue Wiener Tagblatt*. Szeps, an aggressive liberal, intimate friend and ideological mentor of Crown Prince Rudolf, had just spent a month in jail for having libeled the anti-Semitic demagogue Schönerer by referring to him as such. The conviction had, if anything, enhanced the editor's moral stature, which was all the more reason for right-wing fanatics to redouble their efforts at silencing him. They found an ally in Prime Minister Taaffe, Rudolf's sworn enemy, who banned the distribution of Szeps's paper by newsstands or street vendors; it was available only in bookstores and thus faced a serious financial crisis just about the time Szeps made Herzl an offer to join his staff on a probationary basis.

Once again Herzl refused. The fact that both Friedjung and Szeps, two men at opposite poles of the political spectrum, were equally intrigued by Herzl's feuilletons underscores the stylistic appeal as well as the social irrelevance of his work. Herzl, for his part, seems to have been wholly indifferent to the ideological orientation of his potential employers; in both instances, it was his personal pride that was at stake. He would not consent to being put on probation, at this stage in his career, any more than he would placate anti-Semites by hiding behind a Teutonic pseudonym.

The job would in any event have been short-lived: a few months later, Szeps's enemies contrived to drive him into bankruptcy. But the affair was to have an epilogue. Crown Prince Rudolf's financial assistance enabled Szeps, in 1887, to resume the publication of his paper under the slightly modified title of *Wiener Tagblatt*, whose attacks so enraged Schönerer that in 1888 he led a Nazi-style raid on the premises, smashing the presses and injuring several people. The old Emperor, profoundly upset by this breach of etiquette, personally stripped Schönerer of his patent of nobility and banished him from parliament, thus hastening the eclipse of an increasingly paranoid rabble-rouser who, in any event, was about to be replaced by a younger, far more sophisticated, and infinitely more dangerous kind of demagogue.

Right after the New Year, the clouds parted—Herzl fell in love. By what may have been no mere coincidence, the object of his passion happened to be the thirteen-year-old niece of Madeleine Kurz, the girl whom in his early teens he had silently worshipped from afar and whom he had continued to idolize as the only true love of his life. His journal entry of January 10, 1886, speaks for itself:

Since yesterday I'm in love, presumably for a long time to come. I love—a thirteen-year-old child: Magda! Eleven years ago I carried her in my arms, in the days when I loved her then fourteen-year-old, long since deceased Aunt Madeleine, the first and only time in my life that I was truly in love. Between then and now nothing but silly little displays of fake emotions without real substance. Never since have I felt my heart beat quite so anxiously and fast.

It did not beat at all.

A dead period, and yet alive with pain.

In the meantime, I grew rough and raw. My heart, so much in love with love, remained cold and silent.

Then came yesterday! Already the invitation promising HER presence moved me to the quick. Old times intoned a song of memories. I waited for her. She was the last to arrive; they were already dancing at the children's ball. I eagerly rose to meet her. A great small beautiful little lady, very sweet. I wanted to kiss her, but she turned her blond little head. I did not kiss her. Then, taking my arm, she made her entry like a little queen. . . . And from the very first moment she was in charge. I was sad whenever she left me, this precocious flirt. I was jealous of every boy she danced with. . . . I saw nothing but her, the sweet, sweet, sweet one. The little dress still short, the sweet body undeveloped— but this fine, noble, beautiful face. The features recalling old times are still recognizable, but different, more finished. And her dear eyes, her golden, golden hair. . . . I was quite beside myself. I had a hard time not treating her like an adult and telling her that I loved her. . . . In short, I acted like a fool. . . . I'm in love with a child. Ridiculous, stupid. In four years she'll do with me whatever she wants. And she'll never love me. Because her kind only loves rich, crude stock-exchange speculators—a

vulgar pack that catches the most beautiful women. I thought
and dreamed of her at night. And today it was only the greatest
self-restraint that kept me from going to the skating rink, where
I knew her to be.

My God, my God. [YD, 1/10/86]

Three days later, passion won out over self-restraint:

The Night of January 13. Today I took the afternoon off and
went to the skating rink, where I was sure to find my sweet little
beautiful one. And there I stood like an old man at the edge of
the ice and watched red-cheeked youth soar past me. . . . She
saw me and vanished at once in the crowd. I must have displeased
her the other day. . . . Two hours later I saw her taking off her
skates and blocked her way at the small overpass. She saw me
from a distance, hesitated for a moment, then headed straight
for where I stood and wanted to pass by. I asked her to be good,
promised to call her "Miss" and never again to address her in
the second person singular. She nodded in mock acknowledg-
ment and disappeared. I stood there like a ridiculous high-school
student. Once more I tried to waylay her, and once more she
passed right by me. Goodbye, lovely dream. . . . I'll marry her—
if she wants me. I have three years. I need public success. A nest
for the golden bird! [YD, 1/13/86]

This rather disastrous outcome apparently still failed to discourage
Herzl. It was little Magda herself who seems to have shown by far the
greater wisdom, as evidenced by an admission ticket to the rink found
among Herzl's effects, on the back of which he gave vent to his feelings
in flowery French: "There I was, heart swelled with love. She did not
show up, the sweet, the dear one. I shall preserve this ticket as a
souvenir of hours sadly spent, of a childish and painful disappointment.
Will I someday be able to show this little token of my furtive tenderness
to that same beloved one? January 18, '86."

There is an innocence both charming and troubling about this
episode and about Herzl's account of it, an innocence symptomatic
of the times but impossible to credit in our own post-Freudian age.
Herzl, to be sure, was no child molester, any more than the Reverend
Dodgson alias Lewis Carroll. But where the genial Oxford eccentric
might have been vaguely amused by the interpretations to which his

writings lend themselves, the prim Viennese bourgeois would have been deeply shocked by what he unwittingly revealed about himself. The feelings inspired by his glacial Lolita are common enough to have spawned an epidemic of child abuse and a worldwide commerce in child pornography. Herzl, however, was almost certainly unaware of their true nature, and it seems safe to assume that he did not act upon them in any way other than by making a fool of himself. Repression is the price of civilization, and like the Reverend Dodgson, he was an eminently civilized human being—fond of prepubescent girls, wild about visions in the clouds, and afraid of women.

It is remarkable how few among Vienna's artistic and intellectual elite—the only ones to have left some traces of their private lives— were able to outgrow the emotional confusion of their adolescence and develop mature relations combining sex and love. At the same time, however, the vast majority managed to adjust to this arrested development by devising strategies that ranged from compulsive promiscuity and adultery to commercial sex or furtive pederasty. Herzl, on the other hand, found it impossible to envisage any of these commonplace arrangements as a permanent solution. He firmly believed in bourgeois marriage and nearly succeeded in convincing himself that it was something to look forward to.

But the strain of the effort shows up in a play which he had already been struggling with for some time. *His Highness*, conceived as a social satire dramatizing the corrosive power of money in human relations, eventually turned into a four-act comedy whose sophomoric cynicism does not entirely mask the elemental panic aroused in him by predatory grownup females.

On February 28, one month after his adventure with thirteen-year-old Magda—who, as he sadly foresaw, "would one day grow into your average nubile daughter"—he met another golden-haired dream girl. Though five years older than Magda, Julie Naschauer nonetheless seemed full of the playful, childlike innocence he found so immensely appealing. By the time he discovered the truth, it was too late to do either of them much good.

Herzl's courtship of his future bride began rather in the spirit of one of his own boudoir farces. Or so at least it seems, perhaps because his is the only version of the script that survives. The other victim of this farce turned tragedy has left no record of her side of the story. Which may be just as well. Flighty, superficial, intelligent but poorly educated, Julie Naschauer could never have hoped to plead her case successfully against an intellectually far superior opponent who, moreover, was also a trained lawyer and compulsive writer. It is Herzl himself who, in his writings and correspondence, unwittingly makes a strong case on her behalf.

The opening scene is the journal entry of February 28, 1886:

A sweet little kiss from Julie. We're standing out on the balcony. In jest I ask her for a kiss. She refuses—"the reason: I'd tell about it afterward."

"And hope to die, Julie, I'll never tell."

Whereupon her rosy face no longer evaded my own. A kiss of such sweetness! Fragrant, fresh, soft lips.

Rather moved, I stepped back into the room—in love. Incredible. [YD, 2/28/86]

And one month later, on March 21:

Two more bewitching kisses from her.

Ready to leave, I'm standing with her in the window niche. A cautious glance all around—and we embrace. Sweet, sweet!

After the first one, I want another. "How immodest," she says, but grants me yet another, even more sweet, intoxicating, intoxicating.

In the meantime, my darling's repulsive daddy sits there, not two feet away, with two other people.

Unfortunately I have to leave. Unfortunately I still don't have sufficient self-control to put up with the disapproving faces of unpleasant parents.

She whispers: "Stay awhile." I would so like to, little Julie, but I can't.

Staggered out and for some time still sipped the delicious aftertaste. How painful the contact with other people. An indefinable small pang because the lips she kissed now touch a cigar, a glass. . . . The wind, however, quickly dispels it.

She definitely loves me.

That second kiss she savored with something almost like gour-
mandise, the sweet, dear one.

I am quite touched by this innocent little love affair. She
obviously rather likes me. Tomorrow I'll go to see her for the
third time to get my "drop of poison."

A drop of sweetness in the bitter cup of hopeless and unsuccessful ambition. [YD, 3/21/86]

His little Julie may well have been more genuinely innocent than
the precocious little vamp who preceded her in his affections, but as
Herzl began to realize after his third taste of her "sweet poison," she
was nonetheless a woman rather than a child. It was an alarming
thought:

> Postscript May 23: But I must not linger in such charming
> dalliances. The troubles they bring in their wake drive me out
> further and further—out into the void, into obsessive careerism,
> and into a success which, however inevitable, will nonetheless
> come too late. Temper your soft heart on the anvil of a thousand
> obstacles, you poor and last of the troubadours. [YD, 3/23/86]

What Julie wanted was clear from the outset, and Herzl cannot
have entertained any illusions about it: she was looking for a husband.
He had reason to believe that she was in love with him, a thought as
scary as it was flattering, and she derived obvious pleasure from their
furtive little games. But these were the mating rites of the Jewish
bourgeoisie, and he was familiar enough with them to know that if
the "average nubile daughter" from a respectable family let herself be
kissed, what she had in mind was marriage rather than sex. And
marriage, though he viewed it with more than the normal misgivings,
was on his mind as well. Julie embodied all the cardinal virtues he
theoretically wished for in his future wife and mother of his children:
blond hair, blue eyes, easy charm, and a proper family background.
That this background included considerable wealth and the prospect
of a sizable dowry was a complicating but not a decisive factor one
way or another. Unlike chastity, of course, which was taken for granted;
he would never have considered marrying a woman willing to carry
those mating rites to their physiological conclusion.

Yet much as he fantasized about marriage as the ultimate affirmation
of manhood, status, and success, he quite uncharacteristically was in

no hurry to meet that particular challenge. Quite the contrary: he was most anxious to avoid compromising entanglements, and whatever his unconscious motives, he rationalized them by his lack of success as a playwright and his inability to support Julie in the style to which she was accustomed. Being in no position to propose, he decided on the only honorable course open to a man of his principles and embarked on a campaign to "cure" her of her infatuation by an ostentatious display of indifference and a series of deliberate snubs. He told himself—and his journal—that he did so with a heavy heart.

The campaign was unsuccessful. Julie, in the meantime, had mounted one of her own.

What had started as yet another lighthearted flirtation threatened to get out of hand without his quite understanding how and why. And however mixed and mixed up his feelings about it, they merely added a neurotic component to some very realistic problems accentuated by the whole question of marriage. As a playwright, he had thus far been a resounding failure, his sole success a one-shot performance—in some godforsaken dump at the other end of the world—of a play based on someone else's work. And his journalism, despite a prolific output and growing acceptance, still left him financially dependent on his father.

The tentative affair with Julie merely added further pressures; he now believed himself to be in love with her, hence more than ever in need of quick, tangible success. In July—"Julie's month"—having finished *His Highness,* he took off on another trip that again combined escape with a chance to gather fresh material for his newspaper pieces. And once again travel—or distance from home—worked its magic. Full of high spirits after four days in by now familiar Paris, he headed north into Normandy and eventually ended up in Trouville, "the most beautiful, most elegant of all seaside resorts I've ever known. Only in England could there be anything superior." He relished pomp and circumstance, loved the glamour of formal occasions, and threw himself with zest into the social whirl that during the summer months transformed this picturesque fishing village into a playground of the upper middle class. Some of the more daring among the visitors actually bared their ankles and waded out into the ocean during ebbtide; but the principal distractions, apart from the ritual boardwalk promenade and the nightly dances, were provided by neighboring and even more fashionable Deauville, site of a casino and of a famous racetrack.

While making the most of these temptations, Herzl still managed to turn out two feuilletons during his one-week stay. He felt revitalized, full of energy, gave hardly a thought to Julie or to any of the other worries he had ditched back home—and was flat broke by the end of the week. "Sans le sou, literally" (YD, 8/16/86). Living it up in Trouville was obviously expensive, quite apart from Deauville casino with its *"petits cheveaux* that make you lose your money" (YD, 8/21/86). But as always Daddy, like the cavalry, came to the rescue in the nick of time. "Daddy dear, I didn't want to hit you again for a loan, but since you're offering me one, it would be unreasonable to refuse. So please be so kind as to remit another 100 francs c/o General Delivery, Cabourg. There is reason to hope that I'll soon be able to repay part of my debts" (L, 8/15/86). In order to put temptation behind him, he moved twelve miles down the coast to Cabourg, in his day a more modest resort, which has since become one of the world's great literary landmarks—thanks not to Herzl, whose article on the subject has been lost to posterity, but to Marcel Proust, who from 1907 to 1914 spent his summers at Cabourg and immortalized it as the Balbec of his memory.

After barely a month in Vienna, Herzl again took off for Berlin in early October, armed this time with the script of his latest play, in which he invested the usual high hopes. For once they were not to be altogether disappointed. Franz Wallner, his most helpful contact in the Berlin theater, liked *His Highness* well enough to propose extensive revisions that occupied Herzl through much of his three-week stay, though eventually another year and a half were to pass before the play was finally produced. Of more immediate significance for his future career were certain new contacts in the newspaper world, particularly with Arthur Levysohn, the editor in chief of the *Berliner Tageblatt*, Germany's most important liberal daily.

The two had already met earlier during the summer, and Herzl was received with exceptional cordiality.

I've just returned from a visit with the Levysohns. . . . Both gave me a splendid welcome. Levysohn himself heaped so many eulogies and compliments on my head that I felt downright embarrassed. We talked for two whole hours. He is a brilliant conversationalist. They've invited me for dinner tomorrow. Afterward I took him to his office in my carriage, and along the way we agreed that a week from tomorrow I'll turn in a *causerie* [chronicle of the week], with an eye toward making it a regular weekly feature. This first one will be a test. You can well imagine that I'm going to give it my best shot. . . . As he took leave, this uncommonly pleasant man conveyed a feeling of warmth and of friendship that simply delighted me. [L, 10/8/86]

Levysohn, one of the highest-paid journalists in Germany, had been hired in 1876 by the publisher Rudolph Mosse in the wake of a salary dispute at the *Berliner Tageblatt* that led to the resignation of the entire original staff. He was himself of Viennese origin, which may partly account for the extravagant enthusiasm with which he viewed both Herzl's work and his prospects. "Levysohn expects great things from my play. He says he always maintained that I had a great future on the stage. In Gossesass he talked about me with Daniel Spitzer. He says I am already well known in Germany. In short, a hundred things that make me proud and happy" (L, 10/9/86).

Quite aside from admiring Herzl's literary talent, however, Levysohn may have been guided by more personal considerations; there is reason to believe that he saw more in him than just a promising new contributor. At any rate, he strongly encouraged the flirtation that developed between his oldest daughter, Susanne, and the eminently eligible young bachelor. Apparently nothing serious came of it, but even in later years Herzl retained a tone of quasi-filial devotion in all his dealings with the man he always addressed as "Master."

Their professional relationship, on the other hand, got off to a good start. On the basis of Herzl's very first contribution, Levysohn took him on as a regular columnist, giving him complete freedom as to the choice of subject matter. From the fall of 1886 through much of 1887, Herzl contributed a brief feature almost every week or two to the prestigious Berlin daily, thus marking a rather noteworthy advance in his career as a journalist. The features as such covered a broad range of topics, but merely just covered them with a wisp of irony without ever coming to grips with any substantive issue; and though at first the unaccustomed fizz elicited some favorable comments, the novelty soon wore off and it became clear that neither the Berlin literati nor the readership at large shared Levysohn's taste for this exotic import. The column ran with some interruptions for about two years but was discontinued at the end of 1888.

*　*　*

In the end, the high hopes with which Herzl had left for Berlin had once again been dashed; after holding out all sorts of promises, the various powers that be reserved judgment about the much-doctored version of *His Highness* and counseled patience, the one virtue totally foreign to his character. His father for the first time fussed about what seemed to him extravagant travel expenses—a stinging reminder to Herzl of his continued financial dependence. He defended himself by stressing the positive results of the trip. They were real enough; aside from the column for the *Berliner Tageblatt*, he had also linked up with a Hamburg magazine and greatly expanded his contacts. But these partial victories failed to make up for the major disappointment. He still regarded journalism as little more than a temporary expedient, a means of making a living until he had gained a firm foothold in the theater, and the new outlets meant that much more hack work at a time when he least felt up to it.

But again he would not let the depression paralyze him. Determined to live up to his by now overextended obligations, he cranked out his pieces at an ever more frenzied pace, until, by the end of the year, the body rebelled. The tension erupted in an intractable pain afflicting the back of his head and the nape of his neck. The doctors he consulted could provide no relief, but his parents proved more astute: they suggested another trip, this time to Italy, the traditional refuge of all German poets and thinkers.

Instantly recovered and full of enthusiasm, he laid out plans for a series of travel sketches and, in the last week of January 1887, wrote a one-act bedroom farce which he hoped would eventually enable him to repay the 200 guilders his father offered him for the trip. Not that, on the face of it, anything had changed between them. Herzl as always worried aggressively about the health of fifty-two-year-old Jakob and still referred to him as "my golden one," but he could no longer square it with his pride to let himself be supported. Besides, he must have sensed the growing conflict in Jakob Herzl between his paternal love and his tight-fisted bookkeeper mentality.

The potboiler Herzl turned out in less than a week's time was no worse than many of his more ambitious plays. The aristocratic heroine refuses to grant a divorce to her philandering husband. She still loves the charming cad and, by a ruse meant to be vaguely risqué, recaptures her errant playboy—presumably Herzl's idea of a happy ending. The actor-director Ernst Hartmann, to whom *The Fugitive* was first submitted, rejected it out of hand. "Model your characters on real people rather than on plastercasts from a theater museum," he advised Herzl. "You obviously and without a doubt have talent, imagination—everything it takes, but it seems to me that you ought to treat human beings with a little more respect, that you ought to look at them more seriously and at greater depth if you want to portray them" (L. Kellner, p. 69). Despite this blunt critique, the play was accepted a year later by the Burgtheater and had its premiere on May 4, 1889.

Herzl in the meantime had left for Venice on February 15 on the first leg of a leisurely six-week tour that took him via Pisa and Livorno to Rome. After a week in the capital, he headed south, spent time in Naples, Amalfi, and Capri, and returned home via Florence and Bologna, arriving in Vienna on April 2.

The majesty of Rome, the serenity of the Campagna, or the stunning vision of the Gulf of Naples may have been spoiled or wrecked by mass tourism and the infernal combustion engine, but to this day enough of it remains to recapture some of the feelings with which the traveler of a hundred years ago responded to what was then the shrine of European civilization. There was probably no major figure in the arts and letters of the time who failed to make the pilgrimage or, having made it, came away unchanged. For the most part, they were overwhelmed by this sun-drenched landscape in which past and present coexisted in unforced harmony, inspired and ultimately defeated by the challenge to express not only what they saw but what they felt, and Herzl was no exception. What he felt was an inarticulate rapture which resonates even in the banal communiqués to his parents. But what he saw went into a series of feuilletons that far surpassed anything he had ever done before. They revealed his now undisputed mastery of this peculiarly Viennese art form and created a minor literary sensation. He had left for Italy, one among many aspiring young talents. He returned six weeks later with a name and a reputation.

He had earned it; there was nothing fortuitous about this success. From the start he had conceived of this trip as a means to an end, and he let neither the flood of new impressions nor the desire for a well-earned rest distract him from the goals he had staked out for himself. Hard work was part of the secret—ten articles during a six-week vacation. When he ran out of money in Naples—some royalties he had counted on were delayed—he specifically asked his father not to come to his aid. "This is not an affectation on my part, but rather my firm decision. . . . In fact, it is good for me not to be swimming in money, otherwise I wouldn't have the patience to do any work. This is, after all, the place where they invented the *dolce far niente*. Yesterday afternoon I sat down at my desk to write the second feuilleton of the Wanderer. The window was open, and the Gulf of Naples spread out before me, so that I spent hours on end just gazing at it instead of putting pen to paper" (L, 3/4/87). (Two weeks later he was nonetheless forced to ask for a loan of 50 guilders.)

But hard work would have been wasted without astute planning, and Herzl was remarkably adept at finding the right keys to the right doors. "Yesterday I finally finished my 'Emmelfy' feuilleton and will send it by the next regular mail to Kolisch [publisher of the *Wiener Allgemeine Zeitung*]. This because I want to switch to him from the *Pester Journal*, for obvious reasons. The *Neue Freie Presse* (even if those snobs didn't make me beg for it) would at most print one or two of my pieces a year. In Germany, my status is assured by the *Berliner Tageblatt*; for Vienna, the *Wiener Allgemeine Zeitung* will suffice" (L, 3/22/87).

It more than sufficed. His new-won celebrity led to a job offer from Baron Ignaz von Kolisch, which Herzl accepted, though not without misgivings. "I have been hired as feuilleton editor of the *Wiener Allgemeine Zeitung*, starting tomorrow," he recorded in his diary on April 14. "I have arrived as a journalist—and at the same time I am also finished. Or so I fear. Perhaps I am wrong. Which would be all to the good, but I don't believe it" (YD, 4/14/87).

His doubts seem to have been justified; three months later he was fired.

For three whole months I slaved like a coolie and gave good service in return for rank ingratitude. I proved my mettle as a journalist—no one up to then thought me capable of covering a story or writing an obit. Now that I proved I could do it, they're kicking me out. Which does not break my heart. On July 15 I'll be through. What I put up with here in these three months by way of disgust, filth, and excrement would fill the cloaca maxima to overflowing. The charge against me is not having shown proper subservience toward the boss, a man who made his money on the stock exchange and now directs an organ of public opinion. He sees himself as the guardian of public morality. As for myself, I am looking forward to freedom. [L, 6/29/87]

The blow, however, was cushioned by news that the Wallner Theater in Berlin had accepted *His Highness*. At the same time, job opportunities seemed to be opening up everywhere. The *Fremdenblatt*,
a daily sponsored by the Foreign Ministry, published two of his feuilletons and was considering him for an editorial position. A group
planning a new theater magazine in Berlin offered him the editorship,
but the project folded before he could ever make a decision. In the
meantime, the *Berliner Tageblatt* lost its theater critic and feuilleton
editor, and Herzl had high hopes of taking his place. Finally, the
almost equally prestigious *Frankfurter Zeitung* was shopping for a Paris
correspondent, and Arthur Levysohn promised to use the weight of
his influence on Herzl's behalf.

The latter prospect seemed by far the most exciting, but Herzl could
not possibly envisage even a temporary separation from his parents.
"If it does come to pass, my dear daddy, what you'll do is simply shut
down your business and retire in comfort to Paris. The few acquaintances one loses by moving can't hold us back. Heine was a Paris
correspondent. So, after an intermission, were Lindau and Wittmann.
Singer, of the *Neue Freie Presse*, and Blowitz of the *Times* are practically like ambassadors. Levysohn started his big career as Paris correspondent for the *Kölnische Zeitung*. No need, therefore, to fret about
this plan. . . . We would still remain together (L, 8/15/87).

He spent the summer in the Tirolean Alps, dividing his time between
work on another play, discreet self-promotion, and uneasy rest. In
August, a Leipzig publisher brought out his first book, a selection of
eighteen feuilletons. The intriguing title, *News from Venus*, prompted
at least one German newspaper to turn down the advertisement for it,
but the actual contents must have sorely disappointed anyone either
lured or scandalized by the promise of sophisticated lubricity. The
leitmotif is love, nonetheless: just as science and reason stripped the
planet Venus of its mystery and reduced it to merely another heavenly
body moving in predictable orbits, so love—according to Herzl—loses
its magic once it approaches fulfillment and reveals the object of desire
as merely one more human being. The windy, world-weary lucubra-
tions on the theme of love that preempt most of this collection are
proof of a pathetic immaturity; ignorance greatly simplifies issues, and
there was nothing Herzl knew less about than the one subject on which
he was here pontificating. But it also happened to be the subject that
for some time now had both obsessed and disturbed the twenty-seven-

year-old more than any other. He needed love, or felt he did, and nothing in his background, outlook, or psychic structure would permit him to conceive of a love object other than a woman. Yet no woman in the flesh, by the mere fact of being one, could live up to his fantasies of an ethereal companion in the image of his own idealized mother. The dilemma trapped him in a seemingly irreconcilable conflict, but after wrestling with it for nearly two years, he found a solution consistent with his faith in the power of dreams: he endowed Julie Naschauer with the attributes of the ideal woman and proposed marriage.

It is not known what led to their reconciliation in the fall of 1887, after more than a year of separation. Julie was headstrong in her own way, and Herzl's growing fame made him a more desirable catch than ever. He, on the other hand, felt much more confident about his future. True, none of the alluring job prospects had panned out in the end, but he was well on this way to the top, and a vital ingredient of successful manhood in the tradition of his clan and class was the idea of fatherhood and domestic bliss.

I have found my good Julie again—my last love [he exulted on September 7, 1887]. She has always loved me. I am going to marry her. I already told her so. She is sweet, sweet, sweet—

But a few dangerous giants remain to be slain before I can claim my darling little princess.

This was the day of depressing news. I don't have a job. Since July 15 I am no longer with the *Allgemeine*. It looks as though the position with the *Fremdenblatt* won't materialize. If that doesn't work out, I'll once again be shipwrecked, drifting out into the wild sea of the bohème and won't be able to ask for Julie's hand.

True, *His Highness* has been accepted by the Wallner Theater in Berlin, but if it flops, I'll be a poor and broken man. Poorer than ever before, because my youthful courage has deserted me. And then I'll have to say goodbye forever to my much beloved darling. I don't want her to waste her youth on my account. I may never amount to anything. It hurts to have to say that to oneself.

Oh yes—*News from Venus*. Don't make me laugh. Although the publisher talks about a second edition. A fool he who believes it. [YD, 9/7/87]

For a Viennese author or journalist, the ultimate accolade was his byline in the *Neue Freie Presse,* tangible evidence that he had earned his place in the sun. To call it merely the best newspaper in Vienna and one of the best in Europe is to understate the true scope of its influence on the political and cultural climate of Austria-Hungary in the final half century of the Dual Monarchy.

Founded in 1864, it was the first newspaper on the Continent to be printed on a rotary rather than a flatbed press, the first in Vienna to introduce travel sketches, essays, and fiction as an integral part of the editorial contents. Its business section, run by outstanding professionals, quickly gained international recognition. By 1887 the *Neue Freie Presse,* under the joint editorship of Moritz Benedikt and Eduard Bacher, had become a sociopolitical institution, the embodiment of Austro-Hungarian liberalism at both its best and its worst. In literary quality and breadth of overall coverage it had no rival, a fact which regularly led foreign observers to mistake the *Neue Freie Presse* for the authentic voice of Austrian public opinion, when in fact it spoke— however eloquently—for a shrinking minority: it was the voice, the Bible, the Talmud of the liberal bourgeoisie, its one and only window on the world. Whatever the *Neue Freie Presse* featured in its columns was worth knowing about; what it ignored, disdained, or condemned— which took in a large slice of territory, such as sports, fires, routine crimes, and all of avant-garde art—simply did not matter. This elitist attitude, a reflection of Benedikt's personal philosophy, may have been the reason why, despite its qualitative superiority, the paper never attained the circulation—and hence the advertising revenues—of Moritz Szeps's *Neue Wiener Tagblatt,* even if its influence was incomparably greater. Twice a day, six days a week, at the crack of dawn and in the late afternoon, the gospel according to Benedikt rolled off the presses and was faithfully studied even by its most dedicated adversaries.

The paper's dominance of the cultural scene was, in fact, near absolute and, on the whole, pernicious. Its critics ruled supreme as the arbiters of middlebrow tastes, their prejudices being invested with the authority of divine judgment. Eduard Hanslick, a brilliant stylist who, as the paper's chief music critic during the final decades of the century, himself became the center of a minor cult, devoted the full power of his oracular sarcasm to an unrelenting rearguard action against such revolutionaries as Richard Wagner, Anton Bruckner, and Hugo Wolf. The most representative art critic was Ludwig Speidel, a devoted

Makart champion who, during the forty-odd years of his tenure, also reviewed nearly every production of the Burgtheater and, in that capacity, pronounced the verdict that sealed the fate of the play. It was thanks to him that Ibsen and Hauptmann flopped ignominiously on Vienna's most prestigious stage, while one Leo Ebermann became the toast of the town.

Ultimately, the cultural influence of the *Neue Freie Presse* derived from its power to articulate the bias of culture's main consumers, the liberal middle class. For the same reason, however, its influence on national politics appears in retrospect much less significant than Herzl's contemporaries liked to believe. Initially, the paper's consistently liberal, pro-Austrian stance lent intellectual respectability to prevailing trends, but with the end of the liberal era, it soon found itself at odds with both the government and the rising populist movements at either end of the political spectrum. The fact that it was owned and edited by Jews became an added liability following the crash of 1873 and the spread of organized anti-Semitism.

But though its influence declined, the *Neue Freie Presse*, like the liberal bourgeoisie, remained a potent factor in the country's politics. For one thing, it occupied the often strategically crucial middle ground in a field increasingly polarized between right and left—or did so at least until 1897, when it came out in support of Social Democratic candidates as the only credible alternative to right-wing extremism. Much of the credit, however, must go to Moritz Benedikt personally, whose editorials during the forty years of his reign comprise an estimated two hundred volumes of five hundred pages each. A popular saying of the day had it that "after Moritz Benedikt, the most important figure in the realm is Franz Joseph"—an exaggeration, whether prompted by anti-Semitism or wishful thinking, but not without its kernel of truth. Benedikt played a major role in defeating Taafe's electoral reforms; he helped to bring about the end of the Prime Minister's fourteen-year rule, and until the collapse of the monarchy, few ministerial candidates, no matter how they felt about the *Neue Freie Presse* in private, would fail to stop off at its editorial offices for a chat with the great man himself in the hope of obtaining his blessing.

Some years earlier, Herzl had gone to see Benedikt about a job and been informed that the *Neue Freie Presse* had neither time nor room for novices. Thereafter, he avoided all further contact; it was the one paper to which he never ventured to submit any of his early feuilletons, and his snide remarks about its snobbishness lead one to suspect that he not only smarted from the slight but also felt intimidated by this sacred monster and its high priests.

Intimidated or not, it did not stop him from pursuing his goal. The original strategy seems to have called for a cautiously oblique approach: rather than risk another snub, he would wait for his star to rise and for the *Neue Freie Presse* to try to catch it. But in the fall of 1887, with Julie back in the picture and all his job prospects fizzled out, he swallowed his pride and decided to force the issue.

Avoiding a second confrontation with the formidable Benedikt, he chose instead to approach the co-editor, Eduard Bacher, offering his services "just as the young field marshal Moltke once offered his sword to a higher power." The prideful bombast was, however, softened by an admixture of uncharacteristic humility. A year earlier he had contemptuously scorned Moritz Szeps's proposal of a trial period; now he proposed it himself: "I would not, of course, wish this to be interpreted as the pretentious offer of a present on my part. For actual work done, you could compensate me at your usual rates for freelancers, although I would keep regular office hours. This would give you an opportunity to test me in every department. You might even discover that the feuilletonist who proposes himself as a war-and-peace correspondent is, in reality, an editorial writer" (L, 10/14/87 and 1/2/88).

Bacher's answer was friendly but noncommittal. There were currently no openings at the paper, but he would be happy to consider any contributions Herzl cared to submit; this might eventually lead to a more permanent relationship.

Meanwhile, the Berlin premiere of *His Highness*, originally scheduled for the fall of 1887, kept being postponed; in the end, the play first opened not in Germany but at the Prague German Theater on February 12, 1888. The acting director was Heinrich Teweles, a gifted manipulator who in his multiple roles as playwright, critic, and poet had anointed himself the Pope of the German literary establishment in Prague; he later succeeded Angelo Neumann as director of the German Theater. The fast friendship that developed between him and Herzl may not have been the only reason for the favorable notices, but it certainly did no harm, the less so since "Tewelino," as Herzl fondly addressed him, anonymously authored two highly flattering reviews himself. Even so, the play closed after three performances.

The reception in Berlin, where it opened on March 18, was somewhat more ambiguous. According to the author, "the success was *much greater* than in Prague, despite an incomparably worse performance. . . . The first act was a hit and has made my name here in Berlin— according to what everybody tells me—as a dramatist with a great future. The last act was a miss, though not as bad as in Prague" (L, 3/9/88).

The reviews were reserved, most of them mixing praise for "the brilliant feuilletonist" with pointed criticism of the play itself. It was not, in any case, an auspicious moment for a stage debut; Berliners had other things on their mind. Wilhelm I, King of Prussia and first Emperor of the new Reich, had died ten days before the opening, his successor was himself terminally ill with cancer, and the next in line, Queen Victoria's erratic and unstable grandson, aroused much justified apprehension. That, in the circumstances, the press paid any attention at all to a mediocre play by a novice playwright testifies to the prestige the theater still enjoyed as an institution.

Herzl, though seemingly content, took the criticism to heart and once again tried to lure a more experienced hand into collaborating with him. But Oskar Blumenthal, formerly of the *Berliner Tageblatt*, now director of the Lessing Theater in Berlin, turned down the honor, forcing Herzl to finish *The Swan's Neck* all by himself. Regarded as hopeless even by the well-meaning and well-connected Teweles, it was never produced.

At about the same time, however, Herzl's Leipzig publisher brought out the second collection of his essays. Entitled *Book of Folly*, prefaced by a quote from Swift's *A Tale of a Tub*, and dedicated to Arthur Levysohn, it is a typical *fin de siècle* concoction of arch epigrams, synthetic sophistication, and epic banalities decked out in fake irony, but with the same dandyish attention to style which the young author lavished on his wardrobe and which made him a natural enemy of naturalism in literature and on the stage. He attacked the "macrobiotic school" of playwriting, its preoccupation with illness and death spawned by "the ghosts of Ibsen," and freely dispensed lapidary pro-fundities on the nature of love: "True love, pure love free of vanity, selfishness, reservations, free of all petty, narrow-minded and base motives does not exist." Both his books were published in luxury editions, and neither paid its way. *News from Venus* sold 700 copies, the *Book of Folly* only 300. But they endowed the ephemeral products of his journalism with a touch of immortality and thus served to enhance both Herzl's reputation and his self-esteem.

He spent July and August on an extended trip which took him to Brussels, London, Brighton, the Isle of Wight, Boulogne, Trouville, and Ostend. His first contact with England, and with the grandeur of Victorian London in particular, aroused wild enthusiasm: "London is the most beautiful city I ever saw, including Paris. At the moment, working is no effort whatsoever, because there is constant inspiration" (L, 7/18/88). The inspiration yielded no less than fifteen travel sketches, five of which he submitted to the *Neue Freie Presse*. Every one of them was accepted and immediately published, a sure sign of his being well on his way to realizing at least one of his dreams. "If Dr. Bacher takes everything I send him, he will be the first person I'll go to see when I get back to Vienna. I shall then try to establish some kind of regular contact with his paper, just as I now have with the *Berliner Tageblatt*. The sure touch, the self-confidence I still lack will come once the first half dozen feuilletons are published. This is what I am hoping for. If so, I'll have achieved the purpose of my trip" (L, 3/8/88). He also improved his English, learned to smoke a pipe rather than the habitual cigars which he found inordinately expensive, and felt so much at home in the country that "if today the *Neue Freie Presse* needed a London correspondent, I believe they'd think of me."

Although Bacher still resisted any more permanent arrangements, Herzl rightly felt that he had more or less scaled this particular peak and that, as a journalist, he had arrived. In what he still thought of as his true vocation, on the other hand, he had yet to prove himself. The productions of *His Highness* in Prague and Berlin had given him a temporary lift, but their on the whole rather indifferent reception left a bitter aftertaste. In any event, they could never have amounted to more than an ersatz success at best; the only stage that truly counted for him was the Burgtheater, as formidable an institution in its way as the *Neue Freie Presse*. Having reached his first goal, he now zeroed in on the second.

And once again Herzl the dreamer demonstrated his eminently practical streak. Despite his vast capacity for self-deception, his critics had forced him to recognize certain shortcomings in his work for the stage. He took it to be a lack of technical proficiency and know-how that experience would overcome in time, but he was not prepared to wait any longer. If you will it . . . If he couldn't bring it off all by himself, the logical alternative was to seek competent help. And this time he succeeded.

He chose well. Hugo Wittmann, the man to whom he turned, was a many-faceted writer and theater critic who, from 1869 to 1872, had been Paris correspondent for the *Neue Freie Presse* and thereafter one of its most popular feuilletonists. He had written several plays and was also much in demand as a librettist, working with Johann Strauss among others. Wittmann agreed to collaborate, but only on condition that the authorship of this joint effort remain strictly anonymous. Herzl accepted, having no other choice, and proceeded to draft an outline which his prolific partner fleshed out in record time. The result was *The Poachers*, the greatest critical and financial success of Herzl's entire career as a playwright, even if its record of numerous productions throughout both Austria and Germany tells more about the popular tastes of the time than about the quality of the play as such.

The poachers of the title are two worldly aristocrats and one middle-class oaf who regard all women as fair prey. As chance personified by Herzl wills it, their designated victims turn out to be the aristocrat's ex-wife and daughter, and after the usual farfetched twists and turns, one titled twerp remarries his own wife, the other marries the daughter, and the untitled bumbler is left out in the cold, proving that class conquers all—not quite, one assumes, what Herzl had in mind by way of a moral.

Wittmann, however, managed to provide this mangy skeleton of an idea with exactly what Herzl had never been able to supply—humor, deft pacing, and snappy dialogue, and on February 4, 1889, he submitted the finished script to the Burgtheater with a request not to divulge the names of the authors.

It was accepted immediately, although one reference to a "sleeping car reservation" for a lady was deemed obscene and had to be deleted. The play had its premiere barely a month later, on March 19. It received rave reviews, played to packed houses, and for thirteen years remained a stock item in the Burgtheater's annual repertoire for a total of fifty-six performances; the final one took place on October 24, 1904. (In Berlin, on the other hand, where it opened on March 23, it was an instant flop and folded after three performances.)

For Herzl, the taste of glory must have been somewhat spoiled by the contractually enforced anonymity; what was the good of success without the acclaim of your friends and the envy of your enemies? But as a publicity stunt—though probably an unintended one—the secret of the play's authorship worked wonders. Inquisitive reporters had, of course, no trouble tracking down the truth, but among the uninitiated the guessing game continued for some time; it was not until a year later that the authors—at Herzl's insistence—publicly acknowledged their brainchild.

By then, however, he had had his own personal triumph: on May 4, 1889, the Burgtheater staged his one-acter *The Fugitive*. At twenty-nine, he had thus fulfilled his life's ambitions: his byline in the *Neue Freie Presse* and his name on the Burgtheater playbill. He was now at the top of his world, ready to settle down. Or, if not ready, at least not in a position to postpone the inevitable any longer.

He paid a call on Jakob Naschauer and asked for the hand of his daughter Julie.

NINE

*A*ccording to an entry in the marriage registry of the Vienna Jewish community in Leopoldstadt, Tivadar alias Theodor Herzl, son of Jakob, native of Budapest, Doctor of Law, and Julie Naschauer, daughter of Jakob, native of Budapest, were married in Reichenau on June 25, 1889, at 1 p.m.

This is just about the only fact known for certain about the wedding, and it raises questions. Why Reichenau, of all places, a mountain resort some two hours by train from the city where both families were socially prominent in the Jewish community? Was there a religious ceremony? And given the affluence of the bride's parents and their ostentatious vulgarity, the reception at the Rudolfsvilla—a mansion rented for the occasion—should have been an elaborate affair; yet no wedding pictures, descriptions, or references to it seem to have survived.

The circumstances surrounding this unfortunate event have prompted much speculation, but they constitute merely one aspect of a much larger mystery to which Herzl himself alludes almost exactly one year later in a letter to the woman who by then was his wife and the mother of his child:

> You often told me that it would have been better if I had not married you. To which I myself can only add that it would also have been more honorable. Unfortunately, this is something I have come to understand only now. At the time I deemed it

more honorable to live up to my word, although I had already realized the extent to which our characters are incompatible. A higher morality should have stopped me. [L, 6/90]

What fatal flaw locked these two strangers into a lifelong war of attrition in which they ultimately consumed each other and perhaps destroyed their children and grandchild as well?

If a common background assured compatibility, the marriage should have been a happy one. Although the Naschauers had a great deal more money than the Herzls, they were part of the same social stratum, a Jewish bourgeoisie barely two generations out of the ghetto and indelibly marked by the abrupt transition from piety to prosperity. Julie's paternal grandfather Moritz, a native of Bohemia, settled in Budapest in the early years of the century. An observant Jew much like Herzl's grandfather Simon, and widely respected for his learning, he nonetheless sent both his sons to secular schools. Wilhelm, the older, participated actively in the Kossuth rebellion of 1848, moved to Vienna soon thereafter, and went into business with his brother Jakob. Their partnership, however, extended to the private sphere as well: the two brothers married two sisters, whose rather vague lineage created problems for their progeny.

They were the daughters of one Moritz Kollinsky, presumed to have been Jewish despite his Polish surname. In any case, under Talmudic law—the Halakah—the father's credentials as a Jew have no bearing on the status of his children; the mother alone is empowered to pass her tribal membership on to the next generation, and the mother's pedigree, in this instance, seems to have fallen short of perfection. Franziska Kollinsky, Julie's grandmother, lived with the Naschauers until her death in 1897. She probably passed as Jewish and is buried alongside her husband in the Jewish section of Vienna's Central Cemetery, but in the eyes of the purists, her profession of faith would have been recognized as legitimate only if she herself had either been born of a certifiably Jewish mother or undergone a valid and documented conversion. There appears to have been room for doubt on that score, and in the absence of proof to the contrary, neither she nor any of her descendants would have qualified as Jewish under the Talmudic criteria which the state of Israel has adopted for the strictly secular purpose of deciding whom it recognizes as a Jew. As a result, the wife and children of the man it venerates as its founding father would presumably be ineligible for the instant citizenship which, under the Law of Return, the Jewish state extends to any bona fide Jew.

An issue of less than earth-shaking significance and probably beyond any definite resolution, although the discreet silence of the early hagiographers and the curious choice of Reichenau for the Herzl wedding—and for the wedding of Julie's sister the following year—lend added credibility to these rumors. According to the unpublished memoirs of Rabbi Moritz Guedemann, he was asked to officiate at the Herzl–Naschauer wedding but had to refuse due to family business. Guedemann, who in 1893 succeeded Adolf Jellinek as Vienna's Chief Rabbi, was forever trying to trim a zealously Orthodox conscience to the expectations of a less than Orthodox congregation; the effort required nimble footwork, devious compromises, and frequent readjustments of his public stance. He might in fact have been otherwise engaged; he may also have had his doubts about Julie's qualifications for a Jewish wedding ceremony and wished to back out without offending two prominent members of the community.

Jakob Naschauer was not only prominent but also very rich. He and his brother had gone into business in the early 1860s, at a most propitious moment in the country's economic and industrial development, and made the most of the manifold opportunities that presented themselves. The Wilhelm Naschauer enterprises comprised a whole range of activities, from oil drilling, flood control, and reclamation to food and livestock trade. Wilhelm had his headquarters in Vienna, while Jakob remained in Budapest to exploit his local contacts in the eastern regions until 1880, when he followed the general westward drift and settled with his wife, mother-in-law, and five children in a sumptuous mansion in Vienna's Leopoldstadt district.

It is doubtful if the empire builder could have paid much attention to his family even had he wanted to. His marriage was a business arrangement that had long since degenerated into a perpetual feud, although he personally tried to avoid pitched battles with his wife whenever possible and chose instead to distance himself by taking frequent and extended trips—tactics which his son-in-law initially denounced as cowardly and "unmanly," but whose wisdom he himself came to appreciate in due course of time.

Not that Herzl ever changed his mind about Jakob Naschauer; he despised him as an uncouth barbarian, a cultural illiterate with nothing but money on his brain, probably a fair enough assessment even if the observer was far from unbiased. Like most successful businessmen of his time and ours, Jakob Naschauer loved money for its own sake as well as for what it bought—power, status, and the respect he was willing to settle for in the absence of more maudlin sentiments. And in the end, even Herzl developed a certain grudging sympathy for the old brigand and saw him as a fellow victim in the unholy war of women against men.

In the Naschauer castle on Lilienbrunngasse, the mother ruled supreme; the father was not even accorded the nominal deference which usually masked the true balance of power in a Jewish home. He and she both loved money; he made it, she spent it. Very little else is known about Johanna Naschauer, described by friends as high-strung and temperamental and by enemies as a hysterical harridan, except that she could provoke outbursts of savage fury in her ordinarily cool and self-possessed son-in-law. Herzl referred to her as a bitch and an old sow, epithets he did not normally bandy about in his letters or conversation.

In any case, none of this can have been much of a surprise to the unhappy bridegroom. He had had his first taste of the Naschauers while still a student, shortly after his—and their—arrival in Vienna, and been both awed and appalled by the conspicuous wealth, un-abashed ostentation, and vulgar consumerism. These were the typical nouveaux riches he lampooned in his plays, and he despised them with all the arrogance of the self-styled aristocrat. In the real world, of course, the main difference between the Herzls and the Naschauers was merely one between moderate affluence and great wealth. In most other respects—background and origins, status, attitudes, and aspirations—the families were virtually indistinguishable, part of the same alien enclave struggling to break out of their isolation, even though the Naschauers had, if possible, moved even further away from the ancestral faith than the Herzls. But the real world was something Herzl managed selectively to ignore. His own family, as he saw it, had nothing whatever in common with that nest of vipers and vulgarians whom he later satirized in *The New Ghetto* and *Altneuland*.

Knowing all this, and having quite deliberately kept away from Julie for two whole years without any undue suffering on his part, how *did* he end up marrying her?

There seems to be little doubt that it was she who, in one way or another, forced his hand. Eight years younger than Herzl—she was born in 1868, the next to youngest of five children—she had been pre-adolescent when first they met, in spite of which he apparently paid no attention to her until, ripe and due for marriage at eighteen and determined to marry a man of her own rather than her father's choosing, she took the initiative. It is easy enough to believe that she fell in love with the handsome, brilliant, and already well-known bachelor, though how she finally overcame his ambivalence and made him commit himself will never be known. The fact is that in the end he felt honor-bound, as he put it in his letter, to ignore his premonitions and go through with the marriage; one need not question his sincerity to wonder if, over and beyond his word of honor, the 75,000-guilder dowry—a small fortune—did not help him overcome his apprehensions. Besides, he was rather fond of Julie and may, in the early days of their courtship, even have convinced himself that he was in love with her, whatever he took that to mean. Physically, she lived up to his ideal of the blond, blue-eyed child-woman. Trouble began when she stopped being ideal and became all woman.

There were those hot kisses on the balcony, the sweet poison she "slurped," as he put it, with a gusto that clearly prompted his first headlong flight. In 1891, physically separated from her by half a continent, he still panicked at the thought of her womanly wiles. "There is nothing I fear more than to have her get pregnant again," he wrote, as though powerless to do anything about it. And in fact, not only did she bear his second child, but a third one as well, in spite of the separate bedrooms of which he always made a special point in their living arrangements.

Yet his panic, whatever its roots, had to do not with Julie's powers of seduction but with the surge of violent, conflicting, and profoundly upsetting emotions she aroused in him. The great passion of which Herzl was later to prove himself capable certainly found no outlet in his sex life. The make-believe Don Juan, who boasted about the size of his organ and about his exploits with prostitutes, grew up to become an emotionally constipated adult, morbidly repressed and inhibited in the sexual sphere, and the arousal of libidinal urges threatened his precarious adjustment. It is tempting to see his consuming devotion to the Zionist cause as a form of sublimated sexuality, and if one accepts not only the broad Freudian premise of culture as the product of sublimation but conceives of just about every human activity as sexually motivated, the conclusion becomes self-evident as well as totally irrelevant in that it fails to explain why Herzl, of all people, was moved to found Zionism, whereas another man's repressed desires make him practice psychoanalysis. In his ground-breaking biography, Dr. Bein said that the Jewish people owed a great debt of gratitude to Herzl's unhappy marriage, which about sums up all we know about the complex link between his politics and his sex life. On the other hand, the chances of Herzl ever having what passes for a happy marriage were probably minimal to begin with.

Right after the wedding, the couple left for their eight-week honeymoon in Switzerland and France.

It was a catastrophe about which nothing but the outcome is known for certain. Some three hundred letters from Herzl, mostly to his wife, were held back by the family and eventually ended up in the hands of his youngest daughter, who was deported to the Terezin concentration camp and died there in 1942. These letters, which must be presumed lost, might have cleared up certain details, but the outline of what happened in those first few weeks emerges quite clearly from subsequent developments.

The ornate Victorian mythology that surrounded the loss of innocence and the trauma of the wedding night may seem rather quaint and exotic, but it reflected a great deal of suffering no less real for being mostly silent. What led to widespread tragedy was the repression not so much of sex but of woman; the combination of female ignorance and male arrogance is a singularly poor preparation for marriage. In Herzl's case, the bride had been raised by a mother not only coarse and unloving but also stupid in the bargain, a handicap difficult to overcome in the best of circumstances. And the man who was to introduce her to the raptures of love had picked up his knowledge in whorehouses, along with a case of venereal disease.

In spite of which Julie got pregnant almost immediately, proof that the marriage was consummated. It is likely to have been a problematic experience. But regardless of the horror stories peddled by *fin de siècle* novelists, there often was life and even sex after a disastrous wedding night; a bad start did not necessarily leave permanent scars, provided the partners truly cared for one another. Neither Herzl nor his wife had the capacity to care. They were each too narcissistic and self-involved even to listen, let alone reach out to the other.

We have Herzl's story of what went wrong, amply documented and detailed, or at least detailed enough to allow us to fill in the gaps. His characterization of Julie is supported by a great deal of independent evidence and probably accurate as far as it goes. She was quick-tempered, unstable, given to tantrums, a spoiled brat who could not tolerate frustration and would instantly turn any argument into a dramatic life-and-death confrontation, threatening to kill either her unborn child or herself. In the course of that first year alone, Herzl on numerous occasions wrested poison vials out of her grip, cut the sash cord she had wrapped around her neck, stopped her from cutting her wrist or jumping out of the window, and kept her from deliberately trying to induce a miscarriage. Accustomed to the largesse of a home where money was no object, she went on wild spending sprees, refused to economize or keep accounts, and left the running of the household to the servants. But her worst crime by far in Herzl's eyes—as he made plain time and again in his letters—was that she failed to show proper respect for his mother and in fact openly despised her.

This nowhere near exhausts his list of grievances. Julie's own list has not come down to us. But the surviving Herzl letters that touch on the subject make it possible to draw one up on her behalf without unduly straining one's imagination.

Their tone, to begin with, the sententious sermonizing, the patronizing superiority of the male endowed by the laws of God and men with infinite wisdom and all-encompassing power. He had the last word and the first as well in every situation, and the only way she could ever make him listen to what she was unable to articulate was to scream, curse, or start throwing things. He was a miser who put her on a tight budget and doled out the guilders with an eyedropper, as though they were his—which indeed they were, under Austrian law, even though it was her own dowry and her own father who had earned them. And to top it all off, this precocious patriarch, this paragon of all male virtues, had never outgrown his infancy. He had made sure to find an apartment right around the corner from his parents just so he could run home to Momma at least once a day to feel loved, eat her food, complain about his wife, and convince himself that his darling mamakám and the Golden One were all right and not about to drop dead. Julie's primitive instincts and untutored mind were no match for his glibness. He drove her insane, to the point of wanting to kill.

And as if he weren't enough to put up with, there was his mother. Mamakám. Playing the *grande dame*, looking down her nose at the

Naschauers as morally tainted and intellectually inferior, she had strongly disapproved of the marriage, done her utmost to prevent it, and now did what she could to break it up. She had been all set to run her son's new household, being the only one who knew his habits, tastes, and needs, quite aside from the fact that his bride—"the little one," as she snidely referred to Julie while they were still on speaking terms—was manifestly incompetent in every respect. When "the little one," a week after her return from the honeymoon, threw mamakám out of the house and Jeanette Herzl vowed never to set foot in it again, the marriage to all intents and purposes was dead for good and ever.

Her version, no less plausible than his; the full story encompasses both. Like so many women unhappy with their lot, Julie was found to be suffering from hysteria, an at the time highly fashionable ailment to which men were immune by definition. The diagnosis did nothing for her, but it helped the doctors assert their authority and collect their fees. It may also have made them overlook some less fashionable ailments: Julie Herzl was only thirty-nine years old when she died. But the conjectures about a possible link between her premature death and her husband's history of venereal disease are probably unfounded. The most common complication of chronic gonorrhea in women was infertility; Julie gave birth to her third child in 1893, after four years of marriage.

She undoubtedly made life miserable for her husband. He was entitled to feel sorry for himself, and he did so, until success and the adulation he received in later years compensated for an arid home devoid of love.

Julie, on the other hand, had only one consolation, and one small victory: her children adored her, and they detested her mother-in-law.

Herzl summed up the first four weeks of his honeymoon on a postcard to Kana: "I've grown older again—much, much older. Farewell and be happy" (L, 8/1/89).

Thanks to Julie's dowry, he was also a good deal richer and, at long last, financially independent. But he preferred to perpetuate a reassuring sense of dependency by letting his father manage his assets as well as his current income. For the moment, at least, the "account" he maintained with his "dear banker" obviated the need for journalistic hackwork and enabled him to concentrate on what he still considered his true vocation. In October, he settled with his pregnant bride in their first apartment at 1 Stephanienplatz in Leopoldstadt, around the corner from his parents, and by the end of the month he had completed a new four-act play, *What Will People Say*. It was an exercise in misogyny that derived its strained humor from the fundamental incompatibility of men and women and the manifest absurdity of marriage. "What a happy man I'd be," moans the protagonist, "if only I had the courage to run away from her," echoing, one presumes, the author's own sentiments, three months into his marriage.

The inspiration may have been tragic, but the attempt to transmute his personal conflicts into a fashionable farce misfired badly. The Burgtheater turned the piece down cold—a stunning blow which Herzl had trouble absorbing.

> It really surprises me more than ever [he protested, in a letter to the director]. I would have thought that you would at least accept it with some changes, and to changes—or even to cuts—I would have readily agreed. . . . Is it really so much below the level of *The Poachers*? . . . And in addition to these questions, I have another one that is of particular interest, at least to me personally: Am I really incapable of writing a play *all by myself*? In other words, doomed to be the eternal collaborator? That, too, a farce. As you can see, my esteemed director, the humor of it does not escape me. Which should lend me credibility as a major humorist in everything except my work. [L, 10/31/89]

The ironic banter merely underscores the note of genuine anguish, and a production in Prague the following spring as well as another one in Berlin in the fall of 1890 added further to his misery; both were resounding failures.

To make up for the setback and to defend his precarious toehold at the Burgtheater, Herzl teamed up once again with Hugo Wittmann. By the end of the year, the two had knocked out another comedy, which the Burgtheater accepted at once but did not stage until a year later, on February 6, 1891. This time, even Wittmann's magic touch could not redeem a silly plot about village politics and mistaken identities culminating in the triumph of true love; *The Lady in Black* received the critical drubbing it deserved and died after six performances.

Thus the entire winter of 1889–90 was one bleak stretch; domestic misery and the puzzling reverses in what had seemed a well-launched career added up to a state of unquiet desperation, in which the only ray of light was the prospect of impending fatherhood. Already in early September Herzl had expressed his strong preference for a boy. "What I'll do with him I do not yet quite know. He will under no circumstances be allowed to study, and if he wants to become a writer, I'll kill him. Besides, it is bound to be a girl, if for no other reason than that I want a boy" (L, 9/5/89).

Buoyed, as always, by wishful thinking, Herzl's dreams for the future far outdistanced the reality of the here-and-now. In this instance, he incorporated them into one of his better-known feuilletons, the story of a father's saintly love for his son. "When he was born, my world was suddenly complete. . . . Even in the cradle he cured me of many ironic and superficial attitudes. Our children are our greatest teachers. He taught me a meaningful love of life. For he was my life, my boundless immortality, assurance that I would always walk in the sunlight as my son, my grandson" (Der Sohn).

It was a lofty fantasy of parenthood which, in real life, Herzl managed to reconcile with a remarkably distant and detached relationship to his children. Though proud to be a father, and ever ready to wax maudlin about his children in print or in his letters, he gave them little of his time and even less of himself. He loved them for being his children, but never took the trouble to see them as distinct individuals in their own right.

The next blow fell on March 4, 1890, when Julie gave birth to a baby girl. She was named Pauline, after Herzl's sister.

He proclaimed himself the "superhappy father of a delightful little girl" and rushed off to Prague for the premiere of *What Will People Say* on March 10 at the German Theater; as already mentioned, it was a fiasco. Outwardly poised as ever, commenting on this chain of disasters with his usual acerbic aplomb, he slid into an emotional crisis exacerbated by a growing sense of loneliness. "Kana has now also left, gone to Berlin," he wrote a few days later to an unidentified correspondent, probably Julius von Ludassy. "And I am beginning to feel what he meant to me, even though I often did not see him for months. You and Boxer are gone, too. In other words, none of the people with whom I would have been able to talk about myself is here anymore. Yet every so often one does feel the need for a heart-to-heart talk, even without necessarily being an old woman. Writing? Brrrh. However, even this vice has its virtue: one learns to keep one's mouth shut" (L, 3/20/90).

Both Kana and Boxer had moved to Berlin in pursuit of literary laurels. Boxer, uncomplicated, efficient, and outgoing, succeeded almost immediately. His blend of lucidity and rare human warmth might conceivably have been of some help to Herzl, but relations between them had never been truly intimate. (The friendship with Ludassy was even more tenuous.) Kana, on the other hand, was himself already in the throes of a self-destructive despair so virulent that it prompted Herzl, even in the midst of his own troubles, to send him a long letter full of well-meant advice: Pull yourself together, make the most of things. "And if you see that you can't make it in Berlin, come cheerfully back home. Your good parents will welcome you with open arms, and so will I, your brother" (L, 4/10/90).

Just what a man all but paralyzed by depression most wants to hear, but Herzl himself made dogged efforts to live up to his own preachments. It was not easy. A play he had anonymously submitted to the Vienna People's Theater in a competition did not so much as rate an honorable mention. Yet work had always been his escape and salvation, and the latest series of failures merely reinforced his determination to recoup his losses. He had all but given up on journalism, except for an occasional feuilleton in the *Neue Freie Presse*, with which he was anxious to remain on good terms. The cash flow from royalties was rapidly drying up just when, for the first time, money had assumed a real rather than symbolic significance in his life. He now had a family to support, and pride, if nothing else, demanded that he be able to do so out of current earnings. Julie's dowry was to be preserved intact as the foundation of his future estate, but her unbridled extravagance and chaotic housekeeping made any financial planning all but impossible.

Thus, when a commission for a libretto from the Theater an der Wien offered a chance to earn some money, Herzl reluctantly accepted, though he did a thoroughly professional job. *The Devil's Wife*, an operetta based on the play *Madame le Diable* by Henri Meilhac and A. Mortier, with music by Adolf Müller, was a huge success and went through sixty performances, but it did little to assuage Herzl's personal sense of failure.

The accumulated tensions and frustrations of this unhappy year were building up to a climax. Herzl blamed Julie for most of them—understandably and perhaps, up to a point, even justifiably so. Her tantrums and melodramatics might have served an Ibsen or a Strindberg as inspiration; they certainly did nothing for the creative life of a writer like Herzl. Throughout the nine months of her pregnancy, he had done his utmost to exercise restraint, but the unremitting domestic strife was bound to take its toll. And when, instead of the hoped-for son and heir, she carried her spite to extremes by giving birth to a girl, he saw no further reason to maintain the fiction of a marriage which, as far as he was concerned, had ended before it ever began.

The formal break seemed inevitable. It came one afternoon in May, when she assailed him in front of some visitors. He walked out on her, left town, holed up first in Linz, later in Salzburg and Munich, spending much of his time composing long and rueful epistles to his parents. This would never have happened had he followed their advice. "But be assured that, except for the pain I caused you by my unfortunate choice, I shall never again hurt your feelings. I want to live for and with you" (L, 5/21/90). He contemplates divorce, "which, in any case, is merely a matter of time," and in a lucid moment recognizes that the fault may not all be hers alone: "Perhaps my wife is more to pity than to blame if what I miss in her is the devotion and self-sacrifice of a mother" (L, 5/22/90). He regrets having to leave the child, but better now, before any ties were formed, than in six months or a year, "when the separation might break my heart."

By the end of the week, torn between his desire for a divorce and his unease at the thought of it, he decided, for the sake of his child, to give Julie another chance, hoping that this episode had taught her a lesson she would not easily forget. "If she kisses your hand, ma-makám, and asks you to forgive her, and you find it in your heart to do so, I, too, shall forgive her and return. Your prior forgiveness is an absolute must. It will teach her once and for all that there is no other way to my heart than via my parents. If that condition is met, if Julie comes to see you and you take pity on her, I shall come back to my little baby girl. I'll be waiting in Munich for your reply" (L, 5/27/90).

Barely a week later, the reunited couple were cozily ensconced at Reichenau, in the very mansion in which their marriage had been celebrated a year earlier. Herzl's saccharine references to "my beloved Julie" and to her impressive housekeeping skills may have been a charade acted out for the benefit of his parents—not likely to have been deceived—but the reconciliation does seem to have led to a temporary truce that lasted through much of the summer, at the end of which Julie was pregnant once more.

By the end of the year—his parents had already broken off relations with Julie all over again—Herzl completed another play, *The Princes of Geniusland*, a tale of two women, one titled, the other plebeian. Both vie for the position of prima donna at a provincial opera house; the titled one gets the job, the bourgeoise gets the count who runs the opera house. The play, described by Herzl as a "realistic comedy of the more subtle kind," opened and closed at the Carl Theater in Vienna on November 12, 1891.

The premiere of Herzl and Wittman's *The Lady in Black* took place on February 6, 1891.

The reviews the next morning were hostile for the most part, but a letter received in the morning mail proved infinitely more upsetting:

> My dear, good Theodor, your old friend wants to still bid you farewell before dying. Thank you for your friendship and for all your kindness. I wish you and your dear ones all the happiness in the world. I kiss you,
>
> Your Heinrich
>
> Berlin, February 6, 1891

The passionate friendship of their student years had long since given way to a more sober, more distant if still affectionate relationship. Kana had left Vienna for extended periods as early as 1887, although as Herzl had pointed out, they often did not see one another for months on end, even when he was in town. And yet the bond between them remained strong enough to survive not only spatial distance and Kana's often prickly temperament but even the disruptive intrusion of Herzl's marriage. Theirs was a rather unique friendship in that for both of them it represented the only experience of true intimacy which either man was ever to know in his lifetime.

Kana's flight from Vienna may have already been symptomatic of an increasingly severe depression; in the stark misery of his Berlin exile, it rapidly turned suicidal. In answer to Herzl's encouraging platitudes of the year before, Kana told him that he had written quite a bit—"but mostly garbage. I've been living like a dog these terrible past five months, on 130–140 marks a month, painfully eked out. . . . But this moral and physical depression from which I've been suffering drains me of the strength I'd need to put my work into acceptable shape. I am unbelievably tired. . . . I don't know if you've ever experienced that sense of absolute loneliness" (8/3/90).

That Kana envied his handsome, wealthy, and successful friend may be taken for granted; he was also an astute critic keenly aware of Herzl's shortcomings as a writer. But except for the occasional flare-up of petulance, usually induced by one of Herzl's clumsy offers of financial help in one form or another, he was careful not to let either feelings or opinions come between himself and the only friend he had in the world. He initially resented Herzl's marriage, fearing a powerful rival, but the confessions of the unhappy bridegroom soon changed resentment to compassion. "My poor dear Theodor," he wrote, six weeks before he killed himself, "what I gather from your letters—and with an even more painful shock from your facial expression on the picture—has moved me profoundly. I know only too well that here all attempts to offer consolation are in vain" (12/13/90).

Kana's suicide was a blow from which Herzl never quite recovered. It seems more than doubtful that he could have helped his friend even had he tried. But the fact that he didn't try, that he had been too self-absorbed even to realize the gravity of the situation, added a heavy burden of guilt to the enormous sense of loss. For years he struggled with these feelings, trying to exorcise them by writing a novel about his friend's life. The attempt never progressed beyond some preliminary drafts; Herzl was incapable of the relentless self-scrutiny that such an effort would have involved. But in the utopian *Altneuland*—the only novel he ever completed—written near the end of his life, the idealized vision of Kana appears among a cast of characters that includes just about every important person in Herzl's life.

His immediate reaction, however, was the usual one of taking flight and seeking relief in restless motion. He needed to get away from the wife he had come to hate, and deal with his emotions in prideful solitude. Two days after receiving Kana's letter, he was on his way to Italy.

To his parents—"Your happiness is more important to me than anything else"—he sent morbidly cheerful bulletins from along the way. "Once again a wonderful, sun-filled trip, and I am keeping my eyes open—firmly resolved not to write a single word this time. I am through with *that* kind of travel. . . . Fortunately, I no longer have to depend on *that* sort of work" (L, 2/11/89). He saw Duse in a performance at

Milan's Teatro Filodramatico and surprised himself by how much of the Italian dialogue he was able to follow—"although the acting of this (by the way ugly) woman is such that even a deaf-mute would have understood, and a blind man could have seen her—except that he would have imagined her to be beautiful" (L, 2/13/89). He continued via Genoa to Nice, risked a few francs at the Monte Carlo Casino, and, in his reports to his parents, worked hard at maintaining the slightly breathless tone of youthful exuberance that he wanted them to hear. But the strain showed, and every so often a more somber note crept in. "Walking all alone in this superbly magnificent corner of the world tends to stir up thoughts and moods. And those are what I am after. I am in search of myself" (L, 2/20/91). "It would be tempting to follow your advice and my own inclination and stay here in one of these divine little places along the Riviera. You, my dear daddy, would advance me the money even if I didn't have it myself. But above all I want to do what I consider my duty. I am rushing back home, as though the happiest of family life awaited me. I don't want to be the guilty party" (L, 2/21/91).

Backtracking via Milan and Venice, he returned to Vienna on March 1. If the brief fugue had temporarily restored his inner equilibrium, the situation back home was quick to upset it again. He discovered that *The Lady in Black* had folded at the Burgtheater after six performances, and that his other plays had all been rejected wherever they were submitted. Baffled and profoundly disturbed, he dug up *The Swan's Neck* and sent it to Berlin: "I wrote it three years ago, before the advent of the Scandinavian tidal wave." It, too, was turned down; the Scandinavian tidal wave had swamped the country.

Herzl may have sneered at Ibsen and Strindberg, and he regarded naturalism as a passing if abominable fad. But he was far too intelligent not to have realized that the smug middle-class audiences who came to the theater for entertainment rather than intellectual challenges— his audiences—were fading fast, along with their illusions of unbounded progress in the best of all possible worlds. The optimism of the founding fathers was yielding to the pessimism of their sons, and the serious theater had begun to anticipate, explore, and reflect the doomsday mood of a civilization in crisis. The new audiences—still largely middle class, but troubled rather than smug—were younger and far more demanding. They hailed the Scandinavian tidal wave that threatened to relegate the whole repertoire of vapid bedroom farces and insipid comedies to the backwaters of provincial entertainment, of which the Burgtheater, despite its preeminent position in the Austrian capital, long remained an embattled outpost.

As a playwright, Herzl was quite simply passé—not uncritical of his father's generation, but emotionally committed to it and incapable of catching up with his own. Later in life he may have come to suspect as much, but at the time he seemed almost as much puzzled as distressed by this sudden turn of events. His latest plays were not even given a chance to fail; every second- and third-string theater to which he submitted them—and his frenzied efficiency covered a lot of territory—shipped his manuscripts back almost as fast as they received them. He was particularly upset by the universal rejection of his favorite, *The Princes of Geniusland*, which he considered an innovative "natural"—as opposed to naturalistic—look at love; he even went so far as to ask a prominent critic for his frank opinion of the play. The critic's reply is not recorded, but it is usually a mistake for an author to ask for true candor; he may get it.

Undaunted, or perhaps merely beyond despair, he began to outline what, with his ever-resilient optimism, he described as a highly original new comedy. At the same time, however, he was himself playing the lead in a real-life drama sadly lacking in originality.

Although he had dutifully returned to his pregnant wife in order to be present at the delivery, he had nonetheless made up his mind to divorce her right after the birth of the child. Until then, however, he would keep his decision from her so as to cause no undue and potentially harmful excitement.

The elaborate divorce plans hatched by Herzl during the final months of Julie's pregnancy bear a distinct resemblance to one of his more convoluted plots. They reflect a strange ambivalence beneath his manifest resolve, a desperate eagerness to avoid direct confrontations not just with Julie but also with the finality of his own decision. What he most wanted was to erase the past couple of years altogether and slip quietly, without fuss, back into the *status quo ante bellum*, become once again his parents' beloved one and only son. To this end he arranged to take off on a vacation with his mother the moment the child was born and, still without revealing his true intentions to his wife, remain abroad until the lawyers back home had reached a settlement.

In mid-May, however, he decided to give his father-in-law advance notice, after all. In a face-to-face showdown as well as in a long, lawyerly letter expressly written for the record—he was himself a lawyer, after all—Herzl once again laid out his grievances and, after a lengthy preamble, listed the four major grounds for divorce in numerical order:

1. Julie's brash, crude, impertinent conduct toward me. Her temper, lack of restraint, especially the threats of suicide by which she seeks to get her way, for instance to keep me from reading in the evening.
2. Her unloving, insulting conduct toward my parents. (This may not weigh heavily with the judge; to me it is the weightiest of all reasons.)
3. Her incomprehensible carryings-on with the child, so far with only the first one, preventing me, the father, from implementing my wishes for proper care.
4. The sloppy, extravagant housekeeping and the lack of domestic peace, which make it impossible for me not only to work but even to read. [L, 5/16/81]

He then went on to point out that under Austrian law a divorce is obtainable only with the consent of both parties. Should Julie refuse such consent, he would sue for "legal separation of bed and board" and probably be granted custody of both children. In an uncontested divorce, on the other hand, he would be willing to let her have one of them, provided she agreed to raise the child according to his precepts of child rearing.

Finally, at a stormy meeting with his father-in-law a few days later, he threatened to have Julie examined by Professor Theodor Meynert, a prominent Viennese psychiatrist, and to have her committed to an institution unless the Naschauer family agreed to take care of her after the separation. No idle threat, this; being a man, he had both psychiatry and the law on his side.

On June 10, 1891, Julie gave birth to a boy—"and what a boy. He weighed a quarter again as much as his sister when she was born. A solid, beautiful little fellow who on his first day pulled my beard so hard it hurt. . . . This one is not going to be so weak and petty and fragile, he won't have to swallow so much dirt, he will attain unknown greatness" (L, 6/13/91). He was named Hans; considering how Herzl felt about his mother-in-law Johanna, it seems hard to understand why he agreed to it. The child was neither circumcised nor given a Jewish name.

Sorely tempted though he was to abduct this little treasure, the proud father knew enough about law to think better of it. He would, as he explained to his friend Boxer, try to pressure Julie into surrendering the boy to him of her own free will. If she refused, he would have to wait until the boy's fourth birthday, at which time, under Austrian law, the father was automatically awarded custody; girls were left with the mother till age seven.

But it was time now to make good at least on his own escape, and he proceeded exactly as planned. On June 28, he left with his mother for Munich on the pretext of a business trip. From there he notified Julie that he would be gone for some time, destination unknown. And it was only when he felt absolutely safe and beyond her reach that he instructed his lawyer to get in touch with her and deliver the bomb he had carefully primed in advance.

It was a ten-page indictment summarizing once more the melancholy history of their marriage and announcing his irrevocable decision to seek a divorce. Although touching on some of the low points of their life together—"for two whole years my home was hell on earth"— he makes an effort to sound reasonable and fair: "If I wanted to take revenge for the misfortune you brought into my life, I would proceed in a far more aggressive manner. But I bear you no ill will. Nor is the burden of guilt exclusively yours. The fault lies with those who neglected your upbringing, and with our different natures. . . . You are twenty-three, I am thirty-one. We can both still make happier lives for ourselves."

Sweet reason leaves him, though, when called to deal with the two subjects closest to his heart—his parents and his dignity:

My dear, good, beloved parents, whose entire life I am, to whom I owe gratitude and the most tender love till my dying breath, are heartbroken over my marriage. Your conduct toward them was, if possible, even more reprehensible than toward me. . . . You and a hundred thousand of the likes of you I would kick out of my house with ridicule and scorn before I ever deliberately hurt my mother's feelings. . . . If my parents caused me the greatest pain, my children are my greatest worry. Let me tell you why a divorce is best for them as well. . . . Would you ever be able to control yourself in their presence, you who, when I po-

litely asked you in front of the nursemaid to send little Pauline
out for a ride in the mild air, snapped back: "If you say that once
more, I'll spit in your face and hit you." And *this* I put up with
in silence. To this day I don't know how I was able to muster
that much self-control, and if a child capable of understanding
had witnessed this scene, I would probably have demolished you.
I am not a weakling like your father. You, however, are like your
mother. I would rather not see my children for years on end than
have my authority undermined in their eyes. And if I were the
worst person in the world, the most despicable scoundrel—my
children must believe in me and must respect me.

As to the custody of the children, he declared himself ready to take
them both, "but I am not inhuman, after all, and if you agree to my
conditions, I would let you have our little Pauline, even beyond the
term stipulated by law, i.e., her seventh year. . . . I'll leave Hans in
your care until the fall; after that, I'll take him. . . . Do exactly as I
tell you, and it will be good for you and the children. But if you don't
obey, you'll get to know me and the courts" (L, 6/?/91).

After a week in Wiesbaden, "at the peaceful side of my good golden
Momma," he struck out on his own to look for some picturesque,
inexpensive spot as far away from Vienna as possible, where he could
settle down and work on his new play. Disappointed by the French
Atlantic coast, he headed south into the Pyrenees and eventually came
upon the mountain village of Luz, peaceful, picturesque, and still
primitive despite an influx of summer guests from neighboring St.
Sauveur. The two weeks he spent there turned out to be the most
productive he had had in months, if not years. More important, they
were to change the course of his life in rather unexpected ways.

You can imagine my joy at being able to pick up the long-lost
thread of my play again [he wrote to his parents on August 21,
two days after his arrival at Luz]. The very scene I was stuck with
for weeks got written today with ease and no strain. . . . I'd like
to stay here until I finish at least a first draft of the play, even if
it takes till mid-September. Then I'll again travel a little and write
a few feuilletons. . . . The play is the only thing that matters.

The feuilletons will do as fillers and as an antidote to loneliness, but they're not good for much else. [L, 8/21/91]

The inspiration, however, did not outlast the week; and since work was what saved his sanity and kept him from brooding about Kana, his marriage, and his future—he still had no news about Julie and her reaction to his letter—he chose to write instead about the village of Luz itself. The feuilleton appeared in the *Neue Freie Presse* of September 10 and created a minor literary sensation back home.

It was, in effect, a superior piece of its kind, still suffused with the typical Herzlian irony that often teeters between the sophomoric and the supercilious, but ending on a somber note, less self-indulgent and vastly more mature.

The most significant personality in Luz is the barber. When I say barber, I also mean the mailman, who at the same time functions as grocer. Every so often you see a group of men walking about the main square. They are not ordinary loafers, as you can tell from their somber mien. No, these are people who can't make up their mind to enter the barbershop, because they know the barber. He, in turn, waits for them with a cold smile on his face—he knows they can't escape him. Fashion in the Pyrenees dictates that men be smooth-shaven; only some of the women grow mustaches. At last one of the more courageous fellows steps out, exchanges a last handshake with some of his friends, casts one more misty-eyed glance at the mountains of his youth, and enters the barbershop. The door closes on him; the place has no windows. The operation takes place in darkness. . . . At that, a shave is not the worst; it often lasts only an hour. A haircut, on the other hand . . . But since I don't like to dwell on atrocities, permit me to keep silent. . . . There are also baths in Luz. The natives, however, never use them; they only bathe in the pure mountain air.

He then ascends to the source of the mountain brook and finds a bleak and depressing landscape:

It is like the great sadness at the end of every quest. Yet different people see things differently, and perhaps the woman's voice behind me was right. "Isn't it pretty," she said, in English, and another one agreed: "Really very nice." No, I much prefer the village of Luz. No one will find it "very nice." And yet I have friends there: the blacksmith, the shoemaker, the barber, and many others, whom I like because they wear the picturesque dark blue beret. They still gather in silence on the main square. And when they talk, it is in a dialect that sounds like Spanish to me and may be close to it. But the brook—the Gave de Pau or Gave de Bastan—and its marvelous ritornello I understand perfectly. It leads me into many a delightful valley. Follow the Gave. ["Luz, Das Dorf," F, Vol. II]

The editors of the *Neue Freie Presse* were impressed, both by the article itself—the second Herzl feuilleton they ran within a two-week period—and by their readers' response. In fact, Bacher and Benedikt, always on the lookout for fresh talent, had long had their eye on him. His probationary period was nearly over, although he may have been the last to find out.

Every morning he obstinately went back to his play, putting in the hours but making no progress and settling instead for the feuilletons that seemed to flow from his pen with such elegant ease. By the time he left Luz in early September, he had already finished four of them; the fifth one, written in Biarritz, was a vivid and thoughtful piece of reportage about his visit to Lourdes. The staunch agnostic who thought of himself as a rationalist and scoffed at miracles found himself moved, not like Werfel some fifty years later by the Song of Bernadette, but by the unfathomable miracle of a faith that had transformed a tiny village into a flourishing industry and inspired an endless stream of humanity who came by the thousands to seek relief from the torments of body and soul in the harmless waters of a banal spring.

Voltaire knew it well: we leave the world just the way we found it, no better and no worse. And yet, I can imagine a merciful kind of wisdom that would want to erect such grottoes as Lourdes everywhere. . . . There they sit in long rows of carts, one behind the other, their crippled hands folded, devoutly waiting for their turn. Gentlemen doing penance for their sins—they may be knights or counts—wheel the patients from the hospital to here, carry them into the bath, gently, with reverential love, because one has to be very miserable to be treated well. . . . Physical pain has etched deep furrows around the pale mouth and into the greenish yellow skin of the woman now in the cart at the head of the line. They tell of pain-racked nights in the lightless stupor of a peasant hut, of hours, of weeks, of years illumined only by the picture of the good Virgin of Lourdes above her bed. And now she is at long last about to approach her beloved Lady. How humbly she waits, how confident and yet also a trifle ashamed at the fuss that is being made over her. . . .

Not everyone, however, who comes to Lourdes shares this same confident expectation. For a long time I stood there watching an old man who sought a cure for his failing eyesight; this water is effective against every ailment. He caught it in his kerchief, dripped it between his eyelids, kept his eyes closed for a while, then blinked, opened them, and could see no better than before. He tried it a few more times and finally gave up, shrugged and, trembling, reached for his cane. And as he shuffled off, he sighed a deep and heavy sigh. He sighed like a Jew. ["Der Herr Bischof von Meaux," F, Vol. II]

How does the sigh of a Jew differ from that of a non-Jew?
It was a question Herzl had yet to ask himself. All he knew was that it did.

From Biarritz he crossed the border into Spain and stopped off at San Sebastian on his way to Madrid, intending eventually to continue to North Africa. The social whirl of what was then one of the most fashionable resorts on the Continent came as a welcome relief after his hermit's existence in Luz. "I am beginning to feel human once more. I talk to people and, after a long, long time, am once again socializing with a cultured crowd. It also seems that I know how to behave, mamakám; yesterday the Russian ambassador to Madrid, Count Gorchakov, asked to be introduced to me. He to me! True, he was disappointed to find out that I was rather a nobody, but he concealed it well and continues to be gracious still" (L, 9/23/91).

A trivial incident, yet more telling in its way than reams of prose by worshipful followers trying to describe Herzl's regal appearance. He looked and carried himself like a leader of men long before he became one—and even in those pre-television days, the man was very much part of the message.

He kept extending his stay in San Sebastian. It turned out to be an ideal place to work—a room with a view of the sea in a first-class hotel, good food, good weather, an elegant and cosmopolitan crowd. He turned out several more feuilletons and labored conscientiously over his play—"though progress is slow, very, very slow. But that doesn't matter. All good things take time, *and this play is going to be my masterpiece. If I know anything at all,* Germany has never yet seen so profound a comedy as this one" (L, 10/1/91).

Germany and the world were to be deprived of it forever. Just as he was on the point of leaving for Madrid, Herzl received an offer from the *Neue Freie Presse* to become their Paris correspondent, at a starting salary of 1,000 francs a month. He cabled his acceptance on October 5 and left for Paris the following day.

TEN

*W*hen Bacher and Benedikt started to work for the *Neue Freie Presse* in 1872, it was just one more lackluster liberal daily. By the time they jointly took over as editors and publishers in 1881, they had transformed it into Austria's most influential and literate newspaper.

Theirs was a marriage of true minds; they shared not only the top positions but also a concept of journalism bordering on the religious, along with the whole panoply of prejudices and illusions that constituted the ideological arsenal of the liberal middle class. Eduard Bacher, born in 1846 in Moravia, probably deserved the credit for the paper's solid financial standing. He was an astute businessman, but sober and sedate in contrast to his partner's obsessive perfectionism, flamboyant personality, and unflagging energy. Moritz Benedikt, three years younger, also born in Moravia, worshipped the *Neue Freie Presse* as a holy cause to which he devoted himself body and soul until his death in 1920. In due course, the prestige of the paper, far out of proportion to its circulation, provided him with considerable power in Austrian politics but also induced delusions of *ex cathedra* infallibility, reflected in his editorials and editorial policies.

Benedikt was even elected to parliament in 1907, but in later years his entire horizon shrank to the dimensions of the *Neue Freie Presse*, to the point where he increasingly lost touch with the world beyond its hallowed premises. In 1891, however, he still ran the enterprise with verve, imagination, and a gloved fist, an avuncular autocrat who could sound like a rabbinical sage. He expected from his collaborators nothing less than perfection, and a loyalty to the paper equal to his own. Such qualities, he realized, had to be paid for, and he was shrewd enough to spare no expense. The fees he paid for articles and stories by some of the world's most famous writers were astronomical by the standards of the day, and the pay scale at the *Neue Freie Presse* far exceeded that of any competing enterprise.

His offer to Theodor Herzl was typical of his bold and unorthodox style of management. Herzl's entire previous newspaper experience consisted of one three-month stint as feuilleton editor for the *Wiener Allgemeine Zeitung*, which, moreover, had ended in dismal failure— hardly the sort of background that would normally have qualified him for what was one of the most important, difficult, and delicate positions in European journalism. On the other hand, he had studied law, written plays, even made the Burgtheater, and, in his feuilletons and travel pieces, displayed dashing brilliance, versatility, and a lukewarm Germanocentric liberalism that matched the general orientation of the *Neue Freie Presse*. Experience, as Benedikt well knew, can be acquired, unlike talent. He had long had his eye on this promising young man and been impressed by his freelance contributions from France and Spain. And so—prodded perhaps to some extent by Wittmann, himself once the *Presse*'s Paris correspondent—he decided to take a chance on Herzl and offered him a respectable 1,000 francs a month—the equivalent of about $200—during the initial four-month trial period. (By way of comparison, the average monthly pay of a skilled French worker was about 150 francs.) He was henceforth to confine his entire output to the *Neue Freie Presse* and, in return, was to receive an additional 80 francs for each feuilleton. A regular contract and schedule of pay increases would be negotiated if the trial period worked out to everyone's satisfaction.

As for the job itself, it was as simple and straightforward as Benedikt's basic guidelines—the broadest possible coverage of whatever went on in Paris that might conceivably be of interest to the readers of the *Neue Freie Presse*, from politics and culture to crimes of greed or passion, and from social notes to the state of the French economy. To facilitate smooth working relations with French contacts, the editors were even ready to grant their Paris correspondent somewhat more leeway for the expression of Francophile sentiments than the staunchly pro-German *Neue Freie Presse* would normally permit.

It was a job description that would have daunted most veterans, let alone novices. Herzl, however, took it in his stride and never seems to have had a moment's doubt about his ability to meet the challenge, even if he had never filed a dispatch in his life. "If at first I should commit some blunders, I'll expect a friendly hint from you. Of course, I'll be watching like a hawk; still, I may conceivably miss something. I am not used to a regular routine. But three weeks from now I will be" (L, 10/5/91).

As a matter of fact, he had never so much as held a regular full-time job, never worked under a deadline. Now he suddenly found himself putting in some twelve and sixteen hours a day, having to meet at least one, often several deadlines in the course of a single twenty-four-hour period, and yet feeling happier than ever before. It was precisely the sort of work that engaged all his gifts—brains, charm, and a seemingly inexhaustible energy. It was also a heaven-sent solution to all his personal problems. The "most profound comedy in the German language" was laid aside, without regrets and probably without serious loss to German literature; so was the novel about "Samuel Kohn." He had made good his escape, though in ways rather different than planned.

On October 6, 1891, he checked into the Hôtel de Hollande in the rue de la Paix, familiar from previous visits, but after a few days moved to the more luxurious Hôtel Rastadt, in the rue Daunou, around the corner from the Opéra, and settled into his new life with the buoyant enthusiasm of one who still cannot quite believe his good fortune.

> To the left of my desk is the little table on which I eat breakfast and lunch [he wrote to his parents early in November]. I keep writing even between courses. The food is very good, one reason why I stopped lunching in restaurants. Not that I save any money; the hotel's prices match its high quality. Time is what I save, precious time. I am busy from morning to night—without feeling harassed, of course, because even in the first few weeks I was able to get everything beautifully organized. But I am infinitely happier today, racing against a daily deadline, than I ever was on vacation, free to do whatever I wanted. I really believe that I am now in my element. I'll show them what I can do. Ahead of me lies a future I can *work for*—and I don't have time to brood about my misfortunes. [L, 11/10/91]

It was as though a crushing weight had been lifted. Meticulous, efficient, well organized, he threw himself into the task with a concentrated fury that enabled him, within days of his arrival, to file his first thoroughly professional dispatches.

His initiation into the jungle of French politics was the daily session of the Chamber of Deputies he attended at the Palais Bourbon. It was a not unfamiliar territory, a giant stage on which 533 actors of widely varying ability participated in a virtually uninterrupted spectacle oscillating constantly between high drama and low farce. As a critic of this particular kind of theater, he could sum up mood, scenery, and action within a paragraph or two, but it was the actors on whom he lavished his main attention. In a curious reversal he, who had never been able to breathe life into any of his own creations, displayed an uncanny knack for pen portraits that caught the very essence of a French politician and made him palpably real to the readers back home. And where, as a playwright, he had squandered his irony in labored witticisms, he now used it to deflate grandiloquence and absurdity. By thus following his natural bent, he came up with an approach to political journalism that quickly won him a personal following and boosted the standing of the *Presse*.

Contents aside, what distinguished his work was the writing itself. The unaccustomed constraints of space and time taught him to pare his style down to essentials without sacrificing the polished prose that had always been his pride. No story of his ever went back to Vienna unless and until it satisfied his own standards, more rigorous even than those of the *Presse*'s perfectionist editors, so that in the end he had Bacher begging for mercy: "The main thing is food for the wide-open maws of curiosity," the editor wrote to him in December 1892. "If there is no time to bake, then for God's sake send the raw ingredients, no matter how raw."

The job was an education unlike any he had ever received, instant growth through total immersion. Coping with the daily tide of news and new impressions, struggling to make sense of them within the space of a few hundred words, anticipating and evaluating trends in finance and foreign policy while keeping a close watch on the domestic scene and faithfully attending both the Palais Bourbon and the Comédie Française challenged all the ingrained attitudes and preconceived notions of the Central European Jewish intellectual, his contempt for politics and politicians, his hypertrophied aestheticism, and his indifference to social problems. He had always been a fast learner, but the speed with which he overcame the handicaps of his background and acquired an understanding of basic issues—and, not incidentally, of human beings—surprised even Herzl himself. Within a matter of months, the *littérateur dégagé* who found "a peculiarly somber pleasure" in the thought that life, as he put it in one of his early dispatches, was "not just pain, but also a game inspiring homeric laughter in the gods," had evolved into an informed observer of the social scene. He began to appreciate certain fundamental differences between politics as practiced in the French Republic and what passed for politics in the Habsburg autocracy, and a measure of understanding even moderated his contempt for the noisy spectaculars enacted on the floor of the Palais Bourbon.

Corruption, inefficiency, and greed in the Habsburg Empire probably exceeded anything uncovered in France during the *belle époque*; but an absolutist regime was able to bury the bodies, whereas the French press, constrained by neither censorship nor libel laws, was free to follow the stench and to make up what it could not dig up. The daily free-for-all, in which the press itself formed an integral part of the very corruption it denounced, was hardly calculated to dispel Herzl's mistrust of populist rule or to change his essentially elitist bias; the order, discipline, decorum, even pomposity that ruled his personal life extended to his concept of government. Disorder made him uneasy, and French democracy was without a doubt one of the messiest, most chaotic institutions of its kind. But in trying to analyze what made it work, he discovered that this apparent chaos was also the source of an enormous vitality.

He had arrived in Paris at the time of yet another political crisis— almost impossible to avoid, since the Third Republic—third, that is, within a century marked by defeat, rebellion, coups d'état, miraculous recovery, and recurrent attempts to assert the tyranny of the people over the tyranny of self-styled emperors and kings—was itself little more than an unending succession of crises.

This latest experiment in popular rule grew out of the 1870 Franco-Prussian War, a six-week campaign which ended in the disastrous rout of the French Army at Sedan, the loss of Alsace-Lorraine, the abdication of the Emperor Napoleon III, and the revolt of Paris against the provisional Thiers government sitting in Versailles. The ruthless suppression of the Paris Commune in March 1871, at a cost of some 20,000 lives, got the Third Republic off to a bad start, and for the rest of the century its survival remained in doubt. Corrupt, scandal-ridden, often all but paralyzed by the deep divisions between royalists and republicans, clericals and anti-clericals, the republican regime and its vague, minimalist constitution were for many years seen even by its supporters as at most a transitional phase, pending the restoration of the monarchy.

The yearning for another Bonaparte who would avenge Sedan and restore the glory of the empire remained at least as strong in France as the traditions of enlightenment and revolution. And when, in 1889, General Georges-Ernest Boulanger, a hero of the Indochina campaign who had distinguished himself by the wholesale slaughter of civilians during the Paris Commune, called for a military dictatorship and was elected to the Chamber by a nearly two-to-one majority, democracy seemed doomed. But the muddle-headed Boulanger was no Bonaparte, and French democracy turned out to be more resilient than it appeared. The threatened coup d'état was aborted, and Boulanger killed himself, although Boulangism in one form or another continued to harass the Republic until 1940, when the Fascist right was at last able to enthrone another dotty general as the redeemer of fatherland and family.

But the daily brawls at the Palais Bourbon, the conspicuous corruption and the pervasive cynicism that characterized public life, tended to obscure the powerful stabilizing trends at work beneath the troubled surface. Relying on the cadres of an efficient and highly centralized bureaucracy, the clique of insiders who actually ran the day-to-day business of government had proved remarkably adept at restoring economic prosperity, expanding France's colonial empire, and pushing for reforms that revitalized the country's medieval school system. Within a mere two years, France was able to liquidate the indemnity of 5 billion francs imposed by the victorious Germans in 1871; by the time the Paris World's Fair opened in 1879, the economy was booming and industrialization in full swing. Jules Ferry, twice Premier and twice Minister of Education, revamped French education, introduced compulsory schooling as well as secondary education for women, and banished the clergy from all teaching positions in state-run schools, precipitating a struggle that ended with the complete separation of Church and state. Less progressive but hardly controversial at the time were Ferry's imperialist policies, which added Tunisia, Indochina, Madagascar, and large chunks of sub-Saharan Africa to the French colonial empire.

Thus, in a climate of perpetual crisis, and despite periodic threats to its survival, the republican regime gradually consolidated its position, and even the Chamber of Deputies had a part in the process by striving to curb the power of the executive branch—a largely futile effort that nonetheless registered occasional successes and at times came reasonably close to expressing the vague, wobbly, and wavering will of the people.

Initially, the novice correspondent of "Europe's best-informed newspaper" knew less about these issues than many of his readers, but this lack of expertise left him totally unfazed. In fact, it struck him as a distinct advantage; an artist was, in his view, far more qualified to deal with politics than some narrow-minded pedant of a specialist.

> In politics, at least in contemporary politics, one deals with a low level of abstractions: the craftsman, the peasant, the merchant, the employee, the factory worker, the entrepreneur; at the next higher level we have the taxpayer, the voter, the citizen. Literature, on the other hand, deals with human beings. Politics involve the community, the district, the country, but literature embraces a higher abstraction: the world. And should he who can grasp the world be incapable of understanding the state?
> [12/23/91—quoted in Bein, p. 123]

It may seem a somewhat dubious generalization. His own political reporting merely proves that a bad playwright can sometimes get to be an excellent journalist, but it gave him the confidence he needed for a brilliant debut. By year's end it had become evident that he not only met Benedikt's exacting criteria but surpassed them by a wide margin. He signed his permanent contract at 1,200 francs a month, with another raise four months later. The rate of payment for extracurricular feuilletons was increased from 80 to 100 francs. Clearly, the editors and publishers of the *Neue Freie Presse* were impressed. So were their readers.

And for good reason. Quite aside from the intellectual challenge, the sheer volume of work confronting Herzl in the course of a week was staggering. The first reports had to be filed by 10 a.m., in time for the paper's evening edition. Much of the day went into legwork, interviews, and briefings, with a financial summary due each afternoon at the close of the stock exchange. His only assistant was Josef Siklosy, a distant relative who handled some of the clerical work. New plays and other cultural events kept him busy in the evening, not to mention the frequently even more entertaining sessions at the Palais Bourbon, which had a way of running on into the small hours. (He did not always draw a sharp enough line between the two types of entertainment; one of his early reports on the Chamber was turned down by Benedikt as too much like an operetta.) In addition, there were countless social obligations, an indispensable part of making contacts and gaining an insight into the vital areas of French culture, business, and politics. And somehow, time had to be found or made to get it all down on paper, in his impeccably neat handwriting, to be dispatched to Vienna by mail or cable, depending on the urgency of the item.

He always found the time. That he relished the work is only a partial explanation for his astounding productivity; and while the currently fashionable coinage of workaholic may not quite apply, he certainly derived a secondary benefit from leaving no room for introspection and self-pity. Still, he could never have accomplished what he did without an uncanny talent for organizing his life and work so as to waste as little time as possible.

It was a trait acquired in earliest childhood, compulsive no doubt and, like all virtues, reeking of pathology, but it stood him in good stead just the same and may have been the only facet of his personality that reflects the formative influence of his father. Jakob Herzl's starchy pedantry probably grew more pronounced with age, but he had practiced thrift, punctiliousness, and punctuality since he first started scrambling up the ladder of success. They were his guiding principles, a homemade substitute for his lost faith and his lack of formal schooling. A letter he wrote to the son of his deceased brother on the occasion of the boy's bar mitzvah conveys a rather vivid notion of the atmosphere that must have prevailed in the Herzl household during Theodor's childhood.

My dear Hugo, this is the first time that I am writing to you. The occasion for it is your impending confirmation, an epoch of which, as a rule, it is assumed that the youngsters who enter this epoch must break with their boyish behavior and turn to serious strivings which will lead to their future vocation. . . . By way of a confirmation present I am sending you via the mails a silver wind-up watch, which is to be wound up by the *knob at the top*, while the hands are regulated by pressing on the little button to the left of the knob. The reason why I am sending you a watch rather than some other confirmation present is that I want you to get used to making the most of your time. Whenever you look at the watch, or wish to do so, you should remember that the watch is the equivalent of time, and that time is the equivalent of money, if not right away, then later, thanks to the skills and knowledge acquired. On the other hand, he who carelessly squanders his time or wastes it through laziness, wastes money. Therefore mind well, my dear Hugo, what I am writing you, and if you fully and wholeheartedly follow my advice, your uncle Jakob Herzl will always love you and be fond of you.

His own son saw to it that his father always loved him and was fond of him.

The one hundred miles of boulevards, avenues, and squares carved out by Georges Haussmann during his seventeen years as Prefect of Paris changed the profile of the city, opened it up to much-needed air and light, and added new splendor to its vistas; displacing untold thousands of the anonymous poor was presumably then as now part of any planful beautification. But the intrepid baron's most memorable achievement remained largely invisible, hidden beneath the pavement: over 700 miles of sewer lines constructed under his administration between 1853 and 1870, which transformed a still essentially medieval town notorious for its noxious effluvia—a likely reason why the modern perfume industry originated in Paris—into a metropolis on the threshold of modernity. Electricity increasingly powered the lights of the *ville lumière*, and Mr. Eiffel's monster tower, erected to commemorate the centenary of the Revolution, had instead become a proud, albeit still controversial symbol of French technology and craftsmanship. If, in the salons, new money was supplanting the old nobility, the change made no noticeable difference in the gloss and glitter of *tout Paris*. The city's true vitality was in any case rooted in different social strata altogether—its artists, its intellectuals, and a uniquely resilient, resourceful, and assertive working class. Culturally, Paris was the center of the Western world, with a decided head start into the twentieth century.

It was, of course, plagued by much the same blight and misery as all the other great urban centers of the industrial age, and even for those earning an average wage, living was far from easy; the *belle époque* was *belle* only for the rich and mindless. But on a base pay of over

14,000 francs a year one could probably live more agreeably in Paris than almost anywhere else.

Money alone, however, did not account for the ease with which Herzl adjusted to his new environment. To say that he felt at home in Paris would be overstating the case; he felt nowhere at home—not in his native Budapest, to which he never looked back, and certainly not in Vienna. He was an outsider in Paris as well, but for the first time without having to apologize for it, a privileged foreigner whose very job legitimized his natural tendency to keep his distance.

It was an ideal position for him to be in, and within weeks he began to doubt if he would ever return to Vienna—provided, of course, he could persuade his parents to join him. He already missed them terribly, so much so that a whole year's separation seemed impossible to contemplate, nor did the prospect of occasional visits offer much consolation. He needed to be close to them at all times, to live in the same city, preferably in the same house, or at least no farther than the next block. His insistent pleas soon overcame his parents' rather understandable reluctance. By year's end, they had agreed in principle, though in contrast to the precipitous exodus from Budapest, the logistics of this move took five months to complete. They arrived in Paris at the end of May 1892.

By that time, however, Herzl was no longer alone.

The first hint of a warming trend between him and his wife came in November 1891 and may well have been part of what decided his mother to give up her cozy home for exile in sinful Sodom. Shortly after his arrival, with the divorce still on the docket, he received a conciliatory note from Julie inviting his parents to visit their grandchildren; they had never even bothered to inspect the latest arrival. Herzl passed the letter on without replying, but at the end of the month he dropped a bombshell: Julie was coming to Paris to look for an apartment and make the necessary arrangements for bringing the children. To his indignant mother he pointed out that this was something

neither the President of the Republic nor the Emperor of Austria could keep her from doing. She is as free to come and go as I am myself. Whether this is just idle prattle on her part or whether she really means it I cannot tell, nor can I do anything about it either way. It would not bother me if she lived here, since my way of life is such that I need not fear spies or surveillance. On the other hand, I would have the joy of getting to see more of my beloved children. She finds living in Vienna as a divorcee impossible and thinks she would do better in a place where no one knows her. . . . But in order to make it plain why, in spite of behaving toward her with courtesy and forbearance, I do not wish to live with her anymore, I shall cite the two major reasons that make any reconciliation impossible now and forever: (1) Nothing in the world can make me go back into the troubled life that was my marriage and that kept me from working, and (2) it would mean disavowing, hurting, and being ungrateful to you, my dear, good, loving parents. I am citing this as the second reason, although you know that for me it is the first one. I hope, my beloved good parents, that this explanation will serve to dispel your fears and worries. [L, 11/28/91]

Not likely. Julie arrived the following day, checked into the same hotel as Herzl, brought him photos of the children, behaved with rueful discretion, and, after a week of exemplary conduct, broached a proposal for which by then he had been thoroughly prepped but which he did not dare accept without his parents' blessings and consent. To judge from the tone of his letter, an uneasy mix of petulance and legalese, he must have felt rather foolish trying to justify this sudden about-face to the formidable *mamakám* to whom it was chiefly addressed.

She proposes as follows [he wrote]. She will submit to a trial period of whatever duration, during which you, my dear parents, will observe her in daily contact. And only if you are firmly convinced, after months or even years, that she has become an obedient, quiet, thrifty, and fine wife, an attentive, compliant, and loving daughter-in-law, and then only if you so desire, shall I again live with her. The divorce action would not be withdrawn but merely suspended. . . .

The trial period cannot be a short one. . . . There is no question of going back to the previous setup. My bedroom and study have to be on a different floor, or at least completely separate. . . . She can accept these conditions only if she becomes a truly good wife. In any case, they preclude an immediate reconciliation. Please understand, my dear parents: this was the only way to counter her intention of catching me by surprise. I can no longer be fooled by promises. [L, 12/?/91]

Brave words full of firm resolution, but a few days later, by the time Julie returned to Vienna, he had agreed to again share a home with her and the children in a kind of split-level arrangement—separate bedrooms, separate lives lived under one roof. Her evident powers of persuasion raise questions about the simplistic picture of Julie Herzl as a vulgar shrew and brainless ninny. She probably deserves far more credit than she ever got for her candor, courage, and adaptability, and for a certain native intelligence which neither her background nor her marital life ever gave her a chance to develop. She readily agreed to all of Herzl's conditions and was magnanimously granted a pardon or at least parole by her mother-in-law, who by now had little choice in the matter but registered her misgivings by drawing up a list of rules and regulations for Julie to follow. Her son found them truly inspiring. "What can I possibly say about your magnificent rules of conduct for Julie?" he cooed. "You are a writer of the highest rank, mamakám, because you only say what is good, true, and just."

What motivated Herzl himself in this bizarre and sudden turnabout is much more difficult to fathom. A longing for his children and a certain residual affection for Julie may have played a part. But the decisive factor was, in all likelihood, a paradox: the fear and revulsion which the essential components of a real marriage aroused in him. He believed in bourgeois respectability (and no doubt worried about the effect of a divorce scandal on his career), he craved a well-run, peaceful home, and he derived gratification from his role of a father. What he did not want, did not need, and in fact could not bear was emotional and sexual intimacy. And the elaborate scheme of a pseudo-marriage he had devised may have struck him as the ideal solution, holding out the promise of public virtue and private comfort without any painful entanglements. Moreover, he had changed and grown these past few months, shed the truculent arrogance of the struggling playwright for the genuine self-assurance of the successful journalist; he now felt he knew how to assert himself and keep trouble at arm's length.

Predictably, the solution fell far short of the ideal, but their marriage endured, or they endured the marriage and even tried, though with indifferent results, to avoid making each other miserable. Intellectually, they had nothing in common. Julie shared none of her husband's interest to begin with and later came actively to resent his total involvement with Zionism. Emotionally they were equally mismatched, but much as he strove to retain his distance, he could not help getting dragged into Julie's hysterics and into her running battle with his mother. There is no reason to assume that their sex life was any more fulfilling than other aspects of the relationship; the fact that, despite the coy emphasis on separate bedrooms, Julie again became pregnant in the summer of 1892 is no argument to the contrary. Sex, however, seems no longer to have been an issue for Herzl; where that left his wife is another, perhaps not altogether trivial question. One may take it that he channeled his energies into his work and later on into his cause, and although this primitive metaphor fails to do justice to the complex process of sublimation, it adequately describes the effect even if it slights the cause. What matters is that the young buck who used to brag about his irrepressible "philogyn" and got shopgirls into trouble had turned chaste with a vengeance, hard to account for in a strikingly handsome thirty-year-old separated from his wife. That he led a blameless life and had absolutely nothing to fear from spies or surveillance was no idle boast. He made many enemies in later years and stood accused of many wrongs, but in an atmosphere rife with scandal and rumor, there was remarkably little gossip and no tangible evidence whatever of any sexual indiscretion on his part.

The idea of having the entire family, including his parents, live together under one roof was one of Herzl's more outlandish fantasies, and true to form, he proceeded immediately to act on it. He rented a large apartment at the fashionable end of the rue de Monceau, near the park, and had it remodeled and furnished to suit his needs. In the midst of these preparations he received word of Oswald Boxer's death in Rio de Janeiro on January 26. The gifted young journalist had spent several months in Brazil on behalf of a committee for the resettlement of Russian Jews when, already bound for home, he succumbed to yellow fever. Herzl had been in touch with him till the end, and in the obituary he wrote for the paper he quoted passages from Boxer's final letter. It was a tragic loss that cost him the last friend of his youth.

Julie arrived in February with the children and with two of her servants; two more were hired in Paris to complete the staff. Herzl's parents followed in June and moved in with them. He may have envisaged this communal arrangement as a dream come true, a unique chance for him to be husband, father, and son all at once. But as reality began to bear in on him, he seems to have had second thoughts. Already in March he felt constrained to warn his mother:

Your position, mamakám, is so strong, will always be so strong that you can impose your will without being a dictator or a nudge. Whatever you say will naturally be done. But your *wisdom* and your love for me entitle me to hope that you will always consult with Julie even if you don't need her advice, just as a general, though he could simply issue orders, will always first ask the captain for his opinion. I don't want you two ladies to be bothering me all the time with your arguments. I have other things to worry about, and it would only make me nervous. Of Julie I'll *demand* that she give no cause for quarrels; of you, mamakám, I request it. . . . If I may give you one piece of advice, my golden darling: Try to exert your influence less by preaching and more by setting an example. [L, 3/19/92]

The wave of terrorism that erupted in the spring of 1892 may have been among the lesser threats to French democracy, but it was spectacular in its effect on life in the capital. Hysteria swept Paris, fanned by a yellow press run wild, reviving fears of carnage in the streets and the collapse of law and order. According to Herzl, what France needed at this point was *un bon tyran*; many less discriminating Frenchmen seemed willing to settle for a tyrant *tout court* without insisting on an admixture of goodness.

The politically motivated bombings—which, of course, inspired a host of purely criminal imitators—were perpetrated by a handful of dissident anarchists who, a decade earlier, had broken with the mainstream movement over the issue of individual terror. For years, their "propaganda by deed" remained confined to bloodthirsty rhetoric, biting satire, and fiery editorials in crude though often lively publications. How this verbal violence suddenly turned malignant seemed puzzling at the time; a direct connection to the budding flirtation between the French Republic and the czarist government was suspected by only a few cynics, among them the anarchist Prince Kropotkin, who warned the dissidents that "an edifice based on centuries of history will not be brought down by a few pounds of explosives." The head of the Okhrana's foreign section, a colorless functionary by the name of Rachkovsky ensconced in the basement of the Russian embassy at 79, rue de Grenelle—the same basement is still in use today; only the acronyms of its occupants have undergone a number of sea changes—undoubtedly shared the view of his émigré compatriot. So did the French police, which did not hesitate to supply the necessary explosives and, through their agents provocateurs, recruited a few prospective martyrs ready to die for what they believed to be their cause.

The technology of terror was still in its infancy, and the damage to people and property relatively slight by today's standards. But it quite adequately served the purposes of all the parties involved. French and Russian secret services formalized an "anti-nihilist" alliance, the French police jailed and expelled a number of anti-czarist émigrés— Kropotkin among them—and the anarchist radicals achieved fleeting glory and a martyrdom that, at least in their own eyes, vindicated their deeds, their lives, and their deaths.

The first two bombs went off in early March 1892, and with a promptness not above suspicion, the gang leader was identified as a certain Ravachol, a fugitive from justice already sought in connection with an earlier robbery and murder. "The police prefect personally rushed to the scene of the crime," Herzl reported on March 1. "The investigation is being rigorously pursued; the authorities are anxious to catch the perpetrators before the first of May."

The vigor of the police may be open to question, but the Paris public now began what was probably the most intense and certainly the most frenzied manhunt in the city's history. An army of criminals, psychopaths, and practical jokers got in on the act. Homemade bombs went off all over town and were invariably credited to the ubiquitous Robin Hood, purported master of a thousand disguises. Prominent officials and wealthy individuals received death threats signed by Ravachol; so did many a surly concierge who had incurred the enmity of her tenants. Tips by the thousands poured into police headquarters. Ravachol was everywhere and nowhere; he had become a legend larger than life. Those yearning for a knight in shining armor had found their man— except that his armor was an inconspicuous disguise, and rather than restoring law and order, he seemed bent on doing away with them altogether. Fringe lunatics and crypto-radicals, on the other hand, derived orgasmic thrills from vicarious carnage. "Qu'important les victimes si le geste est beau," cried the poet Laurent Teilhade—who, in a rare case of true poetic justice, thereupon lost an eye in the beau geste that leveled the restaurant Foyot.

In his daily dispatches, Herzl reported on the panic with cool objectivity, but the phenomenon of one man holding an entire city hostage obviously fascinated him far beyond its topical significance and inspired at least one feuilleton which, while decidedly among his less memorable efforts, testifies to his preoccupation with the subject.

In a series of brief dialogues, he tries to convey glimpses of life in Paris during the reign of Ravachol: the snooty owner of a luxury hotel being humbled by the precipitous departure of his wealthy guests, the sudden generosity of well-dressed strollers toward any beggar who accosts them, or a little boy being told that Ravachol will come to get him if he doesn't mind his manners. The very name of the mysterious outlaw makes strong men tremble and weak women swoon:

HE: Don't you feel anything for me?
SHE: No, not for you.
HE: Ah, so there is someone else. Is he here (at the ball)?
SHE: (*Sighing*) No.
HE: (*Jealous*) What does he look like? What is so special about him?
SHE: He has what women love. He makes me shiver and dream.
HE: I suppose you won't tell me his name?
SHE: (*With half-open eyes*) Oh yes, I will. (*Breathes rapturously.*) Ravachol. [F, Vol. II, p. 63]

A temporary relapse into juvenilia, but in a concluding paragraph, Herzl dumps the labored irony and tries to imagine the *real* Ravachol, a hunted animal half mad with fear:

Are they waiting for him in the hallway? Because of all those he scared out of their wits, none is more afraid than he himself. . . . And now he is up there, in his miserable garret. Pans, shards, pots, half-empty bottles, old tin cans—his arsenal. He sleeps in his arsenal. The soft rustle of a mouse gives him a start. He jumps up, shaking all over, taking a long time to recover from his fright. Shivering, he crawls into bed, the poor, miserable bogeyman who this very moment is the talk of the entire world on both sides of the ocean, wherever there is a telegraph. He who makes the powerful shake in their boots, he whose very existence is doubted by keen-witted skeptics and who haunts the dreams of great ladies and small children. [F, Vol. II, p. 65]

As it turned out, he could not have been more wrong.
Trying to avenge some of his comrades, Ravachol on March 27 blew up the residence of the judge who had sentenced them and was providentially captured on March 30, well before the potentially ex-

plosive May Day demonstrations and the self-imposed deadline to which the police had publicly committed themselves.

The trial began on April 26. Herzl attended every session, wrote about them in copious detail, and found himself mesmerized by a defendant who made a mockery not only of the law but also of a feuilletonist's puny imagination. For once the man lived up to his legend, and in an article summarizing the proceedings, Herzl speaks of him with undisguised admiration:

> Two men, and two men only faced each other yesterday in the courtroom of the Paris Criminal Court, the only two who had to have respect for one another. And they did. They were like two knights who, in more primitive times, stepped out in front of their respective armies and turned the battle into a duel. On one side Quesnay de Beaurepaire, courageous defender of the state and of society, the personification of justice in its rigid purity, and on the other side Ravachol. . . . Common criminal or political rebel? Dreamer or villain? Robber and assassin out of love for the poor and the downtrodden? For many hours yesterday we studied this hard face, in which fanaticism alternates with cunning. . . . There is something impersonal about this man. His manner is relaxed. With quiet determination he explains that the present state of affairs must be changed, and his voice softens as he describes a better tomorrow, in which the weak will be protected by the strong. . . . And this is the man who committed murder, who dug up corpses to rob their graves, who forged money and blew up houses in which innocent victims died— innocent even by his own lights. What, then, is he—dreamer or villain? . . . Probably the closest we can come to the truth is to assume that he started as a bad man and ended as a good one. Today he believes in himself and in his mission. In committing his crimes, he became an honest man. The ordinary killer rushes off to the brothel with his booty. Ravachol has discovered lust of a different kind: the voluptuous pleasure of a great idea, and of martyrdom. [Quoted in Bein, pp. 126–27]

And in this one concluding sentence Herzl defines not only the subtle nexus between libido and politics but also, for the first time, the object of his own unconscious quest. Still missing was the great idea.

The trial ended on April 29 in a verdict that was not altogether un-expected ever since, on the eve of it, a massive explosion wrecked the restaurant Very, in which Ravachol had been arrested. The jurors, reading it as the warning it was meant to be, cited extenuating cir-cumstances and refused to impose the death penalty. Instead, Ravachol was sentenced to life at hard labor.

Herzl was outraged by the verdict. No sympathy for the defendant could ever blind him to the cause of justice. The Teutonic code of honor and of civic virtue to which he subscribed all his life made it perfectly possible to render homage to an enemy and even to regret the need to kill him; but not to kill him when the need arose was an act of moral cowardice, whether motivated by pity or by fear. "He who lets himself be moved to sympathize with anarchists is disloyal to the state," he declared sententiously, his prose fairly quivering with righteous indignation. "He who lets himself be swayed by pity for them may be a good person, but he is a bad citizen. To pronounce judgment was once deemed a high honor and a noble burden. Those who fear to judge if it may mean risking their lives are unworthy of doing so when it involves no risk." And he went on to predict the imminent collapse of any democracy unable to produce courageous jurors.

That being a good person might be incompatible with being a good citizen was a possibility which nothing in his background had as yet prepared him to accept, but neither did he appreciate the devious efficacy with which the apparatus of the French state compensated for the endemic lack of respect it inspired in the mass of its citizens. Two months later, Ravachol was tried once more, quietly this time, in tiny, godforsaken Montbrison some 300 miles south of Paris, where an eighteenth-century church had been converted into a Palais de Justice. Charged with the murder of an elderly hermit in nearby Chambles the year before, he was sentenced to death and executed on July 11, 1892.

The street theater of the anarchists, the courtroom drama, the whole wild spectacle of dedicated fanatics with the courage to stage their fantasies and act them out all the way to the guillotine touched a raw nerve in the failed playwright who used to trim his own fantasies into mannered plots about adulterous aristocrats. This was the sort of passion that had eluded him.

The object of that passion, on the other hand, the ideas for which they were prepared to give their lives, left him cold. He ridiculed "fashionable comparisons between the socialist upsurge of this *fin de siècle* and the revolutionary mood of a hundred years ago" because large segments of the middle class now had a stake in the economy, and "the same industries that created an army of proletarian malcontents also gave rise to an army of defenders, less noticed because they make less noise." He still put his faith in technology as the ultimate solution of social problems, "a way to reconcile capital and labor. Until then, however, the meager resources of politics will have to make do for the purpose."

But political developments of a rather different kind had, in the meantime, begun to claim his attention. He had lived—and learned to live—with anti-Semitism all his life, ignored it whenever he could, mocked or trivialized it when he couldn't, dealt with it, in effect, only to the extent to which it affected him personally. In Paris he should have been quite safe, not only as a privileged foreigner, but also because here his darkly exotic looks did not give him away in the street. Instead, it became quite impossible that summer for a conscientious journalist to ignore the surge of anti-Semitism in the land of liberty, fraternity, and equality, although the bulk of French Jewry made every effort to do just that. They were a mere 40,000 in the whole of mainland France (45,000 Algerian Jews had also been granted French citizenship in 1887), about .2 percent of·the population; less than a thousand considered themselves strictly observant. They had enjoyed full equality since the Revolution—which their spokesmen hailed as the second Exodus—and, much like their Austrian co-religionists, were for the most part committed to a process of thorough assimilation which, if it did not quite obliterate all distinctions, would at least render them as inconspicuous as possible.

They had much reason to be satisfied but, as it turned out, no reason to be smug. The Rothschilds, the Hirsches, the whole top layer of Jewish finance and banking had a difficult time making themselves inconspicuous, try as they might, and anti-Semitism persisted even if it lacked official sanction and some of the virulence of the German-Austrian variety. Still, the assimilation of the French Jews had progressed much faster and further than anywhere east of the Rhine, and not only because of official tolerance; they had, after all, a fifty-year head start, they constituted a tiny percentage of the total population, and although the influx of Eastern Jews seeking refuge in France gathered momentum after the Russian pogroms of the 1880s, it was still relatively modest compared to the mass migrations pouring into Vienna.

The first serious tensions arose in 1882, when manipulations by the House of Rothschild were blamed for the collapse of a Catholic bank, the Union Générale, in which thousands of small investors lost their savings. The ensuing flood of anti-Jewish pamphlets, many of them by priests still mired in the mentality and the vocabulary of the Inquisition, crested in 1886 with the publication of Edouard Drumont's *La France Juive*, a two-volume phantasmagoria which not only rehashed the traditional venom but deftly combined divergent paranoid trends in an imaginative synthesis of religious, racial, and economic anti-Semitism that appealed equally to both the populist left and the bourgeois right. In Drumont's version, the French Revolution was itself only the most flagrant example of a Jewish plot to take over the country and the world.

But it was in explaining how a mere 40,000 Jews could manipulate 37 million Frenchmen that Drumont's most creative ingenuity came into play. There were, according to him, at least half a million of "them" out there, but like the Marranos of medieval Spain, they concealed their true allegiance. His list of hidden "Jews" who had been masquerading as Frenchmen comprised over 3,000 names and included just about every historical or contemporary figure any malcontent or reactionary had reason to hate. In the prevailing atmosphere of universal resentment, this intriguing revelation, which satisfactorily explained everything that had ever gone wrong in France, held an enormous appeal and chiefly accounts for the book's most disquieting feature—its unprecedented popularity. Most reputable publishers had originally turned it down; it was finally accepted by Marpon Flammarion as a favor to Alphonse Daudet, one of their most popular authors and himself a staunch anti-Semite. To their discreet delight, they found themselves with a runaway bestseller on their hands; the book eventually went through well over two hundred editions.

But it was with *La Libre Parole*, a weekly dedicated "to the defense of Catholic France against atheists, republicans, Free Masons, and Jews" launched in 1892, that Drumont emerged as an important catalyst in the impending showdown between the two major factions in

French society. *La Libre Parole*, financed in part by extortion—even a number of wealthy Jews were said to have bought immunity from attacks—became a peristaltic weekly discharge of venom, innuendo, and slander. (The exact role of Russian agents in Drumont's operations has never been fully explored.) When, in one of its first issues, the paper accused Auguste Burdeau, vice-president of the Chamber, of being in the Rothschilds' pay, Burdeau responded with a libel suit that gave Herzl his first opportunity to observe Drumont in action.

He had already met the man socially at the home of Alphonse Daudet. Jew-baiting French intellectuals have always reserved the right to make exceptions in individual cases; Herzl, who for his part displayed a similarly selective affinity for anti-Semites, passed the test and became a regular visitor to Daudet's literary salon.

At the trial, the prosecutor denounced Drumont as a rank opportunist out to exploit popular superstition for his own profit by labeling a Jew anyone whom he wanted to blackmail—a case more properly dealt with in a mental hospital than in a courtroom, in spite of which he asked for a prison term. Drumont responded with an appeal to the jury to read his writings and thwart the Jewish conspiracy. The three-month sentence imposed by the judge was greeted by the defendant's partisans with cries of "Down with the Jews."

Herzl found himself once again captivated by the accused, but this time as much by his ideas as by his personality. *La France Juive* struck him as a brilliant performance, and—much like Dühring's notorious *Jewish Question* ten years earlier—it aroused powerful and contradictory emotions. Three years later, almost to the day, on June 12, 1895, while in the midst of working on *Der Judenstaat*, he noted in his diary: "Much of my current conceptual freedom I owe to Drumont, because he is an artist." The compliment seems extravagant, but Drumont repaid it the following year with a glowing review of Herzl's book in *La Libre Parole*.

In the meantime, the "artist" caused more than literary mayhem. Few of his victims resorted to the courts; insults were customarily avenged by more direct methods. The injured parties met at dawn in secluded corners of the Bois de Boulogne, where philandering husbands crossed swords with their wives' lovers, and authors got a chance to fire back at their critics. On the whole, the dueling fad during the *belle époque* caused remarkably little damage, a tribute to either good sense or bad aim. But when, in May 1892, *La Libre Parole*, in a premature rehearsal for its role in the Dreyfus affair, declared that "a

Jewish officer by definition is one who has no compunction about betraying military secrets," things took a more serious turn. Of the 40,000 French officers, 300 were Jews, and a Jewish cavalry captain promptly challenged Drumont. The editor was slightly wounded, and one of his henchmen, the Marquis de Morès, thereupon challenged one of the opposing witnesses, Captain Armand Mayer, a brilliant thirty-four-year-old Jewish officer and professor at the Polytechnic Institute. Although Mayer had a crippled right arm and was hardly able to lift a sword, he did not want to lay himself open to charges of "Jewish cowardice" and was stabbed to death moments into the duel.

The funeral on June 26, just ten days after the Drumont trial, turned into one of the most moving protests against anti-Semitism ever held in Paris, with crowd estimates ranging from 20,000 to 100,000 mourners. Defense Minister Freycinet declared in the Chamber that the army knew neither Jews nor Gentiles but only Frenchmen, and even Drumont in his *Libre Parole* publicly deplored the fact that so valiant an officer "had not been given the chance to spill his blood on the battlefield in the service of the fatherland." Herzl seems to have been genuinely impressed by this display of public sympathy, so different from Vienna, where Jews were not even considered *satisfaktionsfähig*, and where the academic youth, in stark contrast to Paris, was always in the forefront of reaction. In his article of June 27, he stressed the positive impact of the affair on the national conscience and consciousness. Mayer's sacrifice, he wrote, would not be in vain if, "from the mists of mourning that now veil it, the banner of France reemerges as the glorious, immortal symbol of fraternity and justice."

Paris changed Herzl.

French anti-Semitism undermined the ironic complacency of the Jewish would-be non-Jew, but it could not have done so if he had not already been open to the experience. He had finally outgrown the carapace of his egocentric arrogance.

The depth of these changes is strikingly evident in his correspondence with Arthur Schnitzler, which began that July and continued sporadically over the next three years. Schnitzler, the son of a prominent Viennese laryngologist, was two years younger than Herzl. He had studied medicine, dabbled briefly in psychiatry, but ended up in laryngology himself. Although his major works were still in the future, he had already published a number of dramatic poems and short plays that revealed great promise and made him one of the rising stars of the "Young Vienna" literary movement. His latest play, A *Fairy Tale*, had been circulating in manuscript and been passed on to Herzl by a common acquaintance. Herzl had met and cordially disliked Schnitzler during his student years, but A *Fairy Tale* moved him to the kind of spontaneous gesture that reveals an altogether novel and hard-earned self-awareness.

Dear Dr. Schnitzler,

I am greatly indebted to Dr. Goldmann for the opportunity to read your *Fairy Tale*. We were sitting in the press gallery of the Palais Bourbon . . . when he mentioned your name. I was— forgive me for saying so—rather startled to hear him praise you the way he did. Though familiar with some of your sparkling dialogue pieces, I did not share his high opinion of your talent. As for you personally, moreover, I downright disliked you. I had lately seen you in the company of some of these professional "Young Viennese," and our earlier meetings had led me to see in you a conceited fellow flogging all sorts of social inanities.

How foolish and superficial we sometimes are in our judgments. You may have had a similar experience—with me, in fact. At any rate, I am full of remorse, and on reading your *Fairy Tale*, I begged your forgiveness.

That you never came to see me, although we lived in the same district, is now a reason for me to feel ashamed, like the fellow who didn't get invited to the party. It would humble me if I were still in need of such reminders. Obviously you never sensed in any of my public scribblings the note that might have touched your heart. . . . And yet it was just the likes of you I wanted to reach. Obviously, I failed.

By the way, I am by now quite in the clear with myself. In the theater, with which I am through for good, I had a bad and foolish time. Plays in which I believed, in which I aimed for art, were never produced. If, on the other hand, out of a certain greedy despair I descended to mere craftsmanship, I got produced—and panned. When I think of my place in German literature—which happens very rarely—I can only laugh. . . . Yet I must tell you that it has not embittered me. Pain is always an education. And when I see the burgeoning of a talent such as yours, I am as delighted as if I myself had never been a *littérateur*, meaning a narrow-minded, intolerant, jealous, and malicious fool. . . . This is meant to be no more patronizing than the admiration of a somewhat older brother. Because your writing feels familiar: this is the way I myself would have liked to write. . . . In a word, my dear Schnitzler, I believe in you. And if you go on writing just to satisfy yourself, you'll give much pleasure to all of us. If you want a frightening example of where compromise will take you, just look at me. I don't think my taste is too esoteric; and if I, as qualified a theater critic as any young fool or failed playwright, read your pieces with pleasure, I venture to believe that the public will also like them. [L, 7/29/92]

The unsolicited tribute from a man not given to undue humility must have come as something of a shock. But Schnitzler was already much too knowledgeable about people to miss the message between the lines, and he responded immediately with warmth and candor.

Dearest Friend [he began, skipping the formal address (to which he ostentatiously reverted in 1901, after distancing himself from Herzlian Zionism)], Somehow I must have always had a feeling that we would one day find the way to each other, because the vividness with which I recall all the details of our shortlived acquaintance is downright curious. [He went on to describe his first impression of Herzl rhetorically demolishing his opponents at the Academic Reading Hall.] How I envied you that ironic smile of yours. If only I could speak and smile that way, I thought. . . . Shortly thereafter I met you personally and read two of your plays in manuscript . . . and again I envied you. If only I could write such plays. . . . But our student years passed without our making any real contact, evidently—as your letter indicates— because you considered me too arrogant! . . . I saw you again in Kammer, surrounded by a bevy of pretty young women, and again I envied you—not without cause, I hope. You smiled your ironic smile, and I felt depressed the way one does when the other is always twenty paces ahead. [CZA, 8/18/92]

It was the beginning of a lively exchange which, though it never ripened into full intimacy, made up to some extent for the loss of Kana and Boxer; it also kept Herzl in touch with the literary scene in Vienna. In October he inquired about a pseudonymous author whose poems had caught his attention: "Who is Loris? One of your pseudonyms? In any case, those few verses are delicious. Tell me who Loris is. Altogether, pick up your good Toledo steel pen and tell me about Vienna in the year of grace 1892. At length, because you have the time, you perhaps lucky fellow. . . . Tell me what is going on in the arts and newspapers of Vienna. All I know is what I read in the magazines (L, 10/10/92).

Schnitzler, a well-placed informant with close ties to both the haut monde and the demimonde, set him straight at once:

No, I am not Loris. Unfortunately. Because for one thing, I would be twelve years younger, and for another, I would have written *Gaston*, the most beautiful German one-act play for a long, long time. You'll be hearing a lot about this strange eighteen-year-old. . . . Actually, his name is Hugo von Hofmannsthal, he graduated from the Gymnasium in July and is now studying law at the University of Vienna; no need telling you that this is not to be taken too literally. . . . The arts in Vienna? Literary life consists of anti-naturalist couplets at the Carl Theater; there are no publishers and no new works but, on the other hand, a great many cafés, to which all the literati who could think of nothing in the morning repair in the afternoon to exchange their thoughts. If two of them share a table, they are called a clique; if three get together, they in fact are one. They believe neither in themselves nor in anybody else—and for the most part they are right. [CZA, 11/12/92]

But when Schnitzler asked to see some of his manuscripts, Herzl balked.

I've left all that behind me [he asserted]. That is why I won't give in to your gracious request, which I can only interpret as an act of kindness. Despite a measure of insight acquired with age, I am still not beyond a certain degree of vanity, and I think you will understand that I do not wish to be read merely as a gesture of reciprocity. . . . If, as you wrote earlier this summer, you always saw me some distance ahead, the head start was paid for with fatigue; today I already sit by the side of the road and watch the others pass me by. [L, 11/16/92]

And when Schnitzler insisted: "My manuscripts? I've forgotten about them. All that remains is a little love for art and an occasional twinge of nostalgia for literature. Being a journalist takes its toll" (L, 1/2/93).

His brief correspondence with the precocious Hofmannsthal, on the other hand, ended on a note of frustration. The *Wunderkind*, conscious of his genius but too young to bear it with grace—he became one of Young Vienna's most authentic voices but never quite fulfilled his early promise—responded to Herzl's overture with a snooty letter full of condescension, in which he faintly praised Herzl's "graceful style" but felt constrained to express his dislike of journalism as a métier, "despite such colleagues as Heine and Anatole France." The indulgent irony of Herzl's reply was probably lost on the youthful prodigy, and matters never went further.

Within less than a year, Herzl had become a seasoned journalist whose dispatches far transcended in both style and content the run-of-the-mill reporting of most of his colleagues. The rules of the game, of "the métier that the delightful little Hofmannsthal so despises," favored the emotional distance that had always come to him naturally, so that slipping into the professional role of objective observer presented no problem. The trouble was that some of the observations made that emotional distance increasingly difficult to sustain and forced him to confront his identity as a Jew—an Austrian Jew writing for a Jewish-owned newspaper with a largely Jewish readership. And whereas back home, inured by lifelong exposure, he had simply lacked the perspective from which to view a phenomenon more or less taken for granted, anti-Semitism now became an aspect—and an ever more conspicuous one—of the French political scene which it was his job to analyze and interpret.

His reports on the Drumont trial and the Mayer tragedy were still impeccably factual and dispassionate. And in his first comprehensive survey of "French Anti-Semites" on August 31, 1892, he lamely tried to defuse a sensitive subject by labored witticisms à la Heine that betray his evident unease:

> French anti-Semites are more kindhearted than those of other countries; they are even willing to admit that Jews, too, are human beings. . . . What the French hold most against the Jews is that they come from Frankfurt—an obvious injustice, since some of them come from Mainz or even Speyer. Their money is resented only if they have any. . . . And if a Jew carries native cunning

to the point of sacrificing his life in a noble and knightly manner, he will earn widespread murmurs of approval. This is more or less what happened to Captain Mayer; even his opponent, the Marquis de Morès, declared that he "regretted the death of this honorable man." A Jew can certainly not ask for more without appearing greedy. . . . [He closed on an obligatory though possibly sincere note of optimism:] There is a core of common sense and love of justice in the French. . . . The movement here will pass, though probably not without excesses and isolated disasters. [Bein, p. 143]

But by November, as the Panama scandal gathered momentum and turned into an avalanche threatening to bury the Republic, he began to have his doubts.

The affair had its origins in a witches' brew of hero worship, credulity, and plain greed. The hero, one of the very few the French had left to worship, was Ferdinand de Lesseps, conqueror of Suez, a man whom Herzl himself had once idolized. Lesseps, born in 1805 but remarkably well preserved—he remarried at sixty-four and fathered another twelve children by his second wife—was a visionary who, lacking all expertise in matters such as engineering or finance, would never be deterred by mere mundane considerations grounded in reality. The Suez Canal testified to the power of the dream and to the magic touch of the dreamer. In popular mythology it represented the triumph not just of French technology but of the French spirit. And when the wizened visionary proposed to cut a sea-level canal across the Isthmus of Panama—Herzl's own secret childhood dream—and appealed for the necessary funds, the response was overwhelming; small investors by the thousands rushed to convert their faith in the miracle worker into cash profits.

What the visionary had failed to envisage—and hence to include in his cost projections—were the harsh realities of digging a ditch across some fifty miles of wild and mountainous territory infested by the deadly mosquito-borne yellow-fever virus. Between 1881, when the excavations began, and their suspension in 1889, untold thousands of native laborers and hundreds of French engineers died of the plague; entire classes of the great French engineering schools were decimated. In addition, the approximately 12-foot difference in tidal waves between the Atlantic and the Pacific defied Lesseps's stubborn insistence on a lockless canal and made the whole concept seem increasingly chimerical.

Inevitably, within a year of starting operations, Lesseps's Panama Canal Company had vastly overshot its budget and run out of funds. But in order to tap further government subsidies and float additional loans, it was vital to keep news of the disastrous reverses from the public, a task utterly beyond the collective imagination of the incompetents who served on the company's Board of Directors. In desperation, they turned for help to a consortium of shady—and predominantly Jewish—speculators, who quickly took matters in hand. In no time at all, the company's affairs were being managed by the likes of Baron Jacques de Reinach, a German-born French national with an Italian baronetcy, and by his deputy, Cornelius Herz, a French-born naturalized United States citizen. Their way of maintaining public confidence in the project was to put a whole network of journalists on their payroll; additional government subsidies were obtained by the old-fashioned and time-tested method of bribing key politicians. As the need grew for ever more substantial sums, so did the greed and number of journalists and politicians determined to get their hands on a share of the loot. By the time the whole scheme collapsed of its own weight in 1889, so many of the top people were implicated that no one seemed anxious to cast the first stone lest he bring the roof down on his own head. The whole Palais Bourbon had, in effect, become a glass house; nor was the press eager to document the widely prevalent view of it as the older of the oldest professions.

It took an outsider to shatter this complicity of silence. It took Edouard Drumont, to be precise, whose *Libre Parole* had been dragging the sewers all along and now triumphantly presented its slimy catch. With understandable glee, Drumont exposed the machinations of that "alien Jew and fake Frenchman," the so-called Baron de Reinach, thereby precipitating the first of the two major *affaires* that were to shake the Republic to its foundations.

Reinach committed suicide, Cornelius Herz skipped town and settled comfortably in England. But public outrage, the rising clamor of defrauded investors, the relentless attacks by the monarchist opposition and venomous recriminations in parliament seemed once again to portend the imminent collapse of the established order. "I think we'll have a revolution here this coming year," Herzl wrote to Schnitzler on January 2, 1893. "And if I don't get away on time, I am liable to be shot as a bourgeois, a German spy, a Jew, or a financier." Reluctantly, the government finally decided to save what was left of its reputation by prosecuting Lesseps, his son Charles, the company directors, and some of the politicians most flagrantly involved. The trial opened in November 1892 and dragged on into May of the following year. Lesseps and company were found guilty; the politicians were acquitted, although one of the most powerful among them fell victim to the scandal: Georges Clemenceau, great white hope of the republican left, symbol of probity and combative editor of *Justice*, was revealed to have run his paper on funds supplied by Cornelius Herz. It took him some fourteen years to work his way back into the Palais Bourbon.

But the juridical verdicts proved largely irrelevant in any case. Acquitted or not, politicians as a whole—and they had by then evolved into a tight-knit fraternity of more or less tenured professionals—were henceforth held in general contempt and regarded as a gang of professional thieves, thereby widening the breach between the people and their government. Something like this must have been what Herzl had in mind when, at the start of the trial in November, he questioned the wisdom of the legal proceedings altogether. "If it were a simple question of right or wrong," he wrote presciently, "it could be decided by any learned judge on the basis of the established facts in the case. . . . But the politician must ponder whether the law in this instance will serve its purpose, whether the community as a whole would not sustain far greater damage from the mechanical application of the relevant statutes" (Bein, p. 153).

And finally, whatever the guilt of those formally charged, the public at large had its own ideas about whom to blame for this blow to French pride, the ruin of countless small investors, the loss of lifetime savings. A *bas les juifs*.

Herzl covered the trial from start to finish, and filed almost daily reports interspersed with periodic overviews that delved more deeply into the background and significance of the affair. As the case slowly unraveled thread by thread, it exposed the whole skein of corruption linking government, finance, and journalism. "Whoever with his own eyes witnessed the raging fury of these latest sessions in the Chamber must have had visions of the seething passions of the *Convent*," Herzl wrote in his year-end survey. "Folly and crime never change, nor do people themselves. Memory insists: this is the way it was a hundred years ago; what followed was a year of blood and gore. Death bells are tolling—'93 all over" (Bein, p. 154).

He had learned more than he had bargained for about the ways of the world. And the more he came to know, the more he wondered about his own place in it. What, precisely, did he have in common with a Baron Reinach or a Cornelius Herz?

ELEVEN

*I*f Herzl's frenzied activities and exhausting daily routine left little time for his family, there is no evidence that he felt unduly deprived. The reconciliation with Julie had obviously gone beyond mere appearances; on May 20, 1893, she gave birth to another girl, originally named Margarethe and later called Trude. But although divorce no longer seemed an issue, nothing substantial had changed in the marriage; it remained a highly problematic compromise, plagued by the same discords and tensions that a year earlier had driven Herzl into virtual exile. What had changed, however, was Herzl himself, eminently successful now and self-assured, no longer needing to prove his manhood in the private sphere and ready to settle for the kind of arrangement common enough in his circles and considerably less troublesome than a messy divorce.

Although he now had his beloved parents living under the same roof with him and could switch roles from husband to father to son without getting his feet wet, the setup had certain drawbacks. Few apartments can ever be large enough for three children and seven adults, including two temperamental women who cordially despised one another and never missed a chance to vent their sulphurous rancor.

Herzl, however, was no longer quite as vulnerable to emotional blackmail. The bickering and the uncivil war still annoyed, exasperated, sometimes even depressed him, but mostly because it interfered with his work. And while he worshipped his mother as much as ever, he was aware now of some of her less lovable attributes and, rather than siding with her automatically, made it a habit to remove himself from the battlefield altogether by leaving the house or retreating to his off-limits study.

Julie, on the other hand, had no such means of escape. Love, or at least sympathy, might have made a difference, but Herzl, hardly less spoiled and self-centered, never made himself available. He did not expect companionship from any woman other than his mother, and what he looked for in a wife was dutiful devotion to *Kinder* and *Küche*. Julie's devotion to her children, though passionate rather than dutiful, was above reproach. When it came to running the household, however, she was a resounding failure.

Nothing in her background had prepared her for the task. By nature scattered and disorganized, she relied on hired help for everything, with often disastrous results. But her most glaring fault, in the eyes of both her husband and his parents, was her reckless extravagance, and if it upset Herzl, it nearly killed his pinch-penny pedant of a father. Julie, raised in an atmosphere of great affluence and conspicuous consumption, thought of money as an ever-renewable resource, and spending it freely was her one pleasure and comfort in a world of unrelieved bleakness.

The arguments about her spending habits never ceased; if anything, they grew more strident in later years. In Paris, however, they were exacerbated by the sullen presence of Herzl's parents. To Jakob Herzl, money was sacred, and extravagance tantamount to sacrilege; frustrated and resentful, he undertook a detailed analysis of the household finances and chose to submit his findings in a formal memorandum headed "Information Concerning the Conduct of Household Affairs," which fairly spluttered with indignation heavily underlined for emphasis: "My observations during my presence in Paris lead me to conclude that *great savings* are possible if, first, the cook is *strictly forbidden* to socialize with peddlers; second, if the fruit merchant is *strictly forbidden* to deliver merchandise *other than* against a written order from Julie," and so on down the line for several pages—reasonable enough suggestions, no doubt, but hardly designed to promote harmony in the family.

It might have made him feel better had he known that the gist of his findings became part of an official dossier. The French Secret Service, which had Herzl under surveillance as a "suspect foreigner," described him in a report of April 1893 as "seemingly in possession of substantial resources. Lives with his parents, who are reported to be extremely stingy and who criticize him for being too spendthrift."

Although the professional paranoiacs of the Quatrième Bureau may have overestimated Herzl's "substantial resources," their suspicions were understandable. He now lived in the manner to which he had always aspired, on a scale that clearly exceeded even the fairly generous income of a *Neue Freie Presse* correspondent. But *noblesse oblige*, and no clear line separated his social from his professional life. He was a smashing success in both spheres, a regular presence at the Comédie Française, at the Opéra and the racetrack as well as in the cafés and salons of the literati. His regal appearance, quick wit, and fluent French soon gained him access to some of the most influential circles in the capital. There were those he cultivated as potential sources, others who, for reasons of their own, made it a point to cultivate the correspondent of one of Europe's leading newspapers. But while social life is seldom devoid of opportunism, it appears that in this instance Herzl's personality was at least as significant a factor as his professional role. Many years later, in an interview with Pierre van Paassen, Georges Clemenceau recalled his impressions of Herzl:

> Daudet told me about him first, and about a book he was going to write. I read that book later. It was, I believe, the best book he ever wrote, and naturally so. Herzl was essentially a man of action, a great man. When I say a great man, I judge greatness not by what a man has said or written. I want to know what he has done. Your own thoughts may astonish you any time. But what are the actions that follow? The world is full of verbal disguise. . . . There is far too much noise for the virtue of simplicity. Herzl looked life in the face. And he went his way, caring little for acclaim and popular approval. In certain things he was a little naïve. But are not all great men naïve, more or less? [THM, p. 25]

He had animated conversations with Rodin, socialized with members of the Chamber as well as with leading personalities of the French theater, and met every Friday with French and foreign journalists at the restaurant Foyot for a luncheon discussion with important or newsworthy personalities. Once a month he dined at the home of Alphonse Daudet. The openly anti-Semitic author of *Lettres de Mon Moulin* and *Tartarin de Tarascon* was charmed by the exotic Viennese Jew, for reasons which his son, the virulent Fascist Léon Daudet, later professed to find incomprehensible. The father, then at the height of his fame as a novelist, introduced his odd friend to some of the leading lights of the literary establishment, including Huysmans and Proust. He also served up a generous helping of his own like-minded bigots; it was in Daudet's salon that Herzl first met Drumont.

Contacts of inestimable value to a journalist, but Herzl socialized for pleasure as well as for business and was by no means insensitive to the flattering attention he elicited everywhere. By the end of the year, he—unlike his wife and parents—felt as thoroughly at home in Paris as he did anywhere, with a wide circle of acquaintances among the intersecting elites in literature, politics, and the arts. Contact, in most cases, was superficial, urbanely cordial but decidedly less than intimate—with one exception. Herzl's relations with Max Nordau, though not as yet a real friendship between equals at this stage, were different in kind from the very beginning.

During his postgraduate studies in Paris in 1885, the young Freud had called on Nordau and—according to Ernest Jones—dismissed the controversial author, who also happened to be a colleague, as vain and stupid.

That Freud, for all his knowledge of the human soul, could be obtuse about people is amply documented by the whole history of the early psychoanalytic movement. Nordau was vain, to be sure, and his prejudices ran far deeper than his ostentatious erudition. A great many of the ideas he peddled with provocative fanfare and much polemical skill were half baked, absurd, or plain wacky, though none anywhere near as wacky as those of Freud's own intimate friend and associate the naso-sexologist Dr. Fliess. But stupid?

Descended from a long line of Talmudists and himself the son of an Orthodox rabbi, Nordau was born Max Simon Suedfeld in Budapest in 1849. (He legally changed his name after his father's death in 1872.) He received a solid Jewish education but, as a concession to the spirit of the Jewish enlightenment, was also permitted to attend a Catholic Gymnasium. At fourteen, he published his first poem, at sixteen he became a theater critic for the *Pester Lloyd*, and two years later he was hired as a regular correspondent and feuilletonist while simultaneously studying medicine. He received his M.D. in 1876 and settled in Paris with his mother and sister, supporting the family by writing for the *Frankfurter Zeitung* and several smaller papers while he continued his medical studies at the Sorbonne.

He had by then become a thoroughly assimilated agnostic, every bit as estranged from Judaism as Herzl, except that unlike Herzl he knew what he was estranged from. In the 1880s, still practicing medicine but with several plays, a novel, and some travel writing already to his credit, he began to publish the series of books that were to establish him as one of the foremost *fin de siècle* prophets of doom. His professional background as a psychiatrist lent a pseudo-scientific veneer to his most flagrantly irrational prejudices—a major asset in an age in which science superseded God as the source of divine revelation.

What distinguished Nordau from the likes of Gobineau, Chamberlain, Dühring, or Drumont, all of whom also invoked "science" on behalf of their paranoid constructs, was an intuitive grasp of the catastrophic potential inherent in the social and political trends of the industrial age. *The Conventional Lies of Civilization* and *Paradoxes*, published in 1883 and 1885 respectively, were pugnaciously rationalist attacks on the superstitions that in his view threatened civilized society, from religion and racism to nationalism and the deification of money. But it was with the publication, in 1892, of *Degeneracy* (the second volume appeared in 1893) that Nordau attained fame and notoriety on both sides of the Atlantic.

The book is a frontal assault on modernity in all its manifestations, arguably the most impassioned and the most comprehensive ever mounted. In popularizing his views, Nordau compiled not only the basic manifesto of cultural reaction but also, in his very title, supplied the slogan which Nazi ideologues used forty years later to justify their lethal vandalism, though understandably without giving him credit.

Degeneracy was inspired by—and dedicated to—the Italian psychiatrist Cesare Lombroso, whose speculations in the 1860s about the link between genius and madness relied heavily on hereditary taint and the "science" of phrenology. But whereas Lombroso distinguished between the genius and his work, Nordau did away with such subtle distinctions. On the contrary, he insisted that a sick artist inevitably produced sick art, just as sick art was incontrovertible proof of the artist's sickness. Any art or artist deviating from the accepted norms of "moral beauty and health" must be regarded as degenerate, hence a clear and present danger to civilization. Dr. Nordau's list of deviates was a long one—the two volumes comprise over a thousand pages—

and includes nearly every innovative and original nineteenth-century writer or thinker along with all his disciples, from Swinburne, Ruskin, Rimbaud, Verlaine, and Baudelaire to Schopenhauer, Nietzsche, Wagner, Tolstoy, Ibsen, and Zola, to mention but a few.

Since the mad genius was genetically flawed and medically beyond help, Nordau saw his own task as one of prophylaxis. If civilization was to be saved, potentially susceptible victims of degenerate art had to be protected from exposure by isolating the contagion. He therefore proposed the formation of a Society for Ethical Culture that would test works of art for their moral content and publicly brand those found wanting as "degenerate."

Nordau, who died in 1923, was fortunate in not having witnessed the practical realization of his far from original proposal. The Militant Confederation for the Preservation of German Culture, founded in 1929, specifically dedicated itself to judging works of art and literature by standards of "moral beauty"—Hitler's standards rather than Nordau's—and followed up on it with the logical next step in 1933, when its president, Alfred Rosenberg, became the Third Reich's arbiter of culture and, as such, proceeded to ban degenerate art and to exterminate its creators. That Rosenberg would have classified Nordau himself as degenerate merely proves that bad ideas never lose their potential for mischief.

There is a profound irony in this aggressively rationalist physician providing the ideological underpinnings for paranoid philistinism at its most extreme. But the instant, sensational, and worldwide success of *Degeneracy* fed on the deep-seated anti-modernist bias of a frightened and disoriented middle class hopelessly bewildered by cultural changes it could neither control nor comprehend. The expensive two-volume opus, a turgid tract for all its polemical vigor, became a stupendous bestseller and was almost immediately translated into most Western languages; the first English translation appeared in 1895 and went through seven editions within the first four months.

Critical reaction was equally swift and extreme, ranging from unqualified adulation to brutal contempt. Nordau found himself likened to Heine, Spinoza, Lassalle, and Disraeli. Karl Kraus called him a philistine butcher. William James referred to *Degeneracy* as "a pathological book on a pathological subject" whose methods, applied to the author, would make him "a degenerate of the worst sort." George Bernard Shaw, a formidable iconoclast in his own right, paid tribute to the "vigorous and capable journalist, shrewd enough to see that there is a good opening for a big reactionary book as a relief to the Wagner and Ibsen booms . . ." while dismissing the tract itself as "a book which has made a very considerable impression on the artistic ignorance of Europe and America. . . . He is so utterly mad on the subject of degeneracy that he finds the symptoms of it in the loftiest geniuses as plainly as in the lowest jailbirds, the exception being himself, Lombroso, Krafft-Ebing, Dr. Maudsley, Goethe, Shakespeare, and Beethoven" (Ben-Horin, p. 21).

The bestseller had not yet come out when Herzl first met him, but Nordau, eleven years older and already well established as a prolific and versatile writer, was initially very much the senior partner in the relationship; there was an unmistakably reverential tremor in Herzl's remark to his parents, in mid-March, that "our family physician will be Dr. Nordau."

The two had much in common—the Budapest connection, literary ambitions, newspaper work, and a fierce devotion to their mothers. Nordau had brought his mother and sister to Paris, shared an apartment with them, and took a long time founding his own household. He eventually married the widow of a close friend, and the marriage seems to have been a success even though Mrs. Nordau was a Danish Protestant and her husband, unlike Herzl, opposed intermarriage on principle; he in fact later cited it as a reason for not assuming the leadership of the Zionist movement after Herzl's death.

But beyond these surface affinities, the two men shared certain fundamental attitudes. Herzl never explicitly discussed Nordau's *chef d'oeuvre*, at least not in print; if nothing else, his lifelong addiction to Wagner's music makes one suspect that he did not see eye to eye with his friend on a number of points. He was, in any case, far too discriminating a reader to have been completely comfortable with Nordau's caveman approach to literature, nor would he ever have condemned a work of art on the basis of the artist's personality alone. Nevertheless, their tastes were shaped by much the same blend of Teutonic Weimar classicism and Jewish Budapest bourgeoisie, and just as they both worshipped their mothers, so they remained faithful to the cultural precepts and ideals of another generation.

Judaism, however, was one common problem they seem to have avoided during these early stages of their friendship. Nordau, having grown up in an intensely Jewish environment, had made a conscious break with the past. Though he never considered conversion and, in fact, brutally ridiculed converts, he adopted a new name after his father's death and emerged as a belligerently cosmopolitan agnostic. Herzl, too, was rapidly moving toward a break with the past, but moving in the opposite direction.

As a reporter on the French scene he had, of course, been forced right from the outset to deal with the spread of anti-Semitism as a social and political phenomenon. But by the end of his first year in Paris it had already become a troubling and intensely personal issue as well. A private letter to Moritz Benedikt, written in the final days of 1892, is interesting for the light it sheds on Herzl's state of mind at the time and on his disingenuous efforts to define his position:

> I do not consider the anti-Semitic movement altogether harmful. It will inhibit the ostentatious flaunting of conspicuous wealth, curb the unscrupulous behavior of Jewish financiers, and contribute in many ways to the education of the Jews. . . . In that respect we seem to be in agreement.
>
> Perhaps also as regards religion. I consider religion indispensable for the weak. There are those who, weak in willpower, mind, or emotions, must always be able to rely on religion. The others, the normal run of mankind, are weak only in childhood and in old age; for them, religion serves as an educational instrument or a source of comfort. . . . God is a magnificent symbol for an enormous complex of moral and legal imperatives, the apparent solution to riddles, the answer to all childish questions. Which religion, or which god, really makes no difference. I regard myself as an average modern Jew, and I would not shrink from a *pro forma* conversion to Christianity. Any Jew who has children and decides to get baptized has my blessings.
>
> I have a son. For his sake I would rather convert today than tomorrow, so that his membership in Christendom may start as soon as possible, and so that he may be spared the hurt and humiliation that I suffered and will continue to suffer as a result of being Jewish. But I cannot do it, for two reasons. First, because I would hurt my father's feelings. Loyalty and gratitude forbid me to trouble our relationship by what to me is a matter of indifference but which he would regard as harsh and alien. In the natural course of events, therefore, my own generation will still remain Jewish. My son, on the other hand, once he grows

up, will have no such considerations to restrain him, the less so
since I myself have no feelings in the matter.

At that point, however, what is today my second reason may
for him become the one that will keep him from converting: one
does not desert the Jews as long as they are being persecuted. A
matter of self-respect. Also, by the way, quite pointless, as demonstrated by the example of those Spanish Jews who converted,
were allowed to remain but continued to be despised and not
permitted to marry Gentiles. Thus the individual solution of the
Jewish Question by converting to the majority faith holds little
promise as long as the Jews are being hated. One would therefore
first have to bring about a state of tolerance, and then proceed
to have all Jews convert in a body to Christianity. [L, 12/27/92
approx.]

The idea that an end to discrimination would do away with Jewish
particularism and—as Herzl spells it out in no uncertain terms—with
Jews altogether was widely shared in liberal circles but of no practical
significance, since anti-Semitism was not about to fade away by itself.
Most Jews—especially in France—preferred dignified silence to the
risk of undignified confrontation, and few Gentile voices were raised
against the proliferating anti-Jewish demagoguery, even among those
who deplored it. In 1891, however, the noted pacifist—later winner
of the 1905 Nobel Peace Prize—Bertha von Suttner organized a Society
to Combat Anti-Semitism in Vienna. Its founders included a number
of prominent Christians and Jews, among them the novelist Peter
Rosegger, the Waltz King Johann Strauss, the renowned gastroenter-
ologist Nothnagel, and the industrialist Friedrich Leitenberger. It was
on their behalf that Regina Friedlaender, widow of the founder of the
Neue Freie Presse, asked Herzl in January 1893 to contribute to the
society's newsletter, Das Freie Blatt.

Herzl flatly refused. Fighting the symptoms, the outward manifestations of anti-Semitism, he told her, seemed to him relatively simple
and could be achieved by brute force; "half a dozen duels would greatly
elevate the social position of the Jews" and accomplish far more than
yet another pious publication. Curing the evil as such, on the other
hand, was infinitely more difficult. "The Jews would have to shed
those peculiarities for which they are rightfully being criticized. . . .
A long, hard, and ultimately hopeless struggle. At best, some of us

may become Special Status Jews." True equality, he continued to believe, was possible only through conversion and intermarriage.

His letter prompted a barbed reply from Baron Leitenberger, to whom Mrs. Friedlaender had passed it on. The industrialist, deploring the absence of any constructive suggestions, minced no words in demolishing Herzl's jejune arguments. "That any Jew who collects a dirty look should go and fight a duel and that all Jews should convert to Christianity may perhaps qualify as sparkling dinner conversation but could hardly be taken seriously by serious men firmly determined to fight the scourge of racism" (Bein, p. 147).

The words drew blood, but it was more than bruised vanity and bleeding self-esteem that made Herzl take time out, in the midst of the Panama Canal crisis, to compose a twenty-two-page epistle, one of the longest he ever wrote in his life. Its six or more drafts mirror the intellectual and emotional confusion which up to this point he had been able to encapsulate in the brittle complacency punctured by Leitenberger. His objections to the baron's well-meaning efforts—too little and too late—were pertinent and sensible, but so was Leitenberger's rejoinder: What do YOU propose to do?

In rising to the challenge, Herzl found himself obliged to confront the Jewish problem in terms of his own personal dilemma—a Jew condemned to an identity he could neither assume nor reject. That on this first try he failed to come up with a plausible solution is not to be held against him; what matters is that, for the first time, he felt compelled to seek an answer rather than beg the question.

"I don't believe there is anything I need to take back," he first truculently asserted, but then went on to elaborate. "Don't think that I carry flippancy to the point of judging the Jews too harshly. On the contrary, I find them rather admirable, considering the age-old oppression they were forced to endure. When I watch the behavior of many a German here in France trying desperately not to be recognized as such, I realize that there is much to excuse in the Jews, who, after all, have been constantly living in enemy territory" (L, 1/26/93).

Enemy territory?

An altogether new note, and a strangely discordant one, a sound from the heart rather like that "sigh of an old Jew" he had noted at Lourdes, yet still very much at odds with his conscious attitude:

When I said that the Jews ought to convert, I meant it half in jest and half in earnest. I, who will not convert, can permit

myself to say it. But what about my son, Hans? The pressures of
Judaism may well teach him a lesson in humanitarianism; but
do I therefore have the right to make life as needlessly difficult
for him as it was, and will go on being, for me? I hope that as
an adult he will be too proud to desert the faith, though he no
doubt will have as little of it as I do myself. That is why Jewish
boys ought to be baptized in infancy, before they have a mind
of their own and while they can do nothing about it one way or
another. Fade into the majority.

He paid tribute to the baron's good intentions and the society's efforts
but insisted that they came too late. "If ten, twelve years ago these
valiant men had spoken out against the first manifestations of anti-
Semitism . . . and even then I am not sure. The Danube would
presumably be a mighty river even if its source were blocked; the
tributaries make it what it is. . . . A movement that can no longer be
suppressed can only be countered by another movement—and by this
I quite simply mean socialism. I am convinced that the Jews, when
cornered, will finally have no other way out. Now as to your question
of what I propose to do . . ."

His proposal, developed with florid imagination and painstaking
attention to detail, came down to nothing less—or more—than a daily
newspaper that would turn the tide, radically different from any other
publication.

Nothing can be done with a "moderate" paper such as the *Neue*
Freie Presse or the *Freie Blatt*. As a reader, I appreciate the
rational, measured tone and high-class attitude of a paper. As a
politician, on the other hand, I am forced to recognize that this
kind of newspaper is not up to the job; it only convinces those
already convinced, which is why they subscribe to the paper in
the first place. This balanced assessment of a newspaper to which
I am dedicating my best talents entitles me to tell you what I
think of your *Freie Blatt*. . . . It is not a newspaper, but a circular
that does not circulate. . . . Using journalism as a weapon in
the fight against anti-Semitism would, in my opinion, require
something altogether different.

One could, he mused, acquire one of the great popular dailies and
adapt it to the purpose, but this would have several disadvantages,

among them the necessity, "to which, as a member of the profession, I would have to take strong exception," of firing the entire present editorial staff because "a newspaper dedicated to fighting anti-Semitism *cannot have a single Jew* on its staff . . . neither Jews nor Jews' vassals— and no 'converts,' either. This means founding a radically new kind of newspaper in Vienna."

Fired by his own combustible enthusiasm, he went on to explore every aspect of the project with the same obsessive attention to detail which later marked his transition from dreamer to activist. "The independent paper must be designed for the common people. It would discuss social problems in original articles—no phrasemongering, but investigative reports about the working conditions of women, child labor, the working day, etc. . . . A few practical points: the price will be two crowns. You should expect a loss of at least 200,000 crowns. . . . Production costs are bound to exceed income. Taxes amount to one crown, half or a quarter crown for distribution, the rest for editorial services, communications, printing, and paper. The greatest danger is the rising cost of paper."

He weighed the feasibility of an evening edition, a humor section, "and caricatures, one of the most effective means of polemicizing. One must make fun of the anti-Semites. Laughter is much more contagious than wrath." There was the question of illustrations—a touchy one, since Count Taaffe, Prime Minister and himself the publisher of an illustrated paper, might not welcome the competition— and of a literary section: "The imagination of ordinary people needs to be stimulated by adventures they will never themselves experience. . . . If modern novels prove too costly, one can always fall back on Dickens, perhaps even Balzac" (L, 1/26/93).

Leitenberger, a hard-nosed businessman, was clearly taken aback by this eruption. On February 1, he thanked Herzl in the most cordial terms for this thoughtful contribution but expressed his regrets; a project on so ambitious a scale greatly exceeded the modest means at his disposal. Herzl must have replied at once; in another letter dated February 8, Leitenberger told him that he was "delighted to learn that you are pregnant with yet another idea for dealing with the Jewish Question. Perhaps fate will be kind enough to let me be among the chosen and anointed who will someday assist at the delivery. You will find me a somewhat sober but enthusiastic midwife" (Bein, p. 151).

*   *   *

The Leitenberger correspondence is clear evidence that, by the spring of 1893, the Jewish Question had become something of an obsession with Herzl, and he set out to tackle it rather in the spirit of the Man of La Mancha. Among the solutions he incubated at the time were some fairly outlandish fantasies combining unconscious self-hatred with a touch of unselfconscious megalomania. The first, a dream of self-immolation and daring deeds, had him challenge one of Austria's leading anti-Semites—Lichtenstein, Schönerer, or Lueger—to a duel.

> Had I been killed, my farewell letter would have told the world that I fell victim to a most unjust movement. In this way, my death might at least have improved people's minds and hearts. But had I killed my opponent, I would have addressed the jury in a magnificent speech, in which I first of all would have deplored "the death of a man of honor"—just as did Morès, the man who killed Captain Mayer. I would then have gone into the Jewish Question and delivered a powerful Lassalle-like oration that would have moved and shaken the jurors, earned me the respect of the court, and led to my acquittal. The Jews would thereupon have offered to elect me as their deputy, but I would have had to turn them down because I would not want to enter parliament over the dead body of a human being. [D, 6/12/95]

An even more elaborate fantasy involved a *coup de théâtre* reminiscent of the Makart spectacular of 1879, nothing less than the mass baptism of all the Jews in Austria.

> The conversion was to take place in broad daylight, Sundays at noon in St. Stephen's Cathedral, with a solemn procession and the ringing of bells. Not furtively, the way individual Jews had gone about it until then, but in dignified pride. And because the leaders would take their people only up to the gates of the church while themselves remaining Jews, the whole enterprise would attain a level of great sincerity. We who stood firm would have marked the last generation, still clinging to the faith of our forefathers. But we wanted to make Christians of our young sons before they reached the age of reason, at which point conversion smacks of cowardice. As usual, I had worked out the entire plan down to the most minute detail. In my mind's eye I already saw myself dealing with the Archbishop of Vienna, facing the Pope—

both of whom regretted my decision to remain with the Jews—and bringing to the world this message of racial fusion. [D, Whitsuntide, 1895]

The most intriguing aspect of these fantasies is the extent to which Herzl took them seriously. There is no reason why a thirty-four-year-old somewhat jaded and cynical newspaperman should not also indulge in self-glorifying daydreams, however childish; but to confuse them even for one instant with practical solutions in the real world suggests a resolute unwillingness—or striking inability—to distinguish between fantasy and reality.

In the long run, these early melodramatic scenarios, so similar in plot and spirit to his plays, were simply too bizarre to stand up to even his own common sense. He never did cease to glorify the duel as a means of redeeming Jewish honor—in the very first pages of his master plan, he stressed the character-building benefits of dueling in his Jewish state and spelled out the applicable rules in great detail—but after Leitenberger's disparaging remarks about faddish claptrap, he dropped his flirtation with martyrdom as the road to redemption. Mass conversion, on the other hand, he continued to regard as the only honorable and effective way for Jews to accomplish what he himself was so obviously conflicted about—to stop being Jewish and thus solve the problem once and for all.

He actually went so far as to discuss this weird proposal in all seriousness with Moritz Benedikt, in part perhaps out of a self-protective impulse—the artist in Herzl never quite hoodwinked the rational skeptic. The ostensible purpose, however, was to gain the support of the *Neue Freie Presse* for his plan.

But I did not enjoy any real authority with the editors [he lamented]. They only take me for a charming *causeur* and feuilleton writer. Thus Benedikt, when I talked to him about it, rejected my idea about the Pope, just as Bacher had earlier rejected my idea about universal suffrage. But one point in Benedikt's response struck me as just. He said: "For a hundred generations, your tribe has remained true to Judaism. You now propose to set yourself up as the end of the line. This you cannot do. You simply have no right to do it. And by the way, the Pope is never going to receive you." . . . Of course, without my newspaper there was nothing I could do. What other authority did I possess? What could I have offered in return? [D, Whit-suntide, 1895]

Even Herzl at his most optimistic can scarcely have expected Bacher and Benedikt to compromise the hard-won prestige of the *Neue Freie Presse* as the voice and echo of the moderate middle class by investing it in cockamamy schemes dreamed up by their gifted but sometimes morbidly imaginative correspondent. At the same time, they were astute enough to realize that this very imagination—and the temper-ament that went with it—were precisely what lifted Herzl's work out of the rut of humdrum reporting and made him one of their most valuable collaborators. They respected him, they always listened to his ideas—and made sure to keep them out of their newspaper.

Inevitably, the euphoria of those heady first months had worn off; elation hardened into routine frenzy and grim resolve. "It is in every respect a most difficult job," Herzl complained to his colleague Hugo Wittmann in March of 1893. "But you learn two things: cool thinking and quick action. Will this lesson be of any value to me in the future? Not likely. It would be different for someone who wants to go into politics. But for me, a Jew in Austria?" (L, 3/30/93).

In a way, he had been successful beyond all expectations. But suc-cess, like any other drug, requires ever larger doses, and anyway, it was the wrong kind of success—success in a field he continued to deprecate, a mere job he did for a living, a high-speed treadmill to which he had let himself be harnessed just to make the money his wife was throwing out the window with such furious abandon. To Schnitzler, who kept asking to see some of his manuscripts, he replied with an edge of despair: "It is merely a proof of the firm resolve that made me bury my plays for good if even your kind and repeated requests cannot move me to exhume them. Please forgive me, but I don't want to have anything more to do with them myself. I am now just a journalist, a retired old cavalry horse put in harness that only sometimes starts prancing a little when it hears a military band" (L, 5/13/93).

He may even have believed what he wrote.

On May 20, Julie gave birth to little Margarethe, later called Trude. After a suitable period of recovery, the family left in mid-June for a holiday in Austria, intending to spend part of it with Julie's parents in Baden near Vienna. In the meantime, however, rioting broke out in Paris, and when it threatened to take a nasty turn, Herzl cut short his vacation. By July 6, he was back on the job.

France was about to elect a new Chamber of Deputies, and the campaign served to enliven the normally near-comatose summer. Two years of rather intimate familiarity with the end product of universal suffrage had, if anything, exacerbated Herzl's skepticism about the blessings of democracy, but he decided to study the process at the source and spent most of August traveling about the country, sampling public opinion and attending election rallies. The result was a series of sketches for the *Neue Freie Presse,* some of them later collected in *Das Palais Bourbon.*

He had, in fact, quite independently hit on the idea of a pre-election poll.

> One hour by train, another hour through the countryside in the high hansom of a voter who also happened to be a coachman, or vice versa. . . . When I told him that I wanted to go to the pre-election rally, he assumed that I was a particularly loyal friend of the deputy; the idea of someone coming all the way from Paris just to see and hear the so-called fellow citizens of Neuville would have been utterly beyond him. I therefore did not even try to explain that I came to sample the attitude of some of the voters as a way of exploring the basic workings of French parliamentarianism. One always tends to refer to voters as an entity—the community, the district, the nation. . . . Politics only deals with the abstract concept of the voter; but what sort of person is he, as an individual? [PB, p. 4]

The confrontation between the close-mouthed, suspicious peasants and the slippery, hyperarticulate deputy up for reelection turned into an object lesson in democracy. French—unlike Austrian—peasants read the same newspapers as the city folk, Herzl noted. They were sufficiently well informed about the issues to give the candidate a hard time, and they did so with obvious relish and sadistic finesse. Yet, in the end, what concerned them infinitely more than the separation of Church and state or the Panama scandal was the abolition of the 70-centime toll on the nearby bridge across the Oise.

In much the same spirit he visited industrial Lille, stronghold of the socialists, and attended a labor rally for Paul Lafargue, husband of Karl Marx's daughter Eleanor. With a few deft strokes he conveyed the almost palpable sense of solidarity and class-consciousness that united the crowd of true believers passionately devoted to the gospel preached by this rather slippery sorcerer's apprentice, who nonetheless managed to rouse them to a pitch of genuine revolutionary enthusiasm. "The scientific revolutionaries," Herzl concluded, "are getting ready to abolish mankind's present miseries and may thereby well be creating new ones. We can already sense what is in store: the application of electric power. But the task of orators such as this one today is to help the suffering masses through a dark night by duping them with fairy tales, promises, and gory or appealing fantasies" (PB, p. 28).

He also sampled public opinion in his own high-class district among the servants, coachmen, butlers, and cooks left to swelter in the city while their masters and mistresses spent the traditional August at the seashore. "All of them voters, of course, voting for the candidates of their employers. Butlers, coachmen, and cooks, I am told, are mostly Royalists; in this district, however, they are Bonapartists. . . . All those I've met so far are Bonapartists and authoritarians; it goes with their occupation. . . . Under universal suffrage, a butler's vote counts no less than that of a miner, and a moron is worth every bit as much as Alexandre Dumas. This, too, a point of view, I suppose" (PB, pp. 31–35).

The elections as such were relatively uneventful. They brought few surprises and no major changes, except that Herzl's friend Clemenceau, a victim of the Panama scandal, lost his seat in the Chamber.

France's growing friendship with what at the time was probably the world's most repressive regime should have caused some consternation and embarrassment among the heirs of the Enlightenment. Yet the only ones embarrassed seemed to be the patriots of Jewish origin, who suddenly found themselves suspected of divided loyalties. Throughout the 1880s, the bloody pogroms in Russia had evoked widespread public protests in France; the aged Victor Hugo headed a rescue committee for Russian Jews, which included Gambetta, Waldeck-Rousseau, Scheurer-Kestner, and many other prominent figures, including the Archbishop of Paris. French Jews could therefore afford to give whole-hearted support to a cause that enjoyed considerable popularity across the entire political spectrum, although even at the time the Rothschilds pressed for caution and restraint.

But the dramatic "opening to the East" that began in 1891 with a ceremonial visit by the French fleet to the Russian naval base at Kronstadt caused a drastic shift in public opinion. Propaganda played its part, to be sure, and the Okhrana's "resident" undoubtedly had a hand in corrupting some of the eminently corruptible French press. In essence, however, the groundswell of sympathy for Mother Russia represented a genuine manifestation of popular sentiment. Germany, the archenemy that had humiliated France in 1871 and robbed her of Alsace-Lorraine, was now trapped between the hammer and the anvil. With Russia's unlimited manpower—Napoleon's nemesis— poised along her eastern border, she would be unable to defend herself against a resurgent France attacking from the west. The shame of Sedan was about to be avenged; Alsace-Lorraine would once again be French.

This atmospheric change confronted French Jews with a delicate choice. Suspected of placing the fate of their Russian co-religionists above the interests of France, accused of conspiring with the Germans to obstruct the alliance, they all but ceased to protest the violations of human rights in Russia. In fact, during the terminal illness of Alexander III in 1894, prayers were said for him in all Paris synagogues, and the coronation of his successor, Nicholas II, was celebrated by Zadok Kahn, Chief Rabbi of France, with a special service (Marrus, p. 157). But it was the visit of a Russian naval squadron in October 1893 that offered the opportunity for a truly fulsome display of patriotism. While public anticipation ran high and preparations for elaborate receptions in Toulon and Paris were in progress, the prominent actor Albin Valabrègue urged his fellow Jews to demonstrate their affection for the new bedfellows of the Republic by generously contributing to a special fund earmarked for the festivities. In an open letter published in most major newspapers on September 14, he warned: "At a time when efforts are being made to besmirch all our co-religionists, accusing them of the faults of a few unscrupulous cosmopolitan Jews, it seems to me that we have a duty to demonstrate our ardent loyalty in a special way. We are not legitimate children of France; we are only her adopted children, and obligated as such to be twice as French as the others" (Marrus, p. 156).

Valabrègue hardly qualified as a spokesman for French Jewry, and his credentials were further tarnished when, following "an inner revelation" a few weeks later, he converted to Christianity. But the sentiments he expressed were probably not uncommon, and in any case, his appeal, once launched, could not decently be ignored in the circumstances. However they may have felt about the emissaries of the world's chief *pogromchik* in their heart of hearts, French Jews actually contributed some 23,000 francs to their welcome, although the ever-eager Rothschilds accounted for almost half the total.

Herzl, though he described Valabrègue's project with his usual dead-pan objectivity, must of course have been well aware of its controversial aspects. But his public dispatches ignore the Jewish angle and reveal his preoccupation with an altogether different phenomenon. Covering the Paris reception of Admiral Avellan, commander of the Russian squadron, he wrote:

> Wild enthusiasm. On the Place de l'Opéra in Paris, beneath the admiral's window, a crowd numbering in the thousands stood for days on end, from morning to night, shouting his name over and over again—Avellan, Avellan—in the intoxicating frenzy that greets the homecoming victor. But listening to them, one thinks of a lonely man in the far-off distance—the Czar. Never has a single human being held so much power. He orders one of his naval officers—a capable man, no doubt, but entirely unknown to the world—to set sail for France, and with this simple command he has the whole French nation fling itself at the feet of his emissary. And what a nation! Highly civilized, artistic, and at the same time rich and well armed. It was a uniquely curious spectacle. And within the glittering framework of the festivities, the resurgent French nation had a chance to demonstrate its recovery from defeat by a display of its vast powers on land and on sea. They say that what it means is peace. [Bein, p. 166]

It was to be his last dispatch for several months.

In Toulon, where he had gone for a firsthand look at the Russian squadron, Herzl came down with a high fever that was diagnosed as malaria. Treatment consisted of subcutaneous quinine injections which, by his account, led to a series of abscesses that all but crippled him for the rest of the year and forced him to resort to a cane. The acute illness was followed by a long period of convalescence extending into the spring of 1894. In fact, Jakob De Haas, Herzl's first biographer and the only one to have had close personal contact with him in his later years, evidently felt that he never completely recovered: "As a Paris correspondent, he [Herzl] was a brilliant success. For four years he had nothing to regret except that duty having called him to witness the reception of the Russian fleet at Toulon he was seized with malaria, from which he was never wholly cured. To recurrent attacks we attribute his many despondent moods, his fits of listlessness, and his frequent spells of fever" (De Haas, p. 39).

These accounts of what was clearly a severe and debilitating illness with long-lasting sequelae raise a number of questions. Malaria, though it has an incubation period of from ten to thirty days and was by then rare in southern France, remains a remote possibility, and quinine, like any medication, can have devastating side effects in susceptible individuals. But a curious note of November 1893, in which Herzl informed a Paris physician that, against his advice, he had decided not to proceed with the surgical removal of an abscess, suggests that at least one member of the medical fraternity had proposed a different, more ominous, and far more plausible diagnosis:

"Dois je vous répéter, mon cher docteur, que votre aimable intention m'inspire autant de reconnaissance que si j'étais véritablement un loup, selon votre mot plaisant? Qu'on ne dise plus des loups en ma présence après que j'ai eu la chance de connaitre un de leurs plus distingués et qui ne me dévorera pas entièrement j'espère" (L, November '93).

If the pun about the "wolf" devouring him seems a bit labored, the meaning is clear: *loup* (wolf) refers to the Latin *lupus*, an inflammatory connective tissue disorder of unknown etiology first named and described in France in 1851, which this particular doctor evidently suspected as the root cause of Herzl's symptoms. It could have been no more than an inspired hunch; a definitive diagnosis of systemic lupus erythematosus is complicated even with modern laboratory techniques. But the state of Herzl's health in what turned out to be the final decade of his life seems entirely consistent with an autoimmune disease that is associated with a broad spectrum of symptoms ranging from recurrent episodes of fever and joint pains to skin disorders and personality changes, eventually involving any one or several of the internal organs, including the heart muscle. No effective treatment was available in Herzl's day.

Though frail and still plagued by mysterious abscesses, Herzl resumed his duties in December, just in time to cover the terrorist attack in the Palais Bourbon, where the anarchist Vaillant tossed a bomb at the speaker's platform. It tore a hole into the rear wall but caused no serious injuries and greatly boosted the standing of the Senate president, who, seconds after the dust had settled, calmly rang his bell to announce that the house remained in session.

The lingering illness, while slowing him down, also seems to have turned him inward, made him more contemplative and introspective. He dutifully reported on political rifts and the increasingly violent class struggle that rent the country, but much of his time was devoted to feuilletons and theater reviews that reveal lassitude, great weariness, and a keen intelligence sharply at odds with its own preconceived ideas. The theater, on which he had so resolutely turned his back, continued to lure him; he almost instinctively saw and interpreted events in terms of their stage effects and dramatic impact. "The art of the theater . . . must turn back from society to the individual human being. It may already be on its way to doing just that. People once again prefer the simple and natural, the plain spirit, the unadorned straight line. It seems to me that the eternal is about to once again become modern" (Bein, p. 169).

In April 1894, bedridden again for a couple of weeks, he ceased to resist the impulse and, "in eight glorious days," completed *The Marginal Comment*, a one-act verse play. The Burgtheater turned it down within the month but softened the blow by requesting permission to stage the ten-year-old *Tabarin*. Whether Max Burckhard, the director, did so out of consideration for the by now well-known and influential journalist and critic, or simply because there was a shortage of suitably insipid material, is open to question, but it revived Herzl's delusions about his talents as a playwright, and he considered the new verse play an artistic breakthrough which, as he wrote to Teweles, "theaters everywhere" would a few years hence be eager to stage.

He was wrong. The thrust of *The Marginal Comment* is of some marginal interest in that it marks a long-overdue break with the juvenile romanticism of Herzl's earlier plays and demonstrates his growing respect for law and order in the life of the individual as well as the nation; it also, incidentally, confirms his inveterate misogyny. The aging libertine in thirteenth-century Bologna trying to seduce the flighty and flirtatious wife of his best friend, a scholarly expert in Roman law, turns out in the end to be a vapid fool, arthritic in the bargain and—impotence at its most cruel—unable even to accept the final challenge to a duel. The jurist regains his wife, and Roman law wins out over dreams of knightly valor and unbridled freedom. Sententious and operatic in the execution, this comedy in doggerel was never performed, and even the few close friends upon whom Herzl saw fit to inflict it were hard put to feign the requisite spark of enthusiasm.

But the job, in any case, left him no time to brood; spring brought another avalanche of front-page sensations. On June 24, the Italian anarchist Santo Caserio stabbed and mortally wounded Sadi Carnot, the President of France, who died the following day. His funeral, the election of his successor, the trial and execution of Caserio in August, and the fierce debate about the new press laws aimed at extremist publications of both left and right often kept him working around the clock, and it was not until the end of August that he was finally able to join his vacationing family in Austria.

Just how eager he was to do so is debatable. The tensions between husband and wife had never really abated. Both continued to make life difficult for each other and themselves, but after five troubled years of marriage they had come to resign themselves to a kind of armed truce punctuated by flurries of open warfare—Julie because, as the aging mother of three, she felt that she had no practical alternative and considered any marriage preferable to none, and Herzl because his passions were otherwise engaged. At this stage, what he suffered in the marriage was irritation rather than deprivation; seeking neither emotional sustenance nor sexual satisfaction, he had no incentive to upset the status quo.

The idyll on the rue Monceau had been predictably problematic from the very beginning, and even Herzl himself had, after some months, been forced to recognize that, in view of the constant squabbles between his mother and his wife, the arrangement was doomed. Jeanette made a point of voicing her disapproval of whatever her daughter-in-law did or said, and whenever they were not arguing, the two women were not on speaking terms. Inevitably, the children were drawn into their skirmishes and soon conceived a fierce dislike of their grandmother that lasted until her death in 1911. In addition, Herzl's parents were utterly lost in Paris. They did not speak the language and missed the familiar ambiance of Vienna, the son they worshipped was far too busy to devote much time to them, the other members of the household were openly or covertly hostile, and they had no other social life. In the summer of 1894, they decided to return permanently to Vienna.

In the meantime, however, the death of Julie's father on January 3 had affected both Herzl's marriage and his finances. He was now able to enjoy unrestricted access to Julie's dowry, without any interference from his father-in-law. More important, Jakob Naschauer had left an estate of nearly half a million guilders, a considerable fortune which, according to his Will, was to be divided equally among his wife and five children, even though three of his four daughters were married and had already received substantial dowries. Austrian law gave the husband full control of his wife's property, and it is not altogether out of the question that this posthumous generosity on the part of a man Herzl had always held in profound contempt might have stirred a twinge of guilt and gratitude. At the same time, however, it introduced further strain into a marriage whose emotional bankruptcy was already causing endless arguments about money. And while the scope of Herzl's own financial sacrifices in the cause of Zionism has received due recognition, no one ever paid tribute to Jakob Naschauer's generous albeit unintended contribution.

Herzl spent part of his vacation at Bad Aussee in the company of Arthur Schnitzler, Hugo von Hofmannsthal, and Richard Beer-Hofmann, three stars of the Young Vienna literary movement. Though they were all of them younger than he—Hofmannsthal, the most prodigiously gifted, had barely turned twenty—they were already getting the kind of serious critical attention that still eluded him, and he would have had to be less than human not to have felt some pangs of envy. Olga Schnitzler, in fact, left a scathing description of his overbearing and downright ridiculous behavior on that occasion, the only trouble being that Olga was all of twelve years old at the time, that she did not meet her future husband until six years later, and that she wrote her memoirs in 1962, at the age of eighty, all of which makes her reliability as a witness questionable, to put it mildly.

What does seem true is that the fall of 1894 was a period of great stress and turmoil in Herzl's life, though as in most such instances it would be difficult to pinpoint any one single cause, the more so since he had always been subject to cyclical mood swings extreme enough to qualify him as manic-depressive. The mystifying illness and unusually protracted convalescence had obviously sapped him emotionally as well as physically, affected his outlook, and blighted the euphoria that had carried him through the first phase of his Paris assignment. The reception of *The Marginal Comment* had once again brutally confirmed his failure as an artist, and the imminent prospect of having to resume his hectic Paris routine with its drudgery and deadlines was almost more than he could face, especially now that his parents had decided to remain in Vienna and relations with Julie had again deteriorated to the point where she, too, did not want to live in Paris anymore. The joint household on the rue Monceau may not have been much of a home to any of them, but it supplied the largely absent Herzl with quite literally a *pied à terre*—one foot on the ground—and sustained the illusion of an orderly, conventional family life. The old hunger for success, the driving ambition to accomplish great deeds and achieve fame and glory, had been temporarily appeased by the recognition he received as a journalist; now it gripped him once again with renewed force. Moreover, his improved finances seemed at least in principle to open up new possibilities; he was no longer wholly dependent on journalism to support his family. But what possibilities are open to a man living in enemy territory?

His experiences in France had provided painful insights into the nature of the Jewish problem in the era of the emancipation, and the lessons were now being reinforced on an almost daily basis by developments in Austria, where Jew-baiting had become an integral part of the academic scene and where the militantly anti-Semitic Austrian Social Party under the leadership of the inspired demagogue Karl Lueger had just won its first major victory in the Vienna City Council elections. But as Herzl perceived it, the problem that had begun to obsess him transcended social and political dimensions; he experienced it as a blow to his pride and self-esteem, a profoundly personal threat to his own future as well as to that of his son. (The future of daughters being taken for granted, and nothing to either dream or fret about.)

Toward the end of his vacation he had a spirited discussion with his colleague Ludwig Speidel, drama critic and literary editor of the *Neue Freie Presse*, the gist of which he recorded in his diary a year later. While some details may have been unconsciously amended in the light of his by then rather radically changed outlook, the thrust of the argument has probably been quite faithfully rendered.

I understand the nature of anti-Semitism [he told Speidel]. We Jews, though through no fault of our own, have maintained ourselves as a foreign body among the various nations. In the ghetto we adopted a number of antisocial traits. Pressure has corrupted our character, and it will take counter-pressure to restore it. Actually, anti-Semitism is the consequence of the emancipation of the Jews. . . . It was an error on the part of the doctrinaire libertarians to believe that people can be made equal by an edict published in the *Official Gazette*. When first we emerged from the ghetto, we were still ghetto Jews; we needed time to get accustomed to freedom. . . . But when the Jews turn away from money and move into professions previously barred to them, they exert terrible pressure on the livelihood of the middle classes. . . . Yet anti-Semitism, a strong and unconscious force among the masses, will not harm the Jews. I regard it as helpful in building the Jewish character, the education of the group by the masses that may perhaps lead to its absorption. Education is accomplished only through hardship. . . . The Jews will adapt. They are like seals swept into the ocean by an accident of nature. . . . Give them a chance to return to dry land for a few generations, and their fins will turn into feet again. [D, Whitsuntide, '95]

Speidel, mumbling something about a broad historical concept, was obviously unimpressed by Herzl's presentation, and it is hard to fault him. But what he missed was the passion that sparked the argument in the first place and that now gave Herzl no peace. Even before returning to Paris, he conceived plans for an ambitious series of investigative reports on the condition of Jews the world over. "I wanted to see all the places where the accident of history had scattered groups of Jews, particularly Russia, Galicia, Hungary, Bohemia, later the Orient, the new Zion colonies, and finally again Western Europe. All these truthful descriptions were to demonstrate the undeserved misfortunes of the Jews, show them as being reviled by people who simply don't know them. After all, I have now acquired the reporter's eye that such a task requires" (D, Whitsuntide, '95).

Yet however much he kept brooding about the problem, he was still far from envisaging any solution other than total integration. Reviewing *La Femme de Claude*, a play by Alexandre Dumas *fils*, on October 6, 1894, he wrote:

The good Jew Daniel wants to find the old tribal home and lead his brethren back to it. But a man like Daniel would know that the Jews have nothing to do anymore with the historic homeland. It would be childish to go looking for its geographic location; any schoolboy knows where to find it. But if the Jews were ever really to "return," they would discover the very next morning that they had long ago ceased to be one people. For centuries they have been rooted in diverse nationalities, different from one another, their similarities maintained only as a result of outside pressure. All oppressed people have Jewish characteristics, and when the pressure lifts, they behave like free men.

Two weeks later, in the studio of the sculptor Samuel Friedrich Beer, he had the epiphany that changed his life.

At least, that was how he later came to see it, although in fact the process of conversion had begun years earlier and was still far from complete on that morning of October 19. Beer, a fellow Jew from Budapest, was a reasonably successful academic sculptor—his bust of Washington Irving survives in New York's Washington Irving High School—who had found Herzl's noble head and striking features a suitable challenge. The experience of being immortalized in stone is a narcissistic gratification bound to arouse conflicting emotions; he felt destined for greatness, yet he had thus far failed to fulfill his destiny. Did he deserve a monument? (The completed bust is now in the Herzl Museum in Jerusalem.)

Whatever the unconscious tensions that precipitated it, the emotional breakthrough came in a lively argument with the sculptor in the course of that particular session.

> We talked about the fact that it did the Jews no good to become artists and to liberate themselves from the money taint. The curse still sticks to them. We cannot break out of the ghetto. I waxed quite emotional on the subject, and the excitement left an afterglow. The outline of this play emerged with the speed of that dream about the water pitcher in the Arabian fairy tale. I think I had not yet covered the distance from the rue Descombes to the Place Pereire when the whole thing was already complete in my mind. [D, Whitsuntide, '95]

And in a letter to Schnitzler, he added: "The next day, I told Beer: You know, if I weren't a day laborer and could hole up in Ravello, above Amalfi, for a couple of weeks, I would write a play. He made a face that seemed to me incredulous. On the third day I skipped the sitting, and I stayed away until the play was finished" (L, 1/9/95).

TWELVE

*H*erzl completed *The Ghetto*—later retitled *The New Ghetto*—in a mere "three weeks of glowing elation and hard work," a gauge of the intense emotions he had invested in it. His parents had remained in Vienna. Relations between him and Julie had hit a new low, and she, too, was going home with the children. Herzl himself, worn out by the pace and pressure of the Paris assignment, had asked for a transfer to the home office. Bacher and Benedikt agreed in principle but stalled in practice, playing for time; he had, to all intents and purposes, become irreplaceable in that particular spot.

Nevertheless, he was able to manage the daily routine with his left hand, so to speak, during the three weeks it took him to get *The Ghetto* out of his system, a catharsis that netted a four-act melodrama which despite its turgid oratory, cartoon characters, and contrived plot comes alive in spots with the author's own puzzlement and wounded pride. And while technically it marked no advance over his earlier plays, there was one significant difference—for the first time he dealt with a serious social issue and dramatized his own inner conflicts.

It would probably be more accurate to say that he used the play as a means of coping with those conflicts, but either way, the autobiographical element constitutes the dominant and sole interesting feature. The hero is a young lawyer blessed with a set of plaster saints for parents. Though still nominally Jewish, he has severed all links to the past and feels totally at home in the world of the Gentiles until snared by the spoiled daughter of a rich Jewish speculator. The marriage quickly disabuses him of his illusions. His best friend, a Gentile lawyer with political ambitions, drops him as a potential liability to his future career, while his wife's unsavory relatives, stereotypical "stock-exchange Jews" à la Naschauer, involve him in a scheme to acquire a coal mine owned by an aristocratic German playboy—the very one who had once figured in an "affair of honor" from which the hero had been forced to back away because of his father's illness; the gratuitous plot twist serves to dredge up a similar traumatic episode in Herzl's own past.

But before the deal can ever be consummated, the mine workers mount a protest against unsafe working conditions in the mine. The socially conscious hero immediately withdraws from the case, returns his fee, and organizes a strike that ends in a mine disaster. Accused by the playboy owner of having been part of a Jewish conspiracy to ruin him, he redeems his honor and his race by getting himself killed in the ensuing duel. "Jews, my brothers," he contrives to murmur with his last breath as the curtain goes down, "they won't let you live until you learn to die. . . . I want out—out of the ghetto."

The basic thrust of this convoluted soap opera still reflected Herzl's tendency to blame the victim, his conviction that the Jews would never be truly emancipated until they had absorbed the values of the Prussian aristocracy and "learned to bow without subservience, and to stand tall without truculence." But he was beginning to search for the causes of what he perceived as the decadence of Diaspora Jewry and even to identify with their struggle to break out of the ghetto they still carried within themselves.

Of far greater significance than the manifest content, however, was the intensity of his emotional involvement with the play and all it meant to him. For the first time he found himself in the grip of an all but irresistible compulsion; and although, as an uncompromisingly agnostic child of the Enlightenment, he might have scoffed at the term, he certainly conceived of *The New Ghetto* as a sacrament rather than mere didactic entertainment and was determined not to compromise its message by authorial vanity or sacrilegious publicity. On November 8, 1894, in the afterglow of his creative outburst, he dashed off a letter to Schnitzler:

> For this enterprise I need a gentleman and artist. I thought of you. The matter is as follows: I have written a new play—in a state of delirious exaltation, as you can tell from the time it took

me to complete it. I started the first act on October 21 and finished the fourth and last one on November 8. Seventeen days, in other words. Whether it is good or bad—who knows? Not I.

But the mood in which I wrote persists and is stronger than ever. And what it inspired, in addition to a passionate desire to bring my work before the world, is the even more passionate wish on my part to hide, to go underground. Make of it what you will—arrogance, cowardice, or shame, but there it is. In the case of this particular play, I more than ever want to hide my sex organ. The play is of a very special nature, as you will see. In other words, I don't want to be known as the author, at least not for some months or years. [L, 11/8/94]

He then went on at great length to explain the elaborate ruse by which, with Schnitzler's help and connivance, the play would be submitted as the work of one Albert Schnabel, art historian. All correspondence on the subject was to be via General Delivery, because "if you sent a registered letter to my home, my wife would subject me to endless interrogations, which would make me very nervous in the long run."

That arrogance, cowardice, and shame all played a part in this rather childish charade was probably an accurate perception on Herzl's part. He wanted the play to be accepted on its own merits rather than as a favor to an influential member of the *Neue Freie Presse* editorial staff. At the same time, he had well-founded misgivings about straining his relationship with Bacher and Benedikt by a potential *succès de scandale* clearly at odds with the paper's editorial policy. And what he experienced as shame—an oddly apposite formulation, especially when paired with his remark about hiding his (circumcised) sex organ—reveals a still powerful ambivalence about being drawn into swift waters of unfathomable depth. He wanted "to do something for the Jews," but being one still made him feel uneasy.

Schnitzler agreed to act as intermediary and patiently carried out the insanely complicated instructions designed to safeguard a secret no one was anxious to know, but he may have taken Herzl's request for candid criticism more seriously than it was meant. Though he paid him some extravagant compliments on having broken new ground in the theater, he clearly had serious reservations about *The New Ghetto*. Even the crooked Jewish speculators, he objected, were a good deal more complex than Herzl made them out to be. "Which brings me to the final sentence, where Jakob Samuel is made to utter: Jews, brothers, they won't let you live until you learn to die. Well, there was a time when Jews were burned at the stake by the thousands. They had learned to die, all right, but for all that they still weren't allowed to live. Thus your play, after a good start, gets off on the wrong track." Far more subtle than Herzl both as an artist and as an explorer of the human soul, he took equally strong exception to the simplistic portraits of the spoiled wife and of the hero's high-minded Gentile friend. And finally: "I miss the figure of the strong Jew in your play. It isn't even true, as you suggest, that all ghetto Jews were either despicable or despised. There were others—precisely the ones whom the anti-Semites hated most of all. Your play is daring. I want it to be defiant" (Schnitzler Briefe, 1981, pp. 237–39).

This may have been more candor than Herzl had bargained for, but in his still lingering state of euphoria he was quite impervious to criticism. Although he incorporated many of Schnitzler's minor suggestions in subsequent drafts, he refused even to consider any major revisions. "Don't forget," he wrote, passing out free advice to Schnitzler on the art of playwriting, "that . . . you have to be more obvious on the stage because there are no subtle minds in your audience, or very few at best. And this play cries out to be staged, it must be produced, it must. That is why I wrote it. It must get to the people. That is also why I am satisfied just to be daring. Were I to be also defiant, they would not hear me out. I am, after all, talking to a nation of anti-Semites" [L, 11/27/94].

To Schnitzler's further comments he replied a week later:

Now that I've relived this piece, I can respond more fully to your objections. I don't agree that there are too few sympathetic characters. But even if I did, should I dissimulate my misanthropy? Should I make myself see and portray lots of marvelously noble human beings in whose existence no one believes? No, my friend, that won't do. Nor shall I emasculate myself for the sake of some potential success. I've already made these characters about as lovable as I see them. I have no intention of mounting either a defense or a rescue action on behalf of the Jews; all I want is to throw the question open to discussion. Let the critics and the people do the defending and attacking. Once the play is staged, I've done my job. The rest is a matter of complete indifference to me. I don't give a damn about the money, though I have next to none. I have no wish to be a popular playwright. What I do want is to speak out—from the heart, and from the gut. When this play reaches its audience, I'll feel a lot more at peace with myself. [L, 12/17/94]

Herzl then went on to acknowledge what Schnitzler had suspected—that writing *The New Ghetto* had revived long-buried ambitions. "Greater songs still slumber on these steely strings. If ever I can free myself from daily drudgery, I'll devote myself to higher things. I still have an entire springtime within me—perhaps someday it will yet burst into bloom" (L, 12/17/94).

On November 17, 1894, only nine days after Herzl finished *The New Ghetto,* an article entitled "Le Nouveau Ghetto" by the publicist Bernard Lazare appeared in the Paris left-wing weekly *La Justice.* What makes the coincidence even more noteworthy, beyond the convergence of the titles and basic ideas, is the fact that both authors arrived at them by different yet equally circuitous routes.

Bernard Lazare was born Lazare Bernard in Nîmes in 1865, into a moderately observant Jewish family of Alsatian background. He settled in Paris in 1886 and quickly made his reputation as a hard-hitting and independent-minded literary critic with pronounced anarchist leanings. By 1892, he was publishing an anarchist periodical and had become a noted and notorious spokesman for intellectual radicalism. Uncompromisingly anti-religious and anti-clerical, he held Judaism in the same contempt as any other religion, but the rise of racial anti-Semitism and the growing influence of Drumont forced him to make more subtle distinctions. He initially tried to solve the problem by drawing a sharp line between *juifs*—German and Eastern Jews driven by "an obsession with making a quick fortune, and for whom money was the only goal in life"—and *israélites,* French Jews "modest in their aspirations" and with deep roots in the country. He specifically denounced any notion of "Jewish solidarity with the immigrant hordes" from the East. French *israélites,* he declared, had nothing in common with these "Frankfurt money changers, Russian usurers, Polish bartenders and Galician pawnbrokers," and he called on them to "kick out these lepers" who arouse anti-Jewish feelings wholly unjustified when misdirected against genuine French *israélites.*

In due course, however, the Jewish Question became something of an obsession with Lazare, much as it had with Herzl. In 1894, he published a study of anti-Semitism in its historical perspective which, though highly praised by Drumont for its "impartiality," actually marked a significant evolution of his ideas in the direction of Jewish nationalism. Modern anti-Semitism, in his revised view, had its roots in social and national conflicts that would vanish with the revolution, and revolution was what he now saw as the essence of the Hebrew spirit, from the Old Testament prophets to Marx and Lassalle.

This was still more or less his attitude when, on November 1, Drumont's *Libre Parole* under a banner headline screaming TREASON triumphantly crowed about the arrest of a Jewish army officer, thereby immediately focusing the spotlight on the one issue that was to turn the case into a cause. Drumont alone, however, for all his polemical skills and the genius of his cartoonists, could probably have done little more than further poison the already polluted atmosphere. What transformed a seemingly banal case of espionage into one of the most divisive scandals in French history was touched off by the intervention of Bernard Lazare.

Lazare's initial reaction to the news of Dreyfus's arrest was one of supreme indifference; the misfortunes of an army captain from a rich Jewish family could hardly have been expected to appeal to his social conscience. But the outbursts of well-orchestrated anti-Semitism, which expanded the charges against Dreyfus into an indictment of Jews in general—with no fine distinctions drawn between *juifs* and *israélites*—aroused his ire and prompted him to protest against the "moral ghetto" being created in France:

> The Jews are no longer confined to their own section of town, the streets where they live are no longer closed off by chains, but they are imprisoned in a hostile atmosphere of suspicion, of latent hatred, of prejudice the more powerful for not being avowed, a ghetto far more terrible than that from which they could escape by exile or revolt. This hostility is generally concealed, but an intelligent Jew has no trouble perceiving it. He senses an obstacle in his path, the wall which his enemies have erected to separate him from those in whose midst he lives. [Le Nouveau Ghetto, *La Justice*, 11/17/94]

Herzl, much like Lazare, also paid scant attention at first to what seemed just another routine case of espionage. That the suspect was a Jew may have intrigued him personally but, like the torrents of swill generated by the anti-Semitic gutter press, it was not the sort of news deemed fit to print by the editors of the *Neue Freie Presse*. In any case, the illness and death of Alexander III of Russia overshadowed all other news in November and provided the French Republic with a splendid opportunity to display its devotion to the new ally. The spectacular public ceremonies mourning the dead Czar and hailing his successor, Nicholas II, including special services in all four Paris synagogues, kept Herzl busy through much of the month. It was not until December 6 that he undertook to sort out the muddle of facts and rumors about Captain Dreyfus. Alerted initially by Nordau, one of the first to suspect an elaborate frame-up, he may already have harbored grave doubts about Dreyfus's guilt by the time the trial opened on December 19, and the court's decision to exclude the public and the press was hardly calculated to allay his suspicions. The unanimous verdict of guilty, rendered on December 22, came as no surprise and was reported by Herzl without comment. But in his dispatch of December 27, he quoted Dreyfus as having told the sergeant of the guard, "I am being persecuted because I am a Jew."

The idea of the defiantly assimilated and acutely status-conscious artillery captain, who never once in the years of his martyrdom publicly raised the issue of his religion, confiding in an enlisted man assigned to guard him is manifestly absurd, as Herzl must have been well aware. If he nonetheless chose to quote this farfetched rumor, he may have wished to make a point: for the first time the *Neue Freie Presse* was tricked into mentioning the one word that defined the central issue in the case.

The ceremonial degradation took place on Saturday morning, January 5, 1895, and the paper's afternoon edition carried Herzl's vivid description of the event:

> The degradation of Captain Dreyfus on this dreary morning drew a crowd of curious onlookers to the neighborhood of the War College, located just behind the terrain of the 1889 World's Fair. There were numerous officers, some with their ladies. Only officers and a few journalists were admitted to the inner courtyard of the Ecole Militaire. Gathered outside was the usual mob of gaping busybodies who make it a point to attend every execution. A large contingent of police had been deployed. By 9 a.m. the huge yard was filled with troops forming an open square, in the

center of which sat a general on horseback. A few minutes later, Dreyfus was led out wearing the uniform of a captain. Four soldiers brought him before the general, who declared: "Alfred Dreyfus, you are unworthy to bear arms. I hereby degrade you in the name of the French people. Let the judgment be executed." Thereupon Dreyfus raised his right hand and shouted: "I swear and declare that you are degrading an innocent man. Vive la France." With that, the drums began to roll, and the military bailiff tore the already loosened buttons and straps from the uniform. Dreyfus maintained his proud bearing, and the procedure was completed within a few minutes.

Now began the ordeal of filing past the troops. Dreyfus marched like a man convinced of his innocence. As he passed a group of officers who yelled "Judas! Traitor!" he shouted back: "I forbid you to insult me." By 9:20, Dreyfus had made the rounds. He was thereupon shackled and turned over to the gendarmes, who will from now on treat him as a civilian prisoner. The troops filed out, but the mob lingered in front of the gate waiting for the prisoner's departure. Bloodthirsty cries filled the air, such as "If they bring him out now, he'll be ripped to pieces." But they waited in vain. Those, however, who had actually witnessed the degradation ceremony left in a curious state of agitation. The strangely resolute attitude of the degraded captain had made a deep impression on many eyewitnesses.

According to his reports as printed in the *Neue Freie Presse* during the days that followed, street mobs kept clamoring for "Death to the Judas," a rather toothless version of the original *"Mort aux juifs,"* for which Herzl had no doubt provided the literal translation. His editors, evidently anxious not to plant ideas in the thick skulls of native Jew-baiters, must have considered *Tod dem Judas* less inflammatory than *Tod den Juden.*

This was the end of Herzl's personal involvement in the Dreyfus case, and for some time it appeared to be the end of the case as such. Dreyfus was about to be shipped off into lifelong exile on Devil's Island. But the director of the Santé prison, where he was being held pending his departure, grew convinced of his prisoner's innocence and put the Dreyfus family in touch with Bernard Lazare, whom he knew as an effective advocate for several of the prison's anarchist inmates. Contact was made at the end of February, just about the time the prisoner left for French Guiana, and the evidence collected by Dreyfus's brother Mathieu persuaded the initially reluctant Lazare that even wealthy Jews needed help if their crime was being Jewish. Though seldom given due credit, it was Lazare who lit the fuse that eventually detonated what came to be known as *l'Affaire*.

For nearly a year, however, the fuse was left to fizzle. The impassioned pamphlet Lazare drafted in the spring of 1895 was shelved by the Dreyfus family, who favored more discreet, backstairs approaches. This struck Lazare as a typical example of ghetto behavior and hastened his conversion to a radical kind of Jewish nationalism that made him engage with unseemly gusto in a two-front battle against Drumont's legions on the one hand and, on the other, against a pussyfooting, Rothschild-dominated Jewish establishment desperately anxious to keep him from making waves. By the fall of 1896, however, Mathieu Dreyfus had exhausted all other recourses and finally authorized Lazare to take the initiative. His opening shot was the publication of the long-delayed pamphlet, a brilliant mix of polemics and documentary evidence that defiantly pointed up the real issue at the heart of the case.

Didn't I tell you that Captain Dreyfus belonged to a class of pariahs? He was a soldier, but he was a Jew, and it was as a Jew above all that he was prosecuted. Because he was a Jew he was arrested, because he was a Jew he was indicted, because he was a Jew he was convicted, and it is because he is a Jew that the voices of truth and justice cannot be raised on his behalf. The responsibility for convicting this innocent man falls squarely upon those who provoked it by their scandalous agitation, their lies, and their calumny. [Lazare, *"Une erreur judiciaire."* Quoted in Marrus, p. 183]

Lazare's attempts to rouse the intellectuals, to exploit his contacts on the left, and to enlist some of his former comrades in the cause were as yet premature and remained largely unsuccessful. Where he did succeed was in outraging the smug and frightening the timid. He antagonized the Jewish establishment by calling for militant action, he fought a duel with Drumont—neither man was hurt—and he was feared as a loose cannon by the as yet tiny nucleus of pro-Dreyfus partisans, who finally prevailed upon him to moderate his attacks. In the later phases of *l'Affaire* he was upstaged by more celebrated figures and played only a minor role. But for him it had been an education as well as a cause, and he emerged from it as a dedicated Jewish nationalist. After the publication of *Der Judenstaat* in 1896, he joined forces with Herzl—the two had apparently not met before—and participated in the second Zionist congress; although he later broke with Herzl for personal reasons, they maintained friendly relations. An outcast to the end, Lazare died in abject poverty in 1903, at the age of thirty-eight. The Catholic poet Charles Péguy, ardently pro-Dreyfus despite his staunch devotion to the Church, felt that Lazare had been shabbily treated in life and unjustly forgotten in death. He was not alone in these sentiments.

Enfant terrible that he was, Lazare compelled the military, the Jewish establishment, and not least Dreyfus himself to deny what they all knew to be the truth—that a man had been condemned for being a Jew. "And where?" Herzl wrote four years later. "In France. In republican, modern, civilized France, one hundred years after the declaration of the Rights of Man" (*Zionismus*, Vol. I, pp. 390 et seq.).

This is one way of looking at it, and it was obviously what Herzl had in mind when, on the same occasion, he oversimplified his ideological evolution by stating that "the Dreyfus trial . . . which I witnessed in Paris in 1894, made me a Zionist." Yet one wonders what Dreyfus's fate would have been if Lazare had not forced the Jewish issue, or if Dreyfus, who to the very end resisted the role of Jewish martyr, had indeed been "just an ordinary Frenchman," as he insisted. Would this particular miscarriage of justice, not the first and certainly not the last in the annals of French jurisprudence, have had anything like the same impact on French society, caused a major upheaval in its institutions, and ultimately led to a reaffirmation of basic republican principles?

In the long-range perspective the Dreyfus Affair, for all it revealed about the persistence of medieval fanaticism, blind prejudice, and murderous hate underneath the veneer of civility and civilization, was one of the brighter chapters in French history. At the time, however, darkness prevailed. The anti-Semitic cartoons that appeared week after week in the popular press, as vicious as anything Streicher served up in his notorious *Stürmer* fifty years later but drawn by artists like

Toulouse-Lautrec and Caran d'Ache, graphically convey the climate of the period and may explain why Herzl later invoked the Dreyfus Affair as the crucial turning point.

It certainly helped push him over the edge, in more ways than one. In his euphoric fantasies he had seen *The New Ghetto* as a historic revelation that would shake Jews and Gentiles alike and bring about the final reconciliation, the emancipation in fact as well as in law. But the inevitable mood swing left him once again depleted and depressed. Cold reason now told him that what he had accomplished fell decidedly short not only of what had to be done but of what, in the aftermath of the Dreyfus trial, he felt the need to do. What that was, however, he could still not decide.

An even more sobering collision with reality was the response to his play. On New Year's Day of 1895, he had sent Schnitzler the final version, told him that he was now counting the hours, and stipulated a telegram code to signify acceptance or rejection. "My impatience requires instant notice by wire." His patience was not to be tried; by mid-February, he had collected summary rejections from the Deutsche Theater and Lessing Theater in Berlin, as well as the Raimund Theater in Vienna, a none too surprising reaction to a play almost guaranteed to antagonize both Jews and anti-Semites alike. It was a blow, just the same, though Herzl assured Schnitzler that he could take it. "If you only knew how much failure and varied misfortune I've already put up with, and always from behind a mask of fortitude and arrogance" (L, 3/19/95). His last lingering hopes were dashed when his old friend Heinrich Teweles, director of the Prague German Theater, also rejected the play as inopportune. (It was eventually performed without incident at Vienna's Carl Theater three years later, on December 27, 1897, and received moderately favorable reviews.)

He felt crushed, lost, and abandoned throughout that dreary spring. Julie and the children had left; he was about to give up the apartment in the rue Monceau.

> Why don't you tell me about your own play? [he complained to Schnitzler in February]. Why don't you send it to me? Hasn't the secret plotting of the past few months brought us close enough to one another? I badly need a good friend. I almost feel like putting an ad in the paper: Gentleman in the best of years looking for friend to whom he can confide all his weaknesses and fatuities without fear. Or, as they put it here: *on demande ami désintéressé.*

I don't know whether I am too suspicious or too shy, or whether my eyesight is too keen—I cannot find a single one among my local acquaintances. The one is too stupid, the other too manipulative, the third offends me by wanting to exploit his contacts for his own advancement. [L, 2/16/95]

The humility, so out of character, hints at the depth of his feelings, but the plea was pathetically misdirected: Schnitzler had no more talent for genuine friendship than Herzl himself. A vastly superior artist—and well aware of it—he paid for his gifts with a clutch of morbid obsessions, anxiety states, and depressions tinged with paranoia that made him notoriously difficult to get along with; his running battles with censors, critics, and outraged philistines further exacerbated his neuroses. His reputation as a compulsive womanizer was well deserved, but his relations with men were hardly less problematic and almost invariably ended in a hostile parting of the ways. Despite his reservations, he probably did what he could for *The New Ghetto.* He sympathized with what it stood for and, in 1908, wrote a considerably more powerful drama on the same subject; *Professor Bernardi* immediately ran afoul of the censors and caused riots in the theater. His genuine respect for Herzl was, however, intertwined with critical condescension; he thought little of him as a playwright and later refused to take him seriously as a prophet of Jewish renewal. By 1901, relations between them had cooled to the point where they once again reverted to the formal *Sehr geehrter Herr Doktor* rather than "dear friend." In a diary entry made long after Herzl's death, Schnitzler asserted with a characteristic mix of perceptiveness and paranoia that while he had always admired Herzl, Herzl in turn had never liked him and knew nothing about him.

That spring, however, Schnitzler was duly supportive even while keeping his distance. The two saw each other briefly at the end of March, when Herzl spent four days in Vienna visiting his parents. Schnitzler's diary entry of March 29 speaks for itself: "Dinner with Herzl and Richard [Beer-Hofmann] at the Riedhof. Can never really warm up to Herzl, never really feel even remotely comfortable in his presence" (Schnitzler, *Correspondence*, p. 802).

Herzl was in Vienna just long enough to witness the electoral triumph of Lueger's anti-Semitic Christian Social Party, which came within a hairsbreadth of obtaining the majority in the municipal elections of April 2. The handwriting was on the wall, and though the Emperor's refusal to read it delayed the inevitable for a little while, Vienna eventually had the distinction of being the first major metropolis to install an avowedly anti-Semitic demagogue as its mayor.

Herzl returned to Paris in a state of wild agitation, turmoil, and confusion. The rejection of *The New Ghetto* had been a major disappointment, but even more painful was his growing realization that the play's basic ideas were flawed or, at the very least, hopelessly inadequate. "I had thought that with this dramatic eruption I would rid myself of the matter, but the very opposite happened: I was drawn into it deeper and deeper. The thought that I had to do something for the Jews gripped me ever more forcefully."

In mid-April he moved into the Hôtel de Castille on the rue Cambon and spent all his free time trying to give some concrete form to whatever it was that would not give him peace. For the first time in his adult life he attended synagogue services and found them "solemn and moving. Much of it reminds me of my youth, the temple in the Tabakgasse in Pest." He again toyed with the idea of documenting the injustices and indignities suffered by Jews all over the world in a magnum opus of investigative reporting. Alphonse Daudet, whom he told about his plan, wanted to know if it was going to be a novel. "No, I replied, I want to write a book for men. But he insisted: A novel has much greater impact. Look at *Uncle Tom's Cabin.*" This piece of expert advice from his anti-Semitic friend apparently led Herzl to reconsider his project and resurrect instead the novel about Heinrich Kana, which he had outlined in Spain just prior to his appointment as Paris correspondent. But where the original version ended on a note of triumphant self-destruction, with Kana, alias Samuel Kohn, tasting a moment of blissful glory as he takes his fate—and his gun—into his own hands, the new version shifts the focus to a new hero altogether, "a man who, through the vicissitudes of life, is led to discover or, more accurately, to found the Promised Land." Kohn-Kana is now relegated to his real-life role as the hero's dearest friend. "Already aboard ship, ready to depart for the distant shore with his group of experts engaged for the explorations, the hero receives Samuel's farewell letter: 'My dear old boy, when you read this letter, I shall be dead.' The hero's fist, crumpling the paper, presses against his heart. But in the next instant, all he feels is rage. He gives the order to weigh anchor. Then, standing at the bow, he gazes into the distance, in the direction of the Promised Land. And he takes the letter, which yet contains so much loyalty and love, and shouts into the wind: Fool, scoundrel, wretch. A life was lost that should have been ours" (D, Whitsuntide, '95).

THIRTEEN

*H*erzl himself never laid claim to divine inspiration. His relationship to God was, at best, distantly respectful, nor did his one visit to the synagogue in the rue de la Victoire signal a change in his essentially agnostic outlook. But rationalist though he was or felt himself to be, he nonetheless refused to account for his epiphany on rational grounds; the seemingly extraneous forces that took hold of him in the spring of 1895 were simply beyond his understanding. "Just how I got from the fictional to the practical ideas," he wrote, "is already a mystery to me, though it only happened during the past few weeks. It all transpired in the unconscious" (D, 6/2/95).

It may be wise to just leave it there. The speculative explorations of his psyche add up to little more than the tautologous truism that personality traits and life experience account for both success and failure. What they invariably fail to capture is the dynamic synergy of manifest pathology, flawed perceptions, and supreme gifts that transformed the thirty-five-year-old journalist into a messianic leader.

In discovering Zionism, Herzl in fact reinvented the wheel. The label itself was of recent coinage—an early product of the "ism" age—but the ingathering of the exiles was a dream as old as exile itself. Herzl's "practical ideas" at this point were in fact far less practical than those propounded by Yehuda Alcalai, the friend and mentor of his Grandfather Simon, in the 1860s. And he himself later asserted that, had he been familiar with the famous *Auto-Emancipation*, in which Leo Pinsker formulated nearly identical ideas as early as 1882, he might never have written his own *Judenstaat.* He knew nothing about his precursors; and as was to happen time and again, his very ignorance, his almost defiant naïveté, proved a paradoxical but abiding source of strength.

There was, however, one characteristic that from the very beginning set Herzl apart from most of the dreamers and schemers who had preceded him: an exalted sense of his own historic mission. In the revised outline of his aborted novel, it was he himself who starred as the Moses of the new Exodus, and his leap from fictional to practical ideas seems far less mystifying than the flash of inspiration that first enabled him to break out of the rigid patterns of the past and freed him to pursue his fantasies with an obsessive energy that moved men, if not mountains. Where Dr. Pinsker, a physician by training, diagnosed the ailment and wrote a prescription, Dr. Herzl assumed personal responsibility for saving the patient and appointed himself the instrument of salvation. "Anointed" might have been a more appropriate word to describe his state of mind at this juncture, but unlike Shabbetai Tsvi, the only one among his precursors with equally sweeping ambitions, Herzl was and remained a child of the Enlightenment.

Child, also, of Jeanette Herzl, a mother who worshiped his every breath, who instilled and nurtured in him the unshakable belief in a unique destiny. He had failed to build the Panama Canal and fallen far short of greatness as a playwright. Now, in his thirty-fifth year, he at last faced a challenge worthy of both his gifts and her ambitions.

The problem, as he saw it, was as simple as the solution. The rise of ever more brutal anti-Semitism in Western as well as Eastern Europe proved the failure of the emancipation; therefore, the only possibility for Jews to live in peace and dignity was to have a country of their own. Once Jewish sovereignty over a suitable territory had been assured, the chaotic migration of Jews in their constant flight from oppression, which merely spread the contagion, had to be channeled into a carefully planned mass exodus directed toward settling the new land and into building the institutions and infrastructure of a Jewish state. Its precise location still seemed to him, at this stage, of secondary importance. Historic ties spoke for Palestine, but its arid soil and the proximity of Russia poised to swallow the moribund Ottoman Empire argued against it, while some of the remote and sparsely settled parts of Canada and Argentina offered much more enticing possibilities.

He took it for granted that the majority of the world's Jews, once acquainted with his plan, would find the prospect of freedom irresistible and head en masse for the New Jerusalem, be it in the desert or on the pampas. The most formidable obstacle, as he saw it, was financial; the acquisition of adequate territory and the logistics of an orderly mass migration required funds on a scale to match the scope and daring of the enterprise itself. But according to his calculations, the combined wealth of Europe's richest Jews far exceeded the treasury reserves of many major powers, and he felt confident that he could convince them to underwrite the venture, all the more so since they were bound to lose their money anyway in the catastrophe which only mass migration could avert. And they would be richly rewarded for their contributions; better a knighted senator of modest means in a Jewish state than a penniless outcast in an anti-Semitic one. Moreover, the host nations, eager to rid themselves of a troublesome minority, could probably also be induced to show their gratitude in tangible ways.

An idea self-evident beyond argument, and Herzl, dazzled by his own persuasiveness, proceeded to take the obvious first step. At the end of April, he "suddenly," as he put it, drafted a letter to Baron Maurice de Hirsch, one of the richest men in the world, "who had shown such conspicuous and millionairish concern for the Jews." The tone of that noteworthy document betrays Herzl's perennial concern with his image; he was anxious to let the baron know right off that he felt himself to be his equal, that he was not the least bit impressed by patents of nobility—at least not Jewish nobility of recent vintage—and that, rather than asking for favors, he was offering the millionaire a chance to finally do something worthwhile with his money.

Dear Sir:

When may I have the honor to call on you? I would like us to discuss the Jewish Question. This is neither a request for an interview nor an attempt, open or disguised, to broach money matters. The demands on you are such that it behooves me to deflect unwarranted suspicions in advance. I merely wish to discuss Jewish politics with you, but our conversation may well contribute toward shaping a future neither you nor I will live to see.

I therefore would like you to name a day when you can devote an undisturbed hour or two to the matter. Because of my regular occupation, I would prefer a Sunday, but it does not have to be the coming one. The choice is up to you. What I have in mind will interest you. But although this does not offer you much of a clue, I would not want you to show this letter to your staff— secretaries, and so forth. Please treat it as confidential. Perhaps you have already come across my name. In any case, you are familiar with the newspaper I represent.

Yours sincerely,

Dr. Herzl

Correspondent of the *Neue Freie Presse*

After hesitating for two weeks, he finally decided to mail the letter to Hirsch's Paris address and, on May 20, received a courteous but noncommittal reply from London asking him to submit his ideas in writing. Ever quick to feel snubbed, Herzl resentfully agreed to "submit to you a plan for a new Jewish policy when I find the time. What you have done up to now was as generous as it was bungled, as costly as it was pointless. So far you have only been a philanthropist, a Peabody. I want to show you the way to be more than that."

Considering the scope of Hirsch's worldwide efforts on behalf of his fellow Jews, the remark bordered on puerile insolence. Yet whether it piqued the baron's curiosity or played into his tribal guilt feelings, it served its purpose; on May 26, he offered Herzl an appointment for Sunday, June 2, at 10:30 a.m., at his residence on the rue de l'Elysée.

The same smoldering aggression manifest in the above note had often come close to paralyzing Herzl in face-to-face encounters with what he referred to as the great and the famous, presumably anyone he suspected of feeling superior to him. Mindful, therefore, of past experiences that had left him tongue-tied, he prepared for the meeting by compiling twenty-two pages of notes divided into three sections— Introduction, Improvement of the Jewish Race, Emigration. He also made sure to dress for the occasion "with discreet care. The day before, I had purposely broken in a new pair of gloves, so that they would still look new but not just off the shelf. The rich must not be shown too much deference" (D, Whitsuntide, '95).

In this particular instance, Herzl's prickly self-absorption led to a total failure of communications. He had simply accepted the popular image of Hirsch as a wealthy and vulgar Jew trying to buy off his conscience by doing good deeds. If, instead of fussing about his gloves, he had made it his business to find out more about his prospective partner, he might have discovered beforehand what, to his regret, he dimly perceived only in the aftermath of the inconclusive meeting: that, rather than being a simpleminded snob with money to burn, Hirsch was an urbane, complicated individual who combined the ruthless pursuit of buccaneering capitalism with liberal leanings and legendary generosity.

Born in Munich in 1831, the son of a banker to the King of Bavaria, Moritz von Hirsch joined the Brussels banking firm of Bischoffsheim & Goldschmid in 1851, married the boss's daughter, and began to demonstrate his entrepreneurial genius in the construction of railroads in Austria-Hungary and Russia. In 1869, the Ottoman government granted him the concession for a rail link between Turkey and the West across the Balkans, a risky but highly profitable enterprise that netted him an enormous fortune. He spent several years in Constantinople baksheeshing his way through the snake-infested underbrush of Ottoman bureaucracy; Herzl's later attempts to charm the Sultan's satraps out of Palestine would no doubt have greatly amused him. Popularly known thereafter as "Turkish Hirsch," he moved to Paris, acquired French citizenship, along with the former palace of the Empress Eugénie, but continued to maintain a far-flung network of estates, castles, and mansions stretching from the English countryside to the forests of Moravia. He was a true cosmopolitan, which is one way of describing a Wandering Jew with a great deal of money, four different nationalities—Bavarian, Belgian, French, and Austrian—in the course of a lifetime, and good friends in high places, including the Prince of Wales, Prince Rudolf of Austria, the King of Bulgaria, and the President of France, his neighbor on the rue de l'Elysée. But the Vienna Jockey Club, which he could have bought lock, stock, barrel, and membership many times over, blackballed him as a Jew.

And that was what he remained, too consciously or perhaps too self-consciously so ever to blend into Gentile high society after the manner of the Rothschilds, one of several reasons for the fierce antagonism between the two houses. Despite an Orthodox upbringing, his links to traditional Judaism were tenuous; he refrained from hunting on Yom Kippur and served kosher meals to religiously observant guests. But the sense of Jewish solidarity ran deep in this restless and rootless autocrat, and in the 1860s, with his growing affluence, he began to subsidize the educational work of the Alliance Israélite Universelle. In 1882, after the wave of Russian pogroms, he offered the Russian government the then enormous sum of 50 million francs for the education and vocational training of Russian Jews; the prompt rejection of his offer convinced him that mass emigration offered the only hope. After a prolonged search for a suitable haven, in the course of which he had extensive contacts with early Zionist circles but eventually rejected Palestine on purely practical grounds—the instability of the Turkish government and the proximity of Russia—he acquired large tracts of land in Argentina and embarked on a settlement project intended, in due course, to absorb the entire 3 million Jewish population of Russia and turn them into landowning peasants. Hirsch, the millionaire radical, despised intellectuals generally, and Jewish intellectuals in particular, as troublemakers forever striving beyond their station in life. He was convinced that only honest labor and a return to the soil could redeem the Jewish soul—Tolstoyan sentiments he shared with Aaron David Gordon and the latter-day Labor Zionists— and, with the inconsistency that is the privilege of either money or genius, he categorically asserted that "a rich Jew ceases to be a Jew."

Yet despite the expenditure of vast sums of money, the ambitious experiment in resettlement was a dismal failure. The four colonies established by 1894 had attracted a total of about 3,000 settlers, 800 of whom had already moved on to the United States; arable land turned out to be much easier to find than ghetto Jews willing and able to work it, and the bureaucrats hired to oversee the enterprise contributed their share by proving as corrupt as they were incompetent.

Hirsch nonetheless persisted up to his death in 1896, trying to learn from his mistakes and convinced—as, ironically, Herzl and Nordau were to be a few years later—of the need for a "night shelter," a refuge for the oppressed Jewish masses of Eastern Europe. But his activities extended far beyond this single obsession. In fact, after the death of their only son at the age of thirty-one, he and his wife devoted themselves almost exclusively to philanthropy on a scale unmatched in his day. It has been estimated that Hirsch spent a total of about 500 million francs on philanthropy; his wife, Clara, continued the work after his death and invested another 50 million in various worldwide relief actions.

This, then, was the plutocrat Herzl set out to enlighten about the Jewish Question.

*　　*　　*

Herzl was, in all circumstances, a man of the theater, and if his account of the meeting, recorded that same afternoon, reads much like the first act of one of his plays, it was because he had conceived and rehearsed it as such. Determined, above all, not to let himself be upstaged, he hired a coach for the four-block ride from his hotel, but the ostentation did not do much for him. Ushered into the palace by a relay of liveried valets, he felt his defensive snobbery giving way to admiration for the imperial splendor and the profusion of exquisite art. "Wealth impresses me only in the guise of beauty," he reassured himself. "And everything about this beauty was authentic. Old paintings, marble, muted Gobelin tapestry. . . . The baron, I thought to myself, must have hired someone to provide good taste."

Kept waiting a few minutes, he immediately suspected a plot to humiliate him. "Do you have a full hour for me?" he bristled when he and Hirsch finally faced each other. "Because if it isn't at least an hour, I'd rather not even get started. That much I need just to tell you how much I have to say."

Hirsch smiled. "Just go ahead."

Herzl pulled out his notes and launched into his lecture. "You may find some of what I am going to tell you too simpleminded, some of it too fantastic. But simplemindedness and fantasy are what move people. It is astonishing—and well known—with what little intelligence the world is being governed."

Given the pressure of time, he decided to skip the capsule survey of Jewish history he had prepared and confined himself to the conclusion: "Our 2,000-year exile has robbed us of a unified political leadership. That strikes me as our most grievous misfortune; it has done more harm than all the persecutions put together." But intent as he was on overcoming shyness and awe, he soon got carried away and became stridently aggressive. "As to raising our new generation, I want to propose methods radically different from those you practice. There is, first of all, the principle of philanthropy, which I regard as completely wrong. You are breeding *shnorrers*. Characteristically, there is more philanthropy and more begging among the Jews than among any other people. . . . Philanthropy corrupts the national character."

"You are absolutely right," Hirsch agreed. But Herzl pressed the attack. "Your Argentine Jews are one sloppy lot, I am told. I was struck by one detail in particular: that the first house they built was a brothel."

"Not so," Hirsch objected. "It was not built by my colonists."

Undeterred, Herzl continued his hectoring and haranguing until he had expressed all his reservations about the baron's perhaps well-meaning but wholly ineffectual efforts.

"But enough now of criticism. What is to be done? Whether the Jews leave or stay put, the first task is to improve the race here and now. The Jews must be made warlike, eager to work, and virtuous. Once that is done, they could leave—should it still be necessary."

When, however, he proposed cash premiums for raising "the moral level" of the Jews, Hirsch cut him short. "No, no, raising the level is precisely what I don't want to do. Our whole misfortune stems from Jews always aiming too high. We have too many intellectuals. I want to keep the Jews from always wanting to get ahead. They ought not to make such big strides. That is what causes all the hate."

The talk degenerated into a verbal skirmish, in the course of which Herzl told Hirsch in effect that he lacked the requisite imagination. Unperturbed, the unimaginative financier replied that as far as he could see, emigration was the only solution. "There are plenty of countries up for sale."

"Who tells you," Herzl shouted, "that I don't want to emigrate? It says so right here, in my notes. I am going to see the German Kaiser. He will understand me, because he has been raised to take the measure of great things."

"Hirsch blinked perceptibly when he heard these words," notes Herzl with evident satisfaction. "Was he impressed by my rudeness, or by my intention to speak to the Kaiser? Perhaps both."

Perhaps. More likely, though, Hirsch was stifling an impulse to laugh. He knew a great deal more than Herzl about the German Kaiser, first cousin to his friend the Prince of Wales, and he presumably differed radically in his evaluation of this impetuous, mean-spirited, and quintessentially incompetent young monarch.

"I am going to tell the German Kaiser: Let us go," Herzl insisted. "We are strangers, they won't let us assimilate, nor are we able to. Let us go."

"Where are you going to find the money?" Hirsch wanted to know. "Rothschild will give you 500 francs," he added, sarcastically.

Herzl quotes the end of that exchange:

"Money?" I said, with a defiant laugh. "I'll raise a Jewish National Loan of ten billion marks."

"You're dreaming." The baron smiled. "The rich Jews won't give. The rich are evil. They don't care about the sufferings of the poor."

"You talk like a socialist, Baron Hirsch."

"Indeed I am one. I am quite ready to give up everything, provided the others do likewise."

The conversation closed on this somewhat strained note, and the two were never to meet again; Hirsch died the following spring.

Summing up his impressions, Herzl patronizingly characterized Hirsch as "on the whole a pleasant, intelligent, unpretentious person, vain, *par exemple!*—but I could have worked with him. For all his obstinacy he seems reliable" (D, 6/2/95).

What Hirsch, in turn, thought of the encounter has not been recorded, but he was not one to be impressed by mere fervor and sincerity, and the half-baked ideas Herzl tossed off with such impassioned naïveté must have struck him as either banal or absurd. The latter-day Zionist version of history tends to portray him as the man who rejected a crown and missed out on his chance to become the new Moses. It is a simplistic view that grossly distorts the picture; on the contrary, rebuffing Herzl was in fact the greatest service Hirsch could possibly have rendered the cause of Zionism and the Jewish people.

Herzl, disdainful as he was of democracy and of what he called mob rule, believed in leadership by an elite bound to be defined by money, as *faute de mieux* it has been—and to a large extent still is—throughout the two thousand years of Jewish exile. And while the link between money and power is not a peculiarly Jewish phenomenon, it had a far greater potential for insidious consequences in a community that lacked countervailing political institutions. Money buys power, but it buys neither wisdom nor integrity, and the moneyed Jewish elite in the Diaspora has, with rare exceptions, been more concerned with preserving status and privilege than with providing effective leadership. Thus if Hirsch—or for that matter the Rothschilds, whom Herzl approached next—had ever seriously considered his proposals, his whole project might at best have ended up as yet another mass rescue operation for Russian Jews. By snubbing him instead, the philanthropic plutocracy unwittingly spurred the creation of the first democratic mass movement in the history of the Jewish exile.

* * *

Objectively, the meeting qualified as a fiasco. But Herzl's critical judgment had always abandoned him in the face of his own plays; in this instance, moreover, he had never envisaged a dialogue, to begin with. In any case, his performance left him both wildly elated and frustrated all at once. He felt that he had failed in part because he had not been given enough time to deliver the message, but failed also because the message itself still lacked clarity and concision.

As soon as he was back in his hotel room, he dashed off a letter to Hirsch that graphically conveys the pent-up fury of a swiftly evolving spiritual and emotional crisis.

Dear Sir:

For the sake of coherence I had made notes before I went to see you. Back home I now find that I stopped on page 6, out of a total of twenty-two pages. Because of your impatience, you only got to hear the beginning; how and where the idea will flower is something you never gave yourself a chance to find out. No matter. First, I didn't expect an immediate conversion, and second, my plan by no means depends on you. True, I would have liked to use you as a known quantity and available force just to speed up matters. But you would only have provided me with the initial momentum. There are others, last but not least the Jewish masses themselves, whom I shall know how to reach. This pen of mine is power. . . . You are the great money Jew, I am the Jew of the spirit. Please note that the reason you could not have known anything about my efforts is simply because you were my first audience. But I am on my way now. . . .

You cut me off with your polite sarcasm. I still tend to let myself be distracted in conversation. I have yet to acquire the poise needed to break down resistance, to shake up the indifferent, comfort the distressed, inspire enthusiasm in a cowardly and demoralized people, and deal with the rulers of this world. I spoke of an army, but you already interrupted me before I could ever start talking about the basic (moral) training. I let myself be interrupted. And yet I have already worked out the entire plan down to its details. I know exactly what it requires: money, money, money. Means of transportation, providing for large masses of people (which involves not just food and drink, as it

did in the simple days of Moses), maintenance of manly discipline, organization of departments, releases from some heads of
state, transit permission from others, formal treaties with all of
them, and the construction of marvelous new residential housing.
To begin with, however, intensive propaganda, popularization
of the idea by means of newspapers, books, tracts, lectures, pictures, songs. And all of it centrally directed, with vision and a
sense of purpose. But in the end I would have had to tell you
about our flag, and how I intend to unfurl it. And at that point
you would have waxed sarcastic: A flag? A flag is nothing but a
rag on a stick. No, sir, a flag is more than that. With a flag you
can lead people wherever you want to, even into the Promised
Land. They will live and die for a flag. It is, in fact, the only
thing for which the masses are prepared to die—if duly educated
in that sense.

Believe me, policy for an entire people—especially one scattered all over the globe—can be made only with lofty imponderables. Do you know what the German empire was made of?
Dreams, songs, fantasies, and black-red-golden ribbons. All Bismarck did was shake the tree planted by the dreamers.

You don't have any use for the imponderables? What, then,
is religion? Just think what the Jews have suffered over the past
two thousand years for the sake of this fantasy of theirs. Yes, it
is fantasy that holds people in its grip. He who has no use for it
may be an excellent, worthy, and sober-minded person, even a
philanthropist on a large scale—but he will never be a leader of
men, and no trace of him will remain.

Still, people's fantasies must be firmly grounded in reality.
What makes you think I don't have eminently practical ideas for
all the details? Details which themselves are nonetheless of enormous complexity.

In practical terms, the exodus to the Promised Land constitutes
a vast transport enterprise without precedent in the modern world.
. . . And even in the initial stages of this enterprise, the masses
of our young people will find employment—all those engineers,
architects, technicians, chemists, physicians, lawyers who
emerged from the ghetto in the last thirty years and thought they
could make an honorable living in ways other than by Jewish
wheeling and dealing. They are now growing desperate and will
soon constitute a terrifying intellectual proletariat. All my love

goes out to them. I want to see their breed multiply, unlike you who want to reduce it, because I see in them the inherent future strength of the Jews. They are, in other words, the likes of myself.

And from this intellectual proletariat I shall choose the general staff and the cadres of armies charged with exploring and conquering the land.

This is only a broad outline. But what makes you think I have not already developed the details? Did you give me a chance to finish?

I'll be in Paris till the middle of July. Then I'll be traveling for a while, in the cause. May I, however, request your absolute silence on this as on all the other points I brought up. At this time, my actions may not as yet seem important to you; all the more reason for me to stress my request for absolute secrecy. [D, 6/3/95]

Throughout the spring of 1895, Herzl had been heading for either a breakthrough or a breakdown. Holed up in his hotel room, without wife or children, cut off from direct contact with his parents, he led a lonely bachelor's existence that imposed few outward constraints, and there are clear hints of panic in the increasingly strident exaltation that ultimately culminated in the Messianic dream. Emotionally, he had reached a flash point long before his visit to the rue de l'Elysée, yet it was probably no accident that what finally sparked the explosion was his encounter with Hirsch.

The baron's cool irony, his pointedly polite refusal to take him seriously, cut more deeply than outright insult; Hirsch may have been "vain, *par exemple*," but Herzl's vanity, if no less monumental, bruised more easily. Moreover, Hirsch's skepticism merely echoed the doubts that Herzl himself had been wrestling with for weeks and months— doubts about his common sense, his very sanity. The long and impassioned letter he fired off within hours of their meeting was therefore a decisive step in his final conversion. It blew the lid off a volcano. Trying to explain himself—to himself as much as to Hirsch—he lost control. Reality receded, and fantasy took over.

In the weeks that followed, he seldom touched ground, soaring in orgiastic ecstasy through a lightning storm of inspiration. His hand could barely keep up with his imagination run amok. During the first few days he still managed the routine of his job, but eventually he had to ask a colleague to fill in for him and spent most of his time scribbling away, in the grip of a creative frenzy that seemed to come from outside himself. Normally overfastidious and wedded to routine, he now neglected food, sleep, and appearance. As he described it a year later, looking back on that wild voyage of discovery:

> I wrote walking, standing, lying down, on the street, at the table, at night when it roused me out of my sleep. The notes are dated. I started a second diary to record the major events of the day and put the slips aside. I am asking my good dad to copy them in chronological order. I now know, and was even aware of it throughout this entire period of turbulent productivity, that much of what I wrote was wild and fantastic. But I refrained from exercising any self-critique so as not to inhibit the flow of this inspiration. Time enough later, I thought, for critical expurgation. In these notes the Jewish state is at times conceived as substantive reality, at others as the subject of a novel, because at the time I had not yet decided if I would dare to publicly advance it as a serious proposal. [D, 4/16/96]

It seems reasonable to assume that what Herzl underwent during those weeks was, in fact, an acute manic episode. Its possible causes—and they range from the frankly physical to the purely emotional, with any variety of combinations in between—can never be known with any degree of certainty, but the speculation itself raises a much more fundamental question: Does it matter?

If one defines pathology as a deviation from the norm, all creative inspiration—Nordau's facile philistinism notwithstanding—is essentially pathological in origin; the epiphanies, the lightning revelations that change the course of a life and culminate in radical conversions are not within the purview of stolid minds simmering in sobriety. No prophet, visionary, or genuine charismatic leader ever conformed to the stereotypical patterns of normality. The true significance of Herzl's manic exaltation, therefore, rests not in its clinical aspects so much as in the vital energies it unlocked and the use to which he put them.

The initial phase of frenzied agitation lasted from June 3 to about the sixteenth of the month, and the jumble of notes he produced during this two-week bout of near-hallucinatory graphomania as subsequently transcribed by his father filled no less than 291 pages of an 8½-by-7 notebook. Though furiously struggling to keep pace with the onslaught of these "idea splinters," as he called them, he maintained—and quite convincingly—that for him "these notes are not work, but rather a relief. By writing them down, I am ridding myself of these thoughts that keep rising like bubbles in a test tube and which, without an outlet, would in the end have burst the vessel" (D, 6/12/95). That he deliberately refrained from self-critique because it would have "crippled his ideas" is, however, much more questionable, even aside from the fact that he later had them transcribed with loving care and used much of the material for his *Judenstaat*. On the contrary, part of the symptom picture was his very inability to exercise conscious control over this eruption of the unconscious. For what these notes document with stunning immediacy are not just Herzl's fantasies but the extent to which he was totally caught up in them, unable and certainly unwilling at the time to distinguish between objective reality and the products of his overwrought imagination. In it, he had cast himself as the founder, enlightened autocrat, and supreme ruler of a modern utopia, and for one brief but glorious and in many ways decisive moment he not only played the role but lived it.

"These candid notes," he wrote on June 12, "will make some people take me for a megalomaniac. Others will say or think that I merely want business or publicity for myself. But my peers, the artists and philosophers, will understand how authentic this all is, and they will defend me" (D, 6/12/95).

Many of his ideas may be hard to defend even by those gifted with uncommon understanding, but it is indeed the indisputable authenticity of the underlying emotions that accounts for the significance of these notes from the unconscious. They afford a unique insight into a nineteenth-century mind trapped in the conflict between reason and revelation, the vatic visionary in the age of steam and electricity.

"The cause now fills me like a lover's passion for his beloved, to the point where everything I do revolves around it," he wrote on June 5. And later that night: "*Tannhäuser* at the opera. We, too, are going to have such resplendent halls, men in formal black tie, ladies in high fashion. Yes, I want to make use of everything, including the Jewish love of luxury."

"We face bitter struggles," he proclaimed the following morning, "with rueful Pharaohs, with enemies, and most of all with ourselves. The Golden Calf. But farsighted and determined, we shall prevail if we have the support of our people and if they understand our lofty aims."

"Keep the army well in hand. All officials to wear uniforms, smart, soldierly, but not ridiculous. A huge public-works program."

By June 7, Herzl had started fantasizing about negotiations with the Rothschilds: "To the Family Council: I am starting with you, because I don't need a major ruckus before I have my cadres in place, and also because it would give me a better chance to lead the exodus of the masses without loss of property or life. If, on the other hand, I first arouse the masses, it will spell danger for the rich."

Thoughts of the Rothschilds led, by more or less free association, to Vienna's Chief Rabbi, Dr. Moritz Guedemann, who was to provide the necessary contacts. "Guedemann! You will be our capital's first bishop." (An innovative step toward ecumenism, though the strictly Orthodox rabbi might have had his misgivings.)

"I have twenty years in which to train my boys to be warriors. Training by patriotic songs, the Maccabees, religion, stage plays on heroic themes, honor, etc."

On June 7, he was beginning to think on an even more grandiose scale:

"The exodus led by Moses bears the same relation to this project as a Shrovetide Play by Hans Sachs to a Wagner opera."

"We shall probably model our constitution on that of Venice and profit from their experience. If the Rothschilds join us, the first Doge will be a Rothschild. I myself shall never be a Doge, because I want to lead the country beyond my lifetime."

"In the Tuileries, before the statue of Gambetta: I hope that when the Jews put one up for me, it will be in better taste."

"The high priests will wear impressive vestments. Our cavalry yellow trousers, white tunics. The officers silver breastplates."

Throughout the next day, he dwelled on loftier moral and political issues: "Track down and give a job to anyone who at any time in the past may have wronged me and therefore does not dare approach me. Because I have to be the first to set an example of magnanimity."

"The Jewish Question will be settled on a final note of reconciliation. We part as friends from our enemies. This will be the beginning of Jewish honor."

"Let the German Kaiser tell me: I'll be grateful to you if you get these unassimilable people out of here. (That would enhance my authority and make a big impression on the Jews.)"

"The first Senator will be my father."

That evening, however, dinner at the home of a colleague briefly broke the spell:

> Dinner at the Schiffs'. Their in-laws from Vienna were visiting. Affluent, well-educated, subdued people. They softly bemoaned anti-Semitism, to which I kept coming back all the time. The husband expects another St. Bartholomew's Night. The wife believes that things can't get worse than they already are. They argued about whether it was good or bad not to have ratified Lueger's election as mayor of Vienna. Their lack of spirit drained me. Though they don't suspect it, they are ghetto natures, quiet, decent, timid. And most of our people are like that. Will they heed the call to freedom and human dignity? On leaving, I was deeply depressed. Once again my whole plan seemed crazy to me. But right then and there I told myself: You've started it, now finish it. [D, 6/8/95]

The following morning, he was back in shape: "Today I am again rock-hard. The lassitude of those people is one more reason for action. Gentiles in similar circumstances would be cheerful and lively. Jews get depressed" (D, 6/9/95).

"First I'll negotiate with the Czar (introduced by our sponsor, the Prince of Wales) about releasing the Russian Jews. . . . Then I'll negotiate with the German Kaiser. After that with Austria. Then with France about Algerian Jews. And then as needed. In order to get proper respect at the imperial courts, I must obtain the highest decorations. English ones first."

"I shall make frequent surprise spot inspections. Imperative if we are to prevent waste and sleeping on the job. Also a secret administrative police, to report abuses."

"Language will be no problem. Switzerland, too, is a federation of different nationalities. We recognize ourselves as a nation by our faith. Besides, in all likelihood German will become the official language, out of necessity. The Jews' German! Like the yellow star as a merit badge. But I have nothing against French or English."

On the way to the annual Grand Prix race later in the day, which he managed quite conscientiously to cover for his paper, he had another series of inspirational flashes about the coronation ceremony and the rules of manly conduct:

"When it occurred to me that someday I might be crowning Hans as the Doge and that, in the Temple before the leaders of the nation, I would address him as 'Your Highness, my dear Son,' I had tears in my eyes."

But the elaborate fantasies of a procession led by "Herzl Cavalry" escorting the new Doge in a medieval Jews' costume, complete with yellow star and pointed hat, are interrupted by a wholly incongruous but significant aside—one of those stray thoughts that bubbled up from deep within and to which he kept coming back several times:

"This is how I shall punish suicide: for an unsuccessful attempt, lifelong confinement to a lunatic asylum; successful suicides will be refused an honorable burial."

Back to more pleasant dreams. "I need the duel," he declared, "in order to raise decent officers and to lend an air of French refinement to high society," and went on at great length about the rules legalizing honorable murder, concluding with the then rather original notion of a patriotic suicide mission as an acceptable substitute.

"To the Family Council: I opted for aristocracy, because I need a flexible form of government for the future. Monarchy would lead to revolution, and we are not sufficiently virtuous to qualify for democracy."

He assured the Rothschilds—and himself—that "I am picking up the thread of our people's traditions and leading it into the Promised Land. Don't mistake this for a fantasy. I am not one to build castles in the air. I am building a real house, using solid materials you can see, touch, test. Here are the blueprints."

After pronouncing himself in favor of a press law with teeth in it, including the pillory for slander, he had a revelation that cut much closer to the truth:

"At bottom I am still the dramatist in all this. I am taking ragged beggars off the streets, dressing them in magnificent costumes and having them perform in a glorious pageant designed by me. But I now manipulate large bodies of people rather than just individuals: the clergy, the army, the government, the academy, etc., all of them mass concepts to me."

Some of his social ideas had an oddly Calvinist flavor:

"Old maids will be used in nursery schools, for the care of workers' orphans, etc. I will draft these 'left on the shelf' girls into a corps of governesses for the poor, with state housing, honors, and pension rights."

"Only children and old people will be permitted to play. The children's play must, however, serve the purpose of physical training: running and ball games, cricket for boys, tennis for the girls. Old people may play cards, but not for money, because that might tempt onlookers and is unseemly for patriarchs. And I want patriarchal families. I shall, however, tolerate exclusive gambling establishments, with a minimum membership age of forty and high taxes for revenue."

"If we go to South America, for which there is much to be said because of its distance from the militarized swampland of Europe, we will conclude our first governmental treaties with South American Republics."

Time and again, he kept picking at the scab of that narcissistic injury that dominated his fantasies and all of his work—the wounded pride of the Jew who keeps looking at himself through the eyes of his enemies and hates what he sees.

"If, by the outbreak of the next war, we have not yet emigrated, every respectable Jew, whether healthy or sick, must volunteer for frontline service even if previously found unfit. If need be, they must drag themselves to the recruiting stations, serve in the armies of their present fatherlands, and, if on opposite sides, shoot at one another. Some may look at this as paying a debt of honor, others as a down payment on our future honor. But everyone will have to do it."

The following day Herzl suffered a severe migraine attack and resolved to learn to ride a bicycle "so as to direct the blood away from the head. Otherwise I won't be able to complete the task." On the sixteenth, he confessed that "I was often afraid of going mad these past few days. . . . An entire lifetime won't suffice to carry it all out. But I am leaving a spiritual legacy. To whom? To all people everywhere. I believe I shall rank among mankind's greatest benefactors. Or is this belief already a symptom of megalomania?

"I think life for me has ended and world history begun."

In freely articulating these fantasies as they arose and committing them to paper, Herzl had instinctively hit upon what was probably the most effective way of coping with a tidal wave that threatened to sweep him over the edge; his "writing cure" was not in substance all that different from the "talking cure" developed at about the same time by his Viennese contemporary.

By the end of the second week, the hailstorm of "idea splinters" was gradually giving way to a more coherent outline of his plans, couched in deceptively businesslike terms and conceived as an address to the Rothschild family. He was still up in the clouds, but there is a crucial difference between the dreamer content to drift with them and the creative fabulist driven to act out his fantasies. It is, in fact, sobering to realize how many of these seemingly mad schemes Herzl actually managed to carry out within the few short years still left him.

Already on June 11 he had taken a tentative first step toward concrete action by writing to Rabbi Guedemann. In a rather peremptory letter full of mysterious allusions, he asked the Chief Rabbi—with whom he had only had the most casual contact—to meet with him in Caux, Switzerland. "You are a spiritual shepherd. A duty awaits you in Caux. This is as much as I can tell you for now."

At the same time, he also considered a somewhat more modest alternative to the immediate exodus. "If I don't obtain the cooperation of the Rothschilds and of the midget millionaires, I'll publish the whole plan in book form as *The Solution to the Jewish Question*."

Guedemann was understandably dumbstruck by this summons from a man so alienated from Judaism that he had not even bothered to have his son circumcised. He pleaded a previous engagement, just as he had done six years earlier on the occasion of Herzl's wedding, but followed up on his cabled refusal with an unctuous note expressing surprise and gratification at the Herr Doktor's sudden interest in Jewish affairs. Thereupon Herzl, in his eight-page reply of June 16, summarized his ideas and explained that he hoped, via Guedemann, to obtain the cooperation of the Rothschilds. "Because I have the solution to the Jewish Question. I know this sounds crazy; in the beginning, people will often take me for a madman, until they see the truth of what I have to say. I have found the solution. And it is no longer mine alone. It belongs to the world at large" (D, 6/16/95).

The following morning, Herzl had second thoughts about that bombastic statement and hastened to reassure both Guedemann and himself:

Why do I write you again? Because in my yesterday's letter— as yet without giving away any details—I said that I had found the solution to the Jewish Question. And I can see your worried expression as you mumble into your patriarchal beard: He's gone completely mad. The poor family. Well, I am neither completely nor even partially mad. Which is why I want to add these few lines, to prove that I am solidly in touch with reality and fully aware of every least little detail. I am afraid that even my loftiest speeches will henceforth have to include casual references to the fact that $2 \times 2 = 4$ . . . and $17 \times 7 = 119$, and that I clearly remember what you and others have told me or even thought of me on various occasions in the past, just so people can see that I still have my wits about me. Not a pleasant prospect—but then again, pleasure does not accomplish great deeds. [D, 6/17/95]

Later that same day, however, Herzl's confidence in his own sanity was badly shaken nonetheless.

That afternoon he had a visit from Friedrich Schiff, by this time his only contact with the outside world, and the man who in his fantasies already figured as his private secretary. Schiff, Paris correspondent for the Wolff Telegraphic Agency, had been covering for Herzl through much of those stormy weeks. A physician by training, he was shocked at the change that had come over his colleague since he had last seen him. The normally so fastidious man-about-town had been transformed into the caricature of the mad inventor, a gaunt and unkempt apparition with a wild look in his eyes. But instead of claiming the invention of the perpetuum mobile, Herzl informed Schiff that he had just written a book that meant more to him than life itself; he wanted to read him the manuscript, which no one else had seen so far, and get his candid opinion.

By the time Herzl had finished reading his Address to the Rothschild Family Council, Schiff was shaken to the point of tears, though not by any visions of the Promised Land. Convinced that his friend had suffered a severe nervous breakdown, he took his pulse, found it disquietingly irregular, and, when asked for his reaction to the manuscript, urged Herzl to burn it; the whole idea was no more than a symptom of nerve fever brought on by overwork. He advised rest and immediate medical attention.

In the course of the argument that followed, Schiff brought up the case of Shabbetai Tsvi, the false prophet who, "a century ago" (actually, Shabbetai Tsvi, 1626–76, was a seventeenth-century figure), had attempted something very similar and ended up in an Ottoman jail, where he converted to Islam. "In the eighteenth century it could not be done," Herzl countered. "In our own time it can be done, because now we have machines." But the vehemence of Schiff's reaction nonetheless upset him profoundly; he had braced himself for objections, not for a medical diagnosis of insanity. The lowest blow came when he told Schiff about his letter to Guedemann. Schiff was aghast: "Guedemann will immediately notify your parents that you've gone crazy."

The mere thought of his parents was enough to send Herzl into a panic. He rushed out immediately and wired the rabbi: "Must request you return non-registered letter mailed yesterday without opening it. One of participating friends, whose consent had been assumed, is irrevocably opposed. Must comply."

He spent a sleepless night, tried to calm his nerves the following morning by a walk in the Tuileries, but was soon joined there by Schiff, even more concerned and insistent than the day before. His arguments in favor of socialism as the only practical solution to the Jewish problem left Herzl supremely indifferent, but what finally "cured" him, as he put it in his diary, was Schiff's remark that "in pursuing this cause, I would either become a tragic figure or else make myself ridiculous."

Tragedy he might have readily accepted. The risk of ridicule was more than he could face.

Acting with his usual impulsiveness—soon regretted, in this instance—he dashed off another letter to Baron Hirsch that very night, informing him that he had given up on the cause of the Jews.

A friend (not a businessman) convinced me that I would either end up as a tragic figure or else make myself ridiculous. Tragedy would not scare me. Ridicule, on the other hand, would ruin not me but the cause. . . . And that is why I am giving up. For the time being, there is no helping the Jews. If someone showed them the Promised Land, they would mock him, because they have degenerated. . . . I cannot break through the wall with just my head alone, and I have no other tools. That is why I am giving up. . . . I am through with the practical implementation, but I still believe in the theory. Which may merely prove my own degeneracy. A Gentile would move mountains for so powerful an idea. But what can I say? I don't want to look like Don Quixote. On the other hand, I refuse to accept token remedies, such as your 20,000 Argentinians or conversion to socialism, because I am no Sancho Panza, either. [D, 6/18/95]

He later likened the crisis triggered by Schiff's intervention to a red-hot body being plunged into a bucket of cold water—"but if that body happens to be made of iron, it will emerge as steel." In going over the postage and cable bills with Schiff the next day, he took great comfort from being able to add faster and more accurately than his colleague; in the simplistic popular notion of mental illness prevalent at the time, insanity precluded such complex mental operations. Thus reassured about his sanity but still sorely conflicted about the exodus and his role in it, he hit upon a rather desperate solution: submit the idea to an outsider, a figure great enough to fully comprehend it, and let him decide. And who more competent than the greatest statesman living, the one man who had himself realized a dream of similar grandeur?

He sat down at once and drafted a letter to Count Otto von Bismarck, his hero and ego ideal since childhood.

For the child in him, the appeal to this father figure made perfectly good sense. In a grownup journalist of unimpaired intelligence and a measure of political sophistication, on the other hand, its blatantly incongruous naïveté can only be ascribed to blinding egocentricity compounded by megalomania.

The eighty-year-old Duke Otto von Bismarck, architect of German unification, was living in forced retirement on his Pomeranian estate. Since the early 1860s he had, by force of will, ruthless cunning, and the aggressive pursuit of well-defined goals, dominated European politics to an extent that made him indisputably the most influential statesman of his age. Moreover, as Germany's first Imperial Chancellor he had also functioned for nearly two decades as the effective head of the newly unified Reich, which in itself constituted his most memorable achievement. His rule ended, to all intents and purposes, in 1888 with the death of Wilhelm I, the Prussian King whom in 1871 he had promoted to Emperor of Germany.

Wilhelm's son Friedrich was a man anathematized in conservative circles for his liberal views, as well as for his marriage to "that Englishwoman," a daughter of Queen Victoria. Already terminally ill with cancer of the throat, he reigned for only ninety-nine days and was in turn succeeded by Wilhelm II, a callow twenty-nine-year-old with impeccably reactionary credentials but few other qualifications for the job, a fact of which he was—and remained—singularly unaware for the rest of his life. Eager to assume absolute rule, obsessed with grandiose plans for German military and naval supremacy, and imbued with an exalted sense of his divine rights, he was eager to rid himself of the meddlesome old man who, as the founding father of the nation, enjoyed a popularity far exceeding his own. In 1890, he raised him from count to duke and, with a tearful farewell speech, sent him out to pasture.

It was the right move for all the wrong reasons. The very talents that accounted for Bismarck's success in foreign policy—his killer instinct and bulldog tenacity, his taste for intrigue and skullduggery—worked against him in the conduct of domestic affairs. His *Kulturkampf* against the Catholic Church ended in an inglorious stalemate, and his all-out war against socialism—the top item on his domestic agenda—ended in total defeat. Yet if Bismarck at seventy-five was past his prime, the young Kaiser and his retinue of sycophants were hopelessly incompetent from the very outset. Circumstances—and parliament—constrained them to somewhat more enlightened realism in domestic affairs, but in the pursuit of their expansionist foreign-policy objectives they displayed a combination of aggressive arrogance, shortsightedness, and lack of diplomatic skill that was bound to end in disaster.

In what he chose to regard as his exile, Bismarck began to dictate his memoirs, a searing indictment of those who, in his view, were about to destroy his life's work. But he was too much the man of action ever to content himself with passive preachments, and up to his death in 1899, at the age of eighty-five, he never ceased to plot his return to power, including, if necessary, the dissolution of the union as a way of stripping the detested Wilhelm of his imperial prerogatives.

Herzl approached this embittered old man with a reverence bordering on obsequiousness; he was, after all, talking to a genuine Prussian Junker rather than a synthetic Jewish baron, and all too keenly aware of the difference. He identified himself as a journalist for the *Neue Freie Presse*—"Some of my literary writings may perhaps have had the good fortune to come to Your Highness's attention"—who, however, was not asking for an interview but requesting an opportunity to talk to Bismarck about the solution to the Jewish Question. "Not *a* solution, but *the* solution, the only one." He confessed that he had revealed his plans to a rich Jew and a poor but highly educated one. The rich Jew rejected it as impractical because, according to him, other rich Jews were worthless and would never cooperate, while the poor Jew considered him mad.

"This leaves me in a moral dilemma in which I appeal to Your Highness. Allow me to present my plan to you. At worst, it will turn out yet another utopia of the sort that, from Thomas More to Bellamy, has been described often enough. A utopia is the more entertaining the farther it strays from the world of reason. In my case, I can promise you a new, hence entertaining utopia" (D, 6/19/95).

By way of a character reference, he enclosed a clipping of his article on a public-works program that was to be one of the basic ingredients of his plan.

> May I request that you just take note of it, for the time being. At least it proves that I am no Social Democrat. [On a positive note, he undertook to inform Bismarck of the failure of the emancipation.] It is pointless to publish an order in the *Official Gazette* stating that as of tomorrow, all men are equal. . . . Might it have been preferable to let the Jews rise gradually toward emancipation and, gently or rudely, make them assimilate along the way? Perhaps. But how? They should have been sluiced through the filter of mixed marriages, and care should been taken to ensure a Christian progeny. But assimilation should have preceded emancipation, not the other way around. . . . Anyway, it is too late. But just try to abrogate the legal equality of the Jews (the only one that exists, anyway). What would be the consequences? Immediately all Jews, not only the poor ones as heretofore, but the rich ones as well, with all their resources, would join the socialists. They would fling themselves on their moneybags the way an ancient Roman would have impaled himself on the point of his sword. [D, 6/22/95]

He obviously took it for granted that Bismarck shared his own jaundiced view of "the Jews." In fact, the old Chancellor, whatever his private feelings, had been a staunch defender of full legal equality for Jews not only in Germany but also in the newly independent Balkan states, a point on which he had publicly clashed with the Russians. Anti-Semitic circles accused him of being pro-Jewish, which may have meant no more and no less than that he refused to lend his name or prestige to anti-Jewish movements or machinations. What, if anything, he thought of Herzl's strange proposal has not been recorded, but he was later reported to have told the British journalist Sidney Whitman that he had been briefed on Herzl's *Judenstaat* and considered it a melancholy flight of fancy. In any case, he never bothered to acknowledge Herzl's letter.

But it no longer really mattered, for by this time Herzl was already wholly committed to his dream. The only one he still needed to convince of his sanity was himself, and the fact that 2×2 still added up to 4 seemed to him proof enough.

This is borne out by a letter he wrote to Arthur Schnitzler later that same day, in which he informed him that *The New Ghetto* had been submitted to Heinrich Teweles in Prague, and that he was still waiting for the decision. "But for me the whole thing has receded into the background. You were right when you predicted at the time that this one eruption would not bring release. Since I last wrote to you, something new and far greater has erupted within me. It now seems to me like a basalt mountain, perhaps because I am still so shaken. . . . A frenzy of productivity that went on for weeks and at times made me fear for my sanity. . . . This work is, in any case, of the greatest significance for myself and my own future, but perhaps also for others. . . . What makes me believe that I have created something of value is the fact that not for one second did I think in terms of literature, but only about people who are suffering." Without going into further details, he told Schnitzler that he needed just a few more days to finish outlining his project, and that he had deposited all his notes in a safe-deposit box. In the event of his sudden death, Schnitzler was to retrieve and publish them. "Do I seem excited to you? I am not; never in my whole life have I been in such a happy, exalted mood. I am not thinking about death but about a life full of manly deeds that will wipe the slate clean of all the baseness, turmoil, and confusion of my past and reconcile others with me, just as this work of mine has reconciled me with all of them" (L, 6/22/95).

The crisis had apparently driven Herzl not only to the brink of madness but also stirred up dangerous suicidal impulses, to judge from the otherwise inexplicable fulminations in his diary, quite out of any context, in which he again grimly decrees cruel and unusual punishment for those stupid and immoral enough to either kill or try to kill themselves in his utopia—locking up survivors in institutions, carving up the corpses of the dead in the name of science, dumping the remains in potter's field, and confiscating their estates. But by now the storm had abated, and the manic frenzy was yielding to euphoric self-aggrandizement. By June 27, he was wondering if Bismarck had ever even received his letter. "But I don't really care whether he did or not. If he did—*tant pis*" (D, 6/27/95). The time of doubts and questions was behind him. The time for action had begun.

It may even have been true, as he told Schnitzler, that he was thinking only of the suffering masses. But those masses—about whom at this point he knew absolutely nothing—were a mere abstraction, hopelessly neglected children badly in need of parental guidance by an educated and emancipated elite. The task of redeeming them, of raising the "degenerate" Jews to the level of a European *Kulturvolk*, devolved upon the likes of himself, born leaders who in every respect were the equals of Gentile nobility and yet found themselves treated like alien rabble in the countries of their birth.

Herzl had been no admirer of democracy to begin with, and after his four years in the press gallery of the Palais Bourbon, skepticism had soured into contempt. "The only way to govern is by aristocracy. I am all for autonomy in communal affairs. . . . But as to the state and its needs, those are things the common people are simply not equipped to understand" (D, 6/28/95). If his plan was to be realized, he himself would have to take full charge—not as a people's tribune, a Jewish Lueger, but as a man called upon by destiny to negotiate on behalf of the Jews with the true leaders of the world's great powers. And Bismarck, as he now convinced himself, was after all a has-been, too old to grasp a bold new idea. A new star had risen. "One man would understand me—the German Kaiser."

A new Herzl had risen as well, a man beyond discouragement, firmly fixed on his goal, and at ease in the role into which fate or fantasy had cast him. "I shall be the Parnell of the Jews" (D, 10/20/ 95). But to a brief note from Baron Hirsch acknowledging his letter, the Jewish Parnell replied with the brusque acerbity of a Prussian general:

Your failure to respond at once to the letter I wrote you after our conversation made me extremely angry. . . . I am still willing to do something FOR the Jews—but not WITH the Jews. If there was one man from whom I was entitled to expect comprehension for my bold idea, it was you. From other Jews I expect even less. The decadence of our once vigorous race is most clearly reflected in its political lethargy. Those people would mock me or suspect the plan of being just a business scheme. I would find myself having to trudge through a disgusting morass, and I am not prepared to make that kind of sacrifice for the Jews. Jews simply cannot understand that a man may act out of motives other than money, that he could disdain money without therefore being a revolutionary. Hence the last, though perhaps the most effective step I propose to undertake is to bring the matter to the attention of the exalted personage I mentioned to you. He is said to be an anti-Semite, but that does not faze me. I have found a channel to him. He will be given my memorandum. If this prompts him to summon me, an interesting conversation might ensue. . . . Just one more thing, by way of clarifying what may have struck you already. In every one of my letters I stressed that I am not in this for business reasons. I did so because it is compromising to write to rich people. I realize that a true gentleman either destroys confidential correspondence or else safeguards it carefully. But through some unfortunate accident some piece of paper might end up in the wrong hands. And if there is one thing I fear, it is the thought that my efforts might cost me a piece of my reputation. [D, 7/5/95]

And, lest he be accused of trying to settle the Jewish Question without letting the Jews know about it, he sent a curt note to Albert Rothschild, head of the Vienna branch of the family, that read rather like a memo from the Supreme Commander:

Let me come to the point at once.
I have drawn up a memorandum about the Jewish Question for the German Kaiser. It will be passed on to him by a reliable intermediary. It is not a fatuous or querulous complaint . . . but rather a comprehensive self-help plan for Jews of all countries. . . . It will be plain from the outset that I want no special favor from him or from anyone else. I therefore hope that this young and active ruler will understand me. I alone am going to sign the memorandum, and I bear exclusive responsibility. But since I am representing the cause of the Jews, I owe them proof of my good intentions. And for this purpose I need a few reputable and

independent witnesses. Mind you: witnesses, not guarantors or mandators. No single person would be qualified to give me a mandate, which by the way I do not need. Will you be one of the witnesses? I am having some trouble finding men I can use. . . . My memorandum will be submitted to the Kaiser at the end of July or the beginning of August. Should you wish to find out about it, I shall read it to you. We can agree on a meeting, and I am prepared to visit you for half a day. You will see to it that we remain undisturbed. . . . If you have no desire to learn any of the details, it will be sufficient if you return this letter to me. [D, 6/28/95]

Albert Rothschild, too, neither replied nor returned the letter, but again Herzl shrugged it off. "Fortunately I did not humble myself by excessive courtesy."

His last few weeks in Paris were strikingly serene, calm waters after the rapids. Herzl was sick of the city, tired of his job, pleased to be winding up his affairs, and looking forward to Vienna, to his new job, and above all to the reunion with his parents. He still regarded Vienna as his home, or at least his pied-à-terre, the model of the New Jerusalem, complete with "*Salzstangl*, coffee, beer, and traditional dishes. . . . Moses forgot to take along the fleshpots of Egypt. We are going to remember" (D, 7/23/95). But there were deeper reasons as well: the euphoric aftermath of a manic episode, and the exhilarating sense of a decisive intellectual breakthrough that gave him the illusion of having resolved conflicts essentially beyond resolution. He had charted the road to freedom; the maps and detailed instructions were now safely deposited at the Comptoir d'Escompte, Window 6, Drawer 2. The historic part of his mission was over, or so he believed. All that remained was one or two years of detail work—some high-level negotiations and the practical organization of the exodus.

Having thus struck a balance of sorts between his as yet secret role and his very public one, he resumed both his social and his professional life with much of the old zest. Early in July he wrote his last three pieces on the French parliament; they rounded out a selection of his political articles, a slim volume published later that year by a Leipzig publisher in a luxury edition under the title *Das Palais Bourbon*. He also discovered his spiritual kinship with the formidable Max Nordau.

I never realized how much we belong together. That has nothing
to do with religion. . . . But we are of the same race. . . .
Moreover, we both agreed that it was only anti-Semitism that
has made Jews of us. Nordau said: "What is the tragedy of the
Jews? That this most conservative of peoples, wanting nothing
so much as to strike roots in its own soil, has not had a home
for the past two thousand years." We were so much of one mind
that I already started to think that the same ideas had led him to
the same results. But no, his conclusion was different: "Anti-
Semitism will force the Jews to destroy the very concept of a
fatherland everywhere." "Or to create a fatherland of their own,"
thought I secretly to myself. [D, 7/6/95]

He was not as yet ready to risk exposing himself to as radical, unpredictable, and vituperative a critic as Nordau.

In Vienna, in the meantime, Lueger had been elected mayor by a
large majority. The election results were, however, subject to ratifi-
cation by the Emperor, and Franz Joseph refused to sanction the
elevation of a vulgar, anti-Semitic rabble-rouser to an office of considerable power and prestige—a move applauded in liberal and Jewish
circles, but whose dangerous consequences and ultimate futility Herzl
had accurately predicted. (Unlike Freud, who is said to have celebrated
with an extra ration of cigars.) The immediate result was an outburst
of anti-Jewish riots throughout the city, to which Herzl, about to
return, reacted with a lack of surprise not devoid of a certain satisfaction;
it confirmed more than just his political sagacity. To Rabbi Guedemann he wrote on July 15:

Today my sole reason for writing is the latest anti-Semitic rioting
in Vienna. I have been watching that movement in Austria and
elsewhere with the closest attention. These are as yet mere re-
hearsals. Much worse is to come. Unfortunately, nothing decisive
can be done at the moment, although my plan, carefully laid,
mild, intelligent, and anything but violent, is already fully outlined. But trying to carry it out at this particular time would—
given the attitude of the Jews—jeopardize its success. This plan
is to be reserved for the even more difficult days ahead. Please
trust me, even though I sound so vague; you will find out all
about it when we meeet. Meanwhile, I just would like to keep
a man I respect from sinking into despair and, amid the current

miseries of Austrian Jewry, hold out hope for the relief which we resolute younger men are preparing for our unfortunate brethren. [D, 7/15/95]

This time the rabbi, badly shaken by the pogrom mood of the Vienna populace, agreed to meet Herzl the following week in Zurich and proposed Dr. Heinrich Meyer-Cohn, a Berlin banker and Jewish activist member, as the third participant and community representative. But five days later he again backed out, this time because of "an upset stomach." He followed up on this lame excuse with a sententious sermon on the duties of a Jewish son, husband, and father to provide for his family and not to risk losing his job. He urged Herzl to use his God-given powers as a writer to move people's hearts by beautiful words rather than rash deeds. Herzl, thoroughly fed up by now but, in the interest of the cause, already a touch more diplomatic than in the past, thanked him for his no doubt well-meant advice and continued to insist on a personal meeting. "You are not going to flirt with me, are you, like a woman who displays her charms only to withdraw? Where the cause of the Jews is concerned, I don't tolerate jokes" (D, 7/25/95).

Two days later he left Paris for good. "Thus ends one chapter of my life. A new one is beginning. Which one?" (D, 7/27/95).

FOURTEEN

*O*n August 2, Herzl joined his family at Bad Aussee, a popular summer resort in the Traun Valley of Upper Austria surrounded by a spectacular mountain chain. The change of scenery presumably proved beneficial, though neither the famous pine forests nor the reunion with his family seems to have distracted him for long from what was now uppermost in his mind. The specter of anti-Semitism pursued him wherever he turned. A doggerel on the wall of a lakeside rest room so struck him that he noted it in his diary, although it is not clear whether it was the prayer or the curse that captured his attention.

> Oh Lord send Moses back again and lend a hand
> Make him lead his tribesmen back to the Promised Land
> And when the whole damn brood is on the high seas
> Scuttle the lot and give the Christians peace.
>
> [D, 7/2/95]

He argued with a Jewish lawyer from Vienna about Lueger's popularity and tried to disabuse two Budapest doctors of their optimism about the situation of the Jews in Hungary. To a Berlin Jew who, not unlike Herzl himself some time ago, saw conversion as the solution to the Jewish problem, he answered that if enough Jews converted, the anti-Semites would simply change their slogan from "dirty Jew" to "dirty convert."

His family was as yet unaware of the transformation he had undergone. He even kept his parents in the dark; as far as they knew, he was spending most of his so-called vacation time working on a novel. Instead, he was busily exploring possible approaches to the German Kaiser, while also keeping up an almost daily correspondence with Guedemann and Meyer-Cohn, his two handpicked but decidedly luke-warm future adjutants, who time and again derailed his plans for a meeting. Herzl finally wore them down by sheer dogged persistence, and the three of them met in Munich on Saturday, August 17.

He had intended to stage the first public unveiling of his plan as a dramatic performance, and he had counted on the majestic backdrop of the Swiss Alps to induce a duly reverential mood in his audience of two. By capitulating to their demand to meet instead in a Munich luxury hotel, he had already lost control over the mise-en-scène, but on his arrival—carefully stage-managed so as to keep the other two waiting in suspenseful expectancy—he quickly discovered that he had also lost half his audience: Meyer-Cohn was definitely not the sort of man he had been looking for. "From the first moment on I knew that he was not the right man. A little Berlin Jew in outward appearance, and inwardly just as little." Guedemann, on the other hand, struck him on this occasion as "a beautiful and open kind of person," an impression he later had reason to revise. In the course of a preliminary dinner conversation, he felt compelled to expound his—in his view—quasi-Spinozistic conception of God:

> I want to raise my children in the so-to-speak historical God. God to me is a beautiful, dear old word that I want to preserve. It is a marvelous metaphor for concepts that would be inaccessible to the mind of a child or a person of limited intellect. God means to me the Will to Good. The omnipresent, infinite, all-powerful and eternal Will to Good, which does not prevail everywhere at once but in the end is always victorious. And for which Evil is also a means to an end. Why, for instance, does the Will to Good permit epidemics? Because they wipe out musty old cities and create bright, healthy new ones in their place for a free-breathing humanity. [D, 8/18/95]

This windy bit of philosophizing, on which Herzl proudly expatiates at some length in his diary, is not likely to have gone over very well with the scholarly, strictly Orthodox rabbi, a man without much of a backbone but with a perfectly functional brain. However, it scarcely mattered; Herzl was, as always, supremely unaware of his listener's true reaction.

He then proceeded to read his Address to the Rothschilds, but the nasty little Berlin banker kept needling him until he lost his composure. There was an interruption; the banker had a business appointment, and Herzl had to finish his reading the next morning. But in the end, according to him, "the effect was great, nonetheless. I saw it in Guedemann's shining eyes." As they were leaving, Guedemann said to him: "You seem to me like Moses."

"I rejected that idea with a laugh," writes Herzl, "and I did so in all candor and sincerity."

Both his listeners vehemently objected to the idea of a Jewish aristocracy, and they were appalled at Herzl's naïveté in counting on the Rothschilds, whom Guedemann characterized as mean, despicable, and selfish. He urged Herzl instead to publish the plan in the form of a novel, which would then perhaps arouse enough popular enthusiasm for a mass movement.

A much sobered and disappointed Herzl saw Guedemann to the train. "As we parted, he said to me with grave enthusiasm: 'Remain as you are. Perhaps you are the one chosen by God.' We kissed each other goodbye. There was a strange gleam in his beautiful eyes as he leaned out of the compartment window, took my hand once more and pressed it firmly" (D, 8/18/95).

This, at any rate, is Herzl's version of what took place, recorded the following day but hotly disputed twenty years later by Rabbi Guedemann in his unpublished memoirs. Guedemann's account of the 1895 Munich meeting and of his relations with Herzl was not committed to paper until 1915; he was by then eighty years old and had, ever since the publication of Herzl's *Judenstaat*, been one of the most vocal opponents of Zionism in Austria. His public stance drew heavy fire from the Zionists, including a particularly vicious personal attack by Max Nordau, past master of the art of vituperation, invective, and innuendo. It seems reasonable to assume that, ostentatious piety and rabbinical unction notwithstanding, the experience colored his recollections.

Nevertheless, it is also true that Herzl tended to get carried away by his enthusiasm, that he saw what he wanted to see, and that much of what he ascribed to others was no more than a reflection of his own feelings. Trotting out his cracker-barrel theology to impress the rabbi was for him a rather typical display of insensitivity. From the very outset, one of Guedemann's chief objections to Herzlian Zionism was its lack of a religious foundation, and in his memoirs he recalls with pursed-lipped disapproval how he had dropped in on the Herzl family one afternoon in late December only to find them gathered around the Christmas tree in the parlor. The description of his utter bewilderment in Munich, of his confusion and boredom in the hotel room as Herzl kept droning on, sounds thoroughly convincing even if it only proves him to have been another consummate actor on the scene. Herzl, at any rate, clearly misjudged him, as he himself was forced to admit a few months later: "The only resemblance between Guedemann and a real man is his beard and his voice" (D, 11/3/95).

Guedemann specifically denied any blasphemous references to Moses, let alone the Messiah, in connection with Herzl and denounced that legend as an out-and-out lie. His true impression of the meeting, he claimed, was evident from a letter written in Munich and addressed to his wife, in which he told her that "Herzl is a poet, but this plan of his, however interesting, is impossible to put into practice."

All of which leads one to suspect that both men deceived themselves as much as each other.

At the beginning of September, the Herzl family settled into an apartment at Pelikangasse 16, in Vienna's Ninth District.

The failed playwright on the run from marriage, fatherhood, and himself, who four years earlier had furtively left town in misery and disgrace, was back in triumph—professionally as a celebrated journalist and the new literary editor of the *Neue Freie Presse,* and personally as the head of a prototypically upper-middle-class Jewish household, with an attractive young wife and three children. The outward changes were obvious; the far more radical inner ones were to become equally obvious in short order.

But the city, too, had changed in his absence, and although heightened sensitivity and sharpened perceptions accounted for some of the differences that struck him as ominous, many of the changes were real enough. The doom of the old order, long since taken for granted, hence trivialized with the lighthearted flippancy on which Vienna prides itself—the situation is desperate but not serious—now loomed visibly close on the horizon. The tribal patchwork of a state precariously held together by a feudal bureaucracy was unraveling at an ever accelerating pace. The Emperor, its single most visible symbol, had ruled for nearly half a century, an old man facing death whose only son had killed himself. The twilight of the gods gave rise to new prophets, who took to the streets to proclaim their faith.

Doomsday was in the air. But so was the resurrection; missing from the stereotypical image of *fin de siècle* Vienna are two dimensions that mark the difference between Herzl's time and our own—innocence and hope. True, there was despair aplenty in the slums of the bloated metropolis. There was fear and fatalism among the Jewish bourgeoisie, a dread nameless until Freud gave it a name, and forebodings of apocalyptic disaster pervaded the frenzied creativity that has shaped our notions of the "Gay Apocalypse." Yet no imagination, however prolific, fertile, or diseased, could have conceived of the realities that in our own *fin de siècle* we take for granted. When Herzl warned Guedemann of "worse things to come," what he had in mind were pogroms. Hundreds of victims.

But innocence aside, this tableau of a city dancing Schnitzler's *Reigen* on the edge of the volcano derives from the archaeological evidence—the arts and literature of the period. Missing is the counterpoint of hope, as ubiquitous in its way as its antithesis, and no less deadly. To ignore this dialectic tension between hope and despair is to succumb to a media myth, a compound of half-truths and kitsch.

It took many forms. Socialism, for one, which brought hope to the slums, inspired a trade-union movement that radically improved the conditions of the working class, gave dignity to the dispossessed, held out the promise of the brotherhood of man, and extended its influence far beyond the industrial proletariat.

More potent and far more poisonous a source of hope was nationalism, a faith to cling to for those cut off from the past and adrift in time. Whether it was the Czechs, Magyars, Poles, or Croats fighting for power over their own lives, or the Germans resolved to perpetuate their dominance, the struggle gave them a sense of belonging and an outlet for their pent-up hate. Marching in lockstep toward the mirage of their own promised land made men feel like giants. Until they came to the end of the road.

The Jews alone were left with no cause to march for. Their hopes had been heavily invested in liberalism, assimilation, and multinational tolerance embodied in the patriarchal Emperor, lost causes all of them by the time Herzl came on the scene. It left them few illusions to feed on, socialism being the only one that seemed to offer a way out. Yet even Jewish socialists were seldom allowed to forget their traditional place in the natural order of things.

The apocalyptic temper of Vienna's *fin de siècle* was, to a degree far greater than commonly acknowledged, the anguish of its Jews—those still defiantly Jewish, those pretending to be what they were not, and those hating themselves for being what they were, yet all of them equally beyond the pale, strangers unto themselves and others, forced to confront their world without the blinkers of faith, hope, or illusions. It was their half-aborted emancipation that swept a tidal wave of energy and talent into the imperial capital, transformed an overgrown village into a metropolis, and made it the center of a cultural revolution. Our image of *fin de siècle* Vienna as the cradle of modernity is both true and false; true in that the work of Freud, Wittgenstein, Mahler, Berg, Webern, Weininger, Reich, Mach, Mauthner, Kraus, Broch, Roth, Hofmannsthal, Schnitzler, Zweig still reverberates in the present, false in that it confounds the achievements of a distinctly marginal minority with the spirit of their time.

A far more representative figure was that cheerful demagogue and nemesis of liberalism Karl Lueger. Despite his petit-bourgeois background, he managed to attend the Theresianum, Vienna's most exclusive preparatory boarding school, as one of a handful of non-residential students. Nine years as a janitor's son among the budding snobs of Austria's top-drawer nobility failed to crush his sturdy ego; like Herzl, he, too, had a mother who worshipped him. Graduating from law school, he went into politics as a liberal, left-leaning populist and, in 1875, was elected to the Vienna Municipal Council. Ten years later he entered parliament, where his vernacular sarcasm and his attacks on corruption, with special emphasis on "Jewish capitalists," gained him wide notoriety and a growing number of fiercely devoted fans. Quick to recognize the political potential of Jew-baiting as a means of mass manipulation, he joined the pan-German Schönerer in a United Christian Front, but backed away in 1888 when the anti-Semitic psychopath ran afoul of the law. He found a home instead in the Christian Social Party, a new creation truculently dedicated to the defense of the middle class and to the protection of the "Little Man." Though nominally pro-Habsburg rather than pan-German, and initially shunned by the Church for its professed anti-capitalism, the politics of resentment deftly pursued by its leaders attracted a mix of German nationalists, disgruntled shopkeepers, radicalized Catholics, and déclassé malcontents of every stripe that very quickly translated into electoral victories, particularly in Vienna, where the charismatic Lueger had become the party's leading spokesman and candidate. The 1894 municipal elections, in which the Christian Socials gained 64 seats as against 66 for the Liberals and 8 miscellaneous, already caused a near-panic among their opponents; the 1895 elections held right after Herzl's return gave them a 92-seat majority, with the remaining 46 split among the Liberals and a few splinter parties.

Some complex reasons accounted for the upset, but the most simple one was also the most compelling: Lueger's immense popular appeal, and the consummate mastery with which he played on the paranoid fears of the petite bourgeoisie. With genuine charm, wit, and coolly deliberate demagoguery he articulated the grievances of the "Little Man," whose language he spoke to perfection, and pilloried the enemies traditionally blamed for his plight, most specifically the Jews. True, he also fulminated against Slavs, Hungarians, and other *Untermenschen*, but Jews were his most visible target—Jewish big business, Jewish speculators, and the Jew-dominated press. The mass appeal of anti-Semitism cut across all segments of Lueger's following, and he made the most of it without, however, letting it divert him from some of the real issues. He turned out to be that rarest of demagogues, a superb administrator who in his sixteen years as mayor provided Vienna with vastly improved public transportation, a reliable water supply, and a municipal gas company. He built bridges, hospitals, orphanages, schools, and playgrounds and greatly expanded social services to the poor, including free school lunches. His personal—as distinct from his official—attitude toward Jews was equivocal, to say the least. *Der schöne Karl*, unlike Schönerer, was not taken in by his own rhetoric. He consorted freely with the same Jewish *haute bourgeoisie* he so mercilessly lambasted in his speeches and defended such inconsistencies with an imperious *Wer Jude ist, bestimme ich*—I decide who is and who is not a Jew. (What this tells about the Jewish *haute bourgeoisie* is another matter.) Austrian anti-Semitism would have flourished even without Lueger; nonetheless, his cynical exploitation of this endemic scourge for propaganda purposes contributed a great deal to its proliferation and legitimized Jew-baiting as evidence of progressive and patriotic sentiments.

But Lueger's stunning victory in the municipal elections of September 19, 1895, confronted Jews and liberals with an agonizing dilemma;

the fact that they failed to agonize merely underscores their demoralization and political ineptitude. Herzl was among the very few who foresaw the inevitable consequences and refused to compromise his principles, in sharp contrast to the vast majority of anti-clerical liberals and impassioned democrats who promptly appealed to the Catholic Church to disavow the Christian Social Party, while at the same time urging the Emperor to stand fast and, by refusing to ratify Lueger's election as mayor of Vienna, in effect to nullify the results of a popular vote. Herzl has left a telling description both of his own mood and of the atmosphere on the eve of the elections:

Municipal elections in Vienna took place the day before Rosh Hashanah eve. The anti-Semites won all the mandates. The mood among the Jews is desperate. The propaganda against them has whipped up a lot of hatred among the Christians.

Actually, though, the movement is not really noisy. In fact, used as I am to the violent demonstrations in Paris, things here seem to me, if anything, rather too quiet. I find this quiet much more ominous. Yet at the same time one sees the look of hatred everywhere, even without the paranoid fear that makes one go around seeking eye contact.

On election day I was in Leopoldstadt outside the polling place, to take a closer look at all the hate and anger. Toward evening I went to the Landstrasse district. In front of the polling place a silent, tense crowd. Suddenly Dr. Lueger stepped out into the square. Wild cheers, women waving white kerchiefs from the windows. The police held the crowd back. Next to me, someone said, with tender warmth but in a quiet voice: "This is our leader."

More, actually, than any declamations and outbursts, it was this phrase that proved to me how deeply anti-Semitism is entrenched in the hearts of these people. [D, 9/20/95]

Considering that almost a century later, with only 7,000 Jews left in all of Austria, 85 percent of Austrians polled in 1987 acknowledged some degree of anti-Semitism, his observation seems as prescient as his attitude toward Lueger's election. As he predicted, the Emperor was ultimately forced to bow to the will of the people and, in 1897, confirmed the rabble-rouser as the mayor of Vienna. He was reelected time and again with huge majorities until his death in 1913.

Herzl's relations with his bosses, though cordial on the surface, were actually much more ambiguous than he let himself realize. For their part, Bacher and Benedikt were guided solely by what they conceived as the best interests of the *Neue Freie Presse*. They valued Herzl highly as an employee, and though understandably loath to lose their star foreign correspondent, they created the post of literary editor expressly for his benefit so as to keep an obviously first-rate talent from joining the competition.

They were also said to have been personally fond of Herzl, a claim impossible to verify, especially since neither man seems to have had much of a personality or personal life apart from the paper. It is true that they resigned themselves to his increasing preoccupation with Zionist activities, but in all likelihood this was simply a matter of putting up with his eccentricities for the good of the paper and the sake of their readers. The fact is that they strung him along with promises they never kept and probably never meant to keep, and later went so far as to forbid any mention of the word "Zionism" in the paper's columns. It made its first appearance in the *Neue Freie Presse* as part of Herzl's obituary in 1904.

Herzl, in turn, had sound and valid reasons for hanging on to his job; above all, it gave him a power base of incalculable value in his dealings with statesmen and politicians. But beyond that, his feelings for Bacher and Benedikt—Bacher in particular—were unmistakably filial in nature. The two men had become father figures to whom, as to his own father, he owed unswerving loyalty. Within weeks of his return, however, that loyalty was put to a severe test.

In June, the two-year cabinet crisis following the fall of Taaffe ended with the appointment of Count Kasimir Badeni as the new Prime Minister. A Polish nobleman of Italian extraction, Badeni was an able and imaginative administrator who enjoyed the Emperor's confidence and boldly set out to defuse the explosive language problem that bedeviled the multilingual monarchy. Keenly aware that any solution depended on broad public support, he acquired the venerable Vienna *Presse*, the by then moribund parent of the *Neue Freie Presse*, on behalf of the government, refurbished its finances and staff, and cast about for an editor in chief.

Herzl was approached as early as September 20—an impressive tribute to the competitive standing of this thirty-five-year-old journalist, and evidence of the close attention with which his work and career had been followed in influential circles. It was also, of course, the chance of a lifetime. But Herzl's ambition at this point no longer centered on professional advancement, and he weighed the offer exclusively in terms of what it might do for his cause rather than his career. A brief conversation on his first day back on the job, which convinced him that Bacher would never waver in his staunchly pro-German, ultra-assimilationist stance, made the unexpected chance of being his own boss seem especially tempting. He therefore signaled his readiness, in principle, to consider the offer, provided he obtained certain firm guarantees.

The elaborately choreographed preliminaries to the preliminary negotiations dragged on for a month, most of which he spent seeking support for his plan wherever he found a willing ear. Although the practical results were negligible, Herzl kept enough distance from reality to avoid discouragement. Thus, on October 18: "Last night talked for three hours with bank president Dessauer—and won him over. He considers financing of exodus through intermediary bank feasible. The Rothschilds cannot be counted on. . . . Like everyone else with whom I spoke, Dessauer said to me: 'Personally I am with you, but I doubt if you'll find one other person in Vienna.' And yet, I noticed how his eyes lit up. I inspire enthusiasm in everyone I talk to about the Jewish cause" (D, 10/18/95). More instructive was his meeting with Narcisse Leven, a Paris lawyer and vice-president of the Alliance Israélite Universelle, from whom he learned that his ideas were not quite as original as he had thought. Leven told him about an Odessa physician named Pinsker and his pamphlet *Auto-Emancipation*, about a British-Jewish colonel named Goldsmid who had wanted to reconquer Palestine by force of arms, and he assured Herzl that Zadok Kahn, Chief Rabbi of France, was himself an ardent Zionist.

A few days later, with the job situation still unresolved, Herzl decided to tackle Benedikt head-on and "win him over to the cause." In the course of a three-hour walk, he outlined his plan and asked outright for the support of the *Neue Freie Presse*. Benedikt, even more rabidly pro-German than Bacher and totally alienated from Judaism, was a most unlikely candidate for conversion, but he reacted cautiously, always mindful of his paper's long-range interests. "You confront us with a monstrous problem," he told Herzl. "The whole paper would acquire a different cast. They always considered us a Jewish newspaper, but we never admitted it. Now all of a sudden you want us to let down our defenses."

"But you won't need those defenses anymore," Herzl replied. "The entire Jewish Question will have been honestly resolved the moment my idea is made public."

The spirited debate ended on what Herzl took for a positive note when Benedikt asked him for a concrete proposal. Herzl wanted a Sunday edition to be put at his disposal, in which he would publish a summary of his plan and invite comments and questions, to be dealt with in a regular column under his editorship. "Never has anything more interesting appeared in any newspaper," he declared. "And I alone shall assume full responsibility. You can preface my article with a disclaimer on the part of the paper." Benedikt responded with sanctimonious indignation, "That would be cowardly. If we print it, we share the responsibility."

"The walk, as I told Benedikt on the way back, was a historic occasion. I must admit that it also marks a decisive turn in my life. I have begun to move. Everything up to now was all dreams and talk. Now the action has started, because the *Neue Freie Presse* will either be with me or against me" (D, 10/20/95).

One week later, on October 27, the Prime Minister's formal offer brought matters to a head. Herzl requested twenty-four hours to think it over and give his employers sufficient notice—though not, as he was most anxious to stress, in order to "obtain pecuniary advantages." Instead, he presented Bacher and Benedikt with an ultimatum: either support his cause or lose him. Much as he would prefer to stay with the *Neue Freie Presse*, his decision was to be based not on personal preferences but solely on its implications for the cause.

Bacher now had no choice but to submit to a complete reading of the Address to the Rothschilds. He complimented Herzl on his idealism but rejected the plan as hopelessly impractical. "It is a great cause, and I can well understand that a decent person would want to devote his life to it. But I doubt very much if you'll find many such Herzls." And to Herzl's objection that, in the long run, the *Neue Freie Presse* could not avoid dealing with the Jewish Question, he replied: "For twenty years we never once mentioned the Social Democrats."

The die was cast. Herzl conveyed his conditional acceptance of

Badeni's offer, subject to a personal interview with the Prime Minister himself.

The interview on October 30, conducted entirely in French, was cordial but inconclusive. Badeni agreed to give Herzl direct access and to receive him any time he wished, *"comme un ambassadeur,"* but failed—or was unable—to offer guarantees beyond his term of office (which, in fact, was to last a mere two years). Herzl nonetheless all but accepted the job and even attended an editorial conference, though still hoping against hope that Bacher would change his mind. "The idea that I might be making an enemy of this man, whom in spite of his stubbornness I revere, was extremely painful and became more unbearable by the hour. Moreover, my officiousness might not even do much for the cause of the Jews" (D, 11/1/95).

In the end it was Herzl, not Bacher, who changed his mind.

Racked by doubt, guilt, and anxiety, he later that same evening rushed out of the house, tracked down Bacher, and told him that the thought of giving up his friendship was more than he could bear. Bacher, placated and visibly delighted, made some vague promises about a pamphlet on the Jewish Question that might be reviewed in the *Neue Freie Presse.* He also agreed to inform Badeni, on his word of honor, that no material compensation of whatever nature had been offered, demanded, or received to influence Herzl's decision. It was to be the only promise he kept, to the letter; Herzl had taken a pay cut on leaving Paris, but his scrupulous probity failed to shame Bacher into precipitate generosity.

By the time Herzl resurfaced at the *Neue Freie Presse* at the end of the week, he had convinced himself that only practical considerations had made him change his mind at the last minute. But Bacher and Benedikt didn't give a hoot about his motives, as they made plain within hours. The one could find no time to discuss the pamphlet, the other wanted to know when Herzl would finally deliver himself of another feuilleton. As far as they were concerned, he had held a trump card and let himself be bluffed out of it. The potential competitor had reverted to the status of an employee, and they once again treated him as such, with cunning and guile, indulging his foibles and eccentricities, but never letting him forget that, for them, the only cause that mattered was the *Neue Freie Presse.*

Herzl, on the other hand, gave little thought or time to anything other than his project. He attended Jewish meetings and dinner parties in the hope of spotting potential disciples, but the only real convert he felt he had made—a gross misjudgment, as it turned out—was Arthur Schnitzler: "When I told him it was to be the Renaissance, the culmination of this classic century of invention in the field of transportation, he was enthusiastic. I promised to put him in charge of the theater" (D, 11/5/95).

Vienna being what it was, the spontaneous mutation of an urbane and seemingly rational journalist soon became a hot item on the café circuit, where tortured witticisms and sarcastic gibes passed for evidence of intellectual superiority. But the "Mahdi of the Pelikangasse," who only a few months earlier had feared ridicule more than failure, remained remarkably unruffled. He seemed to have made his peace with the thought that "if a man was to prove right thirty years hence, he had to put up with being considered mad in his own day." The idea that he may indeed be mad and, for that very reason, turn out to have been right thirty years later did not occur to him.

His parents, whom he now kept fully informed, backed him as a matter of course. Jeanette Herzl had always been certain that her son was destined for greatness; if she preferred a latter-day Goethe to a latter-day Moses, she kept it to herself. As far as she was concerned, her Dori could do no wrong. The pedantic Jakob, on the other hand, closely scrutinized the Address to the Rothschilds and, in a memo dated October 26, 1895, came up with some pertinent and constructive criticism. Unlike his son, he did not believe that anti-Semitism would prevail in Austria; and if Herzl failed to convince his own father, what chance was there for him to convince the Rothschilds—who, in any case, were not famous for taking other people's advice? Moreover, appealing to moguls, magnates, and moneybags hat in hand was not only futile but also undignified. Instead, he advised his son to take his case directly to the people, the little people who, banding together, would form a mighty river that swept away all obstacles. And the way to mobilize the millions was to write a pamphlet that would stir their imagination and propound the idea of a Jewish state throughout the civilized world.

Whatever the influence of his father's suggestions, Herzl had, of necessity, already been moving in the same direction. Bacher and Benedikt were obviously toying with him, stalling on their promises but throwing him just enough crumbs to prevent an open break. They arranged for a meeting with David Gutmann, czar of the Austro-Hungarian coal industry—a Rothschild partner and Jewish philanthropist, he had been knighted and went under the title of David Ritter von Gutmann—which proved a predictable waste of time. ("I unfortunately forgot to tell him how I was going to liquidate the Gutmann coal business," Herzl noted in his diary, by way of sardonic postmortem.) And, since instead of cranking out feuilletons he continued to pester both editors about the Jewish Question, they finally suggested that he take a leave of absence and try to enlist some influential personalities in France and England in an international study group. If anything came of it, the results might perhaps be published in the *Neue Freie Presse*.

Restless and frustrated, Herzl immediately seized on the idea. From the ever more recalcitrant Guedemann he obtained an introduction to Zadok Kahn—it was to be Guedemann's final and most reluctant contribution to the cause—and, by November 16, he was back in Paris.

In his four years as foreign correspondent, Herzl had never once met the Grand Rabbi, an omission which, after the meeting, he felt he had no reason to regret. Kahn struck him as a timid soul in the cloak of an unctuous French patriot, the only grand thing about him being his title. Subsequent discussions with other leaders of French Jewry also went nowhere; they regarded themselves as full-fledged French citizens of Jewish extraction and resented this German interloper knowledgeable—and tactless—enough to raise some awkward questions about their status. But one Paris encounter more than made up for all the disappointments: he got an ecstatic response from his old friend Max Nordau. "Nordau is the second case of instant comprehension. The first was Benedikt. But Nordau is all for it, whereas Benedikt understood it from the viewpoint of an opponent, at least for the time being. Nordau, I believe, will follow me through thick and thin. He would make a good president of our academy, or a minister of education" (D, 11/17/95).

For once his impression was accurate. Though outwardly every bit as Westernized as Herzl, Nordau had retained deep emotional roots in his ancestral culture, and Herzl's contagious enthusiasm evidently rekindled long-dormant feelings. That the by now world-famous author of *Degeneracy* felt compelled to speculate about the anthropological fitness of the Jews to regenerate as a nation was inevitable but irrelevant. What counted was that he had excellent contacts in England and sent

Herzl off with a sheaf of introductions and some very helpful instructions. He never got to be Minister of Education, for which there is reason to be grateful. But he was to become one of Herzl's closest collaborators in the Zionist movement and, as the "silver-tongued orator," its most eloquent spokesman.

It is in fact doubtful if, without Nordau's intervention, Herzl's first appearance on the English scene would have been the success it turned out to be. His English was practically nonexistent at the time, and his ideas about British Jewry were equally primitive. But by the time he reached London on November 20, Nordau had already lined up an interview for him with Israel Zangwill.

Zangwill was born in London in 1864, the oldest son of Russian-Jewish immigrants. Educated at the Jews' Free School and London University, he taught school for a few years before turning to journalism. In 1892, his *Children of the Ghetto*, the fictionalized account of his childhood in the slums of Whitechapel, brought instant fame and modest affluence. Its exotic setting appealed to the Victorian taste for romanticism laced with social concerns, and Zangwill followed up on his success with a series of hugely popular ghetto novels—*Ghetto Tragedies, The King of the Shnorrers, Dreams of the Ghetto*. He thus became the link between the immigrant peddlers of Whitechapel and their British-born children, whose attitudes toward both Judaism and the "host nation" differed substantially from those of Herzl's generation in Central Europe.

Zangwill and his brother—they were both still unmarried at the time—lived in Kilburn, a shabbily genteel London suburb. It may have been an improvement over the Whitechapel slums, but although much of the dreary street scene was veiled by heavy fog, it struck Herzl as utterly depressing. He primly noted the run-down condition of Zangwill's house and the unholy clutter in his study, describing the writer himself as "a long-nosed Negro type. . . . I have read nothing by him, but I think I know him. His manifest lack of concern for his outward appearance is no doubt made up for by the care he devotes to cultivating his style" (D, 11/21/95).

The meeting between the stiffly formal Viennese and the demonstratively informal novelist began inauspiciously. Herzl's English was simply not up to anything beyond an exchange of greetings, and Zangwill spoke no German. He had a smattering of French, but as Herzl launched into his presentation, Herzl kept wondering how much of it actually registered. As it turned out, however, he could have saved himself the trouble; he was preaching to someone long since converted and ardently in favor of territorial independence for the Jews. There was simply nothing to argue about, and with his straightforward lack of pretension, Zangwill passed on instead to practical matters. He drew up a list of possible contacts and promised to get in touch with Colonel Goldsmid, the man whom Herzl had already tagged as a key figure in his enterprise.

It was a heartening surprise, and one he was to have time and again in England. Almost everyone he met seemed to take the basic premises of Zionism for granted and received him with a warmth and cordiality in stark contrast to the open or half-concealed hostility he had thus far encountered everywhere in Austria and France. High tea at Chief Rabbi Adler's house provided some clues: "All very English, but suffused with Jewish tradition. Here I got a strong feeling that Judaism need not seem ridiculous, as it does back home, where the heart has gone out of Jewish practices. And so, like the others, I put on my top hat after the meal and listened to the rabbi's blessings. Of course, I had told him, as I told Zadok Kahn and Guedemann, that I was not acting out of any religious impulse. But after all, I shall certainly honor the faith of my forefathers at least as much as any other."

Adler passed him on to Sir Samuel Montagu, financier, Member of Parliament, philanthropist, and strictly observant Jew, who received Herzl in his palatial mansion for a kosher Sunday dinner served by three liveried footmen. Two years earlier, as an active member of Hoveve Zion—the Lovers of Zion—he had approached the Turkish Sultan about a possible Jewish settlement in Transjordan, and it was clear from the start that he, too, needed no persuading. In strict confidence he told Herzl that he felt more Israelite than English, and that he would settle in Palestine with his whole family but, in view of his age, could not commit himself to any active involvement. One thing, however, he made crystal-clear: Argentina was out. Palestine, or nothing.

In one form or another, Herzl was to hear the same point repeated wherever he went. The mystical appeal of Zionism in England, among Jews and non-Jews alike, was rooted in a deep reverence for the Bible, whether as Holy Scripture, prophecy, mythology, or the wellspring of language and literature. There could be no Promised Land other than Palestine, and no ingathering of the exiles anywhere but in the ancestral home. Herzl himself was still leaning toward Argentina, whether for purely practical reasons, as he maintained, or out of a need to demonstrate his detachment from tribal sentimentality. But in England he was for the first time forcefully made aware that what inspired Jews was not the blueprint of utopia but the dream of Jerusalem; a Jewish state in South America or sub-Saharan Africa struck most of them as absurd. Then again, what he envisaged was a state for the Jews rather than a Jewish state, a distinction not sufficiently appreciated at the time. And for a man with his faith in the power of symbols, stage props, and dramatics, he seemed curiously slow to recognize and harness the mystique of a 2,000-year-old dream.

On November 24, he found himself the featured speaker at a dinner of the Maccabeans, a club founded in 1891 by London professionals to promote Jewish interests. Introduced by Zangwill, Herzl spoke partly in German, partly in French, while a German-speaking rabbi summarized his remarks in English. Yet despite these communications barriers, he seems to have made a profound impression and, by acclamation, was inducted as an honorary member of the club.

The incident is of some significance. For the first time he found himself on stage, facing an audience directly rather than manipulating its emotions from behind the scenes. Nothing in his writings conveys the spellbinding force of his personality attested to by all who knew him, including enemies and opponents. It was in England that he first became conscious of his power to move people as an actor in his own play.

The following day he took the train to Cardiff for a visit with Colonel Goldsmid, commanding officer of the regimental district. It was the emotional high point of his visit.

Albert Edward Williamson Goldsmid was George Eliot's Daniel Deronda in the flesh. Born in 1846 and raised as a Christian, he and his wife converted to Orthodox Judaism upon discovering that his late father had been Jewish. In 1892, he spent a year in Baron Hirsch's Argentine colonies; the experience merely reinforced his belief that the redemption of the Jews was possible only in Palestine. He was fortunate to be serving in an army traditionally hospitable to brilliant eccentrics, religious fanatics, mystics, and plain madmen, from Gordon and Lawrence to Montgomery and Wingate; Goldsmid, though neither quite mad nor quite brilliant, belonged to that same breed of crusaders out of time and place. Enraptured by the mystique and romance of the Bible, he fancied himself something of a Joshua reborn; he had organized the British Hoveve Zion along paramilitary lines and cherished vague dreams of reconquering the land of his reclaimed forefathers at the head of a Jewish army.

Everything about the man, from his military rank and bearing to his romantic personal history, was designed to arouse Herzl's ecstatic admiration. The colonel received him cordially, introduced him to his family, and listened patiently when, after lunch, Herzl mercilessly read him the complete outline of his plan in a language of which his listener had only the most rudimentary knowledge. But it hardly mattered. Once he caught on to the gist of what Herzl was trying to convey, Goldsmid exclaimed: "That is the idea of my life." And while, as a British officer, he could not assume the leadership of a political organization, he was fully prepared to resign his commission once the movement took shape and join the Jewish army. His only objection was to the word "Jews"; he preferred "Israelites" because the term encompassed all twelve tribes.

Back again in London, Herzl met with some of the most active members of the Jewish community. But though they were sympathetic, they refused to commit themselves to any concrete action without first consulting with the real power centers of British Jewry, men like Rothschild, Mocatta, and Montefiore. And yet the incidental result of that particular meeting far exceeded in importance anything Herzl could have hoped to accomplish by organizing a committee. One of the participants was Asher Myers, editor of the *Jewish Chronicle*, the oldest and most widely read Jewish periodical in England. Myers asked Herzl to send him a summary of the pamphlet he planned to write, suitable for advance publication in the *Chronicle*. Herzl promised to get to work on it as soon as he was back home.

He left London on November 28 in high spirits but arrived in Paris with a severe bronchitis, as diagnosed by Nordau, who warned him that "a prophet has to have good lungs." To which Herzl replied that, in that case, no man could be a prophet wearing his kind of a topcoat in the British climate.

Feeling sick and desperately anxious to get started on his pamphlet, he stayed in Paris only long enough to pay another courtesy call on Zadok Kahn but refused to see any other French Jews. "I expect absolutely nothing from them," he told the rabbi.

The time for palavering was over. He now had more urgent things to do.

FIFTEEN

*H*erzl spent the next three weeks laboring over his pamphlet, re-working the ideas of the Rothschild letter, paring them down to fundamentals and, above all, formulating them in a language of lapidary simplicity—an appeal to reason rather than emotion. This, as he was anxious to make clear from page 1, was no utopian romance à la Bellamy, nor did he have anything in common with his colleague and semi-namesake Theodor Hertzke, former financial editor of the *Neue Freie Presse*, who some years earlier had perpetrated a fatuous fantasy about a Central African utopia. What he proposed was a strictly scientific plan of action, the logic of which seemed to him compelling beyond argument.

By the end of the year he had finished the manuscript, extracted a summary for publication in the London *Jewish Chronicle*, and been categorically turned down by two German publishers, one Jewish, the other Gentile. The Jew objected to the contents, the Gentile felt it would not sell. But the Vienna bookseller and occasional publisher Max Breitenstein liked the idea, and though he, too, entertained no great hopes for a commercial success, he agreed to take a chance. On January 19, 1896, they signed the contract for what Herzl, in a last-minute inspiration, decided to call *Der Judenstaat—An Attempt at a Modern Solution of the Jewish Question*.

He had transformed the dream into a blueprint; his job was done. Let others lay the bricks. "Calmly I now return to my literary projects," he noted that night in his diary. "First of all I am going to rework *The*

Ghetto" (D, 1/19/96). A thought probably inspired by anxiety more than relief; in any case, it quickly became evident that oblivion was one thing he would have no cause to fret about.

The London *Jewish Chronicle* of January 17 devoted two full pages to Herzl's summary. Reaction was lukewarm and slow in London, swift and sardonic in Vienna. The secretary of the Jewish community buttonholed Herzl two days later to tell him that he had received an inquiry from London asking if the author of that utopian *Chronicle* piece was identical with the well-known Viennese journalist. "I told him I didn't think so, because I know Dr. Herzl as a thoroughly rational person." The *Schlagobers* wits of the literary cafés were sharpening their fangs, and the hilarity soon spread beyond those esoteric circles when, in mid-February, the *Oesterreichische Wochenschrift*, published by the Jewish politician and ex-deputy Samuel Joseph Bloch, printed a full translation of the *Chronicle* excerpt.

The "Jewish Jules Verne," though he may not have remained entirely unfazed by this explosion of Viennese *esprit*, put up a good front. But on February 1, he distributed the first galley proofs of the complete *Judenstaat*, and the furor it unleashed in the editorial offices of the *Neue Freie Presse* proved much harder to put up with. It also disabused him of any lingering illusions about the value of the promises he had been given. Bacher and Benedikt were incensed; they urged him to desist from what they saw as a potentially devastating blow not *for* but *against* the Jews while there still was time. Bacher accused Herzl of furnishing ammunition to the anti-Semites by subscribing to their view of the Jews as an unassimilable alien element—an argument echoed a few days later in a pained letter from Herzl's old friend Arthur Levysohn, editor in chief of the *Berliner Tageblatt*. Benedikt was less subtle and more insistent; he in effect offered Herzl a bribe to stop printing and scrap all copies. Given his superior intelligence and long-time familiarity with Herzl's intransigent character, his behavior can only be ascribed to a genuine panic reaction on his part. When it failed, he switched to a mix of lofty pieties and veiled threats. No individual, he argued, had a right to start an avalanche likely to endanger a whole community. Furthermore, by wrecking his own reputation, Herzl was also undermining the standing of the *Neue Freie Presse*. Paying lip service to Herzl's "right to publish," he warned him as a friend, counseled him as an experienced editor, and finally, in utter frustration, delivered himself of a non sequitur that tells much about the true state of his soul: "You're not even an Austrian," he spluttered. "You are a Hungarian." The discussion ended on this odd note, with Benedikt suggesting that the pamphlet at least be published anonymously. Which, as Herzl was quick to point out, would have been not only cowardly but futile as well.

It was, of course, clear to all concerned that at stake in these arguments was not the fate of Austrian Jewry but the career of Theodor Herzl, or at least his future on the *Neue Freie Presse*. And while he could remain indifferent to the mockery of fools, the hostility of his mentors troubled him far more than the implicit threat seemed to warrant. Financially and professionally he was no longer dependent on the *Neue Freie Presse*, but his emotional dependence on its editors engendered conflicts of loyalty the more corrosive for being largely unconscious. For weeks he suffered from insomnia, palpitations, and shortness of breath, which he chose to blame on worries over job, family, and the forthcoming publication of *Der Judenstaat*.

Yet not all the responses were hostile. He received a few encouraging messages from London and Paris, qualified praise from a Berlin Jewish periodical, but the most significant support came from within Vienna itself, though its significance still eluded him. On February 9, he was invited to a meeting at the Jewish Academic Reading Hall, where he gave an extemporaneous one-hour speech before an enthusiastic crowd of university students, several of whom called on him the next day to express their admiration. He was pleased, as much by their reaction as by this new proof of his power to sway an audience. But gratification aside, the incident did not provide much comfort; however flattering the acclaim by a group of impetuous and impecunious Jewish students, the men he wanted to inspire and persuade were the elite of wealth and power; they alone were in a position to provide the support he needed.

On February 14, five hundred bound copies of *Der Judenstaat* were delivered to the Herzl apartment, his personal share of the first edition. The publisher, skeptical about the commercial prospects of the booklet, had limited the first printing to three thousand copies. "When I had the bundle dragged to my room, I was deeply shaken. This bundle constitutes the tangible evidence of my decision. My whole life may now take a new turn" (D, 2/14/96).

Der Judenstaat is the vision of a secular prophet claiming science rather than divinity as the source of his inspiration. Much like the author of *The Communist Manifesto,* Herzl presented his version of paradise as a strictly rational proposition, the only alternative to apocalyptic disaster. But unlike Marx, he went out of his way to avoid vatic eloquence and dialectic subtlety; he wanted his language to reflect what he saw as the compelling simplicity of his argument, and in this he succeeded. He even made a point of stressing his academic credentials: all editions authorized in his lifetime gave the author as Theodor Herzl, Doctor of Law—as opposed to the Theodor Herzl who wrote feuilletons for the *Neue Freie Presse.*

Yet despite its tone of measured sobriety and its frequent invocation of popular science, the intellectual content of this lawyer's brief left much to be desired. Herzl's analysis of the Jewish problem was hopelessly superficial, while his proposed solution ignored fundamental social, economic, and political realities. Jews, in his view, were defined as such by anti-Semites rather than by their own background and traditions, which on the whole he dismissed as the burden and baggage of exile. It was because anti-Semitism seemed ineradicable, deeply ingrained in folklore and myth, and, moreover, justifiable as a defense against alien dominance that Jews needed a land of their own in which to become a people like any other. That this was a goal devoutly to be aspired to was something Herzl took for granted.

Not that there was anything specifically Jewish about the "aristocratic republic," which he proposed to model on medieval Venice because "a people anywhere is nothing but a collection of overgrown children, though susceptible to education" and "politics must be handled at the top." The language question would eventually be settled on the Swiss pattern, since "we cannot, after all, talk Hebrew with one another. Who among us knows enough Hebrew to ask for a train ticket? . . . But the language of the ghetto, that stunted and twisted jargon, is something we must get rid of."

He did recognize that "our national community is a peculiar and unique one, and in essence only the faith of our forefathers still holds us together. But does this mean that we will end up with a theocracy? Not at all. We are not going to give our clergy even the slightest chance to assert their whims. We shall confine them to their temples, just as we shall confine our professional army to the barracks. Army and clergy will enjoy high honors. . . . But they will have no business mixing in the affairs of the state, because their interference could only make for trouble both internal and external."

One prediction that certainly came true with a vengeance, and not the only one, either.

The economy of *Der Judenstaat*, a modified mixed welfare state and free-enterprise system with a seven-hour workday, a state-run labor exchange, and strong emphasis on industrialization over agriculture, was to be based on the theories of the then prominent Vienna School, about as remote from any contact with reality as most economic theories anywhere. It was only in discussing the actual mechanics of the exodus that both Herzl's legal background and his organizational talent came into play. The "Society of Jews" was to be "the new Moses," an appointed body charged with acquiring a suitable territory and managing the enterprise, while the "Jewish Company" (Herzl used the English terms in the original) would deal with the financing. In somewhat modified form, this outline actually served as the basic structure of the Zionist organization.

Though at the time he was still vacillating between Palestine and Argentina, a national flag seemed to him among the more urgent priorities. "If you want to lead a crowd, you have to raise a symbol above their heads. I am thinking of a white flag with gold stars. The white field symbolizes the pure new life, the stars represent the seven golden hours of our working day." And finally, as a man weaned on tales of knightly valor and battlefield glory, he knew that "universal brotherhood cannot even be considered a beautiful dream. Man needs the enemy to spur him on to his greatest effort." The competitive spirit, carried to its logical conclusion.

It is easy enough to scoff at the simpleminded naïveté that characterizes so much of *Der Judenstaat*, and many of Herzl's own contemporaries did so with gleeful zest. But the mockery misses its target, and not just because, as prophets go, Herzl's record is better than most: his two major predictions—the ineluctable triumph of anti-Semitism and the establishment of the Jewish state—both came true within the half century following his death. Even thoughtful criticism—of which there was some—is ultimately beside the point, because the measure of a manifesto is not its intellectual profundity but its emotional impact. And while Herzl may have meant to dazzle the rich and persuade the powerful by a scholarly disquisition, what he produced instead was a manifesto.

As such, *Der Judenstaat* was a masterpiece, an impassioned plea on behalf of Jewish nationalism—not the first, but far and away the most persuasive. Giving vent to his own sense of frustration, he told the Jews that after all these years they had never left the ghetto and were not going to unless they did it on their own. The most powerful message of *Der Judenstaat* was one of pride and defiance: Stop trying to be other than what you are; be proud to be a Jew, just as the German is proud to be a German. Simple to the point of banality, but for many Jews it radically changed the way they saw themselves.

This, however, took time to sink in. Meanwhile, the more immediate reaction was embarrassment, indignation, and shock.

Benedikt's frenzied attempts to block the publication of *Der Judenstaat* only proved how keenly the editor was attuned to the sentiments of his readers; Vienna's Jewish bourgeoisie was profoundly upset. What troubled them most about this tract were not its crazy ideas—crazier ones were being peddled along the Graben every night of the week— but its crazy author. With Lueger's Jew-baiting hordes at the gates— in the municipal elections of February 27 they scored another victory, rolling up huge majorities even in the Jewish district of Leopoldstadt— they feared that the prestige of this once brilliant journalist gone mad would lend credibility to arguments all but indistinguishable from those used by the anti-Semites.

Nor were these fears unfounded. One of the first reviews of *Der Judenstaat* appeared on February 25 in the *Westungarischer Grenzbote*, a nasty little rag published in Bratislava by Ivan von Simonyi, a notorious anti-Semite and member of the Hungarian Diet. Simonyi praised both the booklet and its author to the skies and got so carried away by his enthusiasm that, a month later, he paid Herzl a personal visit: "My weird follower, the Bratislava anti-Semite Ivan von Simonyi, came to see me. A hypermercurial, hyperloquacious sexagenarian with an uncanny sympathy for the Jews. Swings back and forth between perfectly rational talk and utter nonsense, believes in the blood libel and at the same time comes up with the most sensible modern ideas. Loves me" (D, 3/30/96).

The major papers, on the other hand, followed the lead of the *Neue Freie Presse* by giving the book the silent treatment, *totschweigen*— silencing to death—being a well-entrenched Austrian tradition of not coming to grips with unpleasantness. An exception was the *Wiener Allgemeine Zeitung*, which ran a derisive cartoon and a review by

Herzl's old pal Julius von Ludassy attacking Zionism as desperate insanity. Most of Ludassy's readers shared this point of view—the main reason, as he admitted to Herzl, why he had felt obliged to adopt it even though it did not represent his personal feelings. On the café circuit, the idea of a Jewish state headed by a *Presse* editor turned Messiah was always good for a laugh, another time-tested recipe for avoiding coherent thought. Hermann Bahr, the erstwhile Jew-baiter turned philo-Semite, declared himself opposed to Herzl because Vienna could simply not do without the Jews, an illusion indulged in by most of the city's Jews themselves until disabused by the *Anschluss* of 1938.

Few, however, actually read the book. Nordau expressed his for once unqualified admiration with uncharacteristic effusiveness, the poet Beer-Hofmann was enraptured, but Arthur Schnitzler raised principled objections to any sort of nationalism, Jewish or otherwise, a sentiment echoed in the highest quarters. "What would have become of this ungrateful Herzl without equal rights for Jews?" the Emperor is reported to have asked one of his ministers. "A curse on all these nationalist movements." Badeni, to whom Herzl had rushed a copy of the book along with a covering letter requesting a private audience, never bothered to reply. The high and mighty whom Herzl had most wanted to impress not only remained unimpressed but clearly dismissed him as a crank. Not a single one responded.

Like most prophets, he found himself preaching to the converted. What he as yet failed to realize was just how many converts were already out there in the wilderness, waiting for the message. Having discovered Zionism, Herzl was about to discover the Zionists.

Nothing comes closer to the miraculous than the speed with which the literary editor of the *Neue Freie Presse* established himself within a matter of months as the leader, spokesman, and standard-bearer of secular Jewish nationalism. He had no mass media to promote instant celebrity and name recognition, no TV screens to project his photogenic image into towns and villages that were anything but global. The people at whom he beamed the modest three thousand copies of his appeal for the most part ignored him. And yet, by the end of the year, Herzl, whether hailed as another Moses or denounced as another madman, was known throughout Europe, from the Pale of Settlement to the slums of Whitechapel.

Objective factors offer a partial explanation, foremost among them the *Judennot*—the misery of the Jews—which Herzl compared to a head of steam that would drive the engine he had designed. The misery was infinitely greater and far more acute even than he realized when he wrote his pamphlet; it took a while for him to revise his parochial notion of the Jews as an essentially middle-class society. But what the poverty-stricken masses of Eastern Europe dreamed of were the flesh-pots of the Western world rather than the arid wastes of their ancestral land—emigration, chiefly to America, averaged 15,000 annually throughout the decade and doubled in the 1890s.

It was, in fact, Herzl's own class of at least moderately affluent Jews who most keenly experienced that other *Judennot*—the emotional privation of the outsider branded as such and unable to come to terms with his fate. Religion was no longer the issue, not for the Jews, and not for their adversaries. They could become Christians; they could never become Germans. The rising tide of nationalism, and the racial anti-Semitism that was its inevitable concomitant, had effectively put an end to the twin hopes of emancipation and assimilation. It had left the Jews stranded in a no-man's-land, cut off from their roots but barred from striking new ones in "enemy territory." However tenuous their links to the values and practices of traditional Judaism, they were identified as Jews—an identification meaningless enough to engender an identity crisis of major proportions, particularly among the younger generation farthest removed from ancestral traditions. This was the *Judennot* which *Der Judenstaat* tapped into with its stirring answer: "We are a *people*, one people."

The second factor contributing to Herzl's rapid if controversial rise was the existence of long-established Zionist trends and movements not only in Eastern Europe but also in the West, specifically including Vienna itself. Aside from individual idealists and activists who through-out the nineteenth century propounded Zionist ideas and, in many instances, actually settled in Palestine, practical efforts included the establishment of an agricultural school as well as a growing movement for the revival of Hebrew as a first step toward restoring not only a national language but a national consciousness. A number of Hebrew newspapers and journals with a strongly nationalist slant had begun to make their appearance as part of the Jewish Enlightenment. Thus, unbeknownst to Herzl, the Hebrew monthly *Ha-Shahar* (*The Dawn*) was being published right in his own Vienna by the Odessa-born novelist Peretz Smolenskin as early as 1869. Smolenskin died in 1885;

not only would he have known how to ask for a railroad ticket in Hebrew but he also wrote Hebrew novels that enjoyed a sizable readership.

But it was the wave of pogroms following the assassination of Alexander II in March of 1881 that created a major upheaval in the attitudes of the Jewish intelligentsia in Russia. That Russian peasants could be induced to kill Jews came as no surprise to them; what shattered their illusions about their own future in a liberal Russia was the eloquent silence of their Russian counterparts; Tolstoy's voice was almost the only one raised in protest.

Part of the response was the rise of the Hoveve Zion—the Lovers of Zion, the first frankly nationalist movement organized to promote Jewish resettlement in Palestine. "Organized" may be too strong a word. The leaders, men like Smolenskin, Gordon, Pinsker, Ahad Ha-Am, Lilienblum, were idealists of great moral and intellectual stature; but while they shared a common passion for the cause, they were just as passionately dedicated to their own often widely divergent views about how best to serve it. Much of their energy was dissipated in polemics and arguments. Nevertheless, by the time Herzl came on the scene, the movement had established nineteen settlements in Palestine. All of them, however, remained heavily dependent on support from either the Rothschilds or independent philanthropy, so that in due course fund-raising came to preempt all other Hoveve Zion activities and sapped its vitality. Even so, its various chapters, factions, and individual followers, scattered throughout Europe, maintained loose contact and formed a ready communications network.

There was, however, another network, informal and generally overlooked but ultimately far more important—the masses of Russian-Jewish students, refugees from czarist oppression and institutionalized anti-Semitism. They were a conspicuous presence at almost every major institution of higher learning in Western Europe, ideologically fragmented but passionate in their commitment to causes ranging from anarchism and socialism to Jewish nationalism. Zionist student groups had in fact been active at all major academic centers in Germany, Switzerland, and Austria since at least the early 1880s. They maintained close contact, not only among themselves, but also with their like-minded comrades back home.

While these developments all played their part in Herzl's cometlike rise to prominence and preeminence, they do not fully explain it. In fact, no strictly rational explanation can fully do justice to the all-important but intangible elements that mark the difference between Herzl and all his predecessors: the impact of his personality and of his background.

Thus Leo Pinsker's *Auto-Emancipation*, published in Germany in 1882, was an in many ways more profound and sophisticated analysis of the Jewish Question than *Der Judenstaat*. ("Too bad I didn't read that pamphlet before I published my own," Herzl noted on February 10, 1896. "On the other hand, perhaps it was just as well; I might never have tackled the job.") The proposed solution was at least equally cogent, and Pinsker himself, a physician and member of the Odessa intelligentsia, had solid Jewish credentials and extensive contacts among the young Jewish activists of the 1880s, yet he never became an effective leader. There were a number of equally prominent figures, more ambitious than Pinsker and eager to assume leading roles. But although they shaped the moral and intellectual orientation of Zionism for generations, not one of them, in a lifetime of dedication to the cause, inspired the fervor and devotion that this newcomer generated in the few brief years left to him.

In Vienna itself, a small, more or less organized Zionist movement had existed for nearly two decades. In fact, Nathan Birnbaum, one of its founders, is generally credited with having been the originator of the word "Zionism," the one solid achievement in a career full of bizarre convolutions that led from traditional piety via Zionism and socialism to venomous anti-Zionism and ultraorthodoxy. Within a little band of uncommonly contentious and opinionated individualists, the hot-tempered and hirsute Birnbaum—he died in 1937—probably qualified as the most volatile and aggressive.

The main focus of Jewish nationalism in Vienna, however, was the Jewish fraternity Kadimah, organized in 1882 with help from both Smolenskin and Pinsker. The original membership consisted almost exclusively of immigrants and expatriates, but with the steady rise of anti-Semitism at the university, the exotic and militant little band began to attract its quota of native students. In 1888, the fraternity adopted dueling, not to ape an inane German custom, but to refute charges of Jewish cowardice. They succeeded so well that an umbrella organization of German fraternities finally felt constrained to declare Jews as by definition *satisfaktionsunfähig*—not worthy of being given satisfaction.

Although the vast majority of students remained indifferent or hostile, the Vienna Kadimah set the pace and pattern for a whole host of similar Jewish student organizations that sprang up all over Germany and Austria in the years just before Herzl's conversion. Disciples awaiting the Master, they were to play a crucial role in spreading the word.

It seems doubtful if Herzl, even had he known more than he did about these developments, would have been able to resist the impulse that drove him. But his innocence had the practical advantage of having kept him clear of prior entanglements with any of the warring factions and personalities within the overall movement, such as he found it. His determination to maintain this distance, to rise above the often petty, sometimes fundamental differences that divided the movement, and to knock heads together when the need arose, was the instinctive reflex of the born leader and one of the secrets of his instant success.

On March 1, he had his first encounter with three top luminaries of Viennese Zionism, come to claim their new convert:

> The Zionists Birnbaum, Jakob Kohn, and Landau paid me a joint visit and squabbled among themselves. Kohn is against Landau, Kadimah against Gamalah [a rival Zionist fraternity]. Birnbaum wants propaganda confined to scholarly weeklies, Landau wants to agitate everywhere, Kohn only in Vienna. It is downright disheartening to see their petty hostility toward one another. Birnbaum is clearly jealous of me. What the coarser Jews openly accuse me of, i.e., that I am in this only for personal gain, is what I hear in the insinuations of this educated and refined person. The predicted rancor within and without is already here. I regard Birnbaum as jealous, vain, and dogmatic. I understand that he was already on his way from Zionism to socialism when my appearance brought him back to Zion. [D, 3/1/96]

Three days later, Birnbaum came begging for money and intrigued against Landau. Herzl gave him 20 guilders, an act of charity he carefully recorded in his diary (and later struck out) "because I am sure he is hostile toward me and will become more so." Landau accused Birnbaum of plotting to become the socialist leader of Palestine. "We don't even have a country yet, and already they want to tear it apart" (D, 3/4/96).

Nevertheless, there were more uplifting experiences, notably a student *Kommers*, a formal reunion of the Vienna Kadimah in his honor, attended by over a thousand people. Herzl went out of his way to preach moderation and urged them to concentrate on their studies. "I did not want to arouse any boozy enthusiasm." The appeal went largely unheeded; from the ranks of Kadimah came some of his earliest and most devoted followers. They formed the nucleus of his personal staff and proved indispensable in the organizational effort preceding the first Zionist congress. Isidor Schalit, one of their leaders, recalls in his memoirs how "we surrounded him, guarded him, did not leave him alone for a single minute. We established contacts with Zionists in other countries, collected thousands of signatures, organized deputations, etc. It was only many years later that we became aware of what we had accomplished with our efforts" (Ms, CZA).

The few but influential Hoveve Zion members in Germany were more restrained in their initial reaction to *Der Judenstaat*. They welcomed the rather sensational evolution of a prominent assimilationist but criticized the elegiac utopianism and the sacrilegious mention of Argentina as a possible alternative to Palestine. Moreover, they were also put off by Herzl's failure to pay tribute to his predecessors, and it was not until they had made personal contact some months later that their reserve gave way to wholehearted support.

The long-embattled veteran Zionists of Russia, however, reacted with frank suspicion and a sense of outrage. Born skeptics, stridently polemical as a matter of course, they fell upon this usurper coming out of nowhere who had the gall to claim credit for an idea to which they had already devoted years of their lives. In the Warsaw Hebrew weekly *Hatsefirah*, Nahum Sokolow launched an attack headlined WONDERFUL RUMORS ABOUT THE ESTABLISHMENT OF A JEWISH STATE ORIGINATING FROM THE MIND OF A DR. HERZL. *Der Judenstaat*, as they read it, contained nothing that had not been said time and again. More important, there was nothing Jewish about this Viennese-flavored Venetian republic, nor, for that matter, its prospective ruler, who displayed such a staggering ignorance of Judaism and the Jews. That this ignorance extended to their own work and accounted for Herzl's failure to give them due credit was, however, something they refused to believe until they met him in person.

To the common people in the ghettos of Eastern Europe, on the other hand, unencumbered by personal vanity and Talmudic sophistry, news of *Der Judenstaat* came as a revelation. Herr Doktor Herzl of

Vienna, famous author and journalist, who from his photograph gazed upon them like Moses incarnate, who spoke High German and consorted with ministers and kings, seemed a far more credible Messiah than *heimish* Dr. Pinsker from Odessa and similar homegrown Yiddish prophets, the likes of whom could be found in every *shtetl* by the wagonload. To them, the twin message of *Der Judenstaat* came across loud and clear: "We are a *people*" and "Next year in Jerusalem." A ray of light in a world of darkness.

The sudden attention he received from enthusiasts, new converts, and veteran Zionists was almost as disconcerting to Herzl as the vituperative hostility with which dominant Jewish opinion in the West greeted his book. The suffering masses of Russia were still an abstraction to him, Pharaoh's slaves waiting in mute passivity to be led out of czarist Egypt by the likes of himself. That the reality was far more complicated he had yet to discover. Student groups in Vienna and Berlin asked him to speak; he turned down all invitations, and he refused to engage in polemics with his critics, still undecided—or so, at least, he told himself—whether to assume an active role in the implementation of his plan. Above all, he was most anxious not to stir up disorder and popular enthusiasm; he still saw "the masses" as a powerful monster, useful when properly harnessed and led, but dangerous when aroused. Moreover, he found himself in fundamental disagreement with the Zionist activists on a question of principle: where they wanted to found Jewish settlements, he wanted to found a Jewish state. Their goal was to bring as many Jews as possible into Turkish-ruled Palestine, in the hope that they would someday form a majority, whereas he was—and remained—adamantly opposed to any devious and partial approaches. "I have grateful admiration for what the Zionists have done so far, but I am opposed to infiltration on principle," he wrote to the German Zionist leader Max Bodenheimer, turning down his invitation to address a Berlin rally. "Infiltration, if allowed to proceed, will only increase the value of the land and make it that much harder for us to acquire. The notion of declaring our independence 'as soon as we are strong enough over there' I regard as illusory, because the great powers would never sanction it even if by then the Porte were to have weakened sufficiently" (D, 5/24/96).

This did not stop students, Zionist old-timers, new would-be disciples, cranks, and *shnorrers* from beating a path to his home and office. Jews in Zemun, Sophia, and Kolomea assured him that they had their bags packed and were ready to follow wherever he led. The adulation flattered him; it did not make up for the conspiratorial silence of the daily press, the stinging attacks by German and Austrian patriots of the Mosaic faith, the snide jokes and ugly rumors about him circulating in what had once been his social set. Above all, it did nothing to advance his cause. What he needed was access to money and power; the rest would follow.

With his eyes still firmly fixed on a political solution from above, he completely missed the significance of what was happening down below.

SIXTEEN

Beginning with the ecstatic June days of 1895 and ending with his last official letter, written in May 1904, seven weeks before his death, Herzl kept a detailed account of his life for, with, and on behalf of the "Jewish cause." These notes, which eventually added up to eighteen volumes of about 280 pages each, filled with his precise, admirably legible handwriting, are now in the Central Zionist Archives in Jerusalem. They offer a unique perspective on the history of modern Zionism as seen by the man instrumental in its genesis.

Though commonly referred to as diaries, they are in fact both more and less—a hybrid mix of reportage, random thoughts, and observations, drafts or copies of letters, pen portraits, forays into fantasy, and occasional literary flourishes. Equally hybrid were the motives that made Herzl persist through nine frenetic years in what was clearly a labor of obsession; drained as he often was by the demands on his time and energy, nothing kept him for long from the notebooks he carried around with him wherever he went.

One of his aims was to assure his proper place in history, a legitimate enough ambition for a writer turned prophet and struggling to translate literary inspiration into practical politics. The diaries are his romance with history, one of the earliest examples of a genuine non-fiction novel, and as in most of his writings, he again cast himself as the hero. But it is this very self-involvement that highlights the ever-ambiguous role of the individual in shaping the course of history.

Yet the diaries, as Herzl conceived them, were also his bid for literary immortality. He arranged for their posthumous publication and deliberately set out to write for posterity; all too many passages reflect his self-conscious attempt to address future generations. The most conspicuous defect of the diaries as literature, however, is once again the narcissistic egocentricity that handicapped Herzl as a playwright. It resulted in a focus narrow to the point of tunnel vision, and in a simplistic perception of people based on their attitude toward him that does not favor subtle character shadings.

Much has been made of his candor, and it may well be argued that he meant to be as unsparing of himself as he often was of others. Many of the passages already cited make it patently obvious that he did not hesitate to express ideas he knew to be farfetched or foolish. But in a man as rigidly defended as he was, devoid of introspection and incapable of genuine self-irony, candor involves no great risk. Thus there are virtually no extended glimpses of his private life, itself a devastating comment on its place in his thoughts and emotions.

In light of this reticence concerning his personal affairs, the all too emphatically casual entry of March 17, 1896, merits special attention: "Dr. Beck, my parents' family physician, examined me and diagnosed a heart ailment caused by excitement. He can't understand why I would want to get involved in the Jewish cause, and no one else in his circle can understand it, either" (D, 3/12/96).

Dr. Bernhard Beck, a retired former military surgeon in the Turkish Army, may not have been the ideal choice, but his diagnosis as such was probably accurate. The heart defect noted as early as 1879 by army medical boards on two separate occasions—possibly a mitral stenosis—had apparently begun to affect cardiac functions. The mysterious illness of the year before may well have triggered a process of decompensation, nor can the possibility of latent lupus erythematosus be excluded. But if stress played a part, as it undoubtedly did, Dr. Beck's flatfooted intervention merely added to an already heavy load. His verdict confronted Herzl with the choice of either giving up the dream or killing himself for it. He never hesitated for a moment; but in addition to all the other pressures bearing in on him from all sides— Zionist politics, public ridicule, constant job worries, and the mounting hysteria of a wife who felt betrayed and abandoned—he was now haunted as well by the sense of living on borrowed time, and there is something both heroic and suicidal in the reckless abandon with which he threw himself into his work, redoubled his efforts, and drove himself relentlessly, draining his physical and nervous resources past any hope of recovery. Among other things, the diaries were the record of his struggle to make sense of his life and to come to terms with his death.

It gradually dawned on him that renegotiating the Covenant was a lost cause; the idea of a Promised Land in Africa or South America struck most of his new followers as utterly absurd. In a sense, this simplified his task; it now came down to buying territory from the Turks and obtaining international guarantees for an independent Jewish Palestine. Two men held the keys to the solution—the Turkish Sultan and the German Kaiser. Herzl felt confident that, given a chance to present his proposals, he could convince both rulers of the enormous advantages that would accrue to them from his solution to the Jewish Question. The problem was how to procure that chance. It meant penetrating the maze of entrenched bureaucracies that protected, isolated, and imprisoned these two autocrats. He was still plotting a number of devious approaches when, late in February, Saul Raphael Landau came up with some eminently practical suggestions.

Though ten years younger than Herzl, the Cracow-born Landau was already a Zionist veteran. A prolific publicist, journalist, and sometime lawyer, gregarious, fluent in Polish, Yiddish, Hebrew, and German, he wrote for a variety of Jewish and Polish publications and maintained extensive contacts among journalists and politicians. He had been closely associated with the volatile Birnbaum, though the partnership of these two prickly and inflated egos was never less than uneasy. While Birnbaum, bent on defending his turf, instantly resented Herzl as an interloper and rival, Landau grasped the potential of this unlikely convert to the cause and let himself be charmed: "On February 16, 1896, Dr. Theodor Herzl, an editor of the *Neue Freie Presse*, invited me to come to see him in his office. I had thus far only known about him through his work. . . . I was most pleasantly surprised when, after a very cordial greeting, Herzl handed me a copy of his *Judenstaat* with a highly flattering dedication" (Landau, *Sturm und Drang*, p. 52). Landau promised to do what he could for the book in the Jewish and Polish press, the net result being a single favorable review in the Lvov *Gazeta Lwowska* on May 7. But it was he who forged the first links between Herzl and the student movement and provided the two contacts that proved crucial to Herzl's plans: he introduced him to the Reverend William Hechler, and to the Polish nobleman Philip Michael de Nevlinsky. Whether, in the long view, he thereby did him a favor may be argued, but it was precisely what Herzl himself most desperately wanted at the time and should be acknowledged in fairness to the movement's first public-relations man. Like so many others, Landau later broke with Herzl over issues both personal and political and was relegated to a footnote in Zionist history.

The most charitable view of the Reverend Hechler—and the one Herzl ultimately seems to have adopted—was of a harmless old crank who had the good fortune of being an ordained Anglican clergyman, a status that allowed for a fairly broad range of amiable eccentricities. And although in Hechler's case the eccentricities probably went beyond the merely amiable, florid madness could also be a distinct asset in certain social circles, then as now. Thus the reverend, born in India, German on his father's side, had at one time been employed as tutor at the court of the Grand Duke Friedrich of Baden, uncle of the Kaiser, and remained in duly deferential contact with his former master—one possible reason why Herzl's English teacher, punning on the name, called him a *Heuchler*, i.e., a hypocrite.

Formally the chaplain of the British embassy, he considered himself a lifelong "humble but impassioned" student of biblical prophecy, and an inspired reading of Revelation 11:2—"The holy city shall they tread under foot forty and two months"—had convinced him that the Second Coming was imminent. Defining a "prophetic month" as thirty years gave him a total of 1,260 years from the destruction to the resurrection of Jerusalem. The destruction of the Temple in A.D. 70 obviously did not fit his calculations, but he hit on the ingenious solution of using the conquest of the city by the Caliph Omar in 637–38 as his point of departure; this revealed 1897–98 as the target date for the Second Coming. When, in the third month of that year of destiny, Landau told him about *Der Judenstaat* and its author, he immediately took it as a sign from above that the action was about to begin.

He was ready. His highest ambition in life was to become Bishop of Jerusalem in time to welcome the Savior at the gate.

Just how ready, Herzl was to find out on a Sunday in mid-March, when he climbed four flights of stairs to a study lined with Bibles from floor to ceiling, where an apple-cheeked gnome with a wispy gray beard welcomed him with organ music. The rapturous reverend proudly displayed a paper model of the ancient Temple and proceeded to unfold four sections of a huge General Staff map of Palestine that covered the entire floor. The town of Bethel, by his calculations, was at the exact center of the country and would therefore have to be the site of the new Temple, whose construction he regarded as a matter of the highest priority. "You see, we prepared the way for you," he exclaimed.

It took Herzl some time before he could interrupt the bouncy little man long enough to bring the conversation around to his own priorities. Hechler, whatever ailed him, was far from stupid. He immediately grasped the issue and offered to talk to the Kaiser's brother, brother-in-law, and court chaplain, provided Herzl was willing to underwrite the trip to Berlin.

> Of course I agreed at once [writes Herzl]. It will come to several hundred guilders, no small sacrifice for a man in my circumstances. But a chance for a talk with the Kaiser is worth the risk. At that I realize that Hechler . . . may just be a penniless clergyman who likes to travel. . . . He is an improbable figure if viewed through the eyes of a cynical Viennese journalist. But I have to take into account the fact that people who are our opposite in every respect may well see him in an altogether different light. He won't have duped me, even if all he wants is to take a trip at my expense. But certain signs lead me to believe that he is sincere in his belief in prophecy. . . . He regards our departure for Jerusalem as imminent and showed me the coat pocket that would hold his big map as we travel about the Holy Land. That, to me, was his most naïve and most persuasive gesture yesterday. [D, 3/26/96]

For a month, the question of Hechler's sincerity remained in suspense. But in mid-April, the Kaiser paid a state visit to Vienna, followed by an overnight stay at the Karlsruhe castle of his uncle the Grand Duke and Hechler's former patron. Herzl attended a gala performance at the opera for the express purpose of studying the Emperor from up close in preparation for an audience, which in the end Hechler failed to obtain for him. But the clergyman, stubbornly determined to "fulfill the prophecy," trailed the Kaiser to Karlsruhe, taking with him a photograph of Herzl. "He obviously fears they might take me for a shabby Jew." The Kaiser himself remained unapproachable and left the next day, but Hechler stayed on until, at the end of the week, he had talked the Grand Duke into receiving the Scion of the House of

David. On April 21, he triumphantly summoned Herzl to Karlsruhe.

The ever-impatient Herzl, who had already written him off as a pious fraud, began in the meantime to have second thoughts about Baron Hirsch. That very morning he asked Nordau to try to repair the damage as best he could, but within an hour of mailing the letter he learned that Hirsch had died suddenly the night before on his estate in Hungary. "The pamphlet has been out for months. I sent it to everyone except Hirsch. The moment I decide to do so, he dies. His cooperation would have brought us success that much sooner. In any case, his death is a loss for the Jewish cause. He was the only one among the rich Jews willing to do something great for the poor ones. Maybe I didn't know how to handle him right. Maybe I should have written to Nordau two weeks ago. It seems to me that our cause is the poorer for the loss, because I kept thinking all the time that I would eventually bring Hirsch around to our side."

And a few hours later: "What a curious day. Hirsch dies, and I am about to deal with princes" (D, 4/21/96).

To deal with princes . . .

He had acquired more poise since the unfortunate encounter with Hirsch, learned to curb his arrogance and his rhetoric, become self-possessed and persuasive. Instead of furtively apologizing for his Jewishness, he now flaunted it in his dealings with ministers and politicians, with financiers and intellectuals of every stripe and persuasion.

But princes, German princes at that, were a different breed altogether. Even the hard-earned cynicism of the veteran journalist could not dispel the murky myths of knighthood and nobility he had imbibed with his mother's milk; the spell they continued to cast threatened to shake his new-won self-assurance. On the train, all the way to Karlsruhe, he suffered from a bad case of stage fright and again resorted to the diary in an effort to master his anxiety.

The fact that the Grand Duke sent for me is the most striking evidence that he—and consequently also the Kaiser, who visited him only three days ago—are taking the matter seriously. This is the most momentous, the most improbable turn of events. If true, it will hit the world like a thunderbolt. . . . The Jews have lost Hirsch, but they now have me. . . . Much will depend on the conversation, and on the impression I make on [the Duke]. Still, I cannot afford to get dizzy up on those heights. I shall think of death, and be earnest. I shall be cool, calm, firm, modest, but resolute in manner and in speech. [D, 4/22/96]

Hechler picked him up at the station, took him to the hotel, and reported on his encounter with the Kaiser, who had greeted him with a jovial "Hechler, I hear you want to become a minister in the Jewish state," adding a moment later, in English: "I wonder if the Rothschilds aren't behind this scheme."

The audience with the Grand Duke was scheduled for the following afternoon, and Herzl, as usual, gave considerable thought to his appearance, deciding against tails because "too formal a dress might be regarded as tactless in the circumstances, since the Grand Duke wished to see me incognito, so to speak. I therefore put on my trusty Prince Albert. Externals assume an ever greater importance, the higher one climbs. Everything becomes symbolic" (D, 4/23/96).

The interior of the castle more than lived up to his expectations. No trace here of effete artistic taste, as in the palace of the Jewish banker, but an Adjutants Hall "that took my breath away, after all. For there they stood in all their glory, the regimental flags, lined up in rank and file, encased in leather holsters, solemn and silent—the flags of 1870–71. On the wall behind them the picture of a military parade: the Grand Duke leading his troops in review past the Emperor Wilhelm I. Only then did it really hit me, so to speak, just where I was" (D, 4/23/96).

The Grand Duke himself, on the other hand, turned out to be a thoughtful and thoroughly unpretentious septuagenarian. He may not have been overly impressed by Hechler's double-entry numerology, but for sentiment's sake he made allowances for the quirks and foibles of his dead son's tutor. Even his unforced informality, however, could not put the overawed Herzl quite at ease, though he gave him ample time to present his case, listened attentively, and in the end raised an objection that did him honor: The Jews in the Duchy of Baden, he told Herzl, had always been exemplary citizens who knew they could count on him as a fair and unbiased ruler. He feared that they might misinterpret an endorsement of Herzl's plan as a change of heart on his part and think that he now wanted to get rid of them.

Herzl countered by saying that not all Jews had to leave, that Baden's Jews might do well to stay put, but that this was merely one more reason for establishing a Jewish state: "If the benevolence of His Royal

Highness toward the Jews becomes generally known, the influx of Jews would soon be on a scale that spells disaster."

The issue remained academic; the Grand Duke's position had become largely symbolic and ceremonial after the unification of Germany. Nor did family ties give him any real influence at the court of his self-willed nephew, as he tried to point out. When Herzl, pressing him to interest the Kaiser in the plan, said, "After all, Your Royal Highness is the Kaiser's adviser," he replied with a smile. "I give him advice, and he does what he pleases."

Objectively, the results of the audience were minimal. Though he turned down Herzl's request for introductions to the Kaiser and the Russian Czar, the Grand Duke graciously granted him permission to keep him informed about the progress of the enterprise. Herzl, however, still dazed and walking on clouds, felt that he had made an important convert. He was deeply grateful to Hechler, "and unless it later turns out that he was a double-dealer, after all, I want the Jews to bestow on him the full measure of their gratitude."

He was not a double-dealer, but he had his own agenda, in which the Jews figured only as unwitting instruments. "It is wonderful," he wrote to the Grand Duke (in English), "how these Jews are unconsciously fulfilling the Scriptures concerning the events, which the prophets tell us are to lead up to the Lord's Second Coming, and they are doing this just as unconsciously as their forefathers fulfilled God's prophecies when Christ came the first time and lived in Jerusalem" (Herzl, Hechler, the Grand Duke of Baden and the German Emperor, p. 44).

He professed a simpleminded faith that has its admirers. In the same letter, written on the way to Jerusalem in 1898, he mentions his visit with the German ambassador in Constantinople, "whose wife was my pupil at Karlsruhe. . . . I purpose telling him all about Mount Nebo and try to persuade him to have that whole district of East Jordan, near the Dead Sea, given to the Emperor of Germany by the Sultan, so that, when the Ark of the Covenant is found, His Majesty will possess it with the two tables of stone with the 10 Commandments written by God on Mount Sinai, and probably the original MS. of the 5 books of Moses, written by Moses, which were hid in the Ark and which will prove how foolishly so called 'Higher Criticism' tries to make out that Moses could not have written this and that, etc. etc." (ibid., p. 41).

Whatever his motives, Hechler undoubtedly opened doors for Herzl, and a monument in his honor was proposed by leading Vienna Zionists in 1934. The events of that faithful decade soon reordered the movement's priorities, and the project was dropped. Which, all things considered, may be just as well.

The man proposed by Landau as a possible conduit to the Sultan was the antithesis of Hechler; piety and naïveté may have been the only vices no one ever imputed to the Baron Philip de Nevlinsky.

The Polish aristocrat struck Herzl as one of the most colorful characters he had ever dealt with, the only problem being that he changed colors as often and as casually as his clothes. Thoroughly at home in the underbrush of diplomatic intrigue, he operated on behalf of at least six governments, all of which he held in equal contempt and from which he drew regular subsidies for confidential missions that could be disavowed if the need arose. His one allegiance, if he is to be believed, was to the lost cause of Polish independence. He had participated in the ill-fated 1863 uprising against Russian rule, lost all his estates as a result, and, at the age of twenty-two, suddenly found himself with no assets other than perfect manners, expensive tastes, and a cynical intelligence devoid of moral scruples, ideal qualifications for a career in politics, which he parlayed into a substantial income. Austrian intelligence sources reported that in 1899 alone he had received 6,000 francs from Serbia, 5,000 from Turkey, 1,200 from Rumania, 4,500 from France, 3,000 from Italy, and 10,000 from Russia. According to the British—the only ones to consider him too corrupt to use—he received a permanent salary of 18,000 francs a year from the Sultan, besides traveling expenses and liberal presents. "Since I cannot shape the politics of my own country," he told Herzl, "I don't give a damn about anybody. I perform in diplomacy like a pianist on the keyboard—that is all."

Nevlinsky's knowledge of Turkish affairs, profound and widely recognized as such, derived from a stint as press attaché to the Austrian embassy in Constantinople from 1874 to 1878, where he had indeed displayed virtuoso-like skills in cultivating intimate ties to the key figures of the Turkish government, up to and including the Sultan himself. He was recalled because of exorbitant gambling debts, worked for some years as a spy, diplomatic agent, and agent provocateur for various European powers, and in 1887 began to publish a daily newsletter on Turkish and Near Eastern affairs. The *Correspondance de l'Est* and its German supplement, the *Oesterreichische Correspondenz*, provided some solid information and intriguing gossip, but their main purpose was to blackmail parties intent on either floating or squelching rumors. His versatility netted him social cachet, a bucketful of medals—he used to present the more impressive ones to friends on their birthdays—and a handsome income that always fell far short of what his tastes and habits required. By 1889 he was once again broke and deeply in debt, saved only by the Turkish connection. He was one of the few Europeans thoroughly familiar with the twists and turns of the Byzantine labyrinth, and through the years he continued to spy both for and on the Turks in a symbiotic relationship of mutual venality. Even Nevlinsky's wife, Marja, a Viennese of Jewish descent, received one of Turkey's highest orders, for services unspecified but giving rise to much speculation.

He was, in short, a multiple agent with no focal commitment who served, defrauded, and despised all his customers impartially and included his own self in that same world-weary contempt, a complex and at the same time tragic figure out of one of the later novels of his compatriot Joseph Conrad. At the same time, he was also a straightforward con man—his *Oesterreichische Correspondenz* turned out, after his death, to have had all of twelve subscribers—who deliberately squandered his considerable gifts for reasons that were probably a good deal less romantic and more self-destructive than the youthful disillusionment he liked to invoke in his defense.

Nevlinsky's relations with Herzl, as they developed over the next few years, were as inscrutable in their ambiguity as everything else about him. To the very end, Herzl could never make up his mind about who had used whom, the most plausible answer being that each used the other to mutual advantage. He knew enough about Nevlinsky's background never to trust him completely, and he often referred to him as a scoundrel, yet he was clearly captivated by the savoir faire and sophistication of this urbane aristocrat, with whom he shared certain affinities. Both men conceived of themselves as artists in their field, and both were gamblers by temperament, though one bet money and the other risked himself.

Whether Nevlinsky, for his part, succumbed to Herzl's persuasive charms, learned to respect him personally, and became a sincere partisan of the Zionist movement, as has been claimed, must be left open; it presupposes a vestigial capacity for disinterested idealism unsupported by anything known about him. It is true that he carried out all his assignments conscientiously and efficiently, that he promoted Zionist aims in his newsletters, and that, beyond providing solid information, he also gave Herzl much sound advice, most of it cavalierly disregarded. It is also true, however, that he was exceedingly well paid for his services, collecting large fees from Herzl personally (a total of 8,049 guilders, 2,000 francs, 7,576 crowns in just the last year of his life) in addition to a subsidy from the Zionist Action Committee. Moreover, though neither he nor, for that matter, Herzl had any real power to influence the editorial policies of the *Neue Freie Presse*, he no doubt found ways of converting his contact with an editor of Austria's most renowned newspaper into cold cash from his other clients. And finally, it would have been totally out of character for him to have kept Herzl up-to-date about the Turks without at the same time passing on to them, in turn, what he learned about the Zionist movement, and about Herzl's plans in particular.

In fact, the *quid pro quo* aspect of the relationship emerged almost immediately. Herzl, buoyed by his success in Karlsruhe and confident of having deployed his forces for a diplomatic offensive in Germany, was now eager to tackle his second objective and charm the Sultan into giving him Palestine. He phoned Nevlinsky right after his return, and on May 7 the two met at his home. No preliminaries were necessary; Nevlinsky informed him right off that he had not only read *Der Judenstaat* but had already discussed it with the Sultan, who had vowed never to surrender Jerusalem; the Mosque of Omar must forever remain in Muslim hands. To Herzl, this did not seem much of an obstacle. "We'll simply extraterritorialize Jerusalem, which will then belong to nobody and yet to everybody, the holy place common to the adherents of all faiths. The great condominium of culture and morality."

Nevlinsky expressed some doubts on that score, but he, too, had an agenda of his own. Money, he claimed, was of no interest to the Sultan; he simply did not understand its value. A far better way of getting into his good graces was to support him in his struggle with the Armenians. Nevlinsky himself, it so happened, was currently engaged in a confidential mission to the Armenian resistance leaders in Brussels, Paris, and London, charged with persuading them to acknowledge the sovereignty of the Sultan, who would then voluntarily consent to the reforms he refused to promulgate under pressure. Herzl avidly agreed to do what he could, and Nevlinsky promised to drag out negotiations with the Armenians until the Jewish problem was settled. "The Jewish cause will net you more than the Armenian one," Herzl assured him in conclusion, adding—since one lie deserves another: "Actually, I have nothing to do with money matters, but I'll recommend you to our financial backers."

By this time Herzl had seriously begun to believe that the goal was well within his reach. "Tomorrow it will be a year since I started the movement with my visit to Hirsch. If within the coming year we make as much progress as we did from those beginnings to our current successes, it will indeed be *next year in Jerusalem*" (D, 5/24/96). The point was to keep pressing on. "Great things don't need a solid foundation. An apple will fall unless put on a table. The earth floats in the air. Thus I may perhaps be able to found and consolidate the Jewish state without any firm support. The secret lies in motion. (I believe that this holds true also for the problem of a dirigible aircraft. Gravity overcome by motion. One directs not the aircraft but its movement)" (D, 5/12/96).

However wobbly the science, the metaphor conveys something of the frenzy with which he drove himself throughout the month of May, a juggler bent on keeping the issues and himself in perpetual motion. His correspondence alone would have taxed a dozen lesser, or at least less determined mortals; the sheer volume of letters—all of them written by hand and as yet churned out without any clerical help—seems awesome even without taking into account his activities as a full-time journalist. In fact, his paper sent him to Budapest for a few days in early May to cover the thousand-year jubilee of his old hometown, but in his article describing the occasion, he rhapsodized about something much closer to his heart: "The nation is beautiful. Not just this or that nation, but any nation. Because the nation consists of what is best in any individual—loyalty, enthusiasm, the joy of sacrifice and the readiness to die for an idea" (Bein, p. 302).

Back in Vienna and preparing for his assault on Constantinople, he came down to earth long enough to suspect that perpetual motion might not quite suffice to retire the Turkish national debt. He asked Nordau to get in touch with Edmond de Rothschild, head of the Paris branch, and while he was at it, to also do what he could for the Armenians. On the Armenian issue, he got an immediate one-word reply by telegram: "No." Four days later, Nordau followed up with a detailed report on his meeting with Rothschild, who categorically refused to have anything to do with Herzl's harebrained schemes. He considered them extremely dangerous in that they called into question the patriotism of the Jews and jeopardized the existing Rothschild colonies in Palestine.

So much for the Turkish national debt. So much, too, for Herzl's paternalistic notion of "leadership from above." As in the case of Hirsch, the Rothschilds' hostility was probably their most valuable contribution to the development of political Zionism. It did not convert Herzl to a belief in participatory democracy. But believer or not, he was forced, step by step, to turn to the masses he had thus far been determined to ignore "until the time was ripe."

Much the same lesson in a different context was driven home to him a few days later at a memorable meeting with the man who was to become his closest friend and associate. David Wolffsohn, a prosperous lumber dealer from Cologne, had come to Vienna for the express purpose of sizing up the author of *Der Judenstaat*. Born and raised in Vilna, the "Jerusalem of the Diaspora," he grew up in an atmosphere of intense Jewish nationalism and traditional learning, rose from peddler to traveling salesman, eventually settled in Germany, and made his fortune in the lumber business. Wolffsohn and his friend the attorney Max Bodenheimer had for years led a tiny "Lovers of Zion" movement in Germany, struggling to resist the assimilationist tide. *Der Judenstaat*, with its "intense visionary faith that leapt from every page," struck him as a revelation, the more so since he had known its author only as a super-assimilated littérateur. Anxious to meet this valuable new convert in person, he immediately took off for Vienna "expecting to find the stereotypical Viennese, corpulent and smooth-shaven. Instead, to my amazement, I was confronted by the magnificent figure of Herzl. His majestic appearance made a profound impression on me from the very first moment" (Bein, pp. 290–91).

The revelation cut both ways. Herzl, equally addicted to stereotypes, found it hard to believe that this cultured and well-spoken German businessman was actually a "Polish Jew"; Wolffsohn in turn was stunned by the depths of Herzl's ignorance about Eastern Jews in general, and about their intellectual leadership in particular. Even so, he reported back to Bodenheimer that Herzl was "very serious about *Der Judenstaat*. He lives in the firm conviction that he will succeed in reaching his goal, and within the near future at that. He has even set up an office of sorts for the purpose and carries on a vast correspondence, about which, however, he does not want to talk at the moment."

Wolffsohn, a levelheaded realist, bluntly told Herzl that the masses of Eastern Europe rather than Western millionaires and politicians would determine the fate of his plan. Herzl still clung to his view that the mobilization of the masses would have to wait until he had created the proper conditions for their orderly exodus. It took some time before he learned to appreciate the common sense and vision of this soft-spoken "Polish Jew," modest and methodical but unyielding in matters of principle. The most loyal of his disciples, Wolffsohn was also the only one within the inner circle who dared to stand up to him when the occasion demanded.

At the moment, however, Herzl was more determined than ever to pursue his goal via his personal brand of diplomacy, and a quixotic plan by Viennese students to invade Palestine with a volunteer army merely intensified his concern about spontaneous mass action. On May 10, he went to see the Papal Nuncio. "I entered his palace furtively, looking around me in every direction like a man sneaking into a house of ill repute. . . . Anyone seeing me go in there might have easily misunderstood the nature of my visit." The papal emissary, Monsignor Agliardi, gave him little encouragement, raised a few objections tinged with traditional anti-Semitism, but obviously did not take either Herzl or his intentions very seriously.

More encouraging was the news from London, where Montagu had given Gladstone a copy of *Der Judenstaat* and received a cautiously complimentary reply from the Prime Minister condemning anti-Semitism. Confronted with the clipping, Benedikt agreed to publish it as a straight news item, "Gladstone on Anti-Semitism," but warned Herzl against adding any editorial comment of his own. "Have I ever made trouble for you? I meekly replied. And thus, on this June 2, 1896, this skimpy notice which I have pasted in here was the first to appear in the newspaper on which I have been working for years. But unless I am very much mistaken, it will have major repercussions. The other papers, all of them convinced that a deep rift exists between the publishers and myself, will take this as a significant token of reconciliation, while the readers of the *Neue Freie Presse* will start talking about *Der Judenstaat*" (D, 6/15/96).

In the meantime, Nevlinsky, unsuccessful in his London venture, had quietly slipped back into Vienna without giving a sign of life. Early in June, Herzl dropped him a brief and peremptory note: "Leaving on June 15. Are you with me?"

The Pole, who obviously had been talking to a lot of people, no longer showed much zeal for a project that everyone laughed off as a crazy pipedream. Herzl once again worked him over, marshaled all his arguments and all his charm, and finally declared that, with or without Nevlinsky, he would leave on the fifteenth for Constantinople. He was bluffing; the trip made no sense without Nevlinsky.

Nevlinsky tried to stall; it was, he asserted, a most unpropitious moment, just when the Sultan had his hands full with the Greek uprising in Crete. But in the end, he gave in, having very little choice. He did not wish to risk losing a potentially lucrative account. Besides, keeping an eye on Herzl for the Turks was almost certainly part of his job.

SEVENTEEN

*H*erzl's trip to Constantinople was an act of truly inspired innocence.

On the eve of their departure, Nevlinsky asked him about the financial arrangements he planned to propose to the Sultan in exchange for Palestine—a not unreasonable question under the circumstances, but one to which Herzl had not yet troubled to give much thought.

> Unprepared as I was, I only told him that I figured we would offer some 20 million pounds sterling. . . . Afterward I went to Baden and from there phoned Reichenfeld, my wife's cousin [a director of the Vienna Union Bank]. He arrived in Baden at nine that same evening, and I asked him to fill me in on the Turkish national debt. While he explained it to me, I worked out the financing. We invest 20 million pounds in settling the Turkish finances, of which we offer 2 million outright for Palestine, based on the capitalization of the current annual revenue of 80,000 pounds. With the remaining 18 million we enable the Turks to get rid of the European Control Commission. The Class A, B, C, and D bondholders will be offered immediate benefits—higher interest rates, an extended amortization period, etc.—sufficient to make them consent to the abolition of the commission. Reichenfeld was impressed by this plan, which I immediately developed down to the last detail and contingency, and wanted to know

who the financier was who had drawn it up. I wrapped myself
in discreet silence. [D, 6/25/96]

The imagination tends to soar when unencumbered by knowledge;
experts from outside the family might have been less impressed. Not
that it mattered. The 20 million he so freely disposed of was as unreal
as the rest of the package. But the creative disdain of mere facts was
typical of his method. Surprisingly enough, it often brought results,
though almost never the ones intended. The Turkish adventure was
no exception.

"Great things do not need a solid foundation; the secret lies in
motion." The real secret, of course, lay in Herzl's blind faith in such
nonsense, and in his readiness to act on it. The whole Turkish adventure was a gravity-defying stunt: by claiming to speak for the Jews,
he would get to deal with the Sultan. By dealing with the Sultan, he
would in fact be speaking for the Jews. By offering millions he did not
have, he would obtain promises from the Turks, and once he had
their promises, he would raise the money necessary to redeem them.
An ingenious conjuring trick, but the only one he successfully fooled
was himself. The Turks had been at this game far too long to be taken
in.

He was too meticulous a dresser ever to travel light, but when he
boarded the Orient Express on the evening of June 15, he was loaded
down with more than the usual baggage. Insisting that presents were
de rigueur in any dealings with the Turkish court, Nevlinsky had drawn
up an elaborate list of gratuities in kind, choice fruits and vegetables
imported from France, and specified that they be purchased nowhere
but at the Hotel Sacher, Vienna's most exclusive establishment. Luckily for Herzl, the hotel could fill only half the order. "Even so, the
basket cost me 70 guilders. . . . My poor Hechler was a much more
modest fellow traveler."

On the other hand, the intellectual baggage he carried with him on
the trip weighed next to nothing—a grasp of politics which he considered exhaustive, and a hefty portion of endemic Central European
culture bias. The Turks were venal, corrupt, and up to their ears in
debt, more than enough information on which to base his campaign.
For the rest, he counted on his personal charm, his gift for improv-
isation, and on the simple justice of his cause. He was, after all, offering

to free Turkey from the foreign yoke in return for a patch of—to them—worthless wasteland.

Nevlinsky had tried to convince him that this was not the way the Turks saw the situation, but Herzl had a rare talent for disregarding viewpoints other than his own; the idea that internationalizing Jerusalem might not meet the Sultan's objections never even entered his mind. For a seasoned journalist with ready access to reliable information, he was woefully—and, one suspects, willfully—ignorant of the true state of affairs.

Palestine had, in fact, been a major concern of the Ottoman rulers for several centuries. On the one hand, their claim to the spiritual leadership of Islam—the Caliphate—rested on possession of the three holiest of Muslim shrines, which included Jerusalem along with Mecca and Medina. On the other, the system of "capitulations," by which the European powers had exacted special privileges and extraterritorial rights for their own nationals in Palestine, threatened to undermine Turkish sovereignty. In essence, every foreigner enjoyed diplomatic immunity and tax-exempt status. But the vast majority of Christians were affiliated with religious institutions which presented no serious challenge to secular authorities, unlike the Jewish settlers, whose land purchases and agricultural settlements left little doubt as to their ultimate intentions. Moreover, Jewish immigration had picked up alarmingly following the 1881 pogroms in Russia. And although czarist authorities persecuted their Jewish nationals at home, they were suspiciously eager to extend consular protection to them in Palestine, an exercise in hypocrisy that the Sublime Porte interpreted—no doubt correctly—as an attempt to establish a Russian beachhead. As early as 1887, fully nine years before Herzl made them the offer he thought they could not refuse, the Turks tried to block Jewish immigration and barred all newcomers from settling in Jerusalem, although the gap between the law and its enforcement always remained wide enough for almost anyone to slip through without serious trouble.

Herzl either remained unaware of Turkey's strategic and religious interests in the region or else blithely chose to disregard them; his own secular outlook and parochial ethnocentricity rendered him peculiarly insensitive to the overarching significance of Muslim faith, law, and tradition in shaping Turkish attitudes and policies. Moreover, he mistook the Sultan for just an Oriental version of Franz Joseph, an old man on a wobbly throne. Nothing could have been further from the truth.

Whether Abdul Hamid II was quite the monster he was made out
to be is difficult to judge; Turks have had a poor press in Europe ever
since they first invaded it in the fourteenth century, and the Viennese
never forgave them for laying siege to the city in 1683. But although
he loved cats and expanded public education, Abdul Hamid was certainly no humanitarian. He had seized power in a coup d'état in 1876
and hung on to it ever since, while at the same time struggling to stave
off the final collapse of his shaky empire. The feat took ruthless cunning, unscrupulous brutality, and extraordinary intelligence, all of
which the Sultan possessed in abundance. An ugly, parchment-
skinned homunculus, atypically abstemious and wildly paranoid—
though with good reason to fear his friends as much as his foes—he
had abandoned the Dolma Bahce Palace, the traditional seat of the
Ottoman rulers with its splendid view overlooking the straits, and
immured himself instead in Yildiz Palace, a retreat once built for a
Sultan's favorite. From this fortress-like compound at a safe distance
from the capital, he guided the destiny of a nation whose survival
hinged on exploiting the rivalries of those eager to move in for the kill
and carve up the corpse.

The Russians, the archenemy to the north, stood poised to seize
Turkey's remaining Balkan provinces and occupy the strategically vital
Dardanelles, a move France and Britain were determined to prevent
at all cost, while themselves coveting slices of the overextended empire
in the Middle East. By skillfully playing off one power against the
other, Abdul Hamid had created a stalemate which none of the major
rivals felt inclined to break, for fear of precipitating an all-out confrontation. For much needed support, the Sultan turned instead to
Germany and found a more than eager protector in the young Kaiser
Wilhelm, who had his own ambitious plans for a German incursion
into Asia Minor and readily agreed to train and outfit the Turkish
Army, in return for concessions to build a railroad link between Berlin
and the Persian Gulf. Having disposed of the external threat by a
conjuring trick more daring than anything Herzl ever dreamed of,
Abdul Hamid was able to concentrate on crushing the internal opposition to his fundamentalist rule, and he proceeded against the rebellious Christian minorities—Bulgarians, Serbs, Rumanians, and,
above all, Armenians—with a brutality unprecedented in its day. The
massacres were on a scale foreshadowing the genocidal fury of our own
century; they spared neither women nor children and aroused vociferous but, as usual, largely ineffectual protest in the West.

To much of the Muslim world, on the other hand, the Sultan had emerged as something of a hero, a for once incorruptible leader who in his austere habits and fanatical piety lived up to the prophetic tradition of the Caliphate. In their eyes, he had reestablished a strong Islamic regime within his own country and stemmed the advance of Western imperialism, which had already nibbled away at major chunks of Muslim territory in North Africa, India, and Central Asia.

It seems inconceivable for this Machiavellian paranoiac, who mistrusted his closest advisers, slept in a different building every night, and sniffed at each spoonful of food with well-founded suspicion, to have taken Herzl and his purported mission at face value. He may, in fact, never have taken him altogether seriously. Nevertheless, it is easy to see why he welcomed the visit. The myths of a worldwide Jewish conspiracy and of its fabulous wealth were almost as current in the Muslim world as in the West, and Herzl's discreet allusions to anonymous backers, the nonchalance with which he referred to what in his day were astronomical sums, may have led the Sultan to at least consider the possibility of his being a bona fide agent of Jewish finance fronting for some sinister imperialist designs. Ultimately, however, Herzl's true status and resources made no real difference in the game plan of this devious old fox. Though he never had the slightest intention of granting Herzl anything other than one of his mass-produced medals, he was quick to perceive the advantage of holding out the lure of unspecified promises long enough to raise the temperature in certain foreign embassies and financial institutions. A purported generous offer from Jewish financiers was bound to strengthen his hand in negotiations with Turkey's European creditors, and it may indeed have been a decisive factor in the unusually liberal terms he was able to obtain from them a few months later.

Still, Herzl possessed one indisputably genuine asset—his position at the *Neue Freie Presse.* Like all despots since at least the invention of printing, Abdul Hamid blamed the press for much of his trouble at home and abroad. The butchery of a few thousand Armenians received what he considered disproportionate and tendentious coverage in newspapers all over the world, stirring up anti-Turkish sentiment and inspiring terrorist acts. If Herzl wanted Turkey to help the Jews, let the Jews first help the Turks by influencing public opinion in their favor. A few pro-Turkish articles and editorials in the *Neue Freie Presse* would be a good start. The extent to which Nevlinsky was an accomplice in this cynical ploy is not clear, but it would be curious if he had failed to see it for what it was.

The Herzl in Wonderland voyage began with a train ride across the Balkan peninsula that took two days and three nights. Seemingly by coincidence, more likely by prearrangement, Nevlinsky boarded the train in Budapest together with three high-ranking Turkish diplomats, who feigned a burning interest in Herzl's plan and drew him out at length, no great feat since he dreamed and talked of little else.

In fact, so set was he on making history that he all but ignored the one truly historic event on that trip. As the train pulled into the Sofia station, a crowd of several hundred Bulgarian Zionists surged forward to hail the new leader, "the heart of Israel." Their wild enthusiasm and the effusive speeches in French and German moved him, of course, and as he surveyed the crowd from the train platform, he caught sight of an old man in a fur hat who reminded him of his Grandfather Simon. But what mainly pleased him about the reception was its effect on Nevlinsky and the Turks. The Pole gave no sign of being impressed, but just so as not to be outdone, he had himself welcomed by the Greek Orthodox Archbishop of Bulgaria.

Yet whatever lingering doubts Herzl may still have had about him were quickly dispelled once they reached Constantinople. Nevlinsky was clearly on intimate terms with everyone of note and immediately headed for Yildiz Palace, from where he returned a few hours later in a foul mood. The Sultan was sick and in seclusion, and his secretary did not want to hear about the matter. Later that night at the opera, Herzl met the son of the Grand Vizier, to whom he explained his proposal. But when he referred to an "aristocratic republic," the young man strongly advised him never to so much as breathe the word "republic" in the Sultan's presence; people had lost their head for less.

The following day, Nevlinsky steered him to the Russian consulate for a meeting with its resident chief, who "listened with rapt attention and thought it a great and humanitarian plan." A strange errand indeed, considering Russia's anti-Semitic policies and her strained relations with Turkey, but Nevlinsky, who was also on the Russian payroll, may have felt it opportune to justify his retainer. A subsequent interview with the Grand Vizier himself dissolved in a banal exchange of pleasantries. The General Secretary of the Foreign Ministry, half French and Paris-educated, proved more to Herzl's taste. He expressed a guarded interest and passed him on to the ministry's influential Chief Dragoman, who turned out to be a Turkish Jew.

Daoud Effendi, one of the few non-Muslims to have risen to high office in the Abdul Hamid administration, was understandably conflicted. He stressed that the Jews were happy in Turkey, but that they had to tread warily. As a Jew he could never permit himself to support Herzl's plan, no matter how he felt about it.

That night Nevlinsky returned from his first face-to-face talk with the Sultan:

> If Mr. Herzl is as much of a friend to you as you are to me [he said], then advise him not to take one further step in this matter. I cannot sell a single foot of this land; it does not belong to me but to my people. My people have won this empire with their blood. . . . We will again drench it with our blood before we let it be wrested from us. . . . The Turkish Empire belongs not to me, but to the Turkish people. Let the Jews save their billions. When my empire is carved up, they might even get Palestine for nothing. But only our corpse will be divided. I will not consent to a vivisection. [D, 6/19/96]

None of this shook Herzl's rock-solid belief that in a man-to-man talk with the Sultan he could make him see the irrefutable logic of his plan and its benefits to Turkey, so that the audience as such, regardless of the outcome, was now becoming an end in itself. If he had nothing else to show for his trip, at least he wanted to legitimize his self-appointed role as spokesman for the Jews.

But the closest he came to Abdul Hamid was a *Selamlik,* the colorful Friday prayer ceremony held inside the Yildiz compound, which included a review by the Sultan of his personal guard and elite army units. As his carriage passed Herzl, who was standing next to Nevlinsky, the despot fixed him with a long, hard stare. "He is a slight, sickly man with a large hooked nose and a medium-length beard that looks as though it had been dyed brown" (D, 6/19/96).

Herzl liked parades, and this one was a particularly colorful blend of Oriental splendor and Prussian discipline. Afterward he went downtown to watch a group of whirling dervishes, but the "grotesque dance" with its "monotonous music, snuffled prayers, quadrille-like walkabouts with deep bows followed by dizzy, senseless whirling" repelled him and evoked invidious comparisons with Loie Fuller and the Folies-

Bergère. In his indifference to alien customs and his contempt for non-Europeans, he was hopelessly typical of his class and generation— a sightseer not only unwilling to look below the surface but convinced that there was nothing worth looking for.

In Constantinople, however, he was in any case much too busy even for sightseeing. Every morning he came up with a new stratagem for breaking the deadlock—"If I come back without an audience, and with a no for an answer, people will think I had dreamed it all up." Nevlinsky, badgered and harassed, dragged him from pillar to post and back again. Herzl pleaded, argued, remonstrated, tried to convince by charm, diplomacy, and reason—as though it mattered. He quite simply refused to grasp the totalitarian nature of a regime where no one in his right mind ever risked his job, and quite possibly his head, by speaking out of turn before the Sultan himself had made his wishes known.

And the wily old codger seemed to be enjoying the cat-and-mouse game. He refused to receive Herzl, but his secretary came up with a suggestion that struck Herzl as truly inspired: Acquire some other Turkish territory from the Sultan, and later exchange it for Palestine. Against additional cash, *bien entendu*. The proposal, like all previous ones, went nowhere, and after another inconclusive round of visits, Herzl finally deduced that "here everybody has the servile spirit of supporting the Sultan in whatever he is already determined to do, and of bravely opposing whatever he has no intention of doing anyway."

A day later, Abdul Hamid declared—if Nevlinsky is to be believed— that in view of his past experiences with the press, including an interview with Bacher, he would never grant an audience to Herzl, the journalist, but would gladly welcome him as a friend once he had demonstrated his sincerity by moderating the anti-Turkish bias of the major European newspapers and by bringing the Armenian rebels to the negotiating table. Herzl eagerly agreed, but insisted that an audience with the Sultan would greatly facilitate his task. "He'll receive you afterward and give you a medal," Nevlinsky told him. "I don't need a medal," Herzl testily replied. "All I want is an audience. Drive the first stake into the ground—that is our only task right now."

At Bacher's request, he took time out to interview the Grand Vizier about the latest troubles with the Armenians. "Troubles? What troubles?" the interpreter relayed, with a broad grin. "A few hundred people dead, that's all."

Then, just as he was ready to leave, the Sultan sent a message asking him to delay his departure; he might yet have something to tell him. Herzl complied, attended another *Selamlik*, filed a mildly pro-Turkish report on the Armenian situation, and was told about one Lufti Aga, Abdul Hamid's personal dreamer, whose dreams provided the guidelines for some of the Sultan's major policy decisions. "If Lufti Aga were to tell him that in his dream the Jews had come back to Palestine," Nevlinsky wearily asserted, "it would do more for the cause than all the diplomatic interventions put together."

On June 28, the morning of his long-delayed departure, Herzl swallowed his pride and asked Nevlinsky to get him a Turkish medal. "I have never given a hoot for medals, and I don't now, either, but I urgently need some tangible proof of the Sultan's favor for my people in London."

He spent the day on an extended sightseeing tour conducted by the Sultan's personal adjutant. Told that this represented a great honor, Herzl lost his cool: "Am I supposed to be moved to tears?" But waiting for him on his return was a case containing the Commander's Cross of the Order of the Mejidiye, Third Class.

By his calculation, it had cost him approximately 3,000 francs, close to three months' salary.

Later, on the train, Nevlinsky filled him in on his final conversation with Abdul Hamid. The Sultan, he maintained, was basically not opposed to the plan, but had to keep up appearances. "The Jews are clever, he told me. In the end, I'm sure they'll come up with a formula that will prove acceptable. He now expects help from you in the Armenian matter." And by way of subjecting Herzl's devotion to an additional test, the exalted ruler of the Ottoman Empire requested the self-appointed leader of the Jews to procure for him a 2-million-pound loan against a lien on the annual revenue from the Turkish lighthouses.

Although the only concrete achievement of the trip was a sort of Good Conduct medal, Herzl declared it a victory, the successful opening in his grandly conceived diplomatic offensive. He had become greatly attached to Nevlinsky, considered him his most loyal associate, "a rare, peculiar person of extraordinary gifts," and promised him friendship for life. "If thanks to him we obtain Palestine, we'll reward him with a fine estate in Galicia as a token of our gratitude." Still in his upbeat mood, he considered the deal as good as concluded, and his associate did his best to reinforce this delusion. "If you succeed in pacifying the

Armenians, raise the 2 million pounds and get Bismarck to write to the Sultan on your behalf, the whole matter can be settled in a week."

Whether Nevlinsky, out of some vestigial romanticism and a certain personal affection for Herzl, really meant what he said and made Zionism his cause as well as his business is open to question, but that in the end, when all is said and done, he did little to help the cause may not have been entirely his fault—in this particular game, Herzl was at best a pawn, never a player.

And yet: if his mission to the Sublime Porte was a resounding failure in practical terms, it nonetheless marked the beginning of a revolution.

Throughout the nearly two millennia of exile, Jewish communities had struggled for survival in their host countries, dealt as subjects with their respective rulers, pleaded for tolerance or civil rights, and applied their financial leverage to philanthropy or personal advancement. Here, for the first time, a Jew in effect proposed to negotiate with a sovereign government on behalf of the Jewish people as a whole. He had no mandate, he had no backing, and there is little question that the Turks merely intended to use him. But in so doing, they implicitly recognized the reality of a secular Jewish nation and his role as its representative. It was a diplomatic recognition of sorts, and the true measure of his victory in Constantinople, even though he was again slow to realize it, slower than either his followers or his opponents.

He might have had an inkling of it on his way back home. They once more stopped in Sofia, where a crowd numbering in the hundreds greeted him in the local synagogue. "I warned against demonstrations and urged calm so as not to arouse popular passion against the Jews. My French and German speeches were translated into Bulgarian and Ladino. I stood on the altar platform, and when I didn't quite know how to face the congregation without turning my back to the Holy Ark, someone shouted: 'It's all right for you to turn your back to the Ark, you are holier than the Torah.' Several people wanted to kiss my hand" (D, 6/29/96). He was soon to discover that many others were ready to bite or slap it.

But he spent a mere two days in Vienna, closeted most of the time in his parents' apartment and seeing no one apart from two Armenian exiles and his banker cousin, who seemed utterly bewildered by the Turkish loan scheme. On July 3, he was on his way again, headed for London and expecting a hero's welcome.

What he found instead was a distinct chill in the air. Colonel Goldsmid apologized for not being able to absent himself from Cardiff.

Montagu was about to leave town, even though Herzl asked him "to sacrifice his Sunday for my sake, because what I brought back from Constantinople was the near-certainty that we would get Palestine back." For reasons not difficult to fathom, the mood in London had changed abruptly from well-meaning support to one of alarm and outright suspicion. On his first visit, Herzl had been the visionary dreamer who appealed to the romantic Zionism popular in Victorian England. None of his upper-class Anglo-Jewish admirers were seriously expecting him to translate his dreams into immediate action. And he had done worse: certainly nothing entitled him to negotiate in their name with a sovereign government, let alone commit them and their money to the intrigues cooked up by a despicable tyrant and his gang of Oriental cutthroats.

But the problem went deeper.

The Anglo-Jewish aristocracy, while subscribing to the idea of Jewish solidarity, felt resolutely British. By presuming to speak for "the Jewish people," Herzl—the *goy* who did not know any better than to send Montagu a postcard written and dated on a Sabbath—threatened to blur the line between religious identity and national allegiance which protected their rights and defined their public image.

Sensitive to the atmospheric change, Herzl scaled down both his demands and his expectations, calling merely for the formation of a Society of Jews to promote the legal acquisition of territory for such Jews as were unable to assimilate. But the Anglo-Jewish Association under the presidency of Claude Montefiore turned down even this modest proposal; a Jewish state, they declared, was "neither possible nor desirable." At a formal dinner of the Maccabean Club, Herzl read his first public speech in English from a carefully prepared text. Neither Montagu nor Nordau showed up for the occasion, but although he was given a polite hearing, the meeting ended in an inconclusive debate about organizing a study group. The speech itself was moderate in tone, an attempt by Herzl to justify his forays into power politics without giving away any details; and while he continued to oppose settlement by infiltration, he rejected the charge that his actions were liable to endanger the existing colonies in Palestine.

The *Jewish Chronicle* printed much of the speech, along with some skeptical but not altogether hostile comments about the "Viennese enthusiast," and Herzl judged his performance a success.

But more was at stake here than his stage presence. His hopes for a deal with the Sultan were predicated on the availability of adequate funds, and the one man on whom he had counted to supply them had not even bothered to attend the dinner. Sir Samuel Montagu, sixty-four at the time, a Liberal Member of Parliament since 1885 and a baronet since 1894, received him the following day in his office in the House of Commons. "At the sight of this imposing parliamentary establishment—externals do, after all, tend to have a dramatic effect— I felt the same touch of giddiness I had felt in the antechamber of the Grand Duke of Baden, but at the same time I came to understand why the English Jews would cling to a country in which they can enter this House as masters" (D, 7/8/96). Herzl reported on the results of his dealings with the Grand Duke and the Sultan, but if Montagu was as impressed as Herzl seemed to think, the admiration was confined to Herzl's personality rather than to his diplomatic initiatives. Despite a number of cogent objections, however, Montagu seemed disposed to consider the proposal, provided the Hirsch estate and Edmond de Rothschild were willing to participate. He would not budge without Rothschild.

It must have been something of a shock for Herzl to discover that he had come full circle, right back where he started from with his Address to the Rothschilds. Neither the Anglo-Jewish plutocracy nor the British Hoveve Zion would move without, let alone against, the ruling Jewish dynasty.

The Rothschild clan as a whole, and Edmond, the uncrowned king, in particular, had come to represent everything Herzl most detested— high finance, stock exchange, philanthropy, paternalism, arrogance, and arrant snobbery. But the cause was greater than any individual, and it outweighed any personal considerations. "It is absolutely essential to win Edmond Rothschild over to our side," he wrote to Zadok Kahn that same evening. "For the sake of obtaining his support, I am offering to withdraw completely from the leadership of the movement so as to allay any suspicion of personal ambition. . . . Together with Sir Montagu and Colonel Goldsmid, we will find a way to offer Edmond Rothschild the presidency of the Society of Jews—and another title later on" (D, 7/8/96).

By morning, though, he had second thoughts and refrained from mailing the letter.

The change of heart may have been due to a tactical error on Montagu's part. Herzl had been invited to speak the following Sunday at a mass rally in Whitechapel, in the auditorium of the Jewish Work-ingmen's Club. Whitechapel happened to be part of Montagu's constituency, and he urged Herzl to cancel his appearance at the meeting. His insistence on this point abruptly highlighted not only his own conflict of interest but also the growing split in Herzl's own constituency. He could no longer afford to ignore the contrast between the clubby skepticism of the rich, who sabotaged his efforts at every turn, and the enthusiasm he inspired among the broad masses. He was still strongly committed to an authoritarian leadership from above, a commitment he, in fact, never abandoned in principle, even though circumstances forced him to modify it in practice. "I replied that I did not want a demagogic movement. But if worse came to worst—if the aristocrats proved too aristocratic—I would start a movement among the masses."

A year earlier, in his confrontation with Hirsch, he had used similar language, with nothing more than delusions of grandeur to back up the threat. Now, with an active and dedicated following, he was in a somewhat different position. Moreover, he had acquired a sure sense of his power to move an audience, though he still firmly resisted what he viewed as the role of rabble-rousing demagogue, incompatible with his political principles as much as with his aristocratic self-image. "The masses" remained a dark abstraction, designed to frighten the recalcitrant haute bourgeoisie into effective cooperation.

The haute bourgeoisie, however, was unimpressed—more frightened, no doubt, of Herzl himself than of the collective wrath of the Jewish proletariat.

The real masses, on the other hand, had been stirring for quite some time without the benefit of enlightened guidance from above. Among the Eastern European immigrants in London's East End, a Zionist movement of sorts had arisen, inspired in part by *Der Judenstaat*, but it lacked authoritative leaders and a clear sense of direction. The Whitechapel rally of July 13 marked a turning point. By putting an end to Herzl's Hamlet-like hesitation, it provided the inchoate movement with one of the most effective leaders in modern history.

The twenty-five-year-old journalist Jakob de Haas, a moving spirit among the young, as yet unorganized and disorganized London Zionists, had been convinced from the outset that Herzl, out of his depth among the Anglo-Jewish aristocracy, mistook evasive courtesy for agreement and support. After witnessing the fiasco at the Maccabean Club, he decided to enlighten Herzl and was given a seven o'clock appointment the next morning at the Hotel Albemarle. "And that next morning had its surprises," writes De Haas, referring to himself in the third person.

> Herzl in a yellow silk dressing gown was writing, but quickly turned to his visitor, who found that the Nationalist leader he had long been looking for knew nothing of the background of the cause he was so boldly espousing. On condition that the "over there" of the "Jewish State" should thereafter read Palestine, and nowhere else, the writer offered his service, and as a means of definite contact he accepted the office of "Honorary Secretary to Dr. Herzl." His field was to be all English-speaking countries. And so it remained to the end. [De Haas, p. 119]

The honorary secretary's most immediate task was to help save the Whitechapel meeting, planned weeks in advance but which had run into serious trouble as a result of Montagu's opposition. No Jewish community leader dared defy the influential Member of Parliament on his own turf and even Colonel Goldsmid felt moved to withdraw the support of the Hoveve Zion. Thus, three days before the scheduled date, the ad hoc Dr. Herzl East End Reception Committee still had no hall for the meeting, and no prominent figure willing to chair it.

In the end, the obstacles were overcome. The Jewish Workingmen's Club had no compunctions about offending the Liberal multimillionaire M.P. who misrepresented their district, and Rabbi Moses Gaster, an outstanding scholar, veteran of the Rumanian Hoveve Zion and Chief Rabbi of the Sephardic Community in Britain, agreed to preside. Posters went up all over the East End publicizing the event in Yiddish and English, and despite a brutal heatwave, the hall was packed to the rafters. De Haas has left a vivid eyewitness account of the scene:

> Thus by the meeting of the Whitechapel Jews held on July 13, at the Jewish Workingmen's Club, Herzl, who less than a year before sought only the good will and support of millionaires, was suddenly changed into the spear head of a phalanx rebelling against the existing Jewish communal organization, and as the leader of a never-ending struggle between Zionists and "Lovers of Zion." But all these phases were not apparent that hot Sunday afternoon when, despite the prophets of the status quo, the masses

surged into the meeting hall, into which only a tithe of the sweltering crowd could gain admission. . . . Moses Gaster, spiritual leader of the Sephardic community, was the only prominent Jew in London who had the courage to preside at the meeting which proclaimed Herzl the leader of Jewry. Herzl was no orator for the masses and amid all that jubilation he permitted himself only one sentence that had the savour of triumph. He said "the East is ours"—meaning the East End of London and not the Orient. But his personality, his glowing eyes, his fine simple gestures, his open deprecating of himself and the natural touch of mystery with which he spoke of diplomatic affairs, won an audience keyed up by its youthful, resourceful, exuberant leaders to the point where they, not he, challenged all Jewry to follow. Doctor Gaster, a romantic victim of Rumanian anti-Semitism, in, but not of, Anglo-Jewry, possessed exactly that oratorical ability which could ably support that challenge. And it was carried with rapidity from mouth to mouth. [De Haas, pp. 120–21]

Herzl himself was overwhelmed by the reception. He spoke extemporaneously for an hour, and if the mostly Yiddish-speaking crowd had trouble following his German, it does not seem to have detracted from their enthusiasm. "I was eulogized by the speakers who followed me. One of them, Ish-Kishor, compared me to Moses, Columbus, etc. The Chairman, Chief Rabbi Gaster, gave a fiery speech. I finally expressed my thanks in a few words, in which I protested against the extravagant comparisons. Wild cheering, hats in the air, hurrahs that followed me out into the street" (D, 7/13/96).

The full significance of this episode did not, however, begin to sink in until a couple of days later:

Last Sunday, on the stage of the Workingmen's Club, I experienced some strange sensations. I saw and heard my legend being born. The people are sentimental; the masses do not see clearly. I think that even now they no longer have a clear image of me. A light mist is beginning to rise all about me, which may condense into a cloud in which I shall walk. But even if they no longer see my features distinctly, they nonetheless sense that I mean them well and that I am the champion of the poor. True, they would probably lavish the same affection on some clever crook or swindler as they do on me, in whom they will not be disappointed.

This may well be the most interesting subject recorded in this book—the birth of my legend.

And while I was listening on that people's stage to the effusive praises of my followers, I inwardly made a firm vow to become ever more worthy of their trust and their love. [D, 7/15/96]

To no one's surprise, except possibly his own, his halfhearted efforts to meddle in the Turkish–Armenian conflict led nowhere. The embattled Armenians had no more use for him as a mediator than they did for the Sultan's overtures, while no self-respecting British politician would compromise himself on behalf of the unspeakable Turks. (The whole project, in fact, collapsed a month later, when an Armenian guerrilla attack in the capital triggered ferocious reprisals on a scale that ended all further hope of a compromise. The events, however tragic, extricated Herzl from a potentially rather embarrassing entanglement.) From Montagu he had obtained a conditional promise. The conditions were of the sort familiar from fairy tales—solve two insolvable conundrums and slay a fire-breathing dragon and you shall have my daughter and my kingdom—but Herzl, like any proper fairy-tale hero, was of good cheer: "I am satisfied with the results of my London trip. The conditional promise by Montagu and Goldsmid to join in if Edmond Rothschild and the Hirsch Foundation go along and the Sultan engages in positive negotiations is sufficient, for the time being" (D, 7/15/96).

Braced by these illusions, Herzl arrived in Paris on July 17 for his crucial confrontation with Edmond de Rothschild. He checked in at the Hôtel Castille and, as fate would have it, was given the same suite in which, almost exactly a year earlier, he had drafted his Address to the Rothschilds. Waiting for him were three telegrams from Nevlinsky, ever generous with other people's money, asking for "two mantel clocks, two top-quality silver candelabra a half meter or more in height, massive, Renaissance style, one Oriental or Moorish style, each two to three thousand francs cash. Urgently needed for His Majesty in person." He also wanted to know how much, over and above expenses, he could offer the British journalist Sidney Whitman for making contact with Bismarck.

More encouraging was a visit from Bernard Lazare. It was apparently their first meeting, and Herzl, favorably impressed, described his visitor as "an excellent example of the good, intelligent French Jew." But the main item on the agenda was the meeting scheduled for the following afternoon at the Rothschild residence on the rue Laffitte, though "meeting" may not be the *mot juste* for what transpired between these two equally headstrong, self-righteous individuals, neither of whom was in the habit of listening to any point of view other than his own.

Before ushering the visitor into the inner sanctum, Emile Meyerson, editor of the Havas News Agency and a Rothschild confidant, felt moved to inform Herzl that the baron was "a human being just like you and I." "This piece of information," Herzl noted dryly, "did not come as a surprise."

Things went rapidly downhill from there. Twenty years later, after the Balfour Declaration, Edmond de Rothschild is said to have admitted that "Herzl was right and I was wrong," but at the time he was manifestly incensed—and not a little frightened—by the temerity of this wild man whose incendiary ideas and dilettantish excursions into power politics spelled potentially big trouble for the Rothschild colonies in Palestine, provided ammunition for the anti-Semites at home, and threatened to undermine the precarious achievements of the emancipation altogether.

His side of the story has not been told—the Rothschild archives are closed—but even Herzl's own account of the interview gives little credit to his diplomatic skills. He felt snubbed by the Rothschilds, he resented being made to feel like a petitioner, and the baron's air of icy superiority provoked an aggressive arrogance that aborted any prospect of rational discourse right from the outset. But it was probably a lost cause in any event; though he stated his objections with disconcertingly calm finality, Rothschild obviously had never given the plan a moment's serious consideration. He dismissed it as a fantasy, mad as well as futile, and Herzl's increasingly vehement rhetoric merely served to reinforce this impression. He did not believe the Turks and their promises, and even if he did, he would not assume responsibility for the hordes of Jewish *shnorrers* pouring into Palestine. "Maybe you can handle it; I can't." Conditional guarantees from the London contingent did not impress him, either. He could well understand, he said, with cutting sarcasm, that Montagu would want the Rothschilds to cover for him. And in a final display of deft marksmanship, he disclosed that he had received a letter from Colonel Goldsmid warning him of Herzl's downright dangerous machinations.

This revelation of treachery in his own ranks—and by a military man, at that—left Herzl momentarily dumbfounded and effectively ended the dialogue between the deaf. In a dramatic gesture, he picked up his umbrella from the floor and rose: "By way of ending this conversation . . . let me ask: What reveals the power of an idea? The fact that a yes is a commitment, and so is a no. You were the keystone of the entire combination. If you refuse, everything I have thus far accomplished will come apart. In that case, I will have to proceed differently. I am going to mount a major propaganda drive, which will make it even more difficult to control the masses. I wanted to turn the leadership of the whole project over to you and withdraw from it myself. . . . I have shown my goodwill and proved that I am not a stubborn obstructionist. You are not willing—I've done my share" (D, 7/19/96).

The very next morning, Herzl sent off a note to De Haas instructing him to "begin organizing the masses." Credit for having sealed the doom of philanthropic Zionism must go to Edmond de Rothschild.

Herzl's entire career testifies to a degree of self-discipline, efficiency, and organization rare in a business tycoon, let alone in a man who —not without justification—regarded himself as primarily an artist by temperament. Work was his way of fighting the inner conflicts and recurrent bouts of depression to which he was subject. Even in the throes of serious physical and emotional stress, he seldom missed a deadline or failed to answer a letter by return mail. Whether this reliance on sheer willpower, the grim determination never to slow down long enough for his demons to catch up with him, denotes pathology or health is ultimately beside the point; but he now appointed himself the leader of a still largely imaginary mass movement and played his role with an imperious authority that created its own reality. Before leaving Paris, he named Nordau the official head of the French Zionists and issued his new guidelines: "Immediate organization of the masses. Our people will already be organized at the point of departure rather than on arrival. No one will be let in without a valid departure certificate." And later that afternoon, at a rally of Russian-Jewish students, he urged them to start organizing cadres. "I am not yet telling you to start marching. But I am asking you to get ready."

On the way back, he stopped off at Karlsbad, where Nevlinsky had arranged for an informal meeting with Prince Ferdinand of Bulgaria, a German princeling handpicked by the Russians for the Bulgarian throne whom Herzl saw as a potential conduit to the Czar. In the course of an animated, peripatetic conversation on the promenade of the famous spa, Ferdinand expressed subversively philo-Semitic sentiments—"I spent my youth with Baron Hirsch; I've often been accused of being half Jewish, in fact"—and keen admiration for Herzl's plans, but broaching the subject in St. Petersburg was out of the question; the whole Russian court, with the possible exception of the Archduke Vladimir, regarded Jews as less than human. "The Greek Orthodox mistrust me as it is. There are certain delicate areas where I have to subordinate my convictions to political imperatives."

After a brief, busy week with his vacationing family at Aussee, Herzl was back in Vienna on August 3 and immediately flung himself into the practical work of organizing an international mass movement. The Vienna general staff formed quickly, its core consisting of the dedicated but hitherto ineffectual Zionist stalwarts who for years had been meeting every Tuesday night at the Café Louvre. They included Kadimah veterans such as the physician Moses Schnirer and the lawyer Ozer Kokesch, along with the Odessa-born engineer Johann Kremenezky, a practical visionary in his own right who had pioneered the electrification of Vienna and already dreamed of reforesting Palestine; he was to found the Jewish National Fund and serve as its first director. Other early recruits were the Galician philologist and Shakespeare scholar Leon Kellner, later Herzl's controversial literary executor, and Leopold Loebl, Herzl's relative and financial expert, who three years later quit a responsible banking position and emigrated to Palestine. By September, Herzl had formally accepted the leadership of the group and transformed it into his kitchen cabinet, a staff of unimpeachable loyalty and personal devotion whom he drove and bullied mercilessly for failing to keep up with his own frantic pace.

He rented office space, recruited a small staff from among his followers, published a series of circulars and pamphlets, made himself available as a public speaker and, in addition, provided most of the financing out of his own pocket. This imposed limitations; what he wanted most of all—a Zionist newspaper—was way beyond his private means, and he had as yet no other source of funds. In a rather reckless move, and much against his principles, he for the first time in his life took a flier in the stock market, buying 150 shares of the *Neue Wiener Tagblatt*, but his plan to acquire majority control fizzled in the end; the leveraged buyout and the hostile takeover had yet to be invented.

At the same time, an international network of sorts began to take shape, with Nordau in Paris, Reuben Bierer in Sofia, David Wolffsohn and Max Bodenheimer in Germany, and the energetic young De Haas in England ready to expand his activities to North America. There were the small but influential and exceedingly active student organizations all over Europe, along with the pro-Herzl groupings and dissident factions within the Hoveve Zion movement, although the leading Russian Zionists still kept their distance and continued to view the Austrian interloper with wary reserve. Gratified by these developments, an increasingly tense and testy Herzl grumbled nonetheless that all these willing *Mitarbeiter*, by their sloth, sloppiness, and procrastination, virtually forced him to assume sole charge of the movement. He had some grounds for complaint; most of the work and practically all of the funding still devolved upon him, and certainly no one could match his energy and dedication. On the other hand, while he may have been eager to delegate some of the routine tasks, he would brook no hint of opposition to his views and insisted on making all major decisions strictly on his own—not by default, but because that was how he conceived his role as a leader. By living up to it, he transformed intellectual inspiration into charismatic leadership, welded inchoate longings into a purposeful political movement, and attracted a core of enthusiastic disciples. He also alienated a fair number of people who, while sharing his broad objectives, had a mind of their own and insisted on voicing their opinions.

The organization, in the meantime, was beginning to acquire a momentum of its own, and his determination personally to keep up with all new developments began to devour more and more of his time and energy. His correspondence swelled to monstrous proportions, yet he answered virtually every letter at length, in his own hand, advising, cajoling, encouraging, issuing detailed instructions, and following up on every lead. A steady stream of visitors from all over the world made the pilgrimage to Berggasse 6, diagonally across the street from another prophet who, at Number 19, had begun to explore a different kind of emancipation. He attended meetings and conferences, gave speeches, and in addition to it all managed somehow to function in a responsible position on a major daily. That this did not leave much time for his family bothered him a great deal less than it did Julie, who made no secret of her contempt for his crazy ideas and for the riffraff that invaded her living room and her life.

Despite these relatively rapid and impressive gains, Herzl began to

Herzl at age six

Herzl and his
sister, Pauline

Jeanette Herzl as a young mother

Jakob Herzl at forty-one

Simon Loeb Herzl, Theodor's grandfather

Contemporary view of the synagogue on Dohany Street in Budapest which Herzl attended with his father (CREDIT: *Ira Brophy*)

Herzl in Vienna, around 1878

The Albia member
with some of his
fraternity brothers

Julie Naschauer, around
the time of her
wedding to Herzl

The *Neue Freie Presse* of January 5, 1895, with Herzl's report on the formal degradation of Captain Dreyfus

Herzl's press pass for the Chamber of Deputies

Eduard Bacher and Moritz Benedikt, editors and publishers of the *Neue Freie Presse*

Title pages of Herzl's manuscript diary, *Der Judenstaat,* and his novel *Altneuland*

Freud's letter to Herzl enclosing a copy of his book *The Interpretation of Dreams*

Prof. Dr. Freud   IX., Berggasse 19.

29 Sept 1902

Hochgeehrter Herr Doktor.

Über Veranlassung Ihres Redaktions-
Kollegen, des Herrn Max Kende
habe ich zur erbauet, Ihnen durch
den Buchhändler fr. Deuticke
ein Exemplar meines 1900 publizierten
Buches über die Traumdeutung
sowie eines kleinen, das aber
schwer beschafften Vortrags
zuzustellen.

Ich kann nicht wissen, ob Sie den
Eindruck angefangen werden
sollte das Buch bei für die Ver-
wendung rechne die Herr Kende
im Auge gehabt hat, aber ich
bitte Sie, es für jeden Fall als
ein Zeichen der Hochachtung zu
behalten die ich mir so viele
kundre. Für Jahren Ihrer
Meister und dem deutschen
für die Nachgeratsten nahen
Roche entgegenbringe.

Ergebenst Ihr
Prof Dr Freud

Max Nordau

The Basel Casino, site of the first Zionist congress

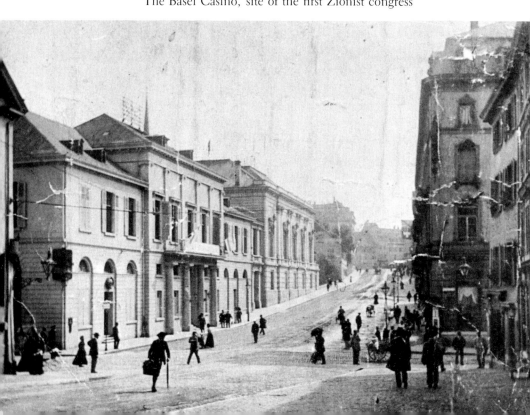

The opening session of the first congress

Herzl and his children

Mother and son

Bound for Palestine: Herzl and companions at the Acropolis

Ew. Kaiserliche Majestät!

Auf den Rath Sr. Königlichen Hoheit des Herrn Grossherzogs von Baden wende ich mich direct an Ew. Kaiserliche Majestät mit der ehrfurchtsvollen Bitte um eine Audienz.

Durch mein anfangs 1896 veröffentlichtes Buch „Der Judenstaat" ist in allen Welttheilen eine Bewegung hervorgerufen worden, welche man die zionistische nennt. Sie hat viele Hunderttausende von Menschen ergriffen.

Unsere heute schon weit verbreitete Bewegung hat überall einen erbitterten Kampf mit den Umsturz-parteien zu bestehen, die in ihr mit Recht einen Feind wittern. Wir brauchen eine Ermuthigung, wäre es auch nur eine sorgfältig geheimzuhaltende. Ich setze alle Hoffnung auf den Kaiser, der mit weltweitem Blick über die Meere schaut und von dessen Thaten die Geschichte gerade diejenigen am höchsten preisen wird, die von kleinen Leuten der Gegenwart nicht ver-standen werden.

Wann und wohin immer Ew. Majestät mich zur Audienz befohlen, werde ich unverzüglich zur Stelle sein.

Ich verharre in tiefster Ehrfurcht
Ew. Kaiserlichen Majestät
gehorsamst ergebener

Dr Theodor Herzl

22 October 1897   Wien IX Berggasse 6

Herzl's letter to the German Kaiser requesting an audience

On the boat, bound for Jaffa

The delegation in Jaffa

The Kaiser as photographed
on horseback

The doctored photograph of
Herzl's meeting with the Kaiser

Herzl with his mother and Israel Zangwill

Herzl with members of the Democratic Faction. Left, second row from the bottom, Chaim Weizmann

Ahad Ha-Am

The last portrait of Herzl

Herzl's funeral

Herzl's tomb on Mount Herzl in Jerusalem

feel less and less hopeful. He persisted in regarding the mass movement as more or less of a side show, but one with potentially explosive consequences unless he could deliver on his promise of an independent Jewish state secured by international guarantees. And that goal seemed more elusive than ever.

Even after the August massacre in Constantinople, which had shocked the world—though not enough to do anything about it— Herzl maintained contact with the Turks via Nevlinsky and the Turkish ambassador. The faint signals emanating from the Sublime Porte were more ambiguous than ever, but he remained convinced that with the proper backing he could have acquired Palestine from the hard-pressed Turks. The Jewish financial mafia, however, godfathered by the Rothschilds, had its own priorities in Turkey, and a Jewish state was not among them; they not only ridiculed his proposals but actively undercut them by helping to consolidate the Turkish debt in a secret deal which Herzl furiously denounced as rank treason. And while, from his point of view, he was indubitably right, the wily Rothschilds once again served the good of the cause by provoking an inspired response: the idea of a Jewish National Fund financed by contributions from the people as a whole.

His initiative on the other fronts had also largely ground to a halt. In September, at the Breslau summit meeting between the Kaiser and the Czar, which he covered for the *Neue Freie Presse,* he again had a chance to observe the German Emperor from up close and to lose himself in speculations about the psychological effect of Wilhelm's withered left arm. But when it came to obtaining a private audience, Hechler was unsuccessful. Efforts to reach the Czar or members of his staff were equally futile. And Bismarck, who had dismissed *Der Judenstaat* as "a melancholy fantasy," resisted all further approaches.

None of it affected Herzl's basic faith in the feasibility of his plan as such, and he continued to explore every chance, however remote, to lay his case before crowned heads, potentates, politicos, and power brokers. His faith in the Jews, on the other hand, was easily shaken, and the mounting irascibility that went with sheer physical exhaustion helped to undermine it still further. But realistic setbacks contributed their share.

At the end of September, Prime Minister Badeni once more offered him the editorship of a pro-government newspaper, this time with full freedom to shape its editorial policy in matters of Jewish concern; like his ex-opponent, now ally, Lueger, Badeni had no objection to the Jews leaving for Palestine. A major daily was up for sale at the bargain price of one million guilders, but the negotiations, conducted in strict secrecy, were extremely stressful for Herzl: "Once again difficult days ahead, much like the ones of a year ago, when I planned on leaving the *Neue Freie Presse* and the discussions gave me such palpitations that my heart has been ailing ever since" (D, 10/5/96). On his own, he was able to raise only 400,000 guilders from within the family, but to accept government slush funds for the balance would have compromised both his principles and his editorial independence. He turned instead to Jewish bankers in Vienna and eventually, via Zadok Kahn, appealed to the Baron Hirsch Foundation in Paris, only to be rebuffed in the end.

He was bitterly disappointed and furious at this new betrayal. For want of a piddling half million, more or less, the Jews lost their one-time chance for an organ that, unlike the *Neue Freie Presse*, would not be afraid to speak up for them. And he personally lost the chance to be his own boss at precisely the moment when he needed both security and independence: his relations with Bacher and Benedikt had again deteriorated to the point where he expected to be fired any day.

Tensions reached their climax early in October, when Bacher summoned him to his office and demanded an explanation for a 3,000-pound bribe he was alleged to have solicited and received on behalf of the *Neue Freie Presse*. Herzl was stunned. "And you actually believed this for even one moment? Don't you know me by now? I should have thought you would at least take me for a gentleman."

Unsettled by his icy calm, Bacher retreated. "All we thought was that Nevlinsky pulled one of his dirty tricks behind your back and ours." But Herzl was not that easily mollified when it came to matters of honor. He traced the rumor back to one Baron Ludwig Doczy of the Austrian Foreign Office and threatened to challenge him to a duel, which precipitated another scene in Bacher's office that degenerated into a noisy row over Zionism. In the end they made up, but the lingering insinuations left Herzl even more uneasy. "I have the impression that I am soon going to be forced out of my job," he wrote. "It would be a disaster, because all the plans for financing my own newspaper have collapsed" (D, 10/11/96).

The buoyant exaltation that had carried him through the summer had also collapsed, giving way to an ever-deepening gloom.

I must frankly admit it to myself [he wrote a few days later]. I am demoralized. No help from anywhere, attacks from everywhere. Nordau writes that in Paris nobody is making a move. The Maccabeans in London are getting more Pickwickian every day, if the faithful de Haas is to be believed. In Germany I only have enemies. The Russians look on in sympathy as I break my back working, but nobody moves a finger. In Austria, particularly in Vienna, I have a few followers. Some—the disinterested ones—are completely inactive, while those who are active just want to further their own interests with the help of the editor of the *N.F.P.* . . . All Jews who are well off are against me. So that I have a right to become the greatest of all anti-Semites. I often think of Levysohn's words: "Those whom you want to help will be the first to nail you painfully to the cross." [D, 10/13/96]

External circumstances offered what may have seemed like plausible reasons for the despair that gripped him as the year drew to a close. "I feel myself getting tired," he wrote on December 20. "I now believe more often than before that my movement is finished. I am fully convinced of its feasibility, but I am unable to overcome the initial difficulties. One single million guilders would be enough to put the movement solidly on its feet. For want of what is a mere trifle, compared to the greatness of the cause, we shall have to go to sleep, although day is breaking" (D, 12/20/96).

The setbacks and disappointments were real enough, but hardly new; what now made them loom so much larger was the darkness within, governed by cycles that followed their own rhythms and drained the world of its colors. "And so we have passed on into 1897, one of my friend Hechler's 'critical years,' " he wrote in January. "I've become lax about keeping this diary. Many a day brings events worth noting, but the general torpor of the movement has gradually settled in my own limbs as well" (D, 1/6/97).

Lax perhaps by his own standards, but despite the acute inner crisis, he did not permit himself the luxury of either respite or self-pity. "I write many letters because I answer everyone. . . . I have many visitors from all over the world. The road from Palestine to Paris is beginning to pass through my study" (D, 1/6/97).

Yet though he forced himself to go through the motions, there was ultimately no way to outrun the fear he had been struggling to ignore, ever since he had been told about his heart ailment. The palpitations were worse than ever; he had dizzy spells, occasional shortness of breath—symptoms that could mean anything or nothing, but which he chose to interpret as warnings of imminent death. His decision to confront mortality by taking the obvious practical measures—he was a lawyer, after all—signals his gradual emergence from the depths of depression. On February 12, he for the first time in his life made a will.

It was the first of three testaments, divided—like the life itself—into two parts. The first, dealing with his literary estate, was meant for the world at large. The second, strictly confidential, deals with his personal and financial affairs; it casts a gruesome light on his marriage and for many years was suppressed by zealous followers intent on promoting the myth of the exemplary husband and father, and of the wife and helpmate who courageously stood by him in his struggles.

He still saw himself as primarily a man of letters, and his "literary testament" was a bid for immortality. It called for the publication of his collected writings as soon as possible after his death, the assumption being that his posthumous reputation would assure a steady flow of royalties to provide for his children.

A man must be prepared for death.

I shall forgo the banalities.

What I was to the Jews, future generations will be better able to judge than the masses of today. . . . My principal estate consists of the diary-like notes concerning my efforts in the Jewish cause. . . . Those memoirs should be published soon after my death. . . . There may also be a demand for a collection of my Zionist articles and speeches. . . . A publisher should be found for my other writings as well. My plays, I think, ought to be published as a collection. My favorite play is *The Ghetto*. . . . Another volume should contain the feuilletons and articles I wrote in France for the *Neue Freie Presse*. The remaining feuilletons not yet published in book form should fill several more volumes.

My name will grow after my death. I therefore believe that a publisher will be found for all my works.

I am proudly conscious of always having wielded my pen as a man of honor, ever since I started to write. I have never sold my pen, never misused it for base ends or even in the service of friendship. This Last Will may be published. Even after my death, no one will be able to call me a liar.

The part not for publication contains no lofty sentiments or language. It rehashes instead Herzl's grievances against his wife, reiterating all the slights and indignities he had collected in the course of their marriage. Charging that her childish demands and irresponsible extravagance had made them live way beyond their means and all but depleted her dowry, he once more expressed the confident hope that the material rewards of his posthumous fame would make up for the loss.

The main thrust of these fulminations, however, was his attempt to brand Julie an unfit mother.

With the arrogance of expertise, the Doctor of Jurisprudence drew up a brief depriving Julie of the custody of her children and appointing his own father and mother as their legal guardians. He urged his parents—as though they needed urging—to protect all three children from the baleful influence of their mother and her clan, but his real concern centered on Hans, his son and heir. While the girls, being girls, would probably have to remain with Julie, Hans was to be immediately removed from his mother—"who does not love but merely spoils him"—either to be brought up in his grandparents' home or to be sent to a boarding school abroad.

These mindlessly cruel but—at least in principle—legally enforceable dispositions may be somewhat difficult to reconcile with the picture Herzl presented to the world. Yet far from being a hypocrite, he seems to have sincerely believed that his children, aged three, five, and six at the time, would be far better off with their carping harridan of a grandmother, whom they loathed, than with Julie, a hysterical and overindulgent but caring and devoted mother, to whom they were deeply attached. That sincerity is in itself one of the more troubling aspects of the picture; it suggests a capacity for self-deception which, however useful in public life, can make ordinary human relations difficult if not impossible.

In any case, none of the crimes of which Julie stood accused—not even *lèse-majesté*, her contempt for his mother—quite explains the kind of visceral passion that would scheme vengeance from beyond the grave. In some manner unknown, which Herzl could not forget, forgive, or probably even admit to himself, she had made him doubt his manhood. And the fact that he plotted posthumously to accomplish what, in life, he had repeatedly threatened to do but never had been man enough to go through with tends to confirm that suspicion. The Will was his way of settling accounts.

Coming to terms with the insidious allure of death involved a much more painful and protracted struggle. It ended in a compromise that combined suicidal fervor with resigned acceptance and enabled him, during what remained of his life, to channel his self-destructive impulses into a self-transcending cause.

A rare glimpse of the inner crisis and its resolution is offered in "The Aniline Inn," a transparently autobiographical tale Herzl wrote in late 1896 and which makes up in artless candor for what it lacks in art. The hero is a learned professor of philosophy whose bitchy wife so torments him that he decides to drown himself. As he repairs to a spot on the river traditionally favored by would-be suicides, he is hailed by a cracker-barrel philosopher in the guise of a fisherman—fisher of souls—who, having himself once contemplated the fatal leap, has come to appreciate the value of what he had been about to throw away. He convinces the hapless philosopher that death needs no helping hand and that even the wilted tag end of a life poisoned by domestic misery can still be put to good use.

Whatever the internal factors, external ones—Herzl's fast-spreading notoriety and fame, the mockery and opposition he aroused along with the fulsome tributes and acclaim—contributed their share to his relatively quick recovery; they helped to revive his self-confidence and reinforced his sense of mission. Playing with fire, he had lit the torch, whether he meant to or not; time for him to shed his ambivalence and accept the role of Moses incarnate. "Hold your arms up high," Wolffsohn implored him, alluding to the biblical account of the battle between Amalek and the Israelites. "Keep up the fight. At the right time the right young men are bound to come to your aid and assure the victory of Israel" (Wolffsohn to Herzl, 8/10/96).

Pride alone would, in any case, never have let him retreat; he had come too far to turn back. But the hard uphill climb had transformed him. Gone were the days when a Burgtheater premiere loomed as life's highest ambition; he had found a cause worth dying for.

His situation in early 1897 was that of a general at the head of an army, with no clear notion of his effectives or of what to do with them. His hopes for a secret top-level conference of the Jewish establishment, originally proposed by Zadok Kahn, had been dashed, his diplomacy had run aground. He had made good on his threat to mobilize the masses—but mobilize them for what? How long would their enthusiasm survive in the absence of concrete results? The moment called for a dramatic gesture, and by coming up with the right one, Herzl proved his genius both as a leader and as a man of the theater.

The idea of convoking an Allgemeiner Zionistentag—a general conference of Zionists—seems to have been a reaction instinctive rather than rational. References to it crop up in Herzl's correspondence shortly after his return from London, but not until January 1897, with all other initiatives blocked, did they jell into a definite plan. He began by notifying various correspondents of his intention to call "a general assembly of Zionists"; a few weeks later, he became more specific about the place and date—Zurich, in late August—but remained conspicuously vague about the agenda, purpose, and other particulars.

This very vagueness, the absence of any clearly defined commitments, gave him the flexibility he needed to seize the first opportunity that presented itself. Early in March, a delegation of Hoveve Zion leaders from Berlin showed up in Vienna, led by Willy Bambus, a veteran activist with a string of practical achievements to his credit. Far less politically inclined than the Cologne contingent of Wolffsohn and Bodenheimer, the Bambus group pursued instead the traditional philanthropic goals of resettling Russian Jews in Palestine, thus avoiding any offense to the delicate sensibilities of the assimilationist majority of German Jews. They had, however, demonstrated impressive competence and dedication and maintained close contact with the Rothschild and Hirsch organizations.

The ostensible purpose of the visit was to discuss ways of jointly organizing an agricultural bank for Palestine, and of turning the Berlin monthly *Zion*—edited by Nathan Birnbaum—into a Zionist weekly or even daily. The hidden agenda, however, was to coopt Herzl and his movement. The Berliners were men of an eminently practical bent; though not in principle opposed to lofty visions, they were primarily interested in practical results on the ground. And Herzl, far and away the most prominent—in fact, the only prominent—figure in Western Jewry to have rallied to the cause, was seen by them as a potentially valuable ally.

The success of the meeting, held on March 6 and 7, 1897, was at least partly due to a mutual misunderstanding. The bank project was shelved as premature. Both sides agreed on the need for a major Zionist organ, and Herzl offered to raise 300,000 guilders, provided the others came up with the remaining 700,000 required. But the most important result was the acceptance of Herzl's proposal for a general Zionist

congress. Bambus, ever the cautious operator and anxious to keep
sensitive issues out of any public discussion, insisted on two distinct
congresses, one open and one closed. Herzl readily agreed, apparently
on the mistaken assumption that all Bambus had in mind were a few
sessions closed to the public. He also agreed to the change in venue
from Zurich to Munich; it was feared that Russian delegates might be
reluctant to travel to Switzerland, notorious as the center of Russian
nihilist activities and under constant surveillance by the Okhrana's
secret agents.

An organizing committee was appointed, headed by Herzl and Bambus, the date was set for August 25, and the two factions parted on
cordial terms, each confident that they had at last found reliable allies
in a common cause.

EIGHTEEN

*H*erzl's quasi-instinctive response to the tactical needs of the moment looms in retrospect as a radical break with the past. By convoking what in effect was a Jewish national assembly with distinctly political goals, he provocatively redefined Jewish identity in terms of a secular nationalism that transcended individual citizenship. Equally far-reaching were the implications for the future: in Basel, the arch-conservative proponent of an "aristocratic republic" unwittingly laid the foundations for the Israeli Knesset, which fifty years later almost to the day erupted on the Asian continent as one of the most vibrantly contentious of democratic parliaments.

But during the frenetic five months of preparing for the event, Herzl was far too preoccupied with the practical problems to ponder the long-range consequences. "Zionism," he declaimed, "is the Jewish people on the march"; and having recognized the need for concrete marching orders, he staked out an attainable interim goal that focused the energies of his followers and challenged both the playwright and the journalist in him. With the same loving attention to detail with which he had once fantasized about the ceremonial mass conversion of the Jews, he now set out to stage the first session of the first Jewish parliamentary body in modern history. It was to be a spectacular demonstration of national solidarity that would fire the imagination of Jews around the world and legitimize their political representatives.

The sheer technical obstacles seemed all but insurmountable, and since none of his followers could meet his standards and match his single-mindedness, the organization of the congress was once again essentially a solo performance. "We consulted, resolved, decided," wrote one of his disciples, "and then we each left and went back to our own business. It was Herzl alone who organized the congress, all by himself, with his own money and his own labor. . . . He saw to every detail, nothing escaped his attention. There were times when he sat up all night with the students, even addressing envelopes" (Thon, p. 26). As always, he complained bitterly about the lack of cooperation from his staff, while at the same time refusing to delegate any but the most trivial of responsibilities. For five crucial months the preparations absorbed every ounce of his energy; toward the end, more often than not, he fell asleep at his desk, drained and exhausted, only to rouse himself again at dawn. "A man who doesn't rise early will never amount to anything." When it came to the climactic mise-en-scène, he had unbounded confidence in his genius as a man of the theater and in his experience as a seasoned political observer. But the effect would, in the final analysis, depend on his assembling a persuasively representative body, an effort tantamount to an election campaign with no constituency, platform, candidates, electoral laws, or parliamentary traditions.

His study became the headquarters of a publicity blitz. The first official notices went out within the week; De Haas's translation, which he began to circulate on March 16, retains the full flavor of the original: "Sir: I am desired to announce that preparations are being made for the holding of a representative Zionist Congress at Munich, on August 25th next. . . . Everything will be done to render this Congress, the first to be held by Jews, as imposing, as its discussions will be of importance to Israel. In order to give the conference a thoroughly representative character delegates will be invited from all Zionist movements, political or philanthropic, local or general, in their aims."

These relatively discreet overtures were soon followed by more formal announcements, complete with a tentative agenda and detailed instructions for prospective delegates. Most prominent personalities, or at least those whose presence Herzl deemed especially desirable, also received a personal invitation. His list included nearly all his contacts in Western Europe, the one conspicuous exception being Edmond de Rothschild—"a man who has consistently been plotting against me." But until late summer, no comparable effort went into wooing Russian Jewry's leading personalities, nor was the neglect accidental. For although Herzl had already drastically revised his attitude toward the *Ostjuden*, he still did not take them seriously; he could hardly hope to impress Western Jews or Gentiles by a display of Hebrew polemicists from Warsaw or a clutch of wild-eyed Odessa literati.

Despite concerted efforts, the initial response to his call was disappointing. His enemies, however, were quick to come to the rescue; their righteous wrath soon more than made up for the equivocations of his friends.

Herzl's *Judenstaat*, whatever its impact on the already converted, did not seriously trouble the largely hostile majority of assimilated Jews, who dismissed it as one more crackpot idea to be ingested, digested, and disposed of. Initiating a public discussion of the Jewish Question, on the other hand, and calling for the establishment of a Jewish state, was a breach of etiquette they could no longer afford to ignore. By impugning the loyalty of Jewish citizens to their respective countries, this self-styled redeemer gave aid and comfort to the enemy. Orthodox believers were outraged by his brazen attempt to pervert religious faith into nationalist idolatry, while secular skeptics tended to detest militant Jewish nationalism even more than most other varieties. The result was an outburst of all-around indignation that gave Herzl far more publicity than his limited means could have bought for him. That it was largely unfavorable hardly mattered; in skilled hands, notoriety can be more useful than fame, and whatever skills he still lacked he was soon to acquire.

The upper-tier Anglo-Jewish circles were understandably alarmed but strove to contain the tremor of the upper lip. Montagu told Herzl that Jews had no business mixing Judaism and international politics. Colonel Goldsmid, beholden to the Rothschilds, opined that "we mustn't talk too loudly of the National Idea" and persuaded the British Hoveve Zion to abstain from "the congress convened by Dr. Herzl." Chief Rabbi Adler, in whose home Herzl had first glimpsed the charms of Jewish life in England, publicly denounced the plan and was characterized by Herzl as "a man who came to England from Germany and would no doubt like to have been of Anglo-Saxon descent." Even more aggressive, in his slippery way, was Vienna's own Dr. Guedemann, who performed a total about-face and weighed in with an unctuously patriotic anti-Zionist pamphlet. "The independence of the Chief Rabbi's position is such as to dispel any suspicion that he, like so many others, could be induced to side with the rich against the poor" (*Zionismus*, pp. 138–47) was Herzl's tart comment; he left the heavy demolition work to Nordau, who a few weeks later acquitted himself with furious gusto.

Nordau himself remained steadfast, but he was the only one among the notables on whom Herzl had counted. Zadok Kahn assured Herzl of his continued interest but excused himself on the grounds that the semiofficial status he enjoyed under French law made it impossible for him to attend the congress. Even in far-off New York, a group of Jews felt compelled to pass a resolution condemning "any formation of a Jewish state in Palestine in such a manner as may be construed as casting a doubt upon the citizenship, patriotism, and loyalty of Jews in whatever country they reside" (De Haas, p. 154).

Still more irksome was the defection of Bambus and of the whole Berlin Hoveve Zion, who, reading the wind, quickly trimmed sail and publicly denied ever having contemplated attending a Zionist congress, much less helping to organize it. Anxious to preserve their respectability and influence in a community seething with indignation, they disavowed Herzl and, in their official publication, joined the protests against the congress that were building up all over Germany. German Jews were quite simply appalled at the prospect of a public spectacle that would call into question their wholehearted allegiance to the German fatherland and, as they saw it, endorse the main postulates of anti-Semitism. The most strenuous opposition arose in Munich itself, where a terrified Jewish community threatened to resort to the courts in order to prevent this outrage.

Herzl parried these blows with as much tact and diplomacy as he could muster, but the growing hostility merely strengthened his resolve. While not above trying to cajole, flatter, and persuade, he made it plain that he would never yield on the main point at issue—the congress must and would take place. There could be no turning back. In April, responding to the clamor in Munich, he simply switched the meeting to Basel, a venue he much preferred in any case. He realized that it might pose problems for the Russian delegates, but even at this stage he still did not give them much thought; their participation, while desirable, would not add much luster or respectability to the occasion.

As the campaign against the congress went into high gear at home and abroad, it helped to publicize it far beyond anything Herzl could have hoped for. In a long history of factionalism, tortuous debates, and paradoxes beyond resolution, the issue dividing Jewish communities and individuals this time seemed clear-cut and simple, a yes or a no. Herzl was in his element. He relished the confrontation, but what increasingly frustrated him was the lack of an independent Zionist organ, essential for propaganda and indispensable in any war of words. Access to Joseph Bloch's *Oesterreichische Wochenschrift*—which published his reply to Guedemann—was a poor substitute for a paper of his own. Early in May, therefore, with the same abruptness that characterized all his decisions, he announced plans for a Zionist weekly; by the end of the month he had resolved all technical problems and was ready to go to press. Together with his father, he personally assumed full financial responsibility for all production costs, estimated at an annual 10,000 guilders, and although he appointed a three-man editorial staff, he would not deprive himself of the opportunity to handle every last detail of the first issue himself, from makeup and contents to reading galley proofs and supervising the press run.

After considerable soul-searching, he had settled on *Die Welt—The World*—as an appropriate name; article and noun were separated on the masthead by the Star of David enclosing a globe with Palestine at its center. The cover of the first issue was a bright yellow, the color of the medieval badge of shame, and the editorial on the front page further stressed the provocative intent:

> Our weekly is a *Judenblatt*. [A Jew rag.]
> We accept this word, meant to be an insult, and will turn it into a mark of honor.
> DIE WELT is a paper of the Jews. Which Jews? Not the strong ones, who are being helped anyway. They don't need our support.
> DIE WELT is the paper of the poor, the weak, the young, and of those as well who, while not themselves oppressed, have nonetheless found their way back to their tribe.
> What we want—to use the words already familiar to our friends—is to create a homeland secured by international law for those Jews unable or unwilling to assimilate in their current host countries. DIE WELT will be the organ of those men who want to lead Jewry out of these times into a better future.

Despite his brave words about the "strong" needing no help, however, he gave in to a joint plea by his three assistants ("who did not explain their motives") and suppressed a news item about the "coal

Gutmanns," one of Vienna's wealthiest families, who had seen fit to appeal their assessment of the Jewish community tax.

On June 1, Herzl ran off the first copy of the first issue, which he dedicated to his parents.

> I am totally exhausted. I'll never forget this Whitsuntide week of 1897. In addition to laboring over *Die Welt*, I still had to force myself into a suitable mood for a *Neue Freie Presse* feuilleton. Not to mention the excitement in the office, where I fear that *Die Welt* is bound to bring about a break with Benedikt. Several times already I was on the point of at least letting him in on the *fait accompli*. He now often drives me home in his car, which would be the best opportunity to talk about everything. But I finally decided to simply place a paid advertisement in the *Neue Freie Presse*. The ad has been accepted by the administration. [D, 6/6/97]

With the appearance of *Die Welt*, the swirl of controversies around the congress and its moving spirit reached a new level of intensity. The paper, which gave the Zionists an effective means of instant counterattack, inevitably widened the breach within the Jewish community worldwide. It set high standards for itself and reached a circulation of 10,000 subscribers within its first year, a respectable figure, though, of course, far from sufficient to cover the deficit. Herzl made the most of this new outlet for his polemical zeal and seldom missed a chance to strike back at his opponents. But there was one confrontation he manifestly dreaded and sought to postpone as long as possible—the showdown with his father figures at the *Neue Freie Presse*.

The storm and stress over *Der Judenstaat* had long since abated, and the truce had evolved into an amiable agree-to-disagree routine that allowed for spirited discussions devoid of rancor. Herzl labored under the illusion that the rise of Lueger had made Bacher and Benedikt more receptive to his own ideas; and when, in early March, they each independently talked about joining him on a trip to Jerusalem, he heard angels' voices in the skies above and began to dream of a pro-Zionist *Neue Freie Presse*. "I am still going to convert you," he told Bacher. "You will be my most noble conquest" (D, 3/17/97).

It is not altogether inconceivable that the catastrophic decline of Austrian liberalism may have temporarily sensitized both editors to problems they had programmatically refused to acknowledge, and that the rising tide of anti-Semitism forced them to confront the ambiguities of their own personal situation. If so, it was a short-lived change of heart. Both men—Bacher died in 1908, Benedikt in 1920—remained lifelong opponents of Zionism and staunch defenders of Austro-German liberalism. More likely, their patronizing indulgence toward Herzl reflected a mix of personal sympathy and ironic condescension. They liked him, they appreciated his work, and they no longer felt threatened by him. The flap over *Der Judenstaat* had passed without serious repercussions for the *Neue Freie Presse*, which was all they ever really cared about. As to his dalliance with the Turks and the murky affair of the suspected bribe, they had successfully contained the damage by assuming an aggressively anti-Turkish editorial stand and could only hope that he would spare them further embarrassment. In short, they treated him like a gifted but sometimes difficult and impetuous young man in need of firm parental guidance, and he responded in kind.

The appearance of *Die Welt*, however, once again upset the delicate balance.

In a letter to Nordau, Herzl describes the *Neue Freie Presse* as his lawfully wedded wife and *Die Welt* as the mistress he feared might ruin him. The remark hints at the heavy emotional charge that invested this particular relationship, and his reference to the obvious mother symbol as a lawful wife makes a Freudian interpretation almost irresistible. In any case, the sneaky, underhanded way, so strikingly out of character, in which he finally broke the news to his bosses via a paid ad in their own paper reveals a tangle of infantile guilt and unresolved conflicts that helps to explain both his irrational behavior and the high anxiety about his job.

He did, of course, have cause for concern. Bacher and Benedikt, though seething at what they considered a flagrant act of disloyalty, initially reacted with the icy calm of parents tried beyond endurance and pondering suitable punishment. Their pointed politeness further unnerved Herzl: "The showdown is due today," he wrote almost hopefully, after a three-day wait. "I don't know how it will end. Perhaps I'll be fired within the next twenty-four hours. I face this possibility with composure, although my heart keeps pounding. But that is just a weakness of the muscle, not of the will" (D, 6/8/97).

As it turned out, he had no reason to worry. During the next few weeks, his editors made a concerted effort to convince him either to sell or to suspend *Die Welt*. An anti-Semitic campaign linking it to the *Neue Freie Presse* and lampooning Benedikt, of all people, as the self-anointed "Benedictus I, King of Zion," lent added weight to their argument. They went so far as to insist that Herzl postpone his vacation until he had made up his mind one way or another. But he remained firm despite the implied threat and promised them his final answer after his return.

On June 23, the night before his departure, he cleaned out his desk at the office "like a good housewife neatly hanging up her bunch of keys as she senses death approaching." He felt an odd sense of relief at leaving "this much-envied position, the admittedly top literary post in Vienna . . . much as I felt when I was leaving school. Death, I thought, must be something like this. The only painful part—psychically more than physically—is probably the agony. Death as such may well be a relief to the dying" (D, 6/24/97).

In the end, however, Bacher and Benedikt backed down. Unlike Herzl, who feared losing their love, they only worried about losing a valued employee. Firing him—and having him snapped up by the competition—would have been a loss to their paper.

The five days he spent at Bad Ischl, a spa in the Salzkammergut mountains, cannot have done much for his frayed nerves. He never stopped working—he now had two newspapers to write for, in addition to his correspondence—nor did the presence of his family contribute to his relaxation. Although he could still wax eloquently sentimental about the joys of fatherhood, he had scant use for real-life children, his own or anyone else's—an attribute which, to be fair, he shared with most fathers of his generation. But he also had to deal with a wife driven to hysterics by the quite justifiable fear that he was about to ruin not only his own life but hers and those of their children as well. Moreover, her social standing as the wife of a prominent author and journalist had to some extent compensated for the miseries of a loveless marriage. Now that he was risking his reputation, not to mention her dowry and their children's future, in pursuit of a cause for which she did not have the slightest sympathy or understanding, her anxiety and frustration erupted in countless scenes which he had trained himself to shrug off with ostentatious indifference, but which nonetheless took their toll.

In July, shortly after his return to Vienna, he faced another frontal attack, this one mounted by the heavy guns of German Orthodoxy. The steering committee of the German Rabbinical Council published a resolution in the *Berliner Tageblatt* condemning the attempt by "so-called Zionists" to convoke a congress "which contravenes the messianic promise and the obligation to serve one's fatherland. Religion and patriotism alike, therefore, compel us to ask all those who cherish the welfare of Jewry to abstain from all Zionist efforts in general and, in particular, from the congress which despite all warnings is still being planned."

Both Herzl and Nordau reacted with barbed sarcasm. "Anyone wishing to turn away from Judaism is free to do so," wrote Herzl. "But to be part of the Jewish people, to practice Judaism professionally, so to speak, and at the same time to fight against it offends anyone's sense of justice. . . . But they do at least enable us to distinguish between real rabbis and those salaried employees of the synagogue who fight against the redemption of their own people. Let us call them Protest Rabbis." Nordau, as usual, went even further in his comments, characterizing the protest rabbis as spineless creatures afraid to rebel against their own servitude. "There are degrees even in degradation," he concluded.

The growing efficacy of Zionist propaganda undoubtedly had much to do with a gradual shift toward more positive views of the congress, but at least equally important was Herzl's flinty resolve to hold it, come what may. He never wavered. He met every obstacle that came his way and managed to turn many of them to his advantage. For all the enthusiasm he inspired among his followers, he alone bore the brunt of the burden, but his notes offer clear evidence that he relished his solitary role. The battle for the congress was his battle, and he emerged from it not only victorious but with enormously enhanced prestige, authority, and self-confidence. By midsummer, as it became definite that the meeting would take place, many of the doubters and opponents—such as Bambus and Goldsmid—changed their mind and decided to attend, after all. The press moderated its sarcasm and adopted a more cautiously respectful tone. At the same time, however, it was also increasingly evident that the glittering assembly of Western notables that Herzl had envisaged was turning into a convention of nobodies, the bulk of them students from Vienna, Paris, and Berlin—predominantly Russian ones, at that—along with a smattering of middle-aged German burghers, a small British contingent from Leeds and the East End of London, and a few individual supporters from various exotic corners of Europe and overseas, Nordau being the only figure of world renown.

It was this sense of isolation that led Herzl, rather late in the day, to change his tactics and redirect his efforts eastward, toward that great reservoir of Jewish life from which he had been largely cut off, as much by his own attitude as by the objective political situation in the Russian empire. As always, he acted swiftly and decisively. He had official invitations to the congress printed in Hebrew and sent to the most prominent personalities in the Russian Hoveve Zion movement. In a flowery letter to Rabbi Mohilever in Bialystock, translated into even more flowery Hebrew, he requested the head of the Orthodox (Mizrahi) Zionists to encourage the participation of his followers. He also wrote to Ahad Ha-Am in Odessa, a deceptively mild-mannered skeptic of incorruptible probity who was already among the most in-fluential voices in Zionism, and whose moral vision of its mission was to make him the great antagonist of Herzl's political approach. And taking the message to the masses was a spirited Russian student, Ye-hoshua Buchmil, who toured the Russian provinces as Herzl's emissary to rally support for the congress.

The Eastern initiative met with a mixed reception among the vet-erans of the movement in Russia. Suspicion of the Westernized out-sider, of the opportunist politician and self-styled prophet, clashed with more positive responses from those who saw in Herzl the dynamic leader needed to revitalize a virtually moribund enterprise. Weighing heavily against him were Herzl's troubles with the Western Zionists and, above all, his rejection by "the Baron," their Lord Bountiful, whom the Hoveve Zion were desperately anxious not to antagonize. Moreover, Herzl's aggressive stance, his provocative nationalist rhetoric and emphasis on bold diplomatic moves, aroused deep-seated fears in the ghettos of Eastern Europe, where people had long since learned that he who asks for trouble is liable to get it in spades.

Nevertheless, Mohilever urged his followers to go to Basel, and when it became clear in July that the congress would be held with or without them, most of those still on the fence fell in line. Lilienblum, Ussishkin, and Sokolow, opinion makers of considerable influence, were personally wooed by Herzl. Only Ahad Ha-Am, though not on principle opposed to the congress, still nursed his doubts about its purpose and effect, although an exasperated Ussishkin pointed out to him that "Herzl has hopes, but he has a program as well. We have hopes, but we don't know what to do." In the end, the great sage also capitulated, though of course not without reservations. "Perhaps I shall be there, after all. I may possibly be of some use, because it is painful to see everything put in the hands of young people whose enthusiasm is greater than their understanding."

The Russian delegates, mainly at Ussishkin's insistence, decided to attend the congress as a united faction—a perhaps inevitable decision that nonetheless presaged many future difficulties—and, at a preliminary caucus on July 28 at Karlsbad, formulated three specific demands: Nothing was to be said at Basel that might offend the Rothschilds or stir up the Turks, and no criticism of the czarist regime was to be voiced. Ideological objections aside, such censorship would have been well-nigh impossible to impose in practice, but Herzl's promise to caution the delegates and to urge voluntary restraint mollified the Russians and removed the next-to-last roadblock. The final one was Bacher, whom Herzl had to ask for an additional week's vacation, but the great man was in a suspiciously benign mood. "What are you up to, anyway?" he grumbled. "Are you about to set yourself up as an itinerant preacher?" He dismissed Herzl with a sarcastic "Give my regards to the Zionists," which Herzl, in the same spirit, promised to do. "Unofficially, of course."

On August 23, he was on his way to Basel, his first chance in weeks to come up for thought. "The fact—and one I keep from everybody— is that all I have is an army of *shnorrers*. I am the leader of a bunch of boys, beggars and *shmucks*. Some exploit me. Others are already envious or disloyal. Still others defect as soon as they sniff a chance for some minor career. The unselfish enthusiasts among them are few in number. And yet, this army would be quite adequate if only we had some success. In that case it would soon become an efficient regular army. We'll see what the immediate future holds in store" (D, 8/23/97).

It takes madness or genius to indulge in such unsparing lucidity without losing sight of the dream.

Stage-managing the congress will involve a rare feat, an egg dance among eggs invisible to all but myself. Egg No. 1: The *Neue Freie Presse*, which I must not compromise or furnish an excuse to for sacking me. 2: The Orthodox. 3: The Secularists. 4: Austrian patriotism. 5: Turkey, the Sultan. 6: The Russian government, against which nothing derogatory is to be said, although the deplorable situation of Russian Jewry will have to be mentioned. 7: The Christian denominations, on account of the Holy Places. In short, it is a summary of all the problems with which I have wrestled until now. Not to mention a few other eggs to watch out for: Edmond de Rothschild, the Russian Hoveve Zion, the colonists dependent on Rothschild's help. Then there are the personality clashes that have to be taken into account—envy, jealousy. I have to run the show impersonally and yet cannot afford to let go of the reins. [D, 8/24/97]

He arrived in Basel on Wednesday, August 25, four days before the formal opening of the congress, and immediately proceeded to take charge of the last-minute preparations. A vacant tailor shop was to serve as congress office; he made sure to have the shop sign covered "so as to forestall bad jokes." The premises rented by his local representative turned out to be a dingy beer cellar; he promptly canceled the lease and rented instead the Municipal Casino, an austere but dignified building that satisfied his need for an appropriate setting, rendered even more impressive by the large blue-and-white flag—the color of the prayer shawl—hung over the entrance. He supervised every last detail, listened to countless complaints and suggestions, paid formal calls on the municipal authorities, sat in on the preliminary meetings, issued a steady stream of orders and instructions. Nothing was left to chance. He was an indefatigable stage director fully in his element, who had designed the whole production, written the script, and was about to play the lead. His attendance at the Saturday-morning services of the local synagogue became the curtain raiser, a sop to the believers, of whom he always stood in secret awe. He managed to memorize the few Hebrew words of the blessing, although he complained that they caused him more sweat than an entire speech.

For the festive opening session on Sunday morning, he had decreed formal dress, tails and white tie. The costume was an integral part of the scenery he had designed long before he ever worried about the actual agenda, and he was thus understandably upset when Nordau, his second in command, showed up in a casual redingote instead and flatly refused to go back and change. "I took him aside and asked him to do it for my sake. I told him: Today the executive committee of the Zionist congress is still an absolute nothing; we have yet to make something of it. People should get used to seeing the congress as a most exalted and solemn authority. He let himself be persuaded, for which I gave him a grateful hug. Fifteen minutes later he was back, in formal dress" (D, 9/3/97).

If some of the delegates were put off by such ostentatious show-manship, their furtive sneers went largely unnoticed. Herzl's concept of politics as theater proved triumphantly effective—a smash hit at long last for the frustrated author of insipid bedroom farces. By staging a spectacle that not only moved people but made them part of the action, he had instinctively hit upon the alchemy of mass manipulation and successfully transmuted fantasy into power. The dramatic trappings may have been mere packaging, not devoid of self-indulgence on Herzl's part; yet it is more than doubtful if, without them, the congress would have lived up to its purpose as the first national assembly of the Jewish people in the Diaspora. By acting out his own fantasy in a *Gesammtkunstwerk* that combined Wagnerian histrionics with a cos-tume drama à la Makart, Herzl successfully transformed a rather hap-hazard collection of Jewish intellectuals, idealists, and opportunists into a representative body imbued with a sense of its own historic role.

The critical opening ceremonies on Sunday morning, August 29, set the tone and left most delegates moved to the point of tears. Dr. Karpel Lippe of Rumania, chosen, as the senior delegate, to pronounce the traditional blessing—though only sixty-seven, he had thirty years on Herzl—rambled on for half an hour in defiance of Herzl's frantic attempts to cut him short, but did not quite break the mood of tense expectancy. The emotional scene that greeted Herzl himself as he at last mounted the rostrum, the wave upon wave of wild applause and the cries of "Long live the King" that for some fifteen minutes kept him from speaking, have long since become part of his legend; they were a spontaneous outburst of hope long deferred, the deep longing for messianic redemption. Many participants have left descriptions of that high point in their lives, but Jakob De Haas's eyewitness report to the London *Jewish World*, despite its stilted journalese, seems more revealing and reliable than the retrospective accounts enhanced by memory:

Sunday morning, and the first session of the first Jewish world wide Congress. An unimpressive hall and a narrow gallery on one side, chairs and tables for the delegates, an L of tables for the journalists. A steep platform, covered with green baize, with a baize covered tribune on its left. To the rear a long narrow room by which the officers could enter the hall. Buzz and buzz for half an hour, of delegates being seated, evening dress and black frock coats the order of the day, the audience in the gallery craning their necks, asking explanations, the programme by no means illuminative, and all expectancy.

Then Dr. Herzl and a few others came out of the side room and stepped on to the platform. The Congress was in being. The gathering leaped to its feet and cheered and cheered, in the acclaiming notes of a dozen nationalities. And then, exhausted by its first burst of enthusiasms, sat down quiet and orderly. The Congress had commenced. Dr. Herzl as he delivered his first address was listened to with spell-bound, tense, ear-straining attention. It was neither the manner nor the method of speech, but something of what he said, and the existence of this tribunal that impressed itself deeply upon all. But for those irregularities that are natural to a large gathering, and are still more natural to men strange to public assemblies, the Congress proceeded in a proper and solemn manner. Herzl received the huzzas of a king, and men climbed over one another to congratulate him. The address of Dr. Nordau, which followed the organization of the Bureau of the Congress, was accorded a reception but a little less royal. Men wept over his new lamentation, which told not so much in tearful accents, but in words that at one moment clashed like an ominous roll of thunder, and at another crossed the horizon like a lightning flash. It stood before the Congress as the tale of the years of woe. For the impression was growing and growing that this was not a mere gathering of practical men, nor yet a mere assembly of dreamers; the inward note was the gathering of brothers meeting after the Diaspora, and every word lent force to the ideas. [De Haas, pp. 173–74]

The actual number of participants is impossible to establish with any degree of accuracy. Clerical foul-ups aside, quite a few used pseudonyms or avoided being listed altogether for fear of repercussions back home; the watchful presence of czarist agents was taken for granted.

The *Präsenzliste*—the official list of delegates—underwent several revisions even in the course of the proceedings. Total attendance, based on these revisions as well as on unofficial counts and retrospective estimates, appears to have been somewhere between 199 and 246 participants, 69 of whom represented communities or organizations, while the rest came as observers, critics, or disciples. As a practical measure this first time around, merely being male and Jewish qualified anyone to cast his vote. Some twenty women were present as either delegates or wives of participants; according to the minutes, Herzl welcomed them as "of course, very distinguished guests, but they do not participate in voting"—a decision reversed at the second congress the following year.

The guest list included Hechler and Nevlinsky, but Zangwill was the only prominent figure aside from Nordau. Still, Herzl's "army of *shnorrers*" turns out, on closer scrutiny, to have been an eminently respectable group of well-educated businessmen and professionals. Roughly a quarter—sixty according to the official count—listed their occupation as business or finance (which does not, of course, preclude the presence of *shnorrers* among them). There were twenty-four lawyers, fifteen physicians, twenty-one writers, thirteen journalists, and thirty-eight students, along with a scattering of other occupations. Most were secularists; none of the eleven rabbis represented anyone or anything beyond their personal convictions. The rather lengthy greetings from Rabbi Mohilever to the congress—all of which Herzl insisted on reading from the rostrum—were the only qualified public endorsement by an Orthodox leader.

They came from twenty countries, ranging from Algeria to the United States, with Russia accounting for the largest contingent (sixty-three), followed by Austria and Germany, although the figures are deceptive in that Russian Jews also predominated in many of the nominally Western delegations. But what perhaps most decisively characterized the assembly as a whole was a common background of active participation in pre-Herzlian Zionism, which lent its prominent veterans an influence far out of proportion to their numbers.

Given the often highly critical attitude of these articulate and contentious Eastern European intellectuals schooled in the unforgiving polemics of ideological combat and organizational infighting, the authority with which Herzl dominated the proceedings was truly impressive. He had certain advantages: he was the only one who knew exactly what he wanted to accomplish, and he had spent four years studying the master manipulators of the Palais Bourbon—"Subconsciously I had absorbed all the subtleties of parliamentary procedure." He ran the show with the autocratic affability of a cunning French parliamentarian, but ultimately it was his charismatic personality, projected by the regal looks, the Assyrian profile, the imperious manners, and the dark-timbred voice that captivated his audience and secured a majority of votes for most of his proposals. So intent was he on maintaining full personal control that he spent as many as twenty-one hours at a stretch in the chair. "Everybody turned to me with everything, relevant or not. There were always four, five people talking at me at once. An enormous mental strain, since they all wanted instant decisions. I felt as if I were playing thirty-two simultaneous chess games" (D, 9/3/97).

Not that all was harmony, by a long shot. Nordau's survey of Jewish misery the world over, delivered with great passion and without notes, caused a sensation, but he seemed visibly piqued at being cast in a supporting role, so that Herzl continually went out of his way to stroke his ego. Running the show with an iron fist in a well-greased glove, he deftly sidetracked a motion to voice collective thanks to Edmond de Rothschild as "an attempt to force upon this body a choice between ingratitude and principle" and foiled an attempted palace coup by Birnbaum aimed at undercutting his presidential powers. The vicious *ad hominem* debate that ensued—chaired by Nordau, since Herzl's chairmanship was itself at issue—prompted a remark by Rosa Sonnenschein, a delegate from New York, which does justice to the high drama of the occasion and seems refreshingly ecumenical, coming from the ardently Zionist editor of *The American Jewess*. "They are going to crucify you," she hopefully warned Herzl, "and I shall be your Mary Magdalene."

Yet within a mere three days—at least one of which was entirely taken up by speeches, announcements, and other routine business— the congress was able to set up the movement's basic institutions and to formulate a program of action, accomplishments for which Herzl deserves most of the credit. The highest authority was to be the annual congress, delegates to which were to be elected on the basis of one per 100 members. Voters qualified by payment of "one shekel," a token amount equivalent to one franc, one mark, one crown, etc. The year-round business between sessions was to be conducted by an eighteen-member Action Committee elected by countries, supplemented by five Vienna residents functioning as the working executive on a day-to-day basis. Local Zionist organizations were granted broad autonomy, but special emphasis was placed on their operating strictly within the laws of their respective countries. This simple and efficient institutional framework was Herzl's personal triumph. It corresponded in all essentials to his grand vision of a representative national assembly and was to serve the movement through the next half century with only minor modifications.

Formulating the Zionist program, on the other hand, proved a much stickier task. Complete unanimity on fundamental aims, deemed of vital importance, necessitated compromises on matters of principle. The most emotional debate raged around the precise phrasing of the movement's ultimate goal. Given the realities of power politics, Herzl himself had quietly dropped the term "Jewish *state*" and used instead "a home secured by international law." The phrase still troubled the moderates, anxious to avoid anything that might arouse Turkish suspicions. At their insistence, the word "international" was deleted, and according to the compromise reported out, Zionism now aimed "at the creation of a home for the Jewish people in Palestine secured by law." This, in turn, struck the radical wing—Herzl's most devoted supporters—as a betrayal of basic principles. Crying foul, they provoked another violent discussion, finally cut short by Herzl's Solomonic proposal to amend the sentence by adding one—essentially meaningless—word. His move was adopted by acclamation, and the preamble of what came to be known as the "Basel program" in its final version called for "the creation of a home for the Jewish people in Palestine secured by public law."

At the closing session on August 31, another tidal wave of emotions swept the by now thoroughly exhausted delegates to the brink of hysteria and beyond. From the rostrum, the Chief Rabbi of Basel proclaimed his conversion to Zionism, provided the Jewish state respected the religious traditions. "Herzl," de Haas reports, "was almost imperial in his reply that religious Judaism had nothing to fear from Zionism, and he reasserted that 'a return to Jewry must precede the return to Zion.' "

He goes on to describe the final moments:

A vote of thanks followed, but it was no ordinary compliment. The Congress was on its feet, the correspondents mounted the tables, and the audience in the gallery grew equally excited. It was not a question of cheering, but of ventilating hearts full of emotion. I have seen bigger crowds and have heard more vociferous outbursts, but the like of this mass of waving handkerchiefs—I made a mental picture of Zangwill's spare figure on a chair, waving a red bandana in the midst of it all—the like of this I have never seen.

The simple words of the president, "The first Congress is at an end," were heard, but not understood; that is to say, no one realized and no one could realize that after so many ages of separation there was to be so speedy a parting. The delegates remained standing, cheering. Some broke out into the Hatikvah; another began singing "The Watch on the Jordan." From side to side of the hall came shouts of "A year to come in Jerusalem." The scene continued for an hour. . . . Perhaps the most self-possessed was the leader, as he bade the delegates farewell in a small side room. [De Haas, p. 177]

Back in Vienna, Herzl at last had a chance to take stock and sort out his feelings. "Were I to sum up the Basel congress in a word—which I shall carefully refrain from uttering in public—it would be this: in Basel I founded the Jewish state. If I were to say this out loud today, everybody would laugh at me. In five years, perhaps, but certainly in fifty, everybody will agree" (D, 9/3/97).

Written on September 3, 1897. It actually took six months longer than he predicted: the Jewish state proclaimed its independence on May 14, 1948.

NINETEEN

*H*erzl was not the only prophet in Basel.

Ahad Ha-Am came as an observer, left as a critic, yet made his presence felt at the congress without ever mounting the rostrum. His vision of the Jewish state differed radically from Herzl's emphasis on politics and power, yet in many ways he proved more prescient than his great antagonist, now rightfully enshrined as the founding father of the state of Israel.

The contrast between them could hardly have been more extreme. The oldest child of a Hasidic family, Ahad Ha-Am was born Asher Ginzberg in 1856 and grew up in Skvira, near Kiev, later described by him as "one of the most benighted spots in the Hasidic districts of Russia." Locked up in the traditional *cheder* at age three, he emerged in his teens as an adept Talmudic scholar but contracted a fatal zest for non-kosher knowledge that eventually turned him into an agnostic of formidable learning. He was married at seventeen to a bride of his rabbi's choosing, whom he met for the first time under the bridal canopy; "she was," as he tartly noted, "neither blind nor deformed," his only known reference to his wife. Having opted for a commercial career, he moved to Odessa in 1886 and soon thereafter was elected to the Central Committee of the Hoveve Zion, which four years earlier had begun to establish settlements in Palestine. His concept of Palestine as the spiritual center of a Jewish national revival led to a clash with Pinsker, who stressed humanitarian needs over abstract ideals and was ready to settle for any territory anywhere.

It was the first of many such conflicts; unfailingly courteous, never stooping to personal attacks, Ahad Ha-Am was every bit as unbending as Herzl on matters of principle but far less circumspect about expressing what he saw as the truth, regardless of consequences. His very first article, a critique of then prevailing trends in Zionism published in the Hebrew monthly *Hamelitz* in 1889 and signed Ahad Ha-Am— One of the People—established his reputation as both a brilliant Hebrew stylist and a seminal if highly controversial thinker. Two visits to Palestine in 1891—the first of several—undertaken on behalf of the Odessa Committee of Hoveve Zion, resulted in a devastating exposé castigating conditions in the settlements, their emphasis on viticulture and philanthropy, and the attitudes of the settlers themselves. Unlike most of his fellow Zionists, who persisted in fantasizing about "a land without people for the people without a land," Ahad Ha-Am from the very beginning refused to ignore the presence of Arabs in Palestine. As early as 1891, he pointed out that, on the contrary, most of the arable land was in fact being tilled by Arabs, "whom we tend to think of as savages who live like animals and don't understand what is going on around them. This, however, is a grave error." And sounding a prophetic warning more pertinent today than any of Herzl's pronouncements on the subject, he urged respect for the native population. "Yet what do our brethren do in Palestine? Just the opposite. Serfs they were in the lands of the Diaspora. Now, as they suddenly find themselves enjoying unconstrained freedom, they become despots themselves. They treat the Arabs with hostility and cruelty, deprive them of their rights, offend them without cause and even boast of their deeds, and none among us opposes this despicable and dangerous trend."

Jewish ethics were the heart and soul of Ahad Ha-Am's brand of nationalism, and to the end of his life he denounced any compromise with political expediency. In 1913, protesting against a Jewish boycott of Arab labor, he wrote to his friend Moshe Smilansky in Rehovot: "Apart from the political danger, I can't put up with the idea that our brethren are morally capable of behaving in such a way to humans of another people, and unwittingly the thought comes to my mind: If this is so now, what will our relations to the others be like if, at the end of time, we shall really achieve power in Eretz Israel? And if this be the Messiah, I do not wish to see his coming."

Nor did he, indeed, see it. He died in Tel Aviv in 1927, and one of his last public statements, a letter to the editor of *Haaretz*, concerns the rumored revenge killing of an Arab boy by Jewish settlers: "What should we say if this really turned out to be true? My God, is THIS the end? Is THIS the goal for which our ancestors have striven and for whose sake all generations suffered? Is this the dream of our return to Zion, that we come to Zion and stain its soil with innocent blood? . . . Do we really do it so as to add yet another small tribe of new Levantines to this corner of the Orient, who will vie with other Levantines in shedding blood, in vengeance and in wrath?"

Ahad Ha-Am's moral absolutism, the reckless compulsion to call the shots as he saw them, made him a lonely figure even within the ranks of his own fellow Zionists and exposed him to constant attacks. But popularity was not his aim in life, though he acknowledged that the age of mass-speak and mass-think was hard on the outsider "who is not part of the crowd and who cannot follow with closed eyes in the footsteps of this or that Messiah." He was a profoundly unhappy man who would settle for nothing less than perfection. But in the course of his doomed quest, he became the conscience of at least a substantial part of the Zionist movement, and one of its most revered and influential figures.

In the end, the contest between Ahad Ha-Am's idealism and Herzl's political approach was decided by forces neither could possibly have foreseen, because both prophets, for all their differences, were shaped and nourished by a belief in nineteenth-century rationalism. Herzl misread anti-Semitism as an understandable and "rational" reaction to alien elements, while Ahad Ha-Am merely took it for granted, being far less concerned with what others did to the Jews than with what the Jews did for and to themselves. Auschwitz was as much beyond the vision of prophets as it was beyond the imagination of ordinary humans.

Modern Zionism claims descent from both Herzl and Ahad Ha-Am, but the link seems more wishful thinking than genuine synthesis. In life, at any rate, these two utterly disparate characters were separated by a wide gap, with Ahad Ha-Am on one side denouncing what struck him as the delusional aspects of Herzl's leadership while, on the other, Herzl chose imperiously to ignore a carping critic without a power base whose isolation made him appear unworthy of serious concern; he is never so much as mentioned in the Diaries. When eventually Ahad Ha-Am drew blood with his devastating review of Herzl's 1902 novel, *Old New Land*, Herzl commissioned Nordau to counterattack, with consequences yet to be discussed.

Ahad Ha-Am attended the congress as a guest, sitting among the delegates "like a mourner at a wedding feast." In a letter to a friend, he recorded his reaction on the morning after:

> Last night the meeting ended. My head still aches, my nerves are on edge, and I do not allow myself to say what I think, because I cannot yet control my feelings. I hate to say it, but one could see how low we have fallen. . . . After the meeting I had a short talk with Herzl, and came to the conclusion that his hints about what he has achieved in Constantinople are worth nothing at all. He got no promise, and there is no doubt that henceforth the Turkish government will be much stricter with us than it has been. [*Essays, Letters, Memoirs*, p. 171]

As editor of the small but influential Hebrew monthly *Hashiloah*, however, Ahad Ha-Am had access to a wider audience, and in his public comments on the congress he took a more balanced though no less critical line. He hailed it as the first "national response to the Jewish Question, delivered fearlessly for all the world to hear," and paid special tribute to Nordau's speech. "We did not, after all, come to Basel to found the Jewish state today or tomorrow, but to let the world know that the Jewish people lives and wants to live. This the Basel congress accomplished in a most edifying manner at its opening session, and for that reason it would have deserved to be inscribed in golden letters in the memory of generations—if it had not attempted to do more."

The "more" he objected to comprised the entire organizational structure set up by the congress, and most particularly the emphasis on political initiatives rather than moral and cultural renewal. "It is prophets rather than diplomats who will bring about Israel's redemption."

This one discordant note in the midst of post-congress euphoria roused a storm of indignation but merely prompted Ahad Ha-Am, in an essay a few months later, to be more specific:

> Since the delegates returned home, they have been gathering the public together and recounting over and over again the wonders that they saw enacted before their eyes. . . . Heads grow hot and hearts beat fast; and many communal workers, whose one care in life had been for years—until last August—the Palestinian settlements . . . have now quite lost their bearings and ask one

another: What's the good of this sort of work? The Messiah is near at hand, and we busy ourselves with trifles. The time has come for great deeds: great men, men of the West, march before us in the van. There has been a revolution in their world, and to emphasize it, they give a new name to the cause: it is no longer "Love of Zion" [Hibbat Zion] but "Zionism."

Hibbat Zion, no less than Zionism, wants a Jewish state and believes in the possibility of the establishment of a Jewish state in the future. But while Zionism looks to the Jewish state to provide a remedy for poverty, complete tranquillity and national glory, Hibbat Zion knows that our state will not give us all these things until "universal Righteousness is enthroned and holds sway over nations and states," and it looks to a Jewish state to provide only a secure refuge for Judaism and a cultural bond for our nation. . . . Dr. Herzl, it is true, said . . . that Zionism demands the return to Judaism before the return to the Jewish state. But these nice-sounding words are so much at variance with his deeds that we are forced to the unpleasant conclusion that they are nothing but a well-turned phrase. . . .

Whoever reads *Die Welt* attentively and critically will not be able to avoid the impression that the Western Zionists always have their eyes fixed on the non-Jewish world, and that they, like the assimilated Jews, are aiming simply at finding favor in the eyes of the nations: only that whereas the others want love, the Zionists want respect. They are enormously pleased when a Gentile says openly that the Zionists deserve respect, when a journal prints some reference to the Zionists without making a joke of them, and so forth. These Zionists do not try to get close to Jewish culture and imbibe its spirit, but, on the contrary, they endeavor to imitate, as Jews, the conduct and procedure of the Germans, even where they are most foreign to the Jewish spirit, as a means of showing that Jews, too, can live and act like all other nations. [*Basic Writings of Ahad Ha-Am*, pp. 66 et seq.]

No movement and few, if any, individuals could ever have lived up to Ahad Ha-Am's ideals. This does not detract from the ideals or invalidate his critical observations; most of what he wrote about Herzl was astute and prescient. But in accusing him, in essence, of having severed his roots—as though he, the ex-Hasid, had not himself lopped off quite a few of them—he vastly underestimated the significance of

Herzl's most conspicuous break with tradition: his will to act. By exalting the deed over the word, Herzl rejected the historic quietism that relied on hope, faith, and charity. Action implies taking risks, and Herzl took large, often foolish ones, but action was the secret of his appeal to the masses of Eastern Europe, and the first Zionist congress demonstrated its revolutionary potential.

The spectacle, by defying popular stereotypes and myths, had aroused the curiosity of the non-Jewish world. It received wide press coverage, most of it fairly objective and favorable; only the *Neue Freie Presse* continued to sulk on principle. Comments by the anti-Semites were markedly respectful at the time, though the congress later came to figure large in their literature as a cabal of Jewish bankers conspiring to rule the world. And even the emphatically philo-Semitic Mark Twain referred to the meeting (which he mistakenly placed in Bern) in terms of mock apprehension:

> Speaking of concentration, Dr. Herzl had a clear insight into the value of that. Have you heard of his plan? He wishes to gather the Jews of the world together in Palestine, with a government of their own—under the suzerainty of the Sultan, I suppose. At the convention of Bern, last year, there were delegates from everywhere, and the proposal was received with decided favor. I am not the Sultan, and I am not objecting, but if that concentration of the cunningest brains in the world was going to be made in a free country (bar Scotland), I think it would be politic to stop it. It will not be well to let that race find out its strength. If the horses knew theirs, we should not ride anymore. ["Concerning the Jews," *Complete Essays*, p. 248]

Unpublicized but at least equally significant were the confidential reports by various agents, diplomats, and spies who attended the meetings. The Austrian embassy characterized the congress as a front for German socialists, while the French consul in Basel ridiculed its aims as the pipe dreams of Jewish journalists. But the German diplomats, themselves no strangers to pipe dreams, took them quite seriously. Von Tottenbach, German ambassador to Switzerland, filed a memorandum that was passed all the way up to the Kaiser, who in a handwritten marginal note added his statesmanlike comment: "Let the kikes go to Palestine, the sooner the better. I am not about to put obstacles in their way."

Herzl's colleagues at the *Neue Freie Presse*, on the other hand, greeted the "future head of state" with gales of laughter and a display of sparkling Viennese wit when he returned on September 2. Bacher refused to engage and seemed to be beating a quiet retreat for the time being, although his coat pocket, as Herzl noted to his satisfaction, was bulging with Swiss newspapers.

One bright spot in an otherwise darkening sky. The emotional binge of the Basel triumph with its drama-filled days and sleepless nights had left Herzl utterly drained, physically and mentally exhausted. But the very success of the congress confronted him with a host of organizational problems, which he alone felt qualified to resolve. However sincere his denial of messianic aspirations, he would have had to be superhuman not to get carried away by the wild enthusiasm of a crowd that hailed him as the King of the Jews. And although good form compelled him to ascribe the tribute to the force of his ideas, in his heart he knew better. It was his personality above all that made him, if not yet the King of the Jews—good form, again—at least their chosen leader and supreme commander, a role for which his fantasies had prepared him since childhood.

He played it to the hilt, running the embryonic organization with a heavy hand and an autocratic temper that brooked no opposition, tolerated no delay, and treated any sign of dissent as incipient treason. His by now fairly sizable staff—the five resident members of the Action Committee, the editorial board of *Die Welt*, clerical help and assorted volunteers—was for the most part sincerely dedicated to the cause as well as to him personally. But he measured their devotion against his own, constantly found it wanting, and conveyed his displeasure with an imperious lack of tact that sparked many a palace revolt.

The streak of aristocratic arrogance, which had long served to cloak self-doubt and fear of rejection, now became the mark and prerogative of leadership. He was beginning to believe in his own legend, and the reverential awe it inspired in him did not facilitate relations with mere mortals, be they followers or members of his family. Complaints and criticism from within what he scathingly referred to as the "Inaction Committee" infuriated him; he suspected Nathan Birnbaum, its secretary, of plotting to oust him, and denounced the rest as incompetent ingrates.

Birnbaum probably did conspire against him—paranoids do have enemies—but what Herzl demanded was nothing short of total submission, and even that did not guarantee his wholehearted approval.

Moreover, he felt he had a right to his grievances. If he himself was working around the clock, running the organization, writing for *Die Welt* at least as much as for the *Neue Freie Presse*, carrying on a huge correspondence, receiving visitors from all over the world and engaging in secret diplomacy while holding on to a full-time, responsible job, sacrificing his health, family, and fortune—why, then, could not his supposed helpers make more of an effort to be like him?

Relations were further strained by money matters. Up to this point, Herzl alone had borne the brunt of expenses, a far from negligible burden which, aside from *Die Welt* and the congress, included clerical salaries, travel, etc. Inevitably it gave him—and, so he felt, entitled him to—certain exclusive rights and a sense of ownership incompatible with an egalitarian atmosphere. At one of the first sessions in September he confronted the members of the "Inaction Committee" with an ultimatum of sorts: "Up to now, I have paid for whatever was necessary out of my own pocket. If the committee wants 'an equal share in the government,' it will first have to pass a test of strength by putting 5,000 guilders into the treasury" (D, 9/24/97).

In the long run, few men of substance could put up with this dictatorial rule, a perennial problem of charismatic leaders. But there was no shortage of sycophants, yes-men, and adoring disciples. There never is; more people by far are eager to trade judgment and independence for the certainties of faith in a supreme authority.

Herzl provided that authority. Yet, to be fair, he also provided a plan of action and much of the energy needed to carry it out. A sound financial basis seemed to him the movement's most pressing need; without it, Zionist policies would forever be hamstrung by the fears and foibles of small-minded financiers. Dusting off his original *Judenstaat* concept of the Society of Jews, he therefore launched a drive in October to raise 2 million pounds sterling as the initial capital for a Jewish Colonial bank. David Wolffsohn, the only member of his inner circle with practical experience in the field, was put in charge of the arrangements, but served mainly as his master's voice. Herzl basically trusted no one but himself when it came to carrying out his intentions—"I myself must forge the tools to fell the tree. The stone age of politics"—and spent himself in ultimately futile attempts to put together a consortium of investors. As usual, his imagination ran way ahead of reality; any vague promise was celebrated as a virtual guarantee, and in order to lend a suitably dramatic flourish to the enterprise, he had already made plans to charter a ship, take all the original investors on a four-week tour of Palestine, and exploit the resulting publicity for a popular subscription drive. In the end, however, none of the individual promises panned out, and the banking houses he approached—Sassoon and Montagu in London, Warburg in Hamburg, Oppenheim in Cologne, and Seligmann in Frankfurt—all turned him down unceremoniously. Only the small German firm of Schaffhausen agreed in principle to underwrite shares; it also happened to be the single non-Jewish one in the lot, a fact which further inflamed Herzl's suspicions of behind-the-scenes intrigues by the dastardly Rothschilds. His fury and frustration contained more than a hint of paranoia; and while, once again, this does not necessarily invalidate his suspicions, it triggered an outburst on his part that would have delighted the troglodytes of the Jew-baiting gutter press but which he published instead in *Die Welt* of October 15, 1897, under the heading of *Mauschel* (Yid, or kike).

Yid is anti-Zionist. We've known him for a long time, and just merely to look at him, let alone approach or, heaven forbid, touch him was enough to make us feel sick. But our disgust, until now, was moderated by pity; we sought extenuating, historical explanations for his being so crooked, sleazy, and shabby a specimen. Moreover, we told ourselves that he was, after all, our fellow tribesman, though we had no cause to be proud of this fellowship. . . . Whenever he perpetrated some dirty deal, we tried to hush it up. Whenever he compromised us all, we felt ashamed but kept silent.

Now at last the Yid has done something that merits praise— he has rejected us.

But who is this Yid, anyway? A type, my dear friends, a figure that pops up time and again, the dreadful companion of the Jew, and so inseparable from him that they have always been mistaken one for the other. The Jew is a human being like any other, no better and no worse. . . . The Yid, on the other hand, is a hideous distortion of the human character, something unspeakably low and repulsive. Where the Jew experiences pain or pride, the Yid feels only craven fear or twists his face into a sardonic grin. . . . The Yid is the curse of the Jews. . . .

In our own day, even a flight from religion can no longer rid the Jew of the Yid. Race now is the issue—as if the Jew and the Yid belonged to the same race. But go and prove that to the anti-

Semite. To him, the two are always and inextricably linked.
. . . And then came Zionism. Both Jew and Yid had to take a
stand, and now, for the first time, the Yid has done the Jew an
unexpectedly great service. The Yid rejects our community. The
Yid is anti-Zionist! . . . This is one of the first and most beneficial
consequences of the movement. We'll breathe more easily, having got rid once and for all of these people whom, with furtive
shame, we were obliged to treat as our fellow tribesmen. [And
Herzl concludes with a snarl worthy of a schoolyard bully] Watch
out, Yid. Zionism might proceed like Wilhelm Tell . . . and
keep a second arrow in reserve. Should the first shot miss, the
second will serve the cause of vengeance. Friends, Zionism's
second arrow will pierce the Yid's chest.

In fact, as these brief excerpts demonstrate, the entire diatribe sizzles
with primitive rage, touched off by a mix of frustration and fatigue
that overrode all restraints. A momentary lapse, a one-time departure
from the cool, ironic prose in which the practiced feuilletonist normally
encased his feelings, but also a glimpse of the still smoldering Jewish
self-hatred, the toxic infection caught in childhood that was so powerful
a motive in his quest.

He was worn out—"too tired, too busy for diary entries . . . and
besides, responsibility inhibits me from freely venting my opinions of
people, since these diaries will obviously someday serve as source
material for the history of the Jews" (D, 10/17/97). Hardly surprising,
given the scope and pace of his activities—"I have been wasteful in
the way I manage energy resources." Whether the bouts of physical
exhaustion signaled or triggered the onset of another depression may
be moot, but they certainly lowered his resistance to the multiple
stresses of his daily routine. He sought comfort in the thought that
"he who brought his peripatetic dreams of June 1895 from the gardens
of the Tuileries and the Palais Royal to the Basel Congress may yet
cross the Mediterranean as a Jew bound for home. Only," he added,
"I am tired like an old man."

He was all of thirty-seven. But he looked at least ten years older,
and though he resolutely refused to pay attention to his health, the
more troublesome symptoms—palpitations, shortness of breath, paralyzing fatigue—were difficult to ignore.

Death was never far from his mind, imparting a special urgency to
his actions and making him drive himself all the more relentlessly. If

the dreams are unrealistic, don't scuttle the dream—change reality.

He revised his plans for the bank. If the moneybags refused to play, he would have to come up with some other solution, but come what may, the bank would be the first item on the agenda of the next congress in August 1898—itself a project that was beginning to absorb more and more of his energy. The first congress had drawn people by virtue of its novelty, the prospect of a happening without precedent, but there was stubborn resistance to the idea of a permanent, quasi-parliamentary body with regular annual sessions, as envisaged by Herzl. It took heroic efforts to build the organizational substructure and create the right climate for a second act that would not only repeat but surpass the success of the first.

Yet all of these, in Herzl's view, were marginal issues, mere technical details, however problematic; he persisted in his belief that the central issue was political. The whole organization had, after all, been conceived mainly as a way to exert pressure on the Jewish plutocracy and to gain leverage in the international power play. If he could obtain reasonable concessions from the Sultan, everything else would fall into place—money, manpower, and eventually statehood. And Zionist diplomacy was his own private domain, an art form in which he fancied himself a virtuoso but which, by its very nature, had to be practiced behind the scenes.

Ever since his return from Constantinople, his offensives had been stalled on all fronts, to the point where even he could not discern any progress, although Nevlinsky fed him a steady diet of inside stories about the progressive deterioration of the Turkish economy. Herzl, for a change, again thoroughly mistrusted the slippery Pole, who, after attending the congress as his guest of honor, betrayed him by going on to Paris for a chat with Edmond de Rothschild. It was obvious that, aside from working both sides of the street, Nevlinsky was also canvassing some of the back alleys as well. But however dubious an ally, the wily con man and professional blackmailer would make a dangerous enemy, capable of doing untold damage—a sobering thought that induced Herzl to put him on a monthly retainer of 200 guilders.

In any event, he had little choice. He had never attempted to expand his contacts in Constantinople, never cultivated other, more objective sources of information, never truly explored the fundamental problems of the Ottoman Empire—in large measure because he conceived of politics in terms of personalities, a game played by powerful individuals trying to outbluff one another. Achieving his goals was, he believed, a matter of bluff and bribery, of making the right contacts and of playing his cards right. Hence his inordinate reliance on Nevlinsky's court gossip and political intelligence, most of which boiled down to speculations about which influential official was up for sale and worth buying.

A broader view of history might have alerted Herzl to the interplay of more complex forces and given him a sounder appreciation of the dynamics as well as the constraints affecting Turkish politicians and their policies. It also might have helped him realize that the Turks were far more sophisticated than his Central European sense of superiority led him to suspect. They were indeed in desperate financial straits, but far too well informed about the true state of Herzl's own resources and about his lack of any substantive backing to be taken in by his grandiose offers of assistance. Moreover, contrary to Herzl's fond belief, opposition to large-scale Jewish immigration into Palestine was not one of Abdul Hamid's personal quirks, subject to change with the proper inducement, but a fundamental tenet of Turkish policy, conditioned by historic, cultural, and political factors which Herzl chose to disregard insofar as he was aware of them in the first place. In fact, Turkish diplomatic correspondence of the period reveals grave concern over Zionism. The Sublime Porte tracked the movement from its inception, closely followed the internal debates, sent observers to the congresses, and received detailed reports on Herzl's progress from numerous diplomatic representatives and agents, Nevlinsky presumably being one of the more prolific sources of information.

It therefore seems more than likely that the three long conversations Herzl had in January with Ahmed Tewfik Pasha, then Turkish ambassador to Berlin but about to become Foreign Minister (he eventually made it to Grand Vizier), were no more than discreet attempts to probe the chinks in his armor. In any event the talks, though cordial and wide-ranging, led nowhere. "I returned to Vienna and told Nevlinsky that Ahmed Tewfik did not yet strike me as ripe for the idea. We would have to wait some more until Turkey was even worse off. On the other hand—and this would by no means be stupid—Tewfik might tell himself: We Turks will have to wait some more until the Jews are still worse off" (D, 2/4/98).

Another potential source of trouble was the Vatican, rumored to have protested in Constantinople against any concessions to the Jews. The rumor proved unfounded in this particular case, although it accurately reflected the Vatican's attitude toward Zionism. Neither Herzl's subsequent discussion with Cardinal Tagliani, the Papal Nuncio in Vienna, nor his 1904 audience with Pope Pius X himself, in both of which he offered assurances about the autonomy of the Holy Places, moved the Vatican to reconsider its opposition to a Jewish state in Palestine.

In addition to his foreign policy concerns, however, Herzl also had to deal with pressing issues of internal Austrian politics, a realm to which he brought much greater depth of knowledge and experience. In April 1897, Prime Minister Badeni introduced an ordinance giving the Czech language equal standing with German in Bohemia and Moravia, in effect making it a second official language, to be mastered by all government employees. Few issues are calculated to arouse as violent a popular reaction as those touching on language. The Germans promptly rebelled, and most Jews living in the predominantly Czech territories joined the rebellion out of a sense of cultural affinity with their beleaguered German compatriots. The stage was set for a showdown. It came in November, when pressure in parliament forced Badeni to revoke the language ordinances and gave the Czechs in turn something to riot about. Czech mobs attacked Germans, the Germans responded in kind, and everybody beat up on the Jews, hated as Germans by the Czechs, as Jews by the Germans, and as competitors by both. In the circumstances, the eminently sensible article Herzl published in the November 5 issue of *Die Welt* under the heading "The Hunt in Bohemia" would seem, in retrospect, to have done no more than labored the obvious; he pointed out that by identifying with either of the hostile camps rather than stressing their own independent identity, the Jews exposed themselves to attacks from both flanks and risked martyrdom in a cause decidedly not their own. But the obvious was as far from obvious to the editors of the *Neue Freie Presse* as it presumably was to the majority of their readers. Unfazed by the increasingly strident anti-Semitism of the German nationalists, they continued to hew to their aggressively pro-German line, and the appeal to an unabashedly Jewish nationalism by one of their own closest collaborators struck them as a stab in the back. The fact that Herzl, at their request, had agreed to sign his *Welt* pieces with the transparent pseudonym Benjamin Seff—his Hebrew name transliterated into German—was small comfort, given the ubiquitous gossip of the coffeehouse circuit that left no one in doubt as to the real author. The fatuity of the *Presse*'s editorial stance was further underlined by the fall of the Badeni government a few days later, which exacerbated the discomfiture of its editors.

Once again they insisted that Herzl relinquish the editorship of *Die Welt,* and once again he refused. In anticipation of his imminent dismissal, however, he decided to resubmit the controversial *New Ghetto* to the Carl Theater while still a journalist in good standing; once he was fired by the *Neue Freie Presse,* no theater director in the country would risk incurring the enmity of that powerful institution for the sake of staging a "Jew play."

Thanks, no doubt, to his fame or notoriety, *The New Ghetto* was immediately accepted this time around, but "in light of the tensions generated by recent national and religious conflicts" the censor demanded extensive cuts, including a less provocative title. On appeal, he was overruled by the governor of Lower Austria, and the play opened on January 5, 1898, to notices that, on the whole, were more favorable than it deserved, although Herzl complained about the treatment he received at the hands of Vienna's "newspaper Jews." In any case, his standing as a public figure overshadowed all other issues and rendered aesthetic criteria irrelevant. Audiences reacted according to their feelings about the "new Moses," and there was sufficient enthusiasm for—or curiosity about—his message to keep the play running for twenty-five performances.

The story was different in Berlin, where, with rare unanimity, every newspaper in town mercilessly panned *The New Ghetto* as crude, clumsy, and lifeless. The judgment of committed Zionist intellectuals was no less harsh. Reuben Brainin, an ardent Herzl disciple who, without first reading it, had agreed to translate the play into Hebrew, subsequently denounced it as a worthless piece of trash and tried in vain to break his contract with the publisher.

While it seems unlikely that success would have made much of a difference, the attacks on his integrity and his ability as an artist helped to precipitate the full-blown depression with which Herzl struggled through much of the winter of 1897–98. He toyed with several literary projects, perhaps not so much to redeem his reputation as to seek refuge in fantasy—a verse play in Renaissance costume, a three-volume novel about an assimilated Viennese journalist rediscovering his Jewish roots, and a biblical drama about Moses, none of which evolved beyond their initial conception; reality gave him no peace.

The Zionist movement was spreading like wildfire, not only in the

East, but all through Europe as well as overseas, in the United States, South Africa, and even Australia. But its explosive growth inevitably spawned internal dissension, which Herzl's haughty disdain for critics and opponents was not calculated to allay. Worse, the major efforts on which he had staked the whole future of the movement and his own role in it—Turkish concessions and the Jewish Colonial Trust— seemed at a dead end. His January trip to Berlin had been a triple fiasco: he had failed as a playwright, he had failed as a statesman in his talks with Tewfik Pasha, and he had been rudely rebuffed by a bunch of parvenu German-Jewish financiers. On his return to Vienna, he felt utterly exhausted, emotionally drained, and turned to Nordau with a plea to give him a year's respite by assuming the leadership of the organization. "It is," he acknowledged, "a big job, and one that has to be done, but fortunately you, too, are a workhorse. And after all, we are talking about just one year, i.e., until the 1899 congress, which you'll prepare just as I prepared those of 1897 and 1898. I don't know if I am being sufficiently explicit, because the matter involves a number of emotional factors as well. I am sure you'll understand my desire for a year's *rest* as well as my concern for the work accomplished thus far, though it nowhere equals the efforts put into it" (D, 2/23/ 98).

At bottom, however, he considered himself indispensable. The very next day he expressed his private reservations: "I don't know if he'd be up to the job. People won't appreciate what I accomplished until they see someone else in my place. Steadfast I was in the worst of days, calm in the best. It was no easy task: to keep silent when one word could arouse enthusiasm, to sustain people's courage when you inwardly despair, to put up with chicanery, consort with scoundrels, be assailed by beggars and snubbed by parvenus. . . . Will Nordau be able to take it, or will he, in his rage, destroy my work?"

Nordau, however, rejected the offer out of hand, for what sounded like perfectly plausible reasons—his work, his marriage to a Gentile, which was bound to upset the Orthodox, and his activism in the Dreyfus case. But he was also much too perceptive not to have sensed Herzl's ambivalence. "Anyone is at liberty not to launch a movement such as Zionism," he wrote. "But once having launched and sent it on its way, no one has the right lightheartedly—or with a heavy heart, for that matter—to abandon it. Death alone can absolve a man from self-imposed obligations" (D, 2/24/98). As to the proposal to transfer the Central Zionist Bureau to Paris, it was obvious that Herzl had not kept in touch with the latest developments in France; Nordau hinted that he himself was under constant surveillance, that the secret police read his mail and tapped his phone.

Back in January 1895, near the end of his term as Paris correspondent, Herzl had witnessed what then seemed the final act in the tragedy of Captain Dreyfus. Even at the time, Nordau—along with many others—had expressed grave misgivings about the verdict, but it was Bernard Lazare, by then one of Herzl's staunchest supporters, who patiently collected evidence of an anti-Semitic frame-up and, in November 1896, opened a campaign to rehabilitate Dreyfus. A few months later, Major Georges Picquart, head of the Statistical Section of the General Staff, independently discovered the identity of the real traitor. Although himself an arch-conservative and avowed anti-Semite, Picquart nonetheless placed justice above personal prejudice and went public with his findings, a breach of military etiquette that earned him a court-martial, exile, and persuasive death threats. Aroused by this blatant assault on human rights and republican virtue, Emile Zola, Herzl's *bête noire* of French naturalism, flung himself into the fray. It was largely his passion that rallied the intellectuals and *hommes de lettres* to the Dreyfus case, for the first time giving these fractious individualists a sense of collective power and responsibility which outlasted *l'Affaire* and became a permanent feature of French politics. On January 13, 1898, his famous open letter, *J'accuse*, appeared in Clemenceau's *Aurore*, followed a few days later by a wave of anti-Jewish riots throughout France and Algeria. On February 23, Zola was tried for libel and sentenced to a year in prison. (The verdict was later set aside.)

These, in outline, were the facts at the time, with which Herzl was undoubtedly familiar. What he failed to appreciate, what he could not possibly have realized, was the abrupt emergence of the Dreyfus case as the paramount issue not only of French politics but of French society altogether. No secondary sources abroad, certainly not the ever-cautious *Neue Freie Presse*, from which he drew most of his information, conveyed the depths to which *l'Affaire* had begun to divide France along fundamental fault lines, with the army, the Church, the old royalist establishment, and the populist anti-Semites on one side, arrayed against a loose coalition of intellectuals, anti-clericals, and left-of-center elements drawing on the vestigial traditions of the Revolution.

The extreme virulence of anti-Jewish feelings, rhetoric, and riots, however, which swept the divided country—and which also went largely unreported in the *Neue Freie Presse*—would scarcely have surprised him, in light of his memories of the first Dreyfus trial three years earlier.

In any event, he was too preoccupied with his own problems to pay much attention to the world at large. Rabbi Armand Kaminka, his sole if lukewarm Orthodox supporter, turned against Herzl in an open letter, accusing him of personal aggrandizement and contempt for Jewish tradition. Opposition to a second congress was gathering momentum in both East and West, and it took all of Herzl's prestige and powers of persuasion to talk the major power brokers into taking what they considered the enormous risk of an anticlimactic fiasco. "Noise is everything," he told the philologist Leon Kellner, the man he had come to regard as "his dearest, closest friend, whose visits are a bright spot amidst all this aggravation." He firmly believed in the need to make oneself heard. "The entire history of the world is nothing but noise. The noise of arms, the noise of progressive ideas. Noise must be made to serve a purpose—and yet should be despised" (D, 5/12/98). And, plagued more than ever by disquieting palpitations, he designated Kellner as his successor on *Die Welt* in the event of his death and charged him with the immediate posthumous publication of his diaries.

In the meantime, he concentrated on both "noise" and action. He had been unhappy with Wolffsohn's impromptu choice of a flag and devised a new one as an item of top priority—"If you want to lead a people, you need flags and trumpets." He also designed a permanent Congress Building in Basel and passed his sketch on to the architect Oskar Marmorek. "The art form now most congenial to me is architecture. Unfortunately I have not mastered its discipline. If I had learned something, I would now be an architect" (D, 7/10/98). No less inspired but a great deal more desperate were his efforts on behalf of the bank which, *faute de mieux*, was to be the centerpiece of the second congress. Since no reputable institution or individual proved willing to negotiate on his terms, he resolved to cut the Gordian knot by launching a popular subscription of one-pound shares, with a 10 percent down payment. "What I am doing is once again a sleight-of-hand, a financial innovation. The provisional subscription drive for a bank about which nothing definite is as yet known is nothing other than founding a people's syndicate for the purpose of issuing shares."

And somewhat dazzled by his own ingenuity in an unfamiliar field, he added a quote from Virgil: *"Flectere superos si nequeo Acheronta movebo"*—If I cannot bend the heavens to my will, I shall move hell.

Those of his followers with some practical experience in matters financial were less than impressed by his innovative schemes, but again he managed to talk them into going along with him. The eventual outcome justified both Herzl's determination and the apprehensions of his critics. The bank—later known as the Jewish Colonial Trust—consumed an inordinate proportion of his time and energy over the next few years and did not reach its stipulated capital base of £250,000 until 1902. On the other hand, its symbolic value transcended even "the rag on a stick" and was part of the grand vision of which Herzl never allowed himself to lose sight, and which sustained him in all his mundane trials and tribulations. He was not afraid to dream big; 2 million guilders, he figured—a mere trifle for the likes of a Rothschild—would enable him to gain control of the *Neue Freie Presse* and turn it into a Zionist organ. "What a shame that we cannot raise this amount, a mere pittance compared to the grandeur of the cause. We are still like the soldiers of the French Revolution, going into battle without shoes or socks" (D, 4/29/98). Unspeakably tired, constantly haunted by the half-acknowledged fear of death, he drove himself all the harder, determined still to see the fruits of his labor.

In addition to the battles for and within the movement he had his private troubles to contend with. The office tempest had once again subsided, followed by an uneasy truce he found almost equally unsettling. Bacher was being demonstratively benevolent, Benedikt's wrath had cooled to mellow mockery: "You have to be careful with that fellow Herzl. He may yet turn out to be right, after all. Every time I see him coming, I feel as if Jesus Christ were making his appearance." In addition to his feuilletons, Herzl was now also writing editorials, about which both his bosses professed great enthusiasm. Nevertheless, his position as an "office slave," a hired scribbler serving masters who opposed his ideas, seemed increasingly onerous and totally inconsistent with his self-image as the messianic leader of a growing national movement; to the end of his life he kept half hoping, half fearing to cut the umbilical cord that tied him to his lucrative servitude. The time never seemed propitious, now less than ever, with *Die Welt* devouring his fortune at an alarming rate, nor was the bank likely to remedy the situation within the foreseeable future.

In May, shortly after the family moved to Karl-Ludwigstrasse 50 (now Weimarerstrasse) in the Eighteenth District, his eight-year-old daughter, Pauline, came down with what appears to have been a bout of rheumatic fever. As is the case with much of the Herzl family's medical history generally, no precise details are known, but the child was critically ill for a number of weeks. By the time Herzl took off for Basel on August 18, she had recovered sufficiently to ease his conscience about leaving her, but the illness seems to have left some permanent damage and may, in the long run, have contributed to Pauline's tragic fate.

In the circumstances, it boggles the mind to discover that somehow, in the course of that troubled spring, Herzl still found time to complete another of those boudoir farces for which he had such an unfortunate penchant and facility. Since June 1891 he had been working, on and off, on a play originally entitled *The Fleshpots of Egypt*, mainly an act of retribution against Julie. It eventually turned into *Our Cathy*, a four-act comedy satirizing "modern marriage" which bore no relation to any of the ambitious literary projects he had been nursing in the depths of his depression. And while—in a letter to Hermann Bahr— he claimed Schopenhauer's misogyny as the source of his inspiration, the more plausible motives were his own marital miseries, along with hopes for a quick, much-needed windfall. On August 10, he sent the piece to Paul Schlenther, a former Berlin theater critic recently appointed director of the Burgtheater, who accepted it at once—a hasty decision, as it turned out, but one which must have buoyed Herzl's spirits as he left for Basel a week later to open the second Zionist congress.

TWENTY

*I*t was manifestly impossible to recapture the emotional intensity of the year before. But if the first Zionist congress had been an event without precedent in post-exilic history, the second made up for what it lacked in novelty and drama by superior organization, more contentious polemics, and much greater attendance.

The stage setting was once again the Basel Municipal Casino, but a much larger hall was needed to accommodate the 349 delegates—almost twice as many as the previous year—along with the 150 journalists covering the proceedings. The accredited delegates had all been duly elected by local Zionist organizations and thus constituted a far more representative body than the first assembly. Moreover, the number of those local organizations itself reflected the phenomenal growth of the movement worldwide. Within that one year, no less than 796 new chapters had been formed, a ninefold increase over the 117 original groups represented at the first congress. Russia alone accounted for 373 of these, followed by Austria-Hungary with 250; the United States registered 50.

One significant new development was the growing participation of women, who either joined existing chapters or formed their own. A special women's caucus was held preliminary to the congress, and this time women were not only seated as delegates but given full voting rights—a break with tradition which the disgruntled Orthodox wing, having already been defeated on a number of other points, chose not to contest. (They got their revenge fifty years later, when the *Judenstaat* incorporated some of their traditional anti-feminism in its basic legislation.)

These were impressive figures, and legitimate cause for pride, the only trouble being that except for Herzl and a few of his intimates, no one knew just what they represented in terms of actual membership (the best estimates range around 100,000). He, in turn, made sure no one would ever find out, just as he adamantly resisted disclosure of the movement's finances. He justified this secrecy by invoking the ultimate goal; bluff was the major weapon in his arsenal, and if his strategy was to succeed, he had to negotiate from a position of apparent strength. Any hint of the less than imposing reality would, he feared, seriously damage his credibility, and he was not about to let a senti-mental hankering for democracy tarnish his image as the supreme commander of a powerful army backed by boundless wealth and a united people. "All the speakers wanted details, facts one cannot reveal because they are too insignificant," he noted, in an entry made at the end of the first day. "The movement is now nine times larger than last year—but it is just that last year it was ridiculously small. This is something we have to fudge. Fortunately the accounts we submitted to the finance committee were in excellent shape" (D, 8/29/98).

His attitude shocked even some of his closest associates, including Nordau, and as it carried over into many other spheres, it gradually opened up what, at this stage, still registered as small fissures, papered over by rhetoric; in due course, however, they were to widen into a deep split between the unconditional Herzl loyalists and their no less intransigent opponents. Early signs appeared at the opening session, when Herzl saw fit to announce from the podium that according to a bulletin just received, Czar Nicholas II had called for a general world disarmament conference—a proposal which Herzl's ever-galloping imagination must have immediately seized upon as a potentially ideal forum for his brand of personal diplomacy; this would seem the only conceivable reason for him to have made the announcement in the first place. That many delegates, especially among the large Russian contingent, greeted this news with a notable lack of enthusiasm should have come as no surprise, but it infuriated him to the point where he found it necessary to denounce their behavior and apologize for it at a press conference, lest it create an unfavorable impression in high places.

The fact that his diplomacy, the main business at hand, was not up for public—or for that matter private—discussion made for some tense moments throughout. A few articulate members of the as yet small Zionist left wing caused him to lose his presidential temper on several occasions. Altogether, he found it much more difficult to control what was beginning to coalesce into a regular parliamentary body deeply divided on many issues of principle and determined to debate them. His own main thrust, on the other hand, was to minimize internal conflict. Thus his opening speech combined a plea for mutual understanding with a call to promote Jewish unity generally by wresting control of communal organizations from secular and religious anti-Zionists. Without modifying his principled opposition to piecemeal infiltration into Turkish Palestine, he expressed his support for the settlements already in place as a conciliatory gesture toward his Hoveve Zion opponents. But it was his concern over their still pervasive influence and its effect on his behind-the-scenes operations that yielded what, from the current perspective, may have been one of the most critical moments in Basel, although—and this, too, is commentary—it passed almost unnoticed at the time.

In a shrewd move to defuse the arguments of the opposition, Herzl earlier in the year had sent one of their most articulate spokesmen, the student leader Leo Motzkin, on a tour of Palestine to investigate the social and economic conditions of the resident Jewish population. Motzkin, a brilliant mathematician, had done an outstanding job under difficult conditions, and his eyewitness report, in which high hopes struggled with a bleak reality shrewdly observed and expertly quantified, was one of the highlights of the congress. But one passage deserves the special attention it failed to receive at the time:

> Completely accurate statistics about the number of inhabitants do not presently exist. One must admit that the density of the population does not give the visitor much cause for cheer. In whole stretches throughout the land one constantly comes across large Arab villages, and it is an established fact that the most fertile areas of our country are occupied by Arabs. . . . According to the usual estimate, based on official reports, Palestine contains at most 650,000 inhabitants, but this seems a questionable figure. [Protocol of the Second Zionist Congress, p. 103]

The bank was the only item on the agenda in which Herzl had a personal stake. Opposition to it was scattered and ineffectual, although the most eloquent opponent turned out to be Bernard Lazare, lionized by all the delegates for his role in the Dreyfus affair. Lazare, in fact, broke with Herzl soon after the congress; he refrained from public statements but, in a private letter, anticipated many of the later objections to his autocratic leadership:

> You are bourgeois in your thinking, bourgeois in sentiment, bourgeois in your social outlook. As such, you want to lead a people, our people, a people of the poor, of the unfortunate, a people of proletarians. You can do this only in an authoritarian manner, by directing them toward what you think is best for them. Thus you act from outside and above: you want to herd them along. Before creating a people you set up a government, you act financially and diplomatically and, like all governments, you find yourself at the mercy of your financial and diplomatic setbacks. Like all governments, you wish to gloss over the truth, to be the government of a people that makes a good impression, and it becomes your highest duty "not to display national disgraces." [Lazare to Herzl, 2/4/99. CZA, H VIII, 479/11. Quoted in Vital, Vol. I, p. 72]

But the bank project won easy approval, although Herzl's choice of Jewish Colonial Bank for the Orient as a deliberately non-specific name revived suspicions about the depth of his commitment to Zion and unleashed a heated four-hour debate, at the end of which he agreed to a Jewish Colonial Bank for Palestine and Syria.

His only defeat came in an indirect confrontation with Ahad Ha-Am, himself not present this time around. In a move which, for the sake of harmony, Herzl had strenuously sought to deflect, the congress resolved to foster a broad program of mass education aimed at intellectual and moral renewal as an integral part of the Zionist ideal. This was an area which the Orthodox contingent regarded as their own exclusive turf. By refusing to accept rabbinical authority, let alone supervision in cultural affairs, the congress majority clashed head-on with the Eastern European rabbinical establishment and set the stage for a bitter struggle that has yet to be resolved.

Many delegates, like the overwhelming majority of their Zionist constituents, were secular in outlook, un-Orthodox if not downright atheist. Yet while they rejected the presumptuous arrogance of a rabbinical authority mired in primitive fundamentalism, they nonetheless retained close emotional and intellectual ties to a traditional Judaism which simply could not be divorced from religion. Moreover, their very claim, their only claim to Palestine as a Jewish homeland was, after all, based on the Bible; when Leo Motzkin informed the congress that "the most fertile areas of *our country* are occupied by Arabs," he merely stated a fact that apparently everyone present, atheist or believer, took for granted.

Herzl himself, with his simplistic concept of the nation-state, was ill equipped to see this as a problem, and his symbolic visits to the Basel synagogue were mainly calculated to impress observant followers. For the others it was, and remains, a basic dilemma. The emotional ties of secular modernists to the traditions of the pre-enlightenment past were a major factor in the massive retreat from Herzl's stated intention of "confining the priests to the temple." Ironically, however, this retreat began with Herzl himself, as will be seen, although in his case expediency seems to have been the only motive.

The congress closed on September 1, after an all-night marathon session that ended at five in the morning. To Herzl's intense regret, the Sultan's wire acknowledging the assembly's greetings arrived too late to be read from the podium. So did a sensational news item: Major Henry, a member of the French General Staff, had admitted forging the documents that incriminated Captain Dreyfus. (He committed suicide the following day.)

On the whole, Herzl had every reason to be satisfied with the outcome, even if, on the morning after, he was still seething with anger at the "filthy machinations of those Galician scoundrels" and left with "a feeling of the most profound exhaustion." He had achieved all he set out to do: obtained legal and moral backing for the bank, and demonstrated to the world at large that the first congress had not been a flash in the pan, that the Jewish National Assembly was now an established fact and a permanent institution. His skill and authority had squelched any serious opposition, and the mise-en-scène, from the opening concert—featuring the "Fantasie" from Wagner's *Tannhäuser*—to the dramatic finale at daybreak, had been superb. More than ever he felt both the weight and the glory of his mission. He *was* the movement, its undisputed leader, irreplaceable, with no challenger and no successor in sight. He certainly was not impressed by the young delegate from Pinsk, a twenty-four-year-old chemistry student named Chaim Weizmann, who intervened in the debate to demand that control of the bank be unequivocally vested in the congress. "Without that guarantee, we cannot go back to our constituents and tell them that we've founded an institute for them, and not just for the capitalists."

Leaving Basel the next morning accompanied by Hechler, Herzl feared the inevitable letdown, a crash landing in the trivia and vexations of everyday reality. Instead, he was about to be taken for a ride in spheres that even he had scarcely dared to dream about.

It began with the short trip to Constance, where the Grand Duke of Baden was spending the summer in his castle on the lake. Herzl had made a point of keeping in touch with him ever since their meeting two years earlier. But while the Grand Duke continued to express His Gracious Interest, he had repeatedly rejected Herzl's pleas to approach the Emperor in a matter which, he felt, did not yet warrant such august attention. Gradually, however, he changed his mind, impressed by *Die Welt*, the congresses, and by the Reverend Hechler's rhapsodic reports; the announcement of plans for the Kaiser's tour of Palestine and the Near East in the fall of 1898 finally persuaded him to broach the subject directly with his imperial nephew. In a long, personal letter of July 28 he told of his first meeting with Herzl, acknowledged initial reservations but expressed his belief that this "interesting movement," its Palestinian settlements and the "consistent, diligent work toward the founding of an Israelite state" had now reached a stage where they deserved "a certain attention" in light of the Kaiser's forthcoming trip. He proposed to have Count Philipp von Eulenburg, German ambassador to Vienna, conduct a study of Zionism and its potential integration into long-range German policy aims.

He also used the occasion to promote one of Hechler's pet projects, the quest for the original Ark of the Covenant. A Swedish geodicist, Henning Melander, speculated that the Jews had buried the Ark in Palestine before leaving for their Babylonian exile, and the Grand Duke enclosed the five issues of *Die Welt* devoted to this chimera. Here was the Kaiser's chance to prove the literal truth of the Bible by subsidizing an expedition and obtaining the Sultan's blessings for this ecumenical enterprise. Nothing came of it, but eventually Herzl contemplated sponsoring Melander. He died before he had a chance to do anything about it.

Encouraged by the Kaiser's response, the Grand Duke asked Herzl to stop off at Castle Mainau, the ducal summer residence, on his way back from Basel. The meeting took place on September 2, setting in motion a chain of events which, in retrospect, seems one of the more bizarre episodes in Jewish history but which, for Herzl personally, may well have been the high point of his life, a moment when the dream seemed within his grasp. The Grand Duke, more affable than ever, ranged freely over the whole of German foreign policy—"If I were to publish [the interview], it would cause a sensation throughout Europe." He informed Herzl that the Kaiser had instructed Count Eulenburg, his closest friend and adviser, to report to him directly on the Zionist movement. Given the Emperor's close friendship with the Sultan, a word from him on behalf of the Jews would carry much weight; moreover, the German ambassador in Constantinople had already been assured of the Turks' essentially favorable attitude toward the Zionists. "You do intend to found a state, don't you," he inquired, launching Herzl into another exposition of his program, with special emphasis on its counter-revolutionary aspects. "When I mentioned the effect of Zionism in Russia, where the socialists and anarchists converted to Zionism because we gave them an ideal, he nodded vigorously and said: Pobyedonostsev ought to know about this. You have to tell him."

To be holding views congenial to one of Russia's most notorious reactionaries and Jew-baiters was hardly a compliment, though meant as such. But the Grand Duke's grasp of politics, national or international, probably did not exceed Herzl's own shallow views; being on good terms with his imperial nephew constituted his major—though by no means negligible—asset, but it gave him no special insight or input into Germany's devious *Drang nach Osten* schemes. He seems, moreover, to have been a genuinely decent person, itself a crippling handicap in the corridors of power. Once again he worried, as he had two years earlier, that German support of Zionism might be misinterpreted as anti-Semitism, a concern Herzl sought to allay: "On the contrary, I pointed out that the Jews would bring a *German* cultural element into the Orient. The proof: German writers—though of Jewish origin—were leading the Zionist movement. The language of the congress was German. The overwhelming majority of Jews are part of German culture. Therefore, since we need a protectorate, a German one would suit us best" (D, 9/3/98).

Probably a case of self-deluding fantasy rather than a conscious lie, but egregious nonsense either way. There were numerous self-styled "writers" in the Zionist movement at the time, but the only two professional ones writing in German were Herzl and Nordau, both of them Hungarians. The congress language was German, because the

Germans and Hungarians had no Russian or Yiddish, while the majority of educated Russian or Yiddish speakers were reasonably fluent in German. This made neither them nor "the overwhelming majority" of Jews a part of German *Kultur*, but the fact that Herzl saw fit not only to record this statement but to repeat it on several later occasions is proof, once again, of his impressionistic ways with reality.

From Unterach, where he was vacationing with Wolffsohn, Herzl wrote to Count Eulenburg, offering his assistance in compiling the dossier on Zionism and requesting an audience with the Kaiser before the latter left for Constantinople and points east. On September 10, the Austrian Empress Elisabeth was stabbed to death in Genoa by an insane self-styled anarchist. Although the unfortunate "Sissy" had spent much of her life trying to keep away from Vienna and its court rituals, the tragedy served as an excuse for a majestic display of imperial pageantry which she was in no position to escape. All European heads of state, including the Kaiser, were to attend the state funeral on the seventeenth, and when Herzl received a summons from Eulenburg for the sixteenth, he immediately left for Vienna in a state of high anticipation.

In Count (later Prince) Philipp von Eulenburg, Herzl for the first time in his life found himself face to face with an authentic representative of that superhuman breed he had idolized since childhood. The gap between his simplistic fantasies and the multifaceted personality of a real-life Prussian aristocrat transcended his imagination to the point where he remained wholly unaware of it. He saw in Eulenburg exactly what he expected to see, a stock character out of one of his own early plays, and in externals the fifty-one-year-old count certainly lived up to the role—a nobleman of ancient lineage, tall and handsome, with the bearing and manners of the veteran courtier, diplomat, and soldier. "He conveys the impression of total self-control, a man locked tight like a steel safe. He looks straight at you, yet there is nothing to be read in the cold blue eyes or in the wrinkled face with its pointed gray beard. Suddenly the safe opens, though he has not moved a muscle in his face; what changed was the look in the hard, blue eyes, which have a way of growing soft" (D, 9/16/98).

The human being locked away out of sight, as Herzl quite astutely observed, was a man of many gifts, not the least of them being enormous charm and a quick, incisive mind. He dabbled in poetry and music, was a knowledgeable lover of the arts, and had the reputation of an exquisite host. He was also a practicing homosexual at a time when homosexuality was cause for dissimulation rather than gaiety.

The existence of an extensive homosexual network in the upper reaches of the imperial German government and the general staff has been amply documented, thanks to the diligence of a metropolitan police force whose proverbial German thoroughness left nothing to the imagination. What makes Eulenburg's case historically pertinent is the presumptive link between his sexual orientation and his unique position as the Kaiser's absolute favorite, his confidant and friend, and the only person able to exert real influence upon the intellectually constricted and emotionally labile Emperor. He was one of the very few people whom Wilhelm addressed in the familiar second person singular, and their relationship can only be described as a love affair, whether or not it included physical intimacy. Bismarck, who knew his Junkers the way Herzl did not, described Eulenburg as "a Prussian Cagliostro . . . a pietist, a romanticizing flatterer . . . especially dangerous in view of the Kaiser's temperamental proclivity for high drama. In the presence of the Lord and Master, he assumes a worshipful pose; maybe he even means it. Whenever the Kaiser looks up, he can be sure to meet this pair of eyes fixed on him in moist adulation" (Ludwig, p. 131).

Regardless of whether Eulenburg's influence was as baneful as Bismarck feared, it certainly gave the "Prussian Cagliostro" a position of power far out of proportion to the office he nominally occupied. He was, as Herzl sensed instantly, a man who made things happen— "about fifty-five, but seems to still have a future ahead of him. Chancellor, maybe?"

Herzl gave his by now standard lecture on Zionism for the Gentiles, and Eulenburg, seemingly impressed, promised to get him an audience with the Kaiser, though not in Vienna, as he had hoped, since the Emperor was already overdue for the hunt in East Prussia. But what, according to Herzl, made the strongest impression on the ambassador was "when I said to him: Our movement exists, I expect that one or the other of the Great Powers will promote our cause. Originally I thought it would be England . . . but I would much prefer it to be Germany. The Jews are now overwhelmingly German in their culture. And I am saying this not because I happen to be in the German embassy but because it happens to be true. Proof: German was the official language at both Basel congresses. My mentioning England . . . was the final hammer blow" (D, 9/16/98).

Devastated no doubt by this blow and by the cunning gamesmanship it demonstrated, Eulenburg arranged for Herzl to see Bernhard von Bülow, the German Foreign Minister, who was also attending the funeral of the Empress. Their meeting took place the following morning at the embassy.

Bülow has been blamed for having frustrated the Kaiser's good intentions on behalf of Zionism, which is no doubt accurate, and for which he deserves both credit and gratitude. Frustrating Wilhelm's intentions, good or bad but always equally foolish and impulsive, was in fact the prime concern of all his ministers, who soon after his coronation divided into two factions—those who considered him insane and wanted him deposed, and the others, who saw him as an unruly, emotionally retarded adolescent with the attention span of an eight-year-old and treated him accordingly. Open defiance sent him into instant tantrums, and no one could match Bülow's skill at contradicting him without appearing to do so. He was the master of the enthusiastic yes, subtly modulated by successive reservations uttered with hypocritical reluctance, until the steady drumbeat of yes-buts induced the flighty Lord of the Realm, if he had not already lost interest in the matter, to change his mind. And, either because this technique was Bülow's way of dealing with people generally, or because he perceived a certain resemblance between Herzl and his boss, he began to ooze paralyzing charm before Herzl ever had a chance to get his bearings.

> He received me in the living quarters, amid open suitcases; he had just arrived. He greeted me with effusive amiability, told me he had already read many of my things, was delighted to make my acquaintance, and so forth.
>
> And that made me weaken. . . . With Eulenburg, who had received me coolly, I was able to be decisive, to speak lucidly and firmly. In Bülow's presence I unfortunately turned into a vain author more intent on tossing off epigrams than seriously talking to the point. It was simply a fit of weakness, caused by his excessive charm. [D, 9/18/98]

This pseudo-intimate *tête-à-tête* robbed Herzl of the chance to deliver his standard lecture, but Bülow in any case proved well briefed

on the subject of Zionism. He volunteered that the Kaiser was no anti-
Semite but merely hated destructive Jews, and Herzl reciprocated by
assuring Bülow that the Jews were not socialists at heart.

> I told him what I had recently read: that pre-Mosaic Egypt had
> been a socialist state. By means of the Decalogue, Moses created
> the social order based on individualism. The Jews have been
> individualists ever since and would remain so. He liked that. He
> quoted Heine's phrase about "egalitarian hoodlums" (a reference
> to America, which Heine had never visited). . . . At any rate,
> on the socialist aspects of the question we were in full agreement.
> He was impressed when I told him that at the Vienna university
> we had lured the students away from socialism. Some of them
> dream of founding a future socialist state "over there," but that
> was not what I had in mind. [D, 9/18/98]

Not until he had been graciously ushered out did Herzl begin to
appreciate the consummate artistry of Bülow's approach: "He never
says no—and he never says yes." The practical results of this urbane
chat were nil. "Looking back on it, I felt I had been had."

Three days later he was on his way again to France, Holland,
England—the Wandering Jew breaking into a sprint as he approaches
the finish line. The new alliance only made the bank project more
urgent than ever, and no one else seemed capable of putting the deal
together. From the Hôtel Castille in Paris, at the same desk at which
he had written *Der Judenstaat*, he wrote once more to Eulenburg,
reiterating the political and strategic advantages Germany stood to gain
from her support of Zionism. "And may my plain and simple words,
thanks to the kindness of Your Excellency, find their way to the genius
of the Kaiser. His journey to the Holy Land is now grandly conceived
as a pilgrimage. It could become more than that; it could attain the
significance of a historic turning point in the Orient if it set in motion
the return of the Jews" (D, 9/21/98).

Words well calculated to appeal to a man with a "temperamental
proclivity for high drama," and faithfully transmitted by Eulenburg.

In all other respects, the stopover in Paris was a waste. France, more
divided than ever over *l'Affaire*, seemed to him in a state of near-total
collapse. Nordau was discouraged, Zadok Kahn discouraging, and in
a financial community dominated by the Rothschilds, there was no

chance of his making headway with his quest for funds. "The French Jews are absolutely useless to us. They are not really Jews anymore. Nor, on the other hand, are they French. They will probably become the leaders of European anarchy" (D, 9/30/98). From Paris he continued to Amsterdam, where the Dutch-Jewish banker Jacobus Kann seemed willing to help raise some of the capital for the Jewish Colonial Trust. But on his arrival at the hotel, he had a surprise waiting for him—a message summoning him to the German consulate, where he was handed a top-secret letter from Eulenburg.

"I read the letter in the cab, and at first I was downright stunned. The colossal triumph I had achieved troubled me at first. I realized at once the serious difficulties it was liable to cause me at the *Neue Freie Presse*. If at the end of my vacation I go to Palestine instead of back to the office, it may quite simply cost me my job. On the other hand, one does not disobey the Kaiser, whose wish is a command" (D, 10/2/98).

His confusion was understandable. The letter promised far more than he could ever have hoped for.

"I have nothing but good news for you," Eulenburg began. "His Majesty has, quite as I expected, shown a full and profound understanding for your movement. I myself was a zealous advocate, convinced as I am of the significance of the Zionist movement. It is an opinion shared also by my friend Bülow, a fact of capital importance." He went on to inform Herzl that the Kaiser was ready "to intercede with the Sultan on behalf of your interests in a manner as exhaustive and as *urgent* as possible. In this he will have the support of Foreign Secretary Bülow, who will be accompanying him."

An audience before the Kaiser's departure might give rise to unwelcome comment, but a Zionist deputation would definitely be received in Jerusalem. "Should *you* lead this deputation, it will afford you an opportunity to present your wishes personally to His Majesty. Finally I must urge you *most emphatically*, dear Doctor, to regard this letter as strictly confidential."

And, in a postscript:

"I have just had another talk with His Majesty. He has asked me to assure you that you will not be deceived in placing your trust in his effort to promote your work for the protection of poor and suppressed Jews. . . . And finally, he wishes you to know that he *is ready* to assume a possible protectorate. In making this statement he is, of course, counting on your absolute discretion. I am very pleased to be giving you this news and hope that you will be able to reach Jerusalem in time, since otherwise His Majesty would be most disappointed."

Eulenburg was not exaggerating. Wilhelm's volatile imagination had indeed caught fire. He, too, conceived of history as theater, with himself always on stage, ordained by God to play the lead, a role for which his most outstanding qualification was a wardrobe of over three hundred uniforms to suit the need or fancy of the moment. The idea of proclaiming himself the Protector of the Jews, and to do so in the setting of the Holy City, greatly appealed to his sense of drama. That it would also annoy his detested British cousins added to the thrill.

From his hunting lodge in East Prussia, where Eulenburg had been stoking his fantasies, the Kaiser on September 29, 1898, dashed off a remarkable letter to the Grand Duke of Baden in his own handwriting, which only surfaced after World War II and which confirms his fleeting enthusiasm, not so much for the Jews as for the prospect of a hero's part in a memorable spectacle.

"My dearest uncle," he began, "a momentary pause in the amorous concert of my deer gives me a chance to devote a few lines to you." He thanked the Duke for calling his attention to a movement with whose basic aims he claimed to have always been in sympathy. He was now convinced that Zionism offered serious possibilities and that the settlement of the Holy Land "by the financially powerful and diligent people of Israel" would not only bring prosperity to Palestine but restore Turkey's finances and prevent a partition of that country.

> Moreover, the energy, creative power, and productivity of the tribe of Shem would be directed toward worthier goals than the exploitation of Christians, and many a Semite addicted to social democracy and busy inciting the opposition will move off to the East, where more rewarding work awaits him that does not, as in the above case, lead to the penitentiary.
>
> Now I realize that nine-tenths of all Germans will be horrified and shun me if they find out at some later date that I am in sympathy with the Zionists and might even place them under my protection if they call upon me to do so. On that point, let me say this: That the Jews killed our Saviour the Good Lord knows better than we do, and He has punished them accordingly.

But neither the anti-Semites nor I nor anyone else has been ordered or authorized by Him to abuse these people in our own fashion *ad majorem Dei gloriam*. . . . And from the viewpoint of secular *Realpolitik* we cannot ignore the fact that, given the enormous and dangerous power represented by international Jewish capital, it would surely be a tremendous achievement for Germany if the world of the Hebrews would look up to our country with gratitude. Everywhere the hydra of the most crude and hideous anti-Semitism is raising its gruesome head, and anxiously the Jews, ready to leave the lands where danger threatens, are looking for a protector. All right, then, those who return to the Holy Land shall enjoy protection and security, and I shall intercede for them with the Sultan, for the Scripture says: "Make to yourselves friends of the mammon of unrighteousness" and "Be wise as serpents, and harmless as doves. [Herzl, Hechler, the Grand Duke of Baden and the German Emperor]

In an effort to master his emotions, Herzl rented a bicycle and went for a ride from The Hague all the way to Scheveningen and back along the North Sea coast. He was overwhelmed by this sudden turn of events, wildly triumphant, yet at the same time filled with anxiety. Now that his bluff had been called, would he be able to make good on his promise, raise the necessary funds, organize the exodus of his ragtag army, persuade the "Galician scoundrels" to accept a German protectorate?

These were major problems, and yet all his worries during those first few hours seemed to focus on his job. The Kaiser was due in Constantinople on October 17 and in Jerusalem on the twenty-ninth. If Herzl was to see him, he would have to leave within three days of his return to Vienna, and the thought of having to confront Bacher on the issue literally terrified him.

After dinner that night, he swore his two companions to secrecy and gave them the news. To Wolffsohn he also confided his private fears; he was by now on sufficiently intimate terms with the stolid, commonsensical businessman to rely on him for emotional support. Wolffsohn came through by pointing out, reasonably enough, that an interview with the Kaiser could only enhance his standing at the *Neue Freie Presse*.

In London, where they arrived on October 2, the excitement of the past few days finally caught up with Herzl. What he referred to as "heart trouble of an unpleasant kind" as well as shortness of breath kept him up for much of the night. Though still feeling far from well the next morning, he nonetheless spent most of the day battling the assembled members of the banking committee, a group given to caution, who failed to share his sense of urgency about the Jewish bank. Angry and frustrated, bound by his pledge to Eulenburg and thus unable to disclose the real reason for his haste, he finally ended the argument with the peremptory announcement that, come what may, the bank would be incorporated at once, with Wolffsohn and himself providing the start-up capital and registration fees.

That same evening he was to address a mass meeting in the East End. Ailing and unprepared, he arrived to find over seven thousand of his followers packing the huge hall, with at least as many more outside. The organizers triumphantly announced from the podium that "one-tenth of the Jewish population of the United Kingdom has assembled in and outside the hall to greet Dr. Herzl."

The reception made him temporarily forget his ailing heart; it also made him forget the caution he had vowed to exercise in dealing with the masses. With Eulenburg's letter burning in his pocket, buoyed by the virtual certainty of imminent success, he let himself get carried away and gave an extemporaneous, uncharacteristically rabble-rousing speech. Although he spoke in German—and without the benefit of either microphone or translators—he held the attention of the audience throughout and finally whipped them into a frenzy when he concluded with what they rightly took to be a hint of great things about to happen: "Our movement belongs above all to the poor, for whom we want to prepare a better future. I won't draw you a picture of our return, because it will soon come about. I can assure you that the day is not far off. I know what I am talking about. I have never spoken with greater conviction. Today I am telling you: I believe the time is not far off when the Jewish people will be on the move."

News traveled fast in those pre-electronic days, unimpeded by the overload of trivia that nowadays passes for information. Within days, the echo of his words resounded throughout the ghettos of Eastern Europe, a message of imminent redemption, the second exodus, although there were always those who remembered Shabbetai Tsvi, the other Messiah who went to Constantinople.

The morning after, Herzl himself had second thoughts. "My speech (German) got a lot of applause, but it was only clever rhetoric. It was not good. Today I can think of things I should have said" (D, 10/4/98).

From London he went straight to Berlin and, on October 8, had another meeting with Eulenburg at the latter's estate, about an hour from the capital. The count was cordial, though without lowering his guard. "Naturally he feels superior to me as a member of a race which he takes to be superior. But how can I hold that against him when I think of how miserably just the 'upper class' Jews, i.e., the very ones with whom he is likely to have had contact, behave toward our idealistic cause? And anyway, he seems to recognize that one can socialize with the Jew Herzl."

Eulenburg took him on a tour of the property, in the course of which he confirmed once more what he had already told Herzl in his letter: "The Kaiser is fire and flame for the matter. I was able to get him really worked up about it. That is the only way. He has to be passionately interested in something, otherwise he quickly loses sight of the matter because there is so much going on." He added that "luckily for you, Bülow, my best friend and a most outstanding statesman, has also been won over to your cause." Herzl, recalling Bülow's snakelike charm, felt impelled to wonder out loud, but Eulenburg dismissed his doubts: "He was reserved. That is understandable at a first meeting. . . . What matters is not what he told you, but what he told me. I convinced him."

If he seriously thought so, and if he sincerely believed Bülow to be his friend, he was far more naïve than he had any right to be.

He stressed the importance of Herzl's presence in Constantinople during the Kaiser's visit, so as to be available for possible negotiations. The idea of a protectorate greatly appealed to Wilhelm, who did not anticipate any objections on the part of his friend the Sultan. Russia would also go along, scandal-ridden France was too weak to cause trouble, and only England might make difficulties.

Toward the end, however, the conversation took a strange turn. As Herzl recounts it:

> I expressed my gratitude in a few warm words. Thereupon Eulenburg remarked, fixing me firmly with his steely eyes: "Perhaps the time will come when I, in turn, will ask you for favors."
> I declared: "Henceforth you have in me a devoted and grateful man."

He said: "I am glad that this is the way you take it."

I: "Your Excellency may count on me. Perhaps you will allow me to give you proof of it right now?"

He waved his hand in refusal. "No, not yet. The occasion may possibly arise someday, but this is not the case at present."

I begged him to take my devotion for granted at any time. [D, 10/7/98]

There is something both poignant and uncanny about this exchange, whose latent content Herzl clearly failed to decipher. "I keep racking my brains over what Eulenburg could possibly have meant by 'favors.' Whatever they may be, he shall get them—whenever, wherever, however. Anyone who deals with me will be left with the opposite of the proverbial impression of the Jews."

That a prominent Viennese journalist might be of some future use to the German ambassador seems obvious—much too obvious to need spelling out by so subtle a diplomat. But as a homosexual in his highly visible position, Eulenburg had to perform a daily balancing act on a tightrope strung across an abyss, in constant danger of blackmail and exposure, and his spontaneous remark may well have been prompted by a sense of vulnerability directly proportionate to the enormous power he wielded in public. Perhaps it also contained a measure of fatalism. Sooner or later he was bound to stumble or be tripped up; his enemies would see to that.

They did. In 1906, lurid details about his liaison with, among others, the commanding general of the Berlin garrison surfaced in a widely read radical monthly. Eulenburg faced the classic dilemma: keep silent and stand condemned, or sue and risk even more damaging revelations. Eulenburg sued but, pleading illness, withdrew the suit and retired to his estate. His friend the Kaiser panicked at the first hint of scandal, fired him, and refused to ever see him again.

By that time, Herzl was no longer around to prove that he was not "the proverbial Jew."

The tenor and substance of their talk fully justified Herzl's belief that German backing was now a *fait accompli*. "It is an extraordinary event which not many people have ever lived to see," he wrote to Wolffsohn. "A dream suddenly come true." He was aware that a protectorate would provoke controversy: "Many will shake their heads, but I believe that the thing to do is to accept the offer gratefully. . . . To live under the protection of this strong, great, moral, splendidly governed, tightly organized Germany can only have the most salutary effect on the Jewish national character. Also, at one stroke we would obtain a completely regularized internal and external status. The suzerainty of the Porte and the protectorate of Germany would surely be adequate legal pillars" (D, 10/8/98).

An unanticipated audience with the Grand Duke of Baden early the next morning at the Imperial Palace in Potsdam further reinforced his illusions. The Grand Duke, who had come to bid godspeed to the imperial pilgrim, received Herzl with downright demonstrative affection. "I can't even remember all the kind things he said to me. All I know is that I love and venerate this wise, great, good man." The Grand Duke confirmed the Emperor's "all-out enthusiasm," mentioned a highly favorable report about Turkish reaction to Zionism by Baron Marschall von Bieberstein, the German ambassador to Constantinople, and firmly urged Herzl, while he was in Potsdam, to go to see Bülow so as to clarify the details of the Jerusalem audience and agree on the wording of a possible communiqué.

Herzl booked a hotel room, sent a message to the palace, and was promptly asked to present himself at 1 p.m. And in Bülow's cramped but elegant quarters he caught his first sobering glimpse of a reality to which he and his fellow dreamers had thus far been stubbornly oblivious.

Present, in addition to Bülow, was the Imperial Chancellor, Prince Chlodwig von Hohenlohe, a Catholic aristocrat and unvarnished anti-Semite. The wizened octogenarian with his shrunken chest full of medals made no effort to disguise his hostility. "Do you really think the Jews are going to quit the stock exchange and follow you instead?" was one of his opening salvos, followed by a series of ironic barbs twisted into questions. How much land did the Zionists want—only as far as Beirut, or beyond? Did they intend to establish an independent state, and what did the Turks have to say about this?

Herzl in his holy innocence replied that Ambassador Marschall's report had described their attitude as distinctly favorable. Whereupon Bülow, who had cast off his snakeskin charm and put on a grim scowl instead for the occasion, interjected that he knew nothing about such a report, leaving Herzl to wonder who was lying. It did not, however, keep him from stretching the truth himself when pressed about the movement's financial resources. He muttered something about various funds, one of which already amounted to 10 million British pounds. "That is a lot," Bülow acknowledged. "Money might do the trick." On this ambiguous note Herzl found himself abruptly dismissed. He drew what cold comfort he could from a fleeting glimpse of the Kaiser, "who today has certainly been talking about me repeatedly and who is very enthusiastic, as the Grand Duke said."

He did not get back to Vienna until October 13, which left him a mere three days in which to take care of pending business, put together a representative delegation, and say hello and goodbye to his family. What he dreaded most of all were the arguments with Bacher and Benedikt, who, after six weeks without their literary editor, were understandably upset about his wanting another month's leave to go chasing Zionist rainbows. "Yesterday the two of them again got me all excited. A curious psychological phenomenon: Bacher causes me more anxiety than Chancellor Hohenlohe. Oddly enough, in his presence I still feel myself to be what I once was, a shy novice journalist, although intellectually he does not impress me at all" (D, 10/12/98).

The other major headache was the makeup of the delegation. He cabled Nordau and Rabbi Gaster. Since he was not free to divulge any details, they suspected one of his sudden inspirations and excused themselves. Professor Mandelstamm, the Kiev ophthalmologist, was willing but could not get a passport on such short notice; however, he contributed 6,000 crowns toward expenses. In the end, Herzl was left with Wolffsohn, Bodenheimer, the engineer Josef Seidener—the only one who had previously visited Palestine—and the Viennese physician Moses Schnirer, all perfectly presentable, but not quite the sort of luminaries he would have wished to have along on this critical mission.

Critical and, he believed, dangerous. From Jerusalem, the Hebraist Ben-Yehuda had conveyed warnings of an assassination plot, and Herzl himself thought the Turks quite capable of either jailing him—shades again of Shabbetai Tsvi, who ended up in a Turkish dungeon—or of contriving a fatal accident. It lent an unusual melodramatic touch to his leave-taking on October 13. For the first time he registered wistful regret at leaving his "beautiful children, whose rosiest childhood is passing without my being able to watch it unfold in its lovely singularity." Both his parents blessed him, shedding bitter tears. "They would be the only ones disconsolate if I failed to return. That I would then be a historic figure would be no comfort to my poor old dears. . . . May God keep them healthy and grant us a happy reunion" (D, 10/14/98).

TWENTY-ONE

*H*erzl arrived in Constantinople on Sunday morning, October 16, 1898, accompanied by Wolffsohn and Bodenheimer; Schnirer and Seidener were to catch up with them two days later.

A steady rain welcomed them. The atmosphere was dank and depressing, and things began to go wrong almost immediately. The indefatigable Herzl, low on sleep but high on adrenaline, took just enough time to change his clothes—he never ceased being particular about wearing the right uniform for every occasion—and made the obligatory rounds of the Turkish dignitaries in the Yildiz, none of whom made themselves available. The snub should have alerted him to a change in the weather, but so sure was he of a resolution at the highest level that he no longer worried about the Sultan's subordinates and their feelings. Much more disquieting was Bodenheimer's encounter with the German ambassador. Herzl had sent him to the embassy to arrange for an interview with Ambassador Marschall, but the same man who supposedly had filed a favorable report on Turkish views of Zionism now curtly declared that he did not know any Dr. Herzl and, moreover, was too busy to receive him.

In the evening, the three of them watched a traveling Yiddish theater group perform Siegmund Feinman's *Gibor Hayil* (*The Great Hero*), which merely deepened Herzl's gloom. "Since this shabby art, such as it be, already represents the highest culture of our Yiddish-speaking masses, their current cultural level must be regarded as deplorably low. I was disgusted" (D, 10/16/98). It seems fortunate that Vienna's *fin de siècle* culture was not judged on the basis of some of Herzl's own plays.

He spent the next morning cooling his heels, increasingly frenetic about seeing the Kaiser, who had arrived the day before. There was no word from him or his staff, and the last boat that would get the delegation to Palestine in time for an audience left on the following morning. They now hesitated even to book passage. Would they still be received in Jerusalem, or had the Kaiser changed his mind altogether?

By noon, a quite desperate Herzl decided to appeal to him directly with "the most humble request for an audience, be it ever so brief and confidential, here in Constantinople," so as to discuss a Jewish Land Company for Syria and Palestine under a German protectorate, which the Kaiser's personal authority and friendship would surely induce the Sultan to accept. "God's secret is upon us in these world-historic hours," he concluded. "There can be no fear when He is with us." Wolffsohn hand-delivered the letter to the Imperial Chamberlain for transmittal, along with a note addressed to Bülow stressing the urgency of the request. And miraculously, the appeal—whether to the Kaiser or to the deity—had an instant effect. Three hours later he was ushered into the presence of the Emperor.

It was a moment he had been fantasizing about for years. Way back in the spring of 1895 he had tried to impress Baron Hirsch with his boast about going to see the German Kaiser. "And he will understand me, because he is trained to judge great things." Not surprisingly, therefore, the encounter with the flesh-and-blood embodiment of Prussian virtue, imperial power, and majestic wisdom had about it the quality of a fairy tale: "I felt as though I had entered a magic forest where the fabled unicorn was said to dwell. Suddenly a magnificent forest creature with a single horn on its forehead materialized before me. But what startled me more than its looks was the fact that it was alive. I had been able to picture its appearance in my mind, but not that it would actually breathe and come to life. And my amazement grew when the unicorn began to talk in a very friendly voice and said: I am the fabled unicorn" (D, 10/19/98).

Despite Bülow's sobering presence, Herzl's first impression lived up to all his expectations. "He has real imperial eyes. They radiate a strange, bold, questing soul." He had forgone the sedative Schnirer had offered him; his heart was racing, and his voice quivered with emotion as he presented his case for a German protectorate. Wilhelm, after listening politely for a while, began to explain his own interest in Zionism, which, as it soon developed, had little in common with the idealistic motives of his royal uncle. "There are elements among your compatriots"—a term he used throughout—"whom it would be a good thing to settle in Palestine. I am thinking of Hessen, where they practice usury among the rural population." Stung by the injustice of libeling all Jews on account of a few usurers, Herzl launched into an attack on anti-Semitism. But Bülow, ever alert to any chance of puncturing the Kaiser's toy balloons, pointedly interjected that the Jews had shown their gratitude for everything the House of Hohenzollern had done for them by joining the left opposition in droves. "Singer," mumbled the Kaiser, as if on cue; Singer, a Jew and leader of the Social Democrats, was his special *bête noire*. Bülow furthermore brought up the fact that neither the wealthy Jews nor the Jewish newspapers supported Herzl's ideas. "[His] intention was unmistakable. He wanted to signal to the Kaiser that I had no real power to back me up. Bülow raised every objection without ever coming straight out with the little word No, which he obviously did not dare to utter because the *voluntas Regis* was Yes. He said Yes, yes, yes but, Yes if only . . . all masked No's."

The conversation shifted to France, the Dreyfus affair, the political turmoil, "all of which," the Kaiser opined, "seems to indicate that the republican form of government is not the best conceivable." Herzl, in turn, though he objected to tarring all Jews with the same brush, was not himself above indulging in a bit of stereotyping for the Kaiser's edification. "A real Frog," he said, "hates the Germans, but he'll gladly take their money."

The audience concluded on what seemed like a note of complete agreement. Wilhelm felt sure that the Turks would raise no objections. "After all, the fact that the German Kaiser has taken up this matter and shown an interest in it is bound to make an impression. I am the only one who still sticks by the Sultan. He holds me in high regard." As for the audience in Jerusalem: "Give Bülow a draft of your speech. I'll go over it with him. And just tell me, in a word, what I am to ask of the Sultan."

"A chartered company—under German protection."

"Very well, then, a chartered company." They vigorously shook hands on it, and a moment later Herzl found himself alone with Bülow. "A genius of a monarch," said the minister, with feeling. He advised

Herzl to go and see Ambassador Marschall right away and ask for a briefing. "I think the Turks are unfavorably inclined at present."

By the time Herzl reached the embassy, the ambassador had left for the state dinner at which the fate of the Jews was to be settled between the Kaiser and the Sultan.

Just exactly what happened at that dinner has never been entirely clarified. According to the Kaiser's own account, he did bring up the Jewish Chartered Company and was told by the Sultan that, while he did not particularly care for the idea, he would nonetheless instruct his Foreign Ministry to look into it and work something out, since anything that had the Kaiser's support could not possibly harm him or his people.

Stripped of the diplomatic verbiage, this amounted to a blunt rebuff and was understood as such. Eulenburg later told Herzl that the Sultan had rejected the Kaiser's suggestion so brusquely that any further discussion became impossible. "We are anxious to remain on good terms with him. As a guest, the Kaiser could not, of course, press the subject." A different version of the conversation was supplied by Nevlinsky. According to his sources, the Kaiser tried to assure the Sultan that the Zionists were no danger to the Turks, but that the Jews were "everywhere a nuisance we would be glad to get rid of"—a rather original sales pitch to which the Sultan supposedly replied that, for his part, he was quite satisfied with his Jewish subjects. The Empress, in turn, was quoted as having said that she enjoyed the journey, the only disagreeable part being the sight of so many Jews. Nevlinsky does not qualify as the most reliable of informants, but the exchange sounds plausible.

In any event, it must have been abundantly clear to both Bülow and Marschall that the Turks, who for years had been fighting the system of Capitulations and chafed under the concessions they had been forced to grant the British and the French in Egypt and Lebanon, would panic at the merest hint of a Jewish Palestine under German protection. Moreover, neither France nor Russia was indifferent to German incursions into the Middle East and would have seen the "German protectorate" as precisely what the Kaiser had in mind—a strategic foothold. Any move in that direction was therefore bound to involve Germany in complications with which she was not—or not yet—equipped to deal. And finally, in the more formal sense, neither

Herzl nor most of his followers were German nationals entitled to the Emperor's protection. Given these self-evident facts, with which the two seasoned diplomats were thoroughly familiar, one can only surmise that they quite deliberately allowed the Kaiser to expose himself to an embarrassing rebuff in order to cure him of his fancy and scuttle the whole project once and for all without having to confront him directly. And in this they succeeded.

Herzl, in the meantime, blissfully unaware of these developments, returned to the hotel in a state of near-total collapse. They were due to leave early the next morning; and while Wolffsohn packed his suitcases for him, Herzl struggled in vain with the draft for the Jerusalem speech he had promised Bülow. By midnight he had to give up and get some rest, with a bottle of Bavarian beer as a sedative. At 4 a.m. he lit all twelve candles in the room, tried again, went back to sleep until six, and then worked until it was time to leave for the pier at half past eight. He sent Bülow the partially completed draft—one of the very few times ever that he missed a deadline, and a measure of the strain under which he was laboring.

Part of it was plain fear. His concern over Turkish designs on his life had ripened into full-blown paranoia. "That my audience (with the Kaiser) cannot remain secret for long, and that the world of diplomacy is already in a major uproar over it is something I believe I can take for granted, without megalomania. Well, we shall see. In any case, today I already represent a troublesome personality to many a party interested in the Holy Land, and I don't know if some plot against me isn't being hatched in Palestine. By whom? I cannot even venture a guess" (D, 10/9/98).

Once safely aboard the *Imperator Nicholas II*, he breathed easier. The Russian steamer took five days for the run from Constantinople to Alexandria, with stopovers in Smyrna and Athens. It was his first look at Greece, and he refused to be impressed. "In clouds of dust up to the Acropolis, which only speaks to us because classical literature was so strong. The power of literature! Then raced through Athens in just a few minutes which, however, seemed enough for the modern city. . . . Hot days in Alexandria and Port Said. Alexandria demonstrates how an intelligent European administration can raise a livable, comfortable city in the hottest of soils. In Port Said I very much admired the Suez Canal. The Suez Canal, this shimmering thread of water drawn into infinity, impressed me much more than the Acropolis" (D, 10/27/98).

In Alexandria they transferred to a small Russian freighter, and two days later, "when it grew light, we began to look for the Jewish coast." On Wednesday morning, October 26, they dropped anchor outside of Jaffa; the harbor, though functioning as the main point of entry into Turkish Palestine, was too shallow to berth larger vessels, and passengers as well as freight had to be rowed ashore. Half expecting to be arrested as soon as he set foot on Turkish soil, Herzl drafted a plea for help addressed to the Kaiser, who was scheduled to arrive a few hours later. It turned out to be an unnecessary precaution. The pier had been all but taken over by a contingent of German police, who quickly whisked him and his party—"the five white tropical helmets"—past the Turkish officials as soon as he invoked the magic name of the Emperor.

Yet his misgivings were not entirely unfounded. Among those waiting for him on the pier was one Mendel Kramer, a Jewish informer in the service of the Turkish secret police. Their choice of this sleazy and inept shlemiel for the job would seem to indicate the low priority they assigned it; nevertheless Kramer, who trailed Herzl more or less successfully throughout his stay, was said to have had a signed-and-sealed arrest warrant in his pocket, with instructions to use it should Herzl cause any disturbances.

Nothing, in fact, could have been further from Herzl's mind. On the contrary, he was most anxious not to draw attention to himself, and to make his visit appear as simply a newspaper assignment. But among the roughly 4,000 Jewish settlers, most of them living in Rothschild-subsidized colonies, his legend was already flourishing; the regal face was familiar, and rumors about the true purpose of his presence spread like wildfire even among the Arabs. And while it was easy enough to avoid mounting a white horse or donkey—a gesture tantamount to messianic pretensions in the ever-explosive atmosphere of religious fanaticism—demonstrations of public support, acclaim, or, for that matter, hostility were much more difficult to control.

In any event, he was in no mood for confrontations of any sort. Although, unlike Moses, he had been allowed to actually set foot in the Promised Land, he may have felt less than grateful for the distinction. For one thing, he was in bad shape physically. He had not yet recovered from whatever it was that ailed him in Constantinople, and, in addition to running a temperature, he had injured his leg in a shipboard accident. For another, the sight of Jaffa, at the time a sun-baked mudhole of a town with few amenities—"poverty and misery and heat in gay colors"—could have inspired rapture only in the already rapturous, to whom, thanks to the narrow-gauge railway that linked it to Jerusalem, it was the gateway to heavenly bliss.

They purposely avoided the one reputable, German-run hotel and checked into a modest rooming house instead. Neither his acute discomfort nor the 110-degree heat could stop Herzl, dressed as always in jacket and tie, from setting off within the hour on a tour of several Jewish settlements in the vicinity. His first stop was Mikve Yisrael, an agricultural school on the main highway to Jerusalem, founded in 1870 by the Alliance Universelle and to this day the major institution for advanced training. The gate was festively decorated in honor of the Kaiser, due to pass the next day on his way to Jerusalem. After a brief round of the grounds and a chat with the director, the party continued "through the in Arab fashion neglected landscape" to Rishon Le-Zion (the First to Zion), the first modern Jewish settlement in Turkish Palestine, established in 1882; it had gone bankrupt within the year and been dependent ever since on Rothschild largesse. The 400-odd settlers living in hardscrabble poverty and subject to the arbitrary rule of the baron's autocratic administrators further confirmed Herzl in his misgivings about both infiltration and philanthropy. Here, too, his reputation had preceded him; overseers and settlers alike were for the most part furtive and guarded, reluctant even to be seen with so notorious an opponent of the great white father in Paris, from whom all blessings flowed. "The poor settlers have swapped one fear for another." They showed off the wine cellars designed to store the mutant Bordeaux that was the colony's only product. "I never for a moment doubted that with enough money you could set up an industry anywhere. The point is that with the millions here being stolen, squandered and poured into the sand, something quite different could have been achieved" (D, 10/27/98).

In the meantime, as news of his arrival spread through the village, a group of younger, more rebellious settlers greeted him in the community hall with music, "unfortunately only well meant," and one of them gave a speech "in which he tried to reconcile their obligations toward the baron with their love for me, an effort no more successful than the conductor's vain attempts to make the flute harmonize with the violin." The worn, weathered faces shocked him, and the colony's physician confirmed that most of them were suffering from malaria, which only a large-scale multimillion-dollar drainage project could hope to eradicate.

After spending the night at Rishon Le-Zion, they toured three more settlements in the morning. Everywhere the population turned out in full force to hail them, but nowhere did they receive a more colorful and enthusiastic welcome than at Rehovot, a settlement founded in 1890 by Warsaw members of the B'nei Moshe who had managed to steer clear of the ubiquitous baron and become self-sufficient by growing diversified crops. Rehovot was the core of Herzl's organizational support in Palestine, and he was moved to tears when their carriage was met by a cavalcade of some twenty young Jewish farmers racing their swift Arabian horses across the fields and welcoming him with boisterous *"hedads."* The miraculous transformation of "pants-peddling Jew-boys" into daring horsemen reminded him of the Wild West cowboys he had once seen in a Paris circus.

The account of this visionary's journey through both past and future is notable for one conspicuous blind spot. As Amos Elon has pointed out, the trip also took him through at least a dozen Arab villages, and in Jaffa itself, Jews formed only 10 percent—some 3,000—of the total population. Yet not once does he refer to the natives in his notes, nor do they ever seem to figure in his later reflections. In overlooking, in refusing to acknowledge their presence—and hence their humanity— he both followed and reinforced a trend that was to have tragic consequences for Jews and Arabs alike.

The party returned to Jaffa late on Thursday afternoon. Herzl, increasingly feverish and totally exhausted by the rigors of the trip, had a reunion with "my good old Hechler." The bouncy, ever-buoyant little clergyman in flowing robes and wearing an Arab *kefiyah* had been busy proclaiming the arrival of the Messiah without attracting undue attention; after several millennia of such proclamations, the native population had developed a certain immunity to both messages and messengers of imminent redemption.

The following morning, already barely able to rouse himself, Herzl left early for Mikve Yisrael, where he had decided to waylay the imperial procession and salute the Kaiser by way of reminding him of his presence. The whole student body, dressed in their holiday best, was lined up along the highway. The Rothschild administrators, visibly miffed and resentful of the intrusion, kept their distance from Herzl, and when he offered to introduce the school's director to the Kaiser, he was reminded of his status as an uninvited guest and told to refrain from what, in the circumstances, might be misinterpreted as a Zionist provocation staged, or at the very least tolerated, by the school. Herzl had trouble enough, anyway, merely keeping on his feet in the grueling heat, but at nine o'clock, when the imperial procession hove into sight preceded by a vanguard of fierce Turkish cavalry, it was he, nonetheless, who conducted the student choir in a rendition of the imperial anthem, "Hail Thee in the Victor's Laurel Wreath." (Sung to the tune of "God Save the King," which, after a somewhat stormy transatlantic crossing, turned into "My Country 'Tis of Thee," an inspiring example of creative recycling.) Then, placing himself conspicuously next to a display of plowshares, he doffed his helmet and hoped for the best.

He was not to be disappointed. The Kaiser on his white stallion recognized him from a distance, reined in abruptly, causing a pileup, stopped dead in front of Herzl, bent down and extended his hand. "How are you?"

"Thank you, Your Majesty. I am having a look at the country. How has the trip agreed with Your Majesty so far?"

The Kaiser blinked rapidly. "Very hot. But the land has a future."

"For the time being it is still sick."

"It needs water," said the Kaiser.

"Yes, Your Majesty. Irrigation on a massive scale."

"It is a land of the future," the Kaiser repeated.

They exchanged a few more words while the Rothschild administrators looked on in sheer disbelief, not trusting their eyes. Wolffsohn pointed his box camera and took two snapshots of the historic meeting, but reverence made his hand shake so badly that all he caught was the Kaiser's silhouette and Herzl's left foot; the second plate was blank altogether. (The widely distributed photograph of the meeting is a fake, subsequently concocted in a photo lab.)

After this uplifting interlude, the five delegates returned to Jaffa and boarded the train to Jerusalem. It was Friday afternoon; for some reason the departure was delayed for an hour while they sat tightly wedged like sardines into a narrow compartment packed with pre-Sabbath travelers and their voluminous bags, bundles, and baskets. Amid the stench and the heat Herzl began to gasp for air. His fever mounted steadily, along with the temperature in the car, while the pious Wolffsohn in turn suffered spiritual agonies when, as a result of the delay, the sun began to sink behind the horizon and darkness fell while they were still en route, thus forcing him to choose between jumping off the moving train or violating the Sabbath.

He opted for sin. But when they reached Jerusalem, with the moon already high above the city, he made Herzl pay for it by insisting that they walk the not inconsiderable distance from the railroad station to the hotel rather than taking a cab, his fear of Jehovah's wrath proving stronger than his pity for the stricken leader, who by this time was altogether *hors de combat* and in no shape for arguments. Leaning heavily on a cane with one hand, the other clutching the shoulder of one or another of his now literal supporters, Herzl dragged his swollen, aching leg and smoldering carcass for half an hour through the sloping, unlit, and unpaved streets to the Kaminitz Hotel, teeming with German and Turkish military personnel. He was given a broom closet of a room, where he collapsed, took a dose of quinine, which he promptly brought back up, and spent a feverish night attended to by Schnirer, who gave him periodic rubdowns with spirits of camphor. His friends feared the worst, but by morning his condition had somewhat improved. Still weak, he spent the day indoors catching up on his diary entries and gazing at the city from the hotel windows. "Even in its decay it is still a beautiful city. When we come here, it could become one of the most beautiful in the world."

From the window he was also able to witness the Kaiser's triumphant entry into the Old City. Wilhelm, for one, had no qualms about being taken for the Messiah; he arrived astride his white horse, and since none of the seven gates in Suleiman's massive wall allowed enough clearance for a mounted rider, let alone one who insisted on wearing a spiked helmet, a fifty-foot section had been broken out of the battlements next to the Jaffa Gate so as to afford the imperial pilgrim access to the holy places without having to humble himself by getting off his horse. Local Zionists had wanted Herzl to welcome the Kaiser in the name of the Jewish community; local anti-Zionists had asked that he not even show his face, and in the circumstances he was reasonably happy to oblige.

Instead, he finished the draft of his proposed address to the Kaiser, had Wolffsohn deliver it to the Imperial Chamberlain for approval, and, at the end of the Sabbath, moved into the hospitable home of Jonas Marx on Mamilla Street, a short block from the Jaffa Gate. Marx, whose descendants still occupy the house, turned the whole second floor over to Herzl and his companions. (The premises have been preserved as a small museum. The house, located in the midst of an area slated for urban renewal, was recently declared a historic landmark and saved from destruction after a protracted battle.) There he received a steady stream of visitors, ranging from ardent Zionists to equally ardent celebrity hunters, until he was finally able to get away for his first walk through the Old City. His impressions fell short of piety.

> When I remember thee in days to come, O Jerusalem, it will not be with pleasure.
>
> The dank sediment of two millennia filled with inhumanity, intolerance, and filth infests the foul-smelling alleys. The amiable dreamer of Nazareth, the one and only human being in all this time ever to pass through here, merely contributed to intensifying the hatred. If we ever get Jerusalem, and if at that time I am still able to do anything about it, the first thing I would do is clean it up. I would clear out everything that does not qualify as sacred. I would build workers' homes outside the city, clear out the filthy hovels, raze them, burn all non-sacred ruins, and transfer the bazaars elsewhere. Then, while retaining the old architectural style as far as possible, I would erect a comfortable, airy city with proper sewage around the holy places. [D, 10/31/98]

Twice he visited what in his day was referred to as the Wailing Wall, but "it stirred no deeper feelings in me because ugly, wretched, speculative beggary has infested the place. At least so it was last night and this morning, when we were there" (D, 10/31/98). In the evening they climbed up to the Tower of David, a massive stone structure dating from the Herodian period, which the Turks used as a jail. "It would be smart of the Sultan to lock me up in here," he joked, a case of whistling in the dark. But the joke fell flat; by now, even his friends feared for his safety. He also insisted on a quick look at the Via Dolorosa, "although it is supposed to be an unwise thing to do for a Jew. Seidener, who used to live here, flatly refused to come along. I would have considered it sheer cowardice not to go, and so I walked up the street to the Church of the Holy Sepulchre. My friends kept me from entering the church itself. One also must not enter the Mosque of Omar or the Temple area; the rabbis punish trespassers by excommunication. This is what happened to Sir Moses Montefiore. So much superstition and fanaticism on all sides. And yet I am not afraid of all those fanatics" (D, 10/31/98).

The view of the Mount of Olives from the Hurva Synagogue in the Old City again inspired the urban planner. "I am firmly convinced that a magnificent New Jerusalem could be erected outside the old city walls. Old Jerusalem would remain Lourdes and Mecca and Yerushalayim. A very handsome, elegant city next to it would be a real possibility" (D, 10/31/98).

On the whole, however, these were the perfunctory impressions of a more or less dutiful tourist who, while no longer acutely ill, was still far from well and who, in any case, had weightier matters on his mind. Herzl had no feeling for the relics of antiquity, be they Greek, Egyptian, or Jewish, and he saw no reason to feign it. On the contrary, he was proud of his progressive mind cast, which disdained the Acropolis and reveled in the miracle of the Suez Canal. Let the "fanatics" have the past; his eyes were on the future. In any case, he had not come to see the sights but to have an audience with the Kaiser, and as the third day passed without word from the imperial encampment, he grew increasingly edgy. Like a drill sergeant he kept lining up his four companions for inspection, checking out their suits, shoes, hats, gloves, and ties, to be ready at a moment's notice. But he concealed from them his one major worry: the weekly mail boat, the only safe connection to Port Said, left Jaffa every Tuesday. He had been most anxious to have the audience done with in time to catch it and leave the country on November 1, "before the Turks had a chance to wake up." But by Monday evening, October 31, it had become clear that they would never make it.

On Tuesday morning, just as he was beginning to lose hope altogether, he was finally called to the imperial compound, where a low-ranking but arrogant diplomat received him with twangy condescension. Herzl was handed the draft of his speech with a number of deletions and told to resubmit a clean copy of the revised text along with the corrected original, a demonstrative display of mistrust which Herzl chose to overlook. The audience was set for 12:30 sharp the following day.

The deletions, though not extensive, were crucial; all references to the Jewish national revival, the Zionist congresses, the Basel program, and, above all, the German protectorate had been crossed out, presumably by Bülow. But in the excitement over the impending audience, nobody paid much attention to such technical details. Herzl tried to convince his jittery crew that the Kaiser, though enormously powerful, was still only human, but this soothing bromide did little to allay the stage fright of these stodgy, authority-oriented, middle-class Jews, who found God in heaven far less unnerving to contemplate than a flesh-and-blood Emperor here on earth. There were last-minute hitches. Bodenheimer's top hat and cuffs did not pass muster. It seemed impossible to scare up a reputable carriage. Herzl supervised their eleven o'clock snack, restricting their intake so as to keep everyone trimly alert, and he rejected the sedative proposed by Schnirer. Hechler popped in to bless them all in the name of the God of Abraham and Jacob.

On the stroke of noon they were off, dressed in their formal best, sweat pouring down their backs. An hour later Herzl was back at the Marx house and already summing up his impressions: "This brief reception will for all eternity be preserved in the annals of Jewish history, and it is not impossible that it may also have historic consequences."

On reaching the imperial compound, twenty-six sumptuous tents supplied by Thomas Cook, Inc., outfitted in Oriental splendor and erected on a rocky slope north of the Old City, they had been ushered into the imperial presence. The members of the delegation were formally presented to the Kaiser, who, wearing a veiled helmet and fidgeting with his riding crop, gave each of them a military salute. Bülow was seated discreetly in the background, and at a sign from him, Herzl began to read his revised speech, while the minister compared it word for word with his own copy of the authorized version, running his finger along the lines.

The speech, purged of its few potentially controversial references, was an exercise in bland banality, and the Kaiser responded in kind. He thanked Herzl, assured him that he found the matter interesting but that it would need further study; he allowed, however, that "your movement, with which I am well acquainted, contains a sound idea." Bülow, no doubt, had done his job, but Wilhelm's enthusiasms never lasted very long, in any case, and it was evident that his romance with Zionism had run its course. After the official exchange, he engaged Herzl and Bülow in a brief chat about Palestine. Everyone agreed that the most urgent need was water.

"That," said Herzl, "we can bring the country. It will cost billions, but it will yield billions."

"Oh well," said the Kaiser, slapping his boot with his riding crop for emphasis, "money you've got aplenty. More money than all of us put together."

"Yes," Bülow eagerly chimed in. "The money that gives us so much trouble is one commodity you possess in abundance."

On this unsubtle reference to international Jewry and its sinister financial power the Kaiser closed the audience, and the five delegates trotted out into the noonday sun. A final humiliation awaited them. The Turkish guards refused to let them out of the compound, and it was Mendel Kramer, the police spy lurking near the gate, who in the end persuaded them to open it.

They got back to find the Marx house swarming with visitors. Most seemed bona fide sympathizers, but Herzl at this point was taking no chances. An invitation from a young Russian farmer provided the opportunity for escape; together with Wolffsohn and Bodenheimer they drove out to Motza, a new colony in the hills west of Jerusalem, where Herzl planted what he thought was a cedar sapling. (It later turned out to be a cypress, cut down during World War I.) They returned to Jerusalem under cover of darkness, caught a few hours of sleep, rose at 2 a.m., stealthily packed their suitcases, slipped out at dawn, and took the first train to Jaffa.

For the moment, Herzl could think of nothing other than getting out as fast as possible. "Things were getting too hot for me in Palestine. If the Turkish government had even an ounce of political awareness, they would have had to stop me in my tracks. When I came to Constantinople, they had a chance they may never have again. All they had to do was expel me. Or they could have taken care of me more easily by just having policemen disguised as bandits attack and kill me. . . . [Instead], they let me continue and complete my journey. And unless I am greatly mistaken, I am now already a political factor to be reckoned with" (D, 11/5/98).

Mistaken or not, he spent most of Thursday out on the water trying unsuccessfully to hitch a ride to Alexandria. There were only a few merchant vessels moored amid the flotilla of German warships, and none was going his way. But the private yacht of the American press lord James Gordon Bennett, publisher of the *New York Herald*, was said to be sailing for Egypt later in the day, and Herzl sent Bennett a note in English:

Dear Sir:

You know perhaps my name as the leader of the Zionist movement. I had to speak with the Emperor in Jerusalem and came yesterday too late back to Jaffa so that there is no ship for me. I wish to go to Alexandria.

Now I understand that your Yacht leaves this evening for Alexandria. If it is so, have you a place for me and only one of my four companions? I could so reach Alexandria tomorrow evening in time for the steamer to Naples, where I am expected. I should be very grateful to get your answer as soon as possible. If you have no place for me, I must try any other combination, and that is difficult in this place. Believe me, Sir,

Yours obediently,

Dr. Theodor Herzl. [D, 11/4/98]

Bennett's refusal finally forced him to spend the night in Jaffa, where Mendel Kramer, along with a host of friends, foes, and stool pigeons, caught up with him. Early Friday morning he and Wolffsohn had themselves rowed out to a flimsy British freighter, the *Dundee*, scheduled to leave at sunset with a cargo of oranges. Herzl decided to remain on board for security reasons and sent Wolffsohn back to shore for the baggage and the rest of the company. Schnirer, Seidener, and Bodenheimer arrived in a mutinous mood. The *Dundee* did not look seaworthy to them, no animal could have survived the trip in the so-called cabins near the boiler room, and, moreover, they did not appreciate Herzl's way of making unilateral decisions without consulting them. But he remained resolute, and in the end they had no choice but to give in.

They turned out to have been right. The heat made the cabins uninhabitable and forced them to sleep on deck. The weather turned stormy, the little nutshell of a boat pitched and rolled in the rough seas, and everybody got seasick. Everybody, that is, except Herzl. He felt well. The irony of the latter-day Moses in headlong flight from the Promised Land back to the fleshpots of Egypt may have been lost on him, but he was conscious of an enormous sense of relief. Sheer survival was a triumph of sorts. As to the concrete results of what he called "the venture of his pretender's journey to Palestine," he had yet to sort them out.

*   *   *

The episode has an epilogue which, far more eloquently than Herzl's own account, testifies to the striking impact of his personality.

The German Kaiser was deposed and rather apologetically sent into exile after the so-called revolution of 1918. He spent his retirement in Holland, chopping wood and dictating his memoirs. His overbearing self-involvement, shallowness, and generally limited vision make this passage from his unpublished memoirs seem all the more remarkable:

> My visit to Istanbul in 1898 gave me an opportunity to meet a very interesting man. Through Count Philipp Eulenburg, the Vienna ambassador, the leader of the Zionist movement, Dr. Herzl of Vienna, a good friend of the Count's, had asked me for an audience in Istanbul, which I granted. A clever, very intelligent man with expressive eyes, Dr. Herzl decidedly was an enthusiastic idealist with an aristocratic mentality. He gave me an absorbing presentation of his ideas, the gist of which is the creation of opportunities for large-scale settlement by his fellow Jews in Palestine, possibly later in Syria. . . . In his recently published memoirs, Dr. Herzl described his audience with me in Istanbul quite accurately and in a very loyal manner for which he deserves much credit. I greeted him on one subsequent occasion, when I passed a Jewish farming settlement in Palestine. [Unpublished Memoirs in the State Archives, Berlin-Dahlem, Quoted in HY, Vol. VI, p. 60]

TWENTY-TWO

*H*erzl and his party spent two days in Alexandria waiting for their connection to Naples, a welcome breathing spell and the last peaceful interlude he was to know for some time. "Wonderful Egypt was for me full of the most delightful surprises. It goes to show what hard work and energy can accomplish even in a hot country." The imperial audience still seemed to him a major triumph, and if the absence of tangible results was disappointing, he found comfort in the thought that "he didn't say yes, and he didn't say no." Somewhat apprehensive because none of the newspapers he was able to get hold of in Egypt carried any mention of the audience, he cabled his father and received a laconic "Audience known" for an answer.

It was only when he landed in Naples that the full extent of the debacle became apparent. The German wire services carried a brief bulletin dated November 2: "Kaiser Wilhelm received a Jewish deputation, which presented an album with pictures of Jewish colonies founded in Palestine. Replying to an address by the leader of the deputation, the Kaiser said that any such endeavors could count on his benevolent interest to the extent to which they aimed at furthering agriculture in Palestine and promoting the welfare of the Turkish Empire while scrupulously respecting the sovereignty of the Sultan."

A plunge into arctic waters; the effect on Herzl's companions was devastating. He himself, suspecting foul play by Bülow, attempted to keep up their morale along with his own by vowing to publish a more uplifting version forthwith. "You see," he told them, "this is why I am your leader. Time and again I prove myself. I am neither smarter nor better than any of you. But I remain undaunted, and that is why I am entitled to the leadership. In moments far more difficult than these I never lost courage. On the contrary, they only spur me on to ever greater sacrifice" (D, 11/15/98).

Courage and fortitude were not, however, his only qualifications; he also had the ability to convince himself that black was white when the need arose: "The fact that the Kaiser did not assume the protectorate in Jerusalem is, of course, excellent for the future development of our cause. My companions, it is true, were greatly disappointed, because the protectorate would have offered obvious and immediate advantages. Not so, however, in the long run. We would later on have had to pay grossly usurious interest for this protectorate" (D, 1/15/98).

Cold comfort, though, and all the more chilling for being absolutely true. Reason should have compelled him, at this point, to cut his losses and drop the notion of a Prussian-sponsored *Judenstaat* once and for all. But reason, as Herzl would have been the first to point out, should have compelled him long ago to give up on the dream altogether.

If his meetings with the Kaiser constituted the high point of Herzl's life, the anticlimactic outcome signaled the onset of a tragic decline, the slow but inexorable ascendance of lucid despair over blind faith.

The causes were many, closely linked, and feeding upon one another—deteriorating physical health, emotional lability, the drama of his marriage, constant stress on the job, and, finally, the political setbacks and internal rifts that sapped the movement and undermined his authority. He was painfully aware of the portents; fever and palpitations aside, the mirror reflected the face of a man looking at least ten years older than his age. But he chose to ignore them and instead drove himself twice as hard to make up for the loss of energy and momentum. He was determined to do what he felt he had to, and willing to pay the price. Too willing, perhaps, but heroism is seldom devoid of self-destructive impulses.

The first task he faced on his return was to render an account of the trip and its results. In *Die Welt*, on November 18, he cryptically informed his readers—and the movement at large—that "we did not go to Palestine as tourists or explorers, but with a definite political purpose. Having accomplished that purpose, we immediately started for home." This left a great deal to the imagination, and the condescending official bulletin, followed by obdurate silence on the part of the Germans, added further disappointment and inspired a spate of rumors about what had and had not taken place. Among the Hoveve Zion veterans of Eastern Europe, the episode revived doubts about Herzl's prudence and judgment; above all, they feared that his open flirtation with German imperialism would lead to Turkish reprisals and compromise the existing settlements. And within the movement as a whole, it reinforced the opposition to Herzl's autocratic methods, his undemocratic secrecy, and his arrogant presumption to speak on behalf of a body that had been neither informed nor consulted. Above all, there was growing impatience with the arch ambiguities, broad hints, and plain bombast which, far from boosting morale, merely aroused premature hopes and unwarranted expectations. Criticism from Ahad Ha-Am and his disciples was to be expected. But even a Herzl sympathizer such as Reuben Brainin wondered publicly in print about the point of the Jerusalem audience and went on to raise a broader question: To what extent were secrecy, back-alley intrigues, and arbitrary one-man decisions compatible with the principles and practices of a democratic movement?

In his somewhat lame response, Herzl maintained that discretion and secrecy were essential to effective diplomacy, and that the Kaiser was "one of the policy makers of our time." It was that very discretion, however, that also handicapped his defense; disclosure of the Eulenburg letter would have gone a long way toward justifying his Palestine junket, as well as his admittedly rash remarks in London. But he had promised not to divulge its contents, and he kept his promise, alluding only to "a colossal achievement" and asking his followers to take his word for it.

More puzzling is the dogged determination with which he persisted in the pursuit of this will-o'-the-wisp long after the "colossal achievement" had proved a dud. In the face of repeated rebuffs—and despite his own rational misgivings—he never quite gave up the hope of reviving German interest in Zionism. Right after his return he sent the Kaiser a copy of his *Palais Bourbon* and requested another audience. Told to see Bülow instead, he refused, having convinced himself that the Foreign Minister was his personal enemy and chiefly responsible for the abrupt shift in German policy. (The latter may have been partly true. As to Bülow's personal feelings, he was quoted as having said that "I had a very good impression of Dr. Herzl, but I don't believe in his cause. Those people don't have any money. The rich Jews won't go along, and with the Polish riffraff you can't do a thing.")

Even his closest collaborators were embarrassed by the effusive encomiums to the Kaiser which Herzl kept publishing in *Die Welt*. Time and again, he tried to enlist Eulenburg and the Grand Duke of Baden in schemes to recapture the Kaiser's attention, and he never really ceased to dream of "resuming relations" with the German Reich. One can only assume that this steadfast refusal to face the facts had to do not so much with his failure to grasp the true nature of German policy and politics as with the depth of his lifelong commitment to German culture, the German spirit, and German power. He meant it when he wrote, in one of the ever more frequent moments of discouragement, that "reaching our goal under a German protectorate" had been his fondest hope, one whose loss he regretted "more than words can express." And in a letter to the Grand Duke, written a month after his return, he could still claim that "our movement is now oriented toward seeking German protection. Ever since I had the good fortune to be allowed to approach Your Royal Highness, it has been my constant thought—a thought that comes naturally to me as a result of my upbringing and in my role as a German author—that we should do everything in our power to acquire the protection of German law and of the German empire."

His status as a "German author" was soon to be put to the test.

Even before he left for Palestine, the cast for his new comedy had been agreed upon. But the premiere of *Our Cathy*, originally scheduled by the Burgtheater for November, was postponed several times, until early in January 1899 the director suddenly demanded extensive cuts. Herzl refused, whereupon the play was abruptly canceled.

The belated discovery of immorality and indecent language served as a clumsy pretext masking weightier objections. *Our Cathy*, while no great play by any means, represented a certain progress over Herzl's earlier farces. The muddled message, delivered by comic-opera characters in libretto prose, stressed the contrast between the corrupt decadence of a bourgeois marriage—modeled on an example close to home—and the comradely virtues prevailing in the unconsecrated union of two noble proletarians. This vaguely "socialist" touch may have given rise to second thoughts at what was, after all, an institution loyally devoted to its imperial sponsor; more likely, the Burgtheater simply did not wish to get involved with an increasingly controversial public figure. But if that was their aim, the last-minute about-face caused precisely the sort of scandal the powers behind the scenes had sought to avoid. There were some lofty arguments over freedom of thought and expression, yet the real issue was clearly not the play—which as yet no one had seen—but its author.

The virulence of Austrian anti-Semitism has been all too readily trivialized by references to the easygoing *Gemütlichkeit* that kept overt physical brutality within bounds. True, Jews were as yet rarely being assaulted in the streets, but some forty years before the triumphant return of the prodigal Nazi son, Vienna's gutter press already engaged in Jew-baiting that rivaled the *Stürmer* for obscenity. The scandal over *Our Cathy* opened the sluice gates to a tidal wave of swill; Herzl was portrayed as a smut peddler, a pervert poisoning the wellsprings of the Aryan soul, a demented Jewish radical bent on undermining the institution of marriage. Cartoons in humor magazines depicted him astride a pig, and even the Burgtheater, for all its caution, found itself under siege for its "initial and incomprehensible tolerance toward a play inspired not by ethical dignity but by Judeo-Gallic frivolity." Another, more inspired satirist saw evidence of "tensions between the Austrian throne and the future throne of Zion; presumably it was their own designs on the crown of Jerusalem that prompted Austrian court circles to derail Herr Theodor Herzl."

The official censor, on the other hand, a policeman of the old school, objected to only a single phrase in the entire play. Speaking of Cathy's mother, "a woman approaching her forties," the protagonists drool at the thought of how *liebesklug*—how well versed in the art of love—her embrace must be. An Austrian woman, the inspector decreed, had no business being *liebesklug* in her embraces, but after deletion of the offending phrase, the play had its premiere at the German Peoples' Theater on February 3, 1899. The reception was as predictably divided as the audience; gangs of anti-Semitic rowdies lined up against militant Zionists, the ensuing fistfights and rioting led to three arrests, and critics split along similar ideological fault lines, devoting more space to the action on the floor than on the stage. None of which did much for Herzl's standing as a "German author," but it helped to enhance his reputation as a Jewish troublemaker.

As such, he soon drew fire from another quarter.

Karl Kraus, born in Jičín, Moravia, in 1874, was the son of an affluent Jewish manufacturer. Transplanted to Vienna at the age of three, he quit school in his teens, failed as an actor, and turned to literature instead. In 1899, after a brief stint as freelance critic, he founded his own satirical monthly, *Die Fackel* (*The Torch*), to which he soon became the sole contributor as well as editor, a dazzling solo performance that lasted from 1911 to his death in 1936 and established him as the preeminent prophet of the Vienna apocalypse.

The label, to the extent to which it applies, is more of a comment on the nature of the apocalypse than on the cramped and crabbed vision of Karl Kraus, whose fulminating self-hatred fueled these more or less monthly eruptions of venom, spleen, and fury. He conducted a relentless campaign of intellectual terror against anything and everything that reminded him of his origins, but the barbed brilliance of his style successfully obscured the essential shallowness of his ideas. In the course of his lifelong crusade against the press, he inevitably skewered many a target that well deserved it, but his anger ranged far beyond the bounds of reason and decency. He attacked nearly every prominent Jewish figure of his time, from Dreyfus to Freud, and very few Jewish writers escaped his invariably scurrilous outbursts and personal invective. Ironically, he was himself the most accomplished practitioner of a style and method characteristic of ghetto polemics and the Yiddish press; to elevate him to the stature of a moralist and social critic is to blind oneself to the morbid bias and strident hysteria that so often perverted his judgment.

What he shared with Herzl was a Faustian energy and a sense of style. A quasi-socialist in his youth, he converted to Catholicism, turned Protestant, and eventually gave up on religion. Even as a somewhat belated pacifist in World War I, he concentrated his fire on the excesses of a chauvinist press rather than on the powers responsible for the carnage. In the thirties he supported the clerical autocracy of the Dollfuss regime, and as to Hitler, he could "think of nothing to say."

Like Herzl, he was a man forever on the run. Unlike Herzl, he remained mired for life in impotent rage against the Jew in himself— a common enough phenomenon among the Vienna intellectuals of his day—and dissipated his talents in spectacular rantings which, for all their verbal pyrotechnics, scarcely deserve the pious reverence they continue to elicit.

And did, from the very beginning.

Although in 1899 he was still an *enfant terrible* rather than a voice from the mountain, his satirical broadside against Herzl and Zionism made a big splash in the cafés and parlors of the Jewish bourgeoisie. Kraus at the time was preparing for his conversion to Catholicism, which took place later that year, and "A Crown for Zion" may thus have been an integral part of his spiritual journey. But Herzl, a feuilletonist as well as a Jew with prophetic pretensions, presented an especially tempting target, and Kraus yielded to temptation with all the punning and passion that distinguished his later diatribes. He diagnosed Zionism as a disease of language promoted by newspapers such as the *Neue Freie Presse* and discovered a clear link between Herzl's corrupting influence as a feuilletonist and his insane notions of a Jewish renaissance. The argument was as sophomoric as the snooty references to Herzl as a bumbling fool, and the essay has been excluded from most posthumous editions of Kraus's writings.

Let it be said in his favor that he himself eventually had the grace to disown it. Upon reading Herzl's diaries, he is reputed to have declared that Herzl was sincere, after all.

Whatever his private reaction, Herzl knew better than to dignify these attacks with a public response; Kraus, in fact, is never even mentioned in the Diaries. But wisdom aside, he had more important issues to deal with, foremost among them being the bank. Without the money to back them, his schemes and dreams did not stand a ghost of a chance in the real world. And just as he had created the movement by an act of faith, he now set out to will the bank into existence— and discovered that founding a bank was a great deal more complicated; faith and fantasy proved not only unhelpful but downright counterproductive. What it took instead—a sound business sense, shrewd judgment of people, and patience, patience above all—were the very qualities in which he was woefully deficient.

This did not stop him from fancying himself an expert in finance. He had several eminently capable businessmen working for him, but in this as in everything else he trusted no one but himself. Every delay, every technical obstacle was seen by him as yet another proof of incompetence, ill will, or deliberate sabotage calling for his intervention; and his intervention, his edgy, impatient hectoring, more often than not took the form of meddlesome interference. In January he complained that "the founding of the bank drags on, painfully and under ridiculous difficulties. Wolffsohn reports that he has completed the formalities" (D, 12/20/98). A week later, he exploded: "I cannot fool myself any longer—the situation of our cause is now truly desperate. After the great success of the Palestine journey, the incompetence of our banking and financial experts is nothing short of catastrophic. Our bank secretary Loewe is pushing the panic button, announcing that he will soon run out of money for the day-to-day expenses. Wolffsohn is coming today. I have to have a serious talk with him. The others are incapable of getting anything done, and I fear that he, too, is not the right man for the job" (D, 12/29/98).

What disqualified Wolffsohn and the other members of the banking committee in his eyes was their conservative approach to a delicate job—nothing less, in essence, than founding a bank without the necessary funds. To Herzl, busy founding a state without a country, this seemed a relatively trivial task by comparison, and their caution infuriated him. The plan of action called for a two-step procedure: incorporation of the Jewish Colonial Trust, Ltd., in London, followed by a public subscription drive. The incorporation, though a mere legal formality, involved an unconscionable amount of red tape and a registration fee of £2,500. Herzl contributed £500 out of his own pocket and accused Wolffsohn of deliberately failing to attend to the paperwork. The real sticking point, however, was the subscription drive, which obligated the trustees to raise £250,000, the minimum required to function as a mutual institution owned by its shareholders. No reputable bank or financial institution in Europe had been willing to participate, whether out of traditional prudence or—as Herzl suspected—because of Rothschild backstairs intrigues. As a result, the money would have to be raised through private subscription among the ideologically committed, the bulk of whom, however highly motivated, were far from affluent.

In light of these difficulties, Herzl's associates pleaded for more time to explore alternate resources and prepare the ground for what, at best, was a risky venture with a potentially fatal outcome for the entire movement. But he bridled at the suggestion. The bank was the key to victory; he wanted it now, in time for the third Zionist congress, and he had no patience with the conservative business approach of his associates. Opposed by the entire banking committee, but with the— at least moral—support of his father, he badgered, threatened, and cajoled until they finally gave in.

The Jewish Colonial Trust was registered with the Bank of England in London on March 20, 1899, and the thirty-day public subscription drive opened a week later. Opening-day subscriptions amounted to a disappointing total of 8,000 one-pound shares. "I am now in one of those moods in which Faust is ready to strike any kind of a bargain with the Devil. If today anyone promised me the success of the subscription drive, I would sell him ten years of my life. This although I yesterday wrote Wolffsohn that I had a feeling, a sort of *flair d'artilleur*, that the subscription would be a success. If I turn out to be wrong, it would be the first—but also the most serious—mistake I have so far committed in the Zionist movement. Those miserable 8,000 shares of this morning have, however, made me drastically trim my expectations" (D, 3/29/99).

In the prospectus for the subscription, on the other hand, he again coupled exhortation with grandiose hints in the manner which his opponents found so disconcerting: "We shall see if the Jewish people is ready to make the effort to help itself. . . . The preliminary diplomatic moves by the leaders of Zionism have advanced to the point where, immediately after the close of the subscription, we can proceed with the first practical steps toward the realization of our great plan" (Quoted in Bein, p. 450).

The Devil did take him up on the ten years—and then some— Herzl had so rashly offered him in his Faustian bargain, but without keeping his part of the deal. The final result of the drive—some 200,000 shares—seems rather respectable, considering that nearly three-fourths were bought by Russia's Jews, but it fell short of the 250,000 needed to open for business and was less than a third of the amount Herzl had projected and hoped for. It took another three months of wrangling, badgering, endless arguments, and negotiations until a consortium organized by Wolffsohn finally came up with the difference, just in time for the third congress.

Once again Herzl had prevailed. He had smitten the rock and made it bleed water. Barely a trickle, but every drop a miracle just the same.

"The bank," he wrote, "has been the most difficult task so far. If it succeeds, no one will ever know how much energy it required" (D, 3/4/99). Most of that energy was supplied by him, and under far from ideal conditions. In addition to a subacute depression and the ever more frequent physical complaints, both of which he valiantly strove to ignore, he constantly wrestled with the conflict between his exalted status as a leader and his subordinate position on the paper. Returning from an audience with the Grand Duke of Baden, he complained that "on the way home, I again went through the same experience I so often had before—the closer I get to the *Neue Freie Presse*, the smaller I feel" (D, 3/4/99).

But frustration and the growing threat of some catastrophic, all-around failure merely seemed to spur him on to ever greater efforts, many of which began to assume the character of desperate improvisations. The bank, for all the trouble and—quite literally—heartache it caused him, was nonetheless a side issue, a means to an end; his overarching preoccupation remained, as always, the struggle on the diplomatic front.

There is something almost heroically simplistic about Herzl's concept of history. Despite a relatively high level of political sophistication, he never acquired a realistic perspective on the forces that shaped his time or, for that matter, his own view of it. A man of unquestionably superior intelligence, professionally in close touch with events and living in an age and place which, however overrated as the cradle of modernism, was nonetheless vibrantly alive with ideas, he managed to remain curiously isolated from the main currents of even nineteenth-century thought. Historical materialism, like any other theory of history, is certainly open to debate, but Herzl knew absolutely nothing about Marxism—his opposition to socialism was simply the gut reaction of a liberal bourgeois—just as he remained amazingly untouched by the winds of change that revolutionized philosophy, psychology, the arts, literature, and the stage in his own generation. For the playwright and littérateur, this isolation proved fatal. For the man of action, it had some distinct advantages, although it also accounted for some of his conspicuous failures.

Time and again he proceeded to act on the assumption that a few men at the top were free to determine the course of events, and that if he could talk to the key players he could convince them to follow his game plan. He felt that he would have succeeded with the Kaiser, had he not been blindsided by Bülow, and it must have been sheer frustration—"Everything has ground to a halt. Something has got to happen"—that made him decide to try his luck with another "man of destiny." In January 1899 he wrote to his well-connected friend, the pacifist Baroness Bertha von Suttner: "I come to you today with a request which means a great deal to me. . . . It would be of the greatest importance for the Zionist movement if I could enlighten the Czar about its aims and purposes. I would have to discuss it with him personally in order to win him over to our cause, just as I succeeded in doing with the German Kaiser. I should therefore like to have an audience with him, and it is my hope that my magnanimous and highly esteemed friend, the Baroness von Suttner, will help me to obtain it" (D, 1/16/99).

It is difficult to conceive of any cogent reason on Herzl's part for seeking an audience with the bigoted and benighted ruler of all the Russias, and the reasons he himself adduces fail to convince. It was true that the ever-vigilant Okhrana had begun to busy itself with the Zionist movement, that the Russian embassy in Berlin had made inquiries about suspected links between Zionists and socialists, and that the Russian Finance Minister had banned publicity for the subscription drive. It is also true that Herzl believed Zionism to be an effective antidote to socialism and other radical ideologies, a point he never failed to stress in his encounters with autocrats and authoritarians. Still, this scarcely warranted a personal meeting with the Czar. Nicholas was an enemy of the Turks, his own interest in Palestine was limited to the holdings of the Russian Orthodox Church, and his undisguised contempt for the Jews made him a rather unlikely patron of their cause.

Chances are that Herzl himself had no clear idea of what he was after, other than yet one more "success" on the order of his audiences with the Kaiser. Success was his addiction. Tell the Czar, he urged the baroness, "that I am the sort of person fit, as it were, to be received in audience, as proven by the fact that the German Emperor granted me no less than *two lengthy conversations*." However he rationalized it, the move was simply a matter of spinning his wheels; the carriage had got stuck in the muck of reality.

Ultimately, however, it was yet another diversionary maneuver; he realized that the one man he had to convert was neither the Kaiser nor the Czar. And so, late in March, he turned his attention back to Turkey and resumed his efforts to gain direct access to the Sultan, convinced that in a face-to-face encounter he could somehow dispose of Abdul Hamid's objection. Despite persistent doubts as to Nevlinsky's true allegiance, if any, Herzl had continued to cultivate him; the man might not be much good, but he could do a great deal of harm. Besides, Herzl had a sentimental—and rather costly—affection for the old roué, who ran up exorbitant hotel bills and kept demanding money for supposed bribes; when all was said and done, he remained Herzl's only real contact at the Sublime Porte.

Nevlinsky had, however, been critically ill for some months, and

when Herzl went to see him on March 14, he found him bedridden
and in very bad shape. Nevertheless, the plucky Pole seemed not only
ready but strangely eager to go to Constantinople, and his doctor raised
no objections. He told Herzl that Nevlinsky was suffering from an
aneurysm of the aorta, liable to burst at any moment; whether he
stayed home or went abroad would make no difference one way or
another. This laid out the situation plainly enough and put Herzl in
a bind, but he felt he had no choice—the Pole was his only hope. To
ease his conscience, he hired a young doctor to accompany Nevlinsky,
and on March 30 the patient, his wife, and his personal physician
boarded the Orient Express. Three days later, Herzl received word of
Nevlinsky's sudden death in Constantinople.

It was a heavy blow to head, heart, and wallet all at once.

First of all, the only link to Yildiz Palace had snapped, with no
prospect of a credible substitute in the offing. Furthermore, the moral
responsibility, real or imagined, which Herzl assumed immediately as
a debt of honor, translated into heavy expenditures that he and the
movement could ill afford at a time when they were desperately trying
to raise money for the bank project. And finally, for all his ambivalence
about the man, Herzl felt a genuine sense of loss.

"Nevlinsky's death has hit me very hard. Although he was terminal,
his wife will hold me responsible for the journey, despite all the pre-
cautions I took. . . . But Nevlinsky is also a heavy loss for our movement. He had the best contacts both in Constantinople and in Rome,
something now almost irreplaceable. With him, the romance of Zionism has lost one of its most colorful characters. He was a *grand seigneur
déchu*, likable despite many questionable qualities, and with truly
charming manners" (D, 4/2/99).

Moreover, his hypertrophied conscience would give him no peace:

> A miserable night. Couldn't get Nevlinsky out of my mind. I
> keep racking my brain about my share of the guilt. Should I have
> kept him from taking the trip? He wanted to go somewhere south.
> He preferred Constantinople, because it was a free trip, with a
> free personal physician, and the possibility of even more lucrative
> results. He was doomed for the past year and a half, ever since
> his first attack. Did the trip cost him months, weeks, days, or
> hours of his life? I told him often enough that he did not have
> to go if he didn't want to. I let him keep the 2,000 florins for

the trip to Rome and said nothing more about it, although he never went. Should I have held him back? [D, 4/3/99]

Nevlinsky's death "in the service of Zionism" briefly became the talk of the town, and from the perspective of a few days later, Herzl began to take a somewhat more detached view of both the dead man and his demise.

The Nevlinsky case is singularly embarrassing and dramatic. The man was never presentable, and all those who used him— princes and governments—always carefully concealed their relations with him. He was the typical "secret agent" portrayed in fiction. Now his corpse lies across our path, and many people seem inclined to charge all his dubious enterprises to our account. Fortunately our accounts are in order, even if we are not going to reveal them, and my conscience, in particular, is clear.

I never had any relations with him other than accepting his offer to intercede with the Sultan. He cost me a great deal of money and also received a subsidy from the committee. To this day I don't know whether he ever did anything for us, or even whether he was in a position to do anything. He never furnished any proof of his contacts other than introducing me to various Turkish dignitaries. Then again, perhaps he only presented me to them as an editor of the *Neue Freie Presse*. This is a secret he took with him into the grave. . . . And yet, my conscience is clear even toward my shekel-payers for having recommended that we pay him a subsidy. . . . With one single paragraph in his *Correspondance de l'Est* he could have depicted us as dangerous enemies of Turkey, or at best dismissed us as inconsequential windbags. [D, 4/7/99]

The body was brought back to Vienna for the funeral, at the expense of the Zionists. The widow, after a heartrending display of public grief at the railroad station, turned out to be remarkably cool and collected when Herzl saw her in private. He promised to take care of her and her children, and to continue the monthly subsidy of 200 guilders, on condition that she go on publishing the *Correspondance de l'Est*, lest it fall into the hands of some other blackmailer. But when, out of either naïveté or cynicism, she revealed that before they ever left for Constantinople a friend had advised her to bury her husband in

Turkey rather than waste money on bringing him back, Herzl at long last caught on to the whole ingenious scheme: "All of them—including the dying man, in this instance still the most honorable of the lot—figured that his death on the trip would place us, the Zionists, under perpetual obligation toward his survivors. He so to speak sold us his corpse. Stranger than fiction. And yet, the only dupe in this sad story is myself, who failed to see through this con game. Nevlinsky himself, on the other hand, showed proof of courage and parental tenderness. In my eyes he posthumously transcends all that riffraff with whom he hung out—the tragic mistake of his life" (D, 4/8/99).

And if anything, his admiration for the well-bred con man soared even higher when, a few days after the funeral, he went over Nevlinsky's records and discovered that the much feared and famous *Correspondance de l'Est* had a total circulation of twelve subscribers, including himself.

In the meantime, he had a visitor drop in on him who, for a change, had some hard-earned firsthand knowledge of the Promised Land and its Turkish rulers.

Eliezer Ben-Yehuda, né Perelman, was born in Lithuania in 1858, studied medicine in Paris, and settled in Jerusalem in 1881, where he edited a number of Hebrew journals and became the most passionate as well as the most effective advocate of Hebrew as the national language of the Jewish population in Palestine. His own practical contribution was the first comprehensive dictionary of ancient and modern Hebrew, a multivolume work only partially completed at the time of his death in 1922. As a "non-religious nationalist," he was under constant attack by the ultra-Orthodox establishment, which objected to his desecration of the holy tongue and went to the extreme of repeatedly denouncing him to the Turkish authorities as a subversive conspirator. But his stubborn pursuit of an ideal which, in his early days, seemed even more elusive than Herzl's own dream also gained him a devoted following among the more progressive elements and eventually made him one of the most influential personalities in Jerusalem.

Ben-Yehuda, like many Eastern European Jewish intellectuals, was critical of Herzl; unlike most of them, he did not succumb to his personal charm. Their meeting on March 18 was a rather chilly affair, and the mutual antipathy may have led Herzl to disregard some potentially valuable suggestions.

The Jerusalem journalist Ben-Yehuda came to see me. A short, red-haired Jew from the Orient. I am beginning to distinguish between the different Jewish types. He is long-winded in his stories and always seems to be holding something back. Still, I learned some things from him about the way the Turks feel about Zionism. In the Orient, he says, everybody is afraid of everybody else. The people are a wild beast that can be unleashed but can also be led in any direction. If the authorities give the signal, the Mohammedans will turn on the Jews—the system of hatchet men, as with the Armenians. This supports my long-held views against infiltration. In the higher baksheesh circles, Zionism is furtively being discussed. Everything depends on the Sultan. Even the Grand Vizier is only a lackey. Ben-Yehuda assures me that Strauss, the American ambassador, secretly favors the Zionists. The Mutessarif (chief regional administrator) of Jerusalem, he said, was an affable gentleman who had asked him why he did not publish an Arabic newspaper. I asked Ben-Yehuda how much he would need for that, and he estimated some 2,000 francs annually by way of subsidy. I told him to remind me of the matter in mid-May; I might be able to get him that amount. (I feel that if the bank is launched, it might be worth that much to have an Arabic voice favored by the Mutessarif and which exerts the right kind of influence on the population.) [D, 3/18/99]

Herzl did not follow up on the idea; his attitude toward the indigenous population was one of benign indifference at best. He never questioned the popular view of colonialism as a mission of mercy that brought the blessings of civilization to stone-age savages. Unlike the more subtle and farsighted Ahad Ha-Am, he fully believed that the Palestine Arabs would welcome the Jews with open arms; after all, they only stood to gain from the material and technological progress imported by the Jews. He committed these views to paper in a famous exchange of letters, which have survived and become something of an embarrassment in the context of the current Arab–Israeli conflict.

Yussef Ziah el-Khaldi was a prominent member of an old, aristocratic Arab family, a man of great culture and political sophistication who, after serving as mayor of Jerusalem, was representing the city in the Ottoman parliament. Alarmed by the Zionist plans, he expressed his apprehension in a letter to the Chief Rabbi of France, whom he assumed to be one of the movement's leaders. He fully recognized the Jews' historical claims to Palestine, he wrote, and he could well appreciate the beauty of Herzl's dream. Unfortunately, however, the destiny of nations is ruled not by abstract concepts, however unassailable in theory, but by harsh reality. And the reality was that "Palestine is now an integral part of the Ottoman Empire, but what is even more serious, it is inhabited by people other than Israelites."

He pointed out that the Holy Places were under the protection of Turks and Arabs, who would never, of their own free will, agree to surrender them to the Jews. A Jewish Palestine, he warned, could never be bought with money but would have to be achieved by force of arms. Did Dr. Herzl have an army? The earth was surely big enough to find some as yet uninhabited territory for the unfortunate Jews, but please, let them keep their hands off Palestine.

Zadok Kahn passed the letter on to Herzl, who replied to it on March 19. He assured el-Khaldi that he had nothing to fear from the Jews.

> As you put it yourself, the Jews have no armed might to back them. They have long since lost the taste for war. They are a peace-loving people, happy to be left in peace. [As for the religious places, they presented no problem; they would be extraterritorialized and administered as the common treasure of mankind.]
> You see another difficulty in the existence of a non-Jewish population in Palestine. But who would want to expel them? Their well-being and individual prosperity will increase as we bring in our own. Do you think that an Arab who owns land or a house in Palestine worth three or four thousand francs will be unhappy about seeing the value of his property rise five- or tenfold? This is bound to happen with the arrival of the Jews, and it is something the natives must be made to understand. . . .
> You ask that the Jews turn elsewhere. This may well happen the day we decide that Turkey will never appreciate the tremendous benefits our movement could bring her. Should we reach that point, we shall look for what we need elsewhere. And believe me, we shall find it. [L, CZA, H III D13]

The last two sentences were meant as a threat. They have since been construed as a promise and cited as proof of Zionist duplicity. Even putting the worst face on them, however, they amounted to no more and no less than the arrogant assumption that Western civilization was an unqualified blessing, and that the natives would gratefully welcome not only Western law, order, and technology but also the people who shouldered the burden of bringing them these goodies.

A rash assumption, as we have since been made to discover. Not everyone, even in Herzl's day, subscribed to the myths and stereotypes of colonialism, but the most that can be held against him was that his imagination did not transcend his background, and that as a prophet he could be blind to what he did not wish to see. In that, however, he was far from unusual.

TWENTY-THREE

*L*e *ressort se fatigue,* he complained in May, the resilience is gone. Hardly surprising, given his schedule: "Yesterday, the Action Committee decided that I should first go to Constantinople. I also have to go to London. I will again be squandering nervous energy if I go to Constantinople in June, from there to The Hague, and on to London to put some order into the bank affairs and revive the comatose subscription. Bitter arguments everywhere, and a standard speech in London. Very exhausting" (D, 5/23/99).

Yet the killing pace was largely his own doing, no matter how much he rationalized it. "The movement requires me to be on the go all the time." The movement, it seemed to him, had stopped moving, and it was this sense of stagnation, the insatiable, inexhaustible need for the ever-elusive "success," however defined, that drove him. Motion, travel, the staggering number of letters, communiqués, and memoranda he kept churning out day and night, the ceaseless efforts to reach the Kaiser, the Czar, the Sultan through channels that ranged from bureaucrats and middlemen to shady spooks and small-time crooks all gave him at least the illusion of action and the hope of some unforeseen and unforeseeable development leading to the decisive breakthrough.

At the same time, his absences, his constant *déplacements,* as he referred to them, caused problems both at home and on the job. "There is no doubt that the *Neue Freie Presse* could fire me for neglect of my office duties, 'with all due respect for our differences of opinion.' This wretched clash of conflicting duties exhausts, unnerves, and grinds me down more than anything else" (D, 4/25/99).

It also involved a far more intimate and, in all likelihood, far more destructive conflict, which went unmentioned in his diaries but set off an eruption of lurid fantasies that inspired what was probably his strangest and most self-revealing play.

Ill, overextended, and exhausted as he was in the spring of 1899, he still found time to rough out a drama of marital misery and a husband's revenge. "What occupies me these days more than my still unfinished congress speech, the congress itself, more than all the princes and my slave drivers at the *Neue Freie Presse*, is the draft of my new play, *The Sinful Mother*, the thought of which delights me" (D, 8/11/99).

Plot and spirit of *The Sinful Mother* are admirably summarized in a police report of March 6, 1900. The police censor, who reviewed every new play before its opening, found nothing to object to. No translation can quite do justice to his Imperial Royal Austro-Hungarian bureaucratese, but it rather faithfully matches the style of the play itself.

The bachelor Edgar Boheim, after many other conquests, has also seduced Marianne, the wife of attorney Dr. Georg Winter. On the stairs leading to Edgar's apartment, Marianne, arriving for her second assignation, runs into Rehborn, one of Edgar's friends. Although Marianne, heavily veiled, has not been recognized by Rehborn, she nonetheless believes that latter now knows about her affair with Edgar. This fear throws Marianne, already exceedingly tense on the way to the assignation, into a panic. She is disconsolate and afraid that her husband would now find out everything. In this state of mind she discovers on Edgar's desk the photograph of her five-year-old daughter, Gretel, which the bachelor had appropriated as a joke. The sight of her much beloved daughter's picture shocks Marianne into full awareness of the enormity of her misstep. Indignantly she rejects Edgar's advances and leaves his apartment, taking the picture with her. Marianne now vows to atone for her sin and henceforth to live only for her husband and child. She is haunted by the constant fear that Rehborn will betray her, and even a talk with him, in which latter attempts to reassure her, remains unsuccessful. When little Gretel suddenly falls ill and is given up by

the doctor, Marianne regards this blow of fate as just punishment
from heaven. By way of expiation, she confesses her infidelity to
her husband. Latter is horrified, decides to separate from Marianne but to take the blame upon himself in the eyes of the world.
Marianne, unaware of her husband's nobility of spirit, thinks that
in the upcoming divorce proceedings she, as the guilty party,
would have to give up the now recovered Gretel. When the child,
on the occasion of a visit with the grandmother, fails to return
on time, Marianne thinks that the child is about to be taken from
her. She cannot accept the thought of the separation, and in her
excitement commits suicide. The husband, rushing in together
with the child, finds her in a dying state. Same forgives his wife,
whereupon the latter dies. [Fraenkel, *Des Schoepfers*, p. 131]

Guilt is a powerful motive for hatred, and Herzl had ample cause
to feel guilty toward his wife. In addition to neglecting her, he had
also by now run through much of her dowry; and no matter how
justified his complaints about her extravagance, it was he who had
spent a substantial part of her fortune on the cause. Whether the "sinful
mother's" extramarital affair was based on suspicions, warranted or
not, or whether his own repressed sexuality stimulated lubricious fantasies is probably impossible to establish—the lost letters might have
furnished a clue—but his daughter Pauline's serious illness of the year
before evidently provided his creative imagination with a "delightful"
way of displacing his own guilt onto his wife.

Unintended self-revelations aside, *The Sinful Mother* is arguably
among the worst of Herzl's plays, awash in soppy sentiment and mind-
boggling banality. Retitled *Gretel*, it opened at the Raimond Theater
in Vienna on April 4, 1900, and received one favorable notice by his
colleague at the *Neue Freie Presse*, as well as some labored applause
by faithful followers. All other reactions were negative, although the
all too blatantly autobiographical aspects may have made for some
lively gossip.

In June, after a week's vacation, Herzl briefly stopped off at The Hague,
where the international peace conference convoked by the Czar had
been in session since May 18. Like most such meetings, it was a purely
social event of no political significance, at which he made the ac-

quaintance of "an intelligent, educated old peddler Jew." Ivan Bloch, Russian State Counsellor, convert to Calvinism who nonetheless had remained attached to his Jewish roots, seemed to have good contacts at the Imperial Palace and promised to arrange an audience with the Czar. Herzl also had extended conversations with the Turkish delegate, Nouri Bey, Secretary General of the Foreign Ministry, who blandly offered to "buy Turkish public opinion" on behalf of the Zionists for 3 to 4 million francs. Herzl deemed the six-day visit a success.

From Holland he went to Paris, checking into the Hôtel Castille. "Sentimental piety always makes me stay at this familiar old hotel, where four years ago I wrote *Der Judenstaat*. What a long road since. And what weariness. My heart is in very bad shape. I am suffering from shortness of breath and an irregular heartbeat" (D, 6/19/99). A talk with the president of the Rothschild-dominated Jewish organizations—the Alliance Israélite Universelle and the Jewish Colonization Association—proved a waste of time, but the Automobile Fair in the Tuileries Gardens revived some of his old faith in the power of technology. "It is as if the automobile had been made just for us. We'll have roads paved with concrete, fewer railroads, and we shall develop a whole new transportation system right from the start" (D, 6/21/99).

The next stop was London. On January 26, he gave a speech at St. Martin's Town Hall in which, mindful of the previous fiasco, he tried to strike a balance between reassurance and restraint; his rather cryptic formulations enabled his audience to hear whatever it wished to hear. But the main order of business was the Jewish Colonial Trust. The minimum legal reserve had finally been collected, and after two days of fierce squabbling—including the resignation of the director—Herzl forced the formal opening on June 29. A rather controversial arrangement, designed to prevent a hostile takeover of the institution by anti-Zionists, provided for 100 founder shares to be assigned to the bank's trustees; while bearing no dividends, they were weighted so as to control 50 percent of the total shareholder vote.

Back in Austria, he just barely managed to spend a weekend with his family at Reichenau—not without trying, while he was there, for an informal chat with his nemesis Bülow, who happened to be vacationing nearby. Bülow begged off, for reasons of health, so he said. On August 6, just before leaving for the third congress, Herzl entered a single sentence in his diary: "My Testament for the Jewish People: Build your state so that the stranger will feel at ease among you." It would make a fitting addition to the monument on Mount Herzl in Jerusalem.

With the third Zionist congress, which opened in Basel on August 15, 1899, the sense of defiant triumph began to give way to a more sober mood. The annual meetings, while still not exactly routine, were no longer mere affirmations of Jewish survival but had become a lively forum for debate and dissent. The congress was, in fact, rapidly turning into what Herzl had both hoped for and feared—a parliamentary body with all the flaws and virtues this implied; at times it reminded him all too painfully of the countless soporific hours he had spent in the Palais Bourbon.

The playwright in him, however, still knew how to build up to a dramatic climax. When his decision to give the bank's trustees a majority vote over the regular shareholders was assailed as a devious and undemocratic maneuver, he abruptly threatened to resign. And despite mounting criticism of his policies, few of the delegates could forget that it was he who, by sheer force of will, had forged a patchwork of little groups and stillborn initiatives into a coherent movement no one could as yet envisage without him. The large majority that ended up endorsing his proposal was a personal triumph as well as the only point on the agenda of any real interest to him. Other, often sharp attacks on his dictatorial practices, his business conduct, his failure to consult the Action Committee, and, most damaging, his constant references to startling behind-the-scenes developments that never materialized did not faze him; he parried them with the skill of a veteran of the Palais Bourbon, stubborn in matters of principle but flexible enough to yield when it seemed strategically sound.

Nevertheless, the tenor and vehemence of the debates clearly signaled trouble ahead. The rift was growing between Herzlian loyalists and the opposition, led by thoughtful but outspoken young men like Motzkin and Weizmann, with the Orthodox faction, the partisans of immediate immigration, and the usual quota of the perennially discontented further complicating the picture. But the lines were still fluid, and Herzl's authority remained sufficiently imposing to paper over the differences, so that the meeting ended once again on a note of harmony.

He declared himself satisfied with the outcome—in part because the undisputed supremacy of his leadership had once again been endorsed even by his most critical opponents, and in part because, with his eyes fixed firmly on grand strategy and the comprehensive political solution, he was contemptuously indifferent to the quasi-Talmudic quarrels about cultural aspects of Zionism, such as the question of language, which he dismissed as "theological beer-hall vapors—*le bois creux des guitares* [the hollow wood of guitars]." What counted was that he had once again won all his points. "The first day I was bored stiff in my presidential chair, the next day I was angry. . . . The third day was somewhat more amusing. . . . On the fourth day I was thoroughly exhausted."

And on the train, heading back for Vienna: "Having once again tasted the feeling of freedom and been a lord for a week, I must now return to my humiliating servitude at the *Neue Freie Presse*, where I am not allowed to have a mind of my own. It is a question of a measly few thousand guilders, which as the head of a family I cannot afford to give up" (D, 8/21/99).

The money worries were justified. By his own calculations, he had up to this point spent more than 50,000 guilders on the Zionist movement, about half of it on *Die Welt*, the rest on travel, clerical salaries, contributions, and bribes in one form or another. *Die Welt* continued to require massive subsidies, which he could simply no longer meet out of his own pocket; at the last moment, the wealthy Rumanian Zionist—and trustee of the Colonial Bank—Heinrich Rosenbaum had come to the rescue. The sumptuous Herzl villa in Waehring with its commensurately large staff would have been a heavy drain on his finances even if Julie had been a more frugal lady of the manor, but her extravagance at least gave him an excuse to blame her rather than himself for the alarmingly rapid depletion of what was left of her dowry. It is tempting to speculate whether without that dowry—and without his marriage—he would have been able to organize the movement in so brief a span of time.

He did, however, feel guilty toward his children. In his feuilletons—"The Empty Nursery," "Little Trude's Tears," etc.—he continued to gush about fathers and children, their joys and bittersweet sorrows. But while his maudlin feelings translated into driblets of sentimental kitsch rather than active fatherhood—for which he had neither time, talent, nor inclination—the thought that he might die without having properly provided for his children kept nagging at him. Concern for their material welfare—the measure of a good bourgeois father's devotion—was what made him dust off some of his old plays and resubmit them under fresh titles; it drove him to write new plays no better than the old ones, even while wrestling with a work load that would have crushed giants. But it was the diaries, above all, that were to assure his heirs a steady income for life. The thought sustained him and kept him filling notebook after notebook almost to his last breath.

Yet no matter how bleak his personal situation, the movement's finances were in even worse shape. Though he had, more or less by magic, created the Jewish Colonial Trust, he was enough of a realist to understand that it would be a long time before he could count on it for any substantial support. And he did not have much time. The next congress would no longer put up with his discreet allusions to unspecified diplomatic triumphs. He knew that unless he came up with some concrete achievements, his leadership—and with it the movement as a whole—would be in serious jeopardy.

The Grand Duke and Eulenburg remained accessible and sympathetic but gently tried to discourage him from expecting any change in the Kaiser's attitude within the near future. This left him no choice but to deal directly with the Turks, and he resolved to resume the offensive interrupted by Nevlinsky's death. At the congress he had deftly modified the original Basel program by proposing a charter recognizing the sovereignty of the Sultan and dropping the international guarantees. The change slipped through almost unnoticed and gave him, so he felt, a more solid basis for negotiations with the Sultan. But he still had to hurdle the first obstacle—getting the chance to make his case in person.

The contact with Nouri Bey, continued in Vienna, seemed to open up new possibilities. Herzl had little use for this shifty-eyed character, the son of a Circassian mother and a French father, who struck him as a crook, a braggart, and a liar. Nevertheless, he agreed to pay him the 40,000 francs he demanded for an audience with the Sultan and went so far as to give him a 10,000-franc down payment in cash. Considering the difficulties he had in raising even this relatively trivial amount, it took a certain amount of courage for him to contemplate settling the Turkish national debt.

Anxious to cover his tracks, Nouri Bey in turn dealt with Herzl through a subordinate bagman, a greasy Levantine named Crespi, who collected his own cut and deluged Herzl with letters announcing important breakthroughs and startling though unspecified developments. On December 10, he asked Herzl to be prepared for an imminent summons to Yildiz Palace. There followed a two-month silence; after repeated inquiries, Herzl was told that the whole country closed down for the month of Ramadan, but that things were progressing splendidly and he would soon have some good news. The fact that for nearly a year Herzl put up with this blatant fraud is a measure of his desperation; in the absence of more reliable intermediaries, he kept hoping against hope that naked greed might somehow work a miracle.

And like most people who put their faith in crooks, he tended to ignore the advice of honest people.

Thus, on December 29, 1899, he had a meeting with Oscar Solomon Straus, the U.S. ambassador to Turkey, who was passing through Vienna on his way back to Constantinople. Straus, "below average height, lean, hook-nosed, with a sparse reddish beard, Jewish pothandle ears, thinning hair, forty-eight years old, wry, smart, and yet [sic] instantly likable because of his honest eyes," was a superbly competent and versatile administrator; he spent most of his life in public service, filling a succession of important posts and, as Secretary of Labor and Commerce under Theodore Roosevelt from 1906 to 1909, becoming the first Jewish member of an American cabinet. He had already served as ambassador to Turkey from 1887 to 1889; when Herzl met him, he was on his second tour. (He was to fill that post a third time from 1909 to 1910.) He not only was thoroughly familiar with the country and its ruling clique but he also brought to the job a great deal of common sense and an outsider's view of the European power game, from which the United States had as yet kept happily aloof. Moreover Straus, in stark contrast to most European Jews in high government positions, had no complexes about his origins and felt no need to dissimulate his sympathies for Jewish causes.

> After five minutes we were on familiar terms, although he began by saying that I had the reputation of being indiscreet. However, he said, he did not blame me for being inconsiderate, because in so great a cause one cannot indulge individuals. He himself was neither for nor against Zionism, being a government official. For good measure he also asked me to give him my word not to let anything about our conversation leak out.
> He considered Palestine beyond our reach. The Greek Orthodox and Roman Catholic Churches would not let us have it. . . . Straus is in favor of Mesopotamia! He said he knew that some years ago a pamphlet about Mesopotamia by Cyrus Adler had been sent to me at the behest of some friends (Judge Sulz-

berger and others in New York). . . . Mesopotamia, he said, was attainable. It involved no Church rivalries and was the original homeland of the Israelites. Abraham came from Mesopotamia, and we could utilize the mystical element. . . . He spoke acidly about the gang of thugs in and around Yildiz Palace. All power was concentrated in the Sultan's mitt. The ministers were idiots and corrupt cowards. The Sultan didn't give a hoot for the whole of Turkey. Talk about "humanity" and such won't get you anywhere with him. If he smelled money, or some other goodies, he might perhaps be won over. But any talk or negotiation with anybody else was a waste. With the Sultan, or not at all. . . . We parted friends. I exacted a promise that he would send me some possibly useful tips from time to time under the code name of "Mesopotamicus." [D, 12/29/99]

For lack of alternatives, Herzl continued to deal with the unscrupulous Nouri Bey and his forty thieves, compared to whom the late Nevlinsky now appeared the essence of probity. It was a frustrating waste of time and money, but he kept up his morale by resorting to the old dreams of diplomatic coups and sensational breakthroughs. The Czar's visit with the Grand Duke of Baden inspired high hopes for an audience with the Russian ruler. "It would be an enormous step forward. On the other hand, I see from the papers that the Czar will be staying at Darmstadt until November 7. We may therefore be on the threshold of a great success for Zionism" (D, 11/2/99). And when the "great success" failed to materialize, he consoled himself with the thought that perhaps "he just does not want to receive me right now and will summon me to Russia. I would actually prefer this" (D, 11/3/99).

Self-deception was a temporary expedient at best, but he could put up with defeat and disappointment; what he could not, and would never, accept was paralysis and surrender. In Rumania, where the Jews were under growing pressure from a ferociously anti-Semitic government, there had been agitation for the Jewish colonization of Cyprus as at least a temporary alternative to Palestine. Herzl secretly favored the plan, but refrained from voicing his support for fear of alienating too many of his followers. But when the audience with the Czar, in which he had quite unaccountably invested so much hope, failed to materialize, he changed his mind.

The imminent future development I see as follows: If, by the time of the fourth congress, I have made no headway with the Turkish government, I shall quietly prepare the Cyprus project, go to London, talk to Salisbury, and persuade the congress to go to Cyprus for the time being. In any case, I believe that after the next congress we shall in fact go somewhere, anywhere. I could, of course, greatly speed things up if I were a free man, able to travel whenever necessary. . . . But I am the clerk of Mssrs. Bacher and Benedikt. I have to put in a daily appearance at the office even if I don't do very much once I get there.

Zionism is costing me money and yet must not yield any returns. On the other hand, I have done myself immense harm as a "German author," and people don't quite dare stage my plays. For the same reason, there is no hope of advancement for me at the *Neue Freie Presse*. From all sides, the demands on me are growing. *Shnorrers* of every stripe come to pester me, from as far away as Persia. I constantly have to give money for *Die Welt*, for the congress, and for the bank. [D, 11/8/99]

A solution to at least one of his problems seemed to present itself in December, when rumors about Bacher's intention to retire began circulating at the *Neue Freie Presse*. The banker Moritz Reichenfeld, Julie's cousin and Herzl's financial adviser, suggested a possible way of acquiring Bacher's shares, and on December 5, Herzl gathered whatever courage he could muster and bearded the lion in his den. His filial fear of Bacher was such that, prior to setting out on his mission, Herzl not only had himself blessed by his parents—"in addition to their blessings, they gave me the good advice to appear self-confident"—but also made a point of memorizing the beginning of his little speech so as not to stumble over his inhibitions.

Bacher confirmed that he wanted to retire but had not thus far found a suitable buyer for his shares. He was in principle ready to sell them to Herzl, but in fairness to Benedikt could not do so without the latter's approval. Herzl thereupon manfully informed him that if Benedikt blocked the transaction and Bacher sold to a third party, he would have no choice but to hand in his resignation.

"He had upset me very much. My legs were like cotton, and I had pains in my heart from the all-out effort to appear firm."

The upshot of the tense negotiations that followed was, on the whole, more favorable than Herzl had expected. Bacher—probably dissuaded by Benedikt—did not retire but acknowledged the justice of Herzl's complaints and granted him a substantial salary increase, which made him the highest paid member of the *Presse* staff. Herzl was also given editorial control over the paper's entire literary section.

He was now one of the highest paid journalists in Austria, and he occupied a position of enormous power and influence in Vienna's literary establishment. None of which, in his mind, made up for his persistent failure as a playwright. In addition to the controversial *Gretel*, he had also revised and recirculated three of his old plays, one of which the Burgtheater finally accepted. *I Love You*, an insipid but totally innocuous one-act farce, had its premiere on January 12, 1900, and lasted seven performances, at least six more than it deserved. Herzl, however, blamed his enemies. "Yesterday at the premiere of *I Love You* in the Burgtheater they again made me pay for my Zionism. At the end of the harmless little piece there was violent hissing, which obviously could not have been provoked by this undemanding play. I must not live on Zionism, I cannot live on literature. Quite a problem" (D, 1/13/1900).

The Jewish Colonial Trust, meanwhile, on which he hoped to rely for his offer to the Sultan if ever he got the chance, staggered along from one crisis to the next. He was sorely tempted to rush off to London to "straighten things out," but he did not dare absent himself again so soon after assuming his new responsibilities at the paper. On the other hand, a potential disaster turned into a stroke of good luck. The governor of Galicia blocked the subscription drive, and the head of the small Vienna firm handling the subscriptions for Austria-Hungary was summoned to police headquarters. Herzl, as was his wont, went straight to the top and requested an audience with Ernst von Körber, the newly appointed Premier and Minister of the Interior. Körber, a relatively enlightened civil servant, was a distinct improvement over the succession of bumbling nonentities who had preceded him following Badeni's fall. He, too, was determined to defuse the nationalities problem and the perennial language conflict by concentrating on the common interest in the economic progress of the empire as a whole, and one of his first steps was to liberalize the censorship regulations and improve relations with the press.

He received Herzl on February 15, already fully briefed on the issue, and promised at once to do everything in his power to let the drive and the bank operations continue without further interference. "I admire the persistence with which you have been pursuing this work of yours," he complimented Herzl. The goodwill of a prominent journalist was of obvious value to the as yet untried newcomer, who had only been in his post since January 18. But while doing favors is a politician's life insurance, Körber seems to have been genuinely impressed by Herzl. It was he who took the initiative in cultivating a relationship that soon transcended mere self-interest and led to numerous far-ranging, off-the-record talks on domestic and foreign affairs. At the end of the year, Körber—like Badeni before him—offered Herzl another chance to edit an independent pro-government newspaper, presenting him with the same dilemma he had failed to resolve the first time around.

Meanwhile, however, the spring of 1900 passed in the stubborn but futile pursuit of his more and more chimerical goals; neither his Turkish "agents" nor the Grand Duke was able to promote an audience with the Czar or the Sultan. Moreover, the Jewish Colonial Trust, on which he had counted to solve his problems, was itself becoming a major problem in its own right, threatening to disrupt relations between him and his closest collaborators.

There had been numerous complaints about slow and sloppy business procedures. Herzl took every one of them personally, a blot on his escutcheon, and began a furious campaign to improve the bank's efficiency. But neither the minuscule London staff nor the Board of Directors could possibly live up to his totally unrealistic expectations, and the stream of angry memos, reproaches, orders, and imperial edicts issuing from Vienna only succeeded in antagonizing and demoralizing the few skilled hands trying to save the operation from imminent collapse. Arrogating unto himself a sort of *droit de seigneur*, he convoked a board meeting in London for April 24 "to straighten things out," a decision which was not his to make under the statutes and which was promptly countermanded by the Amsterdam banker Jacobus Kann, the board's most active and experienced member.

Dissent and disobedience on the part of one of his followers was tantamount to treason in Herzl's eyes, and his response to the mutinous Kann eloquently expressed his feelings: "Dear Mr. Kann, I will not conceal the fact that it costs me a decided effort to write to you. The tone you have repeatedly struck in your letters to me is altogether inappropriate, and recently, when Loewe informed you of the meeting, you countermanded my order" (D, 3/8/1900).

Ignoring all protests, Herzl set off for London on April 16. His main agenda was still the bank, but he was also intent on broadening the scope of his diplomatic offensive by including Lord Salisbury, the British Prime Minister, in his ingeniously disingenuous scheme—something on the order of Salisbury talking to the Kaiser, the Kaiser talking to the Czar, all three agreeing on the blessings of Zionism and persuading the Sultan to grant the Jews a charter in his own best interest.

Nordau, whom he saw on his brief stopover in Paris, procured an invitation for him from Alfred Austin, the British poet laureate. Austin was a pompous old windbag who owed his title not to the twenty volumes of execrable verse he had perpetrated but to his services to Tory journalism as the editor of the *National Review*. The two author-politicians hit it off at once, and the weekend Herzl spent in the Austin home at Ashford, in Kent, gave him further cause to rhapsodize about the British way of life, at least as it was being lived in the rarified air high above the slums and tenements of industrial Britain. "These are the people, this is the environment I need for my well-being. How well I understand them, England's assimilated Jews. If I were living in England, I, too, might well be a Jingo" (D, 4/22/1900).

The table talk revolved almost exclusively around the British reverses in the Boer War. Austin, a frail but fierce armchair warrior, proclaimed Britain's peaceful intentions—it was to her credit that she was not prepared for this war—but in the end she would always prevail, even if she had to take on the whole world. Herzl, not to be outdone in matters of grand strategy, proposed a British–German alliance and went so far as to promise that he would try to influence the Kaiser in this sense. Austin, obviously impressed, immediately asked Salisbury to receive Herzl, but the Prime Minister regretfully declined; at the moment, he had his hands full fighting the Boers.

The exaltation of the visit did not, however, survive the tempestuous negotiations in London. Three board members boycotted the meeting. The absence of Kann and Lourie had been expected, not so that of the ever-faithful Wolffsohn. "For the first time he has let me down." Angry and embittered, Herzl on his own ordered an immediate audit of the bank's affairs, which confirmed both the essential accuracy of its financial statements and the laxity of its overall business practices. Kann, who saw this wholly unauthorized step as a reflection on his probity, handed in his resignation, and the blast of charges and countercharges that followed brought the whole ramshackle edifice to the brink of total collapse. Other board members joined in the protest, and in the end even Wolffsohn got fed up with Herzl's self-willed and self-righteous conduct. "I can now no longer advise you," he wrote. "I know you far too well not to realize that you will not take my advice. My most fervent wish is for you to succeed in your effort to extricate yourself from this affair without suffering too much damage. But as to myself, let me now go as a faithful and devoted friend, so that in addition to my beautiful hopes I do not also have to suffer the loss of your friendship and sympathy. This is for me, as a Zionist, the first truly bleak and desolate day. May God prove me wrong" (Quoted in Bein, p. 476).

To Herzl, this heartfelt plea amounted to rank treason, and he reacted accordingly.

> You wouldn't by any chance be looking for a pretext to desert us? If you have reached that point, don't bother with a pretext. Just simply say: I've had it. And leave. I put up with more impertinence from Mr. Kann than from anyone else in my life, even after I realized his incompetence. . . . We are going to face far greater problems in Zionism, and with God's help we'll solve them. But of course you cannot shit in your pants every time there is trouble. Trouble exists so you can grow strong and overcome it. . . . How you can talk of ingratitude is a total mystery to me. . . . I don't want to be "my own minister," i.e., bank administrator; all I want is to find competent people. . . . I could understand [your resignation] only if you consider Mr. Kann rather than myself the leader of the Zionist movement. In that case, go with him, in God's name, I won't hold you back. But if you are simply tired, like many another, you had better leave it to me to make up a nice, presentable excuse for you, so you don't make yourself ridiculous. [Bein, pp. 476–77]

The fact that after the receipt of this letter Wolffsohn did not break off relations is a credit to his unswerving loyalty, not to mention his angelic temperament (which later made him a poor choice as Herzl's successor). In his firm and dignified reply he told Herzl a few long-overdue truths:

> I am not tired [he wrote], nor am I looking for an excuse. Of my own free will I shall never leave you or Zionism. But if compelling reasons drive me out of the movement, I don't care one bit how it looks to others or what they think of it. I have

never wanted anything for myself from Zionism. . . . You say you don't want to be your own minister, i.e., administrator, but only want to find competent people. But even before you ever find them, you drive out the ones you have. *You* will never find competent people, because you measure everyone against yourself and find them all small, flawed, and wanting. And if they are people like myself—allow me to be immodest—who "would certainly be" capable of getting things done if they had a free hand but who, out of devotion, give in to you all the time, they are also no good, because they cannot create anything out of their own strength. If, on the other hand, they are people like Kann, who have a mind of their own and do what they consider right and proper, they won't suit you. Everything in between these two extremes can only be "wrong" and dangerous. [Bein, p. 478]

At the end of June, Wolffsohn finally came to Vienna for a face-to-face showdown. In a series of blunt talks he told Herzl that, whatever his qualities as a leader, he was incompetent as a businessman and that, unless he stopped meddling in the affairs of the bank, failure and bankruptcy were inevitable. Herzl at first vehemently defended himself and accused Wolffsohn of making common cause with Kann, but in the end prudence won out over vanity; the bank's failure and ensuing scandal would have damaged the whole movement beyond repair. He agreed to let Wolffsohn run the bank as he saw fit, and the two men sealed their reconciliation by agreeing to henceforth address one another in the familiar second person singular.

But the episode took its toll, and it was probably no accident that on June 20, the day after his first confrontation with Wolffsohn, Herzl blacked out in his office. "Yesterday, while talking to people in the *Welt* office, I had an attack of cerebral anemia. I had a sudden blacking out of consciousness and a dimming of perceptions, although I carefully observed myself throughout and even cracked jokes with Schalit and Reich, the secretaries. Then, rather than going to the *Neue Freie Presse*, I drove home and went to bed. The doctor ordered two–three days of rest. Hardly feasible. Constantly fresh excitement. Yesterday with Wolffsohn, who gives me the impression of having gone over to Kann" (D, 6/21/1900).

While stress and excitement may well have precipitated the fainting spell, the underlying causes are unclear, and the diagnosis of "cerebral anemia" is not very helpful. It may just have been the doctor's way of translating the obvious—lack of blood flow to the brain—into Latin jargon, but Herzl may have been suffering from hemolytic anemia, a not uncommon complication of both malaria and lupus erythematosus and a possible cause of the blackouts he experienced with increasing frequency.

The nonchalance, in any case, fails to convince; he felt the swish of wings, too close for comfort.

For months, for years now, he had been living with a sense of doom. He needed no reminders. The sort of man he was and wanted to be looked death in the face unflinching, stiff upper lip contorted into a sick grin, because he was also human, and afraid.

That he needed no reminder is borne out by the fact that on May 23, just a month before the attack, he had made a new Will, superseding the first one dated February 1897—one more weapon with which to strike at Julie from beyond the grave.

He appointed his parents as his universal heirs. In the event of their prior death, the entire estate was to go to his children, in equal parts. His wife was to receive the usufruct, as mandated under Austrian law, only if she could prove total destitution. His literary estate was to be edited by Professor Leon Kellner, jointly with Erwin Rosenberger, his assistant on *Die Welt*, and administered by the Inner Action Committee of the Zionist movement, with the proceeds from the diaries going to his parents or, after their death, to his children.

And in a codicil to the Will, also dated March 23, he further stated that "Of the dowry of my wife, Julie Naschauer, only about 20,000 guilders are still left. The enormous expenditures which she forced upon me consumed during the past eleven years approximately 55,000 guilders, in addition to my hard-earned money." (A statement hard to reconcile with his diary entry of August 24, 1899, according to which he himself spent over 50,000 guilders on the Zionist movement, half of it on *Die Welt* alone.) "Now that my income begins to improve, perhaps I will succeed in replenishing the dowry so that she will receive the original amount at the time of my death. It is my wish that she deposit the above amount with the court and that she receive only the usufruct therefrom until the end of her life."

A few days after the fainting spell, he wrote to Moriz Reichenfeld, his financial adviser:

Dear Friend Moriz,

My illness of last week again brought the thought of death closer to me. Among my friends, you are the only one to whom I confidently entrust the care for the future material welfare of my family. I therefore appoint you, in the appendix to my previous testamentary provisions, executor, if my father should no longer be alive.

Also, in the event of the demise of my father as well as my mother, I appoint you guardian of my children, jointly, that is, with my friends D. Wolffsohn of Cologne and Johann Kremenezky of Vienna. And note that, should my father and mother no longer be alive, you will be the first guardian, Wolffsohn the second, and Kremenezky the third.

While writing this, I have the feeling that you have as sincere a friendship for me as I for you. [HY, Vol. III, pp. 257–68]

TWENTY-FOUR

*T*he quest for an intermediary to take Nevlinsky's place finally ended in Herzl's own native Budapest, and the candidate turned out to be another Hungarian Jew, albeit a rather exotic specimen—quirky, grumpy, and boastful, but nonetheless a man of some substance who knew what he was talking about even if he did not always talk about what he knew.

Arminius Vámbéry, né Hermann Wamberger, was born in 1832 into an Orthodox Jewish family, but lost his father within the first year of his life. Crippled at birth, he was on crutches till age twelve, when the destitute widow chucked him out to fend for himself. He threw away his crutches, apprenticed himself to a tailor, won a scholarship to the prestigious St. George Gymnasium in Bratislava, and discovered his phenomenal gift for languages, of which he eventually mastered a full dozen with amazing fluency—a great asset to a born raconteur who, in his heyday, could charm the maggots out of the cheese. In 1856, he set out on foot for Constantinople, limping across the whole length of the Austro-Hungarian Empire, making a point of always putting up with the local clergy, where "my Latin conversation was sure to cause me some regards and a few Kreutzers for my traveling expenses."

In Constantinople he started out as a cabaret singer but, within the year, rose from French tutor in the Sultan's harem to secretary and adviser to Fuad Pasha, the Grand Vizier, and it was as an intimate of the Turkish ruling clique that he first befriended the then sixteen-year-old prince Abdul Hamid, the current Sultan. Somewhere along the way he switched from Moses to Muhammad, the first of four conversions, all of them strictly a matter of convenience to which, as an inveterate atheist, he attached no undue importance.

In 1861 he received a grant from the Hungarian Academy of Sciences to explore the ancient hunting grounds of the Magyar tribes, and spent the next three years roaming through Central Asia in the guise of a dervish; his colorful adventures in exotic Persia, Samarkand, Turkestan, and Bokhara, rendered even more colorful in the telling, were the subject of his highly successful *Travels in Central Asia*. After a brief guest appearance in Budapest, he went to England, where both his social talents and his firsthand knowledge of a still largely mysterious East gained him access to the top levels of the British establishment. He was consulted by Disraeli and Palmerston, consorted with Edward VII, and acted as a not so secret agent for Britain, as well as for Turkey, where his old friend Abdul Hamid had in the meantime ascended to the throne.

Herzl first heard of him at the second congress, by which time the aging lion had settled into the Chair for Oriental Languages at the University of Budapest, itself a pioneering feat, as he described it in his autobiography:

> The fact that this Hungarian, who had been so much feted abroad, was of obscure origin, without family relations, and moreover of Jewish extraction, spoiled the interest for many, and they forcibly suppressed any feelings of appreciation they may have had. The Catholic Church, that hotbed of blind prejudice, was the first in attack. It upbraided me for figuring as a Protestant and not as a Catholic, as if I, the freethinker, took any interest in sectarian matters. I was the first non-Catholic professor appointed according to Imperial Cabinet orders to occupy a chair at the philosophical faculty of the Pest University. [Vámbéry, *His Life*]

After some unsatisfactory attempts at making contact via Hechler, whom Vámbéry dismissed as an unctuous crackpot, Herzl decided to go and see for himself. On June 16 he traveled to Mühlbach, a resort in the Tirolean Alps where Vámbéry spent the summer. It was a fourteen-hour trip each way, and since Pauline had come down with another severe attack of rheumatic fever, he was anxious to get back, which left only five hours for the actual visit. It more than sufficed for the two compatriots to achieve instant rapport.

I have met one of the most interesting men in this lame, seventy-year-old Hungarian Jew who doesn't know whether he is more Turk than Englishman, writes in German, speaks twelve languages with equal perfection, and has professed five religions, serving two of them as a priest. With this intimate knowledge of so many religions he was naturally bound to end up an atheist. He told me 1001 tales of the Orient, about his intimacy with the Sultan, and so on. He immediately trusted me completely and, after swearing me to secrecy, told me that he was a secret agent for both Turkey and England. The professorship in Hungary, originally a martyrdom because of anti-Jewish hostility, was now merely a cover. He showed me a mass of secret documents, which however I could only admire rather than read, since they were in Turkish, including writings in the Sultan's own hand. . . . "I don't want any money," he began. "I am a rich man. I cannot eat golden beefsteaks. I have a quarter of a million, and I can't use even half the interest I earn. If I help you, it will be for the sake of the cause. . . ." I told him: Vámbéry bácsi [Uncle Vámbéry]—may I call you as Nordau does?—ask the Sultan to receive me (1) because I could be of service to him in the press, (2) because the mere fact of my appearance would raise his credit. I would like it best if you could be my interpreter, I told him; but he fears the hardships of summer travel. My time was up. It remained uncertain if he would do anything, and most particularly, if he would immediately write to the Sultan about my audience. But he embraced and kissed me when we parted. [D, 6/17/1900]

Herzl followed up on this love feast with a letter masterful in its appeal to Vámbéry's vanity:

Dear Uncle Vámbéry:
  There is a good Hungarian word: *zsidóember* [Jewish man]. You are one, and so am I. That is why we understood one another so fast and so completely—perhaps more even at the human than at the Jewish level, although the latter is certainly strong enough in both of us. Help me, no, help us. Write to the Sultan, ask

him to send for me. . . . The details we can discuss after the congress, when I have you along as the interpreter. The audience as such is all I want before the congress. *Takhles* [essentials] later. I don't want to *khokhmetz* [be smart] with you. You would render our cause an enormous service if you could get me the audience now. I well understand what you wish to achieve with your autobiography: a royal tomb. Crown your pyramid with the chapter: How I helped prepare the homecoming of my people, the Jews. Your whole strange life will appear as though it had been leading toward this goal. [D, 6/17/1900]

Vámbéry replied that Turks could never be rushed, and that in any case nothing could be accomplished by mail, but Herzl would not be put off. The fourth Zionist congress was to meet on August 13, and he still had nothing to bring to it by way of a diplomatic coup. "My dear Sir and older brother, that doesn't sound very comforting. You too are saying *yavash* just like the native Turks. But I have no time to lose. . . . Disraeli once told a young Jew: You and I belong to a race that can do everything but fail. My dear Vámbéry bácsi, we can do really everything, but we must be willing. Are you? As you describe your relationship to him, I don't see why you can't write the Sultan and tell him: Now, look here, send for this fellow. He will put an end to your *shlimazel* [misfortune]. Listen to him, look him over, afterward you can always throw him out" (D, 6/21/1900).

Vámbéry finally agreed to write, though he warned Herzl not to expect miracles. In the long run, he might be able to help. But the Turks did things at their own pace and in their own way; he was not even sure the Sultan would ever get to see the letter.

In the long run, Herzl feared, he was going to be dead.

In the short run, he had become not only a prophet but also something like the uncrowned head of a nonexistent state, a position that involved responsibility without power.

For two decades the Rumanian Jews had been persecuted by the government as undesirable aliens, in flagrant violation of the 1878 Berlin treaties. By the end of the century, the pressure had grown unbearable, and in the spring of 1900, they picked themselves up by the thousands as if on a single command and began a mass migration westward which, despite its seemingly organized character, was in fact a wholly spontaneous mass response to sheer desperation. A fair number were able to obtain passage to Canada and the United States, but the vast majority headed for neighboring Austria and Hungary. The arrival of wave after wave of ragged, destitute men, women, and children clamoring for refuge caused a panic among Austrian Jews and provoked strong measures by the government. It sealed off the borders, admitting only refugees in transit for overseas and shipping most of the rest back to their "country of origin." And in their despair, hundreds of these victims, caught between bureaucracy and brutal oppression, appealed to the one man who had pledged to lead them out of this misery.

The heartrending telegrams and letters pouring into the offices of *Die Welt* put Herzl in a difficult position. The Jews of Vienna and Budapest, appalled at the prospect of an invasion by the unwashed hordes from the East, accused him of having instigated this uprising to promote his aims. On the face of it, the charge was ludicrous; these spontaneous, unplanned actions were precisely what Herzl had always warned against. On the other hand, he had predicted that the intensification of anti-Semitism would eventually make life unbearable for large segments of the Jewish population, and now that his prediction had come true, he had to take the blame for it. He was not the first messenger in that classic predicament, nor the last.

He defended himself with great dignity. In a speech before the Austrian Israelite Alliance on May 13, he was sharply critical of attempts to block the influx and urged instead a concerted relief effort on the part of all Jewish organizations, in which the Zionists would be ready to participate. Moreover, he interceded on their behalf with Prime Minister Körber and asked Vámbéry to talk the Sultan into opening the Turkish border. "Make him understand that he would play a beautiful role if he admits the homeless Jews. He will be looked upon as a benefactor of mankind—and his generosity will bear immediate interest. The Jews of the whole world will hail him. It will cause a shift in public opinion" (D, 7/2/1900).

Körber, politician that he was, promised to do what he could and did nothing. Uncle Vámbéry replied that negotiations with "Orientals" could never be rushed, most particularly not with the "arch liar" Abdul Hamid, whom none other than Bismarck had characterized as "the best diplomat of modern times." Have patience, he advised.

*   *   *

At their session of May 25, the members of the Action Committee voted to hold the next congress in London rather than in Basel.

Though initially opposed to the change of venue, Herzl quickly made his peace with the idea. The fantasy of a German protectorate never quite lost its appeal, but there were certain aspects of reality that could not indefinitely be ignored, such as the dominant position of Britain in the Middle East. Moreover, British attitudes toward Zionism, whether inspired by Old Testament romanticism or by imperialist designs, contrasted sharply with those prevailing in Germany and Austria. Thus the center of gravity was definitely shifting, and London loomed as a rather logical choice. "I suddenly realized that we had outgrown Basel. Since then, the idea of London has grown on me. It might give a fresh impetus to the movement."

In July, before going to England, he again stopped off at Aussee, where his family was spending the summer, a by now ritualistic gesture chiefly designed to keep up appearances—the fiction of a busy but devoted husband and father, a contented little wife, and happy, healthy children. In fact, however, the enforced proximity drove both spouses nearly insane; time and again the tension between them erupted in hysterical arguments and bitter recriminations. Their constant sniping, interrupted only by a flare-up of all-out combat or an occasional truce, was further exacerbated by the deadly hostility between Julie and her dominant, domineering mother-in-law. Caught in the cross fire were three sensitive children aged ten, nine, and eight; Herzl's own rare references to them are uninformative, but a causal relationship between these traumatic experiences and the emotional devastation to which all three of them succumbed at an early age seems all too probable.

To make matters worse, Herzl had another episode of "brain anemia," of which, in his usual fashion, he attempted to make light, though the self-mockery sounds hollow. "When you came to see me, I was lying unconscious," he wrote to Kellner on July 11. "Thus the Jewish people is losing—or has already lost—one of the finest forces it ever had at its disposal. And that to no avail, more or less" (HYB II, p. 179).

Nor was this to be the only scare. After an unpleasant channel crossing, he arrived in London a week before the scheduled opening of the congress and promptly came down with a 104-degree temperature. He suspected either malaria or an incipient pneumonia and insisted on concealing the illness from both family and the public at large, but when his condition worsened to the point where his participation in the congress seemed in doubt, he agreed to see a physician, provided he was Viennese-trained and a Zionist. De Haas tracked down the aptly named Dr. Liebster and arranged for round-the-clock nursing at the Hotel Langham, "Two fine English nurses took care of me. The older one, Sister Christine, at night; the younger and very pretty one, whose name I don't know, during the day. They were like Good Fortune and Care in Heine's poem [*"Das Glück ist eine leichte Dirne"*]. Good Sister Care snatched me in the nick of time from the incipient grave illness before I succumbed to it" (D, 8/10/1900).

On August 13, Herzl, still weak and wobbly on his feet, managed by sheer force of will to open the fourth congress with a somewhat rambling address hailing "England, one of the last remaining places on earth where there is freedom from Jew hatred." It was the largest congress so far, with over 400 delegates—at least half of them from the Russian Pale of Settlement—jamming Queens Hall at Langham Place, and Herzl set the tone by urging discipline and restraint. The main purpose, as he made clear, was to demonstrate strength and resolve in the capital of the British Empire. "Britain, free Britain that rules the seas, will understand us and our aspirations. From here, our Zionist idea will take wings and soar ever higher; of that we can be sure."

Extensive coverage by the domestic and foreign press helped to keep the debate within unusually civilized bounds, although the opposition again attacked the vagueness of Herzl's claims—"We are building, we are building, and the edifice is rising" was as far as he would commit himself. Leo Motzkin, Chaim Weizmann, and Martin Buber along with other disciples of Ahad Ha-Am went so far as to organize an official Zionist Democratic Fraction, consisting mainly of students in Swiss and German universities; their demand for greater emphasis on the cultural aspects of Zionism led to some sharp exchanges with the Orthodox wing. In the end, however, Herzl again succeeded in deftly averting an open clash and creating a semblance of harmony and all-around goodwill that earned him the customary encomiums. The congress had served its purpose, even if its practical achievements were nil.

Herzl himself, still far from recovered, was clearly in the trough of a depression, and neither the congress itself nor the festivities connected with it did much to lift his spirits. The congress was "much noise, sweat, and drum beating," and the mass meeting in the East End on Saturday night, at which he shared a platform with Zangwill, "no longer had anything new to offer. The cheers of the crowds mean nothing to me. The only new note was the garden party in the Royal Botanic Gardens on Sunday. The whole crowd kept trailing after me in a compact mass. I would have liked to enjoy the beautiful English garden but was smothered instead under royal honors. They looked on admiringly as I drank a cup of tea. They handed me children, presented their ladies, and old men wanted to kiss my hand. In these situations I am always tempted to ask: Excuse me, but why are you doing this?" (D, 8/14/1900).

The only concrete result—though its significance was not to become apparent for some years—was a luncheon with Eric Barrington, private secretary to Lord Salisbury. Herzl, by his own account, "talked a blue streak" about Zionism, "and it seems that I got him somewhat interested in our cause." For once he was being modest.

He returned to Aussee and spent two more weeks in the heaving bosom of the family, trying to get over the aftereffects of both the congress and the illness. But physical weakness and emotional lassitude continued to plague him throughout the rest of the year and through the winter; in fact, the photographs of the period, along with the increasingly dispirited tone of his diary entries and the morbid gloom of many of his feuilletons, strongly suggest that he never really recovered, and that these undiagnosed or misdiagnosed episodes were part of an insidious and inexorable process undermining his health.

I am now frequently so listless and lacking in energy that I don't register even important and interesting events, which of course are then promptly forgotten. But my situation is a weird one. At the time of the congress I was the lord and master. Now I am a servant once again, like Ruy Blas; and what a master I have to contend with. Every day I report to the boss, Dr. Bacher, who sometimes is gracious and sometimes ungracious. In addition, the huge financial sacrifices I made for the movement are weighing me down. I have done too much, and my lack of psychic energy combined with the awareness of my shaky financial situation, further spoil my mood. [D, 9/20/1900]

A Sunday he spent with Vámbéry in Budapest did nothing for him, either. The old man—only sixty-eight, but suffering from a variety of real and imaginary diseases contracted in the course of his travels— rambled on about his youthful adventures and bored him with stories that lost their punch the second or third time around. Nevertheless, he promised Herzl on his word of honor that the Sultan would receive him some time before the end of May. "I don't quite understand how he can give me his word about something over which he has no control, but so be it. I have to be satisfied with whatever happens. Besides, I am terribly weary" (D, 9/18/1900).

On October 15, he received word from Nouri Bey that the Turkish government "had a pressing need for six to seven hundred thousand Turkish pounds." If Herzl could arrange for a loan at 6 or 6½ percent interest, guaranteed by import duties, he would be rewarded by an audience with the Sultan. The Turkish consul general in Vienna— His Excellency Ladislaus von Dirsztay, né Fischl, another boy from Budapest who had made good—officially confirmed the proposition, and Nouri Bey's bagman Crespi offered his services as an intermediary, against suitable remuneration, *bien entendu*. The news galvanized Herzl into immediate action. He swallowed his pride and got in touch with the "renegade" Jacobus Kann, and through him obtained a binding letter of intent from the Dutch banking house of Lissa & Kann offering an £800,000 loan at 6 percent interest against proper collateral.

The irony, not lost on Herzl, was that while he engaged in matters of high finance and, on paper, dealt in millions, he had no end of trouble raising the 1,000 francs Crespi demanded as "an advance against expenses."

> The treasury of the Action Committee is so empty that, after meeting the December payroll, etc., we are not going to have the 1,000 francs for Crespi. And I have run out of energy; these past few days I have had more serious attacks of weakness than ever before. Actually it is only now that the idea of retiring is beginning to hit me full force. Perhaps I am writing this down in the hope of recalling it in better days ahead, so as to be able to say that when the need was greatest, etc. . . . I am, of course, much too complicated a person to keep a naïve diary, although I am making an effort not to posture. I always feel posterity looking over my shoulder. [D, 11/30/1900]

The negotiations dragged on inconclusively. Crespi, a venal "Levantine braggart and possibly even a con man," came to Vienna, pestered Herzl with countless proposals and counter-proposals, treated him to Yildiz gossip, tried to wheedle further "advances" out of him, and kept him busy with almost daily meetings, while all this time, back in Constantinople, his accomplices were haggling with other eager lenders. It was not until mid-December, when the Turks announced an agreement with the Deutsche Bank, that Herzl realized what, after all these years, should have been obvious to him from the outset—that he had once again been taken for a ride, and made to pay for the trip in the bargain. It marked the second time the Turks had used him as a pawn in their simpleminded but effective ploy, although in this particular instance they were defeated by the overweening greed of their own predatory bureaucracy. The German terms were actually less favorable than those they could have obtained from Herzl, but the German bankers were much more lavish in the distribution of their baksheesh. Crespi, who no doubt had been on their payroll all along, professed outrage and asked for another 10,000 francs to make the Grand Vizier block the deal.

Herzl now turned to Vámbéry for help and advice. The good "uncle," who at their first meeting had so disdainfully sneered at money, declared himself willing to do what he could—against a £5,000 commission. Herzl swallowed hard, refrained from reminding the old man that he could not eat golden beefsteaks, and assured him instead that he had always intended to reward him handsomely for his trouble.

Vámbéry did write to Constantinople, but the only response was an indirect one: at the end of December, the Turkish government imposed further restrictions on Jewish immigration into Palestine. Herzl took it as a good sign: "The whore wants to raise the price by telling us she can't be bought," he wrote Vámbéry on December 28. "Am I right?"

And just to keep his fingers nimble and the ball in play, he offered to settle the Boer War as a favor to the British by publishing the British peace terms in the *Neue Freie Presse*. His friend Austin, the jingo poet laureate to whom he submitted the proposal via the British ambassador, replied that there were no terms, there would be no terms, and that Britain would settle for nothing less than unconditional surrender.

At the beginning of the new year, Herzl went through another emotional roller-coaster ride that ended in a crash.

On January 4, 1901, he received an urgent summons to the Prime Minister's office. Körber informed him confidentially that a group of industrialists headed by Richard von Schöller, the owner of Austria's largest paper manufacturer, planned either to acquire the *Neue Freie*

Presse or to publish a rival pro-government newspaper. He had proposed Herzl as the editor in chief and asked him to get in touch at once with Count Auersperg, the spokesman for the group.

The very first interview with Auersperg left Herzl wildly elated and full of extravagant expectations. As usual, his imagination bounded way ahead of mere facts; he already saw himself as the all-powerful boss of an independent daily, with a huge salary that enabled him to provide generously not only for his immediate family but also for a whole host of poor relations. But a week went by without further word from Auersperg, while Herzl kept replaying the interview in his head and trying to fathom what possible mistakes he might have made. Finally, on January 10, he received another summons for the following morning:

> My hopes revived like parched flowers after a rain. Once again I had my head in the clouds, indulging my fantasies while pacing up and down in the children's room. The children were being bathed and put to bed as on any other night. They made their daily jokes, draped themselves in bedsheets, bounded noisily into the bathroom, danced their way into bed, said their evening prayer, and today, in addition to the German prayer, I also had them say a Hebrew one. All the while they were blissfully unaware that destiny may well pass tonight over their young heads. If tomorrow's conversation results in anything serious, it will once again lead to a major change in my life, and hence also in the lives of my children. [D, 1/10/01]

The discussion, though it took place in Schöller's palatial home, was led by the industrialist Arthur Krupp, a relative of the German Krupps and obviously the brain behind the initiative. Krupp declared right off that they were interested in neither an anti-Semitic paper nor in a *Judenblatt*; what they had in mind was a frankly pro-capitalist organ independent of the pervasive Rothschild influence and designed to improve the climate for large-scale industrial development. This struck Herzl as a reasonable and praiseworthy goal, though he felt compelled to stress that he would "never employ a rude capitalist tone against the workers. Instead, I would try to conduct the debate about social questions in a conciliatory tone and with pointed amiability so as to enlighten the workers about their own true interests, which, after all, are intimately linked to the progress of industry."

The meeting ended in an apparent agreement, and Herzl was left with the impression that the job was his for the asking. His own rather steep demands, which, aside from a 24,000-guilder salary, included a profit-sharing arrangement and shares in either the *Neue Freie Presse* or the new daily, added up to a package worth roughly half a million. When Krupp raised objections, Herzl countered that he had a duty to provide for his children: "This sort of thing you do only once in a lifetime. If you do it, it has to succeed. And if it succeeds, you should get something out of it."

Two weeks later, the talks abruptly collapsed, for reasons unknown. Herzl blamed himself for having made exorbitant demands, but the industrialists—all of them Protestants—might have had second thoughts about hiring the leader of the Zionist movement as their ideological spokesman. In any event, something decided them to drop the whole project altogether, and Herzl found himself once again the slave of Mssrs. Bacher and Benedikt.

It was a bitter disappointment.

Three months ripped out of my life, piece by piece, in Great Expectations. First that scoundrel Crespi, who led me around by the nose, then the bastards from the heavy industry with their newspaper. In the meantime, I stopped work on my novel, which gets worse and ever more insipid the longer I neglect it. Now I have to leave for London, and it will be three weeks before I get back to my desk. The wind blows through the stubble. I feel the autumn of my life approaching. I run the risk of leaving no oeuvre to the world, and no fortune to my children. It would be ridiculous to take up the novel again two days before my departure. But I am giving myself my word of honor to do so immediately after my return. [D, 1/30/01]

He spent the first two weeks of February in Paris and in London, chiefly in pursuit of his latest inspiration. The vast Turkish public debt—190 million pounds at the time of Abdul Hamid's accession in 1876—was held by a consortium of Protestant French and British banks. It was Herzl's plan to purchase that debt at about a quarter of its face value and offer to retire it in exchange for a Palestine charter; all he needed was the cooperation of the Rothschilds. But although he mobilized all his contacts, neither Lord Rothschild in London nor Baron Rothschild in Paris would have anything to do with him.

Nevertheless, despite its frustrations and the eternal squabbles about the affairs of the bank, the week in London turned out to be a blessed relief from the night-and-day grind of Vienna. Life in England—or what little he knew of it—had tempted him enormously ever since his first visit. British Jewry seemed far less fractious than the Viennese community, he had a group of devoted followers, the British upper classes seemed vastly more civilized than their Austrian counterparts, the upper-class Jews were, if not pro-Zionist, at least potentially accessible, and the absence of any overt anti-Semitism in public life greatly facilitated contacts with non-Jews. A rather idealized picture based on very limited exposure, but it had served to inspire vague plans about a permanent move to the British capital. Even as a prominent insider of Vienna's intellectual establishment and, in his current position, the powerful arbiter of literary taste as reflected in the city's most important newspaper, Herzl had never ceased to feel an outsider. The ardent desire to get away from the intrigue, the backbiting and slander, the cloying passion of the Viennese spirit, and, above all, from the humiliating subordinate position at the *Neue Freie Presse* also played their part; and now that, with the failure of the newspaper project, his last great hope of independence had crumbled, he boldly decided to act on his impulse.

Right after his return he broached the subject with Julie, who, much to his surprise, had no objections whatsoever. An even greater surprise awaited him at the *Neue Freie Presse* when, on March 27, he confronted Benedikt with the request for a transfer to London. Benedikt, while expressing formal regrets at losing an irreplaceable literary editor and feuilletonist, assured him that rather than dispensing with his services altogether, they would most certainly post him to London as their foreign correspondent; only the salary question remained to be settled.

But all these plans came to nought on the very next day. Herzl's parents flatly refused to move to London, and that was the end of it. At age forty-one, he was still, to put it charitably, too devoted a son to conceive of life away from Mom and Dad. And so, rather than moving to London, he moved in May to Haizingergasse 29, in Vienna's Eighteenth District. At the same time his parents settled into an apartment just a few houses down the street, at Number 13. It was a cozy

arrangement that was to last for the rest of his life. Poor Julie must
have often dreamed of London.

For well over a year Herzl had sporadically been at work on a novel
that was to meld fantasy, romance, and social thought in a utopian
vision of the Jewish state. On August 30, 1899, he noted in his diary:
"Today, on the bouncing bus going to Waehring, the title of my Zionist
novel occurred to me: *Altneuland* [*Old New Land*]. Allusions to the
Prague Altneuschul Synagogue. It will become a famous word." Progress was slow, but he kept plugging away at it whenever time permitted,
and in the absence of any hopeful prospects in the immediate future,
he welcomed the chance to indulge in dreams about a Jewish utopia
in the year 1920. "I am now hard at work on *Altneuland*. My hopes
for practical success have been dashed. My life now is no novel, and
so the novel has become my life" (D, 3/14/01).

In April, however, Vámbéry at last offered to go to Constantinople
and deal with the Sultan in person. He made it appear a major sacrifice
on his part and demanded 600 francs in traveling expenses; Herzl gave
him 2,000, although—or perhaps because—he had begun to suspect
that the old curmudgeon's loyalty to Zionism ran about as deep as his
devotion to any of the five religions he had professed at one time or
another in his life. But whatever his game, Herzl had no choice but
to trust him. He simply had to see the Sultan. It was, he felt, no longer
just a matter of scoring a diplomatic coup, but a matter of life and
death for the movement.

Vámbéry left Budapest on April 17, and during the next two weeks
Herzl found it almost impossible to bear up under the suspense of
waiting for word from him. He tried to be philosophical, armed himself
with homespun platitudes against the inevitable letdown, played su-
perstitious little games with himself by going for long walks out of
reach of the telephone or letting other people pick up his mail. He
took a nineteen-hour train ride to Aussee, which gave him a chance
to read Moses Hess's *Rome and Jerusalem*—"I was delighted and inspired. What a great and noble spirit. Everything we are trying to do
is already contained in the pages of this book. . . . Since the days
of Spinoza, Judaism has not produced a greater spirit than the faded
and forgotten Moses Hess" (D, 5/2/01). On May 2, he dejectedly
marked his birthday: "Today I am forty-one years old. The wind blows

through the stubble, I must quicken my pace. It will soon be six years since I started this movement that has made me old, tired, and poor."

But on May 7, the call came for him to leave at once for Constantinople via Budapest, where Vámbéry was to give him the details.

TWENTY-FIVE

*I*n the five years since his first visit to Constantinople, Herzl had grown immensely in poise, diplomatic polish, and sophistication. Yet despite wider horizons and a sounder, more comprehensive grasp of technical details, his basic views had undergone very little change.

In fact, he embarked on his second foray into the den of Ali Baba not significantly wiser than he had been the first time around. He had, to be sure, shed much of his naïveté, but he still clung to the same flawed assumptions about the Turks, their policies, principles, and motives. He believed the Sultan to be preoccupied with the national debt, "the thorn in the lion's paw," as he so poetically put it to the despot, and which he proposed to remove, in exchange for a charter. The Yildiz struck him as a nest of vipers, while the whole Turkish civil service was nothing but one huge conspiracy of thugs and drones battened on blackmail and baksheesh. Doing business in this climate of lawless corruption was a nightmare, and Herzl had dropped his illusions about achieving quick results; he had learned that every Yes was a maybe, followed by an equally tentative No intended to raise the ante. But he was convinced that, given the Turks' unbridled greed and venality, they could ultimately be persuaded to sell anything if the price was right, Palestine and their own mothers included.

Despite the ethnocentric bias that inspired it, this was a not inaccurate view of the situation, as far as it went. But it went nowhere far enough, and its blind spots demonstrate a curious lack of imagination on the part of a man who himself exemplified the transcendent importance of symbols and the suprarational in the conduct of politics.

To begin with, the Sultan's real, if not exclusive, concern was not the national debt but the perpetuation of his absolutist regime and of his hold on what remained of the Ottoman Empire. This empire was de facto bankrupt, had been bankrupt ever since he ascended to the throne, and the debt undoubtedly troubled him to the extent to which it limited his ambitions and freedom of action. But what he looked for was a bailout, not a solution. He was shrewd enough to realize that true economic progress involving industrialization would rapidly undermine the foundations of an essentially still feudal society and spell the doom of his reign.

The second miscalculation was even more serious. Unlike the enlightened statesmen of Europe, quick to seal their borders against immigration from the East, the bloody tyrant of the Yildiz had just admitted 15,000 Rumanian Jews and was willing to take all comers. He appreciated the loyalty and commercial talents of his Jewish subjects scattered throughout the realm, but the very last thing he needed was yet another cohesive, militant minority clamoring for independence. And he dealt with Herzl as he dealt with all his problems, in the time-honored devious and convoluted ways that avoided confrontations and in which cunning, intrigue, and delay made up for lack of power. Yet for all his switching, stalling, backtracking, and mixed signals he in the end proved remarkably consistent, faithful to what he had told Nevlinsky when the subject first came up: Palestine was holy to the Muslims and would never be surrendered voluntarily.

Herzl's failure to gauge the depth of passion which Palestine aroused among devout Muslims is ironic but not surprising; for though he catered to the zeal of the equally devout among his own followers and acknowledged the symbolic significance of Jerusalem for the Jews, he was guided by cold reason rather than by any real feelings for the place. And he simply refused to believe that, for the sake of a few sacred shrines which could easily be "exterritorialized," the Turks would turn down a deal promising profits and prosperity.

Then again, even if in his heart of hearts he had known better—what else could he have done? As long as the Turks blocked his way, they had to be dealt with. And dealing with them made sense only on the assumption that they could be moved. The assumption turned out to be facile, to say the least; what he faced was the stalemate of an irresistible force pitted against an immovable object. But like his heirs facing an even more intransigent Muslim power, he had no choice.

On May 7, Vámbéry returned from Constantinople in high dudgeon. Herzl met him at the Budapest railroad station, where he immediately launched into a noisy tirade against the Sultan—"The fellow has gone completely mad. His latest stunt is to confiscate all mail from Europe. He figures they won't go to war over it." It took six meetings to talk the paranoid lunatic into receiving Herzl, although "not as a Zionist, but as leader of the Jews and influential journalist. . . . You must not talk to him about Zionism. That is a phantasmagoria. Jerusalem is as holy to them as Mecca."

The Sultan had insisted on Vámbéry's leaving Constantinople before Herzl's arrival, fearing a conspiratorial link. An official of the Foreign Ministry would serve instead as interpreter. "But you must arm yourself with patience. It may take eight to fourteen days before you are called."

Herzl was overjoyed, "provided I get to talk to the Sultan for at least an hour. If so, I'll promise to cure his ills and gain his confidence. If he now already wanted to sell me Palestine, I would be greatly embarrassed. After all, I first have to raise the money" (D, 5/8/01).

It might have been helpful had he been made privy to some of the confidential information Vámbéry passed on to the British Foreign Office from Constantinople—probably the real purpose of his mission, and one for which no doubt he was also suitably rewarded:

Abdul Hamid is decidedly mentally and physically broken; he is no longer the supreme lord in the palace who is able to impose and command his greedy, dishonest, and cunning servants; he does not unite and keep in his hands any longer the threads of the varied plots, tricks, and foul games upon which his rule was founded. On the contrary, he is now an instrument in the hands of the leading court officials, who exploit him in the interest of their personal affairs, and of whom he is much afraid. Nothing is more interesting than to watch from near the machinations of Tahsin Bey and Izzet Bey, his first and second secretaries, who are in furious enmity against each other, and who, considering the puppet character of the leading statesmen, are his real hands and ministers. The former, a hardworking man from nine in the morning till one or two after midnight, is so to say his pen, whilst the latter may be called his brain, i.e., chief adviser; for Izzet knows french [sic] and has been in Europe, whereas Tahsin does not know any European language. This Izzet, a shrewd Arab, is a bitter enemy to every Christian; he is cruel and reckless in the extreme and all the evil deeds of the latter rule of the Sultan are his own diabolical inventions. Of course the Sultan is quite help-less in the hands of these two servants and manages his affairs only by inciting one against the other and by giving occasionally presents to both of them. [5/12/01. Quoted in Vital, Vol. II, p. 115. The letter has no clear addressee but is marked "Acknowl-edged" and "Seen by Sir N. O'Conor," the British ambassador to Constantinople at the time.]

Whatever his retainer from the British, the sly old "uncle" was livid when told that Nouri Bey and Crespi would share in the generous reward Herzl had promised for the audience, even though they had done little or nothing to bring it about. But no amount of ranting and raving could shake Herzl's principles; he was a man of his word, a promise was a promise, and they parted on distinctly frosty terms.

Herzl arrived in Constantinople on May 13, accompanied by Wolff-sohn and Oskar Marmorek, and began the slow, tortuous—and ex-pensive—crawl through the maze of Byzantine bureaucracy. His guide this time was another Hungarian Jew, Dr. Soma Wellisch, chief of health services in the Turkish Ministry of the Interior and one of Vámbéry's "contacts." Fending off beggars, blackmailers, and spies, Herzl made the obligatory rounds, trying as best he could to sidestep the traps set for him by rival factions in every office. He found time for some sightseeing, but almost every free moment was devoted to rehearsing his interview with the Sultan; even in the bathtub he carried on imaginary conversations and practiced putting his points across without overstepping the limits agreed to.

The summons came on the seventeenth, a Friday morning. On the palace grounds, he first attended another *Selamlik*, the weekly parade with whose pomp and circumstance he was familiar from his last visit. At the conclusion, as he stood around waiting for the audience, he was informed that he had been awarded the Order of the Mejidiye, Second Class. But five eventful years had gone by since his last visit. He now came as something of a sovereign himself, and eager to make this plain right from the outset, he declared that while last time around he had not wanted to refuse the Mejidiye, Third Class, so as not to insult His Majesty, the very least he would now deign to accept was the Mejidiye, First Class, Turkey's highest decoration. The flustered interpreter rushed off to confer with his superiors and returned to announce, with a broad grin, that His Majesty was bestowing the Grand Cordon of the Mejidiye, First Class, upon the distinguished guest.

Having thus made his point, Herzl was ushered into the presence of the exalted monarch—"exactly as I had pictured him, short, skinny, with a large hooked nose, a dyed beard, and a thin, tremulous voice," a poison pen portrait Herzl later fleshed out once he was safely out of Turkey:

> Short, shabby, with the badly dyed beard which probably gets painted only once a week for the *Selamlik*. The hooked nose of a Punchinello, the long yellow teeth with the large gap in the upper right, the fez pulled deep over his probably bald head, the protruding ears—"pants protectors," as I used to call them, to the amusement of my friends, designed to keep the fez from slipping all the way down to the pants. The feeble hands in white gloves too large for them, and the ill-matched, coarse, loud-colored cuffs. The bleating voice, the limited intelligence in every word, the timidity in every glance. And *this* rules. Only in name, of course, and on the surface. [D, 5/21/01]

The passage, a sample of Herzl's famous wit as a stylist, is also highly revealing in other ways. A consummate narcissist, inordinately vain, ever conscious of his own impressive looks and fanatical about the choice of the proper tie, he consistently tended to judge—and mis-judge—people by their outward appearance. Unlike the Kaiser, who with one flashing glance from his steel-gray eyes had reduced Herzl to a jellied pulp, Abdul Hamid did not *look* like an emperor; it took a man like Bismarck, unburdened by petit bourgeois superstitions about Teutonic knighthood to realize that the Kaiser's plumed helmets and ocular acrobatics camouflaged the vapidity of an infantile mind, whereas the Sultan's funny-looking fez covered not only a "probably bald" pate but a cunning intelligence superior to that of most Western leaders. Like Vámbéry, who not incidentally came from much the same background and whose expertise helped to shape official British attitudes, Herzl grossly underestimated Abdul Hamid.

In the long run, this probably contributed to the impasse; it certainly caused Herzl needless headaches and heartaches. But in this first encounter it gave him a considerable psychological advantage, albeit it a wholly illusory one. Filled with the sense of his own superiority, he immediately seized the high ground and took charge of the situation.

After the routine courtesies—the Sultan, who did not speak a word of German, declared himself a faithful reader of the *Neue Freie Presse* and inquired after the health of Emperor Franz Joseph—Herzl expressed the gratitude of world Jewry for the monarch's generous treatment of the Jews and unloaded the well-rehearsed story of Androcles and the Lion. "The thorn, as I see it, is the public debt." The Sultan agreed with a sigh; it was something he had tried to get rid of ever since he ascended the throne. Herzl thereupon offered his services, "but the first and most basic precondition is absolute secrecy," since otherwise the superpowers, anxious to perpetuate Turkey's weakness, would do their utmost to sabotage this effort.

"He understood. I continued—and from that point on I took the reins altogether—that I would have my friends carry out this operation on all European stock exchanges, provided I had His Majesty's support. But that support, at an appropriate time, would have to take the form of some measure particularly friendly to the Jews, and be proclaimed in a suitable manner."

Abdul Hamid, a *faux naif* if ever there was one, eagerly agreed. He had a court jeweler, he told Herzl, who was a Jew. He could say something nice to him about the Jews and have him publicize it in the newspapers. There also was the Chief Rabbi, the Haham Bashi; he might say something to him as well.

Herzl gravely replied that this was not quite what he had in mind, and that he would submit his request for an appropriate manifestation in due time. "All this beautiful country needs is the industrial initiative of our people."

Again the Sultan signified total agreement and asked Herzl to recommend a competent financier capable of "creating new resources," such as new taxes that would not be too onerous, something on the order of the tax on matches.

Herzl promised to look for the right man. Then, with his usual gift for fabulation, he began to frighten the Sultan with audacious plans for electrification, urban renewal, and the construction of a new Stamboul bridge spanning the Golden Horn. But Abdul Hamid demurely asked that he hold off on all these marvelous plans for the time being and concentrate instead on the public debt. It was agreed that, before his departure, Herzl would receive a detailed account of the financial situation, as well as of current efforts at consolidating the debt.

The audience had lasted a full two hours, and while Herzl had kept his word and never mentioned Zionism or Palestine, he felt he had laid out the bait, impressed the Sultan, and established the kind of *quid pro quo* relationship that would sooner or later induce him to swallow it. Flushed with victory, he fought his way out of the palace through a gauntlet of outstretched palms, dropped a small fortune in gold coins, paid off Nouri Bey and his gang as promised, even though they had done nothing for him—"*C'est un art de grand seigneur de se laisser voler*"—and was asked to send the interpreter "a nice carriage and a couple of horses" as a token of his appreciation.

It was a vital first step, but as he soon found out, getting from square one to square two in the Yildiz involved more than just putting one foot in front of the other; the grounds of the palace were riddled with traps. He spent three more nerve-racking, frustrating days in Constantinople, pitting his diplomatic skills against the predatory instincts of bazaar-bred cutthroats disguised as bureaucrats. He studied the details of the proposed debt-consolidation plan, denounced it for the shameless fraud it was, and promptly found himself caught in the deadly rivalry between the Sultan's first and second secretaries described in Vámbéry's report; the mere presence of an honest broker threatened the thieving schemes and machinations of both men.

He requested a follow-up audience with the Sultan, but had to content himself with the gift of a diamond-studded tie pin, and with written communications passed back and forth by intermediaries. Abdul Hamid evidently did not feel up to subjecting himself to a second lecture by this self-possessed infidel with his subversive plans for turning the empire over to Jewish entrepreneurship, but Vámbéry's impression to the contrary notwithstanding, it seemed evident that from somewhere deep within the cave the wizard of the Yildiz was still manipulating his puppets, even though Herzl considered him their prisoner. In the course of the protracted negotiations, he asked for an immediate loan of 4 million pounds to cover defense expenditures and offered the exploitation of five state monopolies in return. And although both sides managed to skirt the focal issue, the Sultan pointedly stressed that, while Jews were welcome in Turkey, they would have to accept Turkish nationality and be subject to the draft. The closest they came to a direct confrontation over the charter was a final argument over dispersal versus the large-scale settlements Herzl insisted on as the only rational means of raising agricultural productivity.

In his farewell note to the Sultan, he promised to keep in touch and to submit definite financial proposals within the next four weeks. On May 20—"the ninth birthday of my daughter Trudel"—he left Constantinople by sea.

Herzl returned to Vienna convinced that "we have now entered into actual negotiations about the charter. Good luck, skill, and money are all we now need to realize everything I have planned. At this stage, the charter would be more in the nature of a favor granted to arouse our sympathies for the Turkish Empire" (D, 5/20/01).

The principle of reciprocity had indeed been established; however, the extent to which the Turks were actually willing to trade political concessions for economic benefits remained to be seen. But as far as Herzl was concerned, finding the money to back up his offers loomed as the only potential stumbling block, and with only four weeks to raise a few million, he stopped at home just long enough to change his clothes, kiss his children, touch base with the Turkish ambassador, and write Benedikt a letter announcing his departure for London and requesting to be relieved of his responsibilities as literary editor. He could no longer put up with the daily office routine and proposed instead to submit his contributions by mail, showing up at the *Neue Freie Presse* only when his schedule permitted—provided, of course, his salary remained the same. On May 29, he was off again.

He first looked up Vámbéry in the Tirolean village of Franzensfeste. A generous bonus mollified the old codger, and Herzl promised him a 300,000-guilder reward for the charter, which Vámbéry now felt sure he could obtain for him by the end of the year. The next stop was Karlsruhe, where he reported to the Grand Duke of Baden on his talk with the Sultan and again requested help in obtaining an audience with the Czar. It was, he explained, mainly a symbolic gesture but might also help to allay possible Turkish fears of Russian opposition to a charter for Palestine. The Grand Duke, though he promised to do what he could, intimated that at the moment the Czar had more pressing problems to deal with.

The triumphant mood of the conquering hero lasted as far as Paris, where it abruptly deflated, turning to rage and disappointment.

Immediately after his arrival on May 31, Herzl summoned the
French financier and Zionist sympathizer Benno Reitlinger and gave
him twenty-four hours to raise 1.5 million pounds sterling. Reitlinger
did his best, but met with no interest in financial circles. Herzl next
approached Edmond de Rothschild and the Jewish Colonization Association via Zadok Kahn and was crudely rebuffed. His effort to enlist the Péreires, Rothschild's competitors and sworn enemies, was
equally unsuccessful. Even more demoralizing was the reaction of
his followers to his exploits in Constantinople. Marmorek informed
him that the Odessa Action Committee members—Ussishkin, Tchlenov, Bernstein-Kohan among others—had protested his wasting bank
money on such futile schemes, and his cup overflowed when Nordau
accused him of irresponsible adventurism. Furious, bitter, and de-
jected, he surrendered to a surge of self-pity:

> With such "helpers" I am forced to work. Once the Jewish
> state has become a fact, everything is going to seem routine and
> perfectly natural. A fair-minded historian may perhaps under-
> stand what an achievement it was for an impecunious Jewish
> journalist in the midst of the deepest degradation of the Jewish
> people, at a time of the most disgusting anti-Semitism, to have
> fashioned a flag out of a rag and turned decadent riffraff into an
> upright people rallying to this flag.
> But neither this nor my skill in negotiating with powers and
> princes seems to mean anything. No one can appreciate what I
> have done and what I have suffered who does not know (1) what
> I had to put up with during these past six years at the *Neue Freie
> Presse*, where I trembled for my children's bread, (2) the toil and
> trouble I had trying to procure the means for propaganda, (3)
> who my helpers were. The best-intentioned among them are
> either too poor, hobbled, or unsuited. [D, 6/1/01]

An even more dramatic reaction to the emotional stress and distress
was another, rather alarming blackout he suffered on June 4: "Last
night again an attack of brain anemia. One of these days I won't come
out of it. I was on a pleasure drive through the Bois de Boulogne when
I fainted in the carriage. I first stretched out on two chairs in the bushes
and then drove home with greatly diminished consciousness. Today
I feel better. But my nerves are shot" (D, 6/5/01).
It was envy and jealousy, he decided, that accounted for Nordau's

incessant carping and criticizing, but he was fed up with it and finally appealed to the eminent physician and mental-health expert, "in the most gentle way possible," to please shut up; what he, Herzl, needed from his friends at this point was support, not criticism. "You don't make a man dizzy when he is balancing on a tightrope." Nordau conceded the point. "All we can do now is run after you with a mattress."

If Paris was a disaster, London at first seemed to justify great expectations. Herzl's speech before an audience of prominent upper-class Jews at the Maccabean Club was a skillful blend of discretion and uplift, but it ended on a blunt note: "As to the question of what was accomplished in Constantinople, let me, in the Jewish manner, answer with another question, a Jewish question: Are you prepared to help the one who wants to help you? . . . We need approximately 2 million pounds in the very near future."

Socially, the visit was a huge success. He had become a celebrity, the papers clamored for interviews, he was being fed, feted, and passed around in both Jewish and non-Jewish high society. "*I am awfully dinnered,*" as he put it in idiosyncratic English, with probably unintended ambiguity. "Society is curious about me. I am now a sight not to be missed, a dish on the table, one comes to *meet Dr. Herzl.*" But the moneyed Jews were as unwilling to invest in any adventures with the Turkish monster as were their French confreres; the practical results of this social whirl amounted to nothing more positive than the advice to try his luck with Andrew Carnegie and Sir Cecil Rhodes. Carnegie never responded. Rhodes helpfully suggested, via the British journalist William Thomas Stead, that "if he wants any tip from me, I have only one word to say, and that is let him put money in his purse."

The upshot was that Herzl returned to Vienna empty-handed, full of gloom and resentment, and all the more anxious to keep the Turks on the line while he went in search of a miracle. From his so-called vacation retreat at Aussee, where he spent the months of August and September, he deployed a feverish activity; like a magician both spellbound and spellbinding, he kept pulling new and ever stranger-looking rabbits out of his head. "The latest figures in my chess game are Cecil Rhodes . . . Roosevelt, the new President (through Gottheil), the King of England (through the Bishop of Ripon), the Czar (through General von Hesse), etc." In blessed innocence of the ways of U.S. politics, he schemed to have Robert Gottheil, professor of Semitic languages at Columbia University and first president of the Federation of American Zionists, appointed U.S. ambassador to Constantinople: "While sitting at the lake, it occurred to me that I could bring Gottheil into play as a knight on the chessboard. I'll tell the Sultan that I know of a way for him to get an ambassador who will be his staunch friend among the powers: he should ask for Gottheil, or accept him" (D, 9/ 23/01). (The innocence extended to Turkish politics as well; he should by then have known better than to expect Abdul Hamid to welcome a notorious Zionist as U.S. representative.)

The four-week deadline had long since passed, and his numerous letters to the Sultan remained unanswered, but he was cheered by a thank-you cable in reply to his birthday greetings. He fired up Vámbéry, urging him to go to Constantinople and reminding him of the 300,000-guilder reward, with the rather startling result that the venerable adventurer, evidently infected by Herzl's way of thinking big, proposed a coup d'état in Constantinople, with himself taking charge of the government. For once Herzl found himself in the curious position of having to talk someone else back down to earth. "I have read your youthfully audacious letter with great joy. You are really a divinely favored man. May God keep you." He even went so far as to study Turkish in the hope of being able someday to dispense with the treacherous interpreters.

Worn out and disgusted, he still never gave in, tempted though he was to "issue a proclamation: All right, Jews, I as a poor and helpless journalist have nevertheless managed, within five years' time, to reach the point where I can negotiate with the Sultan in person. I have done my part, and then some. But you have left me in the lurch. You are a despicable rabble—go to hell." He left nothing untried, yet all his efforts—heroic, quixotic, blunt, devious, sophisticated, or fatuous— added up to nothing. On December 26, the fifth congress opened in Basel; he faced it with a heavy heart, empty hands, and very empty pockets.

Herzl, who had held out for London in August and been outvoted by the obstreperous "Russians," was in a foul mood to begin with, and four days and nights of tense, often vituperative sessions were not calculated to improve his disposition. According to de Haas, present as both a delegate and a journalist, he suffered a "heart attack," whatever that meant; that the strain took its toll may be taken for granted.

The discomfort, physical and emotional, probably played its part in a subtle erosion of his leadership skills. His brief account of proceedings is noteworthy for its significant gaps as well as for the tone of imperious exasperation that may at least partially explain the clashes he fails to mention.

In his opening speech he again hinted at a major breakthrough in Constantinople and concluded by assuring his audience that "the Jewish people has a friend and benefactor in the reigning Caliph. The Sultan has empowered me to announce this in public." His audience was not, however, as easily reassured as in years past. A new, aggressive element of young intellectuals, mainly Russian students, insisted on being heard, and although Herzl still dominated the assembly with an unassailable authority, it no longer shielded him from sharp, often unfair attacks on his methods and motives. Impatient with the lack of tangible progress, his critics charged him with "playing bourgeois games," denounced the use of bank funds for bribes, and agitated for "creating facts on the ground" by infiltration into Palestine.

He had no serious trouble disposing of these strictures and burying his critics under massive votes of confidence. But being so totally focused on practical politics, he was unaware—or at least disdainful—of a much more formidable opposition building up within the movement and challenging not only his methods but his very principles.

At the previous congress, the "cultural Zionists," largely inspired by Ahad Ha-Am's ideas, had already unsuccessfully attempted to put cultural questions on the agenda and been squelched in the interest of unity. Their main opposition to Herzl was grounded in his essentially negative interpretation of Zionism as a reaction to anti-Semitism. In their view, Zionism was more than a movement; it represented a cultural as well as a political renaissance, and rather than concentrating exclusively on long-range political goals in a distant and uncertain future, they wanted to see greater emphasis placed on *Gegenwartsarbeit*, on an active effort to upgrade Jewish education and Jewish culture in the here-and-now. This heretical notion inevitably put them on a collision course with the Orthodox, who felt that Talmud and Torah provided all the education and culture any Jew ever needed. Stirring up that particular hornets' nest was precisely what Herzl had wanted to avoid at all cost, and the fact that most of the rebels were fiery secularists or even outright socialists made a dispassionate discussion of the issues that much less likely.

Since their defeat of the year before, the "culturals" had formed a

452]   E R N S T   P A W E L

Democratic Zionist Faction, which, despite its small representation at the congress—about twenty delegates, for the most part students from nearby universities—exerted a moral and intellectual influence far beyond its numbers. They included some of the most dedicated, most eloquent, and most intelligent among the new generation, men such as Chaim Weizmann, Martin Buber, Leo Motzkin, Berthold Feiwel, the writer Davis Trietsch, and the painter E. M. Lilien. Personally, Herzl rather liked most of these "youngsters," all in their early twenties; he had even entrusted the editorship of *Die Welt* to Feiwel, and after Feiwel's resignation in August of 1901 for reasons of health, he turned the paper over to the twenty-two-year-old *Wunderkind* Martin Buber, giving him full editorial freedom to express his point of view. But his attitude toward them was patronizing and condescending. He had no real quarrel with their ideas; he merely considered them irrelevant as long as the Jews lacked the material and political bases for a state of their own.

It was a view even more forcefully propounded by Max Nordau, whose speech surpassed all his previous performances. He contemptuously dismissed any efforts at raising the spiritual level of the Jewish masses in the Diaspora as a sheer waste of time and energy. "I refuse to even talk about it. Anything said about it is empty prattle as long as we lack the one precondition for a thorough, all-encompassing popular culture, and that precondition is money."

Buber was outraged. He mounted the dais and declared that by reducing the spiritual needs of the Jewish people to a question of money, Nordau had insulted him, his friends, and his people. No mean orator himself but given to esoteric allusions and lyrical flounces, he had to contend with some derisive hooting from the floor. Nevertheless, he managed to submit the "faction's" resolutions, which aside from some rather tired platitudes concerning the "education of the Jewish people in the national sense" included practical demands for a Hebrew university in Jerusalem, a Jewish publishing house, expansion of the cultural committees, and the organization of a statistical commission. When Herzl, ostensibly because of the late hour—it was way past midnight—cut off further debate and blocked the vote on the resolutions, thirty-seven members and sympathizers of the opposition rose from their seats and walked out.

Realizing his tactical error, Herzl quickly made amends the next morning by throwing the floor open to a full-scale debate and by supporting the resolutions, all of which eventually passed, with the exception of the subsidy for a Jewish publishing house. On the surface, peace had been restored.

In fact, however, the underlying conflict continued to smolder; it involved fundamental questions of principle beyond mere priorities, not the least of them being Herzl's own authoritarian leadership, his conduct not only with princes and potentates but with his own followers. The young rebels, while readily acknowledging his achievements, even his greatness, were repelled by the cult of personality that had sprung up around him. Buber probably spoke for most of them when, in later years, he recalled that "we venerated him, loved him, but a great part of his being was alien to our soul." The walkout represented the first massive challenge to his leadership, and despite his outwardly conciliatory attitude, Herzl was quite unwilling to forgive what he experienced as a personal insult, a clear case of *lèse-majesté*.

Moreover, it made him realize that he had greatly underestimated the strength and influence of the newborn Democratic Faction. And it was in order to strangle the baby in the crib and forestall any potential subversion of "his" movement that he resorted to an uncharacteristically devious maneuver which, no doubt in the interest of hagiography, remained a closely guarded secret until 1955.

At a banquet honoring the eightieth birthday of Rabbi Maimon— known as Yehudah Leib Fishman in Herzl's day—the guest of honor revealed that in the wake of the fifth congress he had been approached by Herzl with the suggestion to found a party of religious Zionists to counter the growing influence of the Democratic Faction. The suggestion was passed on to Rabbi Isaac Jacob Reines, the leader of the Orthodox wing, who proceeded to organize the Orthodox Zionist Mizrachi Party at a convention for which Herzl paid the expenses out of his own pocket. Motivated by political expediency and personal vindictiveness rather than any sudden religious conversion, Herzl thus helped to exacerbate the very split he had been so anxious to avert; but given the temper of our times, what had once been buried as a shameful lapse now redounds to his credit in the eyes of the proliferating Jewish fundamentalists and feeds the myth of his late-life return to a faith he never had in the first place.

None of this is so much as alluded to in the diary. For whatever reason, he did not sum up his impressions of the congress until a week later and mainly lists the practical results, the most important of which, in the long run, proved to be the founding of the Jewish National Fund as an instrument for collective land purchases in Palestine. On the whole, his leadership had once more been reaffirmed and his achievements of the past year duly ratified, if not fully appreciated. But he was infinitely weary.

TWENTY ⋈ SIX

*F*rom Basel, Herzl went to Venice, trying to relax for a few days, but the gloom that had settled in his bones would not yield to such simple expedients. He felt old and weary; death was no longer the romantic abstraction he had been flirting with for so much of his life. In January he had another fainting spell in the office. "I did not tell anyone about it. My parents would find out and get excited. Nor would it make my wife any more loving, either. But it will finish me off one of these days. I can imagine death: the slow waning of consciousness, the awareness of this loss being itself the painful part. This morning I thought: Life—in the most favorable circumstances, one is mourned. If I die soon, my parents will be the ones who will mourn me most. My children less so; their youth will console them. And the entire Jewish people. A beautiful funeral procession: the tragic, the lovely, and the sublime" (D, 1/30/02). Thus, in the midst of morbid realism, fantasy—and life—kept reasserting themselves; he was stage-managing his funeral.

And yet, he was only forty-one years old; even while trying to make peace with death, he schemed to outrun it—outrun it at least long enough to taste the fruits of his labor. "Zionism," he wrote during that same desolate month, "was the Sabbath of my life" (D, 1/24/02). So far, he had not even made it to Mount Pisgah.

His situation at the *Neue Freie Presse* remained unchanged. The plea for relief from office duties had been quietly ignored, but his bosses now seemed resigned to his ever more frequent absences. One reason was, quite simply, Herzl's professional competence. He was ideally suited to the job of literary editor in that his own tastes faithfully reflected those of the paper's most representative readers—the educated, liberal Jewish middle class.

He had the final say on what went into the "cultural" pages. Submissions came in by the bushel, in many instances brought in by the authors themselves, who would sit across the desk from him waiting for his decision. To have one's story published by the *Presse* or one's book reviewed in its columns was the gateway to success and put the gatekeeper in a position of inordinate power, which Herzl wielded with remarkable tact and sensitivity—far more so than he normally exhibited in his dealings with his disciples. It also put him in touch with many of Vienna's young writers, but while he instantly recognized the talents of a still adolescent Stefan Zweig, he seems to have paid no attention to a letter he received in September 1902 from one of his former neighbors in the Berggasse:

Dear Dr. Herzl,

At the suggestion of your editorial colleague, Mr. Max Nordau, I took the liberty of having the Deuticke Bookstore send you a copy of my book on the interpretation of dreams, which appeared in 1900, along with a brief lecture dealing with the same topic.

I don't know if you will find the book suited to the purpose which Mr. Nordau had in mind, but I beg you to keep it in any case as a token of the high esteem in which for years now I and so many others have held the writer and fighter for the human rights of our people.

Sincerely yours,
Prof. Dr. Freud

According to Anna Freud's recollections, the two men never met, which is probably just as well—two prophets listening to very different voices and crossing vastly different deserts even while living within a block of each other. Herzl knew nothing about Freud, but Freud was evidently fascinated by Herzl; he went to see *The New Ghetto*, he twice dreamed about Herzl, and although he rejected Jewish nationalism, his own personal experience certainly made him sympathize with Herzl's struggle in the face of ridicule and derision.

His note further suggests that Vienna's Jewish professionals—an important segment of the *Neue Freie Presse* readership—were no longer quite as inclined to dismiss Herzl as a crackpot; anti-Semitism had ceased to be a joke, and the subtle atmospheric change may have helped to make Bacher and Benedikt more tolerant of their eccentric collaborator's eccentricities.

On February 5, Herzl suddenly received a cable from the Turkish Foreign Office asking him to proceed *immediately* to Constantinople "to furnish certain explanations regarding your affairs."

The summons came at a most inopportune moment. He had still not raised the money and would not know what to do with the charter even if he got it. He was physically run down, deep into a depression, and Julie had just taken to bed with a mysterious high fever. But he had no choice. A flood that washed out part of the rail link afforded a brief respite, but on February 14 he was on his way, accompanied by the British businessman and Zionist leader Joseph Cowen.

The reception this time was warmer—he was to consider himself the Sultan's guest for the duration of his stay—and more businesslike. Substantive discussions began the very next day, with the ogre hidden as always in the innards of the Yildiz and represented by two go-betweens who came straight to the point: even though Herzl had done nothing for them since his last visit other than making disconcerting noises in Basel and in London, the Sultan was ready to welcome all Jewish refugees willing to accept Ottoman citizenship and have them settle anywhere in the empire—with the sole exception of Palestine. In return, he asked Herzl to undertake the consolidation of the public debt and to take charge of developing the country's present and future mine resources.

"What mines?" Herzl inquired.

"All mines—gold, silver, coal, or oil. We know you are interested in a strong Turkey, that is why we are not afraid of being exploited by you. However, it has to be done through an Ottoman company with a board consisting entirely of Jews and Muslims."

Herzl asked for time to consider the offers and, next morning, submitted his own counterproposals. He was prepared, in principle, to accept the mine concessions, "which will afford me the opportunity for loyal service to Your Imperial Majesty." On the other hand, it would be all but impossible to mobilize Jewish capital on behalf of Turkey unless immigration was granted without restrictions.

Much of the day went into these arguments back and forth, complicated by the Sultan's unwillingness to show his face and by his insistence on word-for-word written translations of every point raised. He finally repeated his offer, emphasizing that his government would let the Jews settle anywhere throughout his realm—Anatolia, Syria, Mesopotamia, anywhere but in Palestine.

Herzl turned him down. No Palestine, no deal.

That was the end of the talks for now, though Herzl had at least had the satisfaction of openly stating his case, and he made as graceful an exit as possible under the circumstances. Along with a parting letter reiterating his own propositions, he sent the Sultan a presentation copy of his *Philosophical Tales* and announced the impending arrival of an Arabic typewriter, which he was having specially constructed in the United States. The Sultan, in turn, sent him a purse containing 200 pounds sterling in silver coin for travel expenses. Herzl had an impulse to refuse the baksheesh but decided that the Zionist movement had better use for it than some thieving official in the Yildiz.

In the rickety, storm-tossed Rumanian steamer taking him back across the Black Sea he pondered his next step. He suspected that the Turks had once again used him to pressure other creditors, but that was a chance he had to take. If the price was right, they might buy from him in the end, anyway. The sensible thing, it seemed to him— an idea suggested by Izzet, the Sultan's secretary, and which, for that reason alone, should have set alarm bells ringing—was to gain an economic foothold in Turkey by acquiring the mining concessions. He bludgeoned a most reluctant Colonial Trust board into issuing three letters of credit by way of demonstrating his financial solvency to the Turks and signaling his readiness for another round of bargaining. And although officially his hands were tied by the Basel program, with its narrow emphasis on Palestine, he was privately determined to grab whatever he was offered right now, as a temporary expedient. How far was it from Mesopotamia to Jerusalem, anyway?

But the unpredictable Turks didn't bite—perhaps because they had never meant what they said, or because Izzet and Tahsin were trying to trap each other, each using Herzl as a lure, or because one or the other had tried to rob the Sultan, or because the Sultan was playing them off against one another—the possible combinations were infinite, and Herzl would never know the truth, if such there was. At the court of Abdul Hamid he was merely a lamb up for fleecing, if not for slaughter.

After weeks of pleading, scheming, and arm twisting, he finally deposited the 3 million francs, only to be informed by the Turkish consul that Constantinople wanted to know who this Dr. Herzl was and what the money was all about. At this point he began to suspect that he was perhaps out of his depth. The consul himself seemed a bit apologetic: "Between you and me, I must confess that order in our country leaves much to be desired." But a far more serious blow was the announcement that the Sultan had approved a debt-consolidation plan proposed by Pierre Rouvier, a former French cabinet minister, with the backing of his government. On April 4, the Turkish consul got word from Constantinople that the 3-million-franc deposit had been the result of a misunderstanding. "That much, by God, I knew myself," Herzl wrote. "I just wanted to show them the money—so they wouldn't forget me. Thus ends this chapter of my political novel."

The relative calm of the next few weeks enabled him to devote himself instead to a different sort of novel. On April 30, he at long last finished *Altneuland*, that blueprint of a Jewish utopia on which he had been working on and off since 1899. The book was to be published in October.

In the meantime, he tried to salvage what he could of his Turkish contacts. Adapting Weizmann's idea of a Hebrew university, he proposed it to the Sultan as an institution to be staffed by Jewish scientists and academics "anywhere within the Ottoman Empire, for instance in Jerusalem," where young Turks could obtain a higher education without having to study abroad and run the risk of catching infectious ideas. Abdul Hamid had no interest in the education of his subjects, but he slyly inquired if perhaps Herzl could offer better terms than Rouvier. Herzl, burned child or just plain fed up, hinted that he could indeed, but that he was not about to commit himself a second time just so the Turks could play him off against the French competition. Only if they had concrete proposals was he willing to come to Constantinople.

They did not, and he left for Paris instead, morose and discouraged. "Now I am an aging famous man," he wrote on June 4, after settling into the old hotel that had seen the first flush of his inspiration seven years earlier. "I much preferred the days of my youth, despite their melancholy aspects. . . . In the Jewish question I have become world-famous as a propagandist. As a writer, notably as a dramatist, I am considered a nothing. A less than nothing. I am merely referred to as a good journalist. And yet I feel, I know, that I am—or was—a writer of the highest potential who simply did not give his full measure because he became disgusted and discouraged" (D, 6/4/02).

He did not, however, have much time to flounder in maudlin self-pity. Invited to testify before the Royal Commission for Alien Immigration, he packed his bags and eagerly left for London.

Hysteria over what was perceived as a mass influx of cheap labor from abroad had been mounting in Britain throughout the 1890s. The bulk of the immigrants were poor Jews from Russia and Rumania, a fact which tended to exacerbate the tensions; anti-Semitism was by no means as rare in England as Herzl seemed to believe. And although the actual numbers—some 25,000 in a decade—scarcely warranted the excitement, the government found itself in an awkward position, trapped between popular pressure for restrictive measures and the traditional British policy of the open door. Unwilling to act, and unable not to, Parliament appointed a commission in March 1902 to study the question.

Herzl's British followers immediately proposed him as an expert witness, and the commission eventually agreed to invite him, over the strenuous objections of Lord Rothschild, its only Jewish member. Nathan Rothschild had called Herzl a demagogue and a windbag; but faced with a *fait accompli*, he was now anxious to tell the windbag exactly what he should and should not say in public.

Herzl, for his part, immediately grasped the crucial import of the invitation in terms of his own goal: "It is the encounter—strife or reconciliation—with Lord Rothschild, hence of enormous significance. I am instructing my faithful Greenberg and Cowen to arrange a meeting with Rothschild prior to my appearance before the commission" (D, 6/4/02).

Two days later he was in London, but before he could ever get his bearings, fate struck him a devastating blow. On the night of June 9, as he returned to his hotel after the theater, he found a cable from his wife: DAD VERY ILL. COME TO VIENNA IMMEDIATELY. He spent the rest of the night—"one of the darkest of my life"—in a daze, canceling all plans, trying to arrange for transportation, and finally resorted to the diary in an effort to cope with the all but unbearable sense of loss. "I think I was a loyal, grateful, respectful son to my good father, who has done so infinitely much for me. . . . And now that he is closing his eyes, I am not there with him. . . . My darling did not get to read the end of *Altneuland*. How much did I remain in his debt, though I am not a bad son. . . . Like a tree he stood next to me, and now the tree is gone."

Even before boarding the ferry in Dover, he received word that his father had died of a stroke. "Secretly I still nourished a glimmer of hope that it might just be pneumonia." Wolffsohn boarded the train in Cologne, offering to accompany him to Vienna, but Herzl refused. He felt the need to be alone. "After all, he can't help me. During these past twenty-nine hours I have been licking my paws like a dog that has been run over."

Jakob Herzl was sixty-seven years old when he died—a placid, level-headed, pedantic businessman typical of the countless fathers who had worked their way up from ghetto poverty. Quite atypical, however, was the relationship between this particular businessman father and his intellectual son. Jakob never quite lost a lingering sense of social inferiority. He lived in awe both of his wife and of his *Wunderkind* of a son; with the latter, however, he came to identify to a degree which, though touching in its way, greatly complicated Herzl's own emergence as an independent adult. The father's devotion was absolute, unconditional, and utterly submissive; he worshipped the victor in a contest in which he had refused to engage to begin with, knowing that he did not stand a chance.

He gave his son what the child in Herzl most wanted—adulation and unquestioning support, no matter what, practical as well as emotional. And to the child in Herzl the loss came as a natural disaster, the ground heaving under his feet.

After a week of disconsolate mourning, he retreated to Aussee. "Everything passes. Now I am again sitting at the same desk as last summer, and all I have left of my father is his picture facing me. He is completely gone from my life. Only this picture tells me what he looked like, he whom I shall never see again." His mother wanted to move in with him, but he still had the good sense to refuse. "You and Julie would be at each other's throat on the second day, if not the first. After fifteen years we ought to know better." (Jeanette Herzl continued to reside at Haizingergasse 13 until her death in 1911.)

By the end of the month he was ready to return to London, and on July 4 he had the long-delayed confrontation with Lord Rothschild, whose fluent German partially made up for his deafness. Nathan Mayer

Rothschild, son of the first Jewish Member of Parliament and himself the first Jew to enter the House of Lords, headed the British branch of the Rothschild empire; he was a member of the board of the Bank of England, president of the United Synagogue, and the undisputed leader of British Jewry. In addition, he was fabulously wealthy and twenty years older than Herzl—all of which added up to an impression on his part that he was entitled to give orders, and that it was Herzl's place to carry them out.

After delivering himself of some scathing remarks about Zionism and about the intellectual endowment of his fellow commission members, Rothschild began to tell Herzl what he was to say in his public testimony and suddenly found himself shouted at in a tone no one had ever dared use with him, and at a decibel level that more than overcame his handicap. "I'll tell the commission whatever I consider good and proper. I'll state my convictions. That is what I have always done, and that is what I shall do this time as well."

Rothschild, though visibly taken aback, also seemed faintly impressed. He warned Herzl that the commission had invited him merely to publicize their conviction that a Jew could never become a proper Englishman.

Herzl reassured him on this point; he did not feel qualified to lecture the commission on what constituted a proper Englishman. "I'll simply tell them that there is enormous poverty in the East, and that the people face a choice of either dying or getting out. We've known about the Rumanian misery since '97. . . . In Galicia, the situation may be even worse. There are over 700,000 utterly destitute people there; they, too, will start moving westward." Rothschild pleaded with him not to tell this to the commission, "otherwise there will be restrictive legislation. At this point I exploded: You bet I'll tell them. And how I will."

Respect changed to grudging admiration as Rothschild summoned his two younger brothers and made Herzl repeat what he had just said. For good measure, Herzl added that Jewish charity had become "a machine for stifling cries of distress." Whereupon Rothschild invited him to stay for lunch.

After lunch, Herzl got his chance to unpack his own plan, seated close to his host and trumpeting into his one good and by now rather sympathetic ear: "I want to ask the British government for a charter for colonization."

"Don't say charter. The word has a bad ring right now."

"Call it what you will. I want to found a Jewish colony in a British possession."

"Take Uganda."

"No. The only places I can use . . ." And because there were other people in the room, he wrote on a slip of paper: "The Sinai Peninsula, Egyptian Palestine, Cyprus. Are you in favor?"

Rothschild thought it over for a moment. "Very much so."

This was the victory Herzl had long been waiting for. He added to his note: "Prevent the Sultan from getting money (Rouvier)."

Rothschild replied that while he had been able to prevent the Rumanians from getting money, he could do nothing about the Turkish debt, because the Great Powers were pushing the consolidation deal in return for railroad concessions. Herzl then told him that the Sultan had offered him Mesopotamia.

"And you refused?"

"Yes."

On that note they parted, not yet allies, Herzl felt, but no longer enemies. Elated by this first real success in a long time, he had no trouble turning down an urgent summons from the Sultan that reached him that same afternoon via the Turkish ambassador. At the moment, he pointed out, the quarantine measures taken against an outbreak of the black plague in Constantinople made travel difficult. In any case, he was busy in London.

On June 7, he appeared before the Royal Commission, warmly greeted by Rothschild, who introduced him to his fellow members. In his prepared statement, he summed up the Zionist position: the intolerable conditions of their lives made the mass flight of Eastern Jews inevitable. If—as the very existence of the commission seemed to suggest—they were not welcome in the West, a legally recognized homeland had to be found where Jews would no longer be regarded as aliens.

In the oral questioning that followed, Herzl was handicapped both by his limited English and by his fear of unwittingly providing ammunition to the anti-immigration lobby. When Major Evans Gordon, who strongly favored restrictions, sought to have him agree that no anti-Semitism was involved, he replied that he "would not be the crown witness for anything against the Jews." Rothschild brought up the question of dual loyalties, asking if Zionists could still be devoted citizens. "Yes," asserted Herzl truculently, "and more so than those who are not Zionists," a statement that went unchallenged.

On the whole, he acquitted himself creditably, although he himself felt that he had made a bad impression, largely because of his poor English. He later told his son, Hans, "I passed my examination before the Royal Commission pretty well, but my English was not very good. You know that feeling from your Latin. Let it serve as a warning to make up for deficiencies. You and I must do everything with distinction." Throughout his brief and tragic life, poor Hans strove valiantly to live up to this portentous injunction. He did become fluent in English.

At a private lunch with Rothschild the next day, Herzl in strict confidence showed him the 1898 letters from Eulenburg and the Grand Duke of Baden, which all but promised a German protectorate and which, much to his detriment, he had felt honor-bound not to reveal. Impressed with this evidence both of near-misses and of Herzl's discretion, the financier promised to bring the project of a Jewish Company for the settlement of the Sinai, Egyptian Palestine, and Cyprus to the attention of Joseph Chamberlain, the Colonial Secretary. Their only disagreement was over the scope of the enterprise, Rothschild wanting it initially confined to 25,000 settlers, whereas Herzl insisted on "big or not at all." In the meantime, he was to draw up a proposal for official consideration.

Throughout the next week, while Herzl remained in London, Constantinople bombarded him with messages, pleas, cables, and letters, the gist of them being that he should rush down there at once if he could underbid Rouvier. But on July 12, when he was finally about to leave, the Turkish ambassador informed him that the Rouvier consolidation plan had been approved in principle and that Herzl's trip would make sense only if he could beat out the French. On the fifteenth, an "ultimatum" arrived from the Sultan giving him just one day to come up with a better offer. In reply, Herzl pointed to the fiasco of the 3-million-franc deposit; he was prepared to submit a plan that would save the Turks at least 2 million to begin with, but he needed time.

Leaving London, he wrote once more to Rothschild, stressing his hope for closer cooperation. "Who can help our poor people if not you? You are a kind man—now that I have met you, I am sure of that. Be a great one as well."

On the eighteenth he was back at Aussee, where the Turks kept up their barrage, so that on the twenty-second he found himself once more on the Orient Express with Wolffsohn, bound for Constantinople. These trips—it was his fifth—were beginning to settle into a familiar routine, as he noted on his arrival at the Yildiz gate, where the baksheesh collectors joyfully welcomed him with open hands. But even within the palace, the atmosphere was suspiciously friendly. First to receive him with unaccustomed warmth was his enemy Tahsin, the man who had all along been busy plotting against him. He was again to be the Sultan's guest and would even have a court carriage at his disposal.

But although he pleaded fatigue—he had driven to the Yildiz straight from the station after two nights on the train—the Sultan insisted on having a written outline of his proposals at once, or so, at least, Tahsin asserted. With Abdul Hamid a forever unseen presence, it was impossible to know when his underlings were transmitting orders and when they were acting on their own. Either way, Herzl had no choice but to spend half the night on a four-page memorandum, a translation of which was to be in the Sultan's hands early the next morning.

He submitted it in the form of a personal letter, polite but peremptory in tone. He offered to consolidate the debt against a 30 million bond issue, i.e., 2 million less than Rouvier, and to organize the exploitation of Turkey's natural resources—mines, forests, and possibly electric power. In return, he demanded "a charter or concession for Jewish colonization as Y.I.M. deigned to offer me last February, with in addition the territory of Haifa and environs."

The next day was a Friday. He arrived at the palace at noon in time for the *Selamlik*, as he had been told, expecting afterward to have an audience with the Sultan. Instead, after waiting around for several hours, he was dismissed until 6 p.m., ostensibly because the Sultan needed time to study his memo. No sooner was he back at his hotel than he was urgently recalled to the palace, where it turned out that the ever so anxiously awaited document had as yet not even been translated. The elder, somewhat dotty statesman Karatheodory Pasha, whose moment of glory had been the 1878 Berlin conference, was brought in to do the job. Sweating and groaning, he struggled with it till after midnight, interrupting his labors periodically to treat Herzl to well-rehearsed anecdotes about Bismarck and Disraeli.

With the translation finally in the Sultan's hands, Herzl showed up at ten the next morning as instructed, only to be kept waiting once again. "Here time isn't money," he noted—not altogether accurately.

Although in the light of past experience he had come with minimal expectations, it still took him awhile to figure out that the procrastination and delays, the foul-ups, unabashed laziness, and cryptic contradictions were all part of a very deliberate strategy in which even the court carriage had its place. For all the time, even while stringing him along, the Turks were haggling with Rouvier over the final terms of the settlement, and Herzl's conspicuous presence—the more conspicuous the better—was their ace in the hole. They were obviously determined to display him prominently until the deal was concluded.

He spent the morning socializing with Karatheodory, was taken to lunch and told in the afternoon that the Sultan wanted him to see the Grand Vizier, who, however, had a bad cold and an abscessed tooth. The interview was therefore rescheduled for the following afternoon and took place at the Palace of the Sublime Porte, where a pudgy, teary-eyed, but obviously shrewd little old man with a streaming nose received him ceremoniously in his bathrobe and declared that, in his opinion, helping destitute Jews was a worthy humanitarian sentiment. Herzl repeated his proposals, the Grand Vizier with studied casualness asked for the names of his backers—which Herzl, with the same fake nonchalance, refused to divulge—and they parted with mutual compliments.

Back at the Yildiz, he was asked not only to supply a written report on his talk but also to arrange for the translation on his own—a request which Herzl interpreted to mean that the Sultan did not trust his own palace guard, but which posed problems for him in a city where he was a complete stranger. Soma Wellisch finally tracked down a young Sephardic Jew with serviceable French but no experience as a translator, who spent almost twenty-four hours on the job. Herzl carefully checked the accuracy of the Turkish version by having it translated word for word back into French; it seemed to him a precious one-time chance to communicate with Abdul Hamid without having his message deliberately garbled by scheming third parties, and in a postscript he pledged to start studying Turkish immediately if his plan was accepted. In three months' time, he assured the Sultan, they would be able to talk directly with one another.

These nebulous pseudo-negotiations went on for two more days. There was another chat with the Grand Vizier, and yet another letter to the Sultan. He ate a great deal of indigestible "snake food," drank countless cups of black coffee, spent endless hours waiting around in smoke-filled offices. And suddenly, on Thursday night, he was dismissed—told that he would be free to leave after next morning's *Selamlik*. The deal with Rouvier—who, in the meantime, had become the French Minister of Finance—had been concluded.

He was neither surprised nor greatly disappointed. His offer was still on the table. The next time the Turks ran out of money—which was a matter of months or even weeks—they were more likely to take him up on it.

The Sultan, as a token of his appreciation, offered him a hefty subsidy for the *Neue Freie Presse*, which Herzl rejected as politely as he knew how. He could not, however, refuse the purse filled with silver coins he was given to cover expenses. And in a personal letter, the Sultan once again stipulated exactly the same terms for Jewish immigration—dispersal, Ottoman citizenship, military service—he had offered years ago. There was, quite obviously, a method to his inconsistency.

Time to look elsewhere for allies.

Lord Rothschild had been at least partially converted, but he persisted in his belief that exclusively Jewish settlements would only end up as new ghettos and breed the same anti-liberal bigotry. Writing to him after his return from Constantinople, Herzl argued that "I cannot agree that the Jewish commonwealth I intend to organize would necessarily have to be small, Orthodox, and illiberal. I spent three years working on a comprehensive answer to this and similar objections. It turned into a book entitled *Altneuland*, which will appear in a few weeks; you will be among the first to whom I shall send a copy" (D, 8/22/02).

Altneuland, dedicated to the memory of Herzl's father and sister, appeared in October 1902. The title, rendered by Nahum Sokolow, its Hebrew translator, as *Tel Aviv* (*Hill of Spring*), has the distinction of having inspired the name of the first all-Jewish city of modern times, founded in 1912. This of itself is indicative of the book's emotional impact on generations of Zionists, an impact wholly unrelated to its literary merits. Read purely as a novel, *Altneuland* is an insipid and indigestible *fin de siècle* concoction. Herzl considered it his masterpiece, his final bid for recognition as the serious author he felt himself to be, but this conceit merely points up his handicaps as a critic—the taste for kitsch absorbed with his mother's milk, and his role at the *Neue Freie Presse* as purveyor of sentimental mush to the Jewish middle class.

The plot as such is a melodramatic fairy tale that can easily be—and largely has been—ignored in any serious discussion of the book's message. And yet, it is precisely in their fiction that authors tend to reveal their hidden selves, and the cruder the art, the more obvious the clues. Thus the sole but far from negligible interest of *Altneuland*'s blatantly autobiographical storyline, with its paper-thin characters all drawn from life, lies in what it tells about the inner life of a man who quite successfully resisted coming to terms with it in other ways.

The hero, Dr. Friedrich Löwenberg, an unstable compound of Theodor Herzl and Heinrich Kana, courts Ernestine Löffler, the spoiled, birdbrained, but seductive daughter of rich and vulgar parvenus, who are caricatured with the same acid contempt that had already inspired several of Herzl's stage characters patterned after his in-laws. Unlike the real-life hero, Löwenberg gets lucky: Ernestine jilts the sensitive but poor young lawyer and settles instead for an aging, potbellied speculator, one of her father's cronies, who offers her a life of luxury and leisure. This sensible decision frees the heartbroken hero to team up instead with a Prussian nobleman and ex–cavalry officer who had gone to America, changed his name from Königshof to Kingscourt, made a vast fortune, and foolishly married a girl just like Ernestine who promptly cheated on him with the chauffeur. The two men share a violent dislike of women and a taste for the finer things in life, such as "hunting, drinking, eating, sleeping, and playing chess." Fed up with civilization and its discontents, they retire to a Pacific island equipped—thanks to Kingscourt's millions—with all modern conveniences but completely cut off from communications with the outside world.

After twenty years of presumably companionable bliss in this luxurious Garden of Eden—no details are vouchsafed—they for reasons unknown decide to return briefly to Europe. Along the way, Kingscourt's yacht stops off in Palestine, where a miracle awaits them. What on their previous visit twenty years earlier had been arid desert was now a flourishing landscape with thriving cities, vast but smokeless industries, and prosperous cooperative farms. Zionism has in the meantime brought the Jews back home, liberated their long-suppressed genius, and enabled them to create not just another nation-state but a model society, a cooperative commonwealth in which all social problems have been disposed of in a rational spirit of voluntarism. A free-enterprise system without capitalists, crossed with socialism without coercion, this New Society—its official name—learned from Europe's mistakes and was thus able to avoid all the pitfalls of progress while enjoying its blessings.

The bulk of *Altneuland* is devoted to a minutely detailed description of this social fantasy. Meanwhile, the plot that serves as its frail vehicle lurches on to its preordained happy end, along the way giving the author further opportunities to rewrite his own past. Although anti-Semitism has vanished, thanks to the Zionists, most Jews have come to settle in this paradise, re-creating a Vienna without Jew-baiters— or, for that matter, without Jews, most of whom have become indistinguishable from upstanding, self-possessed, and productive Gentiles, except for a few incorrigible *Mauschels* of the old school. Thus Löwenberg runs into perfidious Ernestine and, to his grim satisfaction, finds that twenty years have turned the erstwhile seductress into a matronly, middle-aged blob, while he has preserved his youthful appearance playing chess in the South Pacific. Edifying, on the other hand, is his encounter with an Eastern European family whom he had once befriended and helped when they were starving in the slums of Vienna. David Litvak, alias David Wolffsohn, a little beggar boy when last seen, became one of the pioneers of the New Society and, at the book's end, is elected its president. David's sister, Miriam, whom Herzl consciously modeled on the idealized portrait of his own late sister, Pauline, is a striking beauty selflessly devoting her manifold talents to teaching. Löwenberg falls in love with her, and Miriam's mother on her deathbed does what Herzl's mother had never done for him—she sanctions and blesses this faintly incestuous union. Even Kingscourt decides to rejoin the human race and throw in his lot with these noble Hebrews, who in no way resemble the Jews he once used to know.

But while *Altneuland* confirms Herzl's persistent mediocrity as an artist, it at the same time marks a sharp break with the political platitudes that inspired *Der Judenstaat*. He was finally able to let go not only of the whole childish baggage of flags and fanfares, of costume spectaculars, autocratic tyrants, and aristocratic republics, but of the idea of the nation-state altogether. "We are not a state like the European states of your time," explains David Litvak, "but a *Gemeinschaft*"—a voluntarist community in which Adam Smith's free market

forces are buffered by Peter Kropotkin's mutual aid. The French anarchists, whose doings Herzl so extensively covered in his Paris days,
evidently left a deep and lasting impression. Except for the disparities
of wealth—David Litvak lives in a palatial mansion on Mount Carmel,
attended by liveried Negro servants—*Altneuland* is, more than anything else, an anarchist utopia. The entire coercive apparatus of the
state has been dismantled, along with all the trappings of nationalism.
There is no army, jails are empty because crime has disappeared. Jew,
Gentile, and Arab, native-born and foreigner, live together in freedom
and harmony, and all the creative forces of this cosmopolitan population are harnessed to productive pursuits ranging from industry and
farming to culture and education. Liberty and fraternity are the tenets
of the New Society, hence no friction arises between the Jewish immigrants and the Arab natives. When Kingscourt asks Litvak's Arab
friend—fluent in German—why the Muslims don't oppose the Jews
as intruders, the Arab replies: "Christian, you have strange ways of
speaking. Would you consider him a robber who takes nothing from
you, but gives you something instead? The Jews have made us wealthy.
Why should we scorn them? They live with us as brothers. Why should
we not love them?"

It is not easy, in this century of Holocaust and total war, of unbridled
fanaticism and the mushroom cloud, to recapture the spirit of that
brief moment in history when all problems of the human race seemed
amenable to rational solutions. And though *Altneuland* differs in its
details from other nineteenth-century utopias, the underlying faith in
the power of reason to create an ideal society was part of a common
myth rooted in the Enlightenment.

One is tempted, from the dubious vantage point of the late twentieth
century, to sneer at the prophets of the nineteenth. Having poisoned
our waters and polluted our air, spawned monstrous slums and the
means for a final solution to all the world's problems, we have learned
the cost of progress without being the wiser for it. We have seen Marx's
classless society evolve into the Soviet state, and Herzl's *Altneuland*
into Shamir's embattled Israel. And yet, within his limitations as a
human being, Herzl turned out to be a creditable prophet.

Not because the Jewish state came into existence within the time
he predicted it would, nor because there are now mansions on Mount
Carmel; for every one of his predictions that came true, there are a

dozen that did not. But the spirit that animated *Altneuland* was the spirit that animated Israel's pioneers. Their goal was a democratic and egalitarian society, and with their agricultural communes and cooperatives, with the collective ownership of the land, and with the voluntarism that characterized the early stages of the Jewish settlement of Palestine, they came closer to fulfilling Herzl's vision than did most idealists in pursuit of a dream. That they shared his naïve illusions about the Arabs, that the cooperative society turned into a nation-state, and that coercion, bigotry, and greed sapped the idealism of the New Society does not detract from that unique achievement. Swimming against the tide of history is a noble effort. It is also a losing proposition; at best, one survives.

In terms of political theory, *Altneuland* may have marked a significant advance over *Der Judenstaat*. Within the Zionist movement, however, the book was for the most part greeted with consternation; it reawakened the old misgivings about Herzl's commitment to Zion. Even those close to him were made uneasy by the absence of anything specifically Jewish about this latest version of the Jewish state, but it was Ahad Ha-Am who first tore into the book with the cold passion of the secular Talmudist. His devastating attack, published in the fall of 1902 in his own *Hashiloah*, came perilously close to splitting the movement.

He began by skewering the fairy-tale aspects of *Altneuland*, not on literary grounds—which did not interest him—but because he quite rightly considered them symptomatic of the fantasies which Herzl and the "political" Zionists persistently indulged in. The mere suggestion that within only twenty years the majority of the world's Jews could be resettled in a utopian commonwealth by the Mediterranean struck him as irresponsible demagoguery. "A historical ideal requires a historical evolution, and historical evolution moves at a slow pace." But what, precisely, was the nature of this utopia, and what did it reveal about the mind of its author?

As he pointed out, everything about the New Society was copied from alien models. Moreover, not only did the Jews contribute nothing of their own, they also seemed strangely anxious not to play the dominant role in it. "Without distinction of nationality or religion—that is the spirit that animates the entire story, stressed in almost every chapter with such emphasis that it seems as though the author were chiefly concerned with assuring the 'outside world' that Zionism was a completely harmless enterprise." After criticizing Herzl's failure to even discuss the language question, Ahad Ha-Am, with a prescience noteworthy for its rarity in his day, went on to puncture Herzl's illusions about the Arabs and their attitude toward the new arrivals. "Peace and brotherly love reign between them and the Jews, who took nothing from them and gave them so much. A delightful idyll, indeed. Only, it is not quite clear how the New Society managed to obtain sufficient land for the millions of Jews from all over the world if all the arable land previously in Arab hands, i.e., most of the arable land in Palestine altogether, continues to remain in their hands as before."

He ended with a few sarcastic comments on the Solomonic Temple in Jerusalem, lovingly restored down to its last detail, and where "on Friday nights they sing 'Lecho Dodi' to organ music, just as they do in the Vienna synagogue. . . . But if we were curious, we might ask a more embarrassing question: Just where has this new Temple been built? On the Temple Mount stands, as we know, the Mosque of Omar; would the 'venerable Rabbi Samuel,' the friend of the Liberals, have allowed them to build the Temple elsewhere? But in *Altneuland* one does not wonder; the whole thing is one big wonder."

A German translation of Ahad Ha-Am's Hebrew review was prepared for the periodical *Ost und West*, whose editors as a matter of courtesy sent Herzl advance proofs to afford him an opportunity for rebuttal in the same issue. Herzl, evidently in a blind rage, abused their goodwill by passing the article on to Nordau instead and commissioned him to write a reply, which reached every important German-language Jewish publication before the *Ost und West* issue in question ever appeared.

Where Ahad Ha-Am had used a stiletto, Nordau used a truncheon. He was vitriolic far beyond the bounds of decency, and outrageous in his arrogance. Every inch the Defender of the West, he sallied forth to crush this reptilian specimen of Eastern degeneracy. "Ahad Ha-Am does not want tolerance. Aliens should be slaughtered, or at best chased out as they once were in Sodom and Gomorrah. The idea of tolerance disgusts him. Well, what disgusts us is to have a crippled, round-backed victim of intolerance, the despised slave of intolerant, knout-wielding *pogromchiks*, speak of tolerance in this manner. Ahad Ha-Am reproaches Herzl with aping the customs of Europe. He won't permit us to import academies, opera houses, and white gloves. The only things he wants to take with him to Altneuland are the guidelines of the Inquisition, the customs of the anti-Semites, and the anti-Jewish laws of Russia. Such perversion of the spirit would arouse nausea, if pity did not prevail."

The low point of his fulminations was an abusive personal attack on the man venerated for his probity, decency, and skeptical wisdom. "Ahad Ha-Am's sole merit is a passably good Hebrew. This is praiseworthy. Unfortunately he has nothing, absolutely nothing to say in this pleasant language. His so-called essays are insipid prattle whose presumptuous vapidity simply cannot be conveyed in words. . . . He belongs to the worst enemies of Zionism; for this secular-protest rabbi dares to pose as a Zionist and to distance himself from the real Zionism, the only one that exists, by calling it political Zionism."

The assault on their spiritual leader caused a riot in the ranks of the Democratic Faction. Buber immediately inquired if Herzl had approved of Nordau's piece and if he thought it conducive to harmony in the movement, but Herzl's evasive reply merely added fuel to the fire. Thereupon, Buber, Weizmann, and Feiwel published an open letter of protest in *Ha-Zman*, signed by an imposing number of prominent Zionists, which Herzl correctly construed as a personal attack. The outraged monarch in him now leaped to the defense of his faithful vassal: "Nordau has reacted with a blunt reply to an insidious attack. I don't think I need to point out that Mr. Guenzberg, who stands remote from my literary interests, has left me absolutely cold in his capacity as a literary critic. But the troublemaking enemy who sneaks into our ranks to undermine the morale of our comrades should at least be identified as such. No one, I think, can deny that this is in the interest of the movement."

He was lying, probably to himself more than to anyone else. Had only politics been involved, he would have known how to deal with the issues in his usual calculated and calculating manner. What made him foam at the mouth was the hurt vanity of the author whose dearest offspring had not merely been savaged but dismissed as fatuous, a narcissistic injury he found impossible to forgive. A week later, in reply to another appeal from Buber, he in effect accused him of treason. "Without going further into details," he wrote, "I won't conceal from you my view that the so-called faction has, for reasons unknown to me, fallen into error. My advice to you is: Find your way back to the movement."

It was a piece of advice that squarely joined the issue: since he was the movement, anyone against him was out of bounds. Buber curtly informed him that he and his friends did not need to find their way back, that they were as much a part of the movement as anyone else and, with all due respect, could not permit Herzl to decide otherwise.

The break never healed, although tenuous relations with some of the leaders of the faction—Buber among them—were eventually reestablished.

TWENTY~SEVEN

*T*rimmed of its sound and fury, the flap over *Altneuland* was merely one more dialogue of the deaf. A month earlier, over 500 delegates had attended an all-Russian conference of Zionists in Minsk. The informality of the week-long meetings, the expansive and meandering oratory—mostly in Russian, which even Ahad Ha-Am found himself constrained to use—and the impassioned all-night debates seldom cut short by gavels or bells made for a telling contrast to the rigid formality of Herzl's quasi-parliamentary congresses. Presided over by veterans of Hoveve Zion such as Lilienblum, Tchlenov, and the four-square Ussishkin with his foghorn voice, it was in fact wholly dominated by the schoolmasterly Ahad Ha-Am, whose stress on the cultural over the political components of Zionism constituted the main item on the agenda.

This was becoming an increasingly contentious issue between Herzl and his opponents, and the fact that neither side quite knew what the argument was all about merely intensified the acrimony. Herzl was not against culture, nor was Ahad Ha-Am opposed to a political solution, even if they differed in their priorities. Herzl, who vastly overestimated the influence and power of the rabbis in Eastern Europe, feared that even discussing cultural Zionism—utterly irrelevant anyway; you don't argue about the wallpaper before you've ever built the house—would revive the clash between Orthodoxy and enlightenment and cripple the movement. Besides, just what—aside from Hebrew, to which he was no longer opposed on principle—did these critics of his have in mind when they kept ranting about Jewish culture, considering that they had no use for religion?

Meeting this very challenge and defining the aims of the culturalists was the major purpose of the Minsk conference, and it proved a difficult task, not least because "culture" had become a rallying cry for all those who, while basically opposed to Herzl's autocratic rule, tried to give their personal resentment a veneer of objectivity. Ahad Ha-Am did his best. In a masterful speech, he pleaded for a Jewish education embracing both the secular and the religious branches of Judaism. The Orthodox, with their close ties to tradition, needed to link up with the national spirit, while secular learning had to be infused in all its aspects with the essence of national Judaism, in which the Hebrew language played a preeminent role. How these vague generalities were to be translated into practice he did not specify.

Nor did he need to—and therein lay the crux of the problem.

For Eastern European Jews to define Jewish culture was to define their very selves—the world in which they had grown up, the community of language, customs, and suffering, the traditions they either clung to or rebelled against, and the identity from which, for better or for worse, there was no escape. The differences in background between the Odessa sage and the Viennese journalist were fundamental and could not be reduced to theoretical formulations. Herzl's failure to grasp that fact—a failure of the imagination, above all—was to culminate in the tragic conflict which, if it did not kill him, certainly hastened his end.

After his fifth descent into the Turkish wonderland, Herzl was finally resigned to the futility of further efforts in that direction. There would be no Jewish state in Palestine as long as the Sultan had anything to say about it. In the meantime, another solution had to be found, because, as he put it, "I can wait, but the Jewish people cannot."

It was a half-truth he perhaps half believed in. His struggle against the ever more frequent and alarming manifestations of his physical decline—recurrent blackouts, heart trouble, pain, and paralyzing fatigue—was little short of heroic and made sense only in the context of the larger struggle for the ultimate goal. He knew that his days were numbered and that it was he who could not wait.

But in ascribing his pursuit of at least temporary alternatives to strictly personal ambition, his critics did a grave injustice to the complexities of the man and his motives. He no doubt longed to see some of his work accomplished and to still catch a glimpse of the Promised Land—even if promised by England rather than God—and who could blame him? At the same time, however, he had become the captive of his own legend, thrust into a role which far transcended that of a political leader, and begun to assume the responsibilities of the Messianic spokesman for the Jewish masses. His concern for the plight of East European Jewry was genuine and heartfelt. The desperate situation in Russia and Rumania affected him profoundly, and he was convinced that the Jews in those countries could indeed not wait much longer. "If only you had an idea of the boundless misery of our honest poor—I am not talking about *shnorrers* and rabble—you would listen to me better," he wrote to Rothschild in August. "I am enclosing a random newspaper clipping, the likes of which I could send you every day from any number of countries. I cannot count the number of letters I get from workers, businessmen, academics. With a sigh I have to tell them: I cannot help you. People like these don't want a handout—they wouldn't turn to me for that—but a chance to work, and a life safe from persecution" (D, 8/12/02).

Having reached the ultimate dead end in the Turkish maze, he now began to shift his attention to Britain as the last best hope. Cyprus, El Arish, and Sinai (which he called Egyptian Palestine), exotic names casually invoked to impress Lord Rothschild, suddenly assumed a hard-edged and even tempting reality as alternatives to a Turkish charter; a Jewish homestead in any of these could be rationalized as a temporary expedient, a proving ground and staging area for the eventual move into Palestine. Leopold Greenberg, a British publicist and recent convert to Zionism—he later became publisher of the London *Jewish Chronicle*—had access to Joseph Chamberlain, the Colonial Secretary; both men came from Birmingham and had been flaming radicals in their youth. On September 22, he informed Herzl that Chamberlain was ready to see him, but it took Herzl another month to disentangle himself from the *Neue Freie Presse*, engaged at just that moment in deadly combat with a new and aggressive competitor. In the end, he never did work up the courage to ask for a leave and simply sneaked off instead like a truant schoolboy, feeling guilty and again fretting all through his London stay about whether he would be fired.

The Colonial Secretary received him on October 22. Not quite "the famous master of England," as Herzl apostrophized him, Chamberlain nonetheless was "the man who made the weather," in Winston

Churchill's phrase, and undoubtedly among the most influential politicians of his day. A classic bureaucrat and outstanding administrator,
he subscribed to all the brainless prejudices of his tribe and, while not
averse to socializing with individual Jews, considered the "race" as a
whole—he was big on race—a decidedly inferior breed. This racist
snobbism, however, made him particularly receptive to the arguments
Herzl had advanced before the Royal Commission. An additional
factor was his lifelong ambition to enlarge the frontiers and spread the
blessings of British rule; a reservoir of Jewish manpower, money, and
goodwill which, aside from diverting the flow of immigration from
Britain proper, could also spearhead an eventual British advance into
Palestine struck him as an appealing notion.

Herzl had carefully composed his introductory sentence in English:
"You are accustomed to see rise suddenly before you great historical
questions." Chamberlain's "immobile mask" and his icy formality
apparently made him think better of it, and he improvised his speech
as best he could, disconcerted as much by Chamberlain's impenetrable
gaze as by his own at times equally impenetrable English. But his
account of doing business at Yildiz Palace eventually broke the ice—
"the mask laughed"—and gave him a chance to come to the point:
Cyprus, El Arish, and Sinai.

As Colonial Secretary, Chamberlain explained, he could only discuss Cyprus (which, though ceded in 1878 to Britain as a base for
supporting Turkey against Russia, was theoretically still part of the
Ottoman Empire); the other two came under the jurisdiction of the
Foreign Office. And Cyprus, as he pointed out, was populated by
Greeks and Muslims, whom he could not simply drive out for the
sake of Jewish immigrants. Not that he personally had anything against
Jews, he hastened to add; on the contrary, if he had a drop of Jewish
blood in his veins, he would be proud of it. (But *voilà*, adds Herzl,
"he didn't.") In fact, he found the Zionist idea most appealing, "and
if I could show him a British possession where there were as yet no
white men, one might talk business."

Despair, though it may have exacerbated the blatant naïveté of
Herzl's counterargument, does not excuse it. "We should be invited
[into Cyprus]," he told Chamberlain. "I would have the ground prepared by half a dozen emissaries. Once we establish a Jewish Eastern
Company with 5 million pounds for Sinai and El Arish, the Cypriots
will be eager to have that gold rain on their island as well. The Muslims
will leave, the Greeks will sell their land at good prices and move to

Athens or Crete." A self-serving delusion which all too many of his successors also indulged in.

To his credit, Chamberlain remained unconvinced, but he held out hope for El Arish, though he had no idea where it was and let Herzl point it out to him on the map. Seeing that it was next door to Egypt, he again became doubtful. "But in Egypt we'd have the same problem with the natives."

"No," replied Herzl, "we will not go to Egypt. We have been there."

He summed up his impression of Chamberlain: "Not brilliant. No imagination, a sober screw manufacturer who wants to expand his business. A mind devoid of literary or artistic resources, a businessman, but with a clear, unclouded head" (D, 10/22/02).

No Prussian Junker, in other words. Still, he judged the interview "a colossal success" and, with Chamberlain's blessings, went to see Lord Lansdowne. The Foreign Secretary seemed accommodatingly indifferent; neither personally nor in his official capacity did the Jews and their problems hold the slightest interest for him. But he deftly passed the buck: he could not commit himself without approval from Lord Cromer, nominally Britain's consul general in Cairo for the past twenty years but, in actual fact, the resident monarch. It was agreed that Leopold Greenberg, as Herzl's plenipotentiary, would immediately leave for Egypt to negotiate with Cromer.

The contrast between the cool efficiency and professionalism of British bureaucracy and the red tape, procrastination, and malignant pomposity of Habsburg officialdom made a deep impression on Herzl. Lansdowne, for his part, immediately alerted his formidable proconsul in a memo which suggests that behind the façade of bland amiability, the Foreign Secretary did have some thoughts of his own:

I was interviewed yesterday by Dr. Hertzel [sic], an Austrian Jew who is interested in the Zionist movement. He had made the acquaintance of Chamberlain who asked me to see him. I am told he is respectable, and he impressed me favorably. His idea is to get hold of a tract near El Arish and there to establish a colony of carefully selected Hebrews. I suggested, but without much effect, that they were not likely to make very good settlers and that El Arish might not be exactly the spot upon which to dump Jews from the East End of London or from Odessa.

He told me that he and his friends were sending out at once to Cairo one Mr. Gruneberg [sic] to collect information and I promised that I would mention the matter to you and explain the nature of Gruneberg's mission.

I think he should be civilly received by the authorities, although it is impossible for me to express any opinion as to the merits of this scheme, which seems to be very visionary. [Lansdowne to Cromer, 10/24/02. Quoted in Vital, *The Formative Years*, p. 147]

Once again Herzl, with his seemingly inexhaustible capacity for bouncing back from defeat, was exultant as he left London the next morning: "Yesterday, I think, was a great day in Jewish history." But the trip had nonetheless been a tremendous strain, and on October 28, barely back in Vienna, he faced another ordeal, the annual conference of the Zionist Action Committee. Its members were far less sanguine, and not shy about voicing their misgivings. They objected that El Arish was technically part of Egypt, which in turn was still a vassal state of the Sultan, even though in fact ruled by Britain. Was it worth the risk of becoming yet one more party to this complicated arrangement for the sake of an arid strip of desert in the middle of nowhere?

Herzl, as usual, got his way in the end, but the excitement proved too much. After the meeting he collapsed and this time remained totally incapacitated for a week, unable even to hold a pen. For only the second time in his career at the *Neue Freie Presse* he reported sick and spent two weeks at Edlach, a mountain resort in Lower Austria, where Greenberg reported to him on his way back from Cairo.

The results of his emissary's three days in Egypt proved more therapeutic than the enforced rest. "My heart again beats more regularly." Greenberg had indeed been civilly received by Lord Cromer, by the Egyptian puppet Prime Minister Boutros Gali-Pasha, and by an array of lower-level functionaries, a strictly routine procedure which Herzl, however, took to mean that "they had been won over to our cause." With the help of Greenberg, Zangwill, and Nordau, who persuaded him to cut out some of the more flowery passages, he drafted a formal memorandum for submission to the Foreign Office.

Chamberlain himself, on the first leg of an extended fact-finding trip to East Africa, stopped off in Cairo to discuss the matter with Cromer, who raised no principled objections to the plan but had some legal and technical reservations. He questioned the special status for the colonists implied in the phrase "colonial rights" and, since the Sinai—which he admittedly had never troubled to visit personally—appeared to him quite unsuitable for settlement, he made his final approval dependent on the findings of a commission of inquiry, which should include impartial non-Jewish experts. Finally, the settlers would have to be subject to Egyptian law, "otherwise I do not think that the project should be entertained."

On December 22, the British Foreign Office, in a letter which Herzl qualified as "a historic document," notified him to that effect and invited him to dispatch a commission to the Sinai. And for once the hyperbole was warranted, at least in retrospect; the letter recognized Herzl as a serious partner in negotiations and constitutes the first formal dealings between the British government and political Zionism.

In his euphoria, he immediately let himself get carried away by visions of a flourishing Jewish colony, with highways and railroads taming the desert and linking a great Mediterranean port with the mountainous hinterland, irrigated by Nile water diverted by a system of siphons and pipes running underneath the Suez Canal. But sitting in his office on New Year's Eve and getting ready once again to slink off furtively to Paris and London, he had another of the increasingly severe fainting spells. This time he was unconscious long enough to be frightened, but he nonetheless left the next morning as planned.

No sooner had he arrived in London than Rothschild—"the man who two years ago would not even meet me at Lady Battersea's"—came to see him at his hotel. Herzl briefed him on the latest developments, asked him to raise 3 million pounds for the Jewish Eastern Company, and offered him the financial leadership of the entire project. Rothschild declined. "No, you are the leader, Dr. Herzl. I only want to be your collaborator. I shall be pleased to be of help to you."

Later in the day Herzl and Greenberg met with Sir Thomas Sanderson at the Foreign Office to settle the itinerary and personnel of the proposed Sinai expedition. They chose Leopold Kessler, a South African Zionist and experienced mining engineer, as the leader; the other members were Oskar Marmorek, the Viennese architect; Emile Laurent, a Belgian agricultural expert; Dr. Hillel Joffe, a Jaffa physician; and the seesawing Daniel Deronda, alias Colonel Goldsmid, whose flagging enthusiasm for the cause was once more on the upswing. He had no special expertise to contribute, but Herzl was counting on him for an introduction to King Edward VII and agreed to pay him the £100 over and above traveling expenses he demanded for his participation. Greenberg, who was to go along as liaison to Cromer and the Egyptians, asked for a £500 loan in lieu of compensation.

Two weeks later the explorers assembled in Cairo and, after a briefing by Cromer, mounted their camels and took off on a journey whose very real hardships were greatly eased by Thomas Cook's efficient staff, services, and equipment. Herzl, back in Vienna, had few doubts about the outcome. "I hope the expedition will return safe and sound in a few weeks," he wrote to Rothschild, "and soon thereafter I should be in possession of the charter."

It was this volatile mix of optimism and self-delusion that kept him going in spite of illness and exhaustion. But with his head in the clouds, he was blind to the facts on the ground. On February 16, Greenberg cabled from Cairo that the Sultan's man, acting on instructions from Constantinople, was doing all he could to obstruct the mission. "Do not forget khedive [viceroy] is subject to Sultan." Herzl, conversant with Turkish customs, immediately instructed Greenberg to offer the fellow "two thousand pounds after charter signed by Egyptian government." But the following day Greenberg cabled that it was impossible to obtain a charter, and that, in line with Cromer's instructions, he had prepared an "alternative" then under consideration by the Egyptians.

Baffled and furious, Herzl demanded a full explanation, instead of which Greenberg left Cairo and, without stopping off in Vienna or providing any further information, proceeded directly to London. His evasiveness aroused Herzl's darkest suspicions, which were not allayed by the report of which Greenberg finally delivered himself. Instead of a charter, all he had brought back was a letter from the Egyptian Prime Minister granting the settlers essentially the same rights as enjoyed by other non-Muslims.

Herzl felt betrayed. Always loath to delegate authority, he had from the very outset resented being cast in a passive supporting role and was now convinced that Greenberg had not only failed properly to represent him but was also plotting to usurp the leadership of the project. Adding to the tension were inconclusive interim reports from the expedition still roaming the biblical wilderness. By mid-March he was no longer able to bear the suspense and inactivity; convinced that only he himself could bring matters to a satisfactory conclusion, he took off for Cairo, where he arrived on March 24. The following morning he had his first interview with Lord Cromer, "the most unpleasant Englishman I have ever met."

The dislike was mutual.

In the twenty years of his all but absolute reign, which began with the British occupation of Egypt in 1882, Cromer had skillfully expanded his power and influence far beyond his nominal position and achieved a status largely isolated from the vicissitudes of domestic politics. He was an empire builder of the old school, a cool, immensely capable administrator, ruthless and rigid, but genuinely concerned for the welfare of his subjects insofar as it contributed to the strength and stability of British rule. Herzl's un-English excitability, his wild schemes for building railroads in the desert and diverting Nile water instantly antagonized him, and he made his feelings rather plain by pointedly asking when Mr. Greenberg was coming back. Though ostensibly willing to support the project, he was not going to be rushed. Everything depended on the conclusions of his own expert, but in any case the settlers could expect no rights not granted to the natives. Three days later, reporting to Sanderson on the substance of the interview, Cromer was even more outspoken: "Dr. Herzl is, I understand, going to London. He is a wild enthusiast. Be careful not to pledge yourself *to anything* in dealing with him. Goldsmid is more businesslike" (HY, Vol. I, p. 116).

While waiting for the return of the expedition, Herzl spent three days brooding over the impasse with Cromer, for which he blamed his fatigue and general poor health. Nevertheless, he used the time for a fleeting glance at the country and its people. Attending a boring lecture on the irrigation of Mesopotamia, he was struck by the large number of intelligent-looking young Egyptians in the audience. "They are the coming masters. It seems amazing that the British fail to see this. They think they will forever be dealing with *fellahin*. . . . The British are doing magnificent work. They are cleaning up the Orient, bringing light and air into filthy nooks and crannies, breaking up entrenched tyrannies, and doing away with abuses. But along with liberty and progress they are also teaching the *fellahin* to rebel" (D, 3/26/03). He also forced himself to write a long, lyrical, and rather melancholy mood piece about Egypt for the *Neue Freie Presse* to atone for his latest truancy. And on the way to the pyramids, he caught a glimpse of the native hovels just a few miles beyond the metropolis and was shocked by the "indescribable misery. I am determined to think of the *fellahin*, too, once I am in power."

A few days later the expedition returned with what Herzl considered generally encouraging findings. They had indeed done a thorough job and discovered promising resources in mining and fishing, but their final conclusion would have seemed anything but encouraging to a dispassionate reader:

> The result of the Commission's research has been, that in their opinion, under existing conditions, the country is quite unsuitable for settlers from European countries; but from what they have seen on the spot, and from the experience of individual members of the Commission, they can confidently state that were a sufficient water supply forthcoming, the conditions of soil, hygiene and climate are such, that part of what is now desert, would be capable of supporting a considerable population. In short, the whole question is one of water supply, the furnishing of which would involve great capital expenditure. [HY, Vol. I, p. 135]

This in fact shifted the entire debate from the realm of politics to that of technology, and there was no arguing with facts and figures. Although Herzl, on Cromer's instructions, drew up the draft of a concession to be submitted to the Egyptian government, he was beginning to realize that the ultimate decision rested solely with the proconsul, whose irrigation expert, Sir William Gastin, was not expected to submit his findings before the end of the month. Unable to overcome Cromer's dislike of him, Herzl glumly departed on April 4, leaving Colonel Goldsmid behind as his representative.

With only a three-day stop in Vienna, he continued on to Paris, where he wasted a week haggling for funds from the Jewish Colonization Association and gained the cautious, conditional support of Baron Edmond, one of the French Rothschilds. It was the week of the Kishinev pogrom, a preview of coming disasters; but news of what, by pre-Auschwitz standards, was a particularly gruesome example of government-sponsored brutality was slow to reach the outside world, and Herzl did not learn of it until April 23, when he arrived in London.

Deeply worried about Cromer's intentions, he immediately rushed out to see Chamberlain, who had just returned from his African inspection tour and received him with a great show of cordiality. The commission's report was already on his desk. "Not very favorable," he commented. Herzl was forced to agree. "It is a very poor country, but we are going to make something of it."

Whereupon, with studied casualness, Chamberlain held out a booby-trapped lure.

"On my trip I have seen another country for you—Uganda. It is hot on the coast, but farther inland the climate is excellent, even for Europeans. You could plant sugar and cotton there. So I thought to myself, This would be a country for Dr. Herzl. But of course he only wants to go to Palestine or some nearby place."

Herzl resisted the temptation, this first time around. "I have to," he said. "We must have a base in or near Palestine. Later we might also settle Uganda, because we have masses of people ready to emigrate. But we must build on the basis of nationalism, that is why we need the political appeal of El Arish."

Chamberlain did not argue the point, though he obviously disapproved of mixing politics and sentiment. He foresaw an imminent clash in the Middle East involving France, Germany, and Russia, while England was increasingly committed elsewhere. "What would then be the fate of your Jewish colony in Palestine, even if you had succeeded in establishing it?"

Herzl shrugged. As a small buffer state, he explained, "we shall get it not from the goodwill but from the jealousy of the powers" (English in the original). "And if we are in El Arish under the Union Jack, our Palestine will also be part of the British sphere of influence."

The conversation ended inconclusively; there was no indication that Chamberlain would flout the traditions of British bureaucracy by interfering in the decisions of another department.

Further attempts to raise funds consumed another week in London and in Paris; the financiers were mildly interested but unwilling to commit themselves until all the facts were in. And so, still clinging desperately to a few remaining scraps of hope, Herzl finally returned home on April 29, looking forward to a much-needed spell of domestic peace. Instead, he was welcomed by a long-suffering wife fed up with Zionism and with the self-righteous arrogance of an absentee husband and father who had squandered her own and her children's inheritance while ruining his health and his career. Her rage on this occasion seems to have been truly spectacular, and while over the years Herzl had trained himself to meet these outbursts with stoical and infuriating calm, they nonetheless shook him profoundly.

This latest episode came at a particularly difficult time. By the end of the week it had become clear that the Sinai project was doomed. In the opinion of Cromer's expert, the Nile could not possibly supply enough water for the colony, even if the scheme for diverting and siphoning it under the Suez Canal were technically and economically feasible, which he strongly doubted. The findings provided a justification for Cromer's political objections, and on May 7 he broke off all further discussions, informing the Foreign Office that he was convinced "nothing could be done in the direction of Dr. Herzl's wishes without the exercise, on the part of His Majesty's Government, of a far stronger pressure than the circumstances of the case would, in any degree, justify."

Another dead end.

"I considered the Sinai project so imminent that I did not want to bother buying a family vault in the Doebling cemetery, where my father is temporarily laid to rest," Herzl wrote on May 16. "Now I consider it so hopeless that I have already been to the district office and am acquiring vault No. 28." His secretary, A. H. Reich, who arranged for the exhumation and transfer, strongly advised him to stay away, "and he agreed that it would be better. But after we had finished, Herzl came nonetheless; he had been too restless not to come, he said. He was deeply moved; as he looked down into the grave, his figure swayed. Then, suddenly, he said to me: Soon, very soon, I too shall lie down there" (THM, p. 122).

Earlier in the year, moved by the same dark forebodings, he had drawn up his third and last Will, dated March 5, 1903. It was even more vindictive than his two previous ones. He designated his three children as the heirs to all his property, consisting "of the deposit at the Union Bank, the contents of the safe deposit box at the Länderbank, 1,680 shares of the Jewish Colonial Trust, the now worthless shares of the dissolved Society for Jewish Periodicals, the rights to publication and authorship of all my writings . . . and a one-eighth share in the tuberculosis serum of Dr. Alexander Marmorek in Paris."

He stipulated, however, that "the usufruct of my entire estate go, until her death, to my beloved, good mother Jeanette Herzl, née Diamant, to whom I am indebted with everlasting gratitude. But I ask her to give to my wife, Mrs. Julie Herzl née Naschauer, that part of her income which exceeds her needs. My mother shall be at complete liberty to determine the amount she needs for her living expenses. With the exception of my author's rights, all the property I still own derives from my beloved, unforgettable father, Jakob Herzl."

He still found it incumbent upon him to meet Julie's reproaches by lame counter-charges: "During the nearly fourteen years of my marriage, I, together with my wife, consumed her dowry. I had to use it because my wife made such demands in the household that I was unable to meet these expenditures solely with my income as a writer. I was also justified in using the dowry, not only because it was jointly consumed, but also because, knowing of my parents' fortune, I was certain that her dowry would be repaid later; either to her, or to our dear children."

It was a stunning admission of near-bankruptcy by a man with a substantial income who had married into a great deal of money. Considering the amounts he spent on travel, bribes, *Die Welt*, and various other ventures and adventurers, there was something near-pathological about his need to put the blame on Julie. What happened to his parents' fortune he does not trouble to explain; presumably it was consumed by his mother, who survived until 1911.

He left instructions to be buried in a metal casket and laid to rest next to his father "until the Jewish people transfer my remains to Palestine. Likewise, the coffins of my father, of my sister, Pauline . . . and of members of my immediate family (mother and children) should be brought to Palestine. My wife only if she so declares in her last Will."

His son, Hans, was to be raised in England, if possible; his friend Joseph Cowen had promised to make the necessary arrangements. "Let my children bear my name in honor. I have brought honor to it."

Yet already some months earlier it had become apparent to him that the assets of his estate would be insufficient to provide for his children. In a letter dated November 8, 1901, which he entrusted to Wolffsohn in a sealed envelope to be opened after his death, he declared that he had "poured enormous sums into our dream" and neglected to think of his own children, a statement considerably closer to the truth than the self-serving remarks in his Will. He appealed to Wolffsohn to launch a drive in their behalf under the slogan "The

Nation's Gift to the Children of Dr. Herzl" as soon as possible after his death, while the magic of his name still had the power to make people respond to the call. Wolffsohn, faithful in this as in everything else, carried out his instructions to the letter.

For several more weeks, Herzl persisted in futile attempts to reverse Cromer's decision by appealing to a higher instance. But in this respect also, British bureaucracy differed from the brand he was familiar with. London politicians were much more apt to respect the opinions of the professional civil servants in the field; with the Boer War still an open wound, none would have risked antagonizing a native population in defiance of warnings from the resident administrator. In the event, moreover, no one but Herzl seriously disputed Cromer's conclusions, and on July 16, a letter from the Foreign Office put a definite stop to any further discussion of the matter.

Chamberlain, on the other hand, to whom Herzl had turned for support—and whose interest and goodwill he probably overestimated— had no intention of interfering in the affairs of a fiefdom not his own; it would have been bad form and bad politics. But in an interview with Greenberg on March 20, he repeated his offer of "Uganda." (It soon became clear that the territory in question was part of what is now Kenya, near the Uganda border, but the term has stuck and become part of Zionist history.)

Greenberg reported that the Kishinev pogrom, by bearing out Herzl's prediction, had made of Chamberlain "a convinced Zionist." The tract he was proposing had an excellent climate and could support at least a million settlers. "I did not press it upon Dr. Herzl," Chamberlain told Greenberg, "because I sympathized with his desire to satisfy the sentimental idea in regard to Palestine, and I quite saw that the El Arish plan to some extent did so. But, if that comes to nothing, I do hope Dr. Herzl will consider very seriously the suggestion. At the moment there is nothing in the way of his having the place, but it will not be long vacant as there are undoubtedly large mining prospects, apart from all else."

Greenberg added that in his opinion an offer from the British government would of itself constitute a political coup, and the East African territory "could be used in the nature of a drill ground for our national forces."

Herzl concurred. "Having Goldsmid's report who left yesterday for London," he wired back, "I consider El Arish impossible for next years. We must take therefore Chamberlain's proposition in serious consideration provided it is really advantageous" (D, 5/23/03—English in original).

TWENTY-EIGHT

*I*n retrospect, after nearly a century of unprecedented progress in organized butchery, mass murder, and the technology of genocide, the Kishinev pogrom seems an almost trivial episode in the history of anti-Semitism. By today's standards, the toll—49 dead, 495 injured, a large number of mostly unreported rapes, some 1,500 stores and workshops looted and destroyed, and about 20 percent of the town's Jewish population left homeless—would hardly rate more than a thirty-second spot on the evening news. In 1903, the news traveled more slowly; but when it finally did reach the outside world, it had a devastating impact.

The carnage as such did not differ substantially from the atrocities perpetrated many times before; only ten years earlier, the same drunken mobs had ravaged the ghettos of the Pale, killing, raping, burning, and looting with the same depraved bestiality. And yet, Kishinev signaled a new and ominous stage in the Jewish struggle for survival.

Where, in the past, local authorities had for the most part passively sanctioned mob violence by their refusal to suppress it, the Kishinev riots were actively inspired and supported at the highest levels of the Russian government, a precedent-setting first step down the slope from institutional persecution to physical extermination. Evidence soon emerged which directly implicated Vyacheslav K. Plehve, the Minister of the Interior, and Konstantin Pobyedonostsev, the Procurator of the Holy Synod, two fanatical Jew-baiters whose zeal scarcely required the additional encouragement they received from the Czar, his maniacal German wife, and their entourage of unholy fools and sinister fanatics.

Moreover, what stoked the fires in Kishinev was not only the traditional blood libel but a new and even more insidious kind of lie. The myth of the Jewish world conspiracy in one of its earliest versions was first published and peddled in Kishinev as *The Rabbi's Speech* by P. Krushevan, the editor of an anti-Semitic local rag with contacts in the highest places. It served as model for the notorious *Protocols of the Elders of Zion* fabricated by the Russian secret police a few years later.

Equally disturbing was the reaction of Kishinev's non-Jews to the atrocities and their aftermath. According to an eyewitness account in the semiofficial *St. Petersburg Gazette* that somehow slipped past the censors, "The better class of the Christian public behaved disgracefully. They did not raise a finger to put a stop to the plunder and assaults. They walked calmly along and gazed at these horrible spectacles with the utmost indifference. Many of them even rode through the streets in their carriages in holiday attire in order to witness the cruelties that were being perpetrated" (Quoted in the London *Jewish Chronicle*, May 8, 1903).

This, too, fails to surprise, a century later. But one powerful voice was raised in protest. "When the first news came out," wrote Tolstoy, "I began to grasp the full horror of what happened and felt a deep compassion for the innocent victims, indignation at the bestiality of these so-called Christians, and at the same time disgust for the so-called civilized people who incite these mobs and sympathize with their crimes. But I was especially horrified by the main culprits—our government, its predatory functionaries and its clergy, who whip up fanaticism and bestiality. The crime of Kishinev is the direct consequence of the propaganda of violence and lies promoted with such energy by the Russian government." The protest, needless to say, was suppressed but widely circulated in the underground.

The most significant new element in Kishinev, however, was the reaction of Russia's Jews, a mixture of rage and shame that broke with the centuries-old tradition of plaintive martyrdom and yet found itself powerless in the face of what was no longer a local pogrom but a *national* trauma. Chaim Nachman Bialik, their greatest poet, expressed those feelings in his "Ballad of Nemirov." (The fact that "Nemirov" fooled the censors confirms the general low opinion of their intellectual equipment.)

Great is the pain, but great, too, is the shame
Yours to decide which is the greater.
They beat their breasts, confess their sins,
Proclaim their guilt. The heart cannot believe the mouth.
They ask forgiveness—what is there to forgive? Let them demand
    vengeance instead.

Kishinev further radicalized Jewish youth and strengthened both the Zionist movement and the socialist Bund. It also ended any realistic hopes for a gradual liberalization and stimulated systematic efforts at self-defense, some of them reasonably successful. But above all, Kishinev became a symbol—of impotence, of rage, and of the precariousness of life in the ghettos of Russia.

Herzl, though he had predicted as much and foresaw worse to come, was horrified as the full scope of the tragedy began to emerge. On May 8, *Die Welt* published his "Kishinev and the Sardines," a rather flat-footed and maudlin editorial, but its very flaws attest to the turbulent emotions that inspired it. The two great controversies that clouded the final months of his life were probably unavoidable in any case; but by lending a new, desperate urgency to his efforts, Kishinev defined the issues between him and his opponents more sharply than ever before.

To Herzl, saving the Jews was the supreme task and rationale of Zionism. A Jewish state in Palestine would have been the ideal solution, but as long as Palestine seemed beyond reach, other ways had to be found to rescue the masses desperately in need of immediate help. To the opposition, Zionism meant above all the establishment of a national home in Palestine. It alone could save the Jews; to settle for any other temporary expedient was merely to perpetuate the disasters of the Diaspora. As for the suffering masses, they had suffered for two millennia; a few more years would make little difference.

The argument continued long after Herzl's death. In 1938, Ben-Gurion, soon to be the first Prime Minister of the Jewish state, declared at a central committee meeting of the Labor Party that if he knew he could save either *all* the Jewish children of Germany by transporting them to England or only half of them by bringing them to the land of Israel, he would not hesitate to choose the latter, because "before us lies not only the numbers of these children but the historical reckoning of the people of Israel." Ben-Gurion, as yet ignorant of the true horror of the threat, undoubtedly overstated his case; but where, in the absence of a strong Jewish presence in Palestine, would the survivors of the Holocaust have been welcomed seven years later?

One may disagree with Herzl's position. But however muddled his thinking at times, and however mixed his motives, what predominated at that moment was compassion and a nobility of purpose for which—certainly in his day—he received far less credit than he deserved.

Herzl's enthusiasm for the Uganda project was in any case minimal from the outset. Unlike even El Arish, it failed to stir his imagination, but there were what seemed to him sound and compelling reasons for following up on it, or at the very least for not rejecting it out of hand. For one thing, "Great Joe" Chamberlain was a powerful but capricious and vindictive politician; by turning down his proposal Herzl risked antagonizing a hard-won supporter and key player in any further dealings with Britain. Furthermore, Greenberg's point that it implied "recognition of the necessity of aiding our people as a whole . . . and hence the first recognition of our people as a Nation" seemed well taken. And finally, the sixth Zionist congress, scheduled to meet in Basel on August 23, was almost upon him. His diplomatic initiatives had thus far yielded nothing of substance and drawn increasing criticism over the years; he deemed it imperative this time to come up with some concrete results to silence the opposition. And finally Uganda, while not yet Palestine, was better than nothing and would provide a way station for those eager to escape new and ever more bloody Kishinevs.

True to his usual tactics, he did not cease to explore other possibilities and clutched at whatever straws happened to float within reach. He went to see the Portuguese ambassador about a concession on Mozambique, inquired about a tract in the Belgian Congo, and renewed his contacts with the Turks. He even came up with a quasi-ideological justification for these hopeless schemes: instead of a motherland founding colonies, the Jews would found colonies and go on from there to conquer the motherland.

Yet the fact is that he pursued none of these initiatives with anything like his customary vigor, either because his heart was not really in them or because the illness was rapidly draining his energies. He therefore authorized Greenberg to submit a tentative agreement to the British Foreign Office, formally responsible for the African protectorate. The firm of Lloyd George, Roberts and Co. was hired to draw up the actual document; as a Member of Parliament and a well-connected politician familiar with East Africa, David Lloyd George was a logical and perhaps fortuitous choice; it may not have been wholly coincidental that fourteen years later the Balfour Declaration, with its promise of a Jewish homeland in Palestine, was issued during Lloyd George's tenure as Prime Minister.

In its initial response, the Foreign Office objected to what it saw as an attempt to establish "an empire within an empire." Greenberg agreed to a number of changes, but his most pressing concern at the moment was to obtain a British statement of intent in time for the congress, and in this the Foreign Office obliged. On August 14, Sir Clement Hill, Superintendent of African Protectorates, confirmed the government's readiness, in principle, to grant the Jewish Colonial Trust certain territorial concessions in the protectorate and promised to facilitate any preliminary investigations.

Here at last was the concrete offer that vindicated Herzl's strategy and gave him something to present to the delegates. Yet his uneasy ambivalence about the whole scheme is evident from his correspondence with Nordau, whom he coyly asked at the end of June to deal with "the subject of migration in general" in his annual congress speech. Nordau refused. Migration in general, he pointed out, was the sort of topic good only for windy rhetoric, but the migration of the Jews in particular raised many questions which he did not feel qualified to answer. In his reply, Herzl invoked Kishinev—the Jews simply had to go somewhere, and the Sultan had to be shown that they had other choices. Nordau was unimpressed; what was the point of urging Jews to emigrate if you could not tell them where to go? This rather obvious question at last "reminded" Herzl, as he disingenuously put it in his letter of July 6, to initiate Nordau into the Uganda project.

Nordau was outraged. Attuned far more closely than Herzl to the feelings of the Eastern European Jews and to their attachment to Palestine, he denounced the plan in the sharpest terms as a dangerous folly. The Jews would never follow Herzl to Uganda, no matter how much he waved the blue-and-white flag; if they could neither go to Palestine nor stay where they were, they would head for England, America, or Australia. And anyway, all they could look forward to in tropical Africa was a chance to exploit black labor in the manner of the British colonials; what would this do for the moral regeneration of the Jewish people? He concluded by warning that the proposal could only split the movement, and he urged Herzl to not even think of bringing it up.

It was the first reaction by an outsider not privy to the negotiations, and a mild foretaste of things to come. The uncharacteristically conciliatory, almost apologetic tone of Herzl's reply indicates that for once he was less than certain of his grounds. "Have you suddenly lost all faith in me? Do you take me for a man completely thoughtless in such serious matters? When El Arish failed, I simply had to reconsider the Uganda offer. An English colonist will declare Uganda much better than El Arish, a Zionist will say it is much worse. But it is the task of leadership to point the way to the goal, even by a detour, if necessary. Moses himself went through the same experience. And if there is a rebellion in the ranks, we shall just have to deal with it."

In his next letter, he went so far as to concede that the territory might indeed not be suitable, but even if this turned out to be so, the movement would still have gained a major political asset—"a charter, which is to say, recognition. Our road to Zion will have to be paved with charters. And I can then present this *state treaty* as a model, particularly to the Sultan, and that will carry enormous weight."

Nordau finally agreed not to oppose the plan in public, but the question of his congress speech remained unsettled, because Herzl was about to embark on another venture, equally controversial but far more dramatic. On August 5, he left for Russia.

Over the years, Herzl's repeated attempts to make contact with Russian government circles had been consistently rebuffed. In time, more pressing issues had led him to suspend further efforts in that direction, the more so since it was never quite clear what, exactly, he hoped to achieve in the first place. True, Russia was a powerful neighbor of Turkey, and Herzl thought highly enough of his personal magic to believe that, given a chance, he could persuade the autocrat of St. Petersburg to get rid of his Jewish revolutionaries by pressuring the despot of the Yildiz into letting them settle in Palestine. But these hopes faded in the wake of the Turkish fiasco, and he did not turn his attention back to Russia until after the collapse of the El Arish project, when two facts combined to make it seem imperative: the Kishinev pogrom, and the government's threat to outlaw Zionism in Russia.

Kishinev had provoked a storm of indignation around the world and not only inflamed public opinion but raised grave doubts in political and financial circles about the Russian government's ability—and willingness—to maintain law and order. Herzl shrewdly and correctly judged it an opportune moment to offer its leaders a chance to redeem themselves in the eyes of the West by some propitiatory gesture in the direction of the Jews. It was, however, the mortal threat to Russian Zionism that decided him to intervene at once, and in person; if the ban was imposed before the end of August, no delegates from Russia would be able to attend the congress.

Throughout the nineteenth century, the sum and substance of internal Russian policy was to suppress any and all opposition to the feudal autocracy. One inevitable result was the emergence of the secret police as the most powerful component of the government, and the only one that functioned with any degree of efficiency. Its huge army of spies and informers infiltrated any group ever so remotely suspected of potentially subversive inclinations, and the Zionists were no exception. In the early years, however, the movement was judged harmless enough to be tolerated, although local officials frequently interfered on their own initiative.

But in April 1902 a terrorist bomb killed D. S. Sipyagin, the relatively moderate Minister of the Interior. He was succeeded by Vyacheslav K. Plehve, formerly chief of the Okhrana, a cunning, ruthless, but highly intelligent policeman of rare organizational ability, fanatically dedicated to the defense of the autocracy. His immediate crackdown on the revolutionaries, a disproportionate number of whom turned out to be Jews, led to closer scrutiny of the Zionist movement and convinced him that its goal was no longer simply emigration but— as proved by the discussions at the Minsk conference—the propagation of Jewish nationalism, a decidedly subversive activity. In June 1903, in an order to provincial governors and senior police commanders, he initiated a close surveillance of all Zionist activities pending a ukase outlawing the movement altogether. Its Russian leaders immediately notified Herzl of these developments, though arguments later broke out over whether they had merely meant to keep him informed, or whether they were asking for his personal intervention. In any event, he chose to act.

His earlier requests for interviews, addressed directly to Plehve and Pobyedonostsev right after Kishinev, had remained unanswered. This time he enlisted the help of Mme Korwin-Piatrovska, a Polish writer

residing in St. Petersburg who sympathized with Zionism and socialized with Plehve. Within days she was able to inform Herzl that Plehve
"would be delighted to make the acquaintance of so interesting a
personality as Dr. Herzl, and that he wholeheartedly supported emigration without return [Herzl's own phrase]; he had always been in
favor of this kind of Zionism."

He had to submit to a strict and humiliating customs search at the
border. But although the trip had supposedly been kept a closely
guarded secret even within the movement, sizable crowds gathered at
the stations to greet him in Warsaw and in Vilna. "They are so badly
off that even I, poor devil that I am, look like a liberator to them,"
he noted, in a rare moment of anguished self-doubt. His guide and
traveling companion was Dr. Nissen Katzenelsohn, a banker and leading Russian Zionist, who incessantly plied him with advice; like most
of his colleagues, he feared that Herzl in his self-confident ignorance
of Russia and the Russians would let himself be outmaneuvered and
end up making things worse. Moreover, many Russian Jews, both in
and out of the movement, were adamantly opposed to any dealings
whatsoever with the government, and most particularly with Plehve,
the man seen as the instigator of the Kishinev pogrom.

Herzl had two meetings with Plehve and came away greatly impressed with his intelligence, breadth of knowledge, and businesslike
approach to the subject at hand. The first discussion took place on
August 8, the morning after his arrival. The minister, a man in his
sixties, tall, slightly obese, with "strangely young, energetic brown
eyes," offered Herzl a cigar, which he refused, and immediately made
his opening move; he spoke a reasonably good French.

"I have granted you this interview at your request so that we might
come to an understanding with regard to the Zionist movement, of
which you are the leader. Such relations as may be established between
the Imperial Government and Zionism—and which may become, I
won't say amicable but at least characterized by mutual understanding—will depend on you."

The gambit was far from subtle, as Herzl was quick to realize. "If
they only depend on me, Your Excellency, they will be excellent,"
he said piously, wondering how much Plehve was willing to concede
in return for not having Kishinev discussed at the forthcoming congress.

"The Jewish Question, while not vital, is still a fairly important one for us," the minister continued, stressing that the Russian state needed and wanted a homogeneous population, and although religious and linguistic differences could not be obliterated overnight, the long-range goal was the full assimilation of all nationalities, including the Jews, through education and economic progress. "Of course, we can only admit a limited number of Jews to higher education, otherwise there would soon be no jobs for Christians." He acknowledged that the economic situation in the Pale of Settlement was deplorable, but maintained that the Jews themselves were partly to blame because they were joining subversive organizations in ever-growing numbers.

This much was routine. But as he launched into a discussion of the Zionist movement proper, his intimate familiarity with details and personalities came as a shock. (Herzl might have been less impressed had he known that the secret police had just compiled a 149-page report on Zionism, and that many of its agents and informers, including the two most infamous double agents Gershuni and Azef, were themselves Jews.)

"Initially," said Plehve, "we were in sympathy with your Zionist movement as long as it worked toward emigration. You don't have to justify the movement to me—you are preaching to one long since converted. But ever since the Minsk conference we have been noticing a shift at the top. There is now less talk of Palestinian Zionism than of culture, organization, and Jewish nationalism. This we do not like. We particularly noticed that your leaders in Russia—prominent people in their own circles—don't really follow the orders of your Vienna committee. Actually, Ussishkin is the only man in Russia who backs you."

"They all side with me, all the Russian leaders, Your Excellency," Herzl objected, "even if they sometimes oppose me on certain issues. The most important, after all, is Professor Mandelstamm of Kiev."

"Ah, but Bernstein-Kohan—he is most decidedly against you. Incidentally, we know that he is the one orchestrating the foreign press campaign against us."

"I don't think so," said Herzl. "The man is little known abroad. He has neither the contacts nor the authority. And as regards the opposition of these gentlemen, it is the same phenomenon with which Christopher Columbus already had to contend. When after weeks and weeks there still was no land in sight, the sailors on the caravel began to grumble. What you are seeing, in our case, is a mutiny of the sailors against their captain. Help me reach land sooner, and the mutiny will cease. So will the defections to the socialists."

"What do you want from us?" Plehve asked bluntly.

Herzl had three requests: diplomatic pressure on Turkey, financial support for emigration out of taxes paid by the Jews, and freedom for the Zionists to organize. And much to his surprise, Plehve immediately agreed, without raising any serious objections. He merely asked Herzl for a written memorandum, along with an outline of what he intended to say at the congress. They parted on the most cordial of terms, each convinced that he had outwitted the other.

"I am happy—and please, don't take this for a mere phrase—to have made your acquaintance," said Plehve.

"I, too, Your Excellency, am very happy to have met Monsieur de Plehve, of whom they talk so much all over Europe."

Plehve was not devoid of a sense of humor. "Of whom they say so many bad things."

"Of whom they talk in ways that made me think he was a great man," said Herzl, ever the diplomat.

The following day he went to see Plehve's archenemy and rival, Count Sergei Witte, the Minister of Finance. Witte, a brilliant economist, happened to be one of the few cabinet members both able and honest, but despite his stubborn and partly successful struggle for industrial progress and economic liberalization, his reputation as a liberal was, as he quickly demonstrated, justified only in very relative terms. Physically repulsive, ill mannered unlike his suave policeman colleague, he received his visitor with undisguised hostility and immediately launched into a tirade against the Jews—the rich were arrogant, the poor were disgusting and engaged in all manner of shady dealings, from pimping to usury. This made it hard for friends of the Jews to defend them. "Because you see," he announced, in a rather unexpected about-face, "I am a friend of the Jews."

With such friends, thought Herzl, we don't need enemies.

The other reason, Witte added, that made it hard to defend the Jews was that everyone immediately assumed you had been bought. But he didn't care. "I have this courage. And my reputation for honesty is unassailable." The Jews themselves, however, were now making things ever more difficult by their increasing participation in subversive movements. "There are only 7 million Jews out of a total population of 136 million, but they account for about 50 percent of the revolutionaries."

"To what do you ascribe this?"

"To oppression by the government," Witte replied, without hesi-

500] E R N S T P A W E L

tation, and proceeded to deliver himself of a remark that exquisitely defined his brand of liberalism. "I used to say to the late Czar Alexander III: 'Your Majesty, if it were possible to drown 6 or 7 million Jews in the Black Sea, I would be all for it. But if it is not possible, they must be given a chance to live.' That has remained my opinion. I am opposed to further oppression."

Compared to Hitler, he was indeed a liberal.

On the other hand, the actual purpose of Herzl's visit—a lifting of the ban on the sale of shares for the Colonial Bank—proved easy enough to accomplish. Witte agreed at once, on condition that the bank open a branch in Russia, which was precisely what Herzl had been hoping to do all along.

His second interview with Plehve on August 13 was, at least in his own eyes, even more successful than the first. Plehve announced that the Czar had personally approved Herzl's three requests but that, while doing so, he had complained about the attacks on him in the foreign press following the Kishinev pogrom—a subtle hint that Herzl's position on the *Neue Freie Presse* had not escaped the attention of his host. The Czar was "extremely hurt by insinuations to the effect that the Russian government had instigated the riots or even passively tolerated them. His Majesty, as head of state, is equally well disposed toward all his subjects and, in his well-known great kindness, feels particularly hurt when acts of inhumanity are imputed to him."

The situation of the Jew in Russia was not brilliant, Plehve conceded. "In fact, if I were a Jew, I, too, would probably be an enemy of the government." But while it was easy for other countries to criticize the Russians, "when asked to take 2 or 3 million poor Jews off our hands, they change their tune." From the Russian point of view, the creation of an independent Jewish state able to absorb a few million Jews would be the ideal solution.

In the meantime, he promised to give some thought to easing certain residence restrictions. As for an audience with the Czar: "We'll see—after the congress." First eat your spinach.

They parted on even friendlier terms than the first time. Glancing at the proposed bylaws of the Zionist organization, which Herzl had just handed him, Plehve said: "You are asking me to do exactly the opposite of what I was going to do in October—recommend a total ban on the Zionist movement to the cabinet."

"It will be your decision," said Herzl.

He had no doubts—and no qualms—about the outcome of that

decision being dependent on what happened in Basel at the end of the month. "The situation is clear: either help, administrative and financial as well as intervention with the Sultan—or prohibition of the movement. Thus everything will depend on our people doing nothing foolish" (D, 8/14/03).

Precisely, one assumes, the sort of conclusion Plehve wanted him to draw.

Herzl came away feeling that the talks had been "the greatest of all my accomplishments to date." His elation, though short-lived as usual, seemed justified. He had been received—and most respectfully at that—by a top-ranking member of the cabinet—itself a rare distinction for a Jewish leader. The czarist government, in a written statement approved for publication, had agreed to his three requests and, by so doing, had both implicitly and explicitly recognized the Zionist movement as a partner in negotiations.

But while Herzl himself had boundless confidence in his ability to outbargain the devil, his Russian comrades, familiar with hell and its ways through firsthand experience, shared neither his confidence nor his elation. In their eyes, even by just going to see the butcher of Kishinev, Herzl had compromised both himself and the cause. And as if this were not bad enough, he had committed himself to helping the Russians stifle criticism at home and abroad and to quell revolutionary ferment in return for promises to which—according to the minutes of the Greater Action Committee of August 21, 1903—none of the Russian members gave any credence.

Some of these misgivings surfaced at a private banquet on August 11, the only occasion during his ten-day visit on which Herzl met with a small, select group of his followers. His own speech, in turn, may well have intensified suspicions of a sellout. He warned against repeating the error of the Western Jews, who fought for social progress in their host countries only to end up strengthening anti-Semitism. Jews, he asserted, should confine themselves strictly to Zionism and fight for nothing and no one else until they had a state of their own. "Those who say that my own views are very far from progressive, socialist ideas are doing me an injustice. But here, in the present conditions, it is too early to be concerned with their realization" (*Die Neue Welt*, 7/26/29. Quoted in Vital, *The Formative Years*, p. 259).

The end of that debate was as inconclusive as the outcome of Herzl's deal with Plehve. Both parties to it were dead within less than a year; Plehve was killed by a terrorist bomb on July 15, 1904, eight days after Herzl's funeral.

Herzl's talks with Russia's top policeman, whatever the results, were further proof that in the eyes of the world he had become the chief spokesman for the Jews. But it was "the day of Vilna," as he called it, that demonstrated what he had come to mean to the Jews themselves.

Vilna, the "Jerusalem of Lithuania," had long been one of the most vital centers of Jewish life in all its extremes, from ultra-Orthodox piety to Jewish enlightenment and radical socialism. It was a stronghold of both the Zionists and of the anti-Zionist Bund, and its roughly 140,000 Jews—most of them miserably poor—were among the politically most active elements in the Pale of Settlement. The range of beliefs, ideas, and ideals, all of them held and argued with passionate zeal, made for a rich cultural ambiance but a not always peaceful coexistence, and Herzl had been warned in St. Petersburg that the Bundists of Vilna, outraged at his hobnobbing with Plehve, were planning to assassinate him. In fact, throughout his stay in Russia there had been widespread rumors of his death at the hands of either the government or the revolutionaries.

He scoffed at the warnings and insisted on going through with his plans for the Vilna visit, which the Russian authorities for reasons of their own chose not to oppose outright. Instead, they did what they could to limit his contacts with the local populace by applying the time-tested mix of harassment and brutality. They took the names of everyone entering Herzl's hotel, listened in on his phone calls, kept him from visiting a synagogue, forced him to make last-minute changes in the routing and itinerary, and time and again broke up the huge crowds—some numbering in the thousands—that gathered everywhere in the hope of catching a glimpse of him.

There are many eyewitness accounts describing the events of that day, including some fairly detailed police reports. But the most eloquent and moving testimony by far is Herzl's own, written on the train the following morning.

Yesterday, the day of Vilna, will live in my memory forever. And this is no after-dinner platitude.

Already my arrival in this Russo-Polish town at noon was marked by ovations. I don't much like this sort of thing. These receptions are histrionics on one side and hysteria on the other.

But the situation became more dangerous, hence more real, when the police, which had been favoring me with the greatest attention from the outset, banned all gatherings, even my visit to the synagogue.

I nonetheless later drove through the tumultuous Jewish streets to the offices of the Jewish community, where I was welcomed by a dense crowd of officials and deputations. There was a tone in their greetings that moved me so deeply that only the thought of the news reports enabled me to contain my tears.

The many speeches vastly inflated my importance, but the misery of these sorely oppressed people was genuine. Afterward, all kinds of deputations laden with gifts called on me at the hotel. The crowds that gathered in front of it kept regrouping every time the police dispersed them. I was also warned by the police not to drive around in the city.

Toward evening we drove to Verki, about an hour's distance from the city, where Jews are normally not allowed to reside. There our friend Ben Jacob had illegally rented a small summer house in what is considered way out in the country, the state of the roads in this Russian provincial town being what it is. He had invited about fifty guests. A ghetto, with good ghetto talk. And the meal that went with it was exquisite; they simply could not do enough for me. After many toasts, the host gave a welcoming speech of truly old-Jewish nobility. "All of us here tonight are happy," he said. "But I am the happiest, because I had the good fortune to welcome this guest under my roof."

And yet he was to be outdone by the uninvited guests who suddenly materialized in the darkness in front of the curtained porch—a crowd of poor young people, men and women from Vilna, who had walked all the way out here—about two hours on foot—just to see me at the table. Now they stood out there, watching us eat and listening to the speeches. And they provided the dinner music by singing Hebrew songs. Ben Jacob, noble host that he was, had the goodness of heart to feed these unbidden guests as well.

One of the young workers in a blue smock, whose hard, determined features had caught my attention and whom I took to be one of the revolutionary Bundists, surprised me by proposing a toast to "the reign of Hamelech Herzl" [King Herzl]. An absurdity, and yet uncanny in its effect against the darkness of that Russian night.

We drove back to the hotel, and from there to the station at one o'clock in the morning. The town was wide awake, because the people wanted to bid me farewell. They stood and walked in the streets through which we had to pass and shouted *Hedad* [Hurrah] whenever they recognized me. They were also out on the balconies. But near the railroad station, where the crowds grew denser, they unfortunately clashed with the brutal police, who had been ordered to keep the station clear. It was a routine Russian police maneuver, which I watched with horror as my carriage rushed toward the station at breakneck speed. Cries of *hedad*, brutal shouts of the policemen as they again and again hurled themselves at the running crowds, and my coachman lashing out at the horses.

Three police officers stood in front of the sealed-off station. The white-whiskered senior officer greeted me with deferential courtesy.

A small group of about fifty to sixty of my friends had nonetheless managed to sneak into the station. I was standing there quietly talking to them when, with a mighty jingling of spurs, a police officer trailed by a sergeant marched into the restaurant and posted himself at a table behind us. When I took off my hat to bid my friends goodbye, he respectfully joined in the greetings.

Did he have orders from St. Petersburg to protect me, or were the police officers secretly afraid of the crowd?

Early in the morning at Eydtkuhnen I was met by a group of Zionists from that Russian border town.

Another speech, another bouquet.

That was Russia. [D, 8/17/03]

It was the last and greatest triumph of his life. A coronation of sorts.

TWENTY-NINE

*H*e went directly from Vilna to Basel, with just a one-day stop at Aussee to pick up his mother, who was to accompany him to the congress. A chance meeting on the train with Count Philipp von Eulenburg instantly revived a long-abandoned but still unforgotten dream. "I immediately saw the advantage of getting Germany back into the game. I'll gladly let Wilhelm II have the glory of placing himself at the head, once I've removed one by one the diplomatic obstacles that were in the way the last time around. Eulenburg asked me if he should write Bülow what I had told him. 'Bülow,' I said, 'is an old enemy of our cause, and he will continue to be against it. If you want to write—write to the Kaiser. He understood it at the time.' 'Can do,' he said. We left it at that. What I had accomplished in Russia struck him as fantastic" (D, 8/19/03).

He arrived in Basel on August 21, 1903, two days before the official opening of the congress—a puffy-faced, worn-out old man of forty-three, short of breath, his beard streaked with gray. The change in his appearance since the previous congress shocked everyone who had not seen him in the interim, yet few realized just how desperately ill he was, nor did he himself appreciate the extent to which his physical deterioration affected his conduct. The autocratic manners, the self-righteous faith in his own superior judgment, the secrecy with which he surrounded all his moves were nothing new; but where in the past they had to some extent been offset by tact, diplomacy, and charm, they now stuck out in their naked abrasiveness and helped to turn an in any case inevitable showdown into a major disaster.

Herzl knew that he faced a fight. But with two major achievements to his credit, he felt certain of an easy victory. The letter from Plehve and the tentative commitment from the British Foreign Office would vindicate not only his tactics but his leadership style. So sure was he of their effect that rather than broach these delicate subjects with due caution and discretion, he chose to "explode the two bombs" and put the opposition *hors de combat* before they could even gather their wits.

He did so at a preliminary session of the Greater Action Committee on August 21, but with results exactly opposite to those intended.

The Plehve letter aroused a storm of protest among the Russian committee members. That Russia wanted to get rid of her Jews came as no revelation to them. But they saw no reason to lend moral support to that insidious ambition, nor could they accept the idea of financing emigration out of Jewish communal taxes. On the other hand, they were caught in a trap of Herzl's making; they could not publicly denounce an official Russian document without running the risk of arrest on their return home. They therefore pleaded with him not to make it public, but he remained adamant; Plehve's promise of pressure on the Turks, he maintained, far outweighed all other considerations.

And while they were still in a state of shock, he dropped the other "bomb"—the British charter for East Africa. It was late Friday afternoon, and before they had a chance to react, he adjourned the session in time for the Sabbath services.

It was not quite the reception he had expected. "The same old mess. My heart is acting up from the fatigue. If I were doing this to earn gratitude, I'd be a damn fool. Yesterday I reported to the Greater Action Committee. I told them about England and Russia. And it did not occur to a single one of them that for these greatest of all accomplishments to date I might deserve a word, or at least a smile, of thanks. Instead, Mssrs. Jacobsohn, Belkovsky, and Tchlenov raised all sorts of objections" (D, 8/22/03).

With 592 delegates, the sixth Zionist congress was to be the largest in the movement's first half century. The official agenda seemed routine if not downright dull, but by the time the first session opened on Sunday morning, August 23, an unscheduled and unannounced item was uppermost on everyone's mind and preempted all other issues.

Even Plehve's letter, now made public in the special congress issue of *Die Welt*, shrank into near-irrelevance compared with "Uganda."

This was not the way Herzl had planned it. By briefing the members of the Action Committee in advance, he had hoped to neutralize the opposition; instead, he had sacrificed the element of surprise and given them an extra day to marshal their forces. What he now faced was a major battle. And yet, though he may not have appreciated it at the time, that battle itself was testimony to one of his greatest and most enduring achievements—the establishment of a truly representative, democratically elected body exercising its prerogatives and asserting its independence, even from its founding father.

During his brilliant opening speech there was a brief resurgence of the old self, factual and persuasive, with few rhetorical flourishes, still the dominant figure without a serious challenger in sight. After summarizing his futile dealings with the Sultan and the ultimately unsuccessful negotiations for El Arish, he warned that in the course of the past year, the situation of the Jews had drastically changed for the worse. Kishinev was a portent of things to come. "Kishinev exists wherever Jews are being tortured in body and soul, wherever their self-respect is injured and their property despoiled because they are Jews. Let us save those who still can be saved." It was in light of these developments that the British offer of an East African territory had to be evaluated. "Considering the plight of Jewry and the immediate need to alleviate this plight as soon as possible, I did not feel justified in doing anything other than obtaining permission to submit this proposal to the congress." For Zionists, he acknowledged, the new territory did not have the historic and emotional connotations that even the Sinai Peninsula would have had, but as an interim solution it was better than nothing and ample reason to be grateful to the British government. "I believe the congress can find a way to make use of this offer. The offer was made to us in a manner that is bound to improve and alleviate the situation of the Jewish people without our abandoning any of the great principles on which our movement was founded."

The following morning, Nordau seconded Herzl in one of his masterful perorations, which, if anything, merely added fuel to the fire. It is not clear when, or even whether, he changed his mind about Uganda, but there was no hint of private misgivings in his arguments. Emphasizing that Palestine remained the ultimate goal, he nevertheless considered the Zionist congress "the authorized, legitimate representative body of the Jewish people"; as such, it had the duty and

responsibility to defend Jewish interests everywhere pending the establishment of the state. A *Nachtasyl* (shelter for the night) had to be
provided for the hundreds of thousands in immediate danger and
desperately seeking the kind of refuge that the East African territory
might offer.

Technically, the ensuing debate was to deal merely with the appointment of a committee to study the proposal, but by the time it
formally opened on Tuesday afternoon, over a hundred speakers had
registered, and the argument inevitably degenerated into a passionate
free-for-all. Arrayed with Herzl were most of the Western contingent
and the bulk of the Orthodox, while the opposition consisted mainly
of the Russian delegation, although a few Russians supported Herzl,
while some Westerners, notably Buber and Feiwel, came out against
him. Ironically, some of the most vociferous "Zion Zionists," as they
began calling themselves, were the secularists. Having severed their
ties to tradition, they placed the full burden of their Jewish identity
on the link to the historical past and to the land of their forefathers,
whereas the religious wing was much more amenable to territorial
solutions; the Talmud, after all, can be studied in Uganda just as well.

The impassioned, circular, often fatuous, but always highly emotional argument in half a dozen languages continued through much
of the night until the following afternoon, frequently interrupted by
cheers and boos from the gallery as well as from the floor. Yet the
basic issue was clear-cut and simple—should the movement concentrate all its forces on establishing a Jewish homeland in Palestine or
should it actively engage in the quest for alternate interim solutions
which, as the opposition charged, would compromise its goals, dis-
sipate its strength, and dilute its moral and ideological purity. One of
its chief spokesmen likened the East Africa project to old-fashioned
philanthropy, while Cyrus L. Sulzberger, a self-avowed New York
philanthropist himself, demanded to know what, if anything, the Zionists proposed to do in the here-and-now about the stream of refugees
propelled by present and future Kishinevs while waiting for the gates
of Palestine to open. There already were one million Jews in the United
States, 600,000 of them in New York alone; what if immigration quotas
were to be imposed? How would other governments react if the Jews
turned down the British offer and refused to help themselves? He was,
he said, a Zionist, but he was a Jew first of all. Which rather defined
the opposing points of view.

There was much heat on both sides, but in terms of rhetorical thunder and lightning the opposition clearly outmatched the Herzl loyalists, the more so since many of the latter were themselves shaky in their support and uneasy about this deviation from the original Basel program. Yet when the motion to appoint a committee was finally put to the vote late on Wednesday afternoon, the outcome, on the face of it, was a victory for Herzl. Of the 468 votes cast, 292 were in favor, 176 against. But 143 delegates had abstained, which considerably reduced his actual margin of victory. And when, in the general uproar following the announcement of the final tally, Tchlenov rose from his seat and left the hall, most of the dissidents got up in turn and walked out after him.

Pale and shaken, though outwardly composed, Herzl made a defiant attempt to keep the session going. But Sir Francis Montefiore's disquisition on Zionist propaganda failed to capture the attention of the remaining audience, and the chair was forced to move for adjournment. To a journalist who covered the episode, it seemed as though "the congress suddenly dissolved."

The opposition, in the meantime, moved to an adjoining hall, where the demonstration quickly escalated from drama to sheer melodrama. Chaim Weizmann, one of the leaders, describes the "unforgettable scene. Tchlenov, Kornberg, and others of the older statesmen wept openly. When the dissidents had assembled separately, there were some delegates who, in the extremity of their distress, sat down on the floor in the traditional ritual mourning which is observed for the dead, or in commemoration of the destruction of the temple on the ninth of Ab" (Weizmann, *Trial and Error*, p. 88).

The future first President of Israel himself played a rather ambiguous role in these proceedings. Initially one of the few Russian delegates to speak in support of the East Africa project, he abruptly switched sides as the debate got under way and became a leading critic not only of the Uganda plan but of Herzl personally. In his autobiography, he admits that he had "for a moment" been misled but soon came to see the light. There is an at least even chance that what he really came to see was the all but unanimous hostility to Herzl and to his proposal within the Russian delegation, which Weizmann was anxious to cultivate as his own power base; with the quick reflex of the born politician he not only joined the parade but grabbed the flag.

The weeping and wailing over ravished principles continued into the night, rising to a pitch of out-and-out hysteria, in which genuine distress fused with long-simmering hostility, rivalries, and opportunism. Word of this noisy and spectacular demonstration finally reached Herzl at his hotel, and once more he rose to the occasion. Dead tired as he was, he dragged himself back to the convention hall, where the mutinous crew had locked themselves in; according to some accounts, he was admitted only after a lengthy debate. Adopting the tone of a stern but forgiving father who realizes that his children have strayed out of ignorance rather than malevolence, he tried to reassure them about his love for Zion while again expounding his reasons for at least considering the British offer. He stuck to his guns, but he pleaded for understanding. "I need you to trust me, because without that trust one cannot be a leader," he concluded. "And let me tell you one more thing: in this institution that I have created—allow me to put it this way, because it happens to be the truth—I have always left open the possibility of my stepping down. You can remove me, if you want to. Believe me, I'll gladly return to the longed-for tranquillity of my private life without a murmur of discontent."

Vladimir Jabotinsky, in later years the leader of the hard-line Zionist Revisionists, who was present at the meeting and has left an account of it, remarked that Herzl's words and the reaction of the audience reminded him of a saying attributed to the eighteenth-century Russian scientist Lomonosov: "It is a lot easier for me to expel the Academy of Science than for the Academy to expel me."

Weizmann, for his part, came away with a somewhat different impression, at least if we are to credit his 1946 recollections:

> Meanwhile, as we sat in caucus, depressed, our hearts filled with bitterness, a message was brought in that Herzl would like to speak to us. We sent back word that we would be glad to hear him. He came in, looking haggard and exhausted. He was received in dead silence. Nobody rose from his seat to greet him, nobody applauded when he ended. He admonished us for having left the hall; he understood, he said, that this was merely a spontaneous demonstration and not a secession; he invited us to return. He assured us of his unswerving devotion to Palestine, and spoke again of the urgent need for finding an immediate refuge for large masses of homeless Jews. We listened in silence; no one attempted to reply. It was probably the only time that Herzl was thus received at any Zionist gathering; he, the idol of all Zionists. He left as he had entered; but I think that at this small meeting he realized for the first time the depth of the passion

which linked us with Zion. This was the last time I saw him except from a distance, on the platform." [Weizmann, *Trial and Error*, p. 88]

Missing from this account—and what politicians omit to tell us is always far more interesting than what they choose to reveal—is Weizmann's harsh personal attack on Herzl two days later, significant because in both style and content it reflects the volatile mix of pent-up animosity and personal ambition which motivated both sides in this "historic" affair at least as much as the ideological principles ostensibly at stake.

> Herzl's influence on the people is very great. Even the "no's" have been unable to free themselves of his influence. . . . The truth is that Herzl is not a nationalist but a promoter of projects. He came across the Hibbat Zion idea and aligned himself with the movement for a period. Then, when it failed, he reversed himself. He only takes external conditions into account, whereas the power on which we rely is the psychology of the people and its living desires. We, for our part, always knew that we were incapable of gaining Palestine in the short term and were therefore not discouraged when this or that attempt had failed. It is the people's consciousness that now has to be bolstered. . . . Cultural work must be put before all else. [Hatsofe, Warsaw, 9/3/03. Quoted in Vital, *The Formative Years*, p. 305]

It was a clash of giant egos in which the nominal issues symbolized a struggle for power. But at least for the time being, Herzl prevailed. The fractious rebels returned to the fold the next morning, the intransigent Weizmann had himself elected to the very committee whose appointment he opposed, and Herzl was reelected for his sixth term as president, with only three votes dissenting. In his closing address on the eve of the Sabbath, he once more and for the last time pulled out all the stops and, in a magnificent finale, displayed his mastery of politics as theater:

"When in a difficult moment—which is a not infrequent occurrence—I thought that all hope must be abandoned at least for the span of a normal life, I proposed an expedient to you, and having learned to know your hearts, I also want to offer you a word of consolation, which is at once a pledge on my part." And slowly raising his right hand, he recited the psalmist's "If I forget thee, O Jerusalem, let my right hand forget her cunning" in Hebrew.

It was to be his curtain call.

As he may well have suspected. He had managed to salvage the formal unity of "his" movement by drawing upon the last reserves of his strength, but at a cost to himself, physically and emotionally, that he could ill afford. Bernstein-Kohan, a physician, maintains that on two occasions during that week he treated Herzl for "heart attacks," and Buber, who saw him in private during an intermission, found him struggling for breath in a state of wild agitation. But the furious hostility, the aspersions on his motives, and the vicious personal attacks—he was repeatedly called a traitor to his face—opened up wounds which only his superb skill as an actor enabled him to conceal from his audience. He had chosen his role, and he was determined to play it to the end.

Sitting in the hotel room that night with Cowen, Zangwill, and Nordau, he gave them a preview of the speech he intended to deliver at the next congress, "if I live to see it. By that time I will either have obtained Palestine or else realized the futility of any further efforts." Although he himself was now a Lover of Zion, he did not believe that the movement had a right to withhold relief from thousands of Jews clamoring for a refuge. And since any interim solution would again provoke a clash centered on his person, "I see only one solution: I must resign my leadership."

It was a comforting thought he often toyed with during the coming months, but which he never took seriously, not least because his adversaries continued to gang up on him; he would never resign under fire. In the intervals between ever more frequent bouts of lassitude, depression, and enforced rest, there were stretches when he still seemed nearly his old driven self, working at a furious pace and in total disregard of his health. But the sixth congress had been a brutal ordeal, and though on the face of it both he and the movement had emerged more or less intact, neither was ever quite the same again.

Ailing in body and soul, Herzl went straight back to Aussee, with just a brief stop on the way to visit the Grand Duke of Baden, a man whose genuine humanity and old-fashioned sense of fairness had rendered him increasingly obsolete and irrelevant in the empire of Wilhelm II. And although all the old gentleman had to offer was admiration and approval, Herzl appreciated the balm to his badly bruised ego.

The first two weeks at Aussee—he stayed on for nearly two months—were spent in a state of near-collapse. Yet even so, incapacitated as he was by progressively severe cardiac symptoms, his restless mind kept probing for ways to turn the congress debacle to his advantage. In a long letter to Plehve he cited the episode as proof that Russia's Jews would go nowhere but to Palestine. If Plehve really wanted to get rid of them, it was incumbent upon him to intercede with the Sultan on their behalf as soon and as forcefully as possible.

Whatever Plehve's true intentions—and they probably were nowhere near as unambiguous as Herzl seemed to believe—they had no apparent effect on the way Russian authorities dealt with the Jews. On September 11, another major pogrom broke out in the White Russian city of Gomel, but this time the local Jews—over half the population—broke with the tradition of passivity. Zionists and socialists jointly organized a self-defense force which, after beating off the *pogromshchiki*, was promptly set upon by Russian police and army troops, who killed twelve of the defenders. An investigation by the provincial governor blamed the riot on Jewish radicals; so much for Herzl's impact on Plehve. At the Ministry of the Interior, it was obviously business as usual.

Herzl seemed to be rallying, but it may have been adversity and opposition more than the rest cure that helped to bolster his resistance. And as he became more active, he fired off fusillades of letters, directives, and memos in bursts reminiscent of the early days of his leadership. He kept up the pressure on Plehve, directly and through other members of the Russian bureaucracy; his ministerial ex-policeman friend responded by asking for information about the conduct and attitudes of the Russian delegates to the congress. Eventually, Plehve did instruct the Russian ambassador in Constantinople to speak up for a Jewish Palestine, but the ambassador blithely ignored the instructions. And despite the clear signals he had been given by the congress, Herzl continued to push the East Africa project through Greenberg, Rothschild, and Goldsmid. Informed that the colonel was to be the King's guest at Balmoral Castle, Herzl urged him to win royal support for a combination of El Arish and Uganda, and he declared himself ready to come to England at a moment's notice should His Majesty wish to see him.

There was, in fact, a streak of perverse obstinacy born of desperation in the way he clung to a project manifestly dead beyond any hope of revival—and dead not only because of resistance from within the movement. In East Africa itself, the white settlers mounted a protest as soon as they got wind of the plan; unlike the natives, they had sufficient political clout to make themselves plainly heard in London. The correspondence columns of *The* (London) *Times* were filled with letters on the subject, most expressing strong criticism. And the anti-Zionist Jews, who had long ridiculed Herzl for wanting to lead the Jews back to Palestine, now bemoaned his having given up on the Holy Land in favor of Africa. Herzl himself tended to dismiss these objections with his usual nonchalance as "pinpricks by busy scribblers," but their cumulative effect caused a decided shift in the attitude of British officialdom, reluctant to incur the wrath of such politically well-connected institutions and individuals as the African Settlers' Association, the Bishop of Mombasa, or the commissioner, Sir Charles Eliot, among others.

Everyone concerned was actually having second thoughts, and the negotiations soon turned into an intricate minuet as both parties tried to back away as gracefully as possible without losing face or stepping on each other's toes. To the British, the original notion of earning points for high-minded generosity while reinforcing the white element in their African territories had lost much of its charm once they discovered that, to the resident British colonists, Jews were not really white, after all. And Herzl by the end of the year also no longer had his heart in the deal, though he pursued it in the rather forlorn hope that an unacceptable offer could perhaps still be used as a bargaining chip for El Arish. After prolonged talks back and forth, the British Foreign Office on January 25, 1904, finally came through with a definite offer of some 5,000 square miles near Lake Victoria; when Herzl hesitated, Greenberg virtually forced his hand by accepting it in his name. Further action was, however, deferred until the forthcoming meeting of the Greater Action Committee, scheduled for March 1.

By year's end, the real issue was no longer Uganda but the leadership of the movement itself. If Herzl still nurtured illusions about having restored unity, they were quickly dispelled when, in October, Menachem Ussishkin returned from his tour of Palestine.

Ussishkin was the first in a long line of iron-willed *apparatchiks* with tunnel vision, grossly inflated egos, and an inflexible devotion to the cause, from Ben-Gurion and Golda Meir to Begin and Shamir, who were—and still are—an asset and an affliction to Zionism in about equal proportions. Bialik in one of his letters described him as

> not as solid and hard as people say. Those who know him well find in him a good measure of emotion and sentimentality. There is a little bit of fantasy in him, too. His eyes tend to fill with tears. His supposed hardness stems more from stubbornness and inflexibility. His thoughts move as heavily as a bear and when he is set on an idea he cannot easily move away from it or turn right or left in the slightest degree. He is by nature and in spirit limited; he is straight. And very conservative. . . . He recognizes no colors or shadings. . . . In sum: a man who is not very complicated—but nevertheless a man whose greatness is in his simplicity, his primitivity, and in all his impulses, small as well as big. [Letter to David Rothblum, 9/1/33. Quoted in Vital, *The Formative Years*, p. 187]

The characterization applies with equal force to many Zionist leaders, past and present.

A graduate of the Moscow Technical Institute, possessed of enormous drive, ambition, and organizational talent, Ussishkin pursued all his goals with the tenacity—and some of the manners—of a bulldog, though the ultimate prize eluded him. Chaim Weizmann, who allied himself with him as long as it suited his purposes, beat him out in the final race for the leadership during a period when the precarious state of the movement required suppleness, urbanity, and intellectual brilliance at the top.

In May 1903 he had gone to Palestine and, rather than attending "Herzl's" congress, had organized a "representative assembly" of Jewish settlers, with himself as president. The implicit challenge was rendered explicit in his telegram of greetings "from the representatives of the Jewish people in Eretz Israel to the representatives of the Jewish people in the Diaspora." Herzl dismissed the provocation by thanking "the brethren already settled in Eretz Israel for their good wishes." But Ussishkin, who in his absence had been elected to the Greater Action Committee, lowered his horns and went for the kill. Right after his return, he published an open letter refusing to comply with any resolutions concerning Africa. "A majority of the congress may decide questions of ways and means, but not of principles and ideas."

The sanctimonious declaration reached Herzl, still at Aussee, where he was now detained by his wife's illness rather than his own; Julie had come down with a near-fatal appendicitis complicated by pneumonia, and for some days the outcome seemed in grave doubt.

His answer to Ussishkin was a discursive exercise in heavy-handed Viennese café-style sarcasm, treating "Herr Ussishkin from Ekatarinoslav" as a dim-witted oaf who would either have to learn to behave or else take his marbles and go play by himself. "Many imagined that the moment had arrived when they could step into other people's shoes because my friends and I proposed to send an expedition for the purpose of investigating the splendid offer of the British government. They were in error. Their time has not yet come."

Ussishkin responded by convening the nine Russian members of the Greater Action Committee, who met in Kharkov from November 11 to 14 and resolved to present Herzl with a "final warning" against pursuing the Uganda project or any other not relating to Palestine, and to promote settlement work in Eretz Israel. The ultimatum, to which Herzl was to respond in writing, was to be delivered by a special two-man delegation. If he refused to comply, steps to "organize an independent Zionist Organization without Dr. Herzl" would be taken.

Stunned by their own daring, and perhaps dimly aware of their own vulnerability in any confrontation with a living legend, they vowed to keep the ultimatum secret until it could be delivered, a sure way to guarantee its immediate dissemination.

Herzl's reaction was swift and decisive; righteous anger always had a bracing effect on his health. "The first thing they acquire are all the bad qualities of the professional politicians. I am first of all going to mobilize the masses of the lower class . . . then cut off their funds, etc." He did precisely that, convinced—not without reason—that the main support for the rebels came from middle-class professionals and intellectuals. But the peremptory tone of the secret ultimatum, which he immediately published in *Die Welt*, gained him considerable sympathy even among those who disagreed with him. The controversy reached a climax on December 19 at a Hanukkah ball in Paris, where one Chaim Louban, a demented Russian-Jewish student, drew a revolver and fired two shots at Max Nordau, crying "Death to the East African." He did no serious damage to either Nordau or anyone else and was eventually judged insane, but the incident highlighted the violent passions aroused. Herzl promptly accused the Kharkov cabal of indirect responsibility, which did nothing to calm the waters.

On December 31, the two Kharkov delegates finally appeared on Herzl's doorstep in Vienna to present the ultimatum. Much to their discomfiture, they were cordially received, but only as individuals and visitors. Herzl dismissed the whole Kharkov committee as illegally constituted, refused to recognize any delegations or ultimatums, and instead invited his by now rather befuddled guests to sit in on a meeting of the Vienna Action Committee, where they once more argued the seemingly inexhaustible topic of East Africa. Herzl, from all accounts, was in top form and remarkably high spirits. No minds were changed, there was no reconciliation, but the two delegates slunk back home with nothing to show for their trip. Herzl had once more imposed his authority; and that, in the final analysis, had been the only real issue. A minor victory in a major battle, but it left him free to turn back to politics.

Deeply worried about Herzl's health and wanting to ease his burdens, Wolffsohn, Cowen, and Zangwill conspired to make it financially possible for him to resign from the *Neue Freie Presse,* but he rebuffed their offer with unfeigned indignation. "You are a good fellow," he wrote to Wolffsohn, "but what sort of person do you think I am? You offer me an annuity so that I can live in London and lead the movement from there. Well, what about my self-respect? Why would I accept money from you? Because I act according to my convictions?" And to Zangwill, who had assured him of total discretion, he replied, "You say no one would know. One person would know. I would know."

On January 17, he took off for Italy.

The trip was a gesture of defiance, a challenge to his failing health as much as to the Kharkov rebels, but it also marked the resumption of his grand strategy, the politics of persuasion. The Chief Rabbi of Florence had set up an audience for him with King Victor Emmanuel III, reputedly friendly to Zionism and eager to meet its leader. Herzl hoped to enlist him as another ally in his campaign for a Turkish charter, but there were other considerations as well, notably Italy's expanding interests in Tripolitania, which suggested possibilities for a North African concession not unlike El Arish. It was, in any case, important to build bridges.

As it turned out, a chance meeting in Venice, where he stopped for twenty-four hours to recover from the first leg of his journey, opened up even more exciting perspectives. An Austrian portrait painter who attached himself to him bragged about his friendship with the Pope and offered to make the introductions. Herzl took him for a con man, a gossip, and a name-dropper, all of which he may well have been, but in this particular instance, Berthold Dominik Lippay—he, too, a boy from Budapest—proved as good as his word. By the time Herzl reached Rome on January 22, Lippay was already waiting to take him to the Vatican for a preliminary interview with Cardinal Merry del Val, the Papal Secretary of State.

The cardinal was affable but firm, and their conversation led to nothing more than a restatement of the Church's traditional position. "As long as the Jews deny the divinity of Christ, we cannot pronounce ourselves in their favor. Not that we wish them evil. On the contrary, the Church has always extended protection to them. For us they are the indispensable witnesses of God's term on earth. But they deny Christ's divinity. How, then, can we agree to their regaining possession of the Holy Land without sacrificing our highest principles?"

Neither Herzl's assurances about extraterritorializing the Holy Places nor his rather broad hint that a benevolent attitude on the part of the Church might prove more effective than persecution when it came to making converts seemed to impress the cardinal, but he agreed to recommend a papal audience.

Three days later, Herzl was received by Pope Pius X.

He had agonized over whether or not to kiss the Pope's hand and in the end decided against it. "I think that is how I antagonized him, because everybody who comes to see him kneels and at least kisses his hand." Nevertheless, it seems unlikely that this breach of etiquette accounted for the Pope's refusal to endorse Zionism. Though more blunt in his language, he repeated the same message as his cardinal: "The Jews did not recognize our Lord, and therefore we cannot recognize the Jewish people." Extraterritoriality did not interest him; the whole of Jerusalem must never fall into Jewish hands. When Herzl insisted that *Judennot*—the distress of the Jews—rather than religion was what motivated the Zionists, and that they, in fact, wished to avoid religious issues, he was sharply reminded that maybe *he* could avoid religious issues, not so the head of the Church. If the Jews clung to their faith and denied the divinity of Jesus, the Church could not be expected to help them; if, on the other hand, they went to Palestine "without any religion," the Church would oppose them even more strongly.

Herzl was greatly impressed by the massive dignity of this "good, coarse-grained village priest, for whom Christianity has remained a living faith even in the Vatican," but the Pope's *non possumus* was firm and final. It seems hard to believe that Herzl could have expected anything else.

In between these two somewhat grim encounters, however, he spent a most enjoyable morning at the Quirinale Palace. King Victor Emmanuel turned out to be a remarkably intelligent and delightfully unpretentious man, well informed about Palestine and the Jewish Question, although "here we don't make any distinctions between Jews and Italians. Jews can be anything, and in fact they are everywhere—in the army, the government, even in the diplomatic service." He told Herzl that one of his own ancestors had conspired with Shabbetai Tsvi to become "King of Macedonia, or Cyprus, or some sort of king, anyway. He was a bit crazy, but he thought big."

He promised Herzl that "personally, whenever I meet a Turk, I'll bring up your cause." But as to an official intercession with the Sultan, he referred him to his Foreign Minister, Tommaso Tittoni, because as a constitutional monarch his hands were tied when it came to foreign policy initiatives.

Yet however pleasant the conversation, its practical results were no more encouraging than the talks at the Vatican. Herzl went to see the Foreign Minister, a seasoned bureaucrat who was professionally polite and, like all seasoned bureaucrats, asked for a memorandum, to be duly filed and forgotten. He also met Giacomo Malvono, the Jewish secretary general and real power in the ministry, "a dirty, moth-eaten little man with fetid breath" who had no use for Zionism and refused to talk about it.

On January 28, Herzl returned to Vienna. "The balance sheet for Rome is positive, just the same."

In March, he sent two emissaries to Constantinople—either to test the waters, now that he had all but obtained a British charter, however useless, or else to document his basic pro-Palestine loyalties at the forthcoming session of the Greater Action Committee. As usual, nothing came of it. The emissaries quickly got stuck in the Yildiz maze, and for some weeks he quite seriously contemplated backing a Swedish adventurer, a convert to Islam married to a Turkish princess, who proposed to slip into the Bosporus with two cruisers, bombard the Yildiz, and install a Sultan prepared to give the Zionists a charter for Palestine. All this at a bargain price of half a million pounds—200,000 for each cruiser and 100,000 for miscellaneous expenses. It was not until April 19 that he definitely dropped this insane and potentially disastrous scheme.

A week earlier, from the eleventh to the fifteenth, the Greater Action Committee convened in Vienna to deal with the crisis in the movement. Both sides were fully represented and, on the whole, eager to restore unity. To a certain extent, they succeeded. The debate, while it circled around the same points that had been regurgitated hundreds of times before, was markedly more restrained in tone. The speakers strove to refrain from personal attacks, and even Ussishkin found it in his heart to pay Herzl a backhanded compliment by declaring that "great men have great failings."

Herzl was at his brilliant best at these meetings, his vigor seemingly restored. Throughout the five days he was in complete control, patronizing and paternal, acidly sarcastic and good-humored in turn, his authority utterly beyond question. "You have a hard skull," he told Ussishkin. "And so do I. Maybe that is why I like you." "And why I like you," Ussishkin replied. "But let me tell you something," Herzl went on. "I am stronger than you. That is why I am conciliatory. I know that if we fight, I'll win."

In a formal sense, this was true, and his opponents knew it; he still had the majority of the movement on his side. But on the substantive issue he had already lost the fight. No matter how many more times they still went to battle over Uganda, the plan was dead. And so, Solomonic wisdom—or the instinct of self-preservation— ultimately prevailed in both camps; rather than carving up their child, they made peace, even though they were a long way from loving one another.

Two weeks later, on April 30, Herzl had his last fling at personal diplomacy—a talk with Count Goluchowski, the Austrian Foreign Minister. It was his first attempt to enlist his own country in efforts to further his cause, and he judged it a success, although the count, exceedingly amiable otherwise, would not commit himself in any serious way.

That very day, Herzl underwent an examination by a panel of physicians. They insisted on his immediately dropping all activities and taking at least six weeks of complete rest. He left the following morning for Franzensbad.

THIRTY

*F*or much of his life, Herzl fought self-destructive and even suicidal tendencies, a struggle that itself affirms his overwhelming and at times desperate will to live. To see his conduct during the difficult final years as evidence of a death wish is at best simplistic, and in any case irrelevant—unconscious death wish or not, he also very much wanted to live, no matter how relentlessly he drove himself to the very end. There is a subtle but by no means insignificant difference between suicide and self-immolation.

Although he consistently refused to make any concessions to his failing health, he kept consulting a number of physicians in the hope of staving off the fatal outcome and gaining a reprieve, at the very least. None, however, was able to do much for him. Even their diagnoses, given the technology of the time, were seldom more than educated guesses based on clinical experience, but the best—or at least the most humane—among them tried to keep up his spirits by offering hope where there was none. Thus in December 1903, quite literally fighting for breath as well as for Uganda, Herzl went to see Dr. Gustav Singer, a heart specialist and professor at the University of Vienna, who left a revealing memoir of his professional contacts with him:

> Theodor Herzl came to consult me in December 1903. . . .
> He had long fascinated me as an author to whom I owed many delightful and inspiring hours. The imagery of his travel pieces, the mastery with which he captured the flavor of the Parisian

salons in the German language, the grace and feeling with which he wrote about his children had made me feel very close to him. But now a very different man came to see me, a pale, tired, sick patient. I was soon forced to realize that death was already lurking in the shadows. His pulse was irregular, the heart output greatly impaired as manifested by obvious congestive symptoms. In addition, there were the circles around his once so fiery eyes, and the dark forebodings that assailed him. I believe that I succeeded in deceiving him for a while and to calm him down. But in consultation with Ortner, who was also treating him, we were forced to postulate a disease of the heart muscle, which implied rapidly progressive heart failure. He came to see me whenever he felt bad, or whenever Ortner's prescriptions made him suspect a worsening of his condition. Actually, all I did for him was to provide emotional support. [CZA]

In the circumstances, Herzl's Italian journey in January had clearly been a triumph of mind over matter. But although he mentions taking some time to catch his breath after climbing the stairs to the Quirinale Palace, the psychic benefits probably outweighed the physical strain and may have helped to carry him through another two months of feverishly sustained activity. By the end of April, however, his condition had become alarming to the point where a panel of specialists urgently recommended a course of hydrotherapy combined with a complete and extended rest.

The choice of Franzensbad (now Frantiskovy Lazne) proved less than auspicious. The resort was famous for its twenty-seven mineral springs and radioactive gas baths reputedly effective against ailments ranging from heart and circulatory diseases to rheumatism and dyspepsia. Since the season did not open until May 1, Herzl found himself practically alone in the place. "I am the only guest in the house," he reported to Julie on his arrival. "There still is no bed in my room. The landlady was speechless when I appeared. What is more, I am here not just the only man, but also the only woman." The series of daily hot baths prescribed by the *Kurarzt*, the medical entrepreneur in charge of the establishment, may actually have done more harm than good. In any case, the benefits of a spa, such as they be, bear scant relation to the mineral content of its waters. Whatever relief patients are apt to experience is mainly due to their temporary escape from the stresses of the ordinary day-to-day routine, and Herzl left none of those behind; even his domestic troubles caught up with him in short order.

Within days of his arrival, Nissen Katzenelsohn, his personal representative in Russia, stopped off in Franzensbad on his way back to St. Petersburg from a meeting in Berlin with the American banker and philanthropist Jacob Henry Schiff. Schiff was prepared to finance a loan for Russia, provided the Russians changed their anti-Jewish policies. Herzl spent an entire night composing a memorandum to Plehve, which he wanted Katzenelsohn personally to deliver to the minister. And when, in the morning, Katzenelsohn reproachfully pointed out that this was hardly the way to recover one's health, he shrugged it off. "Why fool ourselves? I've heard the third bell. I am no coward, and I am facing death very calmly, the more so since I did not waste the last years of my life. I was not too bad a servant of the movement, don't you think?" On May 6, he informed Wolffsohn that he was taking "the heart cure. But my mother knows nothing about it. She thinks I am here only for a rest." And he concluded his letter with the curious admonition: "Don't do anything stupid while I am dead."

He spent most of his time writing letters—to friends in the movement, to Plehve, to Austrian and Italian politicians; his last diary entry, dated May 16, breaks off in the middle of a letter to Jacob Schiff. An additional headache was the stream of complaints from the seldom quiescent home front that reached the ailing patient in his supposed retreat. Open warfare had once more broken out between his wife and his mother, who again talked about moving in permanently with the Herzls. "By your meddling you would only make my life miserable," he wrote to her. "I am sick and tired of all the quarrels and the excitement. Above all Julie, as the mother of our innocently involved children, and as a sick woman herself, is entitled to the most tender consideration. Give other people a chance as well to act as they see fit. No dictatorship! Even a general consults with his captain."

In the circumstances, it was no surprise that he not only failed to improve but that his condition steadily deteriorated. Toward the end of May he broke off the pointless cure, briefly returned to Vienna, and on June 3, following his doctor's advice, left for Edlach, an alpine resort near Reichenau. This time he was accompanied by Julie as well as their oldest daughter, Pauline, and by his friend Johann Kremenezky. They rented a small cottage, and contrary to expectations he quite miraculously began to regain some of his strength in the bracing mountain air. Julie seems to have nursed him with genuinely self-sacrificing devotion, even if one discounts the somewhat pointedly ecstatic notes on the subject he wrote to his mother, and legend has it that the two at long last transcended their differences and achieved a few tragically final moments of marital bliss—not altogether impossible, although there is no objective evidence to support it.

He had a steady stream of visitors—his cousin Raoul Auernheimer, Hermann Bahr, the ex–fraternity brother and convert to philo-Semitism, colleagues, movement activists, and friends. The Reverend Hechler came to see him and vowed that they would see Jerusalem again. "Greet Palestine for me," Herzl is said to have replied. "I gave my heart's blood for my people." He was soon able to take walks on the terrace and gradually started to believe in a recovery, or at least a remission; he even made plans to travel to the North Sea shore. But his doctors evidently had no such illusions.

Wolffsohn came to see him on June 19 and left the following day, totally devastated by his confidential talk with the attending physician. In utter despair he appealed for help to his friend and fellow Zionist Dr. Simonsohn, a Berlin physician. "It was only last night that I got the horrible news from Dr. Konried. After long hesitation he told me that there was not much hope. He will start faradization today, but he knows it to be pointless. It is not just a dilatation of the heart, but something much worse. The heart muscle has completely degenerated, and Konried is firmly convinced that the reserves have all been used up. You, as a doctor, will be in a better position to judge what this means. As for myself, all I know is that I am on the verge of madness, that from last night's farewell until noon today I have been writhing in pain and fear. What is to become of us if the doctor is right? And I am afraid he is right" (CZA)

The friend, in turn, got in touch with Dr. Max Asch, a prominent Hamburg cardiologist with the reputation of a miracle worker, who agreed to take on the case and arrived in Edlach on June 26. Reporting to his colleague on his initial examination of the patient, he declared himself "very pleasantly surprised at finding a gentleman who, rather than being moribund and with one foot in the grave, gave me his medical history in a strong voice and with animated eyes." The objective findings were serious but, in his expert opinion, far from life-threatening—a dilatation of the heart, arrhythmia, and probable coronary insufficiency. He thought less than nothing of Dr. Konried, the local physician, "who is not familiar with proper examination techniques and altogether gives the impression of a physician with only the most rudimentary knowledge of routine procedures." He therefore suggested transferring the patient to his own clinic in Hamburg as soon as possible, preferably within the week, with interim rest stops in Vienna and Berlin.

Three days later, he followed up on this first report with an even more cheerful message: "The myocarditis, if any, cannot be significant. I am definitely optimistic. I believe that the arrhythmia and weak heart action are due mostly to nervous disturbances. We'll be leaving for Vienna on Friday. Saturday night we'll presumably be in Berlin."

But the most revealing document in this series is the memorandum Dr. Asch addressed to his Berlin colleague on June 30, marked *Confidential—unofficial*. While testifying to the unbridled arrogance of experts afflicted with delusions of omniscience, the observations of a relatively detached outsider nonetheless provide important clues to the true story of Herzl's final weeks and days, as distinct from the versions destined for public consumption.

Dear Simonsohn,

Having observed Dr. Herzl very closely now for three days and nights, I am absolutely convinced that there is no evidence of a significant, life-threatening myocarditis. He was here in Edlach in April and felt relatively well. Then, in mid-April, there was a ten-day period of difficult committee meetings from early in the morning until eleven at night, without proper nourishment. He collapses. Prof. Ortner diagnoses myocarditis and sends him to Franzensbad, where for three weeks he takes hot 20-minute carbon baths daily. Here he is all alone, reads all sorts of literature about heart disease, and turns into an exquisite hypochondriac. On May 21 he returns to Vienna with shortness of breath, etc. (cardiac dilatation). He spends fourteen days in bed, then comes to Edlach, where instead of taking care of himself he does too much walking. On June 7, the symptoms of heart-muscle insufficiency recur, with edemas which, however, resolve in short order after administration of minimal doses of Digitalis and Diuretin. From June 7 to 24 good convalescence. Even on June 26, when he had a visit from Hermann Bahr, he was still capable of several hours of conversation. He undoubtedly did too much during those days when he felt better; as a result, he naturally suffered a relapse. Last Tuesday a major depression. Yesterday he again felt better all day long, but in the evening there was a wild marital scene. His wife had a fit of hysteria. I was called twice during the night. He did not get any sleep all night and was, of course, checkmate by morning. In the afternoon I sent him back to bed. He slept well for an hour or two, and now things are all right again. Tomorrow morning we are leaving for Vienna, where we have a consultation set up with his physicians. I have repeatedly faradized him, the heart is rather labile. (Artist's heart—Smith.)

All in all, a case of neurasthenia gravis, with a strong admixture of hypochondria, extreme excitability. The crux of the problem is the wife; the constant friction is wrecking him as well as her. This factor is bound to greatly complicate the recovery; further details on the subject orally. My prognosis, as regards survival, is entirely favorable, but I doubt if he will be able to resume work any earlier than six months from now. The man needs a long period of rest. The local physician, Dr. Konried, is a run-of-the-mill country doctor; I have put a stop to his poisoning the patient by overmedication.

As a result of last night's ruckus, we may not reach Berlin before Sunday. . . . Herzl under no circumstances wants to spend more than one night in Berlin. If his wife comes along—and I suppose there is nothing we can do to stop her from doing so—we can look forward to difficult times. My task here was by no means easy or pleasant. It is no joke dealing with two such hysterical heart patients, but I succeeded in imposing my counsel. If, after a night like the last one, a patient does not collapse and develops no significant symptoms of insufficiency, I am willing to hang myself if he has anything like a significant myocarditis.

Well, my dear friend, I believe I have accomplished a historic deed for Zionism, and I now expect to be made an honorary member.

Yours, Asch

In his emphasis on psychogenic factors, Dr. Asch may have been well ahead of his time. In the evaluation of the patient's physical condition, however, it was the "run-of-the-mill country doctor" who turned out to be right in the end.

The very next day, instead of leaving for Vienna, Herzl was confined

528] E R N S T P A W E L

to bed with a bronchial catarrh. An urgent call brought three of his Viennese physicians as well as several close friends to his bedside. One of them—Dr. Siegmund Werner, editor of *Die Welt* and himself a physician—took over the nursing duties and left what amounts to the official account of Herzl's last hours.

The night of July 1 was raw torment. Delirious, running a high fever, and racked by painful coughing spells, Herzl told Werner in one of his lucid moments that he had always thought he knew the meaning of fear and terror, "but whatever you imagine is just a joke compared to that dreadful horror of not being able to draw a breath."

In the morning, somewhat improved, he pleaded to have his mother and the two younger children—the oldest had been with him all along—sent for as soon as possible, and throughout the day he fretted about still getting to see them. Thanks to ample medication he had a more restful night, but on the morning of Sunday, July 3, the bronchitis turned into pneumonia. It was not until noon that he seemed sufficiently lucid for his mother to be admitted to the sickroom. According to Dr. Werner, what followed was

> an unforgettable scene. Herzl, whom a few minutes before I had left bent and broken, unable to catch his breath, the same Herzl was now sitting upright in his bed with eyes wide open. Stretching his hands out to his mother, he said: "It is really good, Mother, that you're here already. You look well. I don't look so well, but that will soon pass." He kissed the mother, who kept her self-control and spoke some encouraging words. When the two younger children, Hans and Trude, came into the room, he seemed almost gay. After a talk of about five minutes, he turned to his mother and said, "Well, my dear ones, you saw me, and I saw you. Now go back." [De Haas, Vol. 2, pp. 241 et seq.]

Moments after they left, he collapsed. Early in the afternoon he briefly rallied once more, but at five o'clock, just as Werner had turned away to prepare an injection, he heaved a deep sigh and gave up the struggle. He was forty-four years old.

His death left many orphans.

Within the Zionist movement, Wolffsohn's desperate "What is to become of us" was echoed not only by Herzl's admirers but also by most of those who had opposed him in life. The shock was all the greater for being wholly unexpected; the gravity of his illness had been a closely guarded secret, kept from all but a few intimate friends. And even the stormy final year of his stewardship had demonstrated once again that there was no one to take his place.

There never would be.

The movement survived, in no small measure thanks to the institutions he had helped to create, and to the momentum he had provided. Among those who succeeded him to the leadership were many able men with a clearer sense of their Jewishness and a better grasp of reality. But none could match Herzl's moral authority, his energy, his imagination, and his unrivaled power to translate sweeping visions into a message of hope for the masses. Demagogues and charismatic leaders—the line that divides them is often far from clear-cut—leave no successors.

In a brief official notice, the Zionist Action Committee on Monday, July 4, announced the death of its president. "The burial will take place on Thursday, July 7, 1904, at 10 a.m. at the Doebling Cemetery (Jewish Section). Services at the home of the deceased, Vienna-Waehring, Haizingergasse 29."

The *Neue Freie Presse* devoted its front page to the death of its most prominent staff member. Under the impact of the tragedy, even Bacher and Benedikt felt compelled to relent; for the first time, an allusion to Zionism was allowed to appear in the columns of their paper:

"His early death deeply shocked all his friends, and these included the many thousands who did not merely honor him as a writer and as a man but also as the leader of Zionism. Through his book about the Jewish state some years ago, it grew from small beginnings into a great movement which absorbed much of his strength, energy, and organizing talent."

The obituaries in the European press ranged from factual reports to lengthy eulogies, but his death was noted everywhere; without the benefit of electronic media he had, within the span of a few brief years, attained the status of an international celebrity.

Ussishkin, the last to fight him, paid him a tribute that sounds sincere and in any case sums up a simple truth: "Herzl brought the Jews unity and courage. . . . Those who came before him carried the ideal in their hearts but only whispered about it in the synagogues. . . . Herzl brought us courage and taught us to place our demands before the whole non-Jewish world."

Weizmann, in a letter to his wife—hence with no apparent motive for hypocrisy—described Herzl's death as a great personal loss. "I have had to experience a heavy blow. . . . At this moment, all the differences between us have disappeared, and I only have the image of a great creative worker in front of my eyes. . . . He has left us a frightening legacy. . . . I feel that a heavy burden has fallen on my shoulders."

Buber was equally shaken. "For him it was, to be sure, the best possible time to die," he wrote to his wife, "before all the unavoidable events, disappointments, and decline, and at the height. What shape the movement will take cannot yet be foreseen. But one can barely think about that, so deeply is one shattered by the personal loss alone." Shortly thereafter he all but withdrew from the movement. "With Herzl, the *grand seigneur*, it was possible to come to an understanding; it is impossible to deal with these pompous nonentities."

Ahad Ha-Am, the most trenchant among Herzl's critics, did not pretend to mourn the man who had systematically snubbed and ignored him all his life. Himself honest to the point of perversity, he mocked the "crocodile tears" shed in an orgy of sanctimonious grief by people for whom Herzl had been an obstacle in the path of self-promotion. His own tribute to the dead leader, however, like his critique of the living one, was among the more thoughtful and pertinent:

"Herzl gave us the Congress, the Organization, the Bank, the National Fund. Whether these are to be reckoned great achievements we cannot yet know. All depends on whether they endure and in what form they continue to exist. But one thing Herzl gave us involuntarily, which is perhaps greater than all he did on purpose. He gave us *himself*, to be the theme of our Hymn of Revival, a theme which imagination can take and adorn with all the attributes needed to make of him a Hebrew national hero, embodying our national aspirations in their true form" (HY, Vol. II, p. 148).

Far more eloquently than any obituaries, however, was the funeral on July 7. It demonstrated the wild sense of loss felt throughout the Jewish world, and most particularly among the masses of Eastern Europe. Movement or no movement, for many of them a dream had died. And they came to pay homage.

On Monday morning the body was brought to Vienna, and for three days and nights the casket stood in Herzl's study, guarded by members of the Zionist student fraternities while mourners filed by in a steady stream. On Thursday morning, as services were being held in the apartment, a huge crowd estimated at anywhere between six and ten thousand people gathered in the streets outside to escort the body to the Doebling Cemetery. In his final Will, Herzl had asked to be buried in a metal coffin next to his father "until the Jewish people transfer my remains to Palestine," and added, with his unfailing flair for the dramatic gesture: "No flowers, no speeches."

But the spontaneous outpouring of emotions was something that defied all stage directions. Stefan Zweig, who attended the funeral along with Vienna's entire literary establishment, gave a vivid account of it in his memoirs:

> A strange day it was, a day in July, unforgettable to all who were there to see it. Because suddenly at every railroad station in the city, with every train, night and day, from every country and corner of the world, masses of people kept arriving, Western and Eastern Jews, Russian and Turkish Jews, from every province and every little town they came streaming in, the shock of the news still marking their faces. What all the arguments and gossip had for so long tended to obscure was here at last revealed to us in all its true significance—that the man being laid to rest was the leader of a great movement. It was an unending procession. Vienna was suddenly made aware of the fact that this was not a mere author or mediocre poet who had died but one of those creators of ideas such as emerge only at the rarest of moments in the history of countries and peoples. At the cemetery, there was a mob scene. The crowds were pressing in on the coffin, weeping, howling, screaming in a wild eruption of despair that turned into a near-riot. All semblance of order broke down, swamped by a kind of elemental and ecstatic mourning such as I have never seen before or since at a funeral. And this immense pain rising out of the depths of an entire people made me realize for the first time how much passion and hope this singular and lonely man had given to the world by the power of his idea. [Zweig, p. 133]

At the graveside, both mother and wife fainted. The thirteen-year-old Hans recited the Kaddish. As the coffin was being lowered, David Wolffsohn spoke a few words: "You willed that at your graveside no speeches be made. To us your wish is sacred. But we swear to you that we will keep your name sacred and that it will remain unforgotten as long as a single Jew lives on this earth. In these heavy hours we recall the oath you took at the sixth congress, and we repeat it. 'If I forget thee, O Jerusalem, may my right hand forget its cunning.' "

On August 17, 1949, Herzl's coffin, along with those of his parents and sister, were transferred to Israel and reburied on Mount Herzl in Jerusalem.

There were the orphans, and then there were the victims.

As Herzl had feared, his wife and children were left with few resources and no income; the appeal Wolffsohn launched on their behalf netted about £9,000 and helped to alleviate some of the most immediate problems. In a statement obviously written *for*, rather than *by* her, published in the *Jewish Chronicle* of July 29 and designed to graft the legend of the faithful helpmate onto the Herzl myth, Julie expressed her gratitude for the innumerable messages of sympathy and was made to explain that

> if I did not take part in the life work of my beloved husband, it was because I feared still further to encourage him in his restless and worrying labors and because I foresaw an end which, unhappily, has come all too soon. His work was, however, and will ever remain sacred to me. I will serve the Zionist movement with all my strength and will do everything possible to initiate my children into the work of their father, and to make them worthy champions in the movement for the deliverance of our people, for which he strove. I hope thereby to act in the spirit of my beloved dead husband, and also to give expression to my love for his life's work.

She most likely bears no blame for the nauseating hypocrisy of this primitive public-relations stunt. But whatever her public statements—and whatever the reasons that induced her to sign them—the fact is that she did not have the slightest interest in her husband's work and that her often embarrassingly outspoken hostility to the movement was widely known. That hostility had nothing to do with principles or ideology; it was simply the fury of a woman wronged. She felt that the Zionists had robbed her of her husband, her fortune, and were now about to rob her of her children. Yet though only thirty-six at the time of Herzl's death, she was ill, and dependent on those same Zionists for support. She spent much of the remaining three years of her life in spas and sanatoria, being treated for unspecified ailments. Spoiled, impulsive, incapable of managing her finances or her life, she constantly assailed Wolffsohn with demands for money, often accompanied by suicide threats, while Wolffsohn tried in vain to convince her that he could not possibly provide "for three people, three apartments, four servants," not to mention the cost of her medical care. In 1906, at the Cohnstamm Sanatorium in Koenigstein, her derogatory remarks about her late husband so outraged the director that he asked her to leave, declaring that "it would be good if, in the interest of Zionism, Mrs. Herzl were to disappear from Koenigstein and from Western Europe" (Stern, p. 26).

She died at Aussee in 1907 at the age of thirty-nine, presumably of heart disease, and was cremated according to her wish. Her son, Hans, is said to have left the urn with her ashes somewhere on a train. The director of the Cohnstamm Sanatorium thus had his way.

But as always, the victims hardest hit were the children. Although Julie up to this point had been a devoted if overprotective mother, she evidently had little contact with them after her husband's death. Pampered, overindulged, raised as junior royalty in a golden cage with only the most minimal and carefully supervised exposure to the outside world, they were educated by governesses and private tutors, did not attend school, and were actively discouraged from playing with other children, one reason—or pretext—being the mother's phobic fear of contagious diseases. This hothouse atmosphere with its sticky intimacy among the siblings would have been a poor preparation for life under the best of circumstances. But the father's death, a shattering event of itself, entailed in this instance the abrupt and total collapse of their entire world. At one stroke they found themselves orphaned, separated, and poor.

Pauline, the oldest, fourteen when her father died, had been sickly ever since the first attack of rheumatic fever at the age of eight left her with a damaged heart valve. With the fairy king father gone and the ailing mother henceforth unavailable and usually absent, the rather plain but physically precocious adolescent was dumped onto a series of more or less complaisant relatives and began to act out with a vengeance. The reports of "unbridled lust" and "nymphomania" may be more descriptive of the temper of the times than of what ailed Pauline, but there is ample evidence not only of numerous liaisons but of a conspicuous lack of discretion and selectivity on her part. Her conduct scandalized the circle of Herzl's intimates and led to many

well-meant but clumsy interventions, including psychiatry and insti-
tutionalization. Her only real attachment and emotional support was
her brother, Hans, but although well aware of her problems and at
least as deeply and unconditionally devoted to her as she was to him,
Hans was living in England and in any case had his hands full trying
to cope with his own problems.

Drifting from town to town and from one affair into another, Pauline
got married in 1911 and divorced a year later. Hans, who in the
meantime had discovered Freud, suggested an analysis with him, but
nothing came of it. Instead, Pauline was repeatedly hospitalized between 1915 and 1924, when she dropped out of sight altogether.
Nothing is known about her life during the next six years, except that
by the time the police picked her up as a vagrant in Bordeaux, she
was both desperately ill and a severe morphine addict. Her brother,
alerted by the authorities, came rushing down from London, spent
four days with her, and left when she seemed to be making a satisfactory
recovery. A month later he received another urgent summons; this
time he arrived in Bordeaux only to find his sister dead of coronary
insufficiency. She was forty years old. With uncanny calm and som-
nambulistic lucidity, he thereupon proceeded to seek what he felt was
his destiny—to share her fate and her coffin.

To be the son of a legend is a heavy burden, greatly complicated
in Hans's case by the trauma of having lost the flesh-and-blood father
on the threshold of adolescence, before he ever had a chance to come
to terms with him. Uncommonly sensitive and highly intelligent, he
was taken to England shortly after Herzl's death and educated at Clif-
ton, where he proved a brilliant student. He went on to read philosophy
and philology at Cambridge, received his M.A. in 1914, and served
in the British Army during the First World War. His father cast a
giant shadow over his life, no doubt one reason for his troubled relationship to Judaism. But the fact that he had not been circumcised
at birth—there is no record of a bar mitzvah, either—probably troubled
his Zionist mentors a great deal more than it did him. At their insistence, he underwent the operation at the age of fifteen, at the height
of a turbulent adolescence. What, if anything, this did to his unconscious we have no way of knowing, but he reported to David Wolffsohn
that he was "ever so happy finally to be a real Jew."

After the war, he lived a life of abstemious isolation devoted entirely
to esoteric and erratic intellectual pursuits. His sex life, if any, seems
to have been confined to a few experiments undertaken on medical

advice. Books were his only intimate companions; he was a voracious reader, fluent in a number of languages and with a passionate interest in religion—"Religion is essential to me; I am not a rationalist." He translated Heine and some of his father's works, took up painting, toyed with the idea of becoming a monk, and finally undertook an analysis with Jung. He also evidently went to consult Freud, who reputedly advised him to "finally bury your father—he was one of those people who have turned dreams into reality. They are a very rare and dangerous breed." There is no authoritative source for this unhelpful piece of advice; it may be apocryphal but, in any case, has obviously been quoted out of context.

Ultimately disappointed by psychoanalysis, Hans turned for succor to religion instead and, on the twentieth anniversary of his father's death in 1924, became a Baptist, the first in a series of conversions in the course of which he in rapid succession turned Catholic, Protestant, Unitarian, Quaker, and finally sought readmission to Claude Montefiore's Liberal Synagogue. It is not difficult to imagine the effect of this apostasy by the "crown prince" on the Jewish community, and on the Zionists in particular. The Jews of Vilna, who once hailed the father as a king, are said to have rent their garments and strewn ashes on their heads.

A perennial exile, totally alienated, isolated and near-destitute, unsuccessful as an author and translator, haunted by excruciating guilt feelings—"I have brought shame upon the memory of my father—one more reason to do away with myself"—he had to beg the Zionist Executive in London for the fare to Bordeaux. When, rushing down for the second time, he found Pauline dead, the last link to life snapped for him. After having been convinced, with some difficulty, that she was truly beyond reviving, he retired to his hotel room and, with the pedantic thoroughness that marked him the descendant of both his father and grandfather, proceeded to settle all his earthly affairs before doing what he felt he had to do.

He addressed a note to the hotel owner apologizing for the mess he was about to make, disposed of his few belongings, wrote a letter to Weizmann, thanked the London Executive for their help, and instructed a Bordeaux attorney to "please see to it that my body be placed in my sister's coffin, where there is ample room, and have us shipped to Vienna. If they do not wish us to rest with our father, this may be a good time to have him transported to Palestine." Finally, he left a suicide note:

The following has been written by me this 14th of September, in full possession of all my faculties, and with the intention of blowing my brains out this very night.

I have lost my beloved sister, and I know that it was due to my own negligence. A man who is guilty in his own eyes should not, I think, leave the execution of the verdict to others. This seems to me a conclusive argument against those who consider suicide a crime. It may, on the contrary, even be a duty, as in this particular instance. Now that I have lost the person dearest to me, I have no further interest in living.

He killed himself hours before Pauline's funeral. Both brother and sister were buried in Bordeaux.

Their younger sister, Trude, was born in Paris in 1893, following her parents' tentative reconciliation. A bright and appealing child, Herzl's "golden Trudel" after his death lived for some years with her maternal maiden aunt, Ella Naschauer. She attended the Gymnasium in Vienna but, though a good student, was forced to quit school at seventeen because of repeated manic-depressive episodes. In 1913 she moved to Cologne and went to live with David Wolffsohn, who died the following year. An unusually attractive woman, she was hospitalized for the first time in 1916 and spent much of the remainder of her life in and out of institutions. The episodes of manic exaltation that offered a relief of sorts from the cyclothymic depressions manifested themselves in what seem almost uncanny parodies of her father's dynamic exuberance and epistolary style, carried to psychotic extremes. Like him, she addressed countless letters to the world's rulers, kings and prominent personalities, often strewn with apposite quotes from classical and modern sources, and there is ample evidence of the hold his internalized image had on her fantasy life. "A healthy Trude Herzl can and will lead the Zionist movement toward new ideas," she announced to Weizmann, and her encouraging words to the recently deposed Duke of Windsor, "You have never been more majestic than now that you no longer are Your Majesty," is the sort of sentence that her father might well have written.

In 1917 she married Richard Neumann, a wealthy textile manufacturer twenty-six years her senior and, a year later, gave birth to Herzl's only grandchild, a son named Stephen Theodor Neumann. Almost immediately following the delivery, she was more or less permanently institutionalized, ending up at Vienna's famous Steinhof Psychiatric Hospital. In 1942, the Nazis deported all patients to Terezin, where Trude died "of hunger and ill treatment" on March 15, 1943. Her husband, also deported to the same camp, had already died there two months earlier.

Their son, Stephen Theodor, was sent to England as a child, studied at Cambridge, and during World War II served as a captain in the British Army, having changed his name to Stephen Norman. Modest, well-mannered, and strikingly handsome, he bore a marked physical resemblance to his grandfather but, at least in his younger years, showed little interest in Zionism or Jewish affairs. In 1945 he was posted to India and on the way, both coming and going, stopped off briefly in Palestine, where the veterans of Zionism enthusiastically welcomed Herzl's sole surviving heir. A rather remarkable unpublished eleven-page essay bears witness to the overwhelming impression made on him, in turn, by the country and its people. He was welcomed in several kibbutzim, accorded the honors due a prince of the realm, and urged to settle in Palestine after his demobilization. Instead, he remained in government service and accepted a position with the British Commonwealth Scientific Office in Washington, D.C., where he arrived in September 1946. Two months later, on November 26, he leaped to his death from the Massachusetts Avenue bridge. No notes were found.

It was an appalling legacy, but the search for causes leads only into dead-end arguments inspired not so much by the need to know as by the compulsion to place blame and to assign guilt. The ancients, in their ignorance, knew better; the end of the Herzl bloodline has about it the inexorable fatality of a Greek tragedy.

His literary legacy did not fare much better. Confident of his genius, he counted on posterity to redeem his reputation and accord him his rightful place as the important playwright and author he felt himself to be. None of his plays was ever staged again, and most of his books went out of print. In literary history he is remembered, if at all, only as a feuilletonist, a brilliant stylist popular in his day but—unlike many of his *fin de siècle* contemporaries—forgotten in our own. The only writings of his that have survived are those linked to his role as the founder of modern Zionism, and even their survival owes more to piety than to merit.

But again fate played its part in this fiasco, fate in the form of bad luck and poor judgment.

In his Will of May 23, 1900, Herzl expressed the wish to have his collected writings brought out as soon as possible in an edition that was to include all feuilletons, editorials, stories, articles, and plays. As literary executors he named Professor Leon Kellner and Dr. Erwin Rosenberger.

Erwin Rosenberger, an early editor of *Die Welt* who, by the time Herzl died, had already switched to medicine, nonetheless managed to put together a volume of Herzl's Zionist articles, which was published in 1905 by the Jewish Publishing House in Berlin and for years remained the only one of his books in print.

Leon Kellner, for his part a renowned Austro-Hungarian Shakespeare scholar from Czernovitz with exalted academic and political ambitions, seems to have put very little time and effort into promoting the publication of Herzl's writings at a time when they might still have found a publisher as well as an audience. For one thing, he was busy with his own affairs, and for another, his once ardent devotion had cooled somewhat during the last years of Herzl's life. As literary executor, his main contribution appears to have been the negative one of sifting the material and censoring anything he deemed offensive.

Herzl was particularly anxious to have his diaries published as soon as possible after his death, in the hope that royalties from this unusual inside view of history in the making would help to support his family. But Kellner, after years of doing little or nothing about them, finally prevailed upon Hans Herzl to edit the eighteen handwritten notebooks for publication, with the result that the first, expurgated edition did not appear in print until 1922. After four years of war, several revolutions, runaway inflation, the breakup of empires, and the Balfour Declaration, the interest of the public at large in these massive volumes and in the events they so painstakingly detailed was understandably limited.

But the measure of a man's life is not the sum of his failures.

It was a life of tragic grandeur that left much wreckage in its wake. In the end, though, his spirit prevailed, and in ways far more substantial than the pious myth, or the ubiquitous icon of the bearded prophet with the burning eyes.

By sheer force of his personality and a will of iron, he welded cantankerous sectarians, youthful rebels, and despairing dreamers into an effective, unified mass movement and improvised the institutions that enabled it to serve as the nucleus of the future state.

He rose above his own elitist bias and his muddled notions of aristocracy in creating the first representative body of the Jewish people, the direct antecedent of the Israeli Knesset.

His political initiatives, however ill conceived and ultimately futile, legitimized the national aspirations of the Jews as a people. In the end, ironically, it was Weizmann who in 1917 was to benefit from the precedent set by Herzl in his dealings with the British government.

Over and above all else, Herzl, by being who he was—a Jew who had stopped apologizing for being Jewish—inspired pride and hope. He was the first Jewish leader in modern times. Thus far, the only one. Those who came after him were politicians.

Still, Jewish politicians in a country of their own.

BIBLIOGRAPHY

Works by Theodor Herzl

In German:

Briefe und Tagebücher. Berlin: Propyläen Verlag.
> A projected seven-volume, unexpurgated, annotated edition of all diaries and correspondence, prepared jointly by German and Israeli experts, to be published in both Hebrew and German. Four volumes have appeared thus far.

Gesammelte Zionistische Werke. (4 vols.) Berlin: Jüdischer Verlag, 1905.
Neues von der Venus. Leipzig: Freund, 1887.
Das Buch der Narrheit. Leipzig: Freund, 1888.
Das Palais Bourbon. Leipzig: Duncker & Humblot, 1895.
Der Judenstaat. Vienna: M. Breitenstein, 1896.
Philosophische Erzählungen. Berlin: Paetel, 1900.
Altneuland. Leipzig: H. Seemann, 1902.
Feuilletons. Berlin: Benjamin Harz, 1903.

In English:

The Complete Diaries of Theodor Herzl. (5 vols.) Trans. by Harry Zohn. New York: Thomas Yoseloff, 1960.
Old New Land. Trans. by Lotta Levensohn. New York: Bloch Publishing Co., 1960.

Secondary Sources

Adler, Joseph. *The Herzl Paradox: Political, Social and Economic Theories of a Realist.* New York: Hadrian Press, 1962.
Adler, Ruth. *Women of the Shtetl.* Rutherford, N.J.: Fairleigh Dickinson University, 1980.

Ahad Ha-Am. *Essays, Letters, Memoirs.* Ed. by Leon Simon. Oxford, England: East
& West Library, 1962.
―――. *Nationalism and Jewish Ethics.* New York: Herzl Press, 1962.
―――. *Am Scheidewege.* Berlin: Jüdischer Verlag, 1913.
Auernheimer, Raoul. *Das Wirtshaus zur Verlorenen Zeit.* Vienna: 1948. Extract under
"Beard of the Prophet," *Herzl Yearbook,* Vol. 6. New York: Herzl Press, 1965.
Ausubel, Nathan. *A Treasury of Jewish Folklore.* New York: Crown, 1948.
Avineri, Shlomo. *The Making of Modern Zionism.* New York: Basic Books, 1981.
Bach, H. I. *The German Jew: A Synthesis of Judaism and Western Civilization.* Oxford
University Press, 1985.
Barber, Noel. *The Sultans.* New York: Simon & Schuster, 1973.
Barea, Ilsa. *Vienna.* New York: Alfred A. Knopf, 1966.
Bakan, David. *Sigmund Freud and the Jewish Mystical Tradition.* New York: Schocken
Books, 1965.
Bein, Alexander. *Theodor Herzl.* Vienna: Fiba Verlag, 1934. (English by M. Samuel)
Philadelphia: Jewish Publication Society, 1942.
Ben-Horin, Meir. *Max Nordau.* New York: Conference on Jewish Social Studies,
1956.
Berend, Ivan T., and Ranki, György. *Economic Development in East Central Europe
in the 19th and 20th Centuries.* New York: Columbia University Press, 1974.
Berlin, Isaiah. *The Life and Opinions of Moses Hess.* London: Jewish Historical Society
of England, 1966.
Bloch, Chaim. *Theodor Herzl and Joseph S. Bloch.* In *Herzl Yearbook,* Vol. 1,
p. 156.
Bodenheimer, Henrietta Hannah. *Am Anfang der Zionistischen Bewegung.* Euro-
päische Verlagsanstalt, 1965.
Bodenheimer, Max Isidor. *Prelude to Israel.* New York: Thomas Yoseloff, 1963.
Boehm, Adolf. *Die Zionistische Bewegung.* Berlin: Jüdischer Verlag, 1925.
Brainin, Reuben. *Hayye Herzl.* New York, 1919.
Bredin, Jean-Denis. *L'Affaire.* Paris: Julliard, 1983.
Bristow, Edward J. *Prostitution and Prejudice.* Oxford University Press, 1982.
Broch, Hermann. *Hugo von Hofmannsthal and His Time.* University of Chicago,
1984.
Brogan, D. W. *The French Nation.* New York: Harper & Bros., 1957.
Chissin, Chaim. *A Palestine Diary: Memoirs of a BILU Pioneer.* New York: Herzl
Press, 1976.
Chouraqui, André. *Theodor Herzl.* Paris: Seuil, 1960.
Cohen, Israel. *Theodor Herzl, Founder of Political Zionism.* New York: Thomas
Yoseloff, 1959.
Crankshaw, Edward. *The Fall of the House of Habsburg.* London: Longmans, 1962.
Dawidowicz, Lucy S. *The Golden Tradition.* New York: Holt, Rinehart & Winston,
1967.
De Haas, Jakob. *Theodor Herzl: A Biographical Study.* (2 vols.) Chicago: The Leonard
Company, 1927.
Diamant, Dr. Paul I. *Theodor Herzl's Väterliche und Mütterliche Vorfahren.* Jeru-
salem: Bamberger & Wahrmann, 1934.
Dubnow, Simon. *History of the Jews.* 4th ed. New York: Thomas Yoseloff, 1973.

Elon, Amos. *Herzl.* New York: Holt, Rinehart & Winston, 1975.

Falk, Avner. "Freud's Herzl." *Midstream.* January 1977.

Fields of Offering. Studies in Honor of Raphael Patai. Ed. by Victor D. Sauna. New York: Herzl Press.

Fraenkel, Josef, ed. *The Jews of Austria.* London: Valentine Mitchell, 1967.

———. *Des Schoepfers Erstes Wollen.* (TH as playwright.) Vienna: Fiba Verlag, 1934.

———. *Lucien Wolf and Theodor Herzl.* London: Jewish Historical Society of England, 1960.

Frankel, Jonathan. *Prophecy and Politics: Socialism, Nationalism and the Russian Jew, 1862–1917.* Cambridge University Press, 1981.

Freundlich, Charles H. *Peretz Smolenskin.* New York: Bloch Publishing Co., 1965.

Friedman, Isaiah. *Germany, Turkey and Zionism, 1897–1918.* Oxford University Press, 1977.

Friedman, Maurice. *Martin Buber's Life and Work: The Early Years, 1878–1923.* New York: Dutton, 1981.

Georg, Manfred. *Theodor Herzl.* Berlin: Höger Verlag, 1932.

Gittman, Sander L. *Jewish Self-Hatred.* Baltimore: Johns Hopkins University Press, 1986.

Gonen, Jay Y. *A Psychohistory of Zionism.* New York: Mason/Charter, 1975.

Gottheil, Richard J. H. *Zionism.* New York: Jewish Publication Society, 1914.

Greenberg, Louis. *The Jews in Russia: The Struggle for Emancipation.* New Haven: Yale University Press, 1965.

Guedemann, Moritz. *Aus Meinem Leben.* Unpublished ms., Leo Baeck Institute, London.

Handler, Andrew. *Dori.* Tuscaloosa: University of Alabama Press, 1983.

Hertzberg, Arthur. *The Zionist Idea, an Anthology.* New York: Harper & Row, 1959.

Herzl, Hechler, the Grand Duke of Baden and the German Emperor. Facsimile letters. Tel Aviv: Ellern's Bank, Ltd., 1961.

Herzl Yearbook. Ed. by Ralph Patai. Vols. 1–7, 1958–71, New York: Herzl Press.

Hess, Moses. *Rom und Jerusalem.* Leipzig, 1862. English ed. New York: Bloch, 1945.

Heyman, Michael. *The Uganda Controversy.* 68 original documents. Jerusalem: Israel Universities Press, 1977.

Hoffmann, Paul. *Die Judenfrage in Ungarn.* Budapest: 1882.

Ignotus, Paul. *Hungary.* New York: Praeger, 1972.

Jósika-Herczeg, Imre. *Hungary After a Thousand Years.* New York: American-Hungarian Daily, 1934.

Kann, Robert A. *A History of the Habsburg Empire.* Berkeley: University of California Press, 1974.

Katz, Jacob. *Out of the Ghetto.* Cambridge, Mass.: Harvard University Press, 1973.

———. *Tradition and Crisis: Jewish Society at the End of the Middle Ages.* Illinois: Free Press of Glencoe, 1961.

Kellner, Anna. *Leon Kellner.* Vienna: Gerold, 1935.

Kellner, Leon. *Theodor Herzls Lehrjahre.* Vienna: R. Löwit Verlag, 1920.

Kinross, Lord. *The Ottoman Centuries.* New York: William Morrow, 1977.

Klausner, Joseph. *Menachem Ussishkin.* New York: Scopus Publishers, 1960.

Klein, Dennis B. *Jewish Origins of the Psychoanalytic Movement.* University of Chicago Press, 1985.

Kohn, Hans. *The Age of Nationalism*. New York: Harper & Bros., 1962.

———. *The Idea of Nationalism*. New York: Macmillan, 1958.

Kornberg, Jacques. "Theodor Herzl: A Reevaluation." *Journal of Modern History*, 52 (June 1980), 226–52.

Kraus, Karl. *Eine Krone für Zion*. Vienna: Die Fackel, 1898.

Landau, Saul Raphael. *Sturm und Drang im Zionismus*. Vienna: Verlag Neue Nationalzeitung, 1937.

———. "Disease and Death of Theodor Herzl." *American OSE Review*, 2 (March–April 1943), 28–32.

Laqueur, Walter. *A History of Zionism*. New York: Schocken Books, 1976.

Lazare, Bernard. *L'Antisémitisme*. Reprint. Paris: Editions de la Différence, 1982.

Lichtheim, Richard. *Geschichte des Deutschen Zionismus*. Jerusalem: Verlag Rubin Mass, 1954.

Listowel, Judith. *A Habsburg Tragedy*. New York: Dorset Press, 1976.

Loewenberg, Peter. "Theodor Herzl: A Psychoanalytic Study in Charismatic Leadership." In *The Psychoanalytic Interpretation of History*, ed. by Benjamin B. Wolman. New York: Basic Books, 1971.

Ludwig, Emil. *Wilhelm II*. Berlin: Rowohlt, 1925.

Macartney, C. A. *The Habsburg Empire*. New York: Macmillan, 1969.

McGrath, William J. *Freud's Discovery of Psychoanalysis*. Ithaca, N.Y.: Cornell University Press, 1986.

Mandel, Neville J. *The Arabs and Zionism Before World War I*. Berkeley: University of California Press, 1976.

Marrus, Michael R. *The Politics of Assimilation*. Oxford, England: Oxford University Press, 1971.

May, Arthur J. *Vienna in the Age of Franz Joseph*. Norman: University of Oklahoma Press, 1966.

Mosse, George L. *German Jews Beyond Judaism*. Bloomington: Indiana University Press, 1985.

Nevlinsky, Philip Michael de. "TH's Envoy." *Herzl Yearbook*, Vol. II, 1959.

Nordau, Anna and Maxa. *Max Nordau—A Biography*. New York: Nordau Committee, 1943.

———. "Nordau." *Judaism*. Vol. 33, No. 3 (Summer 1984).

Nordau, Max. *Zionistische Schriften*. Berlin: Jüdischer Verlag, 1923.

Nussbaum, Dr. T. "Theodor Herzl Before the Military Fitness Commission." *Jüdische Welt*, July 31, 1936.

Oring, Elliott. *The Jokes of Sigmund Freud*. Philadelphia: University of Pennsylvania Press, 1984.

Patai, Jozsef. "Herzl's School Years." *Herzl Yearbook*, Vol. III, 1960, pp. 53–75.

———. *Star over Jordan: The Life of Theodor Herzl*. New York: Philosophical Library, 1946.

Paupié, Kurt. *Handbuch der Oesterreichischen Pressegeschichte*. Vienna: Braumüller, 1960.

Pinsker, Leo. *Road to Freedom*. New York: Scopus Publishers, 1944.

Poliakov, Leon. *Histoire de L'Antisémitisme*. Paris: Calmann-Lévi, 1955.

Pollak, Michael. *Vienne 1900*. Paris: Gallimard, 1984.

Reinharz, Jehuda. *Chaim Weizmann—The Making of a Zionist Leader*. New York: Oxford University Press, 1985.

———. *Fatherland or Promised Land*. Ann Arbor: University of Michigan Press, 1975.

———. "Ahad Haam und der Deutsche Zionismus." Bulletin, Leo Baeck Institute, 61 (1982), 3–27.

———. "Ahad Haam, Buber and German Zionism." In *At the Crossroads, Essays on Ahad Haam*, ed. by Jacques Kornberg. Albany: State University of New York Press, 1983.

Rose, Norman. *Chaim Weizmann*. New York: Viking, 1986.

Rosebury, Theodor. *Microbes and Morals*. New York: Viking, 1971.

Rosenberger, E. *Herzl as I Remember Him*. New York: Theodor Herzl Foundation, 1959.

Rozenblit, Marsha L. *The Jews of Vienna*. Albany: State University of New York Press, 1984.

Ruppin, Dr. Arthur. *Die Juden der Gegenwart*. (4th ed.) Berlin: Jüdischer Verlag, 1920.

Russian Jewry, 1860–1917. Ed. by Jacob Frumkin, Gregor Aronson, and Alexis Goldenweiser. New York: Thomas Yoseloff, 1966.

Sacher, Harry. *Zionist Portraits*. London: Anthony Blond, 1959.

Samuel, Maurice. *The World of Sholem Aleichem*. New York: Alfred A. Knopf, 1943.

Sandler, Aron. *Memoirs*. Unpublished ms, Leo Baeck Institute, London.

Schama, Simon. *Two Rothschilds and the Land of Israel*. New York, Alfred A. Knopf, 1978.

Schechtman, Joseph B. *Rebel and Statesman: The Vladimir Jabotinsky Story—The Early Years*. New York: Thomas Yoseloff, 1956.

Schnitzler, Arthur. *Liebe, Die Starb vor der Zeit*. Correspondence with Olga Wassix, ed. by Therese Nickl and Heinrich Schnitzler. Vienna: Molden, 1970.

———. *Jugend in Wien*. Frankfurt-am-Main: Fischer, 1981.

Schnitzler, Olga. *Spiegelbild der Freundschaft*. Vienna: 1970.

Schorske, Carl. *Fin-de-Siècle Vienna*. New York: Alfred A. Knopf, 1980.

Schulman, Mary. *Moses Hess*. New York: Thomas Yoseloff, 1963.

Simon, Ernst. "Sigmund Freud, the Jew." *Leo Baeck Yearbook* 2, 1957, p. 274.

Sokolow, Florian. *Nahum Sokolow*. London: Jewish Chronicle Publications, 1975.

Sokolow, Nahum. *History of Zionism*. (2 vols.) London: Longmans, 1919.

Stern, Arthur. "The Genetic Tragedy of the Family of Theodor Herzl." *Israel Annals of Psychiatry and Related Disciplines*, April 1965.

Stewart, Desmond. *Theodor Herzl, Artist and Politician*. Garden City, N.Y.: Doubleday, 1974.

Talmon, J. L. *Israel Among the Nations*. New York: Macmillan, 1970.

———. *The Myth of the Nation and the Vision of Revolution*. Berkeley: University of California Press, 1980.

Tapié, Victor. *The Rise and Fall of the Habsburg Monarchy*. New York: Praeger, 1971.

Theodor Herzl, a Memorial. Ed. by Meyer Weisgal. New York: The New Palestine, 1929.

Tietze, Hans. *Die Juden Wiens*. Vienna and Leipzig: E. P. Tal, 1933.

Thon, Yehoshua. *Theodor Herzl*. Berlin: Jüdischer Verlag, 1914.

Toqueville, Alexis de. *The Old Regime and the French Revolution*. Garden City, N.Y.: Doubleday Anchor, 1956.

Vámbéry, Arminius. *Travels in Central Asia*. London: T. Fisher, 1884.

———. *Sittenbilder aus dem Morgenlande*. London: T. Fisher, 1884.

———. *His Life and Adventures*. London: T. Fisher, 1884.

Vital, David. *The Origins of Zionism*. Oxford, England: Oxford University Press, 1975.

———. *Zionism—The Formative Years*. Oxford, England: Oxford University Press, 1982.

Wagner, Renate. *Arthur Schnitzler*. Vienna: Molden, 1981.

Wandruszka, Adam. *Die Neue Freie Press—Geschichte einer Zeitung*. Vienna, 1958.

Waxman, Meyer. *A History of Jewish Literature*. New York: Thomas Yoseloff, 1941.

Weizmann, Chaim. *Trial and Error*. New York: Harper & Bros., 1949.

———. *The Letters and Papers of Chaim Weizmann*. Ed. by Leonard Stein. Oxford, England: Oxford University Press, 1968.

Zweig, Stefan. *Die Welt von Gestern*. Stockholm: Berman-Fischer, 1944.

INDEX